The Handbook of Juvenile
Delinquency and Juvenile Justice

Wiley Handbooks in Criminology and Criminal Justice

Series Editor: Charles F. Wellford, University of Maryland College Park.

The handbooks in this series will be comprehensive, academic reference works on leading topics in criminology and criminal justice.

The Handbook of Law and Society
Edited by Austin Sarat and Patricia Ewick

The Handbook of Juvenile Delinquency and Juvenile Justice
Edited by Marvin D. Krohn and Jodi Lane

The Handbook of Juvenile Delinquency and Juvenile Justice

Edited by

Marvin D. Krohn and Jodi Lane

WILEY Blackwell

This edition first published 2015
© 2015 John Wiley and Sons, Inc.

Registered Office
John Wiley & Sons Ltd, The Atrium, Southern Gate, Chichester, West Sussex, PO19 8SQ, UK

Editorial Offices
350 Main Street, Malden, MA 02148-5020, USA
9600 Garsington Road, Oxford, OX4 2DQ, UK
The Atrium, Southern Gate, Chichester, West Sussex, PO19 8SQ, UK

For details of our global editorial offices, for customer services, and for information about
how to apply for permission to reuse the copyright material in this book please see our website
at www.wiley.com/wiley-blackwell.

The right of Marvin D. Krohn and Jodi Lane to be identified as the authors of the editorial
material in this work has been asserted in accordance with the UK Copyright, Designs and
Patents Act 1988.

Wiley also publishes its books in a variety of electronic formats. Some content that appears in
print may not be available in electronic books.

Designations used by companies to distinguish their products are often claimed as trademarks.
All brand names and product names used in this book are trade names, service marks,
trademarks or registered trademarks of their respective owners. The publisher is not associated
with any product or vendor mentioned in this book.

Limit of Liability/Disclaimer of Warranty: While the publisher and authors have used their
best efforts in preparing this book, they make no representations or warranties with respect to
the accuracy or completeness of the contents of this book and specifically disclaim any implied
warranties of merchantability or fitness for a particular purpose. It is sold on the understanding
that the publisher is not engaged in rendering professional services and neither the publisher
nor the author shall be liable for damages arising herefrom. If professional advice or other expert
assistance is required, the services of a competent professional should be sought.

Library of Congress Cataloging-in-Publication Data applied for

9781118513170 (hardback)

A catalogue record for this book is available from the British Library.

Cover image: Graffiti image © Lorenz Britt / Alamy

Set in 10.5/13pt Minion by SPi Publisher Services, Pondicherry, India
Printed and bound in Malaysia by Vivar Printing Sdn Bhd

1   2015

Contents

Notes on Contributors

Robert Agnew is Samuel Candler Dobbs Professor of Sociology at Emory University. His research focuses on the causes of crime and delinquency, particularly his general strain theory of delinquency. His recent works include *Toward A Unified Criminology: Integrating Assumptions about Crime, People, and Society* (NYU Press, 2001); *Criminological Theory: Past to Present* (Oxford, 2015); *Juvenile Delinquency: Causes and Control* (Oxford, 2012); *Pressured into Crime: An Overview of General Strain Theory* (Oxford, 2006); and *Why Do Criminals Offend: A General Theory of Crime and Delinquency* (Oxford, 2005). He served as President of the American Society of Criminology, is a Fellow of that organization, and is on the editorial board of several criminology journals.

Catrien C.J.H. Bijleveld studied psychology and criminal law, both at Leiden University. Her PhD was on the statistical analysis of categorical time series. After working as an assistant professor at Leiden University she moved to the WODC Research and Documentation Center of the Netherlands Ministry of Justice. In 2001, she moved to NSCR in Leiden, and became professor of Criminological Research Methods at the VU University in Amsterdam. Catrien Bijleveld's main research interests are in the areas of criminal careers, female offenders, the intergenerational transmission of offenders, genocide and sex offending. She is the author of several textbooks, as well as of edited books, on crime and justice in the Netherlands, and on the association between employment and offending.

Arjan A.J. Blokland is professor of Criminology and Criminal Justice at Leiden University, the Netherlands, and senior researcher at the Netherlands Institute for the Study of Crime and Law Enforcement, Amsterdam. He has published on criminal careers, life course criminology and the effects of formal sanctions on criminal development.

Lauretta M. Brennan, MS, is an advanced doctoral graduate student in the Department of Psychology at the University of Pittsburgh. Her research interests focus on developmental trajectories of conduct problems and identifying the precursors and consequences associated with discrepant developmental patterns.

Molly Buchanan earned her MS from Northeastern University and is currently pursuing her PhD in Criminology and Law at the University of Florida. Driven by professional experiences in the criminal and social justice fields, her research interests include evidence-based interventions, developmental and life-course criminology, and intergenerational transmission of antisocial behaviors.

Elena Bystrova is Director of International Programs and Study Abroad at the University of New Haven (CT). She is currently working towards her PhD in criminal justice with primary interests in comparative criminal justice issues as well as criminal justice administration.

Nicholas Chagnon is a doctoral student in Sociology and research assistant in Women's Studies at the University of Hawaii at Manoa. His research interests include violence against women and media and crime. He has also published on non-authoritarian teaching approaches.

Meda Chesney-Lind teaches Women's Studies at the University of Hawaii. Nationally recognized for her work on women and crime, her testimony before Congress resulted in national support of gender-responsive programming for girls in the juvenile justice system. Her most recent book on girls' use of violence, *Fighting for Girls* (co-edited with Nikki Jones), won an award from the National Council on Crime and Delinquency for "focusing America's attention on the complex problems of the criminal and juvenile justice systems".

Kristina Childs is an Assistant Professor in the University of Central Florida's Department of Criminal Justice. Her research interests include juvenile justice system policy, prevention and intervention strategies for juvenile offenders, and increasing access to public health services for adolescent offenders. Recent publications have appeared in *Behavioral Sciences and the Law, Youth Violence and Juvenile Justice,* and *Criminal Justice and Behavior.*

Adam Cooper completed his PhD in Education Policy Studies between Stellenbosch University, South Africa and the Faculty of Education, University of Cambridge, where he was a split-site Commonwealth Scholar. He has conducted research on young offenders, gangsterism and masculinities in South Africa, and produced a toolkit for local government officials working with young offenders.

Andrea Davis is a doctoral student in Criminology & Law at the University of Florida. Her research interests are race and predictors of policy attitudes.

Paulo Ricardo Diniz Filho is a Professor of Sociology and Political Sciences at UNA University Center, Brazil.

Beidi Dong is a doctral candidate in the Department of Sociology and Criminology & Law at the University of Florida. His research interests include developmental and life-course criminology, youth gangs and violence as well as juvenile delinquency and justice in a comparative sense.

John M. Eassey is a Criminology, Law & Society doctoral candidate at the University of Florida. He will be a tenure-track assistant professor at Missouri State University in Fall 2015. His dissertation concerns the mediational role of peer associations in the relationship between employment quality and crime across the life course. His research interests include peers in the developmental study of crime, neighborhood and contextual influences, and statistical and research methodology.

Amanda D. Emmert is a doctoral student in the School of Criminal Justice at the University at Albany. Her research interests include prisoner reentry, weapons, and public policy.

Abigail A. Fagan is an Associate Professor at the University of Florida. Her research focuses on the etiology and prevention of juvenile delinquency, particularly family and community influences on delinquency, the relationship between victimization and offending, gender and delinquency, and the identification and effective implementation of delinquency prevention programs.

Crystal A. Garcia is an Associate Professor of Criminal Justice, Law and Public Safety in the School of Public and Environmental Affairs at IUPUI. Her research interests include community corrections, reentry, the death penalty and crime policy, along with gender-responsive programming and disproportionate minority contact in the juvenile justice system.

Kristin Gardner is a doctoral candidate in Criminology and Law at the University of Florida. While her doctoral research focusses on transfer, graduated sanctions, and recidivism patterns, she plans to expand her program of research to examine juvenile justice and delinquency, and corrections, more broadly.

Chris L. Gibson is Research Foundation Professor and Associate Professor in the Department of Sociology and Criminology & Law at the University of Florida.

Barry Glick received his PhD from Syracuse University in 1972. Trained as a counseling psychologist, Dr Glick has devoted his professional career to the development of policies, programs, and services for adolescents. His specialization is in juvenile delinquency, aggression and violence, youth gangs, as well as the emotionally disturbed adolescent. Dr Glick has worked in both private childcare agencies and state government. He has held positions as childcare worker, psychologist, administrator, manager, and agency executive staff. Previously holding the post of Associate Deputy Director for Local Services, New York State Division for Youth, he is currently a national consultant to juvenile and adult correctional systems, senior editor *of Managing Delinquency Programs that Work*, and author of *Cognitive Behavioral Programs for At-Risk Youth, Volumes I and II*; *No Time to Play: Youthful Offenders in Adult Systems*, and its sequel implementation manual, *Recess Is Over:*

A handbook for managing youthful offenders in adult systems. He co-developed and is co-author of *Aggression Replacement Training®: A comprehensive intervention for Aggressive Adolescents Third Edition;* and *The Pro-Social Gang.* He also co-developed *Thinking for a Change,* a multi-modal cognitive behavior intervention. Dr Glick holds positions on several editorial boards, is a member *emeritus* of the National Gangs Advisory Committee, is a Nationally Certified Counselor and is an Approved Clinical Supervisor by the Center of Credentialing and Education. He is licensed as a Mental Health Professional in the States of New Mexico and New York.

Erich Goode is Sociology Professor Emeritus at Stony Brook University. He has taught at six universities and is the author of 11 books on deviance and drug use, including *Deviant Behavior* (Pearson, 10th edition, 2014), *Drugs in American Society* (McGraw-Hill, 2014), and *Justifiable Conduct Self-Vindication in Memoir* (Temple University Press, 2013).

Courtney Harding is a PhD student in Criminal Justice at Temple University. She received her BA from Rutgers University, New Brunswick. Her research interests include drug treatment and mental health issues in the criminal justice system. Her experience includes working with at-risk juveniles in West Palm Beach, FL, and as a substance abuse counselor at Northern State Prison in Newark, NJ.

John P. Hoffmann is a Professor in the Department of Sociology at Brigham Young University. He received a PhD in Criminal Justice from SUNY-Albany and an MPH from Emory University. His research interests include the etiology of delinquency and drug use.

James C. (Buddy) Howell is a Senior Research Associate with the National Gang Center, in Tallahassee, Florida. His publications on youth gangs include one book, *Gangs in America's Communities* (2012), and work on gang history, gang homicides, drug trafficking, gangs in schools, hybrid gangs, myths about gangs, risk factors, and what works.

Timothy O. Ireland is a professor in the Department of Criminology and Criminal Justice at Niagara University. He received his Master's from Northeastern University and his PhD from Albany's School of Criminal Justice. He has been affiliated with the Rochester Youth Development Study for the past several years, with a research focus on family violence.

Suman Kakar is Associate Professor in the Department of Criminal Justice at the Florida International University. Her interests include juvenile crime, juvenile justice policy, child abuse, domestic violence, human trafficking, and national security threats.

Marvin D. Krohn is a professor in the Department of Sociology and Criminology & Law at the University of Florida. His areas of interest include life course perspectives, gangs, and the impact of official intervention. He is the co-author of three books, including *Gangs in a Developmental Perspective,* which was awarded the Michael J. Hindelang Award for outstanding Scholarship. Professor Krohn is a Fellow of the American Society of Criminology.

Steven P. Lab is a Professor of Criminal Justice at Bowling Green State University and a Past-President of the Academy of Criminal Justice Sciences. He has held visiting appointments at Keele University (UK), the Jill Dando Institute at University College London, and Loughborough University (UK). He is the author of *Crime Prevention: Approaches, Practices and Evaluation* (8th ed., Anderson, also translated into Chinese, Japanese and Korean) and coauthor of *Victimology* (6th ed., Anderson) (with W.G. Doerner) and *Juvenile Justice* (7th ed., Anderson)(with J.T. Whitehead).

Jodi Lane is Professor in the Department of Sociology and Criminology & Law at the University of Florida. Her interests include fear of crime, juvenile justice policy, corrections, and evaluation research.

Lonn Lanza-Kaduce is a professor in the Department of Sociology and Criminology & Law at the University of Florida and serves as director of the Criminology & Law Online Program. His research has focused on juvenile justice issues. He has also collaborated on recent research into the legitimacy of speed trap enforcement and Florida's Stand Your Ground Law.

Michael J. Leiber is Chair and Professor in criminology at the University of South Florida. He earned his doctorate in criminal justice from the State University of New York at Albany. His main research interests and publications lie in juvenile delinquency, juvenile justice, and race/ethnicity. Currently, he serves as the editor of the *Journal of Crime and Justice*.

Andrea Lindsey is a doctoral student at Florida State University. Her research interests include neighborhoods and crime, offender re-entry and recidivism, the prison experience and re-entry, and criminal justice and public policy.

Alan J. Lizotte is dean and professor in the School of Criminal Justice at the University at Albany. He is co-principal investigator on the Rochester Youth Development Study. His substantive interests include illegal firearms ownership and use, and developmental criminology. In 2003, together with his RYDS coauthors, he was awarded the American Society of Criminology's Hindelang Award for the book *Gangs and Delinquency in Developmental Perspective*.

Giza Lopes is a postdoctoral associate at the School of Criminal Justice, University at Albany. Her research interests focus primarily on examining social theories derived from the symbolic-interactionist perspective, such as labeling and medicalization of social problems.

David C. May is an Associate Professor in the Department of Sociology at Mississippi State University. He has published numerous articles and books in the areas of responses to school violence, perceptions of the severity of correctional punishments, fear of criminal victimization, and weapon possession and use among adolescents.

Susan McNeeley is a postdoctoral scholar in the Justice Center for Research at Pennsylvania State University. Her research interests include environmental criminology, victimology, and public opinion. Publications have appeared in *Victims & Offenders*, *Juvenile and Family Court Journal*, and *Handbook of Survey Methodology for the Social Sciences*.

Bryan Lee Miller is an Assistant Professor of Criminal Justice and Criminology at Georgia Southern University. His research has focused on issues of offender reentry, drug policy, and sociology of law. Recent publications have appeared in *Punishment & Society*, *Law & Social Inquiry*, and the *Journal of Drug Issues*.

Jennifer H. Peck is an Assistant Professor in the Department of Criminal Justice at the University of Central Florida. Her research has been accepted for publication in *Crime & Delinquency*, *Youth Violence and Juvenile Justice*, and *Deviant Behavior*. Her research interests focus on the role of race and ethnicity in the juvenile justice system.

James V. Ray is Assistant Professor for Research at the University of New Orleans in the Department of Psychology. His main research interests include juvenile justice and delinquency, juvenile psychopathy, and self-control. Recent publications have appeared in *Psychological Bulletin*, *Journal of Child Psychology and Psychiatry*, and *Criminal Justice and Behavior*.

Allison D. Redlich is Associate Professor in the School of Criminal Justice at the State University of New York, University at Albany, and Executive Director of the Michael J. Hindelang Criminal Justice Research Center. Previously she was a Senior Research Associate at Policy Research Associates and a Research Scientist at the Stanford University School of Medicine. She received her PhD in Developmental Psychology from the University of California, Davis. Professor Redlich is an internationally recognized expert on police interrogations and false confessions, often being asked to present her research abroad and in courts as an expert witness. Professor Redlich also has extensive programs of research on true and false guilty pleas and mental health courts. She has authored more than 75 articles and chapters, including (with J. Acker) the case law book, *Wrongful Convictions: Law, Social Science, and Policy*.

Daniel S. Shaw is Professor and Chair of Psychology at the University of Pittsburgh with primary interests in the development and prevention of early-starting conduct problems. He currently leads four NIH-funded projects investigating the developmental precursors of antisocial behavior and use of the Family Check-Up to prevent its early onset.

Reveka V. Shteynberg is a PhD student in the School of Criminal Justice at the University at Albany. She holds an MA in Criminal Justice from the University at Albany and earned her BA in Criminology, Law and Society from the University of California, Irvine. Prior to entering graduate school, she worked as a research analyst conducting criminal, civil, and media background checks. She also worked as a researcher for a trial and jury consultation firm. Her research interests include plea decision-making; jury decision-making; perceptions of criminal justice actors; the role of gender and age in adjudication; and miscarriages of justice.

Aiden Sidebottom is a lecturer at the Jill Dando Institute of Crime Science, at University College London. His research interests include problem-oriented policing and crime prevention evaluation.

Paul R. Smit joined the statistical unit of the Ministry of Justice in 1995, after having worked on Crime Statistics for Statistics Netherlands. His main research area is international crime statistics. Besides a number of publications in this field, he is secretary of the association European Sourcebook of Criminal Justice e.V. This association has compiled the four editions of the *European Sourcebook of Crime and Criminal Justice Statistics* and is a regular advisor to the UN and the EU. His other research areas are homicide research and judicial forecasting modeling.

Carolyn A. Smith is a professor in the School of Social Welfare at the University at Albany. Smith received her MSW from the University of Michigan, and her PhD from Albany's School of Criminal Justice. A long-time researcher with the Rochester Youth Development Study, her research focuses on family violence and delinquency.

John M. Stogner an Assistant Professor of Criminology at the University of North Carolina at Charlotte. His research interests include the relationship between health and delinquency, novel drug use and policy, and biosocial criminology. His works have appeared in the *Journal of Research in Crime and Delinquency, Substance Use & Misuse,* and *Addictive Behaviors.*

Maria Tcherni is an Assistant Professor of Criminal Justice at the University of New Haven (CT). She got her PhD in Criminal Justice from the University at Albany (SUNY). Her primary research interests are in crime trends and patterns, and the effects of poverty, family characteristics, psychiatric conditions, and psychotropic medications on violence/homicide. Her articles have appeared in the *Journal of Quantitative Criminology* and *Justice Quarterly.*

Nick Tilley is a professor at the Jill Dando Institute of Crime Science, at University College London. His research interests lie in policing, situational crime prevention and program evaluation methodology. He was awarded an OBE for Services to Policing and Crime Reduction in the Queens Birthday Honours in 2005.

James D. Unnever is Professor of Criminology at the University of South Florida-Sarasota Manatee. He has published extensively on race and crime, including his recent *A Theory of African American Offending: Race, Racism, and Crime,* and was the recipient of the Donal A.J. MacNamara Award of the Academy of Criminal Justice Sciences.

Jamie E. Walter earned her Bachelor of Arts in Sociology and her Master's degree in Criminal Justice Administration from Niagara University. Her research interests include exploring racial disparities in sentencing, and the consequences of family violence. She most recently presented some of her research at the Academy of Criminal Justice Sciences national conference.

Elmar G.M. Weitekamp studied social work at the Hochschule Niederrhein in Mönchengladbach, Germany, and criminology at the University of Pennsylvania in Philadelphia, USA. He is the organizer and co-director of the annual course Victimology, Victim Assistance and Criminal Justice in Dubrovnik, as well as one of the founders of the African Victimology course. Together with Jeremy Sarkin and Stephan Parmentier , he is the editor of the book series *Transitional Justice* published by Intersentia in Antwerp, Belgium.

Wayne N. Welsh is a Professor of Criminal Justice at Temple University. His research interests include violence, corrections, and substance abuse. He is author of *Counties in Court: Jail Overcrowding and Court-Ordered Reform* (Temple, 1995), *Criminal Justice Policy and Planning* (4th ed., with P. Harris; Elsevier, 2012), and *Criminal Violence: Patterns, Causes and Prevention* (3rd ed., with M. Riedel; Oxford, 2011). Recent articles have appeared in *Criminal Justice and Behavior, Drug and Alcohol Dependence,* and *Substance Abuse.*

Pamela Wilcox is Professor in the School of Criminal Justice at the University of Cincinnati. She has authored numerous works aimed at developing and testing theories of crime, including *Criminal Circumstance: A Dynamic, Multicontextual Criminal Opportunity Theory.* She also recently edited *The Oxford Handbook of Criminological Theory* and the *Encyclopedia of Criminological Theory.*

L. Thomas Winfree, Jr., retired in 2014. Most recently he had served as a visiting professor in Arizona State University's School of Criminology and Criminal Justice. He has co-authored multiple editions of five textbooks, including *Understanding Crime: Essentials of Criminological Theory*; he has also co-edited two anthologies, including *Social Learning Theories of Crime,* the latter with Christine S. Sellers and Ronald L. Akers. Winfree is co-author of dozens of theory-based articles.

Introduction

Marvin D. Krohn and Jodi Lane

Over the last few decades, major changes have occurred in both the fields of juvenile delinquency and juvenile justice. Our understanding of juvenile delinquency, especially theories, has been refined. The number of youths entering and exiting the system increased dramatically in the 1990s; yet, despite warnings that things would get much worse over time, the population of youths being processed through the system has declined in recent years. Still, policy changes instituted at the height of concern over juvenile crime remain. Theories addressing the reasons for juveniles' delinquent behavior have undergone significant development, and research examining the correlates and causes of delinquency has advanced with the acquisition of longitudinal data and the use of innovative statistical analytical methods.

The 35 chapters in this compendium are intended to address the changes that have taken place in how we deal with delinquency and the evolution of how we think about and study juvenile delinquents and their behavior. We asked the authors to provide some background on where the field has been, what the current state of knowledge is, and where they see practice, research, and theory about juvenile delinquency and juvenile justice going in the future.

The handbook is divided into five distinct sections examining trends in juvenile delinquency, the correlates of youth crime, theories of delinquent behavior, justice approaches (including prevention and treatment), and special issues.

Part I provides eight chapters exploring the current status of juvenile delinquency and juvenile justice in different nations around the world and discusses the processing of juvenile offenders. Most published works focus exclusively on the situation in the US, occasionally comparing it with "sister" nations that are similar in one aspect or another. We were intent upon taking a more global view of the problem and invited scholars from nations in Europe, South America, and Asia to provide a description of the rates of delinquency in their country of interest and to briefly discuss recent changes in laws concerning the processing of delinquents. By including detail about these nations, we are underscoring the notion that juvenile delinquency is a global problem and, more importantly, that scholars and practitioners have much to learn from other countries. Also in this section, Gardner and Lanza-Kaduce write about the processing of juvenile offenders in the US, focusing especially on legal issues and how major court cases have affected the way that youths are treated in the justice system.

In Part II, we turn attention to an examination of the correlates of delinquent behavior to set the groundwork for the theoretical explanations of delinquency reviewed in Part III. Scholars review the state of the research on gender (Chesney-Lind and Chagnon), race and ethnicity (Unnever), genetics (Gibson and Davis), parenting (Hoffman), schools (Welsh and Harding), peers (Eassey and Buchanan) and neighborhoods (McNeeley and Wilcox). Each chapter not only examines our current knowledge but, perhaps more importantly, makes suggestions for future research efforts in their respective areas.

Our field is replete with theories of why juveniles engage in delinquent behavior, and a thorough exploration of all the theoretical positions would constitute a full handbook of its own. For Part III, we have selected six theoretical perspectives to illustrate approaches to explaining delinquency. Scholars well-known for their work on these theories write about the respective points of view on the causes of juvenile crime. The included theories are general strain theory (Agnew), social learning theory (Winfree), social control and self-control theories (Goode), life course theories (Blokland), labeling theory (Krohn and Lopes), and routine activities and opportunity theories (Tilley and Sidebottom).

In Part IV we focus on how the system responds to delinquency. Authors explore three different types of prevention programs to determine what constitutes best practice. Brennan and Shaw look at parental and early childhood prevention, Lab examines programs in schools, and Fagan and Lindsey focus on neighborhood-based prevention. The remainder of this section examines what happens when prevention does not work. Shteynberg and Redlich discuss how the police respond to juveniles. Ray and Childs focus on juvenile diversion. Lieber and Peck examine how juvenile and adult courts deal with troubled teens. Once youths are adjudicated delinquent, different programming and treatment strategies are available. Garcia examines community-based sanctions, and Glick reviews the current state of institutionalization and describes the treatment strategies used in these institutions.

The final section of this compendium covers special issues related to juvenile delinquency. Juvenile or youth gangs have been of considerable policy importance in recent decades both in the US and Europe. Howell examines the current knowledge of the gang problem within the US, while Weitekamp discusses the causes of youth gangs in European nations with a special emphasis on German gangs. Statistics also show that delinquent behavior becomes more problematic when weapons are involved, and Emmert and Lizotte discuss some of the motivations among youth for carrying and using weapons. Drug use constitutes a major form of delinquency among teenagers, and Stogner and Miller identify the different types of prescription and illegal drugs that are commonly used by youths.

Another factor related to delinquency is victimization, and Ireland writes about the connections between child abuse and becoming an offender. Finally, May discusses the broader literature on juvenile victimization and fear of crime among adolescents.

No single compendium can cover the range of relevant issues necessary for a complete understanding of issues regarding juvenile delinquency and juvenile justice. Yet, we believe the current attempt provides a comprehensive examination of many of the most important issues. Including chapters written by scholars who have either established themselves in their respective fields of expertise or are on their way to doing so results in a compendium that provides an up-to-date examination of what we know about juvenile delinquency and the operation of the juvenile justice system.

Part I

Trends in Juvenile Delinquency
Around the World

1

Juvenile Delinquency and Justice Trends in the United States

Jodi Lane

In the US, concern about juvenile crime hit the political forefront in the latter part of the twentieth century, and the policies passed during that get-tough era continue to affect juvenile offenders and the justice system. This chapter briefly discusses the policy and justice system trends of the last few decades, including the way that states tried to curb the incorrectly anticipated rise in juvenile crime and the changes in the number and characteristics of youths who are processed in both the juvenile and adult justice systems. It concludes with a brief discussion of recent policy efforts in American juvenile justice.

Get Tough Movement and Beyond

The US has generally treated juvenile lawbreakers (younger than 18 years old) differently from criminal adults at least since the early 1800s, when Houses of Refuge were established to hold troubled and delinquent children (see New York State Archives, n.d.). At the end of that century, in 1899, the first separate juvenile justice system was formally established, when Illinois created the first juvenile court designed to focus on the children's "best interests" and to help troubled juveniles, rather than punish them as adults (see Illinois Juvenile Court Act of 1899). Soon all states had developed separate juvenile justice systems in which most delinquent youths continue to be processed and punished (about 99% of youths who went to court in 2010) (Griffin, Addie, Adams, & Firestine, 2011).

In the 1980s and 1990s, juvenile crime became increasingly worrisome to policy-makers and practitioners in the US, who scrambled to get out ahead of what they

The Handbook of Juvenile Delinquency and Juvenile Justice, First Edition. Edited by Marvin D. Krohn and Jodi Lane.
© 2015 John Wiley & Sons, Inc. Published 2015 by John Wiley & Sons, Inc.

considered to be a rapidly escalating problem (Lipsey *et al.*, 2010). Specifically, murders (in 1993) and violent crime (in 1994) by juveniles, especially with firearms, were increasing faster than they were for adults and reached new heights (Puzzanchera & Adams, 2011; Snyder, Sickmund, & Poe-Yamagata, 1996). Moreover, population projections were that the numbers of teens generally would skyrocket by the early 2000s, prompting some scholars to worry about even more "teen killers" (e.g., Fox, 1996, p. 3) and young "super-predators" (Bennet, DiIulio, & Walters, 1996, p. 26) preying on the public. In fact, at the time, Bennet *et al.* (1996, p. 21) warned that because they expected a rise in young criminal men soon, America was "a ticking crime bomb". Concerns about rising juvenile crime and these warnings of impending doom prompted policymakers and practitioners to enhance their efforts to combat juvenile crime significantly, including "get-tough" policies, such as increasing the use of gang intervention programs and transfer to adult court as ways to get ahead of the projected coming storm of juvenile crime (Torbet & Szymanksi, 1998).

Even during the get-tough movement the vast majority of youths remained in the juvenile justice system (Lipsey *et al.*, 2010; Snyder *et al.*, 1996), but the system was modified to make it tougher on young offenders. A few adolescent offenders, often chronic, serious or older ones, continued to be processed in the adult court system, and the get-tough movement of the 1980s and 1990s significantly increased the number of youths who were transferred to adult court during that period (Griffin *et al.*, 2011; Snyder and Sickmund, 1999).

Because of concerns about rising juvenile crime, state legislatures across the country rewrote their laws to get tougher on juveniles, including expanding provisions for transfer to adult court (Torbet & Szymanski, 1998). Before the 1970s, juveniles primarily were transferred only after a judge had considered their individual cases, but policies changed drastically through the 1990s. Now, 38 states have automatic transfer laws (sending certain offenders automatically to adult court based on age and/or offense), and 15 allow prosecutors the opportunity to make decisions in some or all cases without judicial review (Griffin *et al.*, 2011). Yet, in the last decade, there has been some policy movement in a few states toward reducing the numbers of youths who go to adult court. For example, ten states recently revised their waiver laws, by making it easier to get reverse waiver hearings (to move a case back to juvenile court), increasing the lower age limit at which a youth can be tried as an adult, allowing the possibility that youths who are transferred can be treated as a juvenile in later hearings, and/or reducing the list of offenses that trigger automatic placement in the adult court process (Arya, 2011).

During the 1990s, states also toughened other policies, including increasing the age at which the juvenile justice system could hold youths for dispositional purposes, enhancing the use of blended sentences (some combination of juvenile and adult options), boosting the emphasis on public safety and accountability (versus the best interests of the child), reducing confidentiality protections for juvenile proceedings and records, and strengthening victim participation in the process (Torbet & Szymanski, 1998). Although juvenile violent crime has decreased significantly since the mid-1990s, most of the get-tough laws remain on the books (Griffin *et al.*, 2011). Delinquent youths in the US primarily face processing and punishment in a tougher juvenile justice system. Currently, the juvenile system focuses on both rehabilitation and public safety as goals, and emphasizes the use of evidence-based treatment programming, or approaches that have been shown to be effective through evaluation research (Brown, 2012). Now we turn to specific information about who goes through the system and what happens to them when they get there.

Juvenile Crime and Punishment Trends: The Statistics

Crime

Almost two million juveniles are arrested each year in the US, but they represent only a small proportion of the total arrested (e.g., 15% of violent crime arrests and 24% of property crime arrests). Very few are arrested for violent index crimes (about 5% of those arrested). For example, in 2009 about 1,170 youths were arrested for murder, but there were over 12,000 people arrested for that offense (Federal Bureau of Investigation, 2010; Puzzanchera & Adams, 2011). In contrast, in 1994 the number of juvenile homicide offenders was over 2,800 (more than double recent numbers) and the overall number of arrests was about 2.7 million (compared with about 1.9 million in 2009) (Snyder *et al.*, 1996). The early 1990s predictions about skyrocketing juvenile violence proved to be misguided, as juvenile arrests for violent crime declined for ten straight years from 1994–2004. Although it increased for a few years after that, juvenile violence has now decreased almost to 1980 levels (Puzzanchera & Adams, 2011). As shown in Figure 1.1, in spite of the dire

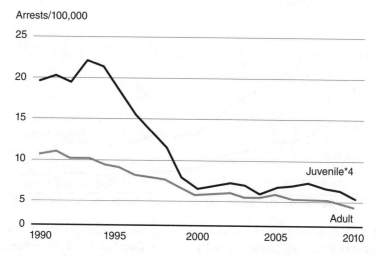

Figure 1.1   US murder arrest rates for juveniles (×4) and adults over 20 years. Reprinted from Snyder (2012, p. 3).

predictions, the juvenile arrest rate for murder declined significantly after 1990, dropping at a much steeper rate than it did for adults. Juvenile arrest rates have also decreased over that 20-year period for forcible rape, robbery, aggravated assault, burglary, motor vehicle theft, weapons law violations, and drug dealing, although juvenile arrests for drug possession and simple assault have not declined compared with 1990 numbers (Snyder, 2012).

Males represent about 70% of arrests, and minorities are disproportionately arrested, especially for violent crimes. African-Americans represented 67% of robbery offenders and 58% of murder offenders, but only 37% of burglary and 25% of drug abuse violations in 2009 (Puzzanchera & Adams, 2011). African-Americans account for only about 13% of the US population, and 16% of the juvenile population (Knoll & Sickmund, 2012; US Census Bureau, 2010).

Another way to examine juvenile crime is to look at victimization rates. Although not all young victims experience crime by juvenile perpetrators, research shows that violent victimization of juveniles often occurs by acquaintances and right after school, meaning it probably involves similar-aged offenders (Snyder & Sickmund, 2006). Victimization rates also show substantial declines in crime, for both juveniles and adults. For example, serious violent crime *against* juveniles declined by 77% from 1994 to 2010 (see Figure 1.2), and the use of weapons and injuries also decreased. The decline in victimization occurred over time for each individual crime type, including rape, robbery, and aggravated assault, and was true for both crimes that happened away from school and at school. Black youths were more likely to be victimized than whites and Hispanics, but victimization has declined for all groups since the 1994 juvenile violence peak. Although males were twice as likely as females to be victimized in the mid-1990s, in 2010 they were equally likely to be the victims of serious violence (White & Lauritsen, 2012).

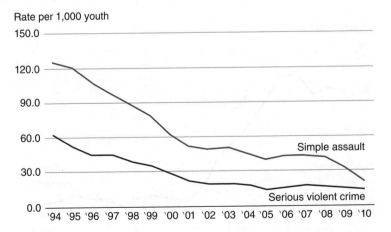

Figure 1.2   Serious violent crime and simple assault against youths aged 12 to 17, 1994–2010. Reprinted from White and Lauritsen (2012, p. 1). Note: Data based on 2-year rolling averages beginning in 1993. See appendix table 1 [in White & Lauritsen, 2012] for standard errors. *Source*: Bureau of Justice Statistics, National Crime Victimization Survey, 1993–2010.

Juvenile and adult court

Recent numbers show that about 1.5 million cases are handled by juvenile courts in the US in a year, meaning that only about a quarter of arrestees are diverted from formal processing. The number of cases in court has declined since the mid-1990s by 20%, but clearly not as steeply as juvenile crime itself. Interestingly, public-order court cases continued to increase over this period, but person and drug cases remained relatively stable. Property cases, however, have steadily declined since 1985 (almost 20%). An examination of trends since the 1960s generally shows increases in cases through the mid-1990s, but decreases in the last few years (see Figure 1.3) (Knoll & Sickmund, 2012).

As shown for crime, generally, minorities are overrepresented in juvenile court. While black youths were 16% of the juvenile population, they represented about 34% of the cases that went to court, and 41% of the person cases. Youths under 16 were involved in about half of the cases overall (52%), but 59% of person cases. Finally, males accounted for 72% of offenders in juvenile court, although the proportion of girls in court has been increasing in recent decades (from 19% in 1985 to 28% in 2009). Most (59%) of those who went to court were adjudicated delinquent (the term for conviction in juvenile court) (Knoll & Sickmund, 2012).

Counting the number of youths transferred to adult court in the US is complicated, because there are three ways a youth can be moved to the adult system, and states do not uniformly count those who face each process or their outcomes. Youths can be judicially waived (a judge reviews the case in a hearing and makes the decision), sent there through direct file by a prosecutor (where there is no judicial review), or legislatively waived (where statute requires certain juvenile offenders – by age and/or offense – automatically go to adult court). In 13 states all 16- and/or 17-year-olds go to adult court automatically via statute, and there may be about

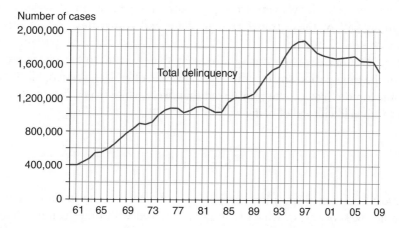

Figure 1.3   Trends in total number of cases in juvenile court. Reprinted from Knoll and Sickmund (2012, p. 1).

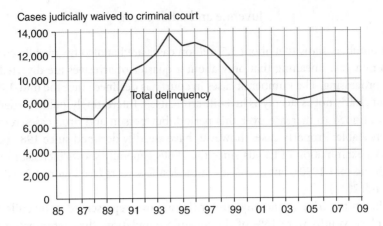

Figure 1.4 Number of cases judicially waived to criminal court. Reprinted from Adams and Addie (2012, p. 1).

175,000 youths in adult court who are statutorily excluded from juvenile court based on age alone (see Griffin *et al.*, 2011).

The best numbers available over time show the number of youths waived by judges. As mentioned above, transfers to adult court significantly increased during the mid–late 1990s, when the get-tough approach was in full swing. The total number waived to adult court was highest in 1994, when 12,100 cases were sent to adult court by judges across the US (Puzzanchera, 2001). By 2009, the number had dropped about 45% to around 7,600, and the rate of transfer had declined (about 14 of every 1000 cases in 1994, to about 9 of every 1000 cases in 2009) (Adams & Addie, 2012; Butts, 1997; see Figure 1.4). Yet, the advocacy organization Campaign for Youth Justice (2012) estimates that about 250,000 youths are sent through the adult system when all mechanisms of transfer are considered. Although theoretically waivers are supposed to apply to the most serious cases, only about half of those transferred in 2009 had committed person offenses (Adams & Addie, 2012).

Males (89% of cases) are much more likely than females to be transferred. For most of the time period since panic about juvenile offenders erupted, black males were much more likely to be transferred than were white males, but in 2009 they faced an equal likelihood of being waived.

Sanctions

The most common disposition for juvenile offenders in the juvenile system is probation (60% of cases), which typically is coupled with other conditions (such as treatment, restitution, or community service). About a quarter of cases (27%) are ordered into residential placement, which means removal from the home into

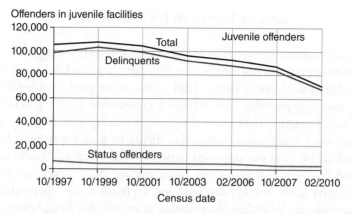

Figure 1.5 Offenders in juvenile facilities, 1997–2010. Reprinted from Hockenberry (2013, p. 5).

any of a variety of programs (group homes, camps, wilderness programs, locked institutions, etc.). The remainder receives a disposition other than probation or institutionalization (Knoll & Sickmund, 2012).

The number of youths in residential placement has decreased 33% since 1997, when juvenile crime was still at the political forefront (Hockenberry, 2013). In 2010, there were over 79,000 youths in residential placement in the US, and the overwhelming majority (about 86%) were there for delinquency (or crimes that would be illegal for adults also). The largest group was person offenders (37%), followed by property offenders (25%), and then public order (11%) and drug offenses (7%). Very few (5%) were locked up for offenses that would not be crimes for adults (skipping school, curfew violations, running away, incorrigibility, etc.) (see Figure 1.5). The remaining few were held for other reasons, such as abuse or mental concerns. In addition, some offenders are detained in custody prior to their court hearings (over 20,000), and combined with those who were committed post-adjudication (conviction), the rate in custody was 225/100,000 juveniles. Again, males (87% of those held) and minorities (only 32% held were white) were much more likely to be in custody. Data show that males and juveniles who committed person offenses are held longer than others (Hockenberry, 2013).

Because of the problems with tracking transfers to adult court (e.g., poor statistics regarding the numbers waived in ways other than by a judge), it is difficult to document what happens to these juveniles once they go through court. In 2012, there were about 4,600 youths held as adults in jails (Minton, 2013), and in 2010, there were 2,295 youths under 18 in prison (Guerino, Harrison, & Sabol, 2012). Yet, there are no good national data on how many juveniles sentenced to adult prison remain there after they turn 18, how long they remain in custody, or what happens to them once they are released. There are also no national data on how many of those transferred to adult court are sentenced to other sanctions like probation or sent back to the juvenile system for sanctions, or how they do while being sanctioned or after (see Singer, 2003).[1]

Recent Trends in Juvenile Justice

Because later chapters address trends in more detail, this section only briefly describes a few of the major juvenile justice efforts now underway in the US. One of the biggest trends in American juvenile justice (and justice more generally) is the push for "evidence-based" approaches. According to Greenwood (2010, p. 1), "the term 'evidence-based practice' refers to a program or strategy that has been evaluated through rigorous scientific study using experimental or quasi-experimental methods." Greenwood (2010, p. 1) distinguished between what he called "brand-name programs" and "strategies". Brand-name programs are those developed by specific researchers over time through research and replication, and they often provide written manuals and/or technical assistance to ensure that practitioners maintain fidelity to the program design. Examples of what Greenwood (2010, p. 9) calls "proven programs" being used in the US include Nurse Family Partnership, Functional Family Therapy (FFT), and Aggression Replacement Training (ART).[2] According to Greenwood (2010), strategies are more general approaches that have been shown in studies, such as meta-analyses, to be effective. Examples of these include cognitive-behavioral therapy, mentoring, teen court, social skills training, and sex offender treatment (Greenwood, 2010).

Another focal point of treatment policy has been to provide gender-specific services, after research showed that the needs and problems of girls differed significantly from those of boys (Chesney-Lind & Bloom, 1997), and scholars argued that girls needed gender-specific programming (e.g., Bloom, Owens, & Covington, 2003; Greene, Peters, & Associates, 1998). The goal of this type of programming is to take into account the needs of girls and use treatment programs that are more suited to their psychological, social and emotional states (Greene, Peters, & Associates, 1998). At least five states – Connecticut, Florida, Hawaii, Minnesota, and Oregon – have passed statutes requiring gender-specific programming (Brown, 2012), but other states are also implementing these types of programs at different points in the system.

In line with the push for evidence-based services, an additional focus has been on addressing the mental health needs of juvenile offenders. Studies show that trauma is a serious issue for youths in the juvenile justice system. For example, the Northwestern Juvenile Project, which is a longitudinal study of youths in detention in Chicago, found that almost 93% of youths had been traumatized, and over half had faced trauma at least six times, often from witnessing violence. About 10% had post-traumatic stress disorder (Abram *et al.*, 2013). One relatively new approach is to use what is called "trauma-informed" care, which hopes to consider the impact of trauma and ensure that treatment does not intensify problems or retraumatize clients (Black, Woodworth, Tremblay, & Carpenter, 2012, p. 192; Miller & Najavits, 2012). States have made some progress in addressing mental health needs of clients. For example, Washington recently allowed counties to increase the sales tax to fund mental health courts, and Idaho also developed mental health courts for youths. Other states, such as Minnesota and Nevada, have focused upon improving mental health assessments that are conducted in the system (Brown, 2012).

Due to children's relative immaturity to adults, there are also efforts to improve their experiences in the system and to ensure due process, thereby moving back to protecting the child. One critical issue in the scholarly literature is whether juveniles have the mental maturity, or competence, to stand trial (e.g., whether they can understand what is happening). Consequently, seven states have allowed developmental incompetence as a consideration in court (see O'Donnell & Gross, 2012). States have also focused on ensuring better defense counsel (e.g., requiring that they be given competent counsel, including youths who cannot afford to hire any themselves). In addition, states have been working to help youths avoid the system entirely, by increasing diversion and community-based services. Interestingly, after many confidentiality safeguards were removed during the get-tough movement, states have now begun reinstituting protections. Since 2007, at least 10 states have done so (Brown, 2012).

Another trend that shows evidence of movement away from the get-tough approach is that some states are expanding the upper age limit of juvenile court jurisdiction (i.e., reducing the number of youths automatically tried in adult court). For example, in 2007, Connecticut raised the upper age from 16 to 18, and in 2009, Illinois raised the age of jurisdiction from 17 to 18 for juvenile misdemeanants. In 2010, Oklahoma allowed for youths in the first half of their eighteenth year to stay in the juvenile system if they committed a misdemeanor. As mentioned before, some states are changing laws pertaining to transfer to adult court. For example, in 2007 Virginia required that a youth be convicted in adult court (not just tried) before being considered as an adult for all future cases. In 2008, Maine allowed younger youth (15 and under) to start serving adult prison sentences in juvenile facilities, and in 2012 Colorado raised the minimum age to be tried as an adult from 14 to 16 (Brown, 2012).

Finally, like in the system more generally, there are increased efforts to improve the reentry experiences of youths returning from correctional programming in hopes of reducing recidivism and improving life chances. There are about 100,000 juveniles released back into the community each year that need help transitioning. Some states (e.g., Oklahoma and Virginia) have passed laws providing mental health services, substance abuse treatment, and other services to youths returning home. Others have made other programs available, such as healthcare, probation programming, and reentry courts (Brown, 2012).

In conclusion, the last 30 or more years have brought major changes for how juvenile offenders are handled in the US. The 1980s and 1990s were riddled with concerns about rising juvenile crime, which led to major get-tough reforms in an effort to get ahead of the anticipated increase in juvenile crime and violence. Yet the warnings were wrong, and the last decade or so has seen declines in crime and juvenile justice system clients. In the last decade, states have slowly begun to make efforts toward reducing the negative effects of the get-tough movement on both offenders and the system. That is, states are starting to increase protections for children and improve rehabilitative services. Consequently, it is likely that the near future will include even more efforts to move back towards the idea of rehabilitation within the confines of maintaining public safety, especially as state budgets continue to tighten and policymakers and practitioners hope to reduce the number of juveniles who return to the system (Lipsey *et al.*, 2010).

Notes

1   The Bureau of Justice Statistics recently funded a survey designed in part to determine what happens to juveniles processed in adult courts, called the Survey of Juveniles Charged as Adults in Criminal Courts (see Griffin *et al.*, 2011).
2   Nurse Family Partnership is a prevention program where nurses work with at-risk mothers in their homes during pregnancy until a child turns two, teaching them child development and providing other important information (see http://www.nursefamilypartnership. org/). FFT is a strength-based intervention program where a therapist works with families to help them solve problems, increase family motivation and engagement, and change problematic behaviors (see http://www.fftinc.com/). ART is an intervention for aggressive youth by a trained staff to help teach interpersonal skills, anger control, and moral reasoning (see http://uscart.org/new/trainings/aggression-replacement-training/–see also Greenwood (2010) for a description of programs).

References

Abram, K.M., Teplin, L.A., King, D.C., *et al.* (2013). *PTSD, Trauma, and Comorbid Psychiatric Disorders in Detained Youth*. Washington, DC: Office of Juvenile Justice and Delinquency Prevention.

Adams, B. & Addie, S. (2012). *Delinquency Cases Waived to Criminal Court, 2009*. Washington, DC: Office of Juvenile Justice and Delinquency Prevention.

Arya, N. (2011). *State Trends: Legislative Changes from 2005 to 2010 Removing Youth from the Adult Criminal Justice System*. Washington, DC: Campaign for Youth Justice.

Bennet, W.J., DiIulio, J.J., & Walters, J.P. (1996). *Body Count: Moral Poverty…and How to Win America's War Against Crime and Drugs*. New York: Simon & Schuster.

Black, P.J., Woodworth, M.J., Tremblay, M., & Carpenter, T. (2012). A review of trauma-informed treatment for adolescents. *Canadian Psychology*, *53*(3), 192–203.

Bloom, B., Owens, B., & Covington, S. (2003). *Gender-responsive Strategies: Research, Practice, and Guiding Principles for Women Offenders*. Washington, DC: National Institute of Corrections. Retrieved from http://www.nicic.org/pubs/2003/018017.pdf

Brown, S.A. (2012). *Trends in Juvenile Justice State Legislation: 2001–2011*. Washington, DC: National Conference of State Legislatures.

Butts, J.A. (1997). *Delinquency Cases Waived to Criminal Court, 1985–1994*. Washington, DC: Office of Juvenile Justice and Delinquency Prevention.

Campaign for Youth Justice. (2012). *Key Facts: Youth in the Justice System*. Retrieved from http://www.campaignforyouthjustice.org/documents/KeyYouthCrimeFacts.pdf

Chesney-Lind, M., & Bloom, B. (1997). Feminist criminology: Thinking about women and crime. In B. MacLean, & D. Milovanovic (eds.), *Thinking Critically About Crime* (pp. 54–65). Vancouver: Collective Press.

Federal Bureau of Investigation. (2010). *Crime in the United States, 2009*. Clarksburg, WV: Federal Bureau of Investigation.

Fox, J.A. (1996). *Trends in Juvenile Violence: A Report to the United States Attorney General on Current and Future Rates of Juvenile Offending*. Washington, DC: Bureau of Justice Statistics.

Greene, Peters, & Associates (1998). *Guiding Principles for Promising Female Programming: An Inventory of Best Practices*. Washington, DC: Office of Juvenile Justice and Delinquency Prevention.

Greenwood, P. (2010). *Preventing and Reducing Youth Crime and Violence: Using Evidence-Based Practices*. Sacramento, CA: Governor's Office of Gang and Youth Violence Policy. Retrieved from http://www.nursefamilypartnership.org/assets/PDF/Journals-and-Reports/CA_GOGYVP_Greenwood_1-27-10

Griffin, P., Addie, S., Adams, B., & Firestine, K. (2011). *Trying Juveniles as Adults: An Analysis of State Transfer Laws and Reporting*. Washington, DC: Office of Juvenile Justice and Delinquency Prevention.

Guerino, P., Harrison, P.M., & Sabol, W.J. (2012). *Prisoners in 2011*. Washington, DC: Bureau of Justice Statistics.

Hockenberry, S. (2013). *Juveniles in Residential Placement, 2010*. Washington, DC: Office of Juvenile Justice and Delinquency Prevention.

Illinois Juvenile Court Act of 1899, 41st General Assembly Laws, Regular Session (Illinois 1899).

Knoll, C., & Sickmund, M. (2012). *Delinquency Cases in Juvenile Court, 2009*. Washington, DC: Office of Juvenile Justice and Delinquency Prevention.

Lipsey, M.W., Howell, J.C., Kelly, M.R., *et al.* (2010). *Improving the Effectiveness of Juvenile Justice Programs: A New Perspective on Evidence-Based Practice*. Washington, DC: Center for Juvenile Justice Reform. Retrieved from http://www.cbjjfl.org/userfiles/files/documents/publications/1-3-11%20Updates/Center%20for%20JJ%20Reform%20Improving%20Effectivenss%20of%20JJ%20Programs.pdf

Miller, N.A., & Najavits, L.M. (2012). Creating trauma-informed correctional care: A balance of goals and environment. *European Journal of Psychotraumatology, 3*, 17246. doi:10.3402/ejpt.v3i0.17246

Minton, T.D. (2013). *Jail Inmates at Midyear 2012 – Statistical Tables*. Washington, DC: Bureau of Justice Statistics.

New York State Archives. (n.d.). *New York House of Refuge: A Brief History*. Retrieved from http://www.archives.nysed.gov/a/research/res_topics_ed_reform_history.shtml

O'Donnell, P.C., & Gross, B. (2012). Developmental incompetence to stand trial in juvenile courts. *Journal of Forensic Sciences, 57*(4), 989–996.

Puzzanchera, C.M. (2001). *Delinquency Cases Waived to Criminal Court, 1989–1998*. Washington, DC: Office of Juvenile Justice and Delinquency Prevention.

Puzzanchera, C., & Adams, B. (2011). *Juvenile Arrests 2009*. Washington, DC: Office of Juvenile Justice and Delinquency Prevention.

Singer, S.I. (2003). Incarcerating juveniles into adulthood: Organizational fields of knowledge and the back end of waiver, *Youth Violence and Juvenile Justice, 1*(2), 115–127.

Snyder, H.N. (2012). *Arrest in the United States, 1990–2010*. Washington, DC: Bureau of Justice Statistics.

Snyder, H.N., & Sickmund, M. (1999). *Juvenile Offenders and Victims: 1999 National Report*. Washington, DC: Office of Juvenile Justice and Delinquency Prevention.

Snyder, H.N., & Sickmund, M. (2006). *Juvenile Offenders and Victims: 2006 National Report.* Washington, DC: Office of Juvenile Justice and Delinquency Prevention.

Snyder, H.N., Sickmund, M., & Poe-Yamagata, E. (1996). *Juvenile Offenders and Victims: 1996 Update on Violence.* Washington, DC: Office of Juvenile Justice and Delinquency Prevention.

Torbet, P., & Szymanski, L. (1998). *State Legislative Responses to Violent Juvenile Crime: 1996– 1997 Update.* Washington, DC: Office of Juvenile Justice and Delinquency Prevention.

US Census Bureau. (2010). *2010 Modified Race Data File.* Retrieved from http://www.census.gov/popest/research/modified.html

White, N., & Lauritsen, J.L. (2012). *Violent Crime against Youth, 1994–2010.* Washington, DC: Bureau of Justice Statistics.

2

Juvenile Delinquency and Juvenile Justice Trends in Europe

Paul R. Smit and Catrien C.J.H. Bijleveld

Introduction

Juvenile offenders are prominent in criminological theory, as well as life-course criminological studies. Much less attention is given to the manner in which the criminal justice system (CJS) deals with underage offenders. On the one hand, most countries have formulated laws for juveniles that emphasize pedagogical principles, and that preclude (long) punishment. On the other hand, imprisonment rates have risen in a number of countries. It is unknown to what extent these reflect increasing trends in incarceration of juveniles.

Research Questions

We will address the following research questions:

1. What is the rate of offending (i.e., number of offenders per capita) for juveniles, overall as well as for distinct crimes?
2. What is the rate of conviction (i.e., number of convicted offenders per number of offenders) for juveniles, overall as well as for distinct crimes?
3. What is the imprisonment rate for juveniles?
4. What is the punitivity rate for juveniles?

All questions will be answered for the years 1995–2013, and data for juveniles will be compared against those for adults.

The Handbook of Juvenile Delinquency and Juvenile Justice, First Edition. Edited by Marvin D. Krohn and Jodi Lane.

Data and Methodology

Data sources

Our main data sources are the five editions of the *European Sourcebook of Crime and Criminal Justice Statistics* (ESB) (Aebi *et al.*, 2006, 2010, 2014; Council of Europe, 1999; Killias *et al.*, 2003). Each edition provides data for a five to seven year period, starting with 1990–1996 in the first edition to 2007–2011 in the fifth edition, with one or two years overlap between editions. In each edition more detailed data are available for one specific year. Since some of the data we use (for juvenile offenders) are indeed only present in this specific year, our trends are based on the years 1995, 1999, 2003, 2006, and 2010. For some missing data (in particular for total crime in 1995, which was missing in the first edition of the ESB), data from the United Nations Crime Trends Survey (UNCTS) (UNODC, 2013) were used, but only where no large differences were found between the two data sources in years where both sources provided figures. Population figures were obtained from the Eurostat demographic statistics (Eurostat, 2013).

The indicators used

In most crime statistics, the main five stages in the criminal justice system where data are collected are (1) the number of crimes as experienced by victims, (2) the number of crimes registered by the police, (3) the number of offenders found (or arrested) by the police, (4) the number of offenders convicted, and (5) the number of prisoners. Since our objective is to look at crimes committed by juveniles, only the last three are applicable for our analysis. Although in most countries crime statistics do indeed provide data for the indicators 3, 4, and 5, they are hardly directly comparable due to differences in procedural law, in definitions, and in the way the statistics are collected and presented. As an example, the number of offenders convicted relate to court convictions only. However, in most countries, and in particular for juveniles, various options are available to the police and/or the prosecution (and these may differ by country) to deal with the offender outside the court. For instance, in some countries juvenile offenders are dealt with only through civil/family law measures. This makes direct comparison of statistics inherently difficult, if not impossible.

Since we restrict ourselves to the analysis of *trends* over a relatively short period (15 years), this inherent incomparability between countries is circumvented for a large part. We assume that procedural law, national definitions and counting rules are reasonably stable within each of the countries we studied during this 15 year period.

After the offending and imprisonment rates we also consider two other indicators in our analysis. The first is the conviction rate – the number of offenders convicted divided by the total number of offenders. The second is punitivity, here defined as the number of prisoners divided by the number of convicted offenders.

The way *punitivity* is defined is not immediately obvious. The rationale is described and discussed in Smit, van Eijk, and Decae (2012). Punitivity is the combination of two factors: Π, the percentage of prison sentences in relation to the total number of sanctions imposed, which is basically the same as offenders convicted (the higher this proportion is, the more severe the punishment) and Λ, the actual average length[1] of prison sentences (again, the longer the prison sentence, the more severe the punishment).

Now it can easily be shown that the product of Π and Λ is proportional to Δ, the number of prisoners, divided by Σ, the number of sanctions imposed.[2] So:

$$\text{Punitivity} = \Pi * \Lambda \approx \Delta / \Sigma$$

Although this is a theoretically valid way of deriving a measure for punitivity, a number of practical issues must be mentioned. The most important issue is whether to include pre-trial detainees in the number of prisoners. Conceptually they should be included (as will be done here) because for most offenders the time spent in pre-trial detention will eventually be regarded as part of the sentence imposed. However, this means that pre-trial detainees who eventually do not get a (unconditional) prison sentence are also counted. Due to lack of data, in Harrendorf and Smit (2010) pre-trial detainees were not included, so only sentenced persons were counted.

We make the usual provision that, for ease of writing, while we will speak of "offending" and "offenders", our data do not permit this in the strict sense, as we have data only on those offenders who became known to the authorities.

Rates and crime types

For the three main indicators: offenders, convicted offenders, and prisoners, the rates per 100,000 inhabitants were computed for both juveniles and adults. Absolute numbers were divided by the population 18 years and older and the population between 12 and 17, respectively.[3] While most statistical offices only provide data for all offenders (with rates as per the whole population), by separating the data for adults we can compare the corresponding findings for juveniles.

For all indicators the number of offenders and prisoners will be presented for all crimes together. In addition, data for four common crime types will be presented, for the offenders and convicted offenders, so that for each of these crime types the conviction rate can be given as well: rape, robbery, theft, and drugs. For prisoners it turned out to be very hard to obtain data per crime type. Therefore only total figures are available for prisoner rates and punitivity.

Countries

Although the ESB provides statistics on 35–40 European countries, only a few countries are used in our analysis. Many countries were not suitable for our trends analysis, mainly because of too much missing data for juveniles, or large differences between editions due to system changes or changes in definitions. The remaining countries where reasonably stable data were available over the whole period 1995 to 2010 were Austria, the Czech Republic, Finland, France, Germany, Italy, the Netherlands, and Switzerland. These are the countries we therefore used to investigate trends in juvenile justice. In total, these eight countries cover about 30% of the population of all European countries (or 45% when Russia, Ukraine, and Turkey are not included).

The data used

Although the data for the eight countries in our analysis were already reasonably complete and stable, some adaptations were still needed. Of a total of 825 data cells,[4] 98 were missing or were clearly out of line with data from other years (and were therefore removed, resulting in missing data). The adaptations were done in two steps as follows.

First, if available, data from the previous or next year from the ESB were inserted (e.g. data from 2002 instead of 2003). If this was not possible, data from the UNCTS were considered as well. In this step, 38 of the 98 missing data were filled in.

In the second step, the remaining 60 missing values were imputed by interpolation and extrapolation, thus resulting in a complete data-set with smoothed data and no missing values.

Computing averages and trends

The average values over the eight countries were computed using weighted averages, where the weighting was done as per the populations. This implies that the contribution on average for large countries (like Germany) was about 10 times the contribution of a small country like Austria. For adults the weighting was according to the adult population, and for juveniles according to the population between 12 and 17.

The trend is computed by fitting an exponential curve over the years and then determining the average percentage change per year. Both the average annual change figures for the whole period (1995–2010) and the more recent period (2003–2010) are given.

Results

Crime patterns

The raw data, per country per year, as well as the data for all eight investigated countries, weighted by population size, are available from the first author and will not be presented here.

Figure 2.1a gives the offender rates (the number of offenders found per 100,000 of the corresponding population), for juveniles as well as adults, for the years 1995–2010 and for all crimes. The picture shows that the offender rate has decreased for juveniles, and has increased slightly for adults. These changes occurred mainly in the years 1995–2003; for the latter years there was virtually no change. For the different crimes, this picture is slightly different. For rape (Figure 2.1b) we see a strong increase for juveniles (amounting to a more than doubling), and a much less strong increase for adults. Robbery offender rates (Figure 2.1c) were stable for adults, but increased for juveniles. Theft offender rates (Figure 2.1d) decreased for both adults and juveniles, but much more strongly so for the latter. Finally, drug offender rates (Figure 2.1e) increased for both juveniles (albeit with a fairly large swing) and adults. This shows that the overall decrease in offender rates for juveniles is likely attributable to a decrease in theft: for juveniles, rape, robbery, and drugs went up, while theft went down, as did the overall rate. However, for adults, a different pattern emerges: total crime went up, as did theft, rape, and drugs, with robbery being remarkably stable.

For all crimes and for total crime, the offender rates for juveniles were always higher than for adults. Overall, the difference by the end of the observation is a factor of a little over 2. Some stark differences emerge for the different crimes: juveniles are five to six times more often involved in robbery than adults, for theft their involvement is about four-fold greater, but for drugs the difference is much smaller.

Conviction rates

Conviction rates for juveniles and adults mirror the offender rates in the sense that where juveniles are more often involved in crime, they are much less convicted. The trends in conviction rates of juveniles and adults look fairly similar in the sense that they show the same humps and dips. However, those for juveniles increased from 13% in 1995 to 21% in 2010; those for adults start and end at the same rate of 45%. All in all, this is a fairly major change: at the beginning of our observation period juveniles were convicted 0.29 times as often as adults, or only a third of the rate; by the end of that period their relative conviction rate was 47%, or almost half (see Figure 2.2a).

For rape, juveniles as well as adults were convicted at the same rate, and their trends are almost identical (Figure 2.2b). For robbery (Figure 2.2c) the rates increased slightly for both juveniles and adults. For theft (Figure 2.2d), juvenile

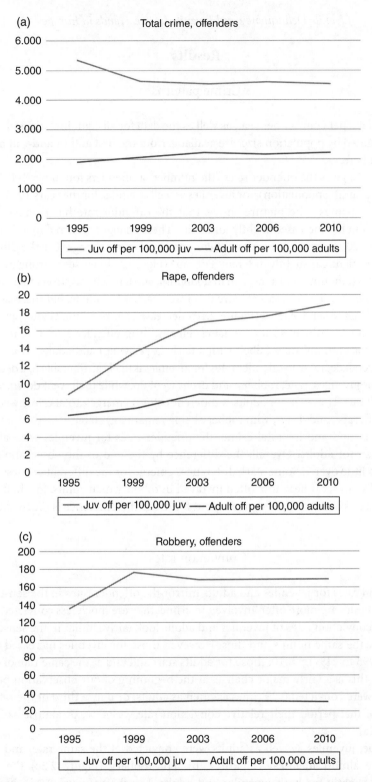

Figure 2.1 Offender rates (offenders found per 100,000 of the corresponding population), for juveniles as well as adults, for the years 1995–2010. (a) Total crime; (b) rape; (c) robbery; (d) theft; (e) drugs.

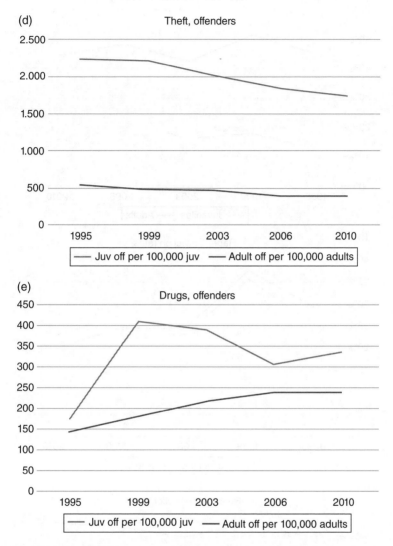

(d) Theft, offenders

(e) Drugs, offenders

Figure 2.1   (*Continued*)

conviction rates increased from 13% to 18%; those for adults increased as well although not as strongly. For drugs (Figure 2.2e), no clear trend is discernible, for juveniles nor for adults.

Again, it appears as if the key, or at least a partial key, to the increase over time in overall conviction rates for juveniles may lie in their increased levels of conviction for theft.

Imprisonment rates

Overall, imprisonment rates for juveniles have decreased (from 25 per 100,000 juveniles in 1995 to 16 per 100,000 in 2010). There are strong swings (a high of 32 per 100,000 in 2003). For adults, the imprisonment rate is almost four times as high, and

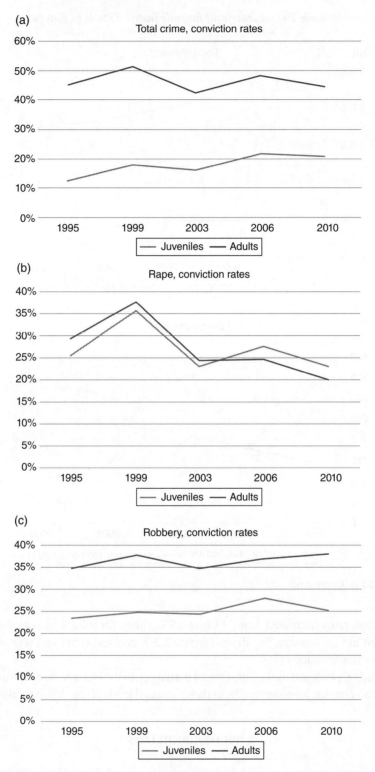

Figure 2.2 Total conviction rates for the years 1995–2010. (a) Total crime; (b) rape; (c) robbery; (d) theft; (e) drugs.

Figure 2.2 (*Continued*)

has increased modestly (see Figure 2.3a). As we saw above, juveniles' crime rates are higher (almost double), but their conviction rates lower (about half). Thus, the imprisonment rate is a fairly singular measure of the lesser extent to which juveniles are committed to prison (about a quarter of adults).

Punitivity

Overall, punitivity trends are different for adults and juveniles (Figure 2.3b). While those for juveniles have decreased (and in fact more than halved) since 1995, those for adults have stayed almost the same (with some fluctuations).

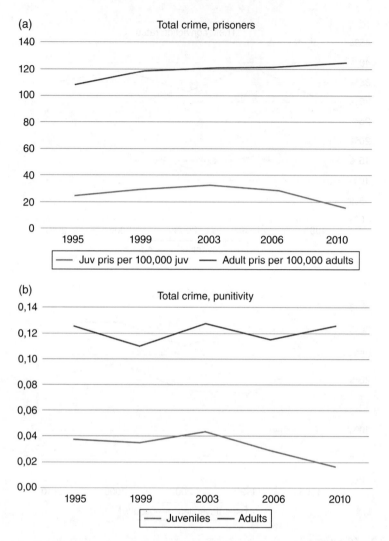

Figure 2.3   (a) Total imprisonment rates (per 100,000 of the corresponding population), for juveniles as well as adults, for the years 1995–2010. (b) Punitivity rates over the same time period, measured by Δ/Σ as explained in the text.

Conclusion

Our analyses showed firstly that the offender rate for juveniles has decreased. We argued that part of this decrease is likely due to their decreased involvement in theft. Violent crime involvement over the same period is up. Juveniles are still involved in crime almost twice as often as adults.

Juveniles are convicted much less often than adults, but the difference has decreased strongly. It appears therefore that policies of restraint when it comes to the conviction of juveniles – which may be due to higher levels of dismissal and higher levels of extrajudicial responses – have waned.

Imprisonment is still only sparingly imposed on juveniles compared with adults. In addition, our analyses of the punitivity measure show that when juvenile imprisonment is imposed, sentences tend to be shorter too. Differences between adults and juveniles have increased over the years.

All in all, we see that with decreasing offender rates for juveniles – a composite measure built from increasing rates of violent crime and decreasing rates of much more common property crimes – conviction rates are going up, reflecting a trend towards more judicial responses towards juvenile norm transgressions. At the same time, our analyses show that these convictions less often lead to imprisonment, and therefore probably increasing parajudicial responses, such as community sanctions or treatment. In the European countries that we studied, we see that when it comes to dealing with juvenile offending, CJS responses are increasingly called for, while custodial sanctions are imposed increasingly less often, and if so, for shorter periods.

Notes

1 Not the imposed sentence, but the actual time spent in prison. This is almost always shorter due to early release or pardon.

2 The number of prisoners at a certain point in time (Δ) is determined by two factors: the number of prison sentences (Pris) and the actual length of the executed punishment (Λ). Or: Δ is proportional to the product of Pris and Λ. Therefore:

$$\Delta \approx \text{Pris} * \Lambda \tag{1}$$

The first factor, the number of prison sentences, is also dependent on two factors, namely the number of convicted offenders (Σ) and the percentage of prison sentences within the convictions (Π). Therefore:

$$\text{Pris} = \Pi * \Sigma \tag{2}$$

And from (1) and (2) it follows that:

$$\Delta \approx \Pi * \Sigma * \Lambda \tag{3}$$

If we now divide the number of prisoners by the number of convicted persons, the result will be the combination of the percentage of prison sentences of the convictions and the length of the executed punishment. Immediately from (3) it follows that:

$$\Delta / \Sigma \approx \Pi * \Lambda \tag{4}$$

This may be an indication of punitivity in a country. To put it briefly: a high outcome is a sign of many and/or long prison sentences.

3 In almost all countries the starting age for being considered an adult is 18 years. The minimum age for criminal responsibility (as a juvenile) is more diverse, although 12 years is often found.

4 For the three main indicators only, the population figures did not have any missing data.

References

Aebi, M.F., Aromaa, K., Aubusson de Cavarlay, B., Barclay, G., Gruszczyñska, B., von Hofer, H., … Tavares, C. (2006). *European Sourcebook of Crime and Criminal Justice Statistics*, 3rd Ed. Den Haag: Boom Juridische Uitgevers, Reeks Onderzoek en Beleid, no. 241.

Aebi, M.F., Aromaa, K., Aubusson de Cavarlay, B., Barclay, G., Gruszczyñska, B., Harrendorf, S., … Þórisdóttir, R. (2010). *European Sourcebook of Crime and Criminal Justice Statistics*, 4th Ed. Den Haag: Boom Juridische Uitgevers, Reeks Onderzoek en Beleid, no. 285.

Aebi, M.F., Akdenik, G., Barclay, G., Campistol, C., Caneppele, S., Gruszczyñska, B., … Þórisdóttir, R. (2014). *European Sourcebook of Crime and Criminal Justice Statistics*, 5th Ed. Helsinki: HEUNI, Publication Series No. 80.

Council of Europe. (1999). *European Sourcebook of Crime and Criminal Justice Statistics*. Strasbourg: Council of Europe PC-S-ST (99) 8 DEF.

Eurostat. (2013). *Eurostat database*. Retrieved from http://epp.eurostat.ec.europa.eu/portal/page/portal/population/data/database/

Harrendorf, S., & Smit, P. (2010). Chapter 6: Resources, performance and punitivity. In Harrendorf, S., *et al.* (Eds.), *International Statistics on Crime and Justice*. Helsinki: HEUNI publication series no. 64, pp. 113–151.

Killias, M., *et al.* (2003). *European Sourcebook of Crime and Criminal Justice Statistics*, 2nd ed. Den Haag: Boom Juridische Uitgevers, Reeks Onderzoek en Beleid, no. 212.

Smit, P., van Eijk, A., & Decae, R. (2012). Trends in the reaction on crime in Criminal Justice Systems in Europe in 1990–2007: a comparison of 4 European regions. *European Journal on Criminal Policy and Research, 18,* 55–82.

UNODC. (2013). *United Nations Surveys on Crime Trends and the Operations of Criminal Justice Systems*. Retrieved from http://www.unodc.org/unodc/en/data-and-analysis/United-Nations-Surveys-on-Crime-Trends-and-the-Operations-of-Criminal-Justice-Systems.html

3

Youth Violence in Brazil: Law, Prevalence, and Promising Initiatives

Paulo Ricardo Diniz Filho and Giza Lopes

Introduction

In the 1980s, a decade marked by the restoration of the democratic regime in Brazil and by a persistent economic instability, crime rates increased significantly in the country, foretelling a pattern that continues today. Zaluar (2007) argued that the 20 years of military dictatorship (1964–1985) virtually eliminated a tradition of warmth in interpersonal relationships, which customarily led individuals to avoid conflict and to seek compromise-based solutions. Brazil's rapid urbanization and the large number of people living in city slums also contributed to the development toward a clear picture of social maladjustment, of which urban violence in general – and youth violence in particular – are the most evident expressions.

As a response to this sharp increase in violence, several research centers dedicated to understanding different aspects of the phenomenon emerged at universities and at non-governmental organizations (hereafter, NGOs) in the 1990s. The analyses generated by these centers, in addition to findings by international researchers, informed the first structured plans of violence prevention implemented by the Brazilian government in the early 2000s (Soares, 2007; see, for instance, the National Public Safety Plans launched in 2000 and 2003, and the 2007 National Program of Public Safety and Citizenship).

It was within this context of both political and activist-based attempts to deal with increasing overall crime rates that Brazil radically restructured its legal approach to delinquency and youth violence. In this chapter, we summarize this legal shift, provide a profile of youth crime and victimization in Brazil, and outline innovative and promising programs focused on the prevention of youth violence.[1]

The Handbook of Juvenile Delinquency and Juvenile Justice, First Edition. Edited by Marvin D. Krohn and Jodi Lane.
© 2015 John Wiley & Sons, Inc. Published 2015 by John Wiley & Sons, Inc.

We conclude by elucidating a few of the barriers to the successful implementation of crime prevention initiatives in the country.

Delinquency and Justice in Brazil: Legal Context and Formal Procedures for Juveniles

Prompted by the guidelines set forth by the United Nations' Convention on the Rights of the Child in 1989, many Latin American countries have since revised their legal systems to respond to the needs of juvenile offenders. Brazil took the lead with the passage of its progressive Statute for Children and Adolescents ("Estatuto da Criança e do Adolescente"; hereafter, SCA) in 1990, two years after the promulgation of the Brazilian Constitution that replaced the 1967 undemocratic charter (Presidência da República, 1990). The SCA was adopted, in part, as a response to international and domestic objections to increasing violence against street children by "death squads" – self-appointed vigilante groups made up of off-duty policemen.[2]

Prior to the passage of the SCA, the law in effect – the 1979 Code for Minors or "Código de Menores" – was widely recognized as a repressive tool and a means "for the wholesale [confinement] of poor youth, often for nothing more than 'vagrancy'" (Hoffman, 1994). The SCA radically reformed the legal status of children, redefined the responsibilities of the State and civil society, and mandated the creation of oversight councils at the federal, state and local levels. It also instituted a "doctrine of full protection"[3] in lieu of the punitive character of previous laws (Adorno *et al.*, 1999). Most importantly, the SCA, in tandem with the country's Penal Code (1940), outlined the rights and freedoms of juveniles in conflict with the law, as well as the age of legal responsibility (18), whereas delinquent children under the age of 12 are treated as children in need of protection.

Rights, procedures, and the law in practice

Brazilian children and adolescents who commit an "infraction" (i.e., behavior that would constitute crime or misdemeanor for adults)[4] are legally afforded a series of protective measures such as foster home or institutional placement, school enrollment, as well as drug, medical or psychiatric treatment (SCA Article 101). The same rights to due process granted to adult offenders are by law extended to juveniles, namely, the right to remain silent; to be formally informed of the infraction of which s/he is accused; to be assisted by an attorney (free legal assistance is provided when the offender is indigent); to confront victims/witnesses; to be personally heard during judicial proceedings; and to request the presence of parents/legal guardian at any point of the process (SCA Article 111). At all stages of legal processing, from police apprehension, the prosecutor's decision to bring charges, and judicial proceedings, children and adolescents are to be processed by specialized personnel, and if temporary or lasting confinement is required, youth, in principle, should be kept separate from older adults.[5]

Once arrested, individuals under the age of 18 should be released to a parent or a responsible adult. The SCA also specifies that detention of juveniles should be used as a last resort and only for the shortest appropriate period of time. Instead, alternatives to incarceration, particularly "socio-educational measures", aimed at the rehabilitation of youth and reintegration into the family and community, are prescribed. These include: warnings;[6] redress of harm caused to the victim;[7] community service;[8] probation;[9] partial deprivation of liberty;[10] and deprivation of liberty in an educational institution.[11] The institutions in charge of dealing with youth who commit infractions are not related to the criminal justice system *per se*. Instead, to achieve their rehabilitative goals, they draw on resources from social services agencies, NGOs, and others.

Despite the SCA's well-intentioned provisions, implementation of the rights and safeguard procedures outlined by the law currently is far from ideal. In a recent report on juvenile justice and human rights in the Americas, the Organization of American States (2011; hereafter OAS) identified the following inconsistencies between the stated legal rights of minors in conflict with the law and its practice in Brazil. First, due to a total absence of public defenders' offices in certain districts, or insufficient numbers of such attorneys in others, legal proceedings are often conducted without defense counsel present. This is also the case in earlier stages of the judicial process; even though the SCA prescribes the presence of counsel at police inquiries, children and adolescents are frequently interrogated with no legal support.

In contrast to SCA's mandate that deprivation of liberty be used sparingly and for the shortest time possible, the OAS found that most juvenile justice systems in the Americas generally resort to this measure both before trial and after conviction – and Brazil is no exception. The rehabilitative goals of socio-educational measures are also systemically jeopardized; the failure to put into practice educational and vocational training programs results in Brazilian youth remaining idle in the "educational detention facilities" where they reside. Besides idleness, living conditions in these facilities are far from adequate – insufficient food, overcrowding, precarious health conditions and substandard medical care, and (violent) mistreatment by guards have been widely documented (see also Bochenek & Delgado, 2006; Human Rights Watch, 2004). To avoid such conditions, juveniles have been known to lie about their age in an attempt to serve time in adult prisons instead of youth facilities (Martins, 2003).

Demographics and Behavior: A Profile of Delinquency and Youth Crime and Victimization in Brazil

Brazil has a population of 190,732,694 inhabitants, and half of them earn less than US$2,500.00 per year (Instituto Brasileiro de Geografia e Estatística, 2010). Roughly a third of Brazilians are children and adolescents: 18.7% are younger than 11; 12.6% are aged from 12 to 18. Due to advances in the implementation of a universal, free public health system, as well as reductions in extreme poverty and improvements of living conditions in urban areas, natural deaths of children and adolescents in Brazil

Table 3.1 Youth homicide rates in Brazil by age group (per 100,000 population)

Age	Year		% change
	2000	*2010*	
0	2.4	2.7	13.8
1	0.8	1.2	36.0
2	0.8	1.0	20.4
3	0.9	0.8	−9.4
4	0.7	0.8	7.6
5	0.7	0.6	−20.1
6	0.5	0.7	36.2
7	0.5	0.7	30.1
8	0.9	0.7	−18.7
9	0.8	0.8	5.2
10	1.1	0.9	−11.9
11	1.4	1.4	0.2
12	1.5	1.8	15.1
13	3.3	4.9	46.4
14	8.7	9.8	13.1
15	16.7	22.2	32.9
16	28.9	37.0	28.1
17	44.2	52.5	18.8
18	51.8	58.2	12.4
19	60.4	60.3	−0.1
0–19	11.9	13.8	15.8

Source: Waiselfisz (2012).

have decreased significantly in the last 30 years: from 387.1 deaths per 100,000 population in 1980 to 88.5 per 100,000 population in 2010 (Waiselfisz, 2012). In contrast, youth death rates due to external causes, which include homicide, suicide, and accidents, increased from 27.9 per 100,000 inhabitants to 31.9 in the same period. Most significantly, between 1980 and 2010, homicide became the top cause of death for those under the age of 19, increasing from 0.7% to 11.5% of all deaths registered (Waiselfisz, 2012).

According to a 2009 study of 92 countries, Brazil had the fourth highest homicide rate among those under 19 years of age (13 per 100,000 population) (Waiselfisz, 2012). El Salvador led the ranking with 18 per 100,000 (Waiselfisz, 2012). However, rates vary within Brazil; in 2010, nine of the 27 Brazilian states had rates higher than those of El Salvador and four had populations larger than that country. Table 3.1 shows a detailed age distribution of victims of youth homicide in Brazil.

The data in Table 3.1 show a marked increase in youth homicide at age 13 as well as a greater rate variation between 2000 and 2010 for those aged 18 and younger. Most victims are male; between 2000 and 2010, female victims ranged from 9% to 10.7% of the total number of homicides (Weiselfisz, 2010).

With regard to victims' race, in 2002 the number of young Afro-descendent homicide victims was 71.1% higher than whites. This disparity increased to 108.6% in 2006 and, in 2010, it reached 153.9%. This overall disproportionate homicide victimization of young Afro-descendents seems negligible when compared with that seen in certain states. For instance, in Alagoas, the proportion is 20 Afro-descendent victims to each white one, and in Paraíba, 19 to 1. In eight states, homicide rates of young Afro-descendent men surpassed the mark of 100 per 100,000 population, reaching 173.1 per 100,000 in Alagoas. In addition, six Brazilian cities have male Afro-descendent youth homicide rates of over 300 per 100,000 (Weiselfisz, 2012). Among White youth, the highest rate is 83.5 per 100,000 in the state of Paraná.

The health service in Brazil, from where the data above originate, is structured as a single system, universal and gratis. Thus, data such as these are typically readily accessible and reasonably reliable.[12] Studies of youth as perpetrators of non-homicidal violence, on the other hand, are much more variable in quality because they are contingent on the accuracy of information maintained by different branches of police in 27 states. Lack of centralization of these data, poor training, and manipulation of statistics are but a few of the obstacles to analysis (Hinton & Newburn, 2008). Therefore, in this chapter we refer to isolated studies on the topic in an attempt to provide a global view of the problem.

According to the national System of Penitentiary Information (INFOPEN, 2012), maintained by the country's Ministry of Justice, the incarcerated population in Brazil totaled 508,357 in mid-2012.[13] Nearly 95% of those behind bars in Brazil are male and 27% of them are young (18 to 24 years old). Accordingly, those in this age group also commit most of the following crimes: homicide (17.56 per 100,000 population), aggravated assault (387.74 per 100,000 population), attempted homicide (22.32 per 100,000 population), kidnapping and extortion (0.34 per 100,000 population), theft (218.23 per 100,000 population), motor vehicle theft (20.24 per 100,000 population), rape (14.57 per 100,000 population), and possession and use of drugs (41.96 per 100,000 population) (Paiva, Ribeiro, & Silva, 2009).

With regard to those under 18 years of age, the nature of the rehabilitative goals set forth by the SCA means that the institutions carrying out the adjudication of minors are often managed by municipal or State governments, or even by non-profit organizations, without the existence of a uniform administrative unit (ILANUD, 2007). Therefore, comprehensive and accurate data on children and adolescents who are "in conflict with the law" are difficult to obtain.

A study conducted in 2002 by the Brazilian Ministry of Health found that 76% of the children and adolescents who were housed in residential facilities were between 16 and 18 years of age, 87% had not completed primary school,[14] and 51% had dropped out of school when they committed the infraction that landed them in the detention center (Ministério da Saúde, 2005). Regarding the nature of the infractions committed by these children and adolescents, 29.6% were housed for committing robbery, 18.6% for homicide, 14.0% for theft, and 8.7% for drug trafficking. The Ministry of Health also found that, in the year 2000, guns were used in 74% of the homicides committed by youth between 15 and 19 years of age, up from 55.7% in 1991. In addition, according to the 2011 Brazilian Yearbook on Public Safety (FBSP, 2011), the number of children and adolescents sentenced to socio-educational corrective measures in detention centers were as shown in Table 3.2.

In 2006, the United Nations Latin American Institute for the Prevention of Crime and Treatment of Offenders (ILANUD, 2007) estimated that 40,356 juveniles were under socio-educational correction measures in Brazil. This figure includes incarcerated youth (i.e., 15.8% in detention centers full-time and 10% in "partial deprivation of liberty" programs), as well as those serving partially restrictive sentences (i.e., 42.8% in juvenile probation and 24.5% in community service). Table 3.3 shows a breakdown of infractions committed by juveniles in state capital cities in 2006.

Finally, Table 3.4 breaks down into age groups the number of juvenile delinquents under socio-educational corrective measures in Brazil in 2007.

A comparison of Tables 3.1 and 3.4 shows a sharp increase in violence involving youth at age 15 as victims and offenders. However, youth between 18 and 19 years of age seem to be the most victimized group, whereas those between 16 and 17 years of age commit most of the violent infractions. The penal system considers the age of the individual at the time when the offense happened for the purpose of defining juvenile status. According to Leal (1996), in recent years there has been growing

Table 3.2 Number and rates of detained youth in Brazil, by sentence type

Type of sentence	*Year*			
	2007	*2008*	*2009*	*2010*
Detention	11,443	11,734	11,901	12,041
Pre-trial detention[15]	3,852	3,715	3,471	3,934
Partial deprivation of liberty	1,214	1,419	1,568	1,728
Total	16,509	16,868	16,940	17,703
Rate per 100,000	81.3	84.3	85.1	85.66

Source: FBSP (2011).

Table 3.3 Socio-educational correction measures and "infractions" committed by juveniles in Brazilian capitals, 2006

Type of corrective measure	*Type of infraction*			
	Property	*Violent*	*Drug-related*	*Others*
Community service	63.1%	14.2%	5.9%	16.8%
Probation	66.6%	10.7%	12.9%	9.9%
Community service and probation	76.2%	7.0%	9.2%	7.6%
Partial deprivation of liberty	73.5%	5.9%	15.7%	4.9%
Detention	68.8%	15.3%	13.4%	2.4%
Redress of harm to victim	60.0%	20.0%	6.7%	13.3%

Source: ILANUD (2007).

Table 3.4   Age of juvenile delinquents receiving "socio-educational corrective measures" in Brazil, 2007

Age (in years)	%
11 and under	0.2
12 to 15	17.6
16 to 17	44.0
18 to 21	34.5
22 and older	0.4
No data	3.4

Source: ILANUD (2007).

popular pressure to reduce to 16 years the age of criminal responsibility. Indeed, a recent poll conducted by the Brazilian Institute of Public Opinion and Statistics (CNI-IBOPE, 2011) indicates that 75% of those surveyed "fully support" reducing to 16 years the age of criminal responsibility (another 11% support the change "in part"). Sixteen is also when Brazilians become eligible to vote.

Youth Violence Prevention in Brazil: Innovative and Promising Programs

Governmental control of the lion's share of Brazil's financial resources falls under the auspices of the federal government. The complex, federated system inaugurated by the 1988 Constitution, however, means that a great number of tasks are actually delegated to the municipal governments for implementation. Between these two levels are the State governments, which are the main parties responsible for managing public safety and criminal justice in Brazil (Diniz Filho, 2006). As a result, even though the Federal government is the political sphere best equipped economically and technically, its role is very limited. Instead, strategies for action on a national scale can occur only indirectly, through the transfer of federal resources to State and local governments, or through the provision of standardized guidelines for action, sponsored by the Federal government and executed by these other entities.

A few states have implemented experimental approaches to violence prevention, mostly focusing on the mitigation of risk factors (e.g., lack of access to education and employment, fragile family units, drug use, etc.) (Branco, 2002). While this approach does not fit well with the electoral interests of Brazilian politicians (Soares, 2000), it has made some strides in the country (Gonçalves de Assis & Constantino, 2005) and two pioneering experiments stood out in the 1990s. First, in 1996, NGOs, local government leaders and residents of a neighborhood in São Paulo (Jardim Ângela), mobilized to create and implement community policing centers (Zacchi, 2002). Second, in 1999, an attempt to reformulate the police force was put in place in Rio de Janeiro State through investments in training, technological improvement and anti-corruption measures (Cerqueira & Lobão, 2004). Although both initiatives showed positive results at first, they ultimately failed either because the outcomes could not be reproduced elsewhere or because they lacked political support.

A recent survey identified a total of 109 violence prevention programs in Brazil – 31 were related to educational activities while the remaining focused primarily on family, community policing and revitalization, drug use prevention, and access to employment (Ministério da Saúde, 2005). In addition, especially promising are a number of youth-centered mediation and conferencing projects throughout the country that incorporate the philosophy and principles of restorative justice (United Nations Office on Drugs and Crime, 2006). Porto Alegre, a southern metropolitan area, is currently piloting this approach and a few schools in São Paulo State have also adopted it as an alternative resolution to petty offenses, gang conflict, robbery, and rape (Prudente, 2008).

Violence prevention programs in Brazil vary in size substantially, serving between 100 and 2,000 people in 2005 (Paiva, Ribeiro, & Silva, 2009). Unfortunately, these programs for the most part have not been systematically evaluated (Gonçalves de Assis & Constantino, 2005). Here we choose to mention the most promising and highly innovative measures implemented by one Brazilian state – Minas Gerais.

With 20.5 million inhabitants, Minas Gerais has the second largest population among the 27 states, houses the third largest metropolitan area in the country, and is ranked third among states in gross domestic product. Even though (by Brazilian standards) Minas Gerais has never had high violence rates, in the past decade the state government has put into practice several measures targeting violence prevention. Especially remarkable, however, have been the policies of violence prevention targeting youth, which at once represented considerable levels of innovation and financial expenditures for a developing nation. Minas Gerais' government has developed three programs focusing on youth violence prevention; two of them are executed by social services agencies and another implemented by the Office of Public Safety of Minas Gerais State. The three programs mainly focus on the social inclusion of at-risk youth.

Implemented in 2003, the "Fica Vivo!"[16] program seeks to reduce homicide rates by reducing opportunities for youth from shantytowns and peripheral neighborhoods to become involved in criminal activity. "Fica Vivo!" operates as a two-tiered community policing program, including both social programs and police efforts. The program creates leisure and work training opportunities for at-risk youth to reduce unstructured time in which they might find themselves on the streets. It also seeks to create local capacity to engage with the police and other state institutions to improve policy implementation, and builds localized integrated criminal justice responses to target the organizations that promote criminal activities in highly violent urban areas (Alves & Arias, 2011). The program targets youth between 12 and 24 years of age who reside in regions with the highest violence rates in the State. By 2012, 39 "Centers of Crime Prevention" had been created in Minas Gerais, serving on average 13,000 youth. The Centers develop cultural activities, sports, and vocational training (SEDS, 2012). An evaluation of crime in the region where "Fica Vivo!" was first developed showed a reduction of 69% in the total number of homicides (Beato Filho, Assunção, & Silveira, 2010).

Another program, the "Plug Minas", began in 2008 and connects a series of actions previously implemented statewide in the area of arts and culture to new actions in the fields of entrepreneurship, languages, and digital and multimedia training. Targeting 14–24 year olds, "Plug Minas" seeks to bolster the self-esteem of adolescents and young adults while better preparing them for employment. 18,000 youth were enrolled in the program in 2012 (Centro de Formação e Experimentação Digital, 2013). Especially noteworthy are the program's activities related to cutting-edge technology, such as the development of video games (Servas, 2011).

Finally, the Youth Savings ("Poupança Jovem") program, in place since 2007, primarily aims at decreasing high school drop-out rates and improving academic performance by awarding US$1,500 to participants who excel in school. The financial incentive is not merely intended to motivate or reward students; it seeks to provide them with the wherewithal to begin a professional career. For instance, there are reports of youth who consolidated their awards to open a small business. Seventy-six thousand young men and women from nine cities and 181 schools have been enrolled in the program, resulting in a cost of US$25 million in assistance to those who met its goals (SEDESE, 2012). As with the other two programs mentioned above, a systematic, comprehensive evaluation of this program is still ongoing.

Conclusion

Over the past 30 years, the linked phenomena of youth violence and juvenile justice in Brazil have undergone profound transformations. Such changes can be observed not only in criminal statistics and trends, but also in the volume of research conducted on the theme, in paradigm shifts in the field of public safety, and in the programmatic actions taken by the State. Because these changes were implemented at different time points in the country's recent history, only now have they begun to show combined effects. Therefore, although it is still too early to outline a clearly defined picture of safety in Brazil, it is possible to forecast the trends in place for the near future.

As we pointed out, there are few evaluative studies about the efficiency of the youth violence preventative programs currently available in Brazil. At the same time, youth violence rates continue to increase, despite the economic improvement experienced in Brazil in recent years. The proliferation of government actions – at Federal, State, and municipal levels – in the past few years indicates that the prevention of youth violence has become increasingly important in the Brazilian political agenda.

That said, the country has yet to overcome significant barriers to fully implement an efficient and rights-based juvenile justice system. For the most part police action in Brazil is still very close to the practices in place during the military dictatorship. Largely based on the use of force (Branco, 2002; Soares, 2000, 2007), "zero-tolerance" practices have permeated Brazil's culture in such a profound way that most citizens tacitly approve police abuse as a legitimate resource to maintain public safety (Zaluar, 2007). Although shifts in this philosophy have gained momentum in the past decade, particularly with attempts at "community policing" in the slums, a paradigm equating police aggression to efficiency is still predominant and this style of policing extends to supervision of youth (see Ungar, 2009).

In addition to the abusive use of force, other factors such as police corruption, the poor condition of detention facilities, extreme economic inequality, and a lack of coordination between the levels of government in tackling crime and violence contribute to the difficulties in meeting the ideals set forth by the SCA. These roadblocks were made apparent in 2006 in São Paulo, when gang-led riots originating in adult prisons quickly spilled over into youth detention centers and onto the streets. Such challenges suggest it is too soon to discuss the "beginning of the end" of youth crime and violence in Brazil. However, the newer trends and efforts towards prevention implemented in the past decade and discussed above allow us to borrow Sir Winston Churchill's expression and assert that one can now see the "end of the beginning" of this widespread problem.

Notes

1   Because most programmatic actions in the field of violence prevention in Brazil focus on populations between 12 and 24 years of age, in providing the data on youth violence we give equal attention to "minors" and those aged between 18 and 24.

2   The issue of death squads captured the attention of NGOs worldwide, as well as of several leaders, including Pope John Paul II. During his visit to Brazil in 1991, he declared: "there cannot and should not be children assassinated and eliminated on the pretext of preventing crime" (Cowell, 1991). Brazil has the largest Catholic population in the world.

3   This doctrine highlights the necessity and duty to address situations of irregularity such as abandoned and abused children, representing a significant advance in the discourse and actions pertaining to the rights of children from previous patriarchal–authoritative models which portrayed such children as threats to National Security to whom punishment and surveillance-based actions were applied as "corrective measures" and forms of social control.

4   The implementation of the SCA inaugurated the use of new terminologies aimed at avoiding the association between youth's self-concept and crime. Therefore, terms like *infraction, infractor* and *minor in conflict with the law* have replaced the traditional crime-related jargon in reference to unlawful actions committed by those under 18.

5   Juvenile detention centers in Brazil may hold both adolescents and young adults up to the age of 21 (SCA Articles 2 and 121).

6   Warnings are imposed by a judge, in a formal hearing where the adolescent, his/her parents or guardian, the prosecutor and the youth's attorney are present.

7   In cases of exclusive property damage, youth may be obliged to redress or compensate the victim for his/her financial loss.

8   Community service cannot take place for longer than six months and for a maximum of eight hours per week. Youth in these situations engage in supervised tasks in schools, hospitals, social services institutions, community programs, and so on. The tasks cannot interfere with school attendance and/or youth's paid employment.

9   The purpose of probation is to provide the youth with assistance and monitoring of school access, employment, and so on.

10   In these cases, the youth are allowed to attend school and/or report to work outside a detention facility, but must spend the night in confinement at the designated detention center. It is limited to three years, with periodic assessments to evaluate the youth's progress.

11   By law, detention is to be used sparingly and limited to three years, with mandatory revisions every six months. Acts of violence or grave threat, recidivism of serious infractions, and/or repeated disobedience of other socio-educational measures automatically warrant detention (Serro, Morais, & Alves, 2012).

12   Due to the difficulty in hiding bodies, homicide statistics are generally considered the most reliable indicator of violent crime rates. In Brazil, however, researchers have found substantial discrepancies between data provided by police and those kept by the Ministry of Health (Hinton & Newburn, 2008). In this chapter, data shown are as recorded by the country's Health Ministry.

13   This number includes pre-trial detention and those who have been sentenced.

14   "Primary school" in Brazil includes the first nine years of compulsory education. It begins in kindergarten and ends when children are 13 or 14 years of age, thus corresponding to the 8th Grade in the US educational system.

15   By law, pre-trial detention should not surpass 45 days.

16   Literally, "Fica Vivo!" means "Stay Alive!", but in Portuguese the expression also connotes "Stay Alert!/Be Smart!".

References

Adorno, S., Bordini, E.B.T., & de Lima, R.S. (1999). O adolescente e as mudanças na criminalidade urbana. *São Paulo Em Perspectiva, 13*(4), 62–74. doi:10.1590/S0102-88391999000400007

Alves, M.C., & Arias, E.D. (2011). Understanding the *Fica Vivo* programme: two-tiered community policing in Belo Horizonte, Brazil. *Policing and Society, 22*(1), 101–113.

Beato Filho, C.C., Assunção, R.M., & Silveira, A.M. (2010). Impacto do programa Fica Vivo na redução dos homicídios em comunidade de Belo Horizonte. *Revista de Saúde Pública, 4*(3), 496–502.

Bochenek, M., & Delgado, F. (2006). Children in custody in Brazil. *The Lancet, 367*(9511), 696–697.

Branco, A.C.C. (2002). Prevenção primária, polícia e democracia. In Gabinete de Segurança Institucional, *Das políticas de segurança pública às políticas públicas de segurança* (pp. 77–88). Brasília: Presidência da República.

Centro de Formação e Experimentação Digital. (2013). Plug minas: metas. *Plug minas.* Retrieved from http://www.plugminas.mg.gov.br/#!/pages/metas

Cerqueira, D., & Lobão, W. (2004). Criminalidade, ambiente socioeconômico e polícia: desafios para os governos. *Revista de Administração Pública, 38*(3), 371–399.

CNI-IBOPE. (2011). *Retratos da sociedade brasileira: segurança pública.* Brasilia: CNI.

Cowell, A. (1991). Protect children, Pope tells Brazil: John Paul laments the fate of the poor and the forsaken. *New York Times,* 21 October, p. A7.

Diniz Filho, P.R. (2006). *Federalismo, indução estadual e cooperação intermunicipal: a experiência de dois consórcios intermunicipais de saúde de Minas Gerais.* Belo Horizonte: Programa de Pós-Graduação em Ciências Sociais PUC-Minas.

FBSP. (2011). *Anuário Brasileiro de Segurança Pública 2011.* São Paulo: Fórum Brasileiro de Segurança Pública.

Gonçalves de Assis, S., & Constantino, P. (2005). Perspectives on the prevention of male juvenile delinquency. *Ciência & Saúde Coletiva, 10* (1), 81–90. doi:10.1590/S1413-81232005000100014

Hinton, M.S., & Newburn, T. (2008). *Policing Developing Democracies.* New Jersey: Routledge.

Hoffman, D. (1994). *The Struggle for Citizenship and Human Rights.* New York: North American Congress on Latin America. Retrieved from http://pangaea.org/street_children/latin/statute.htm

Human Rights Watch. (2004). *"Real Dungeons:" Juvenile Detention in the State of Rio de Janeiro.* Retrieved from http://www.unhcr.org/refworld/docid/42c3bcec0.html

ILANUD. (2007). *Mapeamento nacional de medidas socioeducativas em meio aberto.* Brasília: Instituto Latino-Americano das Nações Unidas para a prevenção do delito e tratamento do delinqüente.

INFOPEN. (2012). Sistema de Informações Penitenciárias. Retrieved from http://portal. mj.gov.br/main.asp?view={d574e9ce-3c7d-437a-a5b6-22166ad2e896}&team=&params= itemid={c37b2ae9-4c68-4006-8b16-24d28407509c};&uipartuid={2868ba3c-1c72-4347-be11-a26f70f4cb26}

Instituto Brasileiro de Geografia e Estatística (2010). Brazil 2010 Census. Retrieved from http://www.ibge.gov.br/english/presidencia/noticias/noticia_visualiza.php?id_noticia=1766

Leal, C.B. (1996). Brazil. In D.J. Shoemaker (Ed.), *International Handbook on Juvenile Justice* (pp. 20–33). Westport, CT: Greenwood Publishing Group.

Martins, M.A. (2003). Território livre da tortura: jovens mentem sobre idade e preferem presídios a internatos do estado. *Jornal do brasil,* 21 September. Retrieved from http://jbonline.terra.com.br/jb.papel/cidade/2003/09/20/jorcid20030920001.html

Ministério da Saúde (2005). *Impacto da violência na saúde dos brasileiros.* Brasília: Ministério da Saúde.

Organization of American States (2011). *Juvenile Justice and Human Rights in the Americas.* Retrieved from http://www.cidh.org

Paiva, A.B., Ribeiro, J.A., & Silva, J.R. (2009). Jovens: morbimortalidade, fatores de risco e políticas de saúde. In J.A. Castro, L.M.C. Aquino, & C.C. Andrade (Eds.), *Juventude e políticas sociais no brasil.* Brasília: IPEA.

Presidência da República. (1990) Estatuto da Criança e do Adolescente, Pub. L. No. 8.069/90.

Prudente, N.M. (2008). Justiça Restaurativa em Debate: Justiça Restaurativa nas Escolas de Porto Alegre: desafios e perspectivas. *Justiça Restaurativa em Debate.* Retrieved from http://justi carestaurativaemdebate.blogspot.com/2008/11/justia-restaurativa-nas-escolas-de.html

SEDESE. (2012). Secretaria Estadual de Desenvolvimento Social. Retrieved from http://www. social.mg.gov.br

SEDS. (2012). *Programa Fica Vivo.* Belo Horizonte: Secretaria de Estado de Defesa Social.

Serro, D.L., Morais, D.T.B.M., & Alves, M.F.R.V. (2012). A aplicabilidade dos princípios e das garantias do processo penal ao direito processual penal juvenil. *Processus, 3*(7), 21–32.

Servas. (2011). *Relatório Plug Minas 2011.* Belo Horizonte: Serviço Voluntário de Assistência Social.

Soares, L.E. (2000). *Meu casaco de general.* Rio de Janeiro: Cia. das Letras.

Soares, L.E. (2007). A política nacional de segurança pública: histórico, dilemas e perspectivas. *Estudos Avançados, 26*(61), 77–97.

Ungar, M. (2009). Policing youth in Latin America. In G.A. Jones, & D. Rodgers (Eds.), *Youth Violence in Latin America: Gangs and Juvenile Justice in Perspective* (pp. 203–224). New York: Palgrave Macmillan.

United Nations Office on Drugs and Crime. (2006). *Handbook on Restorative Justice Programmes.* New York: United Nations.

Waiselfisz, J.J. (2012). *Mapa da violência 2012: crianças e adolescentes no Brasil.* Rio de Janeiro: Cebela/ Flacso.

Zacchi, J.M. (2002). Prevenção da violência: avanços e desafios na ordem do dia. In *Gabinete de Segurança Institucional, Das políticas de segurança pública às políticas públicas de segurança* (pp. 31–43). Brasília: Presidência da República.

Zaluar, A. (2007) Democratização inacabada: fracasso da segurança pública. *Estudos Avançados, 26*(61), 31–49.

4

Juvenile Justice in Russia

Elena Bystrova and Maria Tcherni

History and Evolution of the Law Governing
Juveniles and Juvenile Offending

The system of juvenile justice in Russia has a long history, dating back to Tsarist Russia. Major legal reforms took place during Tsar Alexander II's reign, when he revolutionized the criminal justice system. The Punishment Regulations of 1864 separated minors from adults for sentencing purposes, and special corrective shelters were built for minors. Still, punishment and incarceration had been the main approaches toward juveniles in Russia until the twentieth century. Such approaches did not improve juvenile crime rates and, in the early 1900s, education was introduced as part of the juvenile justice approach. The educational component was aimed at children between ages 10 and 17, and girls were to be taken care of by nuns (Hakvaag, 2009). By 1910, the system of juvenile courts was established, which launched the institution of guardianship. Sentencing tended towards placing children under the supervision of guardians instead of imprisonment (Roudik, 2007). The Communist Revolution of 1917 continued the process of a more rehabilitative approach in juvenile justice. In 1918, local Commissions on Juvenile Affairs were established that operated outside of the criminal justice system. Unfortunately, the initiative stayed mostly on paper for a long time, and by 1920, children between 14 and 18 who committed serious crimes were tried by regular courts (Hakvaag, 2009; Roudik, 2007).

The retributive approach was emphasized during Stalin's rule (1927–1953). The age of criminal responsibility was lowered from 14 to 12, the educational approach towards juveniles dropped, any exceptions for juveniles in sentencing procedures eliminated, and capital punishment of children widely used. Previously established

The Handbook of Juvenile Delinquency and Juvenile Justice, First Edition. Edited by Marvin D. Krohn and Jodi Lane.
© 2015 John Wiley & Sons, Inc. Published 2015 by John Wiley & Sons, Inc.

Commissions were abolished, and thus all juveniles were processed through the regular criminal justice system. Only after Stalin's death in 1953, did a softer approach towards juveniles return, with the reintroduction of the Commissions on Juvenile Affairs, and separation of first-time and repeat juvenile offenders in prisons. While juvenile courts were never reintroduced, juvenile cases were ordered to be tried by specially designated judges. One of the peculiar developments of the system at the time was the dual tracking system for juvenile cases: based on their severity, they were tried either by regular courts or by Commissions on Juvenile Affairs. The Commissions were never designed to be a part of the criminal justice system because they consisted of appointed officials who did not necessarily have a law degree but performed some judicial functions. Those initiatives were the basis of juvenile justice in the Soviet Union until its break-up and separation of Russia into an independent country in 1991 (Finckenauer, 1996; Terrill, 2009).

Russia's independence brought many changes. However, a separate system of juvenile justice was never established. New Criminal Code and Criminal Procedural Code were adopted in 1996 and 2001. These codes were supposed to guarantee the rights and freedoms of Russian citizens. Russia adopted several international documents regarding juveniles, including the Convention on the Rights of the Child. In 2003, the Plenum of the Supreme Court of the Russian Federation in its Recommendation "On the application of universally recognized international standards and norms by judges of general jurisdiction" affirmed that in case of a legal conflict between international laws and Russian laws, international norms would take precedence (Burnham, Maggs, & Danilenko, 2009; Hakvaag, 2009).

Socioeconomic Characteristics and Juvenile Delinquency in Modern Russia

One of the most prominent changes that took place in Russia after the breakdown of the Soviet Union in 1991 was an increase in poverty, especially among households with children (Mroz & Popkin, 1995). The rapid transition from a state-planned to market economy was accompanied by the elimination of most subsidies for food and other basic commodities, and led to drastic increases in the rate of child poverty in Russia. In 1992, 41.4% of all children lived in households below the poverty line, with an additional 24.4% of children living just above the poverty line (101–150% of the poverty line). In 1993, the fraction of children living below the poverty line increased to 47.4%, with an additional 23.4% in the 101–150% of the poverty line category (Mroz & Popkin, 1995, p.13). The staggering statistics on children living in poverty did not improve much through the decade since the study was published. According to the 2005 UNICEF Report (Ovcharova & Popova, 2005), the biggest group of the poor population is still families with children. Over half of them are considered poor and almost 78% of them are at high risk of falling into poverty, according to 2003 data (p. 27). Protein malnutrition stemming from poverty affects about 60% of the population (p. 23).

High poverty levels among families with children persist despite the fact that the majority of these families have two biological parents (the UNICEF Report calls it "favorable demographic composition") and these parents work. Low wages for working adults are an especially prominent problem in some regions of Russia, particularly in rural areas (though nutritional deficiencies of rural dwellers are somewhat ameliorated by subsistence farming that most families rely on). In fact, the differences in child poverty and economic opportunities are especially pronounced when comparing the major urban capital areas (Moscow and St. Petersburg) to some far eastern and southern regions of Russia (for example, the regions bordering Chechnya – Ingushetia and Dagestan – have very high rates of poverty in general and child poverty in particular). A very similar pattern holds for the distribution of crime. Moscow and St. Petersburg – the most privileged locations in terms of financial resources, job opportunities, and the level of education among the citizenry – have relatively low crime rates, more heavily dominated by property crimes than violent crimes compared with most other regions of Russia (Williams & Rodeheaver, 2002).

In addition to the drastic increases in poverty during the period of transition to the market economy in Russia, other social ills have risen as well: divorce and child abandonment, child abuse and neglect, homelessness, alcohol consumption, and homicide rates (Pridemore, 2002a, 2002b; Zohoori *et al.*, 1998). The increase in the already-high level of alcohol consumption was especially astounding. Nemtsov (2005) estimated that, in the Soviet Union during the 1980s, the rate of alcoholism was triple that of the officially registered 2% of the population. During the transition and turmoil of the 1990s, alcohol consumption increased dramatically: the annual rate of deaths due to alcohol poisoning (a proxy for alcohol consumption) jumped from around 20 per 100,000 in the mid-1980s to over 30 per 100,000 in the mid-1990s (Pridemore, 2002b).

These adverse processes, along with legislative changes that allowed children to lose an assigned place of residence (Alternative Report, 2013), led to hundreds of thousands, if not millions, of children finding themselves on the streets. Most situations involved alcoholic parents who neglected or abused their children. Some of these children ended up at orphanages or other state-run institutions for abandoned children, while others were left to fend for themselves at a young age, even with both parents present. They are called *besprizorniki*, which can be translated as "without supervision". These are social orphans – not going to school or skipping school regularly, having no food in the house, and not being cared for by any responsible adults. Available statistics provide widely disparate, though all disturbingly high, numbers: between 420,000 and 716,000 children yearly were in institutional care in Russia in the early 2000s (Alternative Report, 2013; Carter, 2005); between 1 million and 4 million children were among the *besprizorniki* in 2002. According to data from the Federal Agency of State Statistics – a Russian version of Census Bureau (hereinafter referred to by its Russian standard name RosStat) – the share of Russian population aged 0 to 19 years was about 36.5 million in 2002 (breakdown of the 15–19 age bracket is not available in the publicly available RosStat (n.d.) data). Thus, between 1% and 2% of children are in state care and between 3% and 11% of children are effectively on their own. It is not surprising that a lot of them turn to a life of crime to survive. The most common offenses are panhandling, theft, and prostitution (Arefyev, 2003).

Williams and Rodeheaver (2002) provide a comprehensive analysis of juvenile crime in Russia in the 1990s. Their data clearly indicate that, despite some fluctuations reflecting the turmoil of the early 1990s, the pattern of juvenile crime in Russia is comparable to other countries (with theft being the most common offense and the proportion of juvenile crimes among all crimes being around 10–15% on average). The analysis of literature, including sources in Russian (as presented in Williams & Rodeheaver, 2002; Hakvaag, 2009), also shows that some typical correlates of delinquency involvement among juveniles in Russia are similar to what we would find in other developed countries: family instability and adversity, educational failure, unemployment, and substance abuse (mostly alcohol). Specifically, Ivanov (2008) stated that in recent years, illiterate juveniles prevailed in juvenile detention facilities ("reformatory colonies"). In the time before incarceration, 48% didn't work or study and 10% were orphans. The number of juveniles with serious diseases (including mental diseases, substance abuse, and AIDS) has also increased.

Policing, Courts, and Legal Processing of Juveniles

The official age of criminal responsibility in Russia is 16, but in practice it is 14 since the age of responsibility is lowered to 14 for serious crimes (Criminal Code of the Russian Federation, 1996). Serious crimes (felonies) include homicide, robbery, assault, hooliganism under aggravating circumstances, vandalism, and burglary/theft.

Chapter 14 of the Criminal Code (1996) contains specific conditions regarding juveniles and their punishments. Among types of punishments are fines, restriction of employment in certain occupations, mandatory work, and imprisonment. The longest possible terms of imprisonment for juveniles are 6 and 10 years, depending on the seriousness of the crime. Juveniles are eligible for early release if they have served a third of their term (two-thirds in the case of felonies). Judges can also impose a suspended sentence (called a conditional sentence in Russia) in low- and medium-gravity cases (violations and misdemeanors). Usually juveniles have a set period of time during which they have to follow all conditions set by the judge. As a rule, the conviction can be expunged 6 months, 1 year or 3 years after the fulfillment of all punishment conditions, depending on the gravity of the case (Criminal Code, Art 95, 1996).

The Criminal Procedural Code (2001) stipulates the conditions of interrogation of juveniles. A teacher or psychologist must be present and can participate in interrogation for juveniles under 14. If juveniles are between 14 and 18, the investigator makes a decision regarding the presence of teacher. In addition to a teacher, a defense attorney, parent or guardian is also present. The interrogation cannot last more than 2 hours continuously or more than 4 hours a day (Art. 425, Criminal Procedural Code, 2001).

If, during the pre-trial investigation of low-to-medium-gravity cases, the investigator or prosecutor has established that the juvenile can be rehabilitated without the application of criminal punishment, the court can accept a guilty verdict and apply "mandatory educational measures" by sending the juvenile to a specialized "educational facility of closed type" for a term of up to 3 years (Art. 432, Criminal Procedural Code, 2001).

At the end of the preliminary investigation, cases go either to the criminal justice system (justices of the peace or district courts) or the Commission on Juvenile Affairs. This dual tracking system allows many juveniles to stay out of the criminal justice system since the Commission is not a part of it (though its members may perform some judicial functions regarding the rehabilitation and correction of juveniles). If the case is serious enough and the juvenile has reached the age of criminal responsibility, his/her case goes to either a justice of the peace or district court.

The procedures in the Commissions on Juvenile Affairs differ from court procedures since the Commissions are not formal institutions of the criminal justice system. The Commissions handle less serious cases and their role is more preventative rather than guilt-proving.

There is no distinction between adult and juvenile procedures in the court system of Russia. Some juvenile cases can be closed to the public if there are grounds for that. The role of parents in the trial is different, though: their presence at the trial is not necessary but parents can be summoned as witnesses and become financially responsible for damages if their child is found guilty. The courts pay special attention to causes of crime, including social factors. The main stated purpose of sentencing is rehabilitation and deterrence (Terrill, 2009). A judge has several punishment options as stipulated by the Criminal Code (1996), but the death penalty currently cannot be imposed on offenders who committed the crime at the age of 18 or younger.

Approximately three-quarters of motions to imprison juveniles are approved by judges. In 2008, there were 11,700 motions where 9,200 were approved; in 2009, 7,200 (with 5,600 approved); in 2010, 4,500 (with 3,400 approved); and in 2011 (the latest available data), 3,600 (with 2,600 approved) (Judicial Department of the Supreme Court of the Russian Federation, 2009, 2010, 2011).

A similar decrease is seen in the numbers of juveniles confined to reformatory colonies. The numbers dropped substantially from the high of 16,491 in 2003, to 12,752 in 2006, 5,970 in 2009, and 2,808 in 2011, according to the Federal Agency for Punishment Administration, which is a Russian version of the Department of Corrections (hereinafter referred to by its Russian abbreviation FSIN).

Dramatic changes in Russian population structure after the breakdown of the Soviet Union can help to explain this trend. During this transitional period, the country entered a fully-fledged demographic crisis. In the 1980s, according to RosStat, the average annual number of live births approximated the population replacement rate, at about 16.5 per 1000 people. During the 1990s, it dropped to 9.9 per 1000. And it only inched up to 10.5 per 1000 during the 2000s. Thus, the number of adolescents has declined since the late 1990s/early 2000s. According to RosStat, the number of 15–19 year old adolescents dropped from 12.8 million in 2002 to 8.5 million in 2010, and 7.6 million in 2012.

It is not surprising that this demographic trend has contributed to the decline in the number of juvenile delinquents housed in juvenile colonies. However, it is also clear that the 40% drop in the number of adolescents in the general population cannot fully explain the 80% drop in the number of inhabitants of juvenile colonies (from 16,500 juveniles in 2003 to less than 3,000 in 2010 and 2011). Besides the demographic shift, changes in penal policy must have affected the decrease in juvenile incarcerations in the late 1990s and throughout the 2000s. The adoption and amendments to the Criminal Code (1996) and Family Code (1995) have softened the approach towards juveniles. Additionally, the post-Soviet crime wave of the 1990s has subsided as Russia settled into a new way of life.

Juvenile Corrections in Russia

It is illuminating to start the discussion of juvenile corrections in Russia with the results of a survey that asked a representative sample of Russian adults about their opinions on proper punishments for juvenile offenders, assessing people's attitudes towards detention of juveniles in the reformatory colonies (McAuley & MacDonald, 2007). When presented with scenarios of several relatively serious crimes committed by juveniles – robbery, burglary, assault, and sale of drugs on school property – only a small percentage of respondents recommended detention in a colony as a proper punishment. Between 1% and 28% of respondents chose this option, depending on the vignette (McAuley & MacDonald, 2007, p. 16). The explanation for such leniency among Russians probably lies in their understanding of what awaits juveniles in penal colonies. When asked to identify up to three positive and three negative aspects to detention in a colony, the vast majority of respondents perceived the negative aspects outweighing the positives. Thus, only about 10% of respondents identified more positive than negative aspects (p. 18). A positive aspect identified by over two-thirds of respondents was "finish education, get a skill". Deterrence and incapacitation were noted among positives by less than 25% of the respondents. Among the negatives associated with sending juveniles to colonies were high risks of contracting serious diseases like TB or AIDS, a high risk of recidivism upon release, and a high likelihood of being victimized in detention (each of the three negatives was identified by over 50% of respondents).

The conditions of detention in juvenile colonies are just as harsh as would be expected from the Russian public's perceptions. Mary McAuley, who published a book *Children in Custody* (2010) based on her in-depth study of Russian juvenile colonies, describes these institutions as remote, violent places that juveniles often travel to for several weeks (transported under guard). Juveniles there live in barracks, wear uniforms, have highly regimented activities, and are supervised around the clock. Incidents of self-mutilation and riots happen regularly.

According to the most recent Russian official statistics from FSIN (n.d.), there were 46 juvenile colonies in Russia in 2011 (down from 64 in 2002): three are for female offenders (only about 6% to 7% of juvenile offenders in the colonies are female). In 2011, about half of the colony inhabitants were first-timers, in contrast to 92–95% in the early 2000s. Long punishment terms have become more rare as well: in the early 2000s, about 25% of juveniles in the colonies were sentenced to more than 5 years; in 2010–2011, this share fell to about 15%.

McAuley (2010, p. 144) cited Pertsova (then head of the federal department for juvenile colonies in Russia) who said in 2002 about the juveniles released from a colony: "the majority of them have nowhere to go, even those who have parents. No one is waiting for them at home, nor in the factories".

It is also worth mentioning that, due to the geographic location of the colonies, their inhabitants are often very far removed from home (see Moran, Pallot, & Piacentini, 2011, for a detailed analysis of the geography of crime and punishment in Russia). The situation is especially dire for juvenile female offenders. For them, there are only three colonies in Russia so the girls "have to endure particularly long transportations and spatial separation from their families" (Moran *et al.*, 2011, p. 87). After release, the girls are on their own, far from home, with little money, and no clear prospects of putting their lives back on track.

As we mentioned earlier, some juveniles are diverted from the criminal justice system to the Commissions on Juvenile Affairs. One possible outcome for such juveniles is to be sent to "educational institutions of closed type", which are boarding schools for delinquent youths. They are not part of the criminal justice system but instead are under the jurisdiction of the Ministry of Education. Young offenders aged 11 to 13 who committed felonies, or youths aged 14 to 18 who committed minor crimes and were exempted from being sentenced to a colony, are sent to these educational institutions. There are 20 institutions of this type in Russia, housing over 1,000 children (Hakvaag, 2009).

Innovations and the Future

In several Russian regions, there were successful attempts at local reforms of the criminal justice system in handling juveniles (Dutkiewicz, Keating, Nikoula, & Shevchenko, 2009). Especially prominent among them are Rostov Oblast and Perm Krai (Hakvaag, 2009). Interestingly, both areas have historically had very high crime rates.

A new rehabilitative approach towards juvenile justice was initiated in Rostov Oblast in 2000. It was championed by the judge, professor, and children's rights advocate Elena Voronova. The main reforms involved specialization of judges in juvenile cases and establishment of juvenile courts, introduction of social workers in courts, and coordination of approaches among different agencies and actors involved in helping juveniles at risk.

In Perm Krai, juvenile justice reform aimed at implementing restorative justice was launched in 2002 and led by Tatyana Margolina, a deputy governor who later became ombudsman for human rights. The reform involved establishing mediation programs including specialized juvenile court judges, social workers, mediators, and psychologists.

Despite the success of the regional reforms and initial support for juvenile justice initiatives from federal legislators, some powerful forces interested in maintaining the status quo stirred up a media campaign against juvenile justice in Russia, painting it (in the "best" traditions of Soviet propaganda) as attempts by the West, under the auspices of caring for the rights of children, to break apart Russian families and taint Russian traditions of child-rearing involving strict discipline (corporal punishment). The Russian Orthodox Church is one of the most vocal opponents of juvenile justice reform, and even the words "juvenile justice" are now perceived as menacing by the Russian public (based on the authors' personal communication with a wide range of Russian citizens and criminal justice officials).

One of the most prominent advocates of juvenile justice and defenders of human rights is Boris Altshuler, director of the non-governmental organization Right of the Child. In his recent article explaining the resistance to juvenile justice reforms in Russia, Altshuler (2010) argues that the amount of money the state allocates for the institutional care of children is so considerable that the "Russian Orphan Industry Corporation" resists changes with all its might, fearing it may lose this huge source of income.

Considering these recent developments, it is highly unlikely that juvenile justice reforms in Russia will happen any time soon. At the same time, the decrease in crime rates and the enduring demographic crisis that brought incarceration rates down to their current level, the lowest in recent Russian history, make it likely that juvenile incarcerations will continue to decline.

References

Alternative Report (2013). Coalition of Russian NGOs to the UN Committee on the Rights of the Child. Retrieved from http://groups.rightsinrussia.info/archive/right-of-the-child/alternative-report-2013

Altshuler, B. (2010). *Children in Care: the Russian Orphan Industry.* Retrieved from http://www.opendemocracy.net

Arefyev, A.L. (2003). Besprizornye deti Rossii [Children on the streets in Russia]. *Sociologicheskie Issledovaniya, 9,* 61–71.

Burnham, W., Maggs, P.B., & Danilenko, G.M. (2009). *Law and legal system in the Russian Federation.* (4th ed.). New York: Juris Publishing, Inc.

Carter, R. (2005). *Family Matters: A Study of Institutional Childcare in Central and Eastern Europe and the Former Soviet Union.* London: Everychild.

Criminal Code of the Russian Federation. (1996). Retrieved from http://base.consultant.ru/cons/cgi/online.cgi?req=doc;base=LAW;n=144719

Criminal Procedural Code of the Russian Federation. (2001). Retrieved from http://base. consultant.ru/cons/cgi/online.cgi?req=doc;base=LAW;n=145802

Dutkiewicz, P., Keating, A., Nikoula, M., & Shevchenko, E. (2009). *Juvenile Justice in Russia*. Ottawa: Canadian International Development Agency. Retrieved from http://www. juvenilejustice.ru/files/attachements/documents/314_674.pdf

Finckenauer, J.O. (1996). Russia. In D. Shoemaker (Ed.), *International Handbook on Juvenile Justice* (pp. 272–285). Westport, CT: Greenwood Press.

FSIN, or Federal Agency of Punishments Administration of the Russian Federation (n.d.). *The characteristics of persons kept in educational colonies for juveniles* [In Russian]. Retrieved from: www.fsin.su/structure/inspector/iao/statistika

Hakvaag, U.K. (2009). *Juvenile Justice in the Russian Federation* (unpublished Master's thesis). University of Oslo. Retrieved from https://www.duo.uio.no/bitstream/handle/10852/ 33991/Hakvaag.pdf?sequence=1

Ivanov, P.V. (2008). Rol' vospitatelnykh kolonii v sisteme icpolnenija nakazanii [The role of reformatory colonies in the system of punishment administration]. *Voprosy Yuvenalnoi Yustitsii, 19*(5). Retrieved from http://juvenjust.org/index.php?showtopic=1054

Judicial Department of the Supreme Court of the Russian Federation (2009, 2010, 2011). *The review of judicial statistics of federal courts of general jurisdiction and justices of the peace in 2009, 2010, 2011* [In Russian]. Retrieved from http://www.cdep.ru/index.php?id=80

McAuley, M. (2010). *Children in Custody: Anglo-Russian Perspectives*. London: Bloomsbury Academic.

McAuley, M., & MacDonald, K.I. (2007). Russia and youth crime. A comparative study of attitudes and their implications. *British Journal of Criminology, 47*, 2–22.

Moran, D., Pallot, J., & Piacentini, L. (2011). The geography of crime and punishment in the Russian federation. *Eurasian Geography and Economics, 52*(1), 79–104.

Mroz, T.A., & Popkin, B.M. (1995). Poverty and the economic transition in the Russian Federation. *Economic Development and Cultural Change, 44*(1), 1–31.

Nemtsov, A. (2005). Russia: alcohol yesterday and today. *Addiction, 100*(2), 146–149.

Ovcharova, L., & Popova, D. (2005). *Child Poverty in the Russian Federation*. UNICEF Report.

Pridemore, W.A. (2002a). Social problems and patterns of juvenile delinquency in transitional Russia. *Journal of Research in Crime and Delinquency, 39*(2), 187–213.

Pridemore, W.A. (2002b). Vodka and violence: alcohol consumption and homicide rates in Russia. *American Journal of Public Health, 92*(12), 1921–1930.

RosStat, or Federal Agency of State Statistics of the Russian Federation (n.d.). *Demographics* [In Russian]. Retrieved from http://www.gks.ru/wps/wcm/connect/rosstat_main/rosstat/ ru/statistics/population/demography/#

Roudik, P. (2007). *Children's Rights: International and National Laws and Practice*. Library of Congress, Law Library (2007-04112).

Terrill, R. (2009). Russia. In *World Criminal Justice Systems: A Survey*, 7th Ed. (pp. 380–491). New Providence, NJ: Lexis Nexis.

Williams, J.L., & Rodeheaver, D.G. (2002). Punishing juvenile offenders in Russia. *International Criminal Justice Review, 12*(1), 93–110.

Zohoori, N., Mroz, T.A., Popkin, B., Glinskaya, E., Lokshin, M., Mancini, D., … Swafford, M. (1998). Monitoring the economic transition in the Russian Federation and its implications for the demographic crisis – the Russian Longitudinal Monitoring Survey. *World Development, 26*(11), 1977–1993.

5

Juvenile Justice and Juvenile Delinquency in India

Suman Kakar

The juvenile justice system in India envisages an infrastructure in which the legal system has jurisdiction over two classes of children below 18 years of age – those in opposition to the law, and those who require protective care from the state. Currently, the Juvenile Justice Act of 2000 governs the juvenile justice system in India. This act succeeded the original Juvenile Justice Act of 1986 and is modeled to provide care and protection for children. This chapter examines juvenile delinquency and juvenile justice in India from a historical perspective and provides a glimpse of evolution of the laws governing juveniles and legislative efforts intended to provide care and protection to the children in need and children in conflict with law from pre-1850 to 2013. The chapter provides a brief overview of the nature and extent of crimes committed by juveniles, and discusses shifts in public opinion regarding juvenile justice policies. Finally, the future of juvenile justice is discussed.

History of Juvenile Delinquency and Juvenile Justice in India

The history of the juvenile justice system in India can be divided into three time periods with reference to legislative developments in the Indian legal system: (1) pre-1850, (2) 1850–1949, and (3) 1950–2013.

Pre-1850

Although India had been guided by a complex legal system devised by the Hindu and Muslim religions, there were no specific laws or guidelines describing how to deal with children who may violate laws. Consequently, it was left to the families and

The Handbook of Juvenile Delinquency and Juvenile Justice, First Edition. Edited by Marvin D. Krohn and Jodi Lane.

communities to deal with children who violated social and cultural norms, and existing law dealt with child offenders. The law was applied equally to all offenders (adults and juveniles), and all offenders were sentenced to institutions and housed together in prisons. As the societies became more complex, the problem of juvenile delinquency expanded, and a need was felt for formal legislation to address delinquency (Prakash, 2013). This required government to formulate legislation and laws to cope with this issue.

1850–1949

The Apprentices Act of 1850 was the first major legislation in India that attempted to separate offenders by age and introduced the concept of rehabilitation. It stipulated that children between the ages of 10 and 18, if found indulging in crime, must be placed in apprenticeship in a trade (Government of India, 1850). In 1860, the Indian Penal Code (IPC) came into existence, providing guidelines for addressing underage criminals. According to Section 82 of the IPC, a child below seven years of age was considered "doli incapax" – meaning a child below the age of seven does not have the capacity to form a mental intent to commit a crime knowingly. The IPC required that children between the ages of 10–18 convicted in courts should be provided with vocational training as part of their rehabilitation process. IPC Section 83 provided an extension of Section 82 with a rider attached granting qualified immunity to a child aged between 7 to 12 years (Government of India, 1860, Section 82, 83; Vadiraj, 2008).

The Act stipulated that the father/guardian could bind a child between the ages of 10 and 18 up to the age of 21 to an employer to learn a trade. This Act also authorized magistrates to act as guardians in respect of a destitute child or any child convicted of vagrancy or the commission of a petty offense, and could bind him as an apprentice to learn a trade, craft, or employment. This Act was succeeded by the Reformatory Schools Act, 1897 – an Act to amend the law relating to reformatory schools and to make further provisions for dealing with youth offenders (Government of India, 1897).

The Reformatory Schools Act 1897 is one of the most important juvenile legislations in India in the 1850–1949 time period, for two reasons. First, it led to the separation of children and adults, and second, it provided a community alternative to imprisonment. This Act authorized the courts to order the detention of an offender who was less than 15 years and was found guilty of an offense punishable with transportation or imprisonment, to reformatory school instead of sentencing. These reforms played a significant role in providing guidance to subsequent acts and to the states that had no Children's Acts or other special laws dealing with juvenile offenders (Bhardwaj, 2011).

The Criminal Procedure Code of 1898 authorized magistrates to send juvenile offenders to reformatories instead of prisons in specified circumstances, along with provisions relating to the granting of probation and trial of children by the juvenile court. It also addressed the needs of the children of members of criminal tribes under the Criminal Tribes' Amendments Act of 1897, and provided for the establishment of industrial, agricultural, and reformatory schools for children of members of the criminal tribes who were in the age group of 4–18 years. The local governments were given the right to remove such children from criminal tribal settlements and place them in a reformatory (Criminal Tribes' Amendments Act 1897). Another significant development in Indian juvenile justice in this time period came after the release of the 1919–20 report by the Indian Jail Committee (Bhardwaj, 2011). This report made several significant recommendations, namely: provision of aftercare; maintenance of records; and the constitution of children's courts with procedures as informal and flexible as possible. The committee further recommended that regular magistrates should sit at special hours, and if possible in a separate room, to hear charges against juvenile offenders (Government of India, 1920a).

Following the recommendations of the Indian Jail Committee 1919–20, Madras became the first state in India to pass the first Children Act in 1920 (Government of India, 1920b). The Madras Children Act of 1920 specified the age limit of childhood, prohibited the imprisonment of child offenders, created remand homes and certified schools, and enabled adoption of non-criminal children by other states. The example of Madras was followed by Bengal and Bombay in 1922 and 1924 respectively, and Children's Acts for these states were passed (Government of India, 1922, 1924; Prakash, 2013). More states followed suit in the years to follow and passed their Children's Acts (Bhardwaj, 2011).

1950–2013

In 1960, the first Children Act of 1960 was passed by free India. The main objective of this Act was to "provide for the care, protection, maintenance, welfare, training, education and rehabilitation of neglected or delinquent children and for the trial of delinquent children in the Union Territories" (Children Act, 1960). Although this act made a significant improvement over the existing acts in various states, it left several issues unresolved, such as a lack of uniformity in definitions and laws in different states. Each state defined juveniles differently and dealt with delinquency according to the provisions of the Children Act in their state (Rickard & Szanyi, 2010). This lack of uniform provision created disparity in the treatment given to juveniles facing similar situations in different states. The Supreme Court opined that the central Government should initiate parliamentary legislation so that the Children's Act enacted by Parliament should contain not only provisions for investigation and trial of offenses against children below the age of 16 years, but should also contain mandatory provisions for ensuring the social, economic and psychological rehabilitation of children who are either accused of offenses or are abandoned (Government of India, 1960).

The current Indian juvenile justice system and corresponding policy is rooted in the provisions of the Indian Constitution, namely, the "constitutional mandate" as prescribed in Articles 15(3), 39(e) and (f), 45, and 47. Aside from national tenets, the Indian juvenile justice system calls on the directives of many international law covenants, such as the UN Convention on the Rights of the Child (United Nation Organization, 1989), and the UN Standard Minimum Rules for Administration of Juvenile Justice, the so-called "Beijing Rules" (Kumari, 2010; Rickard & Szanyi, 2010). The first Juvenile Justice Act (JJA) in India was passed in 1986. This Act introduced a uniform legal framework for children for the whole of India, with provisions for the care, protection, treatment, development, and rehabilitation of neglected or delinquent juveniles in situations of abuse, exploitation, and social maladjustment (Government of India, 1986). It also provided guidelines for adjudication of certain matters relating to, and disposition of, delinquent juveniles (Bhardwaj, 2011). The JJA was enacted under Article 253 of the Constitution that authorizes the parliament to make any law for the whole or part of the country. It made delinquent and neglected children all over the country a concern of the state at national level, and attempted to reduce the stigma by replacing the word "juvenile" with "child", and modifying the definition of neglected juvenile.

The JJA introduced the following significant improvements over the existing Children's Acts:

1. a uniform definition of juvenile for the whole country, defining the ages for boys and girls;
2. a wider role for voluntary organizations;
3. prohibition of imprisonment of children under all circumstances; and
4. a uniform structure of juvenile justice for the whole country.

It also stipulated provisions for taking charge, adjudication, pre- and post-adjudication care and aftercare for incorrigible children who were brought by their parents or guardians. Under JJA Section 7(2) (Government of India, 1986), police and persons, or voluntary organizations authorized in this regard, could also bring delinquent and neglected children before competent authority. "Competent authority meant the juvenile court with regard to delinquent children and the juvenile welfare board with regard to neglected children, and also included the magistrates specified in Section 7(2) of the JJA" (Bhardwaj, 2011, p. 152). The JJA provided for only one appeal to the sessions court against an order of the competent authority and stipulated that no appeal could be filed against a finding that the juvenile was not neglected or delinquent.

The Juvenile Justice (Care and Protection) Act of 2000 was a formal codification of a system in India that was eclectically drawn previously. Prior to the ratification of the 2000 Act, existing policy was based on the JJA, and various state legislations that dealt with the rights and welfare of children. The problem with the JJA, as discussed earlier, was the lack of a formalized distinction between the aforementioned two classes of children – those in opposition to the law, and those requiring protective care from the state. To this end, one of the key goals of the 2000 Act was to create a separate system, and its related infrastructure, for circumstances where children violated the law, so that it would be separate and apart from the adult criminal justice system. Implicit in the policy behind the 2000 Act was the idea that the juvenile justice system must necessarily incorporate the involvement of informal social arrangements at the level of the family, voluntary organizations, and the community (Government of India, 2000).

So in 2000, JJA (1986) was repealed and replaced by Juvenile Justice (Care and Protection) Act of 2000 (JJ (C&P) Act) in recognition of India's ratification of the UN Convention on Rights of the Child, the Beijing Rules, and other relevant international instruments. The JJ (C&P) Act was amended in 2002, 2006 and 2010. The Act consolidated and amended the law relating to juveniles in conflict with law and children in need of care and protection, by providing for proper care, protection and treatment by catering to their developmental needs, and by adopting a child-friendly approach in the adjudication and disposition of matters in the best interest of children and for their ultimate rehabilitation (Mahrukh, 2006). In 2007, the Government of India passed an updated list of rules to aid in the implementation of the JJ Act (Government of India, 2006). These Model Rules are more expansive than the JJ Act in their guiding principles of "best interests" of the child, the "right to be heard", "speedy trial", and a "fresh start" to be available for all children under the JJ Act. The Indian Constitution has, in several provisions, imposed on the State a primary responsibility of ensuring that all the needs of children are met and that their basic rights are fully protected (Government of India, 2007).

Some of the most important improvements brought about by the Model Rules are:

1. prohibition of "publication of name and/or picture of juvenile or child in need of care and protection involved in any proceeding under the Act" – providing complete privacy and fresh start for delinquents;
2. limitations on the level of police discretion;
3. greater compliance with the rights-based approach;
4. diversion;
5. definitions – a longer list of definitions to prevent ambiguity, which will help in better interpretation of the Act and limiting the discretion of the competent;
6. the inclusion of Child Protection Units;
7. provision of a clear mandate and guidelines for the functioning of the Inspection Committees, enabling greater accountability;
8. Model Rules to provide for an audit for a range of services, institutions and processes;
9. provision for Advisory Boards at the Central, State, District, and city level.

The inherent incapacity to have required mens rea or culpability is now presumed by law in India until 18 years of age, by respecting Article 1 of the UN Convention on the Rights of the Child. Under sections 82 and 83 of the Indian Penal Code, 1860 (IPC), a complete immunity is granted from criminal liability for anything done by a child below 7 years, and it is subjective for a child above 7 years and under 12 depending upon sufficient maturity of understanding to judge the nature and consequences of his/her conduct on that occasion.

Demographics and Juvenile Delinquency

India is the second-most populous country in the world, with its share of the world population amounting to more than 17%. About 29% of the Indian population is in the age group 0–14 years, and 6% are older than 65 years (CIA World Fact Book, 2013). Life in India is influenced largely by its rich cultural traditions, including religion, and it follows the common law system. In terms of applicability to the juvenile justice system in India, defining at what age a person is or ceases to be a child is an important question. The Juvenile Justice Act 2000 defines the age of determination for juveniles – all males and females – as below the age of 18 years

Juvenile crime

Compared with other countries in the world, juvenile crime in India is low. According to the National Crime Records Bureau (NCRB, 2013), IPC crimes committed by juveniles in the country during 2002–2005 remained static at 1.0%, which marginally increased to 1.1% in 2006 and remained static in 2007. This share increased marginally to 1.2% in 2008 and decreased back to 1.1% in 2009. This share further decreased to 1.0% in 2010 and thereafter marginally increased to 1.1 in 2011 and 1.2% in 2012. So the juvenile crime rate has shown a mixed trend during 2002–2012. The crime rate increased from 1.8 per 100,000 in 2002 to 2.3 per 100,000 in 2012 (see Table 5.1 and Figure 5.1).

Table 5.1 Incidence and rate of juveniles in conflict with law under the Indian Penal Code (2002–2012)

Sl. no.	Year	Incidence of:		Percentage of juvenile crimes to total crimes	Estimated mid-year population (millions)	Rate of crime by juveniles
		Juvenile crimes	Total cognizable crimes			
1	2002	18,560	1,780,330	1.0	1,050.6	1.8
2	2003	17,819	1,716,120	1.0	1,068.2	1.7
3	2004	19,229	1,832,015	1.0	1,085.6	1.8
4	2005	18,939	1,822,602	1.0	1,102.8	1.7
5	2006	21,088	1,878,293	1.1	1,119.8	1.9
6	2007	22,865	1,989,673	1.1	1,136.6	2.0
7	2008	24,535	2,093,379	1.2	1,153.1	2.1
8	2009	23,926	2,121,345	1.1	1,169.4	2.0
9	2010	22,740	2,224,831	1.0	1,185.8	1.9
10	2011[#]	25,125	2,325,575	1.1	1,210.2	2.1
11	2012	27,936	2,387,188	1.2	1,213.4	2.3

[#]Actual Census 2011 population (provisional), mid-year projected population for remaining year.
Source: National Crime Records Bureau (2013), Chapter 10, p.51.

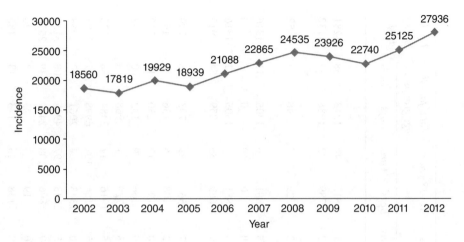

Figure 5.1 Juvenile IPC crime incidence 2002–2012 (National Crime Records Bureau, 2013, Chapter 10, p.133).

Table 5.2 presents data on juvenile crime by the Indian Penal Code (IPC) and Special and Local Laws (SLL) in 2012 by age and gender. This table provides the number of crimes committed in three age groups: 7–12 years, 12–16 years, and 16–18 years by gender.

According to the same report (NCRB, 2013), in 2002 a total of 33,551 juveniles were apprehended. Of these, 31,323 were boys and 2,228 were girls, as compared to a total of 37,764 arrests in 2012 when 35,706 boys and 2,058 girls were arrested. This shows a very small increase by boys over the 10-year period (2002–2012). There was a small increase in the number of boys arrested in 2002 compared with 2012. Among girls, in fact, there has been steady decrease; in 2012, 170 fewer girls were apprehended compared with the number in 2002. The ratio of girls to boys arrested for committing IPC crimes during 2012 was 1:19, whereas this ratio during 2011 was nearly 1:20 (NCRB, 2013) (see Figure 5.2).

According to NCRB (2013), only 2% of the juvenile crime was committed by children below the age of 12, 31% by children between the ages of 12–16, and 67% by children between the ages of 16–18 (see Figure 5.3).

Figure 5.4 presents data on disposition of juvenile cases. In 2012, a total of 39,822 juveniles were apprehended and produced before various courts. At the end of 2012 the percentage of juveniles awaiting trial was 26.9%. Out of the total juveniles apprehended in the country (10,721 out of 39,822), 14.9% (5,927) were disposed of after advice or admonition, 18.3% (7,290) were placed under the care of parents/ guardians, 5.5% (2,183) were sent to institutions, 24.3% (9,677) were sent to special homes, 3.6% (1,452) were dealt with by fines and 6.5% (2,572) were either acquitted or their cases were otherwise disposed of.

Table 5.2 Juveniles apprehended under IPC and SLL crimes by age groups and gender during 2012

Sl. no.	Crime head	7–12 years		12–16 years		16–18 years		Total for all age groups		Total (boys + girls)
		Boys	Girls	Boys	Girls	Boys*	Girls	Boys	Girls	
A. IPC CRIMES										
1	MURDER (Sec 302 IPC)	23	3	373	21	817	44	1213	68	1281
2	ATTEMPT TO COMMIT MURDER (Sec 307 IPC)	11	0	288	12	789	32	1088	44	1132
3	C.H. NOT AMOUNTING MURDER (Sec 304, 308 IPC)	0	0	19	2	29	2	48	4	52
4	RAPE (Sec 376 IPC)	33	0	391	5	881	6	1305	11	1316
	CUSTODIAL RAPE	0	0	0	0	0	0	0	0	0
	OTHER RAPE	33	0	391	5	881	6	1305	11	1316
5	KIDNAPPING & ABDUCTION (Sec 363–369, 371–373 IPC)	3	0	187	19	669	35	859	54	913
	i) OF WOMEN & GIRLS	2	0	140	17	561	29	703	46	749
	ii) OF OTHERS	1	0	47	2	108	6	156	8	164
6	DACOITY (Sec 395–398 IPC)	5	0	48	0	197	10	250	10	260
7	PREPARATION & ASSEMBLY FOR DACOITY (Sec 399–402 IPC)	0	0	26	0	106	0	132	0	132
8	ROBBERY (Sec 392–394, 397, 398 IPC)	9	0	230	8	729	1	968	9	977
9	BURGLARY (Sec. 449–452,454,455,457–460 IPC)	124	4	1444	15	1916	17	3484	36	3520
10	THEFT (Sec 379 – 382 IPC)	304	31	2508	75	4186	101	6998	207	7205
	i) AUTO THEFT	36	3	682	0	1343	4	2061	7	2068
	ii) OTHER THEFT	268	28	1826	75	2843	97	4937	200	5137
11	RIOTS (Sec 143–145, 147–151, 153, 153A., 153B, 157, 158, 160 IPC)	28	2	485	39	1896	108	2409	149	2558
12	CRIMINAL BREACH OF TRUST(Sec.406–409 IPC)	0	0	4	0	19	3	23	3	26
13	CHEATING (Sec 419, 420 IPC)	2	0	33	0	138	13	173	13	186

14	COUNTERFEITING (Sec.231–254,489A–489D)	0	0	11	1	24	1	35	2	37
15	ARSON (Sec 435, 436, 438 IPC)	1	0	30	1	57	7	88	8	96
16	HURT (Sec 323–333, 335–338 IPC)	78	18	1550	115	3931	242	5559	375	5934
17	DOWRY DEATHS (Section 304B IPC)	1	0	9	7	33	23	43	30	73
18	ASSAULT ON WOMEN WITH INTENT TO OUTRAGE HER MODESTY (Section 354 IPC)	1	0	195	1	486	2	682	3	685
19	INSULT TO THE MODESTY OF WOMEN (Sec 509 IPC)	0	0	63	0	174	1	237	1	238
20	CRUELTY BY HUSBAND OR HIS RELATIVES (Sec 498A IPC)	1	2	44	31	129	101	174	134	308
21	IMPORTATION OF GIRLS (Sec 366B IPC)	0	0	0	0	0	0	0	0	0
22	CAUSING DEATH BY NEGLIGENCE (Sec 304A IPC)	2	0	52	1	211	2	265	3	268
23	OTHER IPC CRIMES	177	20	2468	135	5115	353	7760	508	8268
A.	**TOTAL COGNIZABLE CRIMES UNDER IPC**	**803**	**80**	**10458**	**488**	**22532**	**1104**	**33793**	**1672**	**35465**
B.	**SLL CRIMES**									
1	ARMS ACT	1	0	31	0	166	0	198	0	198
2	NARCOTIC DRUGS & PSYCHOTROPIC SUBSTANCES ACT	1	0	19	3	64	5	84	8	92
3	GAMBLING ACT	7	0	75	0	327	0	409	0	409
4	EXCISE ACT	2	0	45	5	242	0	289	5	294
5	PROHIBITION ACT	3	0	42	11	194	87	239	98	337
6	EXPLOSIVES & EXPLOSIVE SUBSTANCES ACT	0	0	3	0	13	0	16	0	16
7	IMMORAL TRAFFIC (P) ACT	0	0	0	1	2	16	2	17	19
8	INDIAN RAILWAYS ACT	1	0	3	0	3	0	7	0	7
9	THE FOREIGNERS ACT	2	0	15	1	16	4	33	5	38
10	PROTECTION OF CIVIL RIGHTS ACT	0	0	0	0	0	0	0	0	0
	(i) PCR ACT FOR SCs	0	0	0	0	0	0	0	0	0
	(ii) PCR ACT FOR STs	0	0	0	0	0	0	0	0	0
11	INDIAN PASSPORT ACT	2	1	1	2	15	10	18	13	31
12	ESSENTIAL COMMODITIES ACT	0	0	4	0	6	0	10	0	10
13	TERRORIST & DISRUPTIVE ACTIVITIES ACT	0	0	0	0	0	0	0	0	0

(Continued)

Table 5.2 (continued)

Sl. no.	Crime head	7–12 years		12–16 years		16–18 years		Total for all age groups		Total (boys + girls)
		Boys	Girls	Boys	Girls	Boys*	Girls	Boys	Girls	
14	ANTIQUITIES & ART TREASURES ACT	0	0	0	0	1	0	1	0	1
15	DOWRY PROHIBITION ACT	0	0	0	0	4	18	4	18	22
16	PROHIBITION OF CHILD MARRIAGE ACT	0	0	0	0	9	0	9	0	9
17	INDECENT REPRESENTATION OF WOMEN (P) ACT	0	0	4	0	0	0	4	0	4
18	COPYRIGHT ACT	0	0	0	0	11	5	11	5	16
19	COMMISSION OF SATI PREVENTION ACT	0	0	0	0	0	0	0	0	0
20	SC/ST (PREVENTION OF ATROCITIES) ACT	0	0	13	1	84	11	97	12	109
	(i) PREVENTION OF ATTROCITIES ACT FOR SCs	0	0	13	1	75	9	88	10	98
	(ii) PREVENTION OF ATTROCITIES ACT FOR STs	0	0	0	0	9	2	9	2	11
21	FOREST ACT	0	0	0	0	5	0	5	0	5
22	OTHER SLL CRIMES	331	52	761	77	1443	76	2535	205	2740
B. TOTAL COGNIZABLE CRIMES UNDER SLL		**350**	**53**	**1016**	**101**	**2605**	**232**	**3971**	**386**	**4357**
C. GRAND TOTAL (A + B)		**1153**	**133**	**11474**	**589**	**25137**	**1336**	**37764**	**2058**	**39822**

*As per the revised definition of the Juvenile Justice Act, the boys' age group of 16–18 years has also been considered as juveniles since 2001.

Source: National Crime Records Bureau (2013), Chapter 10, p. 513.

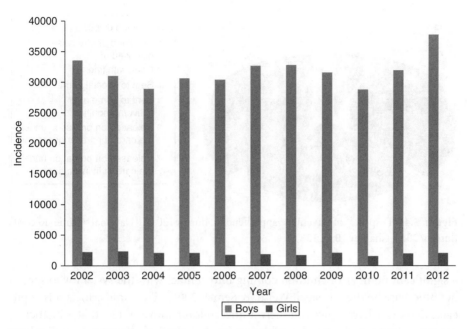

Figure 5.2 Juveniles apprehended under IPC and SLL crimes by gender (National Crime Records Bureau, 2013, Chapter 10, p. 134).

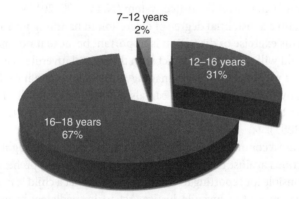

Figure 5.3 Juveniles apprehended under IPC by age group during 2012 (National Crime Records Bureau, 2013, Chapter 10, p. 138).

Police and Juveniles

In India, children entering the juvenile justice system frequently face grave threats to their individual rights. Police abuse is commonplace in some jurisdictions. Police play a crucial role in shaping the child's experience of the juvenile justice system. In Western countries, police are frequently criticized as the weak link in the juvenile justice system. This criticism hinges on the abuse or misuse of the formidable power and discretion afforded to police officers in the juvenile justice system, resulting in

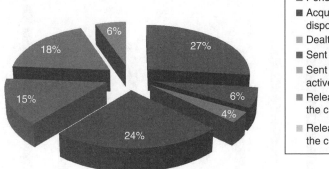

Figure 5.4 Disposal of juveniles apprehended during 2012 (National Crime Records Bureau, 2013, Chapter 10, p. 138).

a significant number of children coming into contact with the system who should not otherwise be there (Siegel, Welsh, & Senna, 2006). The same criticism is applicable to India, where police routinely funnel children into a system that is inefficient and under-resourced, and where false arrests and physical abuse by the police have become a common feature of a child's interaction with law enforcement officials. Therefore, a significant amount of abuse can occur before the child even comes into contact with the formal juvenile justice system (Nair, 2009, 2012).

Police maintain a substantial degree of discretion in handling juveniles in conflict with the law. This exercise of discretion is important because it not only determines whether the child will come into contact with the formal juvenile justice system, but it also serves as a way of effectively managing an incident on an individualized basis (Rickard & Szanyi, 2010). However, it can also "deteriorate into discrimination and other abuses on the part of the police" (National Commission for the Protection of Child Rights, 2007).

False arrests are a common occurrence. When false cases are brought before the JJB, there are no actions against those who fabricate them. When apprehending juveniles, police are responsible for reporting to children's parents that a child is in custody. Police are also obliged under the Juvenile Justice Act to immediately bring apprehended children before a JJB member (National Commission for the Protection of Child Rights, 2007). While this process is theoretically sound, in practice the procedure is not always followed. Particularly in rural areas, there is no monitoring of activity within any given police station, which means that abuse can occur unchecked and unnoticed.

Disposition

The JJA provided for three sets of homes for placing children: an observation home for keeping children while proceedings were pending, unless they were kept with their parents, guardians, or at a place of safety; a juvenile home for housing neglected children; and a special home for delinquents. Children who are adjudicated delinquent are placed in borstal schools. These schools are used exclusively for the imprisonment of minors or juveniles. The primary objective of borstal schools is to ensure care, welfare and rehabilitation of young offenders in an environment suitable for children and to keep them away from the contaminating atmosphere of prisons. Juveniles in conflict with law the detained in borstal schools are provided with various vocational trainings and education with the help of trained teachers (National Crime Records Bureau, 2012). The emphasis is on the education, training and moral influence conducive to their reformation and the prevention of crime. Currently there are 21 functioning borstal schools in India, with a combined total capacity for 2,218 inmates (National Crime Records Bureau, 2012).

The JJ (C&P) 2000 stipulated the creation of Juvenile Justice/Welfare Boards (JJBs). These boards are designed to be a legal body that is responsive to the needs of the children. Each JJB consists of a three-person panel with one magistrate and two social workers. JJBs typically meet one to three times a week, and proceedings generally consist of brief hearings before the child and his or her family, with reports by probation officers and occasional witnesses.

JJBs also offer other due process protections in the amended JJ Act, such as the right to speedy proceedings and the creation of child-friendly police units (Braga, Kennedy, Waring, & Piehl, 2001). The guiding principle of the juvenile justice system is one of accountability on the part of children along with the desire of the system to address the initial cause or causes of delinquency (Dodge, Dishion, & Lansford, 2006).

A full formal processing by the juvenile justice system is not required in all delinquency cases. A child charged with petty theft conceivably should not be subject to the same processes and ranges of punishments as a child who is involved in a violent offense. Thus, some mechanism of classifying juveniles based on the severity of the offense is crucial. The approach to seeking alternative remedies, often "without resorting to formal trial", is known as diversion (Dodge *et al.*, 2006). Effective diversion programs decrease the burden on specific points in the juvenile justice system by directing juveniles to the most efficient and effective resources both inside and outside of the formal system.

Theoretically, the Indian juvenile justice system embraces diversion. However, practically, it falls short on the implementation of this policy. Current practices predominantly fail to realize the benefits of diversion, thereby threatening the development of youth in the system and weakening the system's ability to prevent future offenses. Notwithstanding the negative effects of child detention on a child's welfare, the use of detention in India is pervasive in a number of common scenarios. For instance, processing delays translate to children spending months locked up for no reason other than the fact that the JJB has failed to adhere to legal time requirements. This latitude often allows cases to languish in the system indefinitely (United Nations Organization, 1990).

Bail proceedings also contribute to the misuse of detention. In many cases, children are released on bail to their families, returning every few weeks to stand before the Board (*Calcutta Telegraph*, 2009).

Future of Juvenile Justice in India

Under Indian law, juveniles up to the age of 18 cannot be tried as adults, not even in the cases of serious crimes such as murder or rape. Recent events have triggered a public outcry to curb increasing trends in the incidence of violent juvenile crimes by reducing the age of majority from 18 to 16, and other similar drastic measures such as trying juveniles as adults. In a recent rape case, the court sentenced a teenager to three years in a detention center (Banerji & Mohanty, 2013). Although in response to public rage, the government fast-tracked tougher laws against sex crimes, it resisted calls to change the juvenile law and return the adult age from 18 to 16. The trial was held behind closed doors to protect his identity and media were barred from reporting on any details of the proceedings. During the trial, the juvenile had been held at a detention facility for violent young offenders in Delhi and kept away from other inmates.

India's juvenile justice system is undergoing what the US went through in 1980–1990. During this period, the US felt that there was an "impending doom" due to a rapid increase in violent crime by juveniles. Such fears and perceptions induced major changes in laws and resulted in imposing tougher sanctions on juveniles across the country. Public fear and outrage convinced policymakers to "get tough" and take drastic measures such as trying juveniles as adults, making it easier to transfer juveniles to adult court, using blended sentences, reducing confidentiality protection for juveniles, and putting public safety and accountability ahead of the best interests of the child (Torbet & Szymanski, 1998).

Similarly in India, an increase in violent crimes, especially sexual assault, rape, and murder, has caused public outrage and concerns for policymakers to reconsider juvenile laws. The call has been to reduce the juvenile age from 18 to 16 and to try juveniles as adults. India's Supreme Court is hearing a petition filed for the law to be reinterpreted rather than changed. The petition asks the Supreme Court to consider and assess a young offender's "emotional, intellectual and mental maturity" when deciding whether to try them as a juvenile, rather than basing the decision on age alone (Banerji & Mohanty, 2013).

As discussed earlier, juveniles commit a tiny proportion of total crimes in India and far less than other nations such as the US. Data from the National Crime Records Bureau indicate that although there were about 33,000 crimes committed by juveniles in India in 2012, there has not been a large increase. India should learn from other countries of the world where tougher sanctions have been tried unsuccessfully and focus on efforts to capitalize on the existing infrastructure and resources within the country to yield significant changes for youth in the system. Such reforms have the potential of impacting every facet of the juvenile justice system, which should work for the care and protection of the juveniles and refrain from yielding to public outrage or opinion. The JJ Act is expected to provide proper care, protection and treatment by catering to their developmental needs, and by adopting a child-friendly approach in the adjudication and disposition of matters in the best interest of children and for their ultimate rehabilitation (Subs. by Act 33 of 2006, Sect. 2). India should try to improve on the existing laws by implementing these rather than changing. Other countries including the US provide India with lessons to reflect and learn from.

References

Banerji, A., & Mohanty, S. (2013). Indian teen sentenced to three years in Delhi gang rape case. Reuters (August 31, 2013). Retrieved from http://www.reuters.com/article/2013/08/31/us-india-rape-idUSBRE97U06R20130831

Bhardwaj, D.N. (2011). *Juvenile Justice in India: A Study of Legislative Policies, Judicial Trends and Social Perception.* Retrieved from http://hdl.handle.net/10603/7809

Braga, A.A., Kennedy, D.M., Waring, E.J., & Piehl, A.M. (2001). Problem-oriented policing, deterrence, and youth violence: An evaluation of Boston's Operation Ceasefire. *Journal of Research in Crime and Delinquency, 38*(3), 195–225.

Calcutta Telegraph (2009). *Concern Over Delay in Justice in Juvenile Cases – 168 Accused Still Fighting Legal Battles for "Offences" Committed During Childhood, Reveals Study,* October 7, 2009. Retrieved from http://www.telegraphindia.com/1091008/jsp/northeast/story_11587716.jsp

CIA World Fact Book. (2013). Retrieved from https://www.cia.gov/library/publications/download/download-2013/index.html

Dodge, K.A., Dishion, T.J., & Lansford, J.E. (2006). *Deviant Peer Influences in Intervention and Public Policy for Youth.* Social Policy Report. Retrieved from http://www.sred.org/spr.html

Government of India. (1850). *Indian Apprentices Act of 1850.* New Delhi: Ministry of Home Affairs, Government of India.

Government of India. (1860). *Indian Penal Code, 1860 (Act No. 45 of 1860).* New Delhi: Ministry of Home Affairs, Government of India.

Government of India, (1897). *The Reformatory School Act.* New Delhi: Ministry of Home Affairs, Government of India.

Government of India. (1920a). *Report of Indian Jail Committee, 1919–1920.* New Delhi: Government of India, Ministry of Home Affairs.

Government of India. (1920b). *Madras Children Act (1920).* New Delhi: Government of India, Ministry of Home Affairs.

Government of India. (1922). *Bengal Children Act (1922).* New Delhi: Government of India, Ministry of Home Affairs.

Government of India. (1924). *Bombay Children Act (1924).* New Delhi: Government of India, Ministry of Home Affairs.

Government of India. (1960). *Children Act (1960).* New Delhi: Government of India, Ministry of Home Affairs. Retrieved from http://wcd.nic.in/childrenact1960.htm

Government of India. (1986). *The Juvenile Justice Act 1986.* New Delhi: Government of India, Ministry of Home Affairs.

Government of India. (2000). *The Juvenile Justice (Care and Protection) Act, 2000.* New Delhi: Government of India, Ministry of Home Affairs.

Government of India. (2006). *Building A Protective Environment For Children* (23). New Delhi: Ministry of Women and Child Development, Government of India.

Government of India. (2007). *Model Rules under the Juvenile Justice (Care and Protection of Children) Act 2000.* Gen. S. R. & O. 679(E). New Delhi: Government of India, Ministry of Home Affairs.

Kumari, V. (2010). *The Juvenile Justice System In India: From Welfare To Rights.* Oxford: India Paperbacks.

Mahrukh, A. (2006). *Child and Protection and Juvenile Justice System: for Juvenile in Conflict with Law.* Children India Foundation.

Nair, P. (2009). Procedural delays keep minors at Apna Ghar. *Times of India,* October 9, 2009. Retrieved from http://timesofindia.indiatimes.com/city/goa/Procedural-delays-keep-minors-at-Apna-Ghar/articleshow/5088659.cms

Nair, P. (2012). Apna Ghar is dumping ground for NGOs. *Times of India,* May 10, 2012. Retrieved from http://articles.timesofindia.indiatimes.com/keyword/apna-ghar/featured/4

National Commission for the Protection of Child Rights. (2007). *NCPCR Bangalore Report.* Government of India, Bangalore Visit 6. Retrieved from http://www.ncpcr.gov.in/Reports/Karnataka_Report.pdf

National Crime Records Bureau. (2012). *Prison Statistics in India, 2011.* New Delhi: National Crime Records Bureau, Ministry of Home Affairs.

National Crime Records Bureau. (2013). *Crime in India, 2012.* New Delhi: National Crime Records Bureau, Ministry of Home Affairs. Retrieved from http://ncrb.gov.in/

Prakash, D.H. (2013). Juvenile justice – a hard look. *International Research Journal of Social Sciences, 2*(1), 38–40. Retrieved from http://www.isca.in/IJSS/Archive/v2i1/8.ISCA-IRJSS-2012-067.pdf

Rickard, E., & Szanyi, J.M. (2010). Bringing justice to India's children: three reforms to bridge practices with promises in India's juvenile justice system. *UC Davis Journal of Juvenile Law & Policy, 14*(1), 107–162.

Siegel, L.J., Welsh, B.C., & Senna, J.J. (2006) *Juvenile Delinquency: Theory, Practice, and Law,* 9th ed. Wadsworth Publishers.

Torbet, P., & Szymanski, L. (1998). *State Legislative Responses to Violent Juvenile Crime: 1996–1997 Update.* Washington, DC: Office of Juvenile Justice and Delinquency Prevention.

United Nations Organization. (1989). *Convention on the Rights of the Child.* 1577 U.N.T.S. 3, article 3.

United Nations Organization. (1990). *United Nations Guidelines for the Prevention of Juvenile Delinquency,* art. 11, G.A. Res. 45/112, U.N. GAOR Supp. (No. 49) at 202 (Anne U.N. Doc. A/45/49 (1990); United Nations Standard Minimum Rules for the Administration of Juvenile Justice, G.A. Res. 40/33, Rule 1.2, U.N. GAOR, 40th Sess., Supp. No. 53 at 207, U.N. Doc. A/40/53.

Vadiraj, S. (2008). Juvenile justice in India a far cry. *One World South Asia,* August 8, 2008. Retrieved from http://southasia.oneworld.net/todaysheadlines/juvenile-justice-in-india-a-far-cry/

6

Juvenile Justice in South Africa

Adam Cooper

Introduction

Child[1] justice policies in South Africa – both historically and currently – are inextricably linked to the dominant ideologies within which these policies have emerged. During the colonial period, Roman Dutch and English laws superseded African customary law, leading to increasingly punitive child justice policies and practices (Skelton & Tshehla, 2008). During the repressive apartheid era, legislation divided groups of people racially, resulting in child justice policies becoming increasingly racialized. In the post-apartheid era, the values underpinning the constitutional democracy have shaped child justice policy within a human rights discourse and progressive notions of restorative justice. However, whilst the contemporary policy framework is couched in an admirable restorative justice paradigm, rampant economic and social inequality remains, due to the legacies of colonialism and apartheid. Thus, it is the argument of this chapter that the restorative justice approach can only succeed, in a sustainable fashion, if it forms part of – and is able to contribute towards – a broader redistributive justice strategy in the medium- to long-term future.

Historical Roots

Prior to colonialism, African customary law determined the fate of children who contravened local rules. Disputes and transgressions were dealt with in traditional leaders' courts, and the institutionalization of children did not occur (Skelton, 2007). During the colonial period, Chisholm (1986) linked the birth of the South African reformatory and the creation of separate policies for juveniles as byproducts of

The Handbook of Juvenile Delinquency and Juvenile Justice, First Edition. Edited by Marvin D. Krohn and Jodi Lane.

South Africa's relatively late transition to industrial capitalism, following the discovery of diamonds and gold in the 1880s. To illustrate this point, despite officials stating in the mid-1850s that "juvenile delinquency... in this Colony, as a class of crime may be said not to exist" (Chisholm, 1986, p.484), approximately 25 years later William Porter, the Attorney General at the Cape, established the first South African reformatory in his own name (Skelton & Tshehla, 2008). Boys were predominantly sent to Porter Reformatory for crimes perceived to be reformable, such as property theft, while girls went to Porter for prostitution and childbirth, as well as more serious crimes, such as theft, assault, and murder (Chisholm, 1986). Racial distinctions and segregations began to be practiced at Porter during the 1890s. White boys were directed towards industrial training, whereas black boys were forced into manual labour (Chisholm, 1986).

Welfarist policies saturated in class- and race-based prejudices that delineated which children were "in need of care" dominated South African juvenile justice policies in the first half of the twentieth century (Badroodien, 1999). The definition of children "in need of care" characterized by these policies depicted poor, white young people, who were being subjected to deviant behaviours and undesirable societal conditions, including poverty, racial mixing, illicit liquor trade, and prostitution (Badroodien, 1999; Chisholm, 1986). By 1948, 14 schools of industry had been created, steering the poor, white population away from these societal conditions. Other welfarist legislation included the Prisons and Reformatories Act of 1911, which decreed that children and young adults should not be imprisoned, and the 1913 Children's Protection Act, which allowed courts to release children, ensuring that they were held in a place of safety until their trial (Badroodien, 1999).

During the apartheid era, particularly in the 1970s and 1980s, large numbers of children were detained for their political activities, especially during and after the 1976 uprisings in Soweto, in which young people protested against being schooled in Afrikaans. The lines between political and criminal detentions were therefore blurred during this period, although both contained a similar set of etiological roots, located in the socio-economic conditions created by apartheid. Many children were treated inhumanely, for example in the form of corporal punishment; approximately 30,000 whippings were being dealt out per year in South Africa by the early 1990s (Skelton & Tshehla, 2008). Corporal punishment was banned in 1995.

Juvenile justice in the pre-colonial, colonial and apartheid periods therefore reflected the ideologies and broader societal practices that existed in South Africa during these different eras. As South Africa industrialized, reformatories and schools of industry were established to mould "dissenting" sections of the youthful population to fit the social and economic visions that governors had for the country. Juvenile justice policies and practices increasingly differentiated between race groups as the apartheid state took shape, and when the anti-apartheid struggle began to involve increased numbers of children, young people were often dealt with through violence and repression. The remainder of this chapter will be dedicated to narrating the key events that led to the formation of the Child Justice Bill of 2008 (henceforth referred to as "the Bill"), and summarizing important components of the Bill, before turning to the gaps between the democratic ideals depicted in this policy and the challenges to realizing these ideals.

The Transition to Democracy

Similarities between broader societal developments and child justice policies can again be observed during the South African democratic transition and post-apartheid periods. Child justice policies post-1994 – and the democratic transition more generally – are both characterized by the concepts of "restorative justice" and "Ubuntu". Nobel Peace Prize winner Desmond Tutu has proclaimed that the Truth and Reconciliation Commission (TRC) – a government-appointed group of people that were tasked with determining whether amnesty should have been granted to perpetrators of political crimes that occurred during apartheid – was based on the concept of "restorative justice" (Skelton, 2002).

Similarly, restorative justice is central to the Bill, defined in the final document as: "restorative justice means the promotion of reconciliation, restitution and responsibility through the involvement of a child, a child's parent, family members, victims and communities" (Republic of South Africa, 2008, pp. 9–10). The TRC and the Child Justice Bill were also both encapsulated by the concept of *Ubuntu* – an African worldview and ethos based on recognizing the humanity of others, forgiveness, social harmony and collective action (Skelton, 2002; van der Spuy, Parmentier, & Dissel, 2007). The Bill encourages the promotion of *Ubuntu* in the child justice system through fostering children's sense of dignity and worth, through reinforcing respect for human rights and the fundamental freedoms of others by holding children accountable for their actions, and by involving parents, families, victims and communities in child justice processes (Republic of South Africa, 2008, p. 9).

Parallels between the ideologies of the democratic transition and youth justice policies produced during and after this period are therefore apparent in the concepts of "restorative justice" and *Ubuntu*. This is similar to links between child justice policies and broader government ideological positions during earlier periods.

In terms of the development of new legislation, child justice in the democratic era was catalyzed by South Africa ratifying the United Nations Convention on the Rights of the Child (1989) in 1995. The African Charter on the Rights and Welfare of the Child was also adopted by South Africa in 2000. Thus, the country officially entered into international agreements to establish laws, procedures, and institutions to aid children in conflict with the law. A consultative process produced a draft Child Justice Bill in 2000; however, the Bill could not be passed before the 2004 elections, meaning that it was only reintroduced to parliament in 2007. Civil society organizations and institutions participated in the process, both separately and as a collective under the banner of the newly-formed Child Justice Alliance. The Bill was passed in 2008 and signed and eventually implemented in 2010 (Badenhorst, 2011).

Prior to the implementation of the Bill, other legislation aided children who came into contact with the criminal justice system after the end of apartheid. The 1996 Constitution of the Republic of South Africa states that:

- all the due process rights applicable to arrested, detained and accused persons also apply to children;
- children have the right not to be detained except as a measure of last resort and for the shortest appropriate period of time;
- children have the right, when detained, to be kept separately from persons over the age of 18 and the right, when detained, to be treated in a manner and kept in conditions that take account of the child's age (Republic of South Africa, 1996).

In addition to constitutional legislation, a new Section 29 of the Correctional Services Act of 1959 stated that the detention of children awaiting trial should be minimized as far as possible, and that only children charged with serious offenses, who are between the ages of 14 and 18 years old, should await trial in prisons (Badenhorst, 2011).

The Child Justice Bill

Age of criminal capacity

According to the Bill, children under ten have no criminal responsibility and a prosecutor needs to prove that 10–14 year olds accused of a crime indeed have criminal capacity. One problem is that only 40% of South African children have registered birth certificates (Skelton & Tshehla, 2008). The Bill states that the probation officer can use a list of stipulated documents to estimate the age of the child; the magistrate may also estimate the age of the child or a medical practitioner may be called upon to determine the child's age (Skelton & Tshehla, 2008). Minimum sentencing requirements that apply to adults accused of transgressing the law do not apply to children (Skelton, 2002).

Arrests

The Bill sets out alternatives to arresting the child, and children may not be arrested for a petty offense without compelling reasons. Instead, parents or caregivers should be sent a written letter, or a summons, communicating when the child is required to appear at a preliminary inquiry (Badenhorst, 2011). A probation officer needs to be informed of the arrest or alternative action to an arrest, for example notifying a parent, within 24 hours (Skelton & Tshehla, 2008). Some evidence exists that since the implementation of the Bill, summonses and written notices are not being distributed in an effective manner (Badenhorst, 2011).

Every child who is accused of committing an offense, even those under 10 years of age, must be assessed by a probation officer (these are qualified social workers). Assessment is intended to establish whether the child is in need of care, gather information related to previous cases pertaining to the child, decide whether diversion is possible, and consider whether an adult has used the child in order to commit the crime in question (Skelton & Tshehla, 2008). If a child is indeed arrested, s/he must appear at a preliminary inquiry within 48 hours.

Preliminary inquiry

The preliminary inquiry is an aspect of the Bill observed by international commentators as highly innovative and exemplary to child justice systems elsewhere (Stout, 2006). It is an informal, pre-trial procedure during which the probation officer's assessment, diversion options and the appropriateness of a children's court referral, are considered (Skelton & Tshehla, 2008). Participation of the child and his/her parents at the inquiry should be encouraged (Republic of South Africa, 2008). Upon completing the preliminary inquiry, the magistrate may release or detain the child. A child placed in prison must be brought back to the preliminary inquiry every 14 days, and prison should be seen as a last resort and only enforced for the shortest possible time (Skelton & Tshehla, 2008). In accordance with the United Nations Convention on the Rights of the Child, which South Africa has ratified and echoed in the South African Constitution, incarcerated children are required to be separated from incarcerated adults. There is evidence that this form of constitutional protection is not always upheld, with children continuing to share police and prison cells with adults (Skelton & Tshehla, 2008).

Diversion

Diversion is a core component upon which restorative justice is premised and may be decided upon prior to or during the preliminary inquiry. More specifically, diversion is the process of steering 14–17 year olds away from the criminal justice system, hence avoiding him or her being exposed to the violence that exists in its institutions (Dawes & van der Merwe, 2012). Prior to the implementation of the Bill, Skelton (2002) estimated that if the new law was used effectively, half of the child offenders could be diverted. The Bill outlines three levels of diversion; level one is a set of short, non-intensive programs, with levels two and three comprising longer and more intensive programs. These different levels have been devised in order to encourage practitioners not to perceive diversion as a unilateral process, but as a heterogeneous set of options for minor and more serious offenses (Skelton, 2002). The child is required to accept responsibility in order to be diverted (Dawes & van der Merwe, 2012). Diversion programs include life-skills, peer/youth mentoring, wilderness therapy, skills training/educational or entrepreneurship programs, therapeutic programs, oral/written apologies, community service or multi-modal programs, victim offender mediation, and family group counselling (Dawes & van der Merwe, 2012).

Children's courts

Trials of children are not open to the public. All three levels of courts – district, regional, and high courts – may preside over cases involving children; the level of the court is determined according to the severity of the charge. The court may still recommend diversion, even if the preliminary inquiry found diversion to be inappropriate (Skelton & Tshehla, 2008; Badenhorst, 2011). Children have the right to legal representation in cases where "substantial injustice would otherwise occur" and when the child and his/her family cannot afford legal representation. The legal representative is required to explain to the child what his or her rights comprise, in an age-appropriate manner (Skelton & Tshehla, 2008).

Sentencing

In the case of a child committing a less serious schedule 1 offense (for example, theft to the value of less than US$250, common assault, or possession of illegal narcotics to the value of less than US$50), the Bill encourages that the child is released, either on bail or into the care of a parent or appropriate adult (Republic of South Africa, 2008). The magistrate who presides over the preliminary inquiry is also granted the power to release the child, regardless of the offense. Imprisonment should only be used as a measure of last resort and for the shortest time possible (Republic of South Africa, 2008). The objectives of sentencing child offenders to imprisonment are to help the child take responsibility for harm done to others. The sentence should be appropriate to the particular child and proportional to the offense committed (Badenhorst, 2011).

Children may receive community-based sentences with stipulated diversion options, correctional supervision – which is tantamount to house arrest – or they may be sentenced to imprisonment. Children under 14 years at the time of being sentenced for the offense may not be imprisoned, and children over 14 years of age may only be imprisoned for a schedule 1 offense if they have a record of prior convictions (Skelton & Tshehla, 2008).

Two one-stop Child Justice Centres have been established to enhance cooperation between government departments, NGOs and other civil society organizations, and increase the speed at which children can be processed through the system, hence avoiding cases where children are left awaiting trial for extended periods of time. Initial reports suggest that these centres are operating highly effectively and efficiently (Badenhorst, 2012).

Snapshot of children in contact with the law
- Approximately 10,000 children are apprehended/arrested monthly by the police.
- Between 2,750 and 4,000 appear in court.
- Roughly 1,300 to 1,900 children are diverted from court each month.
- Around 1,000 children are detained in prison awaiting trial.
- In June 2009 there were 908 sentenced children incarcerated and 689 awaiting trial in prison (Parliamentary Research Unit report 2008, in Badenhorst, 2011, p. 8)

Challenges to the Implementation of the Bill

The Bill therefore lays out an extremely progressive set of practices and recommended courses of action, contained within a restorative justice paradigm. However, contemporary South Africa is characterized by rampant inequality and the legacies of colonialism and apartheid, meaning that young people do not experience "justice" in their daily lives and most have yet to reap the material benefits often assumed to accompany democracy. This leads to frustration and, at times, transgressions of the law. What is particularly concerning about law-breaking in South Africa is not the amount of criminal activity, but the violent character of these actions. The homicide rate was 184 per 100,000 amongst 15–29 year olds in the year 2000, which is nine times higher than the international average (Ward, Dawes, & Matzopoulis, 2012). This was twice as high as homicides amongst 15–29 year old men in low- and middle-income countries in the Americas, the region with the highest homicide rate for this cohort globally (Ward *et al.*, 2012). The violent nature of youth crime is also apparent in a Centre for Justice and Crime Prevention study of 12–25 year old young offenders from four provinces ($n = 395$). The research found that 30.9% were incarcerated for armed robbery/robbery, 23.5% for housebreaking, 10.6% for rape and 10% for murder (Burton, Leoschut, & Bonora, 2009); 59.2% stated that they carried a gun, knife, or other weapon for protection, and 48.1% stated that they had used force, threats, or a weapon to steal from another person (Burton *et al.*, 2009).

Part of the reason for these high rates of South African children breaking the law and perpetrating acts of violence is the fact that material and economic transformation and redistribution has yet to occur in the post-apartheid period, leading Samara (2005) to comment that crime is a symptom of unresolved race/class conflict. Inequality is demonstrated through differences in income, unemployment, child poverty, and educational attainment. The Gini coefficient measures inequality by looking at the difference between household incomes for the wealthiest 20% of a country's population versus the same incomes of the poorest 20% of the population. South Africa consistently has one of the highest Gini coefficients globally (Bosch, Rossouw, Tian Claassens, & du Plessis, 2010). Youth unemployment is generally agreed to be the country's greatest challenge (Sparks, 2010), with 51% of 15–24 year old South Africans unemployed (Statistics South Africa, 2010).[2] Even in comparison to other developing countries, the South African youth unemployment rate is extremely high (Bhorat & Oosthuizen, 2007).

South Africa has alarmingly high rates of child poverty, which also demonstrates structural inequalities. Hall and Chennells (2011) calculated that 75% of South African children live in households that survive on less than US$120 income per person per month, 60% live in households with less than US$60 per person per month, and 35% of children lived in households that receive less than US$30 per person per month. Children living in homes that suffer from income poverty are severely unevenly dispersed in terms of geography and race, with urban areas and white[3] children much better off (Hall & Chennells, 2011).

Gross inequalities also exist in the education system. In 2007, amongst the white population of 21–25 year olds, more than 80% had completed at least 12 years of education, yet in the same age group amongst black youth only 35% had completed this level of education (Bhana *et al.*, 2011). Socio-economic level can also be used to predict secondary school completion. Using National Income Dynamics Study data – a national, representative panel study ($n = 28,000$) in which young people are divided into five socio-economic quintiles – Bhana *et al.* (2011) estimated that more than 80% of youth in the wealthiest quintile complete grade 12, in comparison to 23% in the poorest quintile. Finally, as many as three million NEETs – children Not in Education, Employment or Training – are estimated to exist. These descriptive statistics demonstrate that although many new rights and progressive policies, such as the Child Justice Bill, have been crystallized in legislation, young people often do not experience the benefits of the new democracy. Large numbers of children breaking the law may therefore be one symptom of a society that is legally and politically democratic, but economically and socially skewed.

Structural inequality is accompanied by the fact that young people are the most likely age cohort to be victims of criminal activity, in addition to being the most likely perpetrators of crime. Burton (2008) stated that young people are twice as likely to be victims of crime, in comparison with adults. In the period between September 2004 and September 2005, 42% of South African 12–22 year olds experienced crime or violence, with 27% victims of violent crime and 26% falling prey to property crime (Burton, 2008). Even though corporal punishment was made illegal in schools in 1996, seven out of ten primary school children and half of high school youth report having been hit, caned or spanked by educators or the principal (Burton, 2008). South Africa therefore exhibits a situation in which democracy and a set of liberatory legislative measures are combined with gross inequality and violent, illegal actions that have become normalized in everyday settings of the school, home, peer group and community, producing what Pelser (2008) has called a "culture of violence".

Another challenge to realizing the objectives of the Bill is the transformation and capacitation of key institutions and role-players in the child justice system, for example, the police and social workers, such that they have the capacity to practice crime prevention through social development. Historically, police officers in South Africa have been fundamentally punitive in terms of their practice and many have little understanding of child development and what is considered to be in the best interests of children. In one of the first reports since the introduction of the Bill, the Child Justice Alliance states that the number of children entering the youth justice system has decreased substantially and the number of children being diverted has also diminished (Badenhorst, 2012). Badenhorst (2012) attributes these decreased numbers to the lack of police training, meaning that law enforcement officers are unsure how to proceed when encountering children suspected of breaking the law, choosing instead not to apprehend these children.

Restorative justice provides a dynamic framework that encourages police to use a broad reservoir of resources, including communities, families, and grassroots institutions, but the policy requires skilled, well-trained police that are able to utilize these resources and implement this approach (Shearing & Foster, 2007). Children being neglected by law enforcement officers means that those young people who should enter the system and receive early intervention services are denied support. The decreased number of children being dealt with by police may also influence the public to reject the new legislation, as the public is already partial to stricter, more punitive measures, often leading to people taking the law into their own hands, in the form of vigilante justice (Badenhorst, 2012).

Conclusion

South Africa's new Child Justice Bill is a monumental achievement, both in terms of its final form and the persistence of civil society organizations working with government to achieve this end product. The ethos of the South African transition, one that was permeated by a spirit of peaceful reconciliation, combined with the growing momentum of an international restorative child justice paradigm, were structural antecedents that led to the production and particular form of the final Child Justice Bill (Skelton & Tshehla, 2008). The Bill marks a break with previous child justice policies in South Africa, which were used by the state to enforce broader, oppressive regimes. Widespread institutionalization and violence were integral to these earlier child "justice" systems.

However, democratic legislation is only the first phase to constructing a democratic society. This new legislation needs to be followed by work to bridge the hiatus between progressive policy and everyday inequalities that people on the ground experience as unjust. The contemporary South African child justice system therefore demonstrates a tension between some of the most progressive democratic ideals and the realities of massive inequality that exist in a society where violence has become a normal means of problem-solving. In order to treat the "cause" of an unhealthy society, and not merely the "symptoms" that manifest in the form of youth crime, solutions need to be found that are transformative and redistributive at individual, family, school, community, and societal levels. Quality diversion programs that create alternative pathways for young people and, in so doing, stimulate forms of community development, need to be constructed through partnerships that include multiple government departments. Personnel working in the child justice system need to be trained to facilitate these processes using a range of resources, including those that are not directly within their ambit. As former president Nelson

Mandela said, "there can be no keener revelation of a society's soul than the way in which it treats its children". South Africa's "soul" remains in the balance and much work is still required to be done.

Notes

1 This chapter uses the term "child" because the South African Department of Correctional Services (1998) defines children as people under 18 years of age, whilst juveniles and youth are 18–21 and 22–24 years old respectively.
2 This is according to the official definition of work, which means that youth must have sought employment within the past four weeks and may only be working as little as one hour per week. The real rate of unemployment amongst this age group is likely to be much higher.
3 The use of racial classifications in this chapter refers to historically designated categories that continue to have relevance in contemporary South Africa in terms of the likelihood of different forms of deprivation. The use of these categories is not intended to imply that fixed racial categories "exist" in a biological or essentialized manner.

References

Badenhorst, C. (2011). *Overview of the Implementation of the Child Justice Act 2008: Good Intentions, Questionable Outcomes*. Report for the Open Society Foundation for South Africa. Cape Town: Open Society Foundation for South Africa.

Badenhorst, C. (2012). *Second year of the Child Justice Act's Implementation: Dwindling Numbers*. Cape Town: Child Justice Alliance.

Badroodien, A. (1999). Race, crime, welfare and state social institutions in South Africa from the 1940s. *Social Dynamics*, 25(2), 49–74.

Bhana, A., Swartz, S., Taylor, S., Scott, D., Vawda, M., & Dlamini, N. (2011). *Status of youth report 2004–2010: Social cohesion, youth skills, youth work and the national youth service programme*. Draft Report submitted to National Youth Development Agency (NYDA).

Bhorat, H., & Oosthuizen, M. (2007). Young people and the labour market. *Africa Insight*, 37(3), 388–403.

Bosch, A., Rossouw, J., Tian Claassens, T., & du Plessis, B. (2010). *A Second Look at Measuring Inequality in South Africa: A Modified Gini Coefficient*. University of KwaZulu Natal School of Development Studies Working Paper No 58.

Burton, P. (2008). *Merchants, Skollies and Stones: Experiences of School Violence in South Africa*. Centre for Justice and Crime Prevention, Monograph No. 4. Cape Town: Centre for Justice and Crime Prevention.

Burton, P., Leoschut, L., & Bonora, A. (2009). *Walking the Tightrope: Youth Resilience to crime in South Africa*. Centre for Justice and Crime Prevention, Monograph 7. Cape Town: Centre for Justice and Crime Prevention.

Chisholm, L. (1986). The pedagogy of Porter: The origins of the reformatory in the Cape Colony, 1882–1910. *Journal of African History*, 27(3), 481–495.

Dawes, A., & van der Merwe, A. (2012). Interventions for young offenders: what we know about what 'works' in diversion programmes. In C. Ward, A. van der Merwe, & A. Dawes (Eds), *Youth Violence: Sources and Solutions for South Africa*. Cape Town: UCT Press.

Department of Correctional Services. (1998). *Correctional Services Act (Act No. 111 of 1998)*. Pretoria: Government Printer.

Hall, K., & Chennells, M. (2011). *Children and Income Poverty: A Brief Update. Children Count Brief*. Cape Town: Children's Institute, University of Cape Town.

Pelser, E. (2008). *Learning to be Lost: Youth Crime in South Africa*. Discussion paper for the HSRC youth policy initiative, Reserve Bank, Pretoria, 13 May 2008. Cape Town: Centre for Justice and Crime Prevention.

Republic of South Africa. (1996). *The Constitution of the Republic of South Africa (Act No. 108 of 1996)*. Pretoria: Government Printer.

Republic of South Africa. (2008). *Child Justice Act (Act No. 75 of 2008)*. Pretoria: Government Printer.

Samara, T. (2005). Youth, crime and urban renewal in the Western Cape. *Journal of Southern African Studies*, 31(1), 209–227.

Shearing, C., & Foster, D. (2007). Back to the future in South African security: from intentions to effective mechanisms. In E. van der Spuy, S. Parmentier, & A. Dissel (Eds). *Restorative Justice: Politics, Policies and Prospects*. Cape Town: Juta and Co.

Skelton, A. (2002). Restorative justice as a framework for juvenile justice reform: A South African perspective. *British Journal of Criminology*, 42, 496–513.

Skelton, A. (2007). Tapping indigenous knowledge: traditional conflict resolution, restorative justice and the denunciation of crime in South Africa. In E. van der Spuy, S. Parmentier, & A. Dissel (Eds.), *Restorative Justice: Politics, Policies and Prospects*. Cape Town: Juta and Co.

Skelton, A., & Tshehla, B. (2008). *Child Justice in South Africa*. Institute for Security Studies Monograph 150. Pretoria: ISS.

Sparks, A. (2010). Newcastle points the way to beating unemployment. *Business Day*, 10 November 2010.

Stout, B. (2006). Is diversion the appropriate emphasis for South African child justice? *Youth Justice*, 6, 129–142.

van der Spuy, E., Parmentier, S., & Dissel, A. (2007). Editorial preface. In E. van der Spuy, S. Parmentier, & A. Dissel (Eds.), *Restorative Justice: Politics, Policies and Prospects*. Cape Town: Juta and Co.

Ward, C., Dawes, A., & Matzopoulis, R. (2012). Youth violence in South Africa: setting the scene. In C. Ward, A. van der Merwe, & A. Dawes (Eds.), *Youth Violence: Sources and Solutions for South Africa*. Cape Town: UCT Press.

7

Juvenile Delinquency and Juvenile Justice in China

Beidi Dong

Introduction

As the importance of international and comparative criminology has grown over the past two decades (e.g. Bennett, 2004; Howard, Newman, & Pridemore, 2000), the significance of studying China, as a comparison and contrast to American society, has been recognized. To date, there has been limited international literature on China's juvenile delinquency and justice system. Three major reasons account for such scarcity in the literature. First, Chinese society presents unique social and cultural characteristics that differ significantly from American society. While "egalitarianism" and "vigilantism" are two widely discussed features of punishment culture in America (e.g., Miethe & Lu, 2004; Zimring, 2004), Confucianism, as a collectivist culture, teaches individuals to uphold the honor of their family, to think of the consequences of their behaviors to the groups to which they belong, and to be loyal to friends and rulers. Confucianism also shares a number of similarities with socialism today in that it promotes collective interests, self-control and self-sacrifice for the welfare of the community and organization (Yue, 2002). It may be difficult for Western scholars, for instance, to truly understand informal networks of social control in China, which play down individual rights and highlight collective responsibility. Second, the dominant paradigm of criminology in the US emphasizes the use of quantitative methods to achieve an objective understanding of causes of juvenile delinquency and its prevention. For historical and political reasons, the Chinese tradition of studying crime and delinquency tends to be non-empirical. In addition, there are many formidable difficulties to obtain either official or self-reported data on crime and delinquency in China. All of these have resulted in very

The Handbook of Juvenile Delinquency and Juvenile Justice, First Edition. Edited by Marvin D. Krohn and Jodi Lane.
© 2015 John Wiley & Sons, Inc. Published 2015 by John Wiley & Sons, Inc.

limited data available to international researchers. The language barrier is another major obstacle for international communications. Western criminologists rarely read and write in Chinese, and the English of many criminologists in China is also not entirely satisfactory. As a result, discourse between American criminologists and their counterparts in China tends to be sporadic.

Against this backdrop, this introductory chapter aims to provide readers with some basic understanding of juvenile delinquency and justice in China. First, the chapter defines the concept of juvenile delinquency in China and points out that "criminal offenses" and "violations of law" are two different concepts in China. Second, the chapter reviews the nature and scope of juvenile delinquency in post-revolutionary China. The chapter then elaborates on the development of legislation on juvenile justice in China, focusing on the two important national laws. Last but not least, the chapter discusses the reformation of juvenile delinquents.

The Concept of Juvenile Delinquency in China

The legal basis for juvenile criminal responsibility is stipulated by Article 17 of the Criminal Law of China. According to the law, any person who has reached the age of 16 and who commits a crime shall bear criminal responsibility. Juveniles between the ages of 14 and 16 can be held criminally liable only when they have committed certain crimes that are specified by the law, such as homicide, aggravated assault, robbery, or rape. Article 17 further states that juvenile offenders between 14 and 18 years old should receive mitigated punishment and should not be sentenced in the same manner as adult offenders.

It is worth mentioning that "criminal offenses" and "violations of law" are two different concepts in China. Crime is defined as behaviors that reach a certain degree of seriousness according to the Criminal Law and that are treated before criminal courts. "Violations of law", on the other hand, are relatively minor delinquent acts that do not qualify as criminal offenses and that are usually dealt with under the authority of administrative regulations and interventions.[1] It is still common practice in China today to handle a large percentage of minor juvenile delinquent acts as "public order violations" according to the Regulations on Administrative Penalties of Public Security.[2] Chinese authorities typically describe crimes committed by minors between the ages of 14 and 18 as *juvenile* delinquency, and crimes committed by youth under the age of 25 as *youth* delinquency. In this chapter, we use the concept of juvenile delinquency in a broader sense, including not only criminal offenses but also minor law infractions.

The Nature and Scope of China's Juvenile Delinquency

Estimating the extent of China's juvenile delinquency is difficult due to limited access to data. Although Chinese government agencies have released some numbers, many statistics are kept as state secrets for internal use only (Bakken, 2004). Despite these difficulties, several scholars (e.g., Bakken, 1993; Wong, 2001; Yue, 2002) have made efforts to depict the changing reality of juvenile and youth delinquency in China.

China enjoyed a low crime rate after the founding of the People's Republic in 1949. The mid-1950s are still remembered as a golden time when "doors were unbolted at night and no-one pocketed anything found on the road" (Bakken, 1993, p. 29). For instance, the total crime rate per 100,000 population in 1956 was 23, and juvenile delinquency was equally low and constituted an insignificant portion of the overall crime rate. The official viewpoint at that time was that existing crime was a remnant of the "old capitalist society" led by Kuomintang, and characterized by inequalities in wealth, power, and life chances. The establishment of a socialist state was seen to have the capability to eliminate the roots of criminality (He, 1991).

It was not until the period of the Cultural Revolution that juvenile delinquency emerged as a noticeable social problem. In 1966, the radical left in China launched the Cultural Revolution to enforce communism in the country by removing capitalist, traditional and cultural elements from Chinese society, and to consolidate Mao's leadership of the Communist Party. During the Cultural Revolution, youth were encouraged to struggle against their parents, teachers, and authority figures to bring an end to the "Four Old Things" (old customs, old culture, old habits, and old ideas). As a result, traditional family and educational values and practices were downgraded and rejected by young people, many of whom felt at a loss and became involved in antisocial behavior. This was devastating for a society that relied on the social collective to prevent crime. The formal legal system including the public security system and judiciary was also paralyzed at that time. No official crime statistics were collected during that period of time. It was estimated that during the Cultural Revolution, the total crime rate per 100,000 population was between 40 and 60, and youth crime accounted for 40–50% of total crimes (Bakken, 1993).

China experienced something of a "crime boom" beginning in the 1980s. In particular, the upsurge of juvenile and youth crime attracted great attention from both Chinese leaders and researchers. Available statistics indicated that youth delinquency rates rose from 84 per 100,000 young people in 1979, to 195 in 1981. In terms of the percentage of juvenile delinquency of total crime, there was an increase from 7% in 1980 to 20% in 1982 (Bakken, 1993). A campaign of "hard strike" against crime was launched in 1983 to halt this trend. The anticrime campaign particularly targeted juvenile gang leaders with the purpose of getting rid of hard-core criminals through harsh punishment and deterring the rest from criminal involvement. Capital punishment was extensively used during the campaign. A temporary effect of deterrence was observed after the campaign, but the general trend of delinquency remained upwards. Juvenile delinquency rates rose from 106 per 100,000 in 1986 to approximately 190 in 1996, and youth delinquency rates rose from 122 per 100,000 in 1986 to approximately 300 in 1996 (Wong, 2001). Moreover, data published in 2007 showed that the number of juvenile criminals rose from 33,000 in 1998 to an estimated 80,000 in 2007. Juvenile offenders have been growing younger and increasingly violent (Bao & Haas, 2009).

Legislation on Juvenile Justice in China

The Chinese legal tradition centers on Confucian philosophy, and emphasizes moral education and persuasion over rigid penal codes in regulating people's behavior (Zhang & Liu, 2007). Mao, with old-generation communist leaders, assimilated these traditional beliefs about virtue and education in constructing the mechanisms of social control. Under Mao's leadership, China barely established a stable legal system. The routine methods for social control were "continuous revolution" and "class struggle" rather than the enactment and enforcement of legal statutes. After Mao's death, the new leadership realized the importance of law and a stable legal system as China began carrying out economic reforms in the late 1970s. "The new leaders have accordingly taken a series of steps to reconstruct the legal system and have promulgated many laws in order to promote a shift from rule of man to rule of law" (Zhang, Messner, & Lu, 1999, p. 438). It was estimated that the National People's Congress enacted 185 laws between 1978 and 1997, which is about seven times the total number of enacted laws (26 laws) after the founding of the People's Republic in 1949 (Young, Chen, & Gan, 1998).

As part of the legal reform and inspired by the United Nations Standard Minimum Rules for the Administration of Juvenile Justice (the Beijing Rules), and the United Nations Convention on the Rights of the Child, China passed its first national law concerning juvenile justice in 1991.[3] The main purpose of the Juvenile Protection Law (JPL) is to "protect juveniles in all aspects of life" (Yue, 2002, p. 105). The JPL has seven Chapters and 72 total Articles. Chapter I indicates that the guiding principle of the law is to protect the physical and mental health of minors, safeguard their legal rights and interests, and promote their intellectual and moral development. Chapters II, III and IV elaborate on the duties and responsibilities of various institutions, including family, school, government agencies, and other social organizations, on the welfare and legal rights of minors.

Judicial protection is stipulated in Chapter V of the JPL. Several principles have been provided for the first time to protect juvenile delinquents in criminal proceedings (Yue, 2002). For instance, the law regulates that parents or other legal guardians should be present when police or prosecutors interrogate a juvenile suspect (Article 56). Juvenile suspects should be detained separately from adult suspects when in custody, and juvenile offenders should be housed separately from adult offenders (Article 57). There are also provisions that prohibit disclosure of personal information on suspected and accused juveniles by print or other media (Article 58). Chapter VI addresses legal responsibility and accountability if the protection law is violated, and Chapter VII highlights the date the law took effect.

Although the passage of the Juvenile Protection Law marks a milestone for legislations on juvenile justice in China, some provisions contain rather vague principles, and the implementation of the law relies on other laws or regulations such as criminal law, criminal procedure law, marriage law, and so on (Yue, 2002). As an ongoing legal effort to standardize and formalize the practice of juvenile justice in China and further control rising delinquency, a second national law on juvenile justice was enacted in 1999 – the Juvenile Delinquency Prevention Law (JDPL) – which is a development and extension of the JPL. "The JDPL retains the principle of juvenile protection stipulated in the JPL and extends it to delinquency prevention, rehabilitation of juvenile offenders and prevention of recidivism in delinquency" (Zhang & Liu, 2007, p. 545). The JDPL finally sets up an initial framework for the development of juvenile justice in China.

The JDPL consists of eight Chapters and 57 Articles.[4] Chapter I addresses the general principles and guidelines of juvenile delinquency prevention work in China. The law defines "comprehensive management" as the fundamental strategy of delinquency prevention in China; that is, relevant government agencies, judicial organs, relevant social groups and organizations, schools, families, neighborhood committees, and others shall participate in juvenile delinquency prevention under the uniform leadership of the government at all levels (Article 3).

Chapter II of the JDPL emphasizes education as a major measure in delinquency prevention. It stipulates that juveniles should be educated on ideals, morals, legal knowledge, patriotism, collectivism, and socialism. The purpose of such education is to strengthen legal awareness among juveniles, assist them to understand the adverse consequences of delinquency for themselves, their families, and society, and help them to establish law-abiding attitudes (Article 6). Chapter III addresses the prevention of minor delinquency. For the Chinese, "nipping crime in the bud" is always the preferred way of crime control. Accordingly, it is very important to implement early prevention and intervention before minor delinquency develops into full-scale crime. Chapter IV addresses the rehabilitation of juveniles who commit relatively serious law-violating behaviors that do not warrant criminal punishment. Details on these rehabilitative practices are provided in the next section.

As rarely seen in Western legal codes, Chapter V concerns juveniles' self-prevention of delinquency. The law stipulates that juveniles must conform to a variety of laws, statutes, and regulations, and foster a sense of self-respect, self-discipline, and self-development (Article 40). Juveniles also have the responsibility to report those who instigate or induce them to delinquency (Article 42). Chapter VI targets juvenile offenders who have received criminal punishment and addresses the prevention of recidivism. In particular, Article 46 stipulates that criminal trials involving juveniles shall proceed in juvenile courts that are legally formed by judges, or by judges and jurors, who are familiar with the physical and mental characteristics of juveniles. Some provisions in this chapter overlap with those in Chapter V of the JPL but with more details. Chapter VII defines legal liabilities in the case that parents or other legal guardians, police, various social organizations, mass media and others fail to comply with the law. Chapter VIII stipulates the effective date of the law as November 1, 1999.

In summary, compared with Western industrialized nations, the legislation on juvenile justice in China is still in its infancy. The JPL and the JDPL, however, have presented several unique features reflecting Chinese philosophy and thoughts on crime prevention and control (Zhang & Liu, 2007). First and foremost, juvenile justice in China emphasizes delinquency prevention, particularly through legal and moral education. In contrast, Western legal codes are typically created in response to crime and delinquency. In addition, both the JPL and the JDPL promote a "comprehensive management" strategy that requires the entire society to work together in delinquency prevention. This is typically not feasible in Western societies. "Western social organization does not seem to lend itself to the total-society approach to delinquency" (Zhang & Liu, 2007, p. 551). Moreover, the Chinese tend to protect all juveniles as "kids". This paternalistic approach of handling juvenile delinquents has its root in Confucian philosophy that the virtue of fatherhood is to teach children proper behavior. If a child misbehaves, the parents, particularly the father, should be held accountable. This is a different idea from the Western tradition of *parens patriae*.

Reforming Juvenile Delinquents in China

As described above, the Chinese model of delinquency control is quite different from Western models in its intentions and values. This is also true in terms of reforming juvenile delinquents. On the basis of the two aforementioned legislations on juvenile justice in China, a three-stage hierarchy of juvenile delinquent reformation can be identified: (1) educational assistance programs; (2) work–study schools; and (3) juvenile reformatories (Chen, 2000; Curran & Cook, 1993).

Community-based educational assistance programs represent a good example of how formal and informal networks of social control work together to reform juvenile delinquents in China. In general, educational assistance programs target "backward" youth who have committed minor law infractions and are deemed to be beyond the control of their parents. In practice, "education and rescue teams" are formed around juvenile delinquents, which comprised their parents, relatives, teachers, members of local neighborhood committees, and the police. Depending on the nature of the delinquent and his/her acts, appropriate measures are selected in order to "suit the remedy to the case". For different cases, these remedies include victim–offender reconciliation, heart-to-heart talks between juvenile delinquents and representatives of the "education and rescue team", group discussion of juvenile delinquents' problems and offering of criticisms and suggestions, and group study of laws and regulations. As Chen (2000) suggested, the most impressive aspect of community-based educational programs is "the important role played by the masses, not only by monitoring juvenile behavior to maintain social order but also by participating directly in the helping activities" (p. 336). For many Westerners, however, such community-based educational assistance programs may have sacrificed too many individual rights and civil liberties for delinquency prevention and control (Wong, 2001).

Work–study school is another unique mechanism of reforming juvenile delinquents in China. In short, it is a special kind of middle school designed for juveniles who have committed law-violating offenses such as petty theft, fighting or gambling repeatedly. These juveniles are deemed no longer suitable to continue the nine-year compulsory education at their original schools. Admission to the work–study school is recommended by the police or local neighborhood committees, and must have the consent of the parents. Different from regular middle schools, students in the work–study school are required to stay on campus and live together in a strict, collective way. It is believed that this can produce solidarity conducive to the internalization of rehabilitative norms and values.

As an educational institution, the curriculum of work–study schools combines "closely supervised middle-school level academic education and light labor as a means of inculcating social values and teaching self-discipline" (Chen, 2000, p. 338). Specifically, attending a work–study school involves three phases. The first phase is the "awakening" period in which students are guided to understand the nature and harmful consequences of their wrongdoings as well as the philosophy and environment of the work–study school. The second phase is the "relapse-overcoming" period, which emphasizes a blend of academic education, ideological education and vocational training. In the final "consolidating" phase, students continue to live in the work–study school but attend their original schools on some kind of probation. If they behave well, they are officially released from the work–study school. Available statistics indicate that the recidivism rate, for those held in work–study schools, is extremely low (Curran & Cook, 1993).

Although a vast majority of juvenile delinquents in China are handled through the two aforementioned channels, juvenile offenders who have committed serious offenses such as manslaughter, aggravated assault or rape are sentenced to juvenile reformatories, namely, "re-education through labor". In effect, both work–study schools and juvenile reformatories put great emphasis on education and labor, but the nature and intensity of education and labor are different. Unlike students in work–study schools, inmates of reformatories are juvenile offenders who have been officially adjudicated by a court. Students in work–study schools need not wear uniforms, but this is compulsory for inmates of reformatories. In addition, the intensity of labor in work–study schools is stipulated as "light", whereas juvenile reformatories have a "half-day education and half-day labor" schedule.

Conclusion

A number of important issues regarding juvenile delinquency and justice in China were addressed: we defined the concept of juvenile delinquency in China and differentiated "criminal offenses" from "violations of law". The former acts are subject to criminal jurisdiction, whereas the latter are handled under the authority of administrative regulations and interventions. This chapter also provided a picture of the changing nature and concepts of juvenile crime in post-revolutionary

China. From a golden time after the founding of the People's Republic in 1949 to post-reform "crime boom", China experienced a genuine rise in juvenile delinquency. Along with the rising delinquency, the development of legislation on juvenile justice in China is signified by the passage of the JPL and the JDPL.

Despite existing efforts to explore juvenile delinquency and justice in China, several important issues still need to be addressed in future research. First, statistics on juvenile delinquency and juvenile justice are poorly developed in China. Official statistics, particularly police data, are still the main source of data on crime and justice. The limitations of official statistics have been well documented and these concerns also apply to the Chinese context (Liu, 2005; Thornberry & Krohn, 2003). A handful of empirical studies have been conducted in China, but data collected from these studies are usually from convenience samples with a limited number of measures (Zhang, 2008). There is an urgent need to conduct more comprehensive, high-quality surveys and produce more reliable data for analysis. Longitudinal panel studies are of particular interest.

Second, existing international literature on juvenile delinquency and justice in China is mostly descriptive in nature, without much conceptualizing and theorizing. Descriptive information is undoubtedly necessary and useful, but it is more important to understand why and how Chinese adolescents engage in different types of delinquent behaviors and to devise appropriate rehabilitative programs for them. A number of studies have applied Western theories in the Chinese context and concluded that these theories are more or less confirmed in a different social and cultural setting (Zhang, 2008). However, the problem is that Western theories cannot fully accommodate the unique social and cultural characteristics of Chinese society. None of the existing criminological theories, for example, addresses how the rigid population control policy, namely, the "one-child policy", would impact upon juvenile delinquency and justice in China. Developing new concepts and theories would not only benefit Chinese society, but also advance and enrich our knowledge of juvenile delinquency and justice in general. Finally, future studies should broaden the research agenda. For instance, there is little research on female juvenile delinquents and their rehabilitation in China. Evaluation research should also be conducted with respect to the reformation of juvenile delinquents.

Notes

1 "Violations of law" are not equivalent to "status offenses" in the US. "Violations of law" include a wider variety of offenses with varying seriousness.
2 This has been revised and enacted by the National People's Congress as a national act in 2006.
3 Before the 1991 Juvenile Protection Law, there were only a handful of local or provincial regulations on the protection of minors in China.
4 See http://www.novexcn.com/juvenile_delinquency99.html for an English translation of the full text of the law.

References

Bakken, B. (1993). Crime, juvenile delinquency and deterrence policy in China. *Australian Journal of Chinese Affairs*, *30*, 29–58.

Bakken, B. (2004). Moral panics, crime rates and harsh punishment in China. *Australian and New Zealand Journal of Criminology*, *37* (Supplement), 67–89.

Bao, W., & Haas, A. (2009). Social change, life strain and delinquency among Chinese urban adolescents. *Sociological Focus*, *42*(3), 285–305.

Bennett, R.R. (2004). Comparative criminology and criminal justice research: the state of our knowledge. *Justice Quarterly 21*(1), 1–21.

Chen, X. (2000). Educating and correcting juvenile delinquents: the Chinese approaches. *Journal of Correctional Education*, *51*(4), 334–346.

Curran, D.J., & Cook, S. (1993). Growing fears, rising crime: juveniles and China's justice system. *Crime & Delinquency*, *39*, 296–315.

He, B. (1991). Crime and control in China. In H.-G. Heiland, L.I. Shelly, & H. Katoh (Eds.), *Crime and Control in Comparative Perspective* (pp. 241–258). New York: de Gruyter.

Howard, G.J., Newman, G., & Pridemore, W.A. (2000). Theory, method and data in comparative criminology. In D. Duffee, D. McDowall, B. Ostrom, R.D. Cruntchfield, S.D. Mastrofski, & L.G. Mazerolle (Eds.), *Measurement and Analysis of Crime and Justice* (pp. 139–211). Washington, DC: National Institute of Justice.

Liu, J. (2005). Crime patterns during the market transition in China. *British Journal of Criminology*, *45*, 613–633.

Miethe, T.D., & Lu, H. (2004). *Punishment: A Comparative Historical Perspective*. New York: Cambridge University Press.

Thornberry, T.P., & Krohn, M.D. (2003). Comparison of self-report and official data for measuring crime. In J.V. Pepper, & C.V. Petrie (Eds.), *Measurement and Problems in Criminal Justice Research: Workshop Summary* (pp. 43–94). Washington, DC: The National Academies Press.

Wong, D.S. (2001). Changes in juvenile justice in China. *Youth & Society*, *32*(4), 492–509.

Young, Y., Chen, H., & Gan, G. (1998). *The Legal History of the People's Republic of China*. Heilongjiang, China: Heilongjiang Press.

Yue, L. (2002). Youth justice in China. In J. Winterdyk (Ed.), *Juvenile Justice Systems: International Perspectives* (pp. 103–126). Toronto: Canadian Scholars Press.

Zhang, L. (2008). Juvenile delinquency and justice in contemporary China: a critical review of the literature over 15 years. *Crime, Law and Social Change*, *50*, 149–160.

Zhang, L., & Liu, J. (2007). China's Juvenile Delinquency Prevention Law. *International Journal of Offender Therapy and Comparative Criminology*, *51*(5), 541–554.

Zhang, L., Messner, S.F., & Lu, Z. (1999). Public legal education and inmates' perception of the legitimacy of official punishment in China. *British Journal of Criminology*, *39*(3), 433–449.

Zimring, F.E. (2004). *The Contradictions of American Capital Punishment*. New York: Oxford University Press.

8

Putting the Processing of Juvenile Offenders into Context

Kristin Gardner and Lonn Lanza-Kaduce

Introduction – Tensions in Dealing with Juvenile Offenders and Their Processing

Juvenile offenders are not processed in any standard way in the United States. Processing varies from place to place and over time. Several reasons for these variations need to be kept in mind as we review the legal and social context of processing juvenile offenders.

First, under the United States Constitution, police powers were reserved to the states, leaving each state to create its own system of justice and mechanism for processing juvenile offenders. The states set different age jurisdictions for juvenile courts and for juvenile corrections; age 18 is not a uniform cut-off point. Even within each state, the differences can be compounded by local practices, creating enough variation so that scholars recognize the importance of "justice by geography" (see, for example, Feld, 1991).

A second important reason for variations in processing reflects the nature of childhood itself. Maturation, with its lurches forward and retrograde moments, is not easily fit with institutional procedures for dealing with children who break the law. Indeed, Bohannon's (1973) lessons about double institutionalization in the law, leaving law "out of sync" with larger cultural beliefs and practices even as it changes those beliefs and practices, seems particularly telling in areas of law that deal with juveniles (see White *et al.*, 1999, for an example). As law reformulates norms and practices to make them fit within the legal apparatus, the law no longer mirrors the original norms and practices, and it serves as an impetus for

The Handbook of Juvenile Delinquency and Juvenile Justice, First Edition. Edited by Marvin D. Krohn and Jodi Lane.
© 2015 John Wiley & Sons, Inc. Published 2015 by John Wiley & Sons, Inc.

further change and adjustment. Law itself may be one of the reasons the juvenile justice pendulum swings back and forth.

There are competing logics when it comes to dealing with juvenile offenders. Therefore, we organize this review by looking at three inter-related clusters of tensions that have given rise to different experiences across places and over time, as well-intentioned people attempt to deal with juvenile delinquents. We contend that we learn more about the processing of juvenile offenders by considering how law and society manages these tensions in different ways, rather than by cataloging all the variations.

The first longstanding and perplexing set of tensions concerns the nature of children. How different are they from adults? At what age are youth sufficiently adult-like to be processed in the adult criminal justice system?

The second fundamental cluster of tensions relates to issues of autonomy and control. What happens when there is a breakdown in parental control, and what should be the criteria for assessing a breakdown? Who should develop the criteria for assessing a breakdown in control? Who should be responsible for the control of children? When are youths sufficiently adult-like to be autonomous and responsible for themselves and their actions?

The third area centers on the debate over the treatment and punishment of children. Are children so different from adults that rehabilitative treatment rather than criminal punishment is warranted? How effective is treatment and/or punishment in correcting youths? Does punishment require a different kind of due process from that which is required for treatment?

We argue that variations in processing and practices develop through the ways the experience of law tries to resolve these tensions. This chapter will review important issues in processing juvenile offenders using the lens of how the law and its procedures grapple with the resolution of these tensions. We open with a brief history of the tensions themselves, and then examine processing issues at various stages moving from intake to corrections.

The Historical Context of *Parens Patriae* and the Juvenile Court

In Western Europe, it seems that formal differences in processing accused children began with the infancy defense. Beginning in Roman Law and then institutional-ized in England's common law tradition, children below seven years of age were considered to be "infants" and not responsible for their crime-like behaviors. England included a rebuttable presumption in its infancy defense: youths of 7–13 years of age were presumed not to be responsible criminally unless that presumption was rebutted in court by evidence of their maturity and legal capacity. The idea and social role of "adolescent" are relatively recent developments; children were not seen as different from adults in medieval Europe. Many of them were left to fend for themselves or be exploited. In England, a legal tradition developed in the more religiously-oriented Court of Chancery (compared with the more secular King's

Bench) that allowed equitable remedies when dealing with the welfare of children. Equity allowed for individually tailored solutions for "deserving cases". The Chancery Court began to institutionalize *parens patriae*, insisting that the state could assert authority when parents failed to protect children (see Lane & Lanza-Kaduce, forthcoming).

Other developments undercut the *parens patriae* ideal. As Europe's agrarian economy gave way to commerce and industrialization, debtors' prisons and work-houses were legally authorized to house adults and criminals as well as wayward or neglected children. Child labor was legal and could be harsh and dangerous. The law permitted children to be subject to parental discipline and control including very harsh methods, and it allowed children to be indentured to masters who could work them and discipline them (see Myers, 2005).

It was in America that practices began to shift, slowly at first, towards a more complete implementation of *parens patriae*. Already in colonial Philadelphia, the Quaker's Walnut Street Jail segregated women and children from adult male criminals. During the 1800s, American society developed new approaches for dealing with youth in trouble. New York and Boston instituted "houses of refuge" in the 1820s for vagrant and neglected children, an innovation that spread. Separate reform schools were opened. The introduction of probation in the mid-1800s was extended to juveniles, and Massachusetts even experimented with a separate court process for juveniles in the 1870s (see Lane & Lanza-Kaduce, forthcoming).

In nineteenth century America, the "Child Savers" movement took hold to help the many children caught up in that era's rapid growth, migration, and urbaniza-tion. The Child Savers insisted that "children were different" and that they could be "saved". Youth were not so intractable that their wayward behaviors, which often reflected conditions over which they had little control, could not be altered. In other words, they could be treated, and treatment rather than punishment would transform them into law-abiding, contributing members of society. The Child Savers trumpeted *parens patriae* and their influence led to the first separate juvenile court in 1899 in Cook County, Illinois, premised on that philosophy.[1] The Illinois Juvenile Act of 1899 contained provisions obligating probation officers to obtain information in the best interest of the child. The court was premised on civil rather than criminal jurisdiction with its very different processes and proce-dures. The legislation also distinguished between delinquent acts (behavior that would be criminal if committed by an adult), age-related status offenses (like running away or incorrigibility), and dependency or neglect. It barred sending youths under the age of 12 to jails, and established the principle of separation of children from adult offenders.

The Child Savers and the Illinois law had an immediate impact. By 1923, all but two of the states in the US and many countries around the world had moved to a separate justice system for children (Myers, 2005). These separate systems must con-tend with the tensions regarding how different children are from adults, the role of the state, parents, and others in their control, and the relative merits of treatment and punishment when dealing with juveniles.

The Due Process Revolution in Juvenile Law and Juvenile Court Processing

By the 1960s and 1970s, concern was growing that the separate juvenile justice system fell short of the rehabilitative ideals of *parens patriae*. Instead, delinquents received interventions that were tantamount to punishment after court proceedings that curtailed due process procedural rights. In essence, the juvenile offender was receiving the worst of both worlds – punishment without procedural rights. A series of US Supreme Court cases in the 1960s and 1970s, now known as the Due Process Revolution, extended certain due process rights to juveniles that had previously existed only in the adult criminal courts. The Due Process Revolution confronted the tensions about *parens patriae* and the nature of children.

The Revolution began with *Kent v. United States* (1966). *Kent* addressed the issue of whether his judicial waiver to adult criminal court violated due process. The Supreme Court held that Kent's waiver order was invalid and accorded juveniles facing judicial waiver the following due process rights: a hearing; the right to counsel; defense attorney access to all records and reports relied upon by the judge to reach a waiver decision; and a written statement of the reasons for the waiver decision. The Court laid out criteria[2] to guide the waiver decision, including the need to address the "sophistication and maturity" of the juvenile.

The Supreme Court then applied the *Kent* rationale to *In re Gault* (1967) and extended due process rights to juvenile adjudicatory proceedings. The Court noted both that the application of due process requirements for juveniles would not interfere with the *parens patriae* purposes of the juvenile court, and that the history and theory of the juvenile court demonstrated the need for procedural rules and principles. All juvenile court adjudicatory proceedings must comply with the principles of fundamental fairness under the due process clause. Specifically, the Court accorded the following due process rights to juveniles during the adjudicatory phase: notice of the charges; right to counsel; right to confrontation and cross-examination; and privilege against self-incrimination. The right to a transcript of the proceedings and right to appellate review were not extended to defendants in juvenile courts.

The next three cases served to both extend and limit the Due Process Revolution. In *In re Winship* (1970), the Supreme Court considered whether the civil law standard of preponderance of the evidence (used in many juvenile adjudicatory proceedings) was sufficient for delinquency adjudication. The Supreme Court compared the fact-finding phase of juvenile adjudication with that of criminal cases and noted the punitive nature of the consequences for the juvenile (possible loss of liberty and stigmatization). Accordingly, the Court held that due process required proof beyond a reasonable doubt as the standard for delinquency adjudication.

In *McKeiver v. Pennsylvania* (1971), the Supreme Court held that trial by jury is not fundamental to juvenile adjudicatory hearings and is not constitutionally required. The Court remarked that requiring a jury trial in juvenile proceedings would compromise the *parens patriae* orientation of the juvenile court and end the intimate, informal, protective nature of proceedings, something it thought would be undesirable. Furthermore, a jury trial (as opposed to the traditional bench trial) would not strengthen the fact-finding process. The Supreme Court also noted that the states should be free to experiment with how to structure juvenile proceedings to make the system work as well as it can for handling juvenile problems.

Breed v. Jones (1975) dealt with the prosecution of a juvenile as an adult for the same offense for which the youth had already been adjudicated in juvenile court. The Supreme Court held that the double jeopardy protection is applicable to juvenile court adjudicatory proceedings. The treatment ideal would be meaningless if the juvenile court decision could be reconsidered in the more punitive adult court.

Although the Supreme Court did not abandon *parens patriae*, the criminalization of juvenile justice arguably contributed to the de-emphasis of rehabilitation and treatment in favor of punishment of the offender and protection of the public safety. Fear, overblown predictions of a juvenile crime wave, and the growth in the juvenile population fueled the "get-tough" movement in juvenile justice (see Howell, 2009).

> Just desert advocates promoted the use of punitive laws, policies, and practices in the juvenile justice system, including three-strike laws, determinate sentences, longer sentences, sentencing to boot camps, electronic monitoring, drug testing, shock incarceration, and other punitive measures. (Howell, 2009, p. 12)

Incarceration in juvenile prisons and transfer to the adult criminal court became strongly advocated policies for controlling juvenile crime. During the 1980s and 1990s, get-tough policies, which imputed adult-like status to many juveniles, prevailed in juvenile justice and changed processing in various ways.

Intake Decisions and Variations in Practice and Law

Despite the Due Process Revolution in juvenile law, entry into and advancement through the justice system are patterned differently for juveniles than adults. For adults, entry almost always involves law enforcement, something depicted in most criminal justice system flow charts (see, for example, Barkan & Bryjack, 2012, pp. 12–13). The interaction is with the adult suspect; the process is routinized and formal. Certainly, direct contact between law enforcement and juveniles occurs, but other longstanding possibilities exist, some of which are not infrequent (see Krisberg & Austin, 1978). "The variations … make describing this process difficult [but the] process begins when the youth is referred to the juvenile court" (Bartollas & Miller, 2014, p. 16). Complaints and referrals can be made by schools, neighbors, parents, welfare workers, or others, and the official notice does not necessarily funnel through law enforcement. It may go to the parent first instead of the juvenile. The informality of the juvenile court's civil jurisdiction is retained in many cases, and local practices can vary, especially when law enforcement officers are not involved.

The variations in practice reflect the ways in which juveniles are treated differently in the real world; they are emblematic of "common sense" ways in which society recognizes that children are different from adults. The different ways of dealing with youth in trouble also incorporate consideration of the roles that parents and other agents play, including schools, neighborhoods, and welfare officers. Intake officers in juvenile justice generally have broad discretion (Krisberg & Austin, 1978), but their role and procedures may vary from place to place and case to case (see Bartollas & Miller, 2014). They can absorb much of the uncertainty and frame case recommendations as they gather information. Intake officers can devise informal interventions and make influential formal recommendations. Juveniles are not autonomous, and some of the interventions to control and rehabilitate them could not be used with adults. These tensions play out in the processing of juveniles.

The variations and informality in juvenile intake and processing decisions indicate that juveniles are different from adults, that parents and others are important to their supervision and control, and that punishment is not the primary reason for intervening. Informality, however, may be giving way to more formal practices for reasons other than the Due Process Revolution in juvenile law. The US has seen changes in institutional arrangements. Some of them encroach on areas where parents traditionally had broad autonomy. For example, there are hotlines for reporting cases of abuse and neglect; there are reporting requirements (under threat of law) for some people (especially those who hold special relationships with juveniles, such as teachers) to report abuse, neglect, or children in need of supervision (see American Bar Association, 2009).

One major arena for working out the tension between parental autonomy and its relationship to others is the school. Law sets parameters for mandatory attendance, and truancy can be an important status offense for bringing juveniles into court and may serve as grounds in some jurisdictions to reach parents under parental responsibility enactments (see, for example, Ohio State Bar Association, 2013.) Additionally, many schools employ zero tolerance policies that formalize reactions and thereby reduce discretion for handling juvenile offenses.

The traditional informal ways in which schools and parents dealt with problem behaviors in schools have given way to reliance on school resource officers: sworn law enforcement on school campuses. The shifting institutional arrangements have the potential to "criminalize" more juvenile misconduct, for example, through formal charges of disorderly conduct (Theriot, 2009). The threats of drugs and of violence from students or against students that have institutionalized the role of the school resource officer have also affected procedural rules for processing juveniles. For example, traditional standards of probable cause and warrants under search and seizure law are compromised in the school context because of the "special needs" of schools in maintaining discipline and teaching children (*New Jersey v. T.L.O.*, 1985). The warrantless searches and seizures extend beyond those where individualized suspicion can be established and into random drug-testing for school extra-curricular activities (*Board of Education of Independent School District of Pottawatomie v. Earls*, 2002). The differences between children and adults are recognized in law and practice; the responsibility of parents to discipline and control their children is increasingly shared with schools and now sworn law enforcement officers in schools. These changes can lead to formal processing in "criminalized" due process oriented courts where punishment may displace treatment and help.

Arrest and Custody Issues

The most striking way to exert jurisdiction occurs when authorities take juveniles into custody. Although our focus is primarily on arrests for delinquent acts, we should be mindful of the variations found in the juvenile justice system and should underscore several important differences when dealing with juveniles. First, starting in the mid-1920s, many urban police departments developed specialized juvenile units and officers (Bartollas & Miller, 2014). Second, police often exercise informal options with juvenile suspects both on the streets and even at the stationhouse (Bartollas & Miller, 2014; Krisberg & Austin, 1978). Third, in addition to delinquent acts, arrests can be made for "status offenses" (e.g., truancy, running away, curfew violations), so the jurisdictional reach for juveniles is greater than that for adults. Finally, dependent and neglected children may also be taken into custody and removed from their parents (Krisberg & Austin, 1978; Siegel & Senna, 1991).

Arrests can be proactive or reactive. Taking juveniles into custody can be due to pick-up orders or other official processes that the officer uses as legal grounds for asserting custody. Arrests are premised on probable cause – enough evidence so that a reasonable person would believe that an offense was committed by the suspect (Siegel & Senna, 1991). Arguably, probable-cause determinations are similar for adults and children.

Processing differences, however, begin to emerge after that point. Officers routinely give Miranda warnings at the point of arrest, and must give them if there is any sort of custodial interrogation or questioning that occurs to secure the use of any admissions in court (*Miranda v. Arizona*, 1966). Juveniles have Miranda rights, but their juvenile status can bedevil the Miranda analysis, and the US Supreme Court has not always been consistent on whether age matters. In an early case (*Fare v. Michael C.*, 1979), age was not a sufficiently objective factor to warrant a different Miranda analysis for a 17-year-old who requested to see a probation officer rather than a lawyer. Being a juvenile did not mean that the suspect had asserted his Miranda right to silence and it was not interpreted as an imperfect way to request an attorney that should be accepted because of his age. Similarly, in *Yarborough, Warden v. Alvarado* (2004), age and inexperience were not to be used to analyze whether a lengthy interrogation of a juvenile brought to the station by his parents (upon police request and occurring after the parents were excluded from the room) constituted "custodial interrogation" that required Miranda warnings.

In 2011, the court changed direction and indicated that age was an important objective factor in determining whether a 13-year-old was in custody when being interrogated and therefore should have been given Miranda warnings

(*J.D.B. v. North Carolina*, 2011). After the *J.D.B.* ruling, age needs to be considered in determining when someone is in custody.

The US Supreme Court permits custodial interrogations of juveniles outside the presence of their parent or guardian. Some states, however, include parents because juvenile suspects are seen as needing more protection than adult suspects in these inherently coercive contexts.

> In the absence of an attorney, the confession of a juvenile which results from a custodial interrogation may not be used against the juvenile unless both the juvenile and his parent, guardian or adult friend were informed of the juvenile's rights to an attorney and to remain silent, and the juvenile must be given an opportunity to consult with his parents, guardian, adult friend or attorney as to whether he wishes to waive those rights. *In Interest of K.W.D.*, 500 S.W.2d 275 (Mo. App. 973). (see Missouri Juvenile Officer Handbook, 2013)

Because Miranda is a mere "prophylactic" to safeguard important constitutional rights (*US v. Patane*, 2004), legal disputes over confession may go deeper than the Miranda warnings themselves. The basic issue for the admissibility of confessions is their voluntariness. Courts consider whether the defendant's will was overborne by coercive features of the interrogation (see *Lynumn v. Illinois*, 1963). We may expect that age considerations matter in determining whether or how much the questioning procedures overwhelm a juvenile defendant's voluntary waiver of her/his right against self-incrimination.

One other dimension of custody warrants mention. Brief detentions (where subjects are not free to leave) during field stops under *Terry v. Ohio* (1968) allow officers to investigate suspicious activities. Although the basic requirement that officers must articulate reasonable grounds for suspicion to justify these brief detentions applies to circumstances involving suspicious adults and juveniles alike, the overall contexts that make for reasonableness play out differently for juveniles. For example, juveniles hanging out by bars or locations featuring adult activities or in alleys or parks late on school nights (or past curfews where such rules exist) give broader grounds for officers to justify their field stops of juveniles. Miranda warnings are not required in these field stops, even though officers can question the detainee about identity and activities. Inasmuch as these stops can lead to full in-custody arrests once probable cause is established via self-incrimination or plain view/plain feel evidence-gathering, the condition of age affects who can be stopped and, therefore, outcomes.

Booking and Detention Matters

Booking is a necessary processing step after custody. It entails gathering information to move the case from law enforcement to the courts, and often includes fingerprinting and photographing the suspect (see Siegel & Senna, 1991). Questions are asked, but collection of information is routinized and ministerial in nature and does not ask about the offense. Thus, answers are generally not a result of interrogation for Miranda or confession purposes. Bartollas and Miller (2014) note that, for juveniles, booking is sometimes followed by informal interventions (e.g., "talking to", diversion, or release).

Booking is usually done at a designated site, like the police station or local jail. Although booking procedures do not vary significantly for adult and juvenile arrestees (except for the need to notify parents or guardians), the sites may expose juveniles to adult criminals. The commingling of juveniles with adult criminals is a longstanding concern, which culminated in the passage of a series of provisions under the federal Juvenile Justice Delinquency and Prevention Act (hereafter JJDPA), first passed in 1973 and subsequently amended (Pub. L. No. 93-415, 42 U.S.C. sections 5601 et seq.). The JJDPA requires the removal of neglected/abused juveniles from jails and lock-ups. Juvenile status offenders are not to be held in secure conditions but must be kept under supervision while being booked or held for release to parents or guardians. Moreover, sight and sound separation of juveniles from adult offenders must be maintained. Once again, the legal system, in practice, recognizes that juveniles are different and need more protections.

Once booked and still in custody, decisions must be made regarding pre-trial release. State laws and local practices affect release decisions for juveniles. Not surprisingly, the considerations that come into play are different for juveniles. Parental involvement is often a key factor in release decisions for juveniles. The law recognizes that juveniles are different when it comes to release decisions, but practices vary widely. Some states allow bail and bonds, but a few states prohibit bail for juveniles altogether (Bartollas & Miller, 2014).

The differences for children even have constitutional dimensions. Telling are the sentiments expressed in *Schall v. Martin* (1984) to support preventive detention of juveniles who pose a serious risk while awaiting adjudication. The court's due process considerations balanced legitimate state interests in preventive detention against the liberty interests of the juvenile. The state interests included how preventive detention could protect both larger society (applicable to adults and children) and the child from the consequences of the juvenile's delinquency – clearly a *parens patriae* twist. The liberty interests of the child are significantly different from those of adults. The court recognized that juveniles, unlike adults, are always under some form of custody because they are incapable of caring for themselves completely, and that juveniles' liberty interests may be subordinated because of *parens patriae*: the state has an interest in the welfare of the child.

Waiver/Transfer to Criminal Court

In every US state, juveniles are acknowledged to be fundamentally different from adults. That's why, as a rule, they are treated differently when they break the law. But every state makes exceptions to this general rule – prosecuting some juvenile-age offenders "as adults" in criminal court, and sanctioning them in the adult correctional system. (Griffin, 2008, p. 1)

Provisions for the transfer of youths to adult criminal courts were established early on in nearly all states. Waiver to adult criminal court, however, was rarely utilized historically because it was presumed that the processing and punishment of juvenile offenders in the criminal justice system might cause them serious harm (Bishop & Frazier, 2000).

The transfer of juveniles to adult criminal court implicates all three tensions that inform this analysis. Waiver occurs because decisions have been made that a youth is mature enough to be treated as an adult. Transfer to the criminal system is a move toward a punishment emphasis. Whereas parental involvement and authority can be incorporated into juvenile court dispositions, they are largely removed once a juvenile has been transferred to criminal court.

Three major types of waiver laws exist: judicial waiver, legislative waiver, and prosecutorial waiver (Griffin, 2008).[3] Judicial waiver generally focuses on the offender and reflects rehabilitation, whereas legislative and prosecutorial waiver laws emphasize the offense and reflect just deserts or punishment.

Judicial waiver involves a formal hearing before a judge in juvenile court. Most judicial waiver is discretionary, with the discretion structured by the criteria announced in *Kent v. United States* (1966: refer to endnote ii). Some states also allow for presumptive judicial waiver. "If a juvenile meets age, offense, or other statutory criteria triggering the presumption, he or she must present evidence adequate to rebut the presumption in favor of transfer, or the case will be sent to criminal court" (Griffin, 2008, p. 3). The legislative mandates can trump the *Kent* criteria and shift the decision away from the traditional *parens patriae* concerns. Mandatory judicial waiver goes one step further, requiring juvenile court judges to transfer certain cases for criminal prosecution (thereby precluding the import of the *Kent* criteria). In such instances, the primary role of the judge is confirmation that the statutory requirements for mandatory waiver are met (Griffin, 2008).

Legislative waiver (or mandatory or statutory exclusion) utilizes offense and age criteria for the automatic transfer of youth to the adult criminal court. The legislature automatically grants exclusive jurisdiction to criminal courts over juvenile offenders of a certain age (e.g., age 16 or 17) who commit a certain offense (e.g., a violent felony) and/or who meet certain criteria (e.g., criminal record indicates two or more prior felonies). Legislative judgment replaces judicial discretion, and the *Kent* criteria are bypassed. Age often dictates that the juvenile is adult enough and that the juvenile justice system, with its treatment emphasis, is inapplicable.

Prosecutorial waiver (or prosecutorial direct file or concurrent jurisdiction) gives the prosecutor discretion to decide whether to file charges directly in either juvenile or criminal court. There is no formal hearing or specified standards (like those offered in *Kent*) for determining jurisdiction, and the prosecutor's decision is not subject to review or official records (Bishop, 2000; Singer, 1996). The prosecutor's office determines that the accused juvenile is adult enough and that the treatment options in juvenile justice should be foregone.

During the 1980s and 1990s, states implemented a number of transfer policies that expanded the reach of existing laws and made it easier than ever before to waive juvenile offenders to criminal courts (Griffin, 2003, 2008). The new provisions emphasized "prosecutorial direct filing in adult court, lowering the maximum age of juvenile justice jurisdiction to age 15 or 16, and legislative exclusion of certain offenses from juvenile court jurisdiction" (Johnson, Lanza-Kaduce, & Woolard, 2011, p. 757). The expansion of prosecutorial direct filing and legislative waiver led to a substantial increase in the number of youths transferred to criminal court nationwide. While lower, estimates suggest that the numbers of juvenile offenders judicially waived also increased (Stahl, 1999). Despite the intent to get tough on juvenile crime, most of the research shows that transfer makes matters worse – waiver is more likely to result in increased recidivism (see the review in McGowan *et al.*, 2007).

Juvenile Dispositions and Corrections – Punishment and/or Treatment

Under *parens patriae*, dispositions reflect the principle of the offender (Feld, 1987). Such an approach relies on an informal, flexible, individualized justice to meet the needs of the child and permits sentencing decisions to be made based on the particulars of each case. The principle of the offender emphasizes a treatment orientation and typically results in individualized interventions that are indeterminate, non-proportional, rehabilitative, and continued either as long as needed or for the duration of the child's minority.

The Due Process Revolution criminalized the juvenile court and altered its focus "from the Progressives' emphasis on the 'real needs' of a child to proof of the commission of criminal acts," (Feld, 1987, p. 483). During the 1980s and 1990s, the prevailing response to juvenile crime was "get-tough" punitive measures. Many states rewrote their mission statements and revamped their correctional programs to incorporate accountability and punishment (sometimes in addition to, and at other times instead of, the traditional goal of rehabilitation). In that way, the juvenile justice system became more like the criminal justice system and dispositions became more influenced by the principle of the offense (Feld, 1987), with its emphasis on factors such as prior record, seriousness of the offense, proportionality, and retribution. Juvenile courts adopted more determinate and punitive sentences for juvenile offenders.

The tension between treatment and punishment continues to play out in the experiences of juvenile law. Those experiences now show that some get-tough punitive measures like transfer to adult court may do more harm than good (see McGowan *et al.*, 2007) and that treatment "clearly works" (Howell, 2009, p. 190). Research shows that rehabilitation works, even with the most serious juvenile offenders (see the review in Lipsey & Cullen, 2007), and particularly treatment programs that incorporate risk–need–responsivity principles (Andrews, 2006; National Institute of Corrections, 2004). Accordingly, corrections should utilize evidence-based practices that focus on the risks that juvenile offenders pose to the community and others, as well as to themselves, so matters of safety and accountability are included along with rehabilitation. This can be done through the use of validated risk assessment instruments. Such instruments can also help to identify the criminogenic needs of offenders. Matching youth to the relevant evidence-based practices based on assessment results will help individualize treatment so that the youth's needs can be addressed. Evidence-based practices also deal with how well correctional interventions are tailored to, or can be responsive to the youths. Responsivity is best met via "the use of structured social learning and cognitive-behavioral strategies" (Andrews, 2006, p. 598). An important condition of success, of course, is the delivery and implementation of services.

Recent research suggests the importance of a continuum of graduated interventions. "The modern juvenile justice system includes accountability in a continuum of community-based and residential placements, with a corresponding range of therapeutic interventions" (Johnson *et al.*, 2011, p. 758). The goal is to balance the tension between treatment and punishment through graduated sanctions that meet the principles of risk, need, and responsivity. "As offenders progress in the graduated sanctions system, treatments must become more structured and intensive to effectively deal with the more intractable problems that more difficult and dangerous offenders present" (Krisberg & Howell, 1998, p. 358).

The continuum of treatment and accountability also attends to integrating external actors into treatment. For example, school behaviors and performance are often a focus of treatment needs, so that feedback from the school is important. The role of parents and families in treatment is also often incorporated. Many cognitive behavior/social learning approaches involve parenting skills (e.g., multisystemic therapy, functional family therapy). In some states, parental responsibility laws can force parents into the treatment programs (see Brank *et al.*, 2005 for a review of parental responsibility laws).

The "common sense" experiences of the courts have also modulated the swing towards punitive sentencing even for the most serious juvenile offenders facing capital punishment and life without parole. In a series of opinions (*Roper v. Simmons*, 2005; *Graham v. Florida*, 2010; *Miller v. Alabama*, 2012), the US Supreme Court clearly indicated that juveniles are different from adults and should be treated as such. *Roper* reversed directions to hold that murderers could not be executed for homicides committed when they were 16 or 17 years old. *Graham* held that it was unconstitutional to sentence a juvenile offender who neither committed nor intended to commit a homicide to life without parole. In *Miller*, which addressed the constitutionality of a mandatory life without parole sentencing scheme, the Court held that it is unconstitutional to mandate life without parole for juvenile homicide offenders; the sentencing authority must at least be given the option to consider a lesser sanction as the sentencing decision should be individualized to the case at hand. One of the major arguments by the majority in all three cases was that juveniles are less mature and less culpable for their actions than are adults. The character and personality of juveniles are not as formed and are less fixed than those of adults, and youths can be reformed.

Conclusion

This chapter began with the premise that we gain insight into important features and variations in the processing of juvenile offenders by examining how juvenile justice systems grapple with three inter-related tensions: how different or similar children are from adults when it comes to criminal offending; how responsibility and control for juvenile offending should be attributed to or shared among the juvenile, the parent(s), and others; and the relative strengths and weaknesses of treatment or punishment emphases when dealing with wayward children. Our brief review has recounted processing variations in how these tensions play out in practice and identified some unintended consequences that grew out of the efforts to resolve these tensions. In this sense, experiences, rather than explicit logic, shifted the law and practice back and forth.

We have argued that the US Supreme Court's effort to balance due process with *parens patriae* in the Due Process Revolution had the unintended consequence of criminalizing the juvenile court. That criminalization contributed to the get-tough era of the 1980s and 1990s with its emphasis on punishment, which often displaced the treatment emphasis of the original juvenile court. Moving towards a punishment orientation de-emphasizes the differences between children and adults, attributes more responsibility to the youths for their conduct, and diminishes parental authority, sometimes even interjecting the state through parental responsibility laws.

One prominent feature of the punitive get-tough movement was the expansion of juvenile waiver to adult criminal court. In many ways, no other challenge in juvenile justice brings tensions about the nature of children and the transition to adulthood into such graphic relief as the decision to transfer children to adult criminal court. The traditional *parens patriae* orientation of transferring only the worst of the worst gave way to expansive transfer practices authorized via a number of legislatively created mechanisms. Recent research evidence, referred to above, confirms that expansive transfer does not work well for a variety of reasons, so the pendulum has swung back away from the punitive response.

The Supreme Court also swung the pendulum back when it refused to extend the most punitive responses to the most serious juvenile offenders, recognizing that children are different, that they can change, and, therefore, they are less deserving of extreme punishment. Accordingly, it abandoned capital punishment for juvenile murderers, barred the use of life without parole for juvenile offenders who had not committed homicide, and restricted the use of mandatory life without parole sentences for those who had.

We contend that another way in which the Due Process Revolution affected juvenile justice can be seen in the way in which Miranda plays out for juveniles. Whereas considerations of age and maturity were originally too subjective to incorporate into an objective bright-line Miranda application, the Supreme Court has now backed away from that position to endorse the consideration of age in its application. The pendulum has swung in the direction of seeing children as different so that due process protections play out differently for them compared with adults.

We think that it has not only been the Due Process Revolution that contributed to the criminalization of juvenile conduct issues. The drug wars, violence in schools, and school shootings spawned zero-tolerance policies, altered search practices, and encouraged the introduction of school resource officers into our schools. Problem behaviors that were previously more informally dealt with by school officials and parents are now more regularly funneled through more formal channels, often going immediately to law enforcement. This is one development that continues to push practice away from the *parens patriae* orientation.

In many other ways the pendulum has swung back from a heavy punitive orientation. A growing body of research suggests that juveniles are different from adults, and research also suggests that rehabilitation can and does work while punishment does not (see Cullen, 2007). Butts and Mears (2001) concluded that "recent get-tough policies weakened the integrity of the juvenile justice system, but growing evidence about the effectiveness of new ideas in prevention and rehabilitation may save the system yet" (p. 171). Cullen (2007) calls for a new pathway in corrections, one that focuses on offender reformation and relies on the "what works" literature. Recent surveys suggest that the public believes that treatment is important for juveniles and that the public favors early intervention programs. Furthermore, the public is willing to pay for juvenile rehabilitation and early intervention programs (Nagin, Piquero, Scott, & Steinberg, 2006). As Cullen (2007) concludes, the majority of citizens favor "a balanced approach, one that exacts a measure of justice, protects the public against serious offenders, and makes every effort to change offenders while they are within the grasp of the state" (p. 721).

Notes

1   *Parens patriae* concerns extended beyond delinquency. Many states moved to enact child protection laws, but the federal Fair Labor Standards Act of 1938 (29 USC section 212) was not upheld until 1941 (*US v. Darby* 312 U.S. 100 (1941)). Active intervention against child abuse awaited radiological evidence and organizational factors in medicine to offset traditional parental authority (see Pfohl, 1977).
2   The *Kent* criteria are: the seriousness of the offense; whether the offense was committed in an aggressive, violent, premeditated or willful manner; the nature of the offense – offense against person or property, with greater weight to offense against persons, especially if personal injury resulted; the prosecutorial merit of the complaint; whether the juvenile's co-defendants were adults and if it is desirable to try to dispose of the entire case in one court; the sophistication and maturity of the juvenile; the prior criminal history of the juvenile; and the likelihood of rehabilitation and protection of the public safety.
3   In addition to these three basic transfer approaches, many states allow for one or more of the following: "once an adult/always an adult" laws, reverse waiver, and blended sentencing provisions (Griffin, 2008).

References

American Bar Association. (2009). *Mandatory reporting of child abuse*. Retrieved from http://www.americanbar.org/content/dam/aba/migrated/domviol/pdfs/mandatory_reporting_statutory_summary_chart.authcheckdam.pdf

Andrews, D.A. (2006). Enhancing adherence to risk-need responsivity: Making quality a matter of policy. *Criminology & Public Policy, 5*(3), 595–602.

Barkan, S., & Bryjack, G. (2011). *Fundamentals of Criminal Justice. A Sociological View*. Sudbury, MA: Jones & Bartlett Learning.

Bartollas, C., & Miller, S. (2014). *Juvenile Justice in America*. Boston, MA: Pearson.

Bishop, D.M. (2000). Juvenile offenders in the adult criminal justice system. *Crime and Justice: A Review of Research, 27*, 81–167.

Bishop, D.M., & Frazier, C.E. (2000). Consequences of waiver. In J. Fagan, & F.E. Zimring (Eds.), *The Changing Borders of Juvenile Justice: Transfer of Adolescents to the Criminal Court* (pp. 227–276). Chicago, IL: University of Chicago Press.

Board of Education of Independent School District of Pottawatomie v. Earls. (2002). 536 U.S. 822.

Bohannan, P. (1973). The differing realms of law. In D. Black, & M. Mileski (Eds.), *The Social Construction of Law* (pp. 306–317). New York: Seminar.

Brank, E.M., Kucera, S.C., & Hays, S.A. (2005). Parental responsibility statutes: An organization and policy implications. *Journal of Law & Family Studies, 7*(1), 1–56.

Breed v. Jones. (1975). 421 U.S. 519.

Butts, J.A., & Mears, D.P. (2001). Reviving juvenile justice in a get-tough era. *Youth & Society, 33*(2), 169–198.

Cullen, F.T. (2007). Making rehabilitation corrections' guiding paradigm. *Criminology & Public Policy, 6*(4), 717–728.

Fare v. Michael C. (1979). 442 U.S. 707.

Feld, B.C. (1987). The juvenile court meets the principle of offense: Legislative changes in juvenile waiver statutes. *Journal of Criminal Law and Criminology, 78*(3), 471–533.

Feld, B.C. (1991). Justice by geography: Urban, suburban, and rural variations in juvenile justice administration. *Journal of Criminal Law and Criminology, 82*(1), 156–210.

Graham v. Florida. (2010). 560 U.S. 48.

Griffin, P. (2003). *Trying and Sentencing Juveniles as Adults: An Analysis of State Transfer and Blended Sentencing Laws*. Pittsburgh, PA: National Center for Juvenile Justice.

Griffin, P. (2008). *Different from Adults: An Updated Analysis of Juvenile Transfer and Blended Sentencing Laws, with Recommendations for Reform*. Pittsburgh, PA: National Center for Juvenile Justice.

Howell, J.C. (2009). *Preventing and Reducing Juvenile Delinquency: A Comprehensive Framework*, 2nd ed. Thousand Oaks, CA: Sage.

In re Gault. (1967). 387 U.S. 1.

In re Winship. (1970). 397 U.S. 358.

J.D.B. v. North Carolina. (2011). No. 09-11121, slip op. U.S. June 16, 2011.

Johnson, K., Lanza-Kaduce, L., & Woolard, J. (2011). Disregarding graduated treatment: Why transfer aggravates recidivism. *Crime & Delinquency, 57*(5), 756–777.

Kent v. United States. (1966). 383 U.S. 541 (1966).

Krisberg, B. & Austin, J. (1978). *The Children of Ishmael*. Palo Alto: Mayfield.

Krisberg, B. & Howell, J.C. (1998). The impact of the juvenile justice system and prospects for graduated sanctions in a comprehensive strategy. In R. Loeber, & D.P. Farrington (eds.), *Serious and Violent Juvenile Offenders: Risk Factors and Successful Intervention* (pp. 346–366). Thousand Oaks, CA: Sage.

Lane, J., & Lanza-Kaduce, L. (Forthcoming). Juveniles in prison. In J. Wooldredge, & P. Smith (Eds.), *Prisons and Imprisonment*. New York: Oxford University Press.

Lipsey, M.W., & Cullen, F.T. (2007). The effectiveness of correctional rehabilitation: A review of systematic reviews. *Annual Review of Law and Social Science, 3*, 297–320.

Lynumn v. Illinois. (1963). 372 U.S. 528.

McGowan, A., Hahn, R., Liberman, A., Crosby, A., Fullilove, M., Johnson, R., … Stone, G. (2007). Effects on violence of laws and policies facilitating the transfer of juveniles from the juvenile justice system to the adult system: A systematic review. *American Journal of Preventive Medicine, 32*(4), 7–28.

McKeiver v. Pennsylvania. (1971). 403 U.S. 528.

Miller v. Alabama. (2012). 132 S. Ct 2455.

Miranda v. Arizona. (1966). 384 U.S. 436.

Missouri Juvenile Officer Handbook. (2013). Retrieved from http://www.courts.mo.gov/hosted/judedintra/juvenile%20Handbook/Child_Abuse_Neglect/InterInterroJuv.htm

Myers, D.L. (2005). *Boys Among Men: Trying and Sentencing Juveniles as Adults*. Westport, CT: Praeger.

Nagin, D.S., Piquero, A.R., Scott, E.S., & Steinberg, L. (2006). Public preferences for rehabilitation versus incarceration of juvenile offenders: Evidence from a contingent valuation survey. *Criminology & Public Policy, 5*(4), 627–652.

National Institute of Corrections. (2004). *Implementing evidence-based practice in community corrections: The principles of effective intervention*. Washington, DC: National Institute of Corrections.

New Jersey v. T.L.O. (1985). 469 U.S. 325.

Ohio State Bar Association. (2013). Parents must take responsibility for truant students. Retrieved from https://www.ohiobar.org/ForPublic/Resources/LawYouCanUse/Pages/LawYouCanUse-243.aspx

Pfohl, S.J. (1977). The discovery of child abuse. *Social Problems, 24*(3), 315–321.

Roper v. Simmons. (2005). 543 U.S. 551.

Schall v. Martin. (1984). 467 U.S. 253.

Siegel, L., & Senna, J. (1991). *Juvenile Delinquency. Theory, Practice & Law*, 4th ed. St. Paul, MN: West.

Singer, S.I. (1996). Merging and emerging systems of juvenile and criminal justice. *Law & Policy, 18*(1), 1–15.

Stahl, A. (1999). *Delinquency Cases Waived to Criminal Court, 1987–1996*. Washington, DC: United States Department of Justice, Office of Justice Programs, Office of Juvenile Justice and Delinquency Prevention.

Terry v. Ohio. (1968). 392 U.S. 1.

Theriot, M.T. (2009). School resource officers and the criminalization of student behavior. *Journal of Criminal Justice, 37*(3), 280–287.

US v. Patane. (2004). 542 U.S. 630.

White, H.G., Frazier, C.E., Lanza-Kaduce, L., & Bishop, D.M. (1999). A socio-legal history of Florida's juvenile transfer reforms. *University of Florida Journal of Law and Public Policy, 10*(2), 249–275.

Yarborough, Warden v. Alvarado. (2004). 541 U.S. 652.

Part II

Correlates of Delinquent Behavior

9

Gender, Delinquency, and Youth Justice: Issues for a Global Century

Meda Chesney-Lind and Nicholas Chagnon

Classic theorizing about the causes and dimensions of delinquency emerged out of a particular social and economic context. In the early nineteenth century, public and governmental interest in youthful misbehavior in the US was directly tied to explosive immigration and population growth that the country was experiencing. Between 1750 and 1850, the population of the US went from 1.25 million to 23 million. The population of some states, like Massachusetts, doubled, and in New York the population increased five-fold between 1790 and 1830. Beyond sheer numbers, many of those coming into the US during the middle of the nineteenth century were of Irish or German background; the four-fold increase in immigrants between 1830 and 1840 was largely a product of the economic hardships faced by the Irish during the potato famine (Brenzel & Joint Center for Urban Studies, 1983). The social controls of small communities were simply overwhelmed by the influx of newcomers, many of whom were either foreign-born or of foreign parentage.

Cities like Chicago were not only experiencing massive immigration and growth; they were also creating a new urban environment based on manufacturing as well as trade (unlike the cities of the Eastern seaboard, that were largely commercial ports). Ultimately, Chicago would also provide an important setting for the emerging fields of sociology (particularly urban sociology), criminology, and social work (Deegan, 1988). For these early crime researchers like Shaw and McKay (1942), delinquency and crime research provided the perfect venue to develop and demonstrate the utility of a positivist criminology to solve social problems.

Members of what came to be known as the Chicago School also borrowed from ecological approaches, and specifically rejected notions of culture and/or race playing a particular role in the generation of delinquency. They noted, instead, that

The Handbook of Juvenile Delinquency and Juvenile Justice, First Edition. Edited by Marvin D. Krohn and Jodi Lane.

behaviors tended to cluster in particular low-income neighborhoods and stay there through several different ethnic groups (i.e., much like is seen in nature in ecological succession) (Park & Burgess, 1925).

Early research from the Chicago School did come upon some key insights – ones that might travel well into the twenty-first century. Notably, a focus on subcultures, the social organization of urban neighborhoods, and the role played by class and inequality in the production of crime are important ideas. Many other influential delinquency researchers that would follow specifically noted that masculinity was at the core of many delinquent acts (often in rebellion about the confines of their circumscribed world which often included a rejection of things feminine) (Cloward & Ohlin, 1966; Cohen, 1956). Overall, though, this literature produced delinquency theories that were curiously untethered from the real consequences of boys' and men's violence. There was also the fact that not only other boys but also girls were among their victims. Oddly, even the work that was initially done on women's victimizations during the second wave of feminism[1] largely left the delinquency literature more or less untouched, mostly because the earliest work on women's victimizations focused on adult women, not girls.

Meanwhile, thinking about girls and their misbehavior, if it occurred at all, was left to an intellectually isolated collection of researchers. Many of these researchers assumed that most female misbehavior was extremely aberrant, concluding it was likely produced by extreme maladjustment. Therefore, if it existed at all, it was either expressive of women's deep venality (Lombroso & Ferrero, 1895), or shaped by girls and women's anatomies, particularly their sexuality, and their ability to be devious (Pollak, 1950).

Ironically, some of the earliest feminist work on female delinquency focused on exactly what *had* been happening to girls during the same historic period that shaped classic legal and social responses to the delinquency problem. While the earliest researchers had clearly ignored girls, the same could not be said of the founders of the juvenile justice system. Literature critically analyzing the activities of the earliest years of the juvenile court found evidence of intense focus on the policing of young girls' sexuality (Chesney-Lind, 1973; Odem, 1995; Schlossman & Wallach, 1978). This work revealed evidence of considerable discrimination against girls charged with such offenses as "sexual immorality", "waywardness" and later "incorrigibility", the status offenses of that day – non-criminal offenses that would result in the incarceration of vast numbers of young girls during most of the twentieth century (Chesney-Lind & Shelden, 2003).

The real limitations of theories born at the turn of the last century are now becoming more apparent. Despite the deeply problematic role of race in US history, no classic delinquency theories thoughtfully engaged the role of race and racism. These theories also stereotyped and celebrated masculinity, while ignoring girls, gender violence, and sexism. Finally, there was no mention of sexual orientation or homophobia, though some of the early ethnographies clearly documented extreme forms of gender violence (Thrasher, 1927). In short, classic delinquency theory tended to normalize male violence, ignore delinquent girls while trivializing their victimizations, and privileged class over other forms of oppression, particularly racial oppression and homophobia.

In this essay, we will first critically explore masculinity and gender, with a focus on the role that gender, race, class, and sexual orientation have played in male delinquency and responses to same. Following that, we will explore the role that gender and sexism has played in girls' delinquency, along with the roles that class, race, and sexual orientation have played in both girls' pathways into crime as well as the official response to girls' defiance, sometimes called "offending".

Boys' Crime and Gender: A Neglected Topic

As an established subfield of criminology, feminist criminology has generated important critiques of mainstream criminology and provided novel insights into criminal offending and victimization (Chesney-Lind, 2006). Unsurprisingly, feminist criminological inquiry often focuses on female experiences with offending and victimization (Brownmiller, 1975; Chesney-Lind & Pasko, 2013; Dragiewicz, 2011; Schwartz & DeKeseredy, 1997). However, feminist criminology also illuminates previously ignored or missed elements of male delinquency, especially by using masculinity as an analytical framework. In the near future, such inquiry promises to further delinquency research in relation to several important topics including: teen dating violence; racialized masculinities; global organized violence; and privileged delinquent offenders. Furthermore, by identifying common threads among various masculinities, feminist criminology offers a valuable counterweight to classic theories that conceptualized delinquency as a result of deviant subcultures (Hagedorn, 1998).

Dating violence

Perhaps the most prominent body of feminist criminological research is that examining violence against women (VAW). Feminist researchers have brought substantial attention to the pervasive occurrence of sexual assaults on college campuses (Koss, Gidycz, & Wisniewski, 1987; Schwartz & DeKeseredy, 1997). Additionally, these scholars have produced a large body of research examining the gendered and/ or patriarchal aspects of violence between intimate partners (Dobash & Dobash, 1979; Dragiewicz, 2011; Messerschmidt, 1986; Renzetti, 1994; Schwartz & DeKeseredy, 1993). This research often focused on adults, specifically college students and married couples. More recent research, though, has pointed out that violence – sexual, physical, and emotional – is a substantial problem among adolescent dating couples (Dichter, Cederbaum, & Teitelman, 2010; Glass *et al.*, 2003; Lewis & Fremouw, 2001; Molidor & Tolman, 1998; Mulford & Blachman-Demner, 2013). While reviewing the literature, Lewis and Fremouw (2001) stated that though most estimates are flawed, ranging from 9–45%, probably the most accurate estimate is that 30% of teens experience dating violence.

Mirroring the "gender symmetry" argument so common among studies of adult partner violence, much research on teen dating violence (TDV) finds few, if any, gender differences in prevalence (Glass *et al.*, 2003; Molidor & Tolman, 1998). Such research often measures violence with versions of the Conflict Tactics Scale (CTS) (Dragiewicz, 2011; Molidor & Tolman, 1998; Renzetti, 1994; Schwartz & DeKeseredy, 1993). CTS-based research on TDV has significant shortcomings, often merely counting acts of violence, but failing to adequately consider the severity of acts, injuries suffered, and/or the reasons for using violence (e.g., coercing a partner vs self-defense). Moreover, studies examining TDV prevalence among different racial/ethnic groups have often failed to control for important factors such as class, raising validity concerns (Dichter *et al.*, 2010). Thus, some argue that the current CTS-style research is contextually inadequate, missing the gendered elements of TDV (Dichter *et al.*, 2010; Lewis & Fremouw, 2001; Molidor & Tolman, 1998; Mulford & Blachman-Demner, 2013).

While counts of violent acts may indicate equal rates of dating violence among boys and girls, a nuanced examination of TDV illuminates clear gendered patterns. Girls are more likely to hit in self-defense, are more likely to be injured, and are more likely to suffer sexual violence (Glass *et al.*, 2003; Lewis & Fremouw, 2001; Molidor & Tolman, 1998). Boys are less likely to perceive the violence as serious or injurious, and they are more likely to be hit after making unwanted sexual advances (Molidor & Tolman, 1998). Essentially, boys' and girls' experiences with dating violence differ fundamentally; girls tend to suffer more serious consequences and use dating violence in self-defense, while boys tend to suffer less serious consequences and use dating violence to control their partners (Dichter *et al.*, 2010).

While researchers now understand that TDV is a gendered phenomenon, intensive qualitative and observational studies are needed to intimately examine the dynamics and roots of TDV (Mulford & Blachman-Demner, 2013). One way to conduct such research is to examine adolescent masculinities. Masculinities theory holds that men evaluate their manliness in relation to various normative ideal types, or masculinities (Connell, 2002; Kimmel, 2007). In Western (and many other) societies, manhood is founded upon maintaining an image of "toughness", control, and separating oneself from anything considered feminine. This distance from any femininity leads men to consider women as alien and less human than men, making it easier to harm them (Schwartz & DeKeseredy, 1997). Furthermore, many masculinities entail the idea that controlling women, especially one's partner, is a desirable method for demonstrating dominance (Hagedorn, 1998; Totten, 2003). Thus, masculinities are often a primary causal factor in violence against women, and more specifically TDV.

Qualitative research employing masculinities as an analytical framework can allow researchers to scrutinize the various masculinities employed by men and boys, and how this leads them to assault their partners. Performing such research with adolescents is particularly important in that it can illustrate the development of masculinities among boys (Kimmel & Mahler, 2003). Moreover, this inquiry can help to identify not only the diversity among masculinities, especially as employed by various class, ethnic, and racial groups, but also the commonalities among them (Hagedorn, 1998; Mayeda & Pasko, 2012; Totten, 2003).

Racialized masculinities

A key point in masculinities theory is that men's identities are not founded upon a singular masculinity common among all men, but diverse masculinities which are a product of various factors such as patriarchal ideology, structural constraints, and personal experiences[2] (Connell & Messerschmidt, 2005; Hagedorn, 1998). Much attention has been paid to the violence-producing facets of masculinities among urban black youth in the US (Hagedorn, 1998; Mayeda & Pasko, 2012). Researchers have pointed out that young black men, structurally denied legitimate avenues for demonstrating manliness, employ masculinities that deviate from the masculine models of white, middle-class men. Black men's sense of manhood is often based upon physical presence and the willingness to use violence (Anderson, 2000; Hagedorn, 1998; Miller, 2008). Such attitudes facilitate the pervasive violence experienced in poor urban communities disproportionately populated by African-Americans. While this includes the gun violence that makes homicide the leading cause of death for young black men, it is also important to note that this masculinity-borne violence is also suffered by black women (Centers for Disease Control, 2009; Miller, 2008). Miller (2008) pointed out that the ghettos are not just dangerous for black men, but also black women, who are frequently at risk of sexual assault and other forms of physical violence from the men in their community. Moreover, this danger is often under-recognized by criminologists reluctant to further vilify young black men.

Because they are the primary criminal folk devil in America, disproportionately represented in the criminal justice system, and at such high risk for interpersonal violence, black men get copious attention from criminologists, including masculinities researchers (Mayeda & Pasko, 2012; Miller, 2008). However, more research examining masculinities among other economically and racially marginalized groups in America, such as Latinos, Asian-Americans, and Pacific Islanders is needed (Mayeda & Pasko, 2012). One might refer to the masculinities employed by marginalized people of color as racialized masculinities. These masculinities are both racialized – they are imputed with racial connotations – and racializing – individuals employing them are subject to racial stigma (Omi & Winant, 2004). Research examining these masculinities among adolescents promises to build knowledge of the racializing elements of delinquency.

Global organized violence

Gangs are a significant problem in the US, especially in large cities (Decker & Pyrooz, 2010). However, they are only part of a larger global problem, also involving militias and drug cartels, which some scholars call organized violence (Dowdney,

2005). These groups are a significant presence in all regions of the world, though they are particularly problematic in Latin America and Africa (Decker & Pyrooz, 2010; Dowdney, 2005). They are a major cause of youth violence and homicide worldwide. It is difficult to quantify the consequences of such violence, but even imperfect and partial estimates clearly indicate a serious problem. For example, there were at least 7,800 US gang homicides between 2002 and 2006 (Decker & Pyrooz, 2010). Death tolls are not available globally, because many nations do not keep such records. However, the World Health Organization estimated that 199,000 youths died as a result of violence in the year 2000, and that 10 people, aged 10 to 29, die each day from interpersonal violence (Krug *et al.*, 2002). Though it is clearly a significant global problem, organized violence and its consequences for youth are under-researched.

Gender analyses promise to make important contributions to organized violence research going forward. Masculinities are an integral part of why youths join gangs, drug cartels, and militias (Bevan & Florquin, 2006). Like the experiences of American urban black youth, boys in many developing nations have few options for success. This results in a strain-like adaptation in which these youths turn to violence to prove their manhood and establish a sense of identity prestige. Youths who join these violent groups subscribe to extreme masculine ideals that associate severe violence, such as gun violence and abuse of women, with manliness (Bevan & Florquin, 2006).

It is important to note the transnational character of the masculinities associated with organized violence groups. They are not merely a product of local or national cultures – many elements of these masculinities are Western. For example, Utas (2009) acknowledged that rap music, a distinctively African-American cultural product, is quite popular among child soldiers in Sierra Leone. Rap music is rife with ideas connecting violence and manliness (Hurt, 2006). Additionally, Mara Salvatrucha, the infamous El Salvadoran gang, originated in Californian prisons, not Central America (Dowdney, 2005). Masculinities employed in these settings are surely distinctive. However, it is important to recognize their transnational and local character. Child soldiers are not merely an African problem, nor is MS-13 solely a Central American one. Both are, at least partially, products of global capitalism, militarism, the legacy of Western colonialism, and transnational notions of manhood.

Privileged delinquents

Criminologists recognize that marginalized boys are not the only boys who commit crimes – privileged white ones are involved in delinquency too (Richards & Berk, 1979). One of the most visible forms of privileged delinquency is school shootings. Media coverage of recent shootings, such as those in Newtown, CT, and Aurora, CO, has drawn much public attention to mass shootings, especially in schools. There has been no crime wave of mass shootings, yet the public may get that impression from copious and sensational media coverage (Kimmel & Mahler, 2003).

Much of the media frenzy over these shootings has centered on finding an explanation for such heinous violence. Mental pathologies, access to guns, and particularly violent media (e.g. the videogame Grand Theft Auto) have frequently been offered as causes (Kimmel & Mahler, 2003). However, few media sources have pointed out that such shootings are almost exclusively the province of young, suburban, white males. Furthermore, the perpetrators of these crimes are almost always framed as extreme deviants, suffering severe psychological pathologies. Such framing individualizes the problem of mass shootings, ignoring any culpability that mainstream culture may have.

Kimmel and Mahler (2003) have been highly critical of such discourse, offering an alternative explanation for these crimes that directly implicates mainstream culture. These scholars pointed out that school shooters are nearly all white suburban males who have been tormented by their peers for not measuring up to masculine norms. Most often, their peers barraged these boys with homophobic slurs and insults. There is no evidence that any of these boys was gay, but they tended to be quiet, artistic, introverted, or "nerdy" – all traits antithetical to the "jock" cultures of their schools. In response to perpetual and vicious affronts to their masculinity, these young men eventually lashed out in extreme violence in an effort to regain their sense of manhood (Gilligan, 1997). Ultimately, Kimmel and Mahler argued that it is not guns, psychological pathology, or violent media that cause school shootings (though they are surely issues worth addressing). Instead it is the rigid and punitive regime of gender roles in the US, which marginalizes boys who do not meet masculine norms to the point that they may respond with unthinkable violence.

Beyond school shootings, numerous problematic behaviors associated with privileged boys might be linked to masculinity. For example, the torment that drives some school shooters is essentially bullying perpetrated by more "masculine" peers (Kimmel & Mahler, 2003). This bullying, though perhaps not criminal, is clearly a form of violence perpetrated by some men against others in an effort to police masculinity (Kimmel, 2007). Also, cases like the Steubenville rape have drawn attention to the issue of sexual assault among privileged high school boys, often athletes (Bennett-Smith, 2013). Thus, we must recognize that masculinity-borne violence is not a common behavior among only marginalized men, but also among some of the most privileged.

Deviant subcultures or dominant culture?

Many classic delinquency studies looked for the causes of delinquency in deviant subcultures (Hagedorn, 1998). For example, Walter Miller's (1958) classic paper, "Lower class culture as a generating milieu of gang delinquency", located the roots of gang delinquency in particularly lower-class values, such as the normatization of "trouble", "toughness", "autonomy", and "fate", among others. Miller's argument provides useful insight. Surely there are particularities in lower-class culture, and they likely influence delinquent behavior. However, deviant subculture theories implicitly conceptualize delinquency as antithetical to dominant cultural values (Hagedorn, 1998). One might ask, is delinquency all that contradictory to mainstream values? Are criminogenic values really sub- or counter-cultural?

If we consider the insights provided by feminist criminology, we might answer these questions in the negative, at least in relation to some forms of boys' violence. Feminist criminology shows that extreme adherence to masculinities plays a causal role in violence (Connell, 2002). Furthermore, masculinities are an integral part of the dominant patriarchal culture. They provide the necessary socialization to produce men who act as hegemonic patriarchal agents. As we discussed above, there are numerous, diverse masculinities, employed by various groups. Yet, they share one common thread: the requirement that men be dominant and invulnerable. It is this need to be invulnerable and dominate which so often leads to violence, against men and women (Kaufmann, 2003). Considering this, it seems that masculine violence springs from dominant ideas about manhood, not subcultural modifications to masculinity.

Criminalizing Victimization: Girls' Lives and the Criminal System

The amount of violence against girls and women worldwide is truly staggering. The World Health Organization recently reported that "overall, 35% of women worldwide have experienced either physical and/or sexual intimate partner violence or non-partner sexual violence" and that globally "as many as 38% of all murders of women are committed by intimate partners" (World Health Organization, 2013). Since violence against girls and women is such a vast problem, and the site of such violence is frequently the home, one wonders whether classic theorizing about delinquency and crime applies at all to girls' and women's victimization, let alone girls' offending. Recall that much of this theory and research was really built upon notions of urban youth subculture, the slum, and the streets – so the field saw its role as basically predicting and explaining public male crime and mostly male victimization. Note that Shaw and McKay (1942), in their classic work on delinquency, only reported male crime rates (p. 356).

Since the abuse of so many girls and women persists, one has to ask hard questions not only of crime researchers but also the system that promises justice and the prevention of victimization: the police, the courts, and the prisons. Certainly, if the goal of criminal justice systems worldwide is public safety, it has failed girls and women spectacularly. While there are some encouraging signs globally (Hadi & Chesney-Lind, 2014), there is mounting evidence that girls and women cannot count on the criminal justice system to provide them with protection from male violence or to resist the endorsement of male privilege in patriarchy.

Indeed, there is ample evidence globally that many girls and women who start off as victims are often punished as criminals, particularly when they are victimized within the family. In Afghanistan, for example, approximately 600 women and girls are imprisoned for "moral crimes", according to a report by Human Rights Watch

(2013); this represents a 50% increase in the last year and a half. The report indicated that almost all the girls in juvenile detention and about half of the women in Afghan prisons had been arrested for "moral crimes". These "crimes" usually involved flight from unlawful forced marriage, domestic violence, or an alleged relationship outside of marriage where in reality the women had been raped or forced into prostitution.

The judicial enforcement of patriarchal authority is not simply a concern among girls and women in Afghanistan and other economically marginalized parts of the world – what some might characterize as the global south (Lee & Laidler, 2013). In the US, arrests of girls account for nearly a third of all arrests of young people (Federal Bureau of Investigation, 2011), and many of these girls are being held for a wide range of behaviors that violate parental authority: "running away from home", being "a person in need of supervision", "a minor in need of supervision", "incorrigible", "beyond control", "truant", or in need of "care and protection". Although not technically crimes, these offenses can result in a youth's arrest and involvement in the criminal justice system. In 2009 (the last year for which there are complete data on runaway arrests in the US), status offenses accounted for 15% of arrests for girls, and "running away" accounted for 10% of girls' offenses. Comparatively, status offenses account for only 9% of boys' arrests, and only 3% of boys' arrests are for running away.

Girls and status offenses

For many years, statistics showing large numbers of girls arrested for status offenses were taken to be representative of the different types of male and female delinquency. However, self-report studies of male and female delinquency (which ask school-age youth if they have committed delinquent acts) do not reflect the dramatic differences in misbehavior found in official statistics. Specifically, it appears that girls charged with these non-criminal status offenses have been, and continue to be, significantly overrepresented in court populations (Chesney-Lind & Pasko, 2013).

Researchers have known for years that many girls are in the juvenile justice system because their parents insisted on their arrest. Who else would report a youth as having "run away" from home? The fact that parents are often committed to two standards of adolescent behavior is one explanation for these disparities – one that should not be discounted as a major source of tension even in modern families. Despite expectations to the contrary, gender-specific socialization patterns have not changed very much, and this is especially true for parents' relationships with their daughters around issues of sexuality, boyfriends, and dating (Ianni, 1989; Kamler, 1999; Katz, 1979; Orenstein, 2000; Thorne, 1993). Girls can also clash with their parents around issues of gender identity in families committed to heteronormative[3] sexuality, a concern that is surfacing in recent research on girls on the streets in the juvenile justice system (Irvine, 2010; Schaffner, 2006).

There are other more profound reasons for girls running from home. Girls are, for example, much more likely to be the victims of child sexual abuse than are boys (Smith, Leve, & Chamberlain, 2006). In nearly eight out of ten sexual abuse cases, the victim is female (Flowers, 2001). Girls are more likely than boys to be assaulted by a family member, often a stepfather (De Jong, Hervada, & Emmett, 1983; Russell, 1986). For example, in 2008, 57% of sexual assaults on females were committed by someone they knew (Catalano *et al.*, 2009). As a consequence, their abuse tends to last longer than boys' over time (Bergen *et al.*, 2004; De Jong *et al.*, 1983), and all of these factors can cause more severe trauma and dramatic short- and long-term effects in victims (Adams-Tucker, 1982; Hennessey *et al.*, 2004).

The effects of sexual abuse in girls include "fear, anxiety, depression, anger and hostility, and inappropriate sexual behavior" (Browne & Finkelhor, 1986) as well as behaviors that include running away from home, difficulty in school, truancy, drug abuse, pregnancy, and early marriage (Browne & Finkelhor, 1986; Widom & Kuhns, 1996). In addition, girls who have experienced sexual abuse in their families are at greater risk for subsequent sexual abuse later in life (Flowers, 2001).

Despite histories of victimization, and evidence that girls may be running away from home because of abuse, the response of the juvenile justice system in the US to such non-criminal behavior has been harsh. This pattern persists despite efforts in the 1970s to reform the official response to status offenses and reduce detention and incarceration for these non-criminal offenses (American Bar Association, National Bar Association 2001). A 2001 study of gender and juvenile court processing by the American Bar Association found that girls are far more likely to be detained for relatively minor offenses, especially violation of court orders, various misdemeanor charges associated with running away, charges of escape, absconding, and being AWOL (absent without leave), the latter of which suggests that in some situations girls are treated as military personnel who technically are the "property" of those in authority. The report also noted the growing tendency to re-label family conflicts that girls are involved in as "violent" offenses, which affects minority girls in particular (American Bar Association, National Bar Association, 2001).

Jailing girls

Conditions for girls held in the juvenile equivalents of jail and prison are also a huge problem, since there is little effective monitoring of the conditions of youthful confinement in the US (Gruver, 2009). A Department of Justice investigation of the Mississippi training schools holding girls, 75% of whom were committed for status offenses, probation violations, or contempt of court, provides horrific evidence of abuse (Boyd, 2003). In their letter to the Governor of Mississippi, the investigators detailed the conditions they found at Columbia Training School. They specifically detailed "unconstitutionally abusive practices such as hog-tying, pole-shackling, improper use and over use of restraints and isolation, staff assaulting youth, and OC spray abuse" (Boyd, 2003, p. 5). Hog-tying was described in detail in the report:

> Approximately 10–15 boys and girls consistently described the practice, where youth
> are placed face down on the floor with their hands and feet shackled and drawn

together. That is, youths' hands are handcuffed behind their backs. Their feet are shackled together and then belts or metal chains are wrapped around the two sets of restraints, pulling them together… several girls in Hammond Cottage told us that either they had been hog-tied or they had witnessed other girls being hog-tied. They reported that girls are typically tied for three hour periods in the corners of the cottage and stated that girls are also hog-tied in the SIU [Special Intervention Unit]. Girls also reported being hog-tied in a SIU cell called the "dark room". (Boyd, 2003, p. 6)

The report also detailed examples of girls being "shackled to poles in public places" if they were "non-compliant" during military exercise (Mississippi uses a "military model for delinquent youth" stressing "vigorous" physical fitness((Boyd, 2003, pp. 2–5). Girls at Columbia reported being placed in the dark room for "acting out or being suicidal". The windowless isolation cell has lighting controlled by staff; it is also stripped of everything but a drain in the floor which serves as a toilet. When in use, the room is completely dark, and the girls are placed into the room naked. One girl reported being placed in the room for three days with "little access to water as her requests for water were largely ignored" (Boyd, 2003, p. 7). The report concluded: "The conditions in the SIU are particularly inhumane. The cells are extremely hot with inadequate ventilation. Some girls are naked in a dark room where they must urinate and defecate in a hole that they cannot flush."

Upcriming girls' defiance

More recently, the criminal justice system has become involved in criminalizing women's victimization through a more circuitous route than the direct arrest and detention of runaway girls just discussed. Over the last decade, arrests of girls and women for crimes of "violence" have been surging, while male arrests for these types of offenses have dropped (Chesney-Lind, 2002). Consider the case of young girls who used to account for about one juvenile arrest in five; in 2010 they constituted a third of juvenile arrests (Federal Bureau of Investigation, 2011). Much of this increase has been due not to girls' arrests for running away from home, but instead to arrests of girls for "violent" offenses like simple assault. These offenses are now among the most common reasons to arrest girls, and not because girls are getting "meaner" and "wilder" as the corporate media claim (Chesney-Lind & Irwin, 2007). Instead, research has shown that girls are increasingly likely to be arrested in the context of domestic violence, often arguing with their family members (Buzawa & Hotaling, 2006).

Criminalizing girls' sexuality: a global perspective

As a recent high-profile rape of a Norwegian woman in Dubai has made clear, women who are raped in Islamic countries and attempt to report their rapes to police risk arrest and detention (Murphy, 2013). In Pakistan, rape is dealt with under the strict Islamic law known as the *Hudud* Ordinances (Plett, 2006). These criminalize all sex outside marriage, known as *Zina* (Anonymous, n.d.; Plett, 2006). However, the Ordinance excludes marital rape from the definition of that offense.

The *Hudud law* puts all the burden of proof on the rape victims, the women who report that they have been raped. The victims could be charged for *false* accusation and incarcerated if unable to provide proof, which involves producing four male witnesses of the rape. The inability of the rape victims to produce four male witnesses will result in the presumption of them committing *Zina,* while the rapists go free. In these cases, women and non-Muslims cannot be called as witnesses. According to the Human Rights Commission of Pakistan, every two hours a woman is raped in Pakistan and every eight hours a woman is subjected to gang rape (Anonymous, n.d.; Plett, 2006). In such circumstances, a combination of social taboos, discriminatory laws such the *Hudud*, and victimization at the hands of the police are key reasons in Pakistan for many rapes remaining unreported (Anonymous, n.d.).

Sometimes, the matter of punishing women for a "crime" as perceived by society does not even get reported to the legal authorities. The local community takes matters into their own hands. In Bangladesh, despite the banning of *Fatwa*, a form of religious sanction issued by informal village councils to resolve local disputes, local authorities can still sentence women to be publicly beaten when accused of adultery or having a child out of wedlock (Anonymous, 2011). Recent incidents include the public lashing of a 14-year-old girl and a 40-year-old woman, both accused of adultery in two different villages of Bangladesh. Both the victims died after battling severe injuries from their beatings.

Taken together, these examples suggest that violence against women and the criminalization of girls' and women's survival strategies are related and are crucial global problems. Compared with beating, killing, public humiliation, imprisonment, or mutilating women as a form of punishment in the countries reviewed earlier in this section, the practices in the US and other countries in the global North seem less extreme. Yet, from a human rights perspective, it is likely many of the girls in the juvenile justice system worldwide are victims, not criminals, as is the case for many runaway girls not only in the US, but also in countries like Afghanistan (Federal Bureau of Investigation, 2011; Human Rights Watch, 2013; Lee & Laidler, 2013).

The evidence presented here suggests that criminal justice systems appear to have long been enmeshed in the normalization of even extreme forms of male violence, and at a minimum, complicit in the legal enforcement of traditional gender norms (including sexual constraints). International pressure on the most extreme forms of governmental complicity with patriarchal practices that harm girls and women is essential. We must resist efforts to encapsulate such extreme misogynistic practices as "cultural" or "religious" differences, and continue to re-frame them as human rights violations. We must also continue to gather data on the dimensions of male violence against women and we must understand that in virtually all countries the criminal justice system provides girls and women with virtually no justice or safety, and instead is often complicit in the further victimization of girls and women by criminalizing their survival strategies.

Conclusion

This chapter has explored both the historic roots of classic delinquency theory, and the key voids that developed as a result of that history. While this discussion has focused largely on gender, it has also attempted to call attention to issues of race, and more importantly, it has focused on theorizing gender and delinquency as a global phenomenon. Particularly in the areas of violence against girls as well as in the area of gangs or globalized organized violence, it is becoming increasingly clear that national boundaries, while important, no longer "contain" the delinquency or crime problem. Likewise, such boundaries can no longer characterize our thinking about the causes and consequences of boys' and girls' delinquency.

In the case of masculinity and delinquency, we have argued that key theories of delinquency causation contained core elements of masculinity without properly recognizing that actually some forms of delinquency, particularly among privileged youth, might even been considered normal behavior (e.g. sexual and dating violence). Indeed, Schwarz and DeKeseredy (1997) have theorized that privileged males learn key lessons about how their class insulates them from the consequences of illegal behavior while engaging in dating violence, particularly sexual assault. Among youth of color, masculinity continues to be a theme, often informing and supporting various street behaviors that further criminalize the boys and put young girls of color at risk.

For girls our key themes have been the theoretical neglect of the causes of female delinquency, which in turn missed the crucial role played by victimization in girls' acting out (particularly running away), as well as the crucial role that the juvenile justice system has played in backstopping patriarchal systems of control. While such complicity has long been present in the US juvenile justice system, it is perhaps far clearer in global systems of jurisprudence, particularly in religiously conservative countries.

In sum, classic delinquency theory focused more or less exclusively on the role of class and urban subculture as the generating milieu of delinquency. This had the effect of normalizing male violence, missing racism, and ignoring both girls' victimization and the role it plays in traditional female "delinquency". Such a myopic focus on the misbehavior of boys also permitted researchers to miss completely the racism and sexism that permeated the juvenile justice system. The insights of critical feminist criminology point to the need for a delinquency theory that consciously theorizes both gender and patriarchy, and to do so on a more global stage. Hopefully, this modest effort has begun that important conversation.

Notes

1   Feminist history is often conceptualized as entailing three waves. The first wave refers to the push for women's suffrage; the second to feminist activism and thought during the 1960s and 1970s (mostly dominated by middle-class, white women); and the third refers

to recognition and inclusion of diverse women's experiences (e.g., varying across race, class, and sexual orientation) in feminist thought.

2   Patriarchal ideology refers to ideas that promote male dominance, such as the normalization of violence against women. Structural constraints are social-structural limitations on individual boys' lives, such as being born into a poor, socially disorganized neighborhood. Personal experiences refer to the lived events in boys' lives, such as exposure to violence in the home.

3   Heteronormativity refers to seeing a heterosexual orientation and behavior as natural and desirable, while seeing any non-heterosexual orientations as deviant and undesirable.

References

Adams-Tucker, C. (1982). Proximate effects of sexual abuse in childhood: A report on 28 children. *American Journal of Psychiatry, 139* (10), 1252–1256.

American Bar Association, National Bar Association. (2001). *Justice by gender: The lack of appropriate prevention, diversion and treatment alternatives for girls in the justice system: A report.* Washington, DC: National Bar Association.

Anderson, E. (2000). *Code of the Street: Decency, Violence, and the Moral Life of the Inner City.* New York: W.W. Norton.

Anonymous. (2011). Bangladesh court lifts fatwa ban. Retrieved from http://www.bbc.co.uk/news/world-south-asia-13379016

Anonymous. (n.d.). Hudood ordinances: The crime and punishment for Zina. Retrieved from http://asiapacific.amnesty.org/apro/aproweb.nsf/pages/svaw_hudoo

Bennett-Smith, M. (2013). Steubenville high school students joke about rape in video leaked by Anonymous. *Huffington Post.* Retrieved from http://www.huffingtonpost.com/2013/01/02/steubenville-high-school-joke-rape-targeted-anonymous-video_n_2398479.html?utm_hp_ref=steubenville-rape

Bergen, H.A., Martin, G., Richardson, A.S., *et al.* (2004). Sexual abuse, antisocial behaviour and substance use: gender differences in young community adolescents. *Australian and New Zealand Journal of Psychiatry, 38*(1–2), 34–41.

Bevan, J., & Florquin, N. (2006). Few options but the gun: Angry young men. In *Small Arms Survey 2006: Unfinished Business.* Geneva: Small Arms Survey.

Boyd, R. (2003). CRIPA investigation of Oakley and Columbia training schools in Raymond and Columbia, Mississippi. Retrieved from http://i.cdn.turner.com/cnn/2008/images/04/01/oak.colu.miss.findinglet.pdf

Brenzel, B.M., & Joint Center for Urban Studies. (1983). *Daughters of the State: a Social Portrait of the First Reform School for Girls in North America, 1856–1905.* Cambridge, MA: MIT Press.

Browne, A., & Finkelhor, D. (1986). Impact of child sexual abuse: A review of the research. *Psychological Bulletin, 99*(1), 66–77.

Brownmiller, S. (1975). *Against Our Will: Men, Women, and Rape.* New York: Ballantine Books.

Buzawa, E.S., & Hotaling, G.T. (2006). The impact of relationship status, gender, and minor status in the police response to domestic assaults. *Victims & Offenders, 1*(4), 323–360.

Catalano, S., Smith, E., Snyder, H., & Rand, M./ US Department of Justice. (2009). Female victims of violence. Retrieved from http://digitalcommons.unl.edu/usjusticematls/7

Centers for Disease Control. (2009). Men's health: Leading causes of death for males. Retrieved from http://www.cdc.gov/men/lcod/

Chesney-Lind, M. (1973). Judicial enforcement of the female sex role: The family court and the female delinquent. *Issues in Criminology, 8*(2), 51–69.

Chesney-Lind, M. (2002). Criminalizing victimization: The unintended consequences of pro-arrest policies for girls and women. *Criminology & Public Policy, 2*(1), 81–90.

Chesney-Lind, M. (2006). Patriarchy, crime, and justice feminist criminology in an era of backlash. *Feminist Criminology, 1*(1), 6–26.

Chesney-Lind, M., & Irwin, K. (2007). *Beyond Bad Girls: Gender, Violence and Hype*, 1st ed. New York: Routledge.

Chesney-Lind, M., & Pasko, L. (2013). *The Female Offender: Girls, Women, and Crime*. Thousand Oaks, CA: Sage.

Chesney-Lind, M., & Shelden, R.G. (2003). *Girls, Delinquency, and Juvenile Justice*, 3rd ed. Belmont, CA: Wadsworth Publishing.

Cloward, R., & Ohlin, L. (1966). *Delinquency and Opportunity*. New York: Free Press.

Cohen, A.K. 1956. *Delinquent Boys: The Culture of the Gang*. London: Taylor & Francis.

Connell, R.W. (2002). On hegemonic masculinity and violence response to Jefferson and Hall. *Theoretical Criminology, 6*(1), 89–99.

Connell, R.W., & Messerschmidt, J.W. (2005). Hegemonic masculinity rethinking the concept. *Gender & Society, 19*(6), 829–859.

Decker, S.H., & Pyrooz, D.C. (2010). Gang violence worldwide: Context, culture, and country. In Small Arms Survey (pp. 128–155). Geneva: *Small Arms Survey*.

Deegan, M.J. (1988). *Jane Addams and the Men of the Chicago School, 1892–1918*. New Brunswick: Transaction Books.

De Jong, A.R., Hervada, A.R., & Emmett, G.A. (1983). Epidemiologic variations in childhood sexual abuse. *Child Abuse & Neglect, 7*(2), 155–162.

Dichter, M.E., Cederbaum, J.A., & Teitelman, A.M. (2010). The gendering of violence in intimate relationships. In M. Chesney-Lind, & N. Jones (Eds.), *Fighting for Girls: New Perspectives on Gender and Violence* (pp. 83–106). New York: SUNY Press.

Dobash, R.E., & Dobash, R. (1979). *Violence Against Wives: A Case Against the Patriarchy*. New York: Free Press.

Dowdney, L. (2005). *Neither War nor Peace. International Comparisons of Children and Youth in Organized Armed Violence*. Retrieved from http://resourcecentre.savethechildren.se/library/neither-war-nor-peace-international-comparisons-children-and-youth-organised-armed-violence

Dragiewicz, M. (2011). *Equality With a Vengeance: Men's Rights Groups, Battered Women, and Antifeminist Backlash*. UPNE.

Federal Bureau of Investigation. (2011). Crime in the US 2010. Retrieved from http://www.fbi.gov/about-us/cjis/ucr/crime-in-the-u.s/2010/crime-in-the-u.s.-2010

Flowers, R.B. (2001). *Runaway Kids and Teenage Prostitution: America's Lost, Abandoned, and Sexually Exploited Children*. Westport, CT: Greenwood Press.

Gilligan, J. (1997). *Violence: Reflections on a National Epidemic*. New York: Vintage Books.

Glass, N., Fredland, N., Campbell, J., *et al.* (2003). Adolescent dating violence: Prevalence, risk factors, health outcomes, and implications for clinical practice. *Journal of Obstetric, Gynecologic, & Neonatal Nursing, 32*(2), 227–238.

Gruver, M. (2009). Some states ignore juvenile justice law; 34-year-old federal law says runaways are not supposed to be put in jail. *Dayton Daily News*. Retrieved from http://www.highbeam.com/doc/1P2-19857910.html

Hadi, S.T., & Chesney-Lind, M. (2014). Silence and the criminalization of victimization: On the need for an international feminist criminology. In B. Arrigo, & H. Bersot (Eds.), *Routledge Handbook of International Crime and Justice Studies* (pp. 33–52). London: Routledge.

Hagedorn, J.M. (1998). Frat boys, bossmen, studs, and gentlemen: A typology of gang masculinities. In L.H. Bowker (Ed.), *Masculinities and Violence* (pp. 152–167). Thousand Oaks, CA: Sage.

Hennessey, M., Ford, J.D., Mahoney, K., *et al.* (2004). *Trauma Among Girls in the Juvenile Justice System*. Los Angeles, CA: National Child Traumatic Stress Network.

Human Rights Watch. (2013). Afghanistan: Surge in women jailed for "moral crimes": Prosecute abusers, not women fleeing abuse. Retrieved from http://www.hrw.org/news/2013/05/21/afghanistan-surge-women-jailed-moral-crimes

Hurt, B. (2006). *Beyond Beats and Rhymes*. God Bless the Child Productions.

Ianni, F A.J. (1989). *The Search For Structure: A Report on American Youth Today*. New York: Free Press.

Irvine, A. (2010). We've had three of them: Addressing the invisibility of lesbian, gay, bisexual, and gender nonconforming youths in the juvenile justice system. *Columbia Journal of Gender and Law, 19,* 675–702.

Kamler, B. (1999). *Constructing Gender and Difference: Critical Research Perspectives on Early Childhood*. Cresskill, NJ: Hampton Press.

Katz, P.A. (1979). The development of female identity. *Sex Roles, 5*(2), 155–178.

Kaufmann, M. (2003). The construction of masculinity and the triad of men's violence. In M.S. Kimmel, & M.A. Messner (Eds.), *Men's Lives*, 6th ed. (pp. 4–16). Boston, MA: Allyn & Bacon.

Kimmel, M.S. (2007). Masculinity as homophobia. In N. Cook (Ed.), *Gender Relations in Global Perspective: Essential Readings* (pp. 73–82). Toronto: Canadian Scholars' Press.

Kimmel, M.S., & Mahler, M. (2003). Adolescent masculinity, homophobia, and violence random school shootings, 1982–2001. *American Behavioral Scientist, 46*(10), 1439–1458.

Koss, M.P., Gidycz, C.A., & Wisniewski, N. (1987). The scope of rape: Incidence and prevalence of sexual aggression and victimization in a national sample of higher education students. *Journal of Consulting and Clinical Psychology, 55*(2), 162–170.

Krug, E., Dahlberg, L., Mercy, J.A., Zwi, A., & Lozano, R./World Health Organization (2002). *World Report on Violence and Health*. Retrieved from http://www.who.int/violence_injury_prevention/violence/world_report/en/

Lee, M., & Laidler, K.J. (2013). Doing criminology from the periphery: Crime and punishment in Asia. *Theoretical Criminology, 17*(2), 141–157.

Lewis, S.F., & Fremouw, W. (2001). Dating violence: A critical review of the literature. *Clinical Psychology Review, 21*(1), 105–127.

Lombroso, C., & Ferrero, G. (1895). *The Female Offender*. Hein Publishing.

Mayeda, D., & Pasko, L. (2012). Youth violence and hegemonic masculinity among Pacific Islander and Asian American adolescents. *Critical Criminology, 20*(2), 121–139.

Messerschmidt, J.W. (1986). *Capitalism, Patriarchy, and Crime*. Rowman & Littlefield Publishers.

Miller, J. (2008). *Getting Played African American Girls, Urban Inequality, and Gendered Violence*. New York: NYU Press.

Miller, W.B. (1958). Lower class culture as a generating milieu of gang delinquency. *Journal of Social Issues, 14*(3), 5–19.

Molidor, C., & Tolman, R.M. (1998). Gender and contextual factors in adolescent dating violence. *Violence Against Women, 4*(2), 180–194.

Mulford, C.F., & Blachman-Demner, D.R. (2013). Teen dating violence building a research program through collaborative insights. *Violence Against Women.* Retrieved from http://vaw.sagepub.com/content/early/2013/07/11/1077801213494705

Murphy, B. (2013). Dubai pardons Norwegian woman jailed for being raped. MercuryNews.com. Retrieved from http://www.mercurynews.com/nation-world/ci_23707473/dubai-pardons-norwegian-woman-jailed-being-raped

Odem, M.E. (1995). *Delinquent Daughters: Protecting and Policing Adolescent Female Sexuality in the United States, 1885–1920.* University of North Carolina Press.

Omi, M., & Winant, H. (2004). Racial formations. In P.S. Rothenberg (Ed.), *Race, Class, and Gender in the United States,* 6th ed. (pp. 13–22). Worth Publishers.

Orenstein, P. (2000). *Schoolgirls: Young Women, Self-esteem, and the Confidence Gap.* New York: Anchor Books.

Park, R.E., & Burgess, E.W. (1925). *The City.* Chicago: University of Chicago Press.

Plett, B. (2006). How Pakistan's rape reform ran aground. Retrieved from http://news.bbc.co.uk/2/hi/south_asia/5346968.stm

Pollak, O. (1950). *The Criminality of Women.* University of Pennsylvania Press.

Renzetti, C.M. (1994). On dancing with a bear: Reflections on some of the current debates among domestic violence theorists. *Violence and Victims, 9*(2), 195–200.

Richards, P., & Berk, R.A. (1979). *Crime as Play: Delinquency in a Middle Class Suburb.* Cambridge, MA: Ballinger Pub. Co.

Russell, D.E.H. (1986). *The Secret Trauma: Incest in the Lives of Girls and Women.* New York: Basic Books.

Schaffner, L. (2006). *Girls in Trouble with the Law.* New Brunswick, NJ: Rutgers University Press.

Schlossman, S., & Wallach, S. (1978). The crime of precocious sexuality: Female juvenile delinquency in the progressive era. *Harvard Educational Review, 48*(1), 65–94.

Schwartz, M.D., & DeKeseredy, W.S. (1993). The return of the 'battered husband syndrome' through the typification of women as violent. *Crime, Law and Social Change, 20*(3), 249–265.

Schwartz, M.D., & DeKeseredy, W.S. (1997). *Sexual Assault on the College Campus: The Role of Male Peer Support.* Thousand Oaks, CA: Sage.

Shaw, C., & McKay, H.D. (1942). *Juvenile Delinquency and Urban Areas.* Chicago, IL: University of Chicago Press.

Smith, D.K., Leve, L.D., & Chamberlain, P. (2006). Adolescent girls' offending and health-risking sexual behavior: The predictive role of trauma. *Child Maltreatment, 11*(4), 346–353.

Thorne, B. (1993). *Gender Play: Girls and Boys in School.* New Brunswick, NJ: Rutgers University Press.

Thrasher, F. (1927). *The Gang: a Study of Gangs in Chicago.* Chicago: University of Chicago Press.

Totten, M. (2003). Girlfriend abuse as a form of masculinity construction among violent, marginal male youth. *Men and Masculinities, 6*(1), 70–92.

Utas, M. (2009). Trapped in the game: Militia and gang members in war and post-war Sierra Leone. Retrieved from http://www.graduateinstitute.ch/webdav/site/ccdp/shared/5039/Utas-Trapped-in-the-Game.pdf

Widom, C.S., & Kuhns, J.B. (1996). Childhood victimization and subsequent risk for promiscuity, prostitution, and teenage pregnancy: A prospective study. *American Journal of Public Health, 86*(11), 1607–1612.

World Health Organization. (2013). Global and regional estimates of violence against women: Prevalence and health effects of intimate partner violence and non-partner sexual violence. Retrieved from http://www.who.int/reproductivehealth/publications/violence/9789241564625/en/index.html

10

Causes of African-American Juvenile Delinquency

James D. Unnever

Data collected by the US Department of Justice indicate that African-Americans are overrepresented in juvenile arrests for violent, property, and drug abuse violations. For example, the data reveal that:

- In the 1980s, the violent crime index arrest rate for African-American juveniles was six times the white rate. This ratio declined during the 1990s, holding at 4-to-1 from 1999 to 2004. After 2004 the racial disparity in the rates increased, reaching 5-to-1 in 2009.
- The black-to-white ratio in murder arrest rates for juveniles varied substantially during the 30-year period. In 1993, the African-American rate was nearly nine times the white rate. This ratio declined during the late 1990s and early 2000s, falling to about 5-to-1 in 2004. However, between 2004 and 2009 the racial disparity in the rates increased, reaching nearly 7-to-1 in 2009.
- The black–white disparity in juvenile arrest rates for robbery peaked in 1984, when the African-American rate was nearly 13 times higher than the white rate. The disparity declined through the late 1990s, when the African-American rate was seven times the white rate. Yet, by 2009, the African-American rate had increased to about ten times the white rate.
- In 2009, the black–white disparity in property crime index arrest rates was much smaller than the disparity in violent crime index arrest rates (2.5 vs. 5.2).
- Since 1980, drug abuse violation arrest rates for white juveniles generally declined until 1991, while the African-American rate soared. Between 1980 and the peak year of 1996, the African-American arrest rate for drug abuse violations increased nearly 350%. Despite the substantial decline between 1995 and 2002 for black juveniles, the African-American rate was nearly twice the white rate in 2009.

The Handbook of Juvenile Delinquency and Juvenile Justice, First Edition. Edited by Marvin D. Krohn and Jodi Lane.

Where Have We Been?

Scholars have focused on the causes of juvenile delinquency since the origin of US criminology. Indeed, most of the leading "general" theories of crime were formulated and grounded in analyses of data gathered from young adolescents. General theories of crime assume that their findings are generalizable across crimes and groups (i.e., class and racial/ethnic groups). For example, Hirschi's (1969) classic *Causes of Delinquency* was generated from an analysis of data collected from high school students – the Richmond Youth Project. Similarly, the origins of social disorganization theory emerge from Shaw and McKay's seminal work *Juvenile Delinquency and Urban Areas* (1969). And perhaps the most prominent qualitative study in criminology, *The Jack Roller* (Shaw, 1966), was an analysis of a juvenile delinquent. Thus, it is apparent that the etiology of the general theories of crime emerged through analyses of the causes of juvenile delinquency.

The general theories of crime have revealed that there are many factors that predict juvenile delinquency. For example, Hirschi's (1969) social bond theory found that youths are most likely to engage in juvenile delinquency when they have weak attachments, involvements, and commitments – weak social bonds – with their guardians (i.e., parents) and with conventional institutions. Thus, juveniles are most likely to become delinquent when they are weakly bonded to their parents, their schools, and, more generally, to authority (e.g., do not respect the criminal justice system and the law).

Learning theory or differential association highlights how the adolescent's peer group choice impacts their rate of offending, with those who associate with delinquent peers having higher rates of offending. With these delinquent peer groups, juveniles learn the techniques and rationales for offending (Akers, Krohn, Lanza-Kaduce, & Radosevich, 1979).

Gottfredson and Hirschi's (1990) general theory of crime argues that *the* cause of delinquency – low self-control – is set into motion as a result of neglectful parent–child interactions in the first eight years of a child's development. This low self-control becomes a rather intransigent trait, causing the child to engage in delinquent and other analogous behaviors (e.g., smoking, unstable relationships) across their life span. Agnew's (1992) general strain theory argues that delinquency is related to noxious stressors or strains that youth encounter, such as being victimized in school, having relationship problems, or family-related problems.

On a macro-level, social disorganization theorists have clearly found that rates of delinquency vary across geographical areas. The highest rates of delinquency occur in areas that are the most socially disorganized. These areas are characterized by high rates of poverty, a preponderance of female-headed households, and high rates of unemployment. The cumulative consequence of these debilitating forces is that these neighborhoods have little collective efficacy, which can be defined as social cohesion among neighbors combined with their willingness to intervene on behalf of the common good. In the absence of these informal mechanisms of social control, juveniles feel less constrained to engage in juvenile delinquency. Thus, areas with the least amount of collective efficacy have the highest rates of juvenile delinquency (Sampson, Raudenbush, & Earl, 1997).

Most notably, these "general" theories of crime assume that African-Americans and whites engage in crime for exactly the same reasons. Thus, according to these rival-competing theories of juvenile delinquency, African-American youth are more likely to offend than whites because they are overly exposed to the particular crime-causing force highlighted by the general theories. For example, general theorists would argue that African-American juveniles disproportionately offend because they have weaker bonds than whites with conventional institutions (social bond theory), experienced more neglect from their guardians in the first eight years of their lives and thus have less self-control (Gottfredson and Hirschi's general theory of crime), were exposed to more delinquent peer groups (learning theory), encounter more strains (e.g., are victimized more often) (Agnew's strain theory), and overly reside in areas with the least amount of collective efficacy (social disorganization theory).

Where Are We Now?

The basic thesis of this chapter is that the general theories of crime can never fully understand the reasons why African-American youth engage in juvenile delinquency. I argue that while African-Americans and whites share similar reasons why they engage in delinquent behavior (e.g., weak social bonds, poor parenting), black youth encounter inimitable – peerless – experiences in their daily lives and that these unique experiences substantially add to the reasons why they have a disproportionate rate of official arrests especially for index crimes (i.e., violent and property offenses). These arguments are more fully developed in Unnever and Gabbidon's (2011) *A Theory of African American Offending: Race, Racism and Crime.*

The core assumption of Unnever and Gabbidon's (2011) theory of African-American offending is that black juveniles share a peerless worldview that informs their perceptions and behaviors. This lens or worldview is nearly uniformly shared by all African-American juveniles. This worldview was borne out of the lived experiences with chattel slavery, the Jim Crow era, violent oppression by the criminal justice system and other white-dominated institutions, and their continued struggle to achieve the same rights and privileges afforded to whites. Thus, the core belief of their worldview is the knowledge that the US is a racialized stratified society. Consequently, African-Americans assume that their race matters and that racism constrains their life chances.

This worldview becomes a lens through which African-American juveniles situate their lives. They recognize that their race is a "master status" and they are fully aware that most whites perceive them as "less than". In addition, this collective identity or linked fate includes the belief that racism is a prevalent force impacting their lives. Indeed, the research supports this contention. In a national survey, Kessler, Mickelson, and Williams (1999) found that over 90% of African-Americans reported experiencing some form of day-to-day discrimination, with the vast majority (89.7%) attributing these encounters to race or ethnicity. And, analyzing daily diaries kept by African-American college students, Burrow and Ong (2010) reported that, on average, the students reported almost six racist encounters during a two-week span, with having one's ideas minimized or ignored being the most often reported offense.

Unnever and Gabbidon hypothesize that the African-American juveniles who are most likely to offend are those that react to their everyday experiences of racial injustices with negative emotions such as shame, anger, defiance, hostility, aggression, and depression. Unnever and Gabbidon (2011: 205) argue that:

> Together, these debilitating feelings exhaust their emotional capital leaving them vulnerable to engaging in impulsive behaviors, which is a chief factor related to offending. Experiencing racial injustices also cause African Americans to offend because they undermine their capacity to build strong bonds with conventional white-dominated institutions. That is, African Americans are confronted with the paradoxical task of building strong bonds with "conventional" white-dominated institutions that many of them perceive to be racist, such as the criminal justice system.

Unnever and Gabbidon (2011) also argue that the worldview that informs the perceptions and behaviors of African-Americans includes the collective wisdom that has allowed the majority of blacks to maintain their resiliency despite hundreds of years of, at times, violent oppression. Unnever and Gabbidon contend that African-Americans who are infused with this collective conscience – this collective wisdom – are the ones least likely to offend as they have the wherewithal to fend off their everyday encounters with the nearly endless forms of racism. Thus, for some blacks their master status of being "less than" is not debilitating but rather a challenge that must be overcome. In sum, this worldview, which nearly all African-Americans share, can enhance or diminish the probability that black juveniles will engage in delinquent behavior.

Below, I illustrate and add to Unnever and Gabbidon's (2011) theory of African-American offending. For the purposes of this chapter, I will primarily focus on how delinquency is affected by the relationship that African-American juveniles have with their education. Note that this is just one component of Unnever and Gabbidon's (2011) overall explanation of African-American offending. That is, their theory is much more elaborate than what is presented below. As this discussion unfolds, for juxtaposition, remember that the general theories of crime argue that African-American juveniles are less likely to be bonded to their education because they were poorly parented (i.e., low self-control), associate with delinquent peer groups, encounter more strains (e.g., are bullied), or live in resource-depleted neighborhoods.

A Race-Centered Analysis of African-American Juvenile Delinquency

Education and African-American juvenile delinquency

Unnever and Gabbidon (2011) posit that the relationship that African-American juveniles have with their education is a core predictor of their likelihood to engage in delinquent behavior; that is, African-American juveniles are more likely to offend if they are less successful in school. However, their theory situates African-American delinquency within an educational system that they argue is race-based; they posit that the educational system within the US was purposefully constructed to limit or constrain the educational successes of blacks. Indeed, they suggest that racialized educational opportunities constitute a core foundation of the maintenance of the US's racialized stratification system. Jones (1972: 283) described the concept of institutionalized racism:

> It is clear that prejudice functions to create immediate and direct discrimination based on race. [It is also clear] that discrimination is all the more meaningful when it co-occurs with a societal structure that aligns choice and chances with racial group membership. When this alignment privileges one race over another, and does so over centuries with the accompaniment of theories, rationales, and beliefs, this recurring dynamic transcends simple race prejudice. Thus, the cumulative effects of race prejudice over time combine with the cultural rationales and beliefs about racial essences to enable the institutions' implementation of racism.

Racial disparities in schooling

The data are unequivocally clear that a student's sense of school belonging is related to their motivation to do well, whether they believe school is useful and enjoyable, and to their educational persistence (Freeman, Anderman, & Jensen, 2007; Gillen-O'Neel & Fuligni, 2013). However, the data are also unequivocally clear that African-American juveniles struggle to build strong bonds with their schools. Gamboa (2012) reported that 52% of African-American males who entered ninth grade in the 2006–7 school year graduated in four years, compared with 78% of whites. Thus, the research is correct in highlighting that a "pipeline-to-prison" for many African-American youth is their inability to bond with their school (Gonsoulin, Zablocki, & Leone, 2012; Metze, 2012; Shippen, Patterson, Green, & Smitherman, 2012).

There are two related components of a racialized educational system that propel some black youths to offend. First, the ability of African-American juveniles to build strong bonds with the educational system is diminished because of racial segregation, that is, the racial disparities between or across schools. Second, the likelihood that African-American juveniles will build strong bonds is constrained by the racism they encounter within their schools.

Racial segregation across schools   Studies show that racialized inequalities across schools are becoming more entrenched and institutionalized. Flashman (2012) reported that the racial and ethnic segregation of schools has steadily increased since the 1990s, resulting in African-American students experiencing a very different schooling environment than they did only a few decades ago. In fact, in 2000 the average white child attended a school that was 78% white, while the average black student attended schools that were 57% African-American (African-Americans are roughly about 13% of the US population).

Research indicates that these racial disparities are related to the well-noted achievement gap across race (Harber *et al.*, 2012). Hanushek, Kain, and Rivkin's (2009) analysis of the achievement of Texas students disentangled racial composition effects from other aspects of school quality, and from differences in student abilities and family background. They reported that while controlling for the other key predictors of educational success, the racial composition of the schools explained nearly a quarter of the 7th grade achievement gap between blacks and whites. Notably, Hanushek *et al.* found that the racial segregation of Texas schools most profoundly negatively impacted African-American youth who were in the upper half of the ability distribution.

Data from the National Longitudinal Study of Adolescent Health suggest that race-based segregated schools disproportionately negatively impact the academic success of black students (Flashman, 2012). The research indicates that the self-reported grade point averages of students in the schools attended by African-American adolescents are significantly lower than those attended by whites. The average African-American adolescent attends a school where 18% of all students have a GPA over 3.5 (on a 4.0 scale), whereas the average white adolescent attends a school where 27% of all students have a GPA over 3.5. Flashman (2012) further notes that the average white youth attends a school where 30% of the white students have GPAs over 3.5. In comparison, the average African-American youth attends a school where only 12% of black students have GPAs over 3.5. Thus, these racial disparities suppress black achievement because educational successes increase when students – whether black or white – associate with higher-achieving friends and are immersed in a higher-achieving school (Flashman, 2012).

Racial segregation additionally impacts upon the ability for cross-race friendships to develop (Hallinan & Williams, 1989; Quillian & Campbell, 2003). Although segregation is normative – that is, most children associate with peers of the same race/ethnicity – the research indicates that many children have significant cross-ethnic affiliations, and having such relationships is associated with positive adjustment at school, self-confidence, and leadership potential. Yet studies indicate that preferences for cross-race friendships decline as the size of a particular race within a school declines (Moody, 2001; Mouw & Entwisle, 2006; Quillian & Campbell, 2003). It is also notable that the research indicates that segregated friendships tend to heighten the dislike of the out-group (Wilson & Rodkin, 2012). Flashman (2012, p. 902) concludes that: "The racial/ethnic and economic segregation of schools and tracking schemes within schools, disadvantage the already disadvantaged by shaping their opportunities to choose friends."

Racism within schools   The data indicate that the racial segregation of schools impacts African-American juvenile delinquency by diminishing their ability to achieve academic successes. Unnever and Gabbidon (2011) equally emphasize that a chief reason why black juveniles engage in delinquency is because they confront a reality largely unknown to whites: racism *within* their schools (Snyder, 2012).

Studies reveal that African-Americans report that they perceive racism within their schools. Research indicates that 46% of African-American juveniles reported that they were given a lower grade than they deserve because of their race (Rivas-Drake, Hughes, & Way, 2009). Gregory and Weinstein (2008) found that African-American students behaved more defiantly and less cooperatively when interacting with teachers that they perceived as being untrustworthy. Research also shows that African-American juveniles are more likely to worry about their study skills, academic workload, time management, and adjustment to their school if they perceive racism (Chao, Mallinckrodt, & Wei, 2012). Other research indicates that minority status stressors such as racial discrimination are linked to adverse school outcomes, such as low grade point average, poor psychological health, low social involvement, and decreased academic motivation (Greer & Brown, 2011).

Unnever and Gabbidon (2011) highlight a number of ways that race-based discrimination pervades schools, including, but not limited to, white peers rejecting blacks because of their race (not allowed access to the "in-group"), being called racist epithets (the "N" word), being told racist jokes, being bullied because of their race, being physically attacked, teachers only calling on white students, teachers belittling black students, teachers assuming that they are "lazy" or prone to violence, incidents of hate crimes targeting African-Americans (e.g., a display of a white doll dressed in a Ku Klux Klan robe and a black doll with a noose around its neck), racially biased texts and curricula, racial tracking, discriminatory penalties (whites get detention while blacks get suspended from school for the same incident), disproportionately placing African-American students in special education classes, lowered teacher expectations, less encouragement to take advanced courses, and the school authorities' denial and refusal to acknowledge that there is racism within their schools (Alliman-Brissett & Turner, 2010; Benner & Graham, 2012; Rosenbloom & Way, 2004; Wong, Eccles, & Sameroff, 2003). Research also reveals that racial segregation is institutionalized within schools. Scholars report that African-American students are often separated into different classrooms and more informal tracks than white students, and that there is a strong relationship between course taking and academic performance (Flashman, 2012; Holland, 2012).

Stereotypes

One of the most toxic forms of racism that pervades school environments is the negative stereotyping of African-American juveniles (Trawalter, Todd, Baird, & Richeson, 2008; Wood & Chesser, 1994). Bobo and Charles (2009) noted that negative racial stereotypes remain the norm in white America, with between half and three-quarters of whites in the US expressing some degree of negative stereo-typing of African-Americans. Devine and Elliot (1995, p. 1142), in a follow-up to the classic Princeton trilogy studies, provided 147 white students with a checklist composed of 93 adjectives and asked them to mark those that "make up the cultural stereotype of blacks". Note that, based on exploratory analyses, they decided to add the concepts of "criminal" and "hostile" to the original checklist of 84 adjectives. Devine and Elliot found that, from 1933 to the mid-1990s, a consistent and negative stereotype of African-Americans has endured. Devine and Elliot (1995) found that the top nine list of adjectives that whites checked to describe African-Americans were, in order: athletic, rhythmic, low in intelligence, lazy and poor (these were tied), loud, criminal, hostile, and ignorant. In contrast, *no* whites checked, for example, that African-Americans are ambitious, tradition-loving, sensitive, or gregarious. Research further indicates that, in the late 1980s and early 1990s when the crack epidemic was reaching its zenith, a particularly toxic stereotype of African-American juveniles crystallized – that is, the stereotype that black juveniles are violent, dangerous superpredators who kill with no remorse (Dilulio, 1994; Unnever & Cullen, 2012).

Studies show that children develop a stereotype consciousness – an awareness of others' stereotypes – in middle childhood (between the ages of 5 and 10) (McKown & Strambler, 2009). McKown and Weinstein (2003) found that between the ages of 6 and 10, African-American juveniles were more likely to express knowledge of broadly held stereotypes than white and Asian students, and they concluded that the different lived experiences of minorities influences the age of onset of stereotype consciousness. McKown and Strambler (2009) found that by the age of 11 African-American children have mastered all aspects of stereotype consciousness. Brown and Bigler (2005) stipulate that stereotype consciousness causes African-American juveniles to perceive that they and other blacks will be the target of discrimination, and that these beliefs have deleterious consequences across social situations. Thus, it is clear that the worldview shared by African-American juveniles includes an explicit awareness of the pejorative stereotypes that depict them as less intelligent and prone to violence.

Stereotype threats and the pipeline to prison   The research indicates that pejorative stereotypes of African-American juveniles are a salient form of racism within schools, and that these toxic stereotypes are directly and indirectly related to delinquent behaviors. Noxious stereotypes are indirectly related to juvenile delinquency because they cause African-American juveniles who endorse the racist stereotype that they are low in intelligence to hold lower perceptions of their own academic abilities than those who do not hold such beliefs (Copping, Kurtz-Costes, Rowley, & Wood, 2013). Pejorative depictions also indirectly cause delinquency because they become "stereotype threats" that further undermine the academic performance of African-American juveniles. Steele and Aronson (1995: 797) defined stereotype threat as "being at risk of confirming, as self-characteristic, a negative stereotype about one's group".

In their classic stereotype threat study, Steele and Aronson (1995) randomly assigned both African-American and white college students from Stanford University to either an experimental (that elicited stereotype threat) or a control condition. In the experimental condition, the students were told that they would be given a test of intellectual capacity. The control group was told that they would be participating in an "exercise". African-Americans in the experimental condition, in which the stereotype of underperformance was activated because of the negative stereotype that blacks are low in intelligence, performed significantly worse compared with African-Americans in the control group. No performance differences were observed across race in the control group. Thus, Steele and Aronson (1995, p. 808) reported that "making African-American participants vulnerable to judgment by negative stereotypes about their group's intellectual ability depressed their standardized test performance relative to White participants".

Schmader, Johns, and Forbes (2008) described how and why stereotype threats measurably diminish the accomplishments of African-American juveniles. They argued that stereotype threats:

> … pose significant threat to self-integrity, the sense of oneself as a coherent and valued entity that is adaptable to the environment [Steele, 1988]. This self-integrity threat stems from a state of cognitive imbalance in which one's concept of self and expectation for success conflict with primed social stereotypes suggesting poor performance. This state of imbalance acts as an acute stressor that sets in motion physiological manifestations of stress, cognitive monitoring and interpretative processes, affective responses, and efforts to cope with these aversive experiences. (p. 337)
>
> … for those who contend with negative stereotypes about their abilities, the chronic experience of stress, heightened vigilance, self-doubt, and emotional suppression not only can impair performance directly but also can lead them to avoid situations where these aversive phenomena reside. (Schmader *et al.*, 2008, p. 352)

Steele (1997, p. 613) argued that African-American youths develop strong bonds with their school when they identify with their school achievement as being a part of their self-definition, a self-identity to which they hold themselves accountable. In other words, African-American juveniles are likely to be motivated when they perceive that they have the interests, skills, resources, and opportunities to succeed in school. Their motivation to do well in school is also related to believing that they are accepted, valued, and that they belong in school. However, Steele (1997) argued that negative stereotypes of African-American juveniles threaten their ability to perform well in school. Furthermore, he argued that poor performances because of stereotype threats spiral into sustained patterns of failures, especially among adolescents who initially desired to develop strong bonds with their schools. That is, strings of failures over time undermine the enthusiasm that African-American juveniles initially had toward their schools. Steele (1997: 614) defined this process as "disidentification", whereby African-American students reconceptualize their self and their values to remove performing well in school as a basis for self-evaluation. This disidentification offers the retreat of not caring about doing well in school as a basis of self-evaluation.

Yet, Steele argues that as it protects in this way, it can undermine sustained motivation, and that this new self-identity can be costly when doing well in school is important. In fact, scholars argue that racial differences in educational achievement can be accounted for by the relationship between stereotype threats and the underperformance of African-American juveniles rather than any alleged differences in lack of ability or incompetence (Haslam, Salvatore, Kessler, & Reicher, 2008).

Steele (1997) argued that disidentified African-American juveniles – those with weak social bonds with their school – engage in behaviors that allow them to create a self-identity within "domains in which their prospects are better" than academic-related activities (Steele, 1997: 623). Unnever and Gabbidon (2011) assert that one of the domains that disidentified African-American juveniles are likely to choose is delinquency: a behavior that most often does not demand a high level of competence (Gottfredson & Hirschi, 1990). Thus, delinquent behavior offers an opportunity for disidentified African-American juveniles to gain a sense of self-importance: an identity that is not diminished by their tenuous relationship with their school. This assertion is consistent with Steele's (1997) thesis that as African-American students retreat from their attachment, commitment, and involvement in their schools, they may engage in compensatory behaviors (e.g., acting in grandiose ways) in order to bolster their sense of their self-worth.

Pejorative stereotypes and offending   Unnever and Gabbidon (2011) also argue that negative stereotypes of African-American juveniles can directly contribute to their delinquency beyond undermining their ability to bond with their schools. Unnever and Gabbidon argue that some African-American juveniles internalize the negative depictions that are embedded in racist stereotypes – more specifically, the stereotype that they are unremorseful superpredators – and take on that label as their self-identity (Harrell, 2000). Research on negative stereotypes "have depicted a fairly standard sequence of events: through long exposure to negative stereotypes about their group, members of prejudiced-against groups often internalize the stereotypes, and the resulting sense of inadequacy becomes part of their personality" (Steele, 1997, p. 617). Thus, it is likely that some African-American juveniles – especially disidentified youths – may simply say to themselves: "Why bother? I might as well be a superpredator if that is the only thing people think that I am." This argument is consistent with labeling theory's "secondary deviance" hypothesis (Bouffard & Piquero, 2010; Winnick & Bodkin, 2008, 2009).

In addition, Unnever and Gabbidon (2011) hypothesize that pejorative stereotypes, particularly when there is chronic exposure, are debilitating. They deplete ego resources as African-American juveniles are continually confronted with the negative emotions that arise from being "dissed" or insulted by stereotypes that "put them down". Brunson and Weitzer (2009, p. 879) succinctly capture how stereotypes that associate blacks with crime can create a sense of hopelessness (i.e., depressive symptoms) among African-American juveniles: "Black respondents expressed hopelessness regarding the situation because they felt that officers would never see them as anything other than symbolic assailants, even when they were engaged in entirely lawful activity."

The research also suggests that the anger caused by being "dissed" or insulted should be related to offending. Brezina (2010) argues that anger is related to offending because it strengthens aggressive attitudes, weakens the belief that crime is wrong by fostering the belief that delinquency is justifiable, and increases the likelihood that individuals will associate with criminal peers. Research reveals that both anger and depression are related to conduct problems and crime, after controlling for other correlates of offending including the person's current level of social bonding, prior criminal activity, nurturant-involved parenting, affiliation with prosocial peers, and school efficacy (Agnew, Brezina, Wright, & Cullen, 2002; Mazerolle, Burton, Cullen, Evans, & Payne, 2000). Thus, African-American juveniles who respond to racial stereotypes with humiliation–depression and anger–defiance should have higher rates of delinquency because it energizes them to action, lowers their inhibitions, increases their felt injury, increases their likelihood of associating with other delinquent peers, and creates a desire for retaliation and revenge (Agnew, 1992; Brezina, 2010). Alexander (2012, p. 166) adds that some African-Americans embrace the stigma of criminality because it is "an attempt to carve out a positive identity in a society that offers them little more than scorn, contempt, and constant surveillance". Thus, "up in the air" derogatory stereotypes of black juveniles weaken their social bonds, are ego-depleting, and increase the likelihood that they will injuriously express anger/hostility/defiance/depression. In short, juvenile delinquency among African-American youth can be characterized as an ill-fated attempt to reestablish a sense of control and status in their life, which is lost when they are confronted by toxic racist stereotypes.

Thus, the data show that the ability of African-American juveniles to feel a strong sense of commitment to their education is significantly compromised when they report that they are being discriminated against in their schools. The research shows that experiences with racial discrimination are related to declines in school self-esteem, school bonding, grades, academic ability, self-concepts, academic task values, and increases in school detentions and suspensions (Thames *et al.*, 2013). Scholars also have found that the more that African-American students perceive their school's racial climate as a "toxic environment", the weaker their attachment and commitment to their school and the more likely they are to report higher rates of delinquency (Unnever, Cullen, Mathers, McClure, & Allison, 2009). Furthermore, research has found that the negative impact that racial discrimination has on African-Americans is exacerbated when the perpetrator is of a different race (Thames *et al.*, 2013).

In summary, the research is unequivocally clear that racist stereotypes of African-American juveniles can directly and indirectly enhance their likelihood of delinquency. They can directly impact their probability of delinquency when African-American juveniles take on the label that they are unremorseful super-predators as their self-identity. Toxic racist stereotypes can indirectly impact African-American delinquency when juveniles internalize the racist stereotype that they are low in intelligence and, consequently, lower their perceptions of their academic abilities. This possibility is compounded when African-American juveniles experience the deleterious consequences of being exposed to stereotype threats. Together, these effects undermine the ability of African-American juveniles to do well in school, which in turn enhances their probability of dropping out of school. Ultimately, these African-American juveniles may find themselves on the "pipeline to prison", since being a high school dropout is strongly correlated with engaging in delinquent behavior.

Coping with racism

Unnever and Gabbidon (2011) argue that African-American delinquency is most likely to occur among juveniles who encounter chronic and persistent forms of racism. Additionally, they suggest that juveniles who are most likely to engage in delinquency are the least prepared to effectively cope with their experiences of racism and discrimination. In general, coping behaviors are categorized as emotion-focused (i.e., strategies used to manage and/or alleviate emotional reactions), problem-focused (i.e., strategies used to resolve problems), or avoidant (i.e., strategies used to deny or minimize problems) (Greer & Brown, 2011). Unnever and Gabbidon contend that the African-American youth who are the least effective in coping with racism are those who are the most inadequately racially socialized; that is, their parents/guardians did not provide them with a compilation of coping skills that allow them to effectively manage their encounters with racism across a multitude of social situations. In short, African-American juveniles are most likely to engage in delinquent behavior if they are not adequately socialized to cope effectively with their everyday encounters with racism.

Unnever and Gabbidon (2011) hypothesize that a lack of coping skills is undermined if African-American juveniles are inadequately prepared for racist encounters and are socialized to distrust whites and white-dominated institutions. They contend that parents/guardians who racially socialized their children to be highly distrustful of whites and ill-prepare them for racist experiences intensify their likelihood of perceiving and negatively reacting to racial discrimination. Henson, Derlega, Pearson, Ferrer, and Holmes (2013) characterize this outcome as having a *race-based rejection sensitivity*. They define this sensitivity as having a chronic hypervigilance and hypersensitivity about being rejected based on race. Henson *et al.* (2013) found that African-American students with this sensitivity become highly upset when they perceived racism. These individuals show more negative affect (including anger, anxiety, and depression), less positive affect, and less willingness to forgive the perpetrator. In addition, they found that African-American students with this sensitivity have more thought intrusions (i.e., uncontrollable thoughts and feelings) associated with being the target of racial discrimination, and the individuals' preoccupation with having been the victim of the racist event prolongs its negative affect. These scholars further found that a race-based sensitivity undermines the ability of African-American youths to positively make sense about what happened to them because they are less likely to process it with their social support network. Thus, African-American juveniles who are hypersensitive to racism are unlikely "to deal with and/or habituate to emotionally-charged memories associated with a discriminatory event" (Henson et al., 2013, p. 508).

In sum, African-American delinquency is related to the lived experiences of black juveniles living in a conflicted, racially stratified society. The worldview that African-American juveniles have continues to be shaped by experiences with racial discrimination and racist stereotypes. These experiences have deleterious consequences that are related to delinquency. They cause African-American juveniles to experience negative emotions that are related to delinquency, including anger, hostility, aggression, defiance, and depression. These debilitating feelings exhaust their emotional capital, leaving them vulnerable to engaging in impulsive behaviors, which are a chief factor related to delinquency, and they undermine their capacity to build strong bonds with conventional white-dominated institutions such as their schools.

Where Do We Go From Here?

Disentangling the relationship between a racialized society with its racist institutions and African-American juvenile delinquency is a complex and daunting task. What makes it particularly daunting is that discussions that begin with the assumption that the US is a racialized society can be polarizing. This is especially the case when many believe that we have finally created a post-racial society where race no longer matters, as symbolically represented with the election and re-election of the first black President (Kinder & Dale-Riddle, 2012). Indeed, Unnever, Gabbidon, and Higgins (2011) report that 37% of whites and 28% of African-Americans perceived that an open national dialogue on race would cause greater racial division. At the same time, regardless of how painful and potentially divisive a national dialogue on race may be, the data indicate that the majority of whites and the vast majority of blacks believe that it would be restorative by bringing the races together. This dialogue needs to take place in order to decrease African-American juvenile delinquency.

Schools must be on the front line in implementing this national dialogue on race. This means educators must openly acknowledge the racist history of schooling in America. In addition, school administrators and faculty must acknowledge and confront the racist practices and stereotypes that pervade schools. This requires that educators initiate dialogues within the classrooms that discuss the nature of racial prejudice and discrimination. As stated earlier, there is a plethora of ways in which racism permeates the schools. These practices can range from administrators failing to embrace racial diversity (e.g., within the curriculum and in the hiring of African-American faculty), to teachers lowering their expectations for African-American juveniles, and to white students embracing racial prejudices and engaging in racist behaviors (e.g., hanging black dolls in public areas).

An associated problem that educators need to dismantle is the overt and nuanced consequences of the toxic stereotypes of African-Americans that are "in the air". Racist stereotypes can have nuanced and profound negative consequences. For example, they enhance the likelihood that African-Americans will perceive discrimination and they, in the context of schools, increase their likelihood of experiencing "stereotype threats", which in turn increase their probability of disengaging from their education. Thus, educators must take seriously the issue of exposing and eviscerating all of the myriad ways in which African-Americans juveniles are negatively stereotyped. This can be facilitated by African-American juveniles being exposed to a curriculum that embraces and promotes a positive racial identity (e.g., by celebrating black achievements) and by being exposed to more African-American teachers. It is noteworthy that African-American youth report less stress if they attend historically black schools rather than white-dominated institutions (Greer & Brown, 2011).

I also assert that researchers have underestimated the true extent to which negative stereotypes, stereotype threats, and personal experiences with racial discrimination negatively impact African-American juveniles. Scholars should measure the *degree* to which African-American youths experience these forms of racism similarly to how they measure the severity of child abuse. Thus, I recommend that researchers, for example, ask at what age were African-American juveniles exposed to the negative depictions of them and had personal experiences of being mistreated because of their race; who exposed the child to the toxic stereotypes and who discriminated against them because of their race (was it people in positions of trust and authority?); to what degree was the child socialized into believing negative depictions of them; how often was the person exposed to pejorative stereotypes and to racial discrimination (did it happen in daily interactions, did it happen sporadically or chronically?); and, over what length of time was the person exposed to these deleterious racist behaviors (did it persist across their life span)? It is hypothesized that delinquency increases with the *degree* to which African-American juveniles experience negative stereotypes, stereotype threats, and racial discrimination.

I conclude with a larger, more macro issue. The research indicates that race-based inequalities within and across schools are becoming more entrenched and institutionalized. This intensification of the racial polarity in and between schools, I believe, can only further exacerbate the likelihood that whites will continue to associate being African-American with underachievement and crime. These stereotypes will be rather immutable because the racial segregation of schools will undermine African-American youth achievements, and, as a result, further cement the "pipeline-to-prison". Thus, African-American juvenile delinquency will remain inextricably related to the degree to which the US educational system remains racist.

References

Agnew, R. (1992). Foundation for a general strain theory of crime and delinquency. *Criminology, 30,* 47–88.

Agnew, R., Brezina, T., Wright, J.P., & Cullen, F.T. (2002). Strain, personality traits, and delinquency: extending general strain theory. *Criminology, 40,* 43–72.

Akers, R.L., Krohn, M.D., Lanza-Kaduce, L., & Radosevich, M. (1979). Social learning and deviant behavior: A specific test of a general theory. *American Sociological Review, 44,* 636–655.

Alexander, M. (2012). *The New Jim Crow: Mass Incarceration in the Age of Colorblindness.* New York: New Press.

Alliman-Brissett, A.E., & Turner, S.L. (2010). Racism, Parent Support, and Math-Based Career Interests, Efficacy, and Outcome Expectations among African American Adolescents. *Journal of Black Psychology, 36,* 197–225.

Benner, A.D., & Graham, S. (2012). The antecedents and consequences of racial/ethnic discrimination during adolescence: Does the source of discrimination matter? *Developmental Psychology, 49,* 1602–1613. doi:10.1037/a0030557.

Bobo, L.D., & Charles, C.Z. (2009). Race in the American mind: From the Moynihan Report to the Obama candidacy. *Annals of the American Academy of Political and Social Science, 621,* 243–259.

Bouffard, L.A., & Piquero, N.L. (2010). Defiance theory and life course explanations of persistent offending. *Crime and Delinquency, 56,* 227–252.

Brezina, T. (2010). Anger, attitudes, and aggressive behavior: exploring the affective and cognitive foundations of angry aggression. *Journal of Contemporary Criminal Justice, 26,* 186–203.

Brown, C.S., & Bigler, R.S. (2005). Children's perceptions of discrimination: a developmental model. *Child Development, 76,* 533–553.

Brunson, R.K., & Weitzer, R. (2009). Police relations with black and white youths in different urban neighborhoods. *Urban Affairs Review, 44,* 858–885.

Burrow, A.L., & Ong, A.D. (2010). Racial identity as a moderator of daily exposure and reactivity to racial discrimination. *Self & Identity, 9,* 383–402.

Chao, R.C.L., Mallinckrodt, B., & Wei, M. (2012). Co-occurring presenting problems in African American college clients reporting racial discrimination distress. *Professional Psychology: Research and Practice, 43,* 199–207.

Copping, K.E., Kurtz-Costes, B., Rowley, S.J., & Wood, D. (2013). Age and race differences in racial stereotype awareness and endorsement. *Journal of Applied Social Psychology, 43,* 971–980. doi:10.1111/jasp.12061.

Devine, P.G., & Elliot, A.J. (1995). Are racial stereotypes really fading? The Princeton Trilogy revisited. *Personality and Social Psychology Bulletin, 21,* 1139–1150.

Dilulio Jr, J.J. (1994). The question of black crime. *Public Interest, 117,* 3–32.

Flashman, J. (2012). Different preferences or different opportunities? Explaining race differentials in the academic achievement of friends. *Social Science Research, 41,* 888–903.

Freeman, T.M., Anderman, L.H., & Jensen, J.M. (2007). Sense of belonging in College freshmen at the classroom and campus levels. *Journal of Experimental Education, 75,* 203–220.

Gamboa, S. (2012) High School Graduation Rate For Black Males Trails White Students. *Huffington Post.* Retrieved from http://www.huffingtonpost.com/2012/09/19/black-male-hs-graduation-_n_1896490.html.

Gillen-O'Neel, C., & Fuligni, A. (2013). A longitudinal study of school belonging and Academic motivation across high school. *Child Development, 84,* 678–692.

Gonsoulin, S., Zablocki, M., & Leone, P.E. (2012). Safe schools, staff development, and the school to prison pipeline. *Teacher Education and Special Education: The Journal of the Teacher Education Division of the Council for Exceptional Children, 35,* 309–319.

Gottfredson, M.R., & Hirschi, T. (1990). *A General Theory of Crime.* Palo Alto, CA: Stanford University Press.

Greer, T.M., & Brown, P. (2011). Minority status stress and coping processes among African American college students. *Journal of Diversity in Higher Education, 4,* 26–38.

Gregory, A., & Weinstein, R.S. (2008). The discipline gap and African Americans: Defiance or cooperation in the high school classroom. *Journal of School Psychology, 46,* 455–475.

Hallinan, M.T., & Williams, R.A. (1989). Interracial friendship choices in secondary schools. *American Sociological Review, 54,* 67–78.

Hanushek, E.A., Kain, J.F., & Rivkin, S.G. (2009). New evidence about Brown v. Board of Education: The complex effects of school racial composition on achievement. *Journal of Labor Economics, 27,* 349–383.

Harber, K.D., Gorman, J.L., Gengaro, F.P., Butisingh, S., Tsang, W., & Ouellette, R. (2012). Students' race and teachers' social support affect the positive feedback bias in public schools. *Journal of Educational Psychology, 104,* 1149–1161.

Harrell, S.P. (2000). A multidimensional conceptualization of racism-related stress: implications for the well-being of people of color. *American Journal of Orthopsychiatry, 70,* 42–57.

Haslam, S.A., Salvatore, J., Kessler, T., & Reicher, S.D. (2008). How stereotyping yourself contributes to your success (or failure). *Scientific American, April/May.*

Henson, J.M., Derlega, V.J., Pearson, M.R., Ferrer, R., & Holmes, K. (2013). African American students' responses to racial discrimination: How race-based rejection sensitivity and social constraints are related to psychological reactions. *Journal of Social & Clinical Psychology, 32,* 504–529.

Hirschi, T. (1969). *Causes of Delinquency.* Berkeley, CA: University of California Press.

Holland, M.M. (2012). Only here for the day. *Sociology of Education, 85,* 101–120.

Jones, J.M. (1972). *Prejudice and Racism.* Reading, MA: Addison-Wesley.

Kessler, R.C., Mickelson, K.D., & Williams, D.R. (1999). The prevalence, distribution, and mental health correlates of perceived discrimination in the United States. *Journal of Health and Social Behavior, 40,* 208–230.

Kinder, D.R., & Dale-Riddle, A. (2012). *The End of Race? Obama, 2008, and Racial Politics in America.* New Haven, CT: Yale University Press.

Mazerolle, P., Burton, V.S., Cullen, F.T., Evans, T.D., & Payne, G.L. (2000). Strain, anger, and delinquent adaptations specifying general strain theory. *Journal of Criminal Justice, 28,* 89–101.

McKown, C., & Strambler, M.J. (2009). Developmental antecedents and social and academic consequences of stereotype-consciousness in middle childhood. *Child Development, 80,* 1643–1659.

McKown, C., & Weinstein, R.S. (2003). The development and consequences of stereotype consciousness in middle childhood. *Child Development, 74,* 498–515.

Metze, P.S. (2012). Plugging the school to prison pipeline by addressing cultural racism in public education discipline. *UC Davis Journal of Juvenile Law and Policy, 16,* 203–311.

Moody, J. (2001). Race, school integration, and friendship segregation in America. *American Journal of Sociology, 107*, 679–716.

Mouw, T., & Entwisle, B. (2006). Residential segregation and interracial friendship in schools. *American Journal of Sociology, 112*, 394–441.

Quillian, L., & Campbell, M.E. (2003). Beyond black and white: The present and future of multiracial friendship segregation. *American Sociological Review, 107*, 540–566.

Rivas-Drake, D., Hughes, D., & Way, N. (2009). A preliminary analysis of associations among ethnic–racial socialization, ethnic discrimination, and ethnic identity among urban sixth graders. *Journal of Research on Adolescence, 19*, 558–584.

Rosenbloom, S.R., & Way, N. (2004). Experiences of discrimination among African American, Asian American, and Latino adolescents in an urban high school. *Youth and Society, 35*, 420–451.

Sampson, R.J., Raudenbush, S.W., & Earls, F. (1997). Neighborhoods and violent crime: A multilevel study of collective efficacy. *Science, 277*, 918–924.

Schmader, T., Johns, M., & Forbes, C. (2008). An integrated process model of stereotype threat effects on performance. *Psychological Review, 115*, 336.

Shaw, C.R. (1966). *The Jack-Roller: A Delinquent Boy's Own Story*. Chicago, IL: University of Chicago Press.

Shaw, C. R., & McKay, H.D. (1969). *Juvenile Delinquency and Urban Areas*. Chicago, IL: University of Chicago Press.

Shippen, M.E., Patterson, D., Green, K.L., & Smitherman, T. (2012). Community and school practices to reduce delinquent behavior: intervening on the school to prison pipeline. *Teacher Education and Special Education: The Journal of the Teacher Education Division of the Council for Exceptional Children, 35*, 296–308.

Snyder, C.R. (2012). Racial socialization in cross-racial families. *Journal of Black Psychology, 38*, 228–253.

Steele, C.M. (1997). A threat in the air: How stereotypes shape intellectual identity and performance. *American Psychologist, 52*, 613–629.

Steele, C.M., & Aronson, J. (1995). Stereotype threat and the intellectual test performance of African Americans. *Journal of Personality and Social Psychology, 69*, 797–811.

Thames, A.D., Hinkin, C.H., Byrd, D.A., Bilder, R.M., Duff, K.J., Mindt, M.R., Arentoft, A., & Streiff, V. (2013). Effects of stereotype threat, perceived discrimination, and examiner race on neuropsychological performance: simple as black and white? *Journal of the International Neuropsychological Society: JINS, 19*, 583–593.

Trawalter, S., Todd, A.R., Baird, A.A., & Richeson, J.A. (2008). Attending to threat: race-based patterns of selective attention. *Journal of Experimental Social Psychology, 44*, 1322–1327.

Unnever, J.D., & Cullen, F.T. (2012). White perceptions of whether African Americans and Hispanics are prone to violence and support for the death penalty. *Journal of Research in Crime and Delinquency, 49*, 519–544.

Unnever, J.D., Cullen, F.T., Mathers, S.A., McClure, T.E., & Allison, M.C. (2009). Racial discrimination and Hirschi's criminological classic: A chapter in the sociology of knowledge. *Justice Quarterly, 26*, 377–409.

Unnever, J.D., & Gabbidon, S.L. (2011). *A Theory of African American Offending: Race, Racism, and Crime*. New York: Taylor & Francis.

Unnever, J.D., Gabbidon, S.L., & Higgins, G.E. (2011). The election of Barack Obama and perceptions of criminal injustice. *Justice Quarterly, 28*, 23–45.

Wilson, T.M., & Rodkin, P.C. (2012). Children's cross-ethnic relationships in elementary schools: Concurrent and prospective associations between ethnic segregation and social status. *Child Development, 8,* 1081–1097.

Winnick, T.A., & Bodkin, M. (2008). Anticipated stigma and stigma management among those to be labeled "ex-con". *Deviant Behavior, 29,* 295–333.

Winnick, T.A., & Bodkin, M. (2009). Stigma, secrecy and race: An empirical examination of black and white incarcerated men. *American Journal of Criminal Justice, 34,* 131–150.

Wong, C.A., Eccles, J.S., & Sameroff, A. (2003). The influence of ethnic discrimination and ethnic identification on African American adolescents' school and socioemotional adjustment. *Journal of Personality, 71,* 1197–1232.

Wood, P.B., & Chesser, M. (1994). Black stereotyping in a university population. *Sociological Focus, 27,* 17–34.

11

A Biosocial Perspective on Juvenile Delinquency

Chris L. Gibson and Andrea Davis

Introduction

Adolescence is a developmental period when delinquent behavior is common. The age–crime curve provides evidence of this by showing that criminal offending starts to accelerate around the age of 14 and rapidly increases to age 19 (Blumstein, Cohen, & Farrington, 1988). Results from longitudinal studies provide evidence that the upswing in delinquent behavior is due to more adolescents participating in offending, and not a consequence of active offenders committing more offenses (Piquero, Farrington, & Blumstein, 2003). With few exceptions (Krohn, Gibson, & Thornberry, 2013), involvement in delinquency and offending is short-lived, with most desisting shortly after emerging adulthood (Moffitt, 1993). This trend has led criminologists to look for explanations during adolescence, and they have largely emphasized socialization and learning processes as being most important. Criminological research continues to inform us that parenting and peer group affiliations are responsible for non-trivial amounts of explained variance in delinquency and substance use (Akers, 1998; Thornberry & Krohn, 2005; Warr, 2002). However, the lion's share of empirical research on socialization has been one-sided. Historically, parenting and peer influences on juvenile delinquency have almost exclusively been examined in the absence of biological variables.

Genes have too often been left out of sociological-based theory and research on parenting, peers, and juvenile delinquency. This is problematic because research consistently reveals that biology matters for understanding child and adolescent antisocial behaviors, including delinquency. The collective results from genetic studies are robust and unlikely to be explained away by environmental influences.

The Handbook of Juvenile Delinquency and Juvenile Justice, First Edition. Edited by Marvin D. Krohn and Jodi Lane.

Additionally, it also makes sense for biological processes to be considered in theories and research on juvenile delinquency because adolescence is a stage of the life-course when rapid biological change occurs (e.g., puberty and brain development), which has been related to involvement in antisocial behavior, risk-taking, and impulsive behavior (Ellis, Boyce, Belsky, Bakermans-Kranenburg, & Van Ijzendoorn, 2011). Taking nature seriously is a necessary next step if criminologists are to understand how social forces such as parents and peers influence juvenile delinquency.

In this chapter we highlight the particular role of genetics for understanding two social influences on juvenile delinquency – peers and parents. Our focus does not imply that other biological processes are less important (e.g., puberty or brain development), nor does it mean that genetic research is the most relevant biological research for understanding juvenile delinquency. We decided to focus on genetics because of the recent influx of this research in criminology focused on offending and delinquency relative to other biological variables. In doing so, we first provide an overview of sociological-based theory and research that has emphasized the importance of parent and peers, with more attention given to those that underscore both during the transition from childhood to adolescence. Second, we highlight two limitations of sociological-based theories and research on parenting and peers: (1) a lack of serious attention to genetics; and (2) research designs which have discounted or excluded genetic influences. Third, we review research that integrates genetic factors in explaining how peers and parents influence adolescent involvement in juvenile delinquency.

Peers, Parenting, and Juvenile Delinquency: An Overview of Sociologically Based Theory and Research

Peers and delinquency

Research suggests that social changes occurring during adolescence correspond to increased involvement in delinquency (Warr, 2002). One particularly important change is the increasing importance that children place on peer groups during the transition from childhood to adolescence (Krohn, 1986; Simons, Wu, Conger, & Lorenz, 1994; Warr, 2002). Among the most prominent sociologically based theories with strong empirical support are those that highlight the role of peers in delinquency. Interrogating the relationship between peers and delinquency has been a key part of delinquency research for quite some time, and understandably so (Haynie, 2002; Short, 1957). During adolescence, peers are more influential than at any other time in the life-course (Brown, 1990; Haynie & Osgood, 2005; Warr, 2002). A long line of research has also shown that delinquent activity almost always involves co-offenders (Haynie, 2002; Hindelang, 1976; McGloin & Shermer, 2009), is more likely to occur in unstructured activities with peers (Anderson, 2013; Maimon & Browning, 2010), and that it typically occurs in small groups during adolescence but is more likely to be committed alone in emerging adulthood (Warr, 2002).

One of the strongest and most consistent findings in the criminological litera-ture is the relationship between adolescents' own delinquency and the delinquent behavior of their peers (Agnew, 1991; Akers, Krohn, Lanza-Kaduce, & Radosevich, 1979; Elliott, Huizinga, & Ageton, 1985; Elliott & Menard, 1996; Kandel, 1978; Krohn, Waldo, & Chiricos, 1974; Matsueda, 1982; Matsueda & Anderson, 1998; Matsueda & Heimer, 1987; Short, 1957). In fact, a recent meta-analysis revealed that the association between peer delinquency and one's own delinquency has a moderate to strong effect on delinquency (Pratt *et al.*, 2010). Demonstrated by self-report studies, observational studies, and official records data, results have shown that adolescents with few or no delinquent friends exhibit less delinquent involvement compared with those who have more delinquent friends (Haynie & Osgood, 2005; Krohn *et al.*, 1974).

Theories such as social learning (Akers, 1973) and differential association (Sutherland, 1947) posit that the influence of delinquent peers on an adolescent's own delinquency operates through modeling of delinquent behavior and the adop-tion of definitions favorable to delinquency (Akers, 1998; Haynie, 2002). Social learning theory posits a unidirectional relationship in which pro-social adolescents are socialized into delinquency by associating with delinquent peers (Haynie, 2002; Pratt *et al.*, 2010). While much of the discourse on both differential association and social learning theories involves assessing the influences of delinquent versus non-delinquent peer groups (and whether so-called birds of a feather flock together), there is research to suggest that peer groups are often a mix of both delinquent and non-delinquent members (Haynie & Osgood, 2005). Contact with both delinquent and non-delinquent influences is the focal point of differential association theory, as it suggests that exposure to both groups (within an intimate network) will shape definitions of delinquency and thereby affect involvement in delinquent behavior (Haynie & Osgood, 2005; Pratt *et al.*, 2010; Sutherland, 1947).

Other prominent criminological theories offer additional explanations of the link between peers and delinquency. For instance, Thornberry's (1987) interactional theory and Gottfredson and Hirschi's (1990) control theory challenge the main peer relationship tenets of learning theories – mainly the concepts of unidirectional rela-tionships and normative peer influences. Interactional theory rests on the assump-tion that a primary cause of delinquency is the weakening of social constraints on an individual's behavior (Thornberry, 1987; Thornberry, Lizotte, Krohn, Farnworth, & Jang, 1991, 1994). Moreover, interactional theory suggests a developmental process in that the relationship between delinquent peers and delinquency is reciprocal (see Krohn, Lizotte, Thornberry, Smith, & McDowall, 1996; Thornberry *et al.*, 1994); that is, associating with delinquent peers leads to more delinquency, and delinquency leads to more associations with delinquent peers. According to Thornberry and colleagues, delinquent attitudes in childhood are linked to associating with delinquent peers (Thornberry *et al.*, 1994). In adolescence, however, delinquent beliefs, associations, and behaviors are reciprocally related.

The debate over the directionality of delinquent peer affiliations and delinquency is not the only unsettled matter in attempts to explain juvenile delinquency. Learning theory interpretations of normative peer influences have been refuted by Gottfredson and Hirschi (1990), who argued that delinquents self-select into delinquent peer groups rather than delinquent peer groups playing a causal role in explaining delinquency (i.e., delinquent behavior comes before the selection of delinquent friends) (Haynie, 2002).

Moffitt (1993) identified two theoretically distinct pathways to antisocial behavior and juvenile delinquency, and suggested that learning from and mimicking peers is more closely associated with adolescence-limited delinquency rather than life-course persistent offending. She suggests that to understand adolescent-limited delinquency one must understand the developmental period in which it emerges. Her explanation focuses primarily on the difference between biological and social age during adolescence, social mimicking, and access to resources that symbolize adult status.

Despite a large body of research that finds a consistent association between delinquent peer affiliations and delinquency, much about the relationship between peers and delinquency remains either unknown or unclear (Haynie & Osgood, 2005). Unresolved research issues include how peer delinquency should be measured, projection of one's own behavior into self-reports of peer measures, and changes in peer social networks over time, to name but a few. The biological process related to peer formation and influences have been absent from these mainstream topics, and it is rarely mentioned that genetics may be important for understanding when and how peers matter for understanding delinquency.

Parenting and delinquency

Sociologically based delinquency theories (Gottfredson & Hirschi, 1990; Hirschi, 1969) have also recognized the important role that parents play in the lives of children and adolescents. For instance, it has been theorized that the quality of parental attachments, parental supervisions, and control are instrumental to understanding adolescents' deviant behavior (Deutsch, Crockett, Wolff, & Russell, 2012). Control theory (Gottfredson & Hirschi, 1990) asserts that juveniles who are close to their parents will consider their parents' response to deviant behavior whenever the opportunity for such behavior arises (Deutsch *et al.*, 2012). Control theory further claims that parents can exercise control through monitoring their children and punishing bad behavior (Deutsch *et al.*, 2012; Gottfredson & Hirschi, 1990). Research findings on control theory have indicated that supportive parenting (e.g., parental involvement and warmth) practices are associated with lower levels of delinquency among adolescents, independent of parental supervision or punishment (de Kemp, Scholte, Overbeek, & Engls, 2006; Demuth & Brown, 2004; Gorman-Smith, Tolan, & Henry, 2000, cited in Deutsch *et al.*, 2012). Research also has indicated that parental control alone can influence adolescent antisocial behavior (Deutsch *et al.*, 2012).

Adolescents' delinquent peer associations have also been examined to explain ways that parenting may influence delinquency. Parental control has been found to affect an adolescent's involvement in delinquency via influence on deviant peer affiliation (Brody et al., 2001; Chung & Steinberg, 2006). Research has also found that supportive parenting with moderate amounts of behavioral control reduces both the selection and the influence of deviant peers (Brown & Bakken, 2011; Parker & Benson, 2004, as cited in Deutsch *et al.*, 2012).

Developmental theories provide explanations for when parenting may be most important. For instance, interactional theory offers a useful theoretical framework for examining reciprocity and for when the effects of parents on delinquency might be the most salient. As mentioned above, a core idea of interactional theory is that the relationship between informal social control and delinquency is reciprocal. Not only does weakened social restraints cause adolescents to engage in delinquent behavior, but involvement in delinquency can further weaken social restraints (Thornberry *et al.*, 1994). What this means for the effect of parenting is that low levels of parental attachment can lead to delinquency, and delinquency can also lead to lower levels of parental attachment (Liska & Reed, 1985; Thornberry *et al.*, 1994). The importance of parental attachment is not theorized to remain stable throughout childhood and adolescence, however. Instead, interactional theory claims that the effects of parental attachment on delinquency will become weaker as the child ages and becomes more independent (Thornberry *et al.*, 1994).

In summary, this section has provided an overview of how sociological-based criminological theories and research portray the influence of parent and peers on juvenile delinquency. While highlighting socialization and learning from childhood into adolescence, what remains unclear is the role of biology, and particularly genetics. Although reference is sometimes made to biologically related influences on juvenile delinquency, none of these theories or studies actually provide theoretical details or methodological frameworks on how a focus on genes can offer important information towards explaining juvenile delinquency, nor do they provide any detail on how genes may interact with parenting or peers to predict involvement in juvenile delinquency. The remaining sections will shed light on why and how genetic findings and research designs should be better incorporated into criminologists' explanations of juvenile delinquency.

A Biosocial Perspective: Genetics and Juvenile Delinquency

Juvenile delinquency is frequently studied by criminologists as if nature and nurture are separate entities. The latter has almost always taken center-stage and is often seen as most deserving of empirical attention, while the former has been largely dismissed as if a fundamental part of human development plays no role in explaining involvement in crime and delinquency. Of course, if you ask a criminologist whether genes matter, he/she will likely say yes (see Beaver, 2013), but this is inconsistent with what is found in most criminological theories and research.

The marginalization of genetics in criminological research has hindered the understanding of juvenile delinquency. Scholars have shown that by not accounting for genetic influences, criminologists run the risk of inflating the importance of social factors, such as parenting, on aggression, delinquency, and related traits and behavior (e.g., self-control) (see Moffitt, 2005; Moffitt & Caspi, 2006; Wright & Beaver, 2005). Ultimately, this neglect has had the consequence of criminologists attributing more explanatory power to parenting and other social influences than should be, and has resulted in an incomplete picture of juvenile delinquency.

It is inevitable that some criminologists will continue to believe that nurture is *the* causal agent responsible for heterogeneity in juvenile delinquency. This is concerning, and most importantly goes against decades of scientific evidence that runs counter to such beliefs. Hundreds of empirical studies summarized in six well-known meta-analyses have revealed that genes, in conjunction with environment, play a non-trivial role in understanding antisocial behavior (Burt, 2009a, 2009b; Ferguson, 2010; Mason & Frick, 1994; Miles & Carey, 1997; Rhee & Waldman, 2002), with juvenile delinquency being one of them. In spite of the overwhelming evidence suggesting that a better understanding of the human genome will provide rich information on human behavior (e.g., Carey, 2003; Pinker, 2002; Turkheimer, 2000), some criminological researchers will continue to approach biological risk factors with caution.

Doubt among some criminologists, and the hesitancy to embrace biological explanations, is often due to historical misuses of research and unethical treatment of individuals in the name of science. One particularly important era of research responsible for this is eugenics. Eugenics focused largely on the biological inferiority of particular ethnic and racial groups in society. Nearly a century ago eugenicists thought that society's social ills could be solved if criminals, racial and ethnic minorities, and those possessing inherent traits such as low intelligence could be stopped from reproducing. Many eugenicists desired to improve the human species through sterilizing and eliminating individuals that were labeled as biologically inferior, under the cloak of scientific investigation. Eugenics has since produced a lasting scar on the scientific community, leading some social scientists to believe common myths that modern biosocial research has an agenda of genetic determinism and racially driven policies (see Rukus & Gibson, 2011).

Contemporary biosocial criminologists do not endorse the political agendas, crime prevention strategies, or policy implications from theories and research from the eugenics era. The biosocial approach we describe embraces the fact that social environments are very important for understanding involvement in crime, delinquency, and related behaviors. That is, criminologists who now adopt a biosocial framework examine human behavior in ways that allow for both nature and nurture to be considered as predictors of crime and delinquency, and find that both are important. The same cannot be said for those embracing only sociological perspectives – at least this appears to be the case when we closely examine the research designs that are commonly deployed.

Present-day biosocial criminologists have developed a clear and focused research agenda that calls into question the extant criminological theory and research on juvenile delinquency by showing that both genetic and environmental factors are important sources of phenotypic variation – or observable differences in human behaviors and traits (Beaver, 2013; Benson, 2013; Raine, 2013; Simons *et al.*, 2011, 2012). Before describing evidence of how genes are related to juvenile delinquency, it will be helpful to provide readers with a brief genetic primer.

Imagine DNA as a library of books arranged in an unambiguous order (see Champagne & Mashoodh, 2009). Like books stored on library shelves, DNA that is contained in a nucleus of a cell is waiting to be read. DNA is read by enzymes called ribonucleic acid (RNA) polymerase, which result in messenger RNA (mRNA) through a process called transcription. mRNA is a copy of a gene, or a DNA sequence, that is converted into a protein. The translation of DNA into protein is how genes are expressed. Once DNA is read it can affect the functioning of a cell and a human organism. It can increase individual risk for mental illnesses, disease, and antisocial behavior.

Technically speaking, a gene is a sequence of deoxyribonucleic acid (DNA), or a sequence of nucleotide base-pairs (guanine, thymine, cytosine, adenine), and can be found at a particular locus on chromosomes contained in the nuclei of billions of cells in the human body. The human genome is estimated to have roughly 23,000 genes wrapped around chromatin, and if stretched out like a ball of yarn, DNA would equal roughly six feet in length. Genes contain the instructions used to code for the production of proteins and enzymes, and can be thought of as the information used to instruct cells in which functions to perform.

With mapping of the human genome achieved, researchers now have a great amount of information about some genes involved in the etiology of antisocial behavior. Genes that aid in the production, transportation, and regulation of neurotransmitters in the brain are of particular importance to the study of crime and delinquency. Neurotransmitters are chemical signals that allow brain cells (i.e., neurons) to communicate with each other. They cross a synaptic cleft to send a signal to a neighboring neuron. Genes are involved in the neurotransmission code for proteins that assist in the transport, reuptake and enzymatic breakdown of neurotransmitters after communication between neurons.

Genes involved in the dopaminergic and serotonergic systems have been linked to alcoholism, violence, aggression, conduct disorder, delinquency, and victimization to name but a few (see Beaver, 2013; Simons & Lei, 2013). As with all genes, neurotransmission-related genes are inherited maternally and paternally. However, unlike all genes some of these have multiple copies or variants that exist in a population, hence the label "genetic polymorphism". The term *allele* is used to describe when a gene has one or more alternative forms, and alleles of particular genes involved in neurotransmission have been linked to antisocial behavior among children, adults, and adolescents. It is also important to note that genetic influences are probabilistic. A person who possesses a particular variant of a gene may have a greater probability of engaging in antisocial behavior compared with a person who does not possess that variant of the gene, but this is almost always conditional on environmental circumstances that individuals encounter or experience, especially those environments that are in a non-normal range of a population's distribution. A genetic predisposition alone is not enough to cause juvenile delinquency, violence, or any other form of antisocial behavior. Finally, genetic influences are often thought of as having polygenic effects on human behaviors, meaning that multiple genes can influence a phenotype.

With some of the basics now covered, we first review and discuss methodologies and empirical evidence that have shaped the current genetic biosocial perspective in criminology. Second, we discuss how genetic research is providing new insights to questions regarding the relationships between delinquent peer affiliations, parenting practices and juvenile delinquency. In the following sections we particularly focus on behavior genetics and molecular genetic approaches for examining juvenile delinquency and related outcomes.

Behavior genetics: similar environments, unique experiences, and delinquency

After decades of theorizing and research, it would seem that criminologists have a tight handle on the nuanced ways that parents influence adolescent involvement in juvenile delinquency. But, one important observation leads to questions about what can or should be concluded. Many studies on parenting have been carried out in the absence of controls for genetic factors (see Moffitt, 2005; Moffitt & Caspi, 2006). This issue raises the specific concern of to what extent has bias been introduced into sociologically based studies examining the association between "bad" parenting and juvenile delinquency. Research that excludes genetics makes it difficult to know the unbiased influences of parenting because of genetic confounding and the inability to separate distinct sources of environmental influence. The scenario described below illustrates this problem.

Imagine identical twins that share 100% of their DNA and were reared by both of their biological parents. The parents were happily married and were very involved in the twin's lives. They provided them each with affection, attention, support, and warmth. They also disciplined them using similar strategies when they misbehaved. The twins faced the challenges associated with being raised in a disadvantaged neighborhood and having parents whose incomes are below the poverty level. When they began to achieve more independence in the transition from childhood to adolescence, twins A and B started to explore different peer groups in the neighborhood and at school. Twin A associated with peers who got him into trouble and he consequently ended up in a juvenile correctional facility. He witnessed violence and engaged in it himself; he smoked and drank alcohol, and eventually dropped out of high school. Twin B took a different path by associating with a prosocial peer group, was committed to school, made good grades, did not drink or smoke, and engaged in civic activities in his community. In sum, twins A and B were different in the activities they participated in and the company they kept, which in part explains why twin A ended up in a juvenile detention facility and twin B on a trajectory of success. However, when they visited each other after twin A was released from a correctional facility, it became quickly apparent that they share many behavioral and personality characteristics, even though they have had so many different or unique experiences. They are both extroverts and are willing to take risks (but in different ways); they show signs of impulsivity by interrupting each other often; and they are quite fidgety and have limited attention spans.

Can traditional criminological research on juvenile delinquency provide an explanation for the differences and similarities between twin A and twin B's personalities, attention spans, and involvement in juvenile delinquency? The simple answer is no. The lion's share of criminological research providing support for strong parenting and peer influences has done so without considering the different or unique environments experienced by siblings raised in the same household. Furthermore, most criminological research has not controlled for the degree of genetic relatedness among siblings when measuring parenting and peer influences. Why does this matter? It matters because of the high risk for confounded relationships between parenting, peers, and juvenile delinquency, giving more weight to parenting influences than should be given (see Harris, 1998).

Most studies on parenting and peer influences have relied on the Standard Social Science Methodology (SSSM). The SSSM can be defined as any method of data collection or analysis that does not take into account genetic influences (Harris, 1998). In criminological studies examining family/parenting influences on juvenile delinquency, the SSSM is often used because data are typically collected on only one child per household. By using this approach, criminologists often make the statistical assumption that genetic influences are near zero.

The SSSM is ill-equipped for understanding three primary sources of variation in juvenile delinquency – shared environmental, non-shared environmental, and genetics. The shared environment is any environment that two or more siblings share that would make their behaviors or personality characteristics more similar. The non-shared environment includes the unique experiences or environments that siblings encounter that influence their behaviors and traits, or make them less similar. The genetic contribution is accounted for by sampling sibling dyads that possess varying degrees of genetic relatedness (e.g., identical twins, fraternal twins, half siblings, etc.). Although other designs have been used (e.g., adoption studies), genetic influences are most often determined in behavior genetic studies by analyzing identical and fraternal twin dyads. Equipped with this additional information, it is now important to revisit twins A and B to illustrate how sociological studies that use the SSSM are ill-equipped for arriving at unbiased estimates of parent and peer influence.

By sampling only one child per household, an SSSM approach emphasizes, and actually favors, shared environmental influences on juvenile delinquency. Such designs place limits on examining why children in the same household exhibit differences or similarities with regard to juvenile delinquency, personalities, and peers they hang out with. Further, the SSSM's inability to control for genetic influences results in a conclusion that the association between parenting (or peers) and delinquency is entirely due to socialization, while disregarding heritability or genetics.

We know that individuals inherent genetic information from their biological parents. If bad parenting is one manifestation of a parent's antisocial behavior, which is partly due to genes, then it could be that the association between bad parenting and a child's involvement in delinquency share a common genetic source. To date, various studies have shown that a non-trivial amount of variance in parenting practices is attributed to genetics, and that the influence of bad parenting on at least some types of antisocial behaviors among offspring (e.g., aggression) is partly explained by genetics (see Moffitt & Caspi, 2006).

Criminological theories and research on parenting and peers should be able to explain why children in the same family turn out to be different in their delinquent involvement. Is it because they perceive parental treatment differently (or are actually treated differently by parents), have different peer groups, or do they possess different criminal propensities? The same should be important for understanding when siblings in the same family turn out to be very similar. Could it be due to genetics, shared environments, or something else? Behavior genetic studies have shed light on the answers to these questions, but most sociologically based studies have not.

Behavior genetic studies examine identical twins (100% genetically similar), fraternal twins (50% genetically similar), and other pairs of siblings that vary in genetic relatedness. Behavior genetic studies provide valuable information on the percentage of variance in antisocial behavior attributable to genetics, the shared environment, and non-shared environment, including externalizing behaviors, aggression, conduct problems, self-regulation, behavioral disorders (e.g., ADHD), early onset/starter delinquency, and substance use (see Arseneault *et al.*, 2003; Moffitt & Caspi, 2006; Taylor, Iacono, & McGue, 2000). Results from meta-analyses of behavior genetic studies reveal three primary findings: (1) approximately 40–60% of the variance in antisocial behavior is attributable to genetics; (2) the majority of the variance attributable to environmental influence is due to non-shared environments (environmental influences that individuals may differently experience or that they do not share); and (3) the shared environment explains the least amount of variance (e.g., Ferguson, 2010; Mason & Frick, 1994; Miles & Carey, 1997; Rhee & Waldman, 2002).

Multiple informants have also been used in behavior genetic studies to gauge whether the estimated genetic influences found in studies on youth's antisocial behavior is dependent on the rater who reports on a child's behavior (Arseneault *et al.*, 2003; Kendler & Baker, 2007). Genetic influence is uncovered regardless of the person who rates the behavior (teacher, parent, or child). For instance, using data from the Environmental Risk Longitudinal Twin Study, Arseneault and colleagues (2003) examined teacher, parent, and child reports. Taken together, findings from behavior genetic studies hold up across historical periods, countries, and various antisocial outcomes of children and adolescents.

A particularly important finding derived from behavior genetic studies is the strong support for non-shared environmental influences that has been gleaned. As noted earlier, traditional sociologically based studies hardly ever account for genetics or non-shared environmental influences in determining how socialization, learning, and social control processes explain similarities and differences in juvenile delinquency. To be fair, though, studies using the SSSM to examine juvenile delinquency attempt to rule out potential sources of selection bias that may account for a correlation between a sociological predictor variable (e.g., corporal punishment or spanking) and delinquency (e.g., Gibson, Miller, Jennings, Swatt, & Gover, 2009; Gibson, Swatt, Miller, Jennings, & Gover, 2012; Morris & Gibson, 2011).

Behavior genetic studies are not without limitations. First, one criticism has centered on the equal environments assumption. That is, some have argued that identical twins are treated more similarly than fraternal twins, thus leading to the possibility that behavior genetics studies have attributed more explained variance to heritability than they should, and have provided biased estimates of environmental influences. This possibility has been examined in various studies and minimal support for it has emerged (Kendler, 1983; Kendler, Neale, Kessler, Heath, & Eaves, 1993). In spite of the equal environment criticism, other types of genetic designs have analyzed samples of adopted children and identical twins reared apart to find that genetic influences are robust (Plomin, 2011).

Second, environmental influences are often estimated differently in behavior genetics studies compared with those that employ the SSSM. Research using the SSSM approach typically estimates influences of observed measures of shared environments on delinquent outcomes, whereas behavior genetic studies provide a latent estimate of the shared environment and not one or several particular shared environments, although this can be accomplished (see Feinberg, Button, Neiderhiser, Reiss, & Hetherington, 2007).

Third, non-shared environmental influences have been more difficult to pinpoint in behavior genetic studies, thus not allowing for detection of which types of non-shared environmental influences are most important, although exceptions do exist (e.g., Beaver, 2008).

Fourth, behavior genetic designs commonly employed by biosocial criminologists have not allowed for the examination of the association between particular genes and juvenile delinquency, but rather have provided estimates of how much variance in delinquency or other types of antisocial behavior is heritable.

Finally, results from behavior genetic studies are less helpful in guiding policy discussions on juvenile delinquency (Rukus & Gibson, 2011), but such findings may still be useful for policymakers and prevention specialists in determining how much of an effect should be expected by targeting a known shared environmental factor for intervention purposes.

Although biosocial criminologists are interested in the interactions between genes and known environmental factors that include parenting, family socio-economic conditions, and peer group affiliations in the prediction of juvenile delinquency and antisocial behavior, behavioral genetic designs are not best equipped for measuring such interactions. Some exceptions do exist. For instance, Feinberg and colleagues (2007) used a behavioral genetic model to examine gene–environment interactions with parental warmth and negativity to find that parenting influences on child aggression and delinquency were moderated by genetic factors. Gene–environment interactions have also been examined using stratification methods to estimate heritability of a behavior or trait across samples of twins categorized by two or more groupings (e.g., low SES neighborhoods or families vs. high

SES neighbors or families). Such studies show that heritability estimates vary depending on environmental category (Asbury, Wachs, & Plomin, 2005; Rose, Dick, Viken, & Kaprio, 2001).

Molecular genetics, parenting, peers, and delinquency

As a result of the unveiling of the human genome, the social sciences have witnessed a recent influx of molecular genetic studies that center on how particular gene variants are associated with the involvement of children and adolescents in delinquency and antisocial behavior, including substance use, violence, conduct problems, and serious delinquent acts (e.g., Beaver *et al.*, 2007; Beaver, Gibson, DeLisi, Vaughn, & Wright, 2012; Beaver, Gibson, Jennings, & Ward, 2009; Caspi *et al.*, 2002; Simons *et al.*, 2012; Stogner & Gibson, 2013). These studies examine genetic polymorphisms, which as mentioned earlier are genes identified as having two or more alleles in a population. Observed and measurable genetic variability (i.e., alleles) between individuals allows researchers to examine how genes predict variation in antisocial behavior and delinquency.

Biosocial criminologists have played a role in analyzing molecular genetic data and have found that functional genetic polymorphisms involved in the coding and production of proteins and enzymes related to neurotransmission are important for predicting juvenile delinquency and related phenotypes such as low self-control, cognitive processes, emotional states and fear responses, decision-making, and aggression (e.g., Bakermans- Kranenburg & Van Ijzendoorn, 2011; Belsky & Beaver, 2011; Simons & Lei, 2013; Simons *et al.*, 2011). Genetic polymorphisms that are commonly analyzed by biosocial criminologists include the MAOA gene, DRD4 dopamine receptor gene, and the 5HTTLPR serotonin receptor gene, to name a few. These genes play important roles in the reuptake, transport and metabolic breakdown of neurotransmitters in the brain.

Research examining candidate gene–environment interactions move beyond some criticisms of behavior genetic studies by allowing for analysis at a molecular level, and looking at how such differences interact with environmental factors such as parenting and child maltreatment, harsh neighborhood environments, delinquent peer associations, and stress-enhancing circumstances to predict antisocial and delinquent behavior. This section provides examples of studies that show evidence of how particular genetic polymorphisms, in interaction with parents and peers, predict involvement in antisocial and delinquent behavior. Before doing so we describe two frameworks that currently guide these investigations – diathesis-stress and differential susceptibility.

The diathesis-stress model suggests that carriers of genetic risk alleles are at a heightened risk for engaging in violence and related behaviors, but only in the presence of stressful environmental contexts that may trigger a gene's expression. The first study to show an association between a particular gene and antisocial behavior centered on the MAOA gene, a functional genetic polymorphism found on the X chromosome. The MAOA gene has low and high activity alleles present in the population. Caspi and colleagues (2002) found that the low-activity MAOA alleles which confer low levels of MAOA expression (an enzyme responsible for regulation of serotonin and dopamine in the brain) increase the likelihood of conduct problems and violence during adolescence and adulthood, but only among those who reported experiencing severe maltreatment in childhood (Caspi *et al.*, 2002). This finding has since been replicated and confirmed in numerous studies. Other studies have found that the correlation between cumulative stress-inducing experiences during adolescence and substance use is modified by the MAOA low-activity alleles. For instance, Stogner and Gibson (2013) analyzed the Add Health data to examine the interaction between MAOA and a stressful experiences index in predicting adolescents' self-reports of substance use. After accounting for numerous risk factors (e.g., peer substance use, parenting, and low self-control) they found that the relationship between stress-inducing experiences and adolescent substance use (e.g., marijuana use) was stronger for male adolescents who possess a low-activity risk allele for MAOA.

Genes related to the reuptake and transport of dopamine (including DAT1, DRD2, and DRD4) have also been examined in gene–environment interaction studies in predicting childhood and adolescent problem behaviors. For example, DeLisi, Beaver, Wright, & Vaughn (2008) analyzed the Add Health data to examine the dopamine receptor genes DRD2 and DRD4 to predict age of first police contact and first arrest. The DRD2 and DRD4 risk alleles predicted onset in the low family risk sample, but did not reach statistical significance for the high family risk sample (DeLisi *et al.*, 2008). Further, the DAT1 dopamine receptor gene has been studied in children with ADHD (attention deficit hyperactivity disorder) to predict conduct disorder behaviors (Lahey *et al.*, 2011). A gene–environment interaction was found between maternal parenting (both positive and negative) and DAT1 to predict conduct disorder symptoms five to eight years later. Those youth who possessed at least one copy of the 9-repeat allele showed more symptoms of conduct disorder.

Most research studies on candidate gene–environment interactions have operated from a diathesis-stress framework, and have shown that various adverse environmental conditions, such as child maltreatment and parental negativity, can trigger the expression of antisocial phenotypes among children and adolescents who possess genetic risk alleles. However, recent criticisms grounded in evolutionary theory have been launched against this perspective (Belsky, Bakermans-Kranenburg, & van Ijzendoorn, 2007; Belsky & Pluess, 2009; Ellis *et al.*, 2011). From an evolutionary perspective, genes that are dysfunctional should over time be reduced in a population because they serve no advantage to humans. Alleles that confer risk have been theorized to have no benefits, yet they remain highly prevalent in human populations, with some studies showing as high as 50% of subjects being carriers of so-called risk alleles (Ellis *et al.*, 2011). Such findings have been used to argue that these alleles remain in the population because they provide some advantage. This is where the differential susceptibility framework has come into play (Belsky & Pluess, 2009).

The differential susceptibility model proposes that genes thought to place individuals at risk for engaging in delinquency actually make them more sensitive to environmental stimuli, whether they be stressful or supportive environments (Belsky & Pluess, 2009; Belsky & Beaver, 2011; Simons *et al.*, 2011). Carriers of "risk alleles" are not only more at risk for exhibiting maladaptive behaviors when paired with stressful environments, but carriers of the same genetic variants will exhibit substantially less maladaptive outcomes when experiencing supportive environments.

Molecular genetic studies examining differential susceptibility are growing at a rapid pace. For example, in a recent meta-analysis published in a special issue of *Development and Psychopathology* (February 2011), the 7-repeat allele of the DRD4 dopamine receptor gene was related to much lower externalizing of problems among youth in supportive rearing environments. Those who carry the so-called risk alleles for DRD4 reaped the most benefits from positive environments when compared with those who did not possess these alleles. It has also been shown that the more sensitivity alleles that youths possess, the more susceptible they are to supportive or adverse rearing/learning environments. For instance, Belsky and Beaver (2011) analyzed a cumulative measure of genetic sensitivity that included DAT1, DRD2, DRD4, 5-HTTLPR, and MAOA to examine how it modified the relationship between parental support and self-control. They concluded that youth who are most genetically susceptible, or had the greatest number of sensitivity alleles, benefited the most from supportive parenting environments (they had the most self-control), but had the lowest self-control in unsupportive parenting environments. Simons and colleagues (2011) also found support for cumulative genetic sensitivity (an index of sensitivity alleles consisting of DRD4, MAOA, and 5HTTLPR) in a longitudinal study of African-American children. Specifically, they concluded that supportive family factors were related to much lower involvement in delinquency for those possessing heightened genetic sensitivity, when compared with those who were less genetically sensitive. Delinquency outcomes were worse for those possessing heightened genetic sensitivity and residing in adverse family environments.

Studies on the diathesis-stress and differential susceptibility explanations of gene–environment interactions are not without limitations. Most studies do not examine within-person change in exposure to environmental contexts that may produce change in gene expression and, consequently, phenotype. Candidate gene–environment interaction studies that examine intra-individual change and stability can provide novel insights into both perspectives. For instance, they may help facilitate a better understanding of whether adolescents who carry more genetic sensitivity/risk alleles are more likely to change phenotypes in response to moving from a harsh social environment (e.g., hostile parenting) to a more nurturing social environment (e.g., warm, loving, or supportive parenting) when compared with a child who is less genetically sensitive. We are unaware of studies that capture such intra-individual change and inter-individual differences simultaneously when testing differential susceptibility and diathesis stress explanations.

Peer delinquency has also been examined using genetic biosocial frameworks. An important finding regarding delinquent peers is the high degree of homophily in peer groups – that is, individuals tend to associate with others who possess similar traits and characteristics (Krohn, 1986). The idea of homophily has been extended into a biosocial context in that some have suggested that humans will seek out friends who share their own underlying genetic predispositions (e.g., Beaver, Wright, & DeLisi, 2008). Recent research supports this claim as it pertains to delinquent peers. For instance, Beaver and colleagues (2011) found that stability in delinquent peers during adolescence was partly attributable to genetics. In fact, several studies confirm that variance in associating with delinquent peers is partly due to genetics (Cleveland, Wiebe, & Rowe, 2005; Kendler & Baker, 2007). Finally, in a recent study published in the *Proceedings of the National Academy of Sciences*, Fowler, Settle, and Christakis (2011) analyzed the Add Health and the Framingham Heart Study data to examine genetic similarity among friendship networks. Although not focused on delinquent peer associations, they found that particular alleles of the DRD2 genetic polymorphism were related to homophily in friendship networks. Scholars will continue to debate whether peers cause delinquency, or whether the relationship between delinquent peers and one's own delinquency is due to selection (see Warr, 2002). It will be important for future research to examine the causation and selection arguments using research designs that can control for genetic influences on peer associations and delinquency.

A smaller number of recent studies have also shown that genetic polymorphisms are related to reporting having delinquent peers. For example, a recent study analyzing the Add Health data has shown that the 10-repeat allele of the DAT1 genetic polymorphism plays a role in delinquent peer group selection (or having peers who drink, smoke, or do other drugs) (Beaver, Wright, & DeLisi, 2008). The 10-repeat allele only exerted an influence on delinquent peer associations for male adolescents residing in high-risk families that lacked affection, warmth, and disengaged mothers. Yun, Cheong, and Walsh (2011) confirmed these results with a measure that asked peers to report their own involvement in delinquency. Less research has examined how genetic polymorphisms moderate the association between delinquent peer affiliations and one's own delinquent involvement. This seems to be a ripe area for investigation because various genes have been said to make individuals more sensitive to learning experiences and the reward and punishment system of the brain. It stands to reason that certain genes will modify this relationship, given that delinquent peer groups are contexts for learning from peers in ways that provide individual rewards that include social acceptance by similar age peers and status in peer groups. It will be important for future research to further understand the role that genes play in the relationship between delinquent peer associations and delinquency, especially when individuals possess heightened genetic sensitivity to learning environments.

Summary and Conclusions

This chapter has provided evidence for the need to incorporate a biosocial perspective into theories on juvenile delinquency that emphasize parenting and peers as sources of socialization and learning during adolescence. Specifically, we reviewed some genetic research designs and numerous studies on how and why accounting for genetic variation can help solve puzzles connecting socialization, learning, and juvenile delinquency. The behavioral and molecular genetic studies reviewed show that biology is likely to matter most in particular circumstances that youth experience, which include the formation of peer associations, harsh parental treatment, and perhaps very supportive parenting contexts. Those who desire to understand how parents and peers influence adolescent behavior should embrace the large amount of genetic evidence that has emerged over the last decade.

New areas of research on genetics and antisocial behavior are beginning to emerge. One of these is epigenetics, which will likely prove to be a mediating process involved in gene–environment interactions. Differential exposures to toxins, stress, social interactions, and levels of social support may produce epigenetic effects that determine whether or how much some genes are expressed (see Francis, 2011). This occurs through outside instructions from methyl groups made from carbon and hydrogen that chemically bind to genes. Methyl groups communicate to express a gene or not to express a gene. Proteins that determine how DNA is wrapped also affect epigenetics. If tightly wound, genes will tend to express less, and if more loosely wound genes express more. While one's DNA does not change, epigenetic tags can change gene expression over periods of development to produce behavioral and health differences among children and adolescents, even between identical twins sharing 100% of their genomes. Not only can gene expression change in response to environmental triggers beginning in the womb and continue over time, but epigenetic influences may also be responsible for turning off genes that are then inherited by future generations (Francis, 2011). A better understanding of epigenetic influences holds promise for understanding the intergenerational transmission of violence and delinquency.

In closing, the more we come to know about the complex interactions between genetics, peers, and parenting, the better our intervention efforts can target social factors that increase or decrease risks for juvenile delinquency. This will also equip criminologists and prevention specialists with more complete evidence about which children are sensitive to particular interventions and less responsive to other interventions. Recent research does suggest that children who carry particular genetic alleles are more responsive to intervention and prevention efforts (Beach, Brody, Lei, & Phillibert, 2010; Brody *et al.*, 2009, 2013a). It is important to confirm such results in other longitudinal studies that have incorporated preventive interventions tailored to reduce and prevent delinquency and substance use. It is equally important for researchers to design studies that test interventions on twins and other pairs of genetically related siblings to better understand how the shared treatment/intervention may affect children differently or in similar ways in reducing risk factors and antisocial behavior.

References

Agnew, R. (1991). The interactive effect of peer variables on delinquency. *Criminology, 29*, 47–72.
Akers, R.L. (1973). *Deviant Behavior: A Social Learning Approach*. Belmont, CA: Wadsworth.

Akers, R.L. (1998). *Social Learning and Social Structure: A General Test of Crime and Deviance.* Boston: Northeastern University Press.

Akers, R.L., Krohn, M.D., Lanza-Kaduce, L., & Radosevich, M. (1979). Social learning and deviant behavior: A specific test of a general theory. *American Sociological Review, 44,* 636–655.

Anderson, A.L. (2013). Adolescent time use, companionship, and the relationship with development. In C. Gibson, & M. Krohn (Eds.), *Handbook of Life-Course Criminology* (pp. 111–127). New York: Springer.

Arseneault, L., Moffitt, T.E., Caspi, A., Taylor, A., Rijsdijk, F.V., Jaffee, S.R., Abow, J.C., & Measelle, J.R. (2003). Strong genetic effects on cross-situational antisocial behaviour among 5-year-old children according to mothers, teachers, examiner-observers, and twins' self-reports. *Journal of Child Psychology and Psychiatry, 44,* 832–848.

Asbury, K., Wachs, T.D., & Plomin, R. (2005). Environmental moderators of genetic influence on verbal and nonverbal abilities in early childhood. *Intelligence, 33,* 643–661.

Bakermans-Kranenburg, M., & Van Ijzendoorn, M. (2011). Differential susceptibility to rearing environment depending on dopamine-related genes: New evidence and a meta-analysis. *Development and Psychopathology, 23,* 39–52.

Beach, S., Brody, G., Lei, M., & Phillibert, R. (2010). Differential susceptibility to parenting among African-American youths: Testing the DRD4 hypothesis. *Journal of Family Psychology, 24,* 513–521.

Beaver, K.M. (2008). Non-shared environmental influences on adolescent delinquent involvement and adult criminal behavior. *Criminology, 46,* 341–369.

Beaver, K.M. (2013). *Biosocial Criminology: A Primer.* Dubuque, Iowa: Kendal/Hunt.

Beaver, K.M., Gibson, C.L., DeLisi, M., Vaughn, M.G., & Wright, J.P. (2012). The interaction between neighborhood disadvantage and genetic factors in the prediction of antisocial outcomes. *Youth Violence and Juvenile Justice, 10,* 25–40.

Beaver, K.M., Gibson, C.L., Jennings, W.G., & Ward, J.T. (2009). A gene X environment interaction between DRD2 and religiosity in the prediction of adolescent delinquent involvement in a sample of males. *Biodemography and Social Biology, 55,* 71–81.

Beaver, K., Gibson, C., Turner, M., DeLisi, M., Vaugn, M., & Holand, A. (2011). Stability of delinquent peer associations: A biosocial test of Warr's sticky-friends hypothesis. *Crime & Delinquency, 57,* 907–927.

Beaver, K.M., Wright, J.M., & DeLisi, M. (2008). Delinquent peer group formation: Evidence of a gene x environment correlation. *Journal of Genetic Psychology, 169,* 227–244.

Beaver, K.M., Wright, J.P., DeLisi, M., Daigle, L.E., Swatt, M.L., & Gibson, C.L. (2007). Evidence of a gene x environment interaction in the creation of victimization results from a longitudinal sample of adolescents. *International Journal of Offender Therapy and Comparative Criminology, 51,* 620–645.

Belsky, J., Bakermans-Kranenburg, M.J., & van Ijzendoorn, M.H. (2007). For better and for worse: Differential susceptibility to environmental influences. *Current Directions in Psychological Science, 16,* 300–304.

Belsky, J., & Beaver, K. (2011). Cumulative-genetic plasticity, parenting, and self-regulation. *Journal of Child Psychology and Psychiatry, 52,* 619–626.

Belsky, J., & Pluess, M. (2009). Beyond diathesis-stress: differential susceptibility to environmental influences. *Psychological Bulletin, 135,* 885–908.

Benson, M.L. (2013). *Crime and the Life Course: An Introduction,* 2nd ed. New York: Routledge.

Blumstein, A., Cohen, J., & Farrington, D.P. (1988). Criminal career research: its value for criminology. *Criminology*, *26*, 1–35.

Brody, G.H., Beach, S.R.H., Hill, K.G., Howe, G.W., Prado, G., & Fullerton, S.M. (2013a). Using genetically informed, randomized prevention trials to test etiological hypotheses about child and adolescent drug use and psychopathology. *American Journal of Public Health*, *103*, s19–s24.

Brody, G.H., Beach, S.R.H., Philibert, R.A., Chen, Y.-F., & Murry, V.M. (2009). Prevention effects moderate the association of 5-HTTLPR and youth risk behavior initiation: Gene × environment hypotheses tested via a randomized prevention design. *Child Development*, *80*, 645–661.

Brody, G.H., Ge, X., Conger, R.D., Gibbons, F.X., Murry, V.M., Gerrard, M., et al. (2001). The influence of neighborhood disadvantage, collective socialization, and parenting on African American children's affiliation with deviant peers. *Child Development*, *72*, 1231–1246.

Brown, B.B. (1990). Peer groups and peer cultures. In S.S. Feldman, & G.R. Elliott (Eds.), *At the Threshold: The Developing Adolescent*. Cambridge, MA: Harvard University Press.

Brown, B., & Bakken, J. (2011). Parenting and peer relationships: Reinvigorating research on family-peer linkages in adolescence. *Journal of Research on Adolescence*, *21*, 153–165.

Burt, S.A. (2009a). Are there meaningful etiological differences within antisocial behavior? Results from a meta-analysis. *Clinical Psychology Review*, *29*, 163–178.

Burt, S.A. (2009b). Rethinking environmental contributions to child and adolescent psychopathology: A meta-analysis of shared environmental influences. *Psychological Bulletin*, *135*, 608–637.

Carey, G. (2003). *Human Genetics for the Social Sciences*. Thousand Oaks, CA: Sage.

Caspi, A., McClay, J., Moffitt, T.E., Mill, J., Martin, J., Craig, I.W., Taylor, A., & Poulton, R. (2002). Role of genotype in the cycle of violence in maltreated children. *Science*, *297*, 851–854.

Champagne, F.A., & Mashoodh, R. (2009). Genes in context gene–environment interplay and the origins of individual differences in behavior. *Current Directions in Psychological Science*, *18*, 127–131.

Chung, H.L., & Steinberg, L. (2006). Relations between neighborhood factors, parenting behaviors, peer deviance and delinquency among serious juvenile offenders. *Developmental Psychology*, *42*, 319–331.

Cleveland, H.H., Wiebe, R.P., & Rowe, D.C. (2005). Sources of exposure to drinking and smoking friends among adolescents: A behavioral-genetic evaluation. *Journal of Genetic Psychology*, *166*, 153–169.

de Kemp, R.A.T., Scholte, R.H.J., Overbeek, G., & Engls, R.C.M.E. (2006). Early delinquency: The role of home and best friends. *Criminal Justice and Behavior*, *33*, 488–510.

DeLisi, M., Beaver, K.M., Wright, J.P., & Vaughn, M.G. (2008). The etiology of criminal onset: the enduring salience of nature and nurture. *Journal of Criminal Justice*, *36*, 217–223.

Demuth, S., & Brown, S.L. (2004). Family structure, family processes, and adolescent delinquency: The significance of parental absence versus parental gender. *Journal of Research in Crime and Delinquency*, *41*, 58–81.

Deutsch, A.R., Crockett, L.J., Wolff, J.M., & Russell, S.T. (2012). Parent and peer pathways of adolescent delinquency: Variations by ethnicity and neighborhood context. *Journal of Youth Adolescence*, *41*, 1078–1094.

Elliott, D.S., Huizinga D., & Ageton, S.S. (1985). *Explaining Delinquency and Drug Use*. Thousand Oaks, CA: Sage.

Elliott, D.S., & Menard. S. (1996). Delinquent friends and delinquent behavior: temporal and developmental patterns. In J.D. Hawkins (Ed.), *Delinquency and Crime: Current Theories*. Cambridge: Cambridge University Press.

Ellis, B., Boyce, W.T., Belsky, J., Bakermans-Kranenburg, M., & Van Ijzendoorn, M. (2011). Differential susceptibility to the environment: An evolutionary–neuro-developmental theory. *Development and Psychopathology, 23*, 8–28.

Feinberg, M.E., Button, T.M., Neiderhiser, J.M., Reiss, D., & Hetherington, E.M. (2007). Parenting and adolescent antisocial behavior and depression: Evidence of genotype x parenting environment interaction. *Archives of General Psychiatry, 64*, 457–465.

Ferguson, C.J. (2010). Genetic contributions to antisocial personality and behavior: A meta-analytic review from an evolutionary perspective. *Journal of Social Psychology, 150*, 1–21.

Fowler, J.H., Settle, J.E., & Christakis, N.A. (2011). Correlated genotypes in friendship networks. *Proceedings of the National Academy of Sciences, 108*, 1993–1997.

Francis, R. (2011). *Epigenetics: The Ultimate Mystery of Inheritance*. New York: W.W. Norton & Company.

Gibson, C.L., Miller, J.M., Jennings, W.G., Swatt, M., & Gover, A. (2009). Using propensity score matching to understand the relationship between gang membership and violent victimization: A research note. *Justice Quarterly, 26*, 625–643.

Gibson, C.L., Swatt, M.L., Miller, J.M., Jennings, W.G., & Gover, A.R. (2012). The causal relationship between gang joining and violent victimization: A critical review and directions for future research. *Journal of Criminal Justice, 40*, 490–501.

Gorman-Smith, D., Tolan, P.H., & Henry, D.B. (2000). A developmental-ecological model of the relation of family functioning to patterns of delinquency. *Journal of Quantitative Criminology, 16*, 169–198.

Gottfredson, M.R., & Hirschi, T. (1990). *A General Theory of Crime*. Stanford University Press.

Harris, J.R. (1998). *The Nurture Assumption: Why Children Turn out the Way They Do*. New York: Touchstone.

Haynie, D.L. (2002). Friendship networks and delinquency: The relative nature of peer delinquency. *Journal of Quantitative Criminology, 18*, 99–134.

Haynie, D.L., & Osgood, D.W. (2005). Reconsidering peers and delinquency: How do peers matter? *Social Forces, 84* (2), 1109–1130.

Hindelang, M.J. (1976). With a little help from their friends: Group participation in reported delinquent behavior. *British Journal of Criminology, 16*, 109-125.

Hirschi, T. (1969). *Causes of Delinquency*. Berkeley, CA: University of California Press.

Kandel, D.B. (1978). Interpersonal influences on adolescent illegal drug use. In E. Josephson, & E. Carroll (Eds.), *The Epidemiology of Drug Abuse*. Winston.

Kendler, K.S. (1983). Overview: A current perspective on twin studies on schizophrenia. *American Journal of Psychiatry, 140*, 1413–1425.

Kendler, K.S., & Baker, J.H. (2007). Genetic influences on measures of the environment: A systematic review. *Psychological Medicine, 37*, 615–626.

Kendler, K.S., Neale M.C., Kessler, R.C., Heath, A.C., & Eaves, L.J. (1993). A test of equal-environment assumption in twin studies of psychiatric illness. *Behavior Genetics, 23*, 21–27.

Krohn, M.D. (1986). The web of conformity: A network approach to the explanation of delinquent behavior. *Social Problems, 33*, S81–S93.

Krohn, M.D., Gibson, C.L, & Thornberry, T. (2013). Under the protective bud the bloom awaits: A review of theory and research on adult onset and late blooming offenders. In C. Gibson, & M. Krohn (Eds.), *Handbook of Life-Course Criminology* (pp. 183–212). New York: Springer Verlag.

Krohn, M.D., Lizotte, A.J., Thornberry, T.P., Smith, C., & McDowall, D. (1996). Reciprocal causal relationships among drug use, peers, and beliefs: A five-wave panel model. *Journal of Drug Issues, 26,* 405–428.

Krohn, M.D., Waldo, G.P., & Chiricos, T.G. (1974). Self-reported delinquency: A comparison of structure and interviews and self-administered check-lists. *Journal of Criminal Law and Criminology, 65,* 545–553.

Lahey, B., Rathouz, P., Lee, S., Chronis-Tuscano, A., Pelham, W., Waldman, I., & Cook, E.H. (2011). Interactions between early parenting and a polymorphism of the child's dopamine transporter gene in predicting future child conduct disorder symptoms. *Journal of Abnormal Psychology, 120,* 33–45.

Liska, A.E., & Reed, M.D. (1985). Ties to conventional institutions and delinquency: Estimating reciprocal effects. *American Sociological Review, 50,* 547–560.

Maimon, D., & Browning, C.R. (2010). Unstructured socializing, collective efficacy, and violent behavior among urban youth. *Criminology, 48,* 443–474.

Mason, D.A., & Frick, P.J. (1994). The heritability of antisocial behavior: A meta-analysis of twin and adoption studies. *Journal of Psychopathology and Behavioral Assessment, 16,* 301–323.

Matsueda, R.L. (1982). Testing control theory and differential association: A causal modeling approach. *American Sociological Review, 47,* 489–504.

Matsueda, R.L., & Anderson, K. (1998). The dynamics of delinquent peers and delinquent behavior. *Criminology, 36,* 269–308.

Matsueda, R.L., & Heimer, K. (1987). Race, family structure, and delinquency: A test of differential association and social control theories. *American Sociological Review, 52,* 826–840.

McGloin, J.M., & Shermer, L.O.N. (2009). Self-control and deviant peer network structure. *Journal of Research in Crime and Delinquency, 46,* 35–72.

Miles, D.R., & Carey, G. (1997). Genetic and environmental architecture of human aggression. *Journal of Personality and Social Psychology, 72,* 207–217.

Moffitt, T.E. (1993). Life-course-persistent and adolescence-limited antisocial behavior: A developmental taxonomy. *Psychological Review, 100,* 674–701.

Moffitt, T.E. (2005). The new look of behavioral genetics in developmental psychopathology: Gene-environment interplay in antisocial behaviors. *Psychological Bulletin, 131,* 533–554.

Moffitt, T.E., & Caspi, A. (2006). Evidence from behavioral genetics for environmental contributions to antisocial conduct. In P.H. Wikstrom, & R.J. Sampson (Eds.), *The Explanation of Crime* (pp. 108–152). Cambridge, MA: Cambridge University Press.

Morris, S.Z., & Gibson, C.L. (2011). Corporal punishment's influence on children's aggressive and delinquent behavior. *Criminal Justice and Behavior, 38,* 818–839.

Parker, J.S., & Benson, M.J. (2004). Parent-adolescent relations and adolescent functioning: Self-esteem, substance abuse, and delinquency. *Adolescence, 39,* 519–530.

Pinker, S. (2002). *The Blank Slate: The Modern Denial of Human Nature.* New York: Penguin Books.

Piquero, A., Farrington, D.P., & Blumstein, A. (2003). The criminal career paradigm. In M. Tonry (Ed.), *Crime and Justice: A Review of Research,* Vol. *30* (pp. 359–506). Chicago: University of Chicago Press.

Plomin, R. (2011). Commentary: Why are children in the same family so different? Non-shared environment three decades later. *International Journal of Epidemiology, 40*, 582–592.

Pratt, T.C., Cullen, F.T., Sellers, C., Winfree Jr., L.T., Madensen, T.D., Daigle, L.E., Fearn, N.E., & Gau, J.A. (2010). The empirical status of social learning theory: A meta-analysis. *Justice Quarterly, 27* (6), 765–802.

Raine, A. (2013). *The Anatomy of Violence: The Biological Roots of Crime*. New York: Pantheon.

Rhee, S.H., & Waldman, I.D. (2002). Genetic and environmental influences on antisocial behavior: A meta-analysis of twin and adoption studies. *Psychological Bulletin, 128*, 490–529.

Rose, R.J., Dick, D.M., Viken, R.J., & Kaprio, J. (2001). Gene–environment interaction in patterns of adolescent drinking: regional residency moderates longitudinal influences on alcohol use. *Alcoholism: Clinical and Experimental Research, 25*, 637–643.

Rukus, J., & Gibson, C. (2011). From petri dish to public policy: A discussion of the implications of biosocial research in the criminal justice arena. In K. Beaver, & A. Walsh (Eds.), *The Ashgate Research Companion to Biosocial Theories of Crime* (pp. 413–436). Farnham: Ashgate.

Short, J.F. (1957). Differential association and delinquency. *Social Problems, 4*, 233–239.

Simons, R.I., Wu, C., Conger, R.D., & Lorenz, F.O. (1994). Two routes to delinquency: Differences between early and late starters in the impact of parenting and deviant peers. *Criminology, 32*, 247–275.

Simons, R., & Lei, M.K. (2013). Enhanced susceptibility to context: A promising perspective on the interplay of genes and the social environment. In C. Gibson, & M. Krohn (Eds.), *Handbook of Life-Course Criminology* (pp. 57–67). New York: Springer Verlag.

Simons, R.L., Lei, M., Beach, S., Brody, G., Philibert, R., & Gibbons, F. (2011). Social environmental variation, plasticity genes, and aggression: Evidence for the differential susceptibility hypothesis. *American Sociological Review, 76*, 883–912.

Simons, R.L., Lei, M., Beach, S., Brody, G., Philibert, R., & Gibbons, F. (2012). Social adversity, genetic variation, street code, and aggression: A genetically informed model of violent behavior. *Youth Violence and Juvenile Justice, 10*, 2–24.

Stogner, J.M., & Gibson, C.L. (2013). Stressful life events and adolescent drug use: Moderating influences of the MAOA gene. *Journal of Criminal Justice, 41* (5), 357–363.

Sutherland, E.H. (1947). *Principles of Criminology* (4th ed.). Philadelphia: J.B. Lippincott.

Taylor, J., Iacono, W.G., & McGue, M. (2000). Evidence for a genetic etiology of early-onset delinquency. *Journal of Abnormal Psychology, 109*, 634–643.

Thornberry, T. (1987). Towards an interactional theory of delinquency. *Criminology, 25*, 863–891.

Thornberry, T.P., & Krohn, M.D. (2005). Applying interactional theory to the explanation of continuity and change in antisocial behavior. In D. Farrington (Ed.), *Integrated Developmental & Life-Course Theories of Offending. Advances in Criminological Theory* (pp. 183–209). New Brunswick, NJ: Transaction Press.

Thornberry, T.P., Lizotte, A.J., Krohn, M.D., Farnworth, M., & Jang, S.J. (1991). Testing interactional theory: An examination of reciprocal causal relationships among family, school, and delinquency. *Journal of Criminal Law and Criminology, 82*, 3–33.

Thornberry, T.P., Lizotte, A.J., Krohn, M.D., Farnworth, M., & Jang, S. (1994). Delinquent peers, beliefs, and delinquent behavior: A longitudinal test of interactional theory. *Criminology, 32*, 47–83.

Turkheimer, E. (2000). Three laws of behavior genetics and what they mean. *Current Directions in Psychological Science, 9,* 160–164.

Warr, M. (2002). *Companions in Crime: The Social Aspects of Criminal Conduct.* Cambridge: Cambridge University Press.

Wright, J.P., & Beaver, K.M. (2005). Do parents matter in creating self-control in their children? A genetically informed test of Gottfredson and Hirschi's theory of low self-control. *Criminology, 43,* 1169–1202.

Yun, I., Cheong, J., & Walsh, A. (2011). Genetic and environmental influences in delinquent peer affiliation: from the peer network approach. *Youth Violence and Juvenile Justice, 9,* 241–258.

12

Parenting and Delinquency

John P. Hoffmann

Introduction

The notion that parents are responsible for or otherwise influence their children's positive and negative behaviors has existed for thousands of years. Ancient Greeks, Romans, Chinese, and others considered the roles of parents in ensuring that children become responsible, productive, and law-abiding adults. And this emphasis continues today, perhaps more so now that at any point in human history. The large number of popular parenting books, media, and academic research attest to its depth and breadth.

Although the literature on parenting and juvenile delinquency is voluminous, meta-analyses indicate that certain parenting characteristics are particularly important for understanding the development of delinquent and related behaviors. Moreover, advances in our ability to study, at the individual-level, genetic markers and physiological processes and, at the macro-level, neighborhood and community effects, have led to a more thorough view of the way that parents affect various behaviors among youths.

In this chapter, I provide an overview of what contemporary research has shown about parenting and delinquency. After briefly considering the historical context, some aspects of how we conceptualize parenting and delinquency are provided. This is followed by an examination of research on some of the aspects of parenting that have been linked to delinquent behaviors. Since a review of these aspects can provide only part of the etiological picture, the next section discusses a few models that have been used to explain why parenting affects delinquency. The final section discusses directions for future research.

The Handbook of Juvenile Delinquency and Juvenile Justice, First Edition. Edited by Marvin D. Krohn and Jodi Lane.
© 2015 John Wiley & Sons, Inc. Published 2015 by John Wiley & Sons, Inc.

The Historical Context of Parenting and Adolescent Behavior

But praise and reproof are more effectual upon free-born children than any such disgraceful acts [such as whipping]; the former to incite them to what is good, and the latter to restrain them from that which is evil. (Plutarch, 110 CE [1927])

Correct thy son, and he shall give thee rest; yea, he shall give delight unto thy soul. (Proverbs 29:17, King James Version)

Relatively little is known about day-to-day childrearing activities of the ancient world. Much of what we do know comes from religious texts or the musings of philosophers, such as Plato, Plutarch, and Confucius. The picture that emerges is strongly class-based, with free people instructed to focus on the education of their children's minds and spirits. Slave and servant families were either ignored or considered barbaric in the way children were treated. For example, Plutarch's *On the Education of Children* discussed the children of upper-status Roman citizens as "inherently impressionable … constantly shaped to a desired end with appropriate incentives towards, and rewards for, good behavior" (Bradley, 2013, p. 19). Corporal punishment was to be avoided; it was suitable only for slaves and servants. Moreover, parents were warned to keep their children away from "evil men" who would lead them to "drunkenness", "slothfulness", and "lasciviousness" (Plutarch, 110 CE [1927]). This view of parenting is reminiscent of Locke's blank-slate view of human nature, wherein young people must be taught in all ways to become productive citizens. Yet slave families were viewed more in terms of the Hobbesian natural man: nasty and brutish.

The rise of Christianity subtly changed these general views of parenting (Horn & Martens, 2009). An emphasis on teaching children to avoid sin emerged; this often required the use of corporal punishment and isolation of the sexes (Chrysostom, 407 CE [1986]). Spanking and whipping were used frequently to correct misbehaviors. Moreover, during the Protestant Reformation there was an emphasis on training children to be virtuous, deferential to authority figures, and selfless (Ozment, 1983). The best methods for accomplishing this were debated, though, since the source of human nature was an evolving concept. Yet physical punishment remained a common tool for keeping children in line.

By the colonial period in North America, various disciplinary measures were normative. Calvinists, who argued that original sin and depravity infected all, relied on physical means of discipline. A goal of this parenting approach was to "break the will" of children so they would learn to obey their elders, and, indirectly, their God (Grant, 2013). Yet a developing standard among others emphasized affection more than strict discipline in the rearing of the young. This was influenced in the seventeenth and eighteenth centuries by Continental philosophers such as Jean-Jacques Rousseau and John Locke. Although Locke (1693) advocated firm control by parents of their children, he also advised against severe punishment, dishonesty, or any means of socializing youth that might lead them away from developing a genteel and honest manner. In one of his best-known works, *Emile*, Rousseau (1762 [1979]) argued that children are born innocent. Any untoward conduct from them was the result of poor parenting, bad teachers, and a marred environment. Physical punishment should be avoided since it merely teaches youth that violence is a fitting response to another's disobedience.

By the nineteenth and early twentieth centuries, these various approaches to childrearing continued, with some arguing that corporal punishment was necessary to instill a sense of obedience in children, and others emphasizing the development of a close, affectionate relationship between parents and their offspring. By the latter half of the twentieth century, the professional norms had swung to stressing the importance of close bonds with one's children as the best way to prevent misbehaviors. The psychology of parenting movement stressed reasoning, explanation, and rewards as the most effective means of encouraging normative behaviors. And these could be made all the more effective by promoting warm relations between parents and children.

Criminological thought on the subject of parenting has largely paralleled these various historical patterns. There has also been an ebb and flow regarding whether parents influence their children's behaviors via physiological processes. During the early twentieth century, for example, Charles Goring (1913: 372) claimed that the "genesis of crime ... must be tied to heredity"; or the passing of physiological traits – including those that affect delinquency – from parents to their offspring. Several decades later, Sheldon and Eleanor Glueck (1950) maintained that most delinquent behavior was caused by poor parental supervision, erratic discipline (especially by fathers), and low affection between parents and children. But this concern with parental influences diminished as research began to emphasize sociological influences on behaviors. In particular, studies in the 1960s and 1970s focused largely on how communities, the economic system, culturally defined norms and needs, and official reactions to adolescent misconduct were the main causes of delinquent behavior (Hirschi, 1983). The tide began to turn back towards studies of parental and family influences, however, as social learning and control models were modified and advanced as key micro-level theories of adolescent behaviors. Moreover, with the increasing understanding of genetics and biological mechanisms, there has been a resurgence of research on physiological influences on delinquent behavior. There are now several hundred published studies of parenting and delinquency, with more emerging on a regular basis.

Conceptualizing Parenting and Juvenile Delinquency

Before addressing specific research on parenting and delinquency, it is important to consider what we mean by these two concepts. The concept of parenting has biological, legal, and social aspects. The notion of a biological parent has been complicated in recent years by advances in reproductive technology, which, in turn, have affected the legal status of parenting. Although a subsequent section on family structure will return to some biological and legal characteristics of parenting, at present the most important aspect involves the social. Parenting as a social endeavor involves various facets of childrearing responsibilities, including relations between parents, with children, and with the broader social structure that has concerns about socializing children (e.g., educational institutions). Childrearing is also seen as entailing moral responsibilities. Parents are accountable for making decisions that are in the best interests of their children, protecting them from harm, and providing resources that allow their children to develop physiologically, mentally, and socially (Archard & Benatar, 2010).

The notion of juvenile delinquency has a complicated history. A simple legal definition is that it involves violations of the criminal law by those under a certain age, usually 18. However, this includes violations of behaviors that would not be illegal for adults, such as status offenses (e.g., violating curfew in some jurisdictions), or even some vague sets of behaviors that define a youth as incorrigible or otherwise unmanageable. Yet an important issue, especially if one wishes to understand the research on parenting and delinquency, is that many studies do not rely on legal definitions. Rather, numerous studies examine behaviors that fall under terms such as misbehavior, antisocial behavior, psychopathology, aggression, and externalizing behavior; or even related mental health diagnoses such as conduct disorders (CD) and oppositional defiant disorders (ODD). In general, researchers who study youth use a variety of terms when examining their behaviors.

Aspects of Parenting that Affect Delinquency

As mentioned earlier, the literature on parental influences on delinquency and related behaviors is vast. Fortunately, recent years have seen several efforts to organize the results of this literature either through general reviews (e.g., Farrington, 2011; Maughn & Gardner, 2010) or meta-analyses designed to summarize the statistical associations among parenting factors and delinquency (e.g., Derzon, 2010; Hoeve *et al.*, 2009).

Combining the results of these reviews provides a useful summary of what appear to be the most important parenting-related predictors of delinquency. As shown in Table 12.1, the strongest and most consistent predictors include childrearing skills/disciplinary practices, parenting style (neglect, permissiveness), parental rejection, monitoring/supervision/child disclosure, psychological control, maltreatment, parental stress, parent–child relationship quality, and parent antisocial behavior. It is difficult to judge which set of parenting factors is truly most important, however, because studies use different terms and measurement strategies for these concepts. Nonetheless, the factors that emerge from these meta-analyses provide a useful list for the discussion that follows (see, however, Chapter 34 in this volume for a discussion of maltreatment and adolescent problems). In addition, the association between family structure and delinquency is included in this discussion since a relatively large number of studies have addressed it. Other potential influences, such as parental age, mental health, socio-economic status (SES), and employment patterns are not reviewed since they have only modest effects on delinquency once other characteristics are considered (Derzon, 2010).

Table 12.1 Effect sizes of parenting concepts on delinquency from selected meta-analyses

Parenting concept	Hoeve et al. (2009)	Derzon (2010)	Loeber & Stouthamer-Loeber (1986)
Childrearing skills/disciplinary practices	0.20	0.26 (childrearing) 0.17 (discipline)	73.5
Parenting style			
Neglectful	0.29		
Indulgent/permissive	0.09		
Parental rejection	0.26		62.6
Monitoring/supervision	0.23	0.06	66.3
Child disclosure	0.31		
Psychological control	0.23		
Parent–child relationship quality	0.21	0.18	61.5
Maltreatment		0.21	
Family stress		0.21	
Parent antisocial behavior		0.15	34.5
Family structure		0.10	27.7

Notes: The effect sizes (shown as absolute values) from the first two meta-analyses are represented as correlations. The effect sizes from the Loeber and Stouthamer-Loeber (1986) meta-analysis are measures of relative improvement over chance (RIOC). This index is expressed as a percentage and has a range from 0 to 100. Higher values indicate greater improvement in prediction of delinquency over chance.

The concepts are not defined consistently across studies, which may help explain the variation in effect sizes across the studies.

Childrearing skills and disciplinary practices

It is problematic to clearly identify what the term "childrearing skills" implies, even though meta-analyses often use this term to describe a particular aspect of parenting. A related term that is used is "parental management" (Fagan, Van Horn, Hawkins, & Jaki, 2013). Because these concepts typically denote a combination of specific parent–child interaction strategies, this section addresses the question of how parents react to the behavior of their children. In particular, what types of disciplinary or reactive practices are utilized by parents? For example, when a young child takes a toy or otherwise acts aggressively toward other children, do parents react with anger, acceptance, unconcern, or reasoning? When children or adolescents engage in prosocial or helpful activities, do parents offer praise or do they ignore them? Are disciplinary practices consistent or capricious? Do parents use harsh forms of punishment?

As mentioned earlier, Sheldon and Eleanor Glueck (1950) were early proponents of the claim that erratic discipline increases the risk of delinquency. Subsequent studies have supported this point of view (e.g., McCord, 1991). In recent years, attention to disciplinary methods has been sensitized by addressing the actual types of practices that lend themselves to consistency or capriciousness.

Studies suggest that when mothers and fathers are inconsistent, such as when only one parent disciplines as the other ignores or downplays infractions, the risk of delinquency is higher (Smith & Farrington, 2004). Immediacy of discipline may also have ameliorative effects, with children more apt to recognize rules for which they are punished – and consequently follow them – when it occurs closer to the infraction. Moreover, when mild discipline is combined with reasoning, it seems to have a more beneficial effect.

Yet, harsh forms of physical punishment are positively associated with delinquency (Evans *et al.*, 2012). Although maltreatment is discussed in another chapter (see Chapter 34), some studies indicate that even a nominal amount of physical reprimand, such as spanking, increases the likelihood of delinquency and other maladaptive behaviors (Gershoff, 2002). However, this effect may be conditional; research suggests that when spanking is accompanied or followed up with demonstrations of parental affection, the risk of subsequent misbehaviors is attenuated (Bartkowski & Wilcox, 2000).

Parenting style

The child and adolescent development literature includes a rich and substantial set of studies on parenting style. Although there had been studies of various aspects of parenting for many years, it was not until Diana Baumrind (1967) developed a parenting style typology that the research became consistent. Based on the amount of support and control provided by parents, Baumrind (1967) identified four parenting types: authoritative, authoritarian, indulgent, and neglectful. *Authoritative* parents offer their children high levels of affectionate support and control by supervising activities and maintaining a consistent and mild disciplinary style. They are demanding and provide clear rules and direction, but also are responsive, warm, and offer regular praise. *Authoritarian* parents are high on control but low on support. They closely supervise their children's activities, but offer little praise and warmth. *Indulgent* parents are highly supportive, but they do not provide much direction or discipline and engage in relatively low levels of supervision. Finally, *neglectful* parents offer little support and do not provide direction, rules, or monitoring. As discussed later, an advantage of the parenting style approach is that it combines two important aspects of parenting, rather than attempting to isolate one concept as more important than another.

Studies indicate that indulgent and neglectful parenting places adolescents at the highest risk of delinquency (e.g., Schaffer, Clark, & Jeglic, 2009); although meta-analyses suggest that neglect is a stronger predictor than indulgence or permissiveness, and it leads to more serious long-term involvement in delinquency (Hoeve *et al.*, 2009). On the contrary, authoritative parenting is associated with a relatively low risk of delinquency (Simons & Conger, 2007). Interestingly, having even one authoritative parent may be sufficient to attenuate the risk of delinquency.

Parental rejection

Although parental rejection is similar to a neglectful parenting style, there are differences. Whereas neglect typically represents indifference towards one's child, parental rejection is demonstrated not only by a lack of love or affection, but also an absence of support and overt displays of hostility. Being overly critical of an adolescent, showing resentment, and consistently dismissing his or her views are also indicators of parental rejection.

Given the research on parenting style, it is not surprising that parental rejection is positively associated with delinquency (e.g., Trentacosta & Shaw, 2008). Moreover, parental rejection can be especially acute if it occurs at an early age. For example, one study determined that maternal rejection at one year of age was associated with an increased risk of violent behavior at age 18 (Raine, Brennan, & Mednick, 1994).

Monitoring, supervision, and child disclosure

One of the most widely studied aspects of parenting and child behaviors involves monitoring and supervision. These twin concepts, though sometimes distinguished, concern whether parents know what their children are doing and who they are with. This might include knowing where one's children are after school or on weekends; or who they have in the home when parents are away. At least one meta-analysis suggested that supervising adolescents' whereabouts and behaviors was among the most effective mitigators of delinquency risk (Loeber & Stouthamer-Loeber, 1986). In general, research has found that better monitoring by parents reduces the likelihood of delinquency and other adolescent problems (e.g., Barnes, Hoffman, Welte, Farrell, & Dintsche, 2006). In addition, better supervision may lead to a lower risk of delinquency because it attenuates involvement with deviant peers (Keijsers *et al.*, 2012). However, some parents also increase their monitoring in response to adolescent misbehavior.

Recently, researchers have called into question the role of monitoring and supervision, especially the way these concepts are measured. A key critique is that most studies assess parents' knowledge of their children's presumed activities, but not the source of this knowledge. Although parents may actively monitor their children's behaviors by asking questions, requiring regular telephone calls, or contacting the parents of friends, only some adolescents freely disclose their activities. Studies comparing active parental monitoring to offspring disclosure have found that the latter is more strongly related to delinquency and other behaviors (e.g., Hoeve *et al.*, 2009). Yet, it is probable that youths engaged in delinquency or other misbehaviors are less likely to disclose their whereabouts voluntarily to their parents (Smetana, 2008).

Psychological control

Research on delinquency has frequently examined various aspects of direct and indirect parental controls, including supervision and disciplinary practices (Demuth & Brown, 2004). Consistent with the practice of parenting styles, these types of activities are often categorized as authoritative, authoritarian, and behavioral controls. A relatively understudied aspect of parenting, however, is psychological control (Bean, Barber, & Crane, 2006). This type of parental control involves manipulation and intrusion into an adolescent's psyche, including attempts to limit their ability to discuss important matters, invalidating their point of view, or manipulating their judgments.

The few studies that have examined the effects of psychological control on delinquency or aggressive behaviors have found a positive association (e.g., Loukas, Paulos, & Robinson, 2005). Nonetheless, some research indicates that behavioral controls, such as discipline and monitoring, are more important predictors of delinquent conduct, whereas psychological control is more strongly related to internalizing problems, such as depression and anxiety. Moreover, considering the paucity of research on this topic and the lack of uniformity across studies, there remain concerns about how psychological control should be measured (Steinberg, 2005).

Parent–child relationship quality

Among the hundreds of studies of parenting and adolescent misbehaviors, no topic has garnered as much attention as the emotional relationship between parents and children. The literature has often used the term *parent–child attachment* to describe this concept. The meta-analyses discussed earlier included more than 50 studies that examined particular qualities of attachment such as parental support, affection, positive communication, and praise. Moreover, as discussed earlier, affection and praise are two of the characteristics that Baumrind (1967) used to define the four parenting styles.

Research has determined that adolescents who have stronger affectionate relations with their parents and experience parental warmth and praise are less likely to be involved in delinquent activities (e.g., McCord, 1991). They are also less likely to be stigmatized by a delinquent label or become involved with delinquent peers (Jackson & Hay, 2013). Moreover, indicators of poor parent–child relations, such as conflict and arguments, predict greater involvement in delinquency (e.g., Fagan, Van Horn, Antaramian, & Hawkins, 2011). There is contradictory evidence, though, concerning whether other aspects of parenting, such as monitoring and disciplinary style, attenuate or otherwise account for the effects of parent–child attachment on delinquency (cf. Farrington, Loeber, Yin, & Anderson, 2002; Sampson & Laub, 1994). This may point to the need to consider distinct cross-classifications of parent–child attachments and parental monitoring in order to determine more precisely how parents affect adolescent behaviors (Hoeve *et al.*, 2008). This has been a goal of the research on parenting styles discussed earlier.

Family and parental stress

There are several parenting and family-related characteristics that are stressful, such as maltreatment, family conflict, corporal punishment, parental rejection, and psychological control. However, stress is also indicated by daily hassles, living in risky environments, mental health problems (e.g., depression), lack of social support, financial insecurity, or other stressful life events experienced by parents (Deater-Deckard, 2004). When parents face substantial stress, their child-rearing skills tend to suffer, discipline may become erratic or overly harsh, and the general quality of their relationship with their children often diminishes. Thus, as discussed in earlier sections, a higher risk of delinquency ensues.

Studies have shown that there are direct and indirect effects of parental stress on delinquency and other misbehaviors. For example, Conger, Patterson, and Ge (1995) determined that stressful life experiences among mothers and fathers lead to a higher risk of experiencing depressive symptoms, more erratic discipline, and more deviant activities among adolescents. A path model demonstrated that both maternal and paternal stress lead to more problematic parenting, which, in turn, increases the risk of delinquent behaviors.

Parent antisocial behavior

Parental antisocial and criminal behaviors are associated with a higher risk of offspring problems, including difficulties in school, developmental delays, and delinquent conduct (e.g., Bijleveld & Wijkman, 2009). As mentioned earlier, concern with this association has existed for many years, leading many observers to posit that criminal and delinquent behaviors are inherited propensities.

Although there is a certain degree of intergenerational transmission of these behaviors, it appears to be conditioned in part by the relationship that youth have with parents – including their presence during childhood – and the parenting style utilized in the family (Farrington, Coid, & Murray, 2009). Intergenerational transmission is more likely when parents are absent or their presence is intermittent, when they are neglectful, or when they have low attachment with their children. Moreover, the positive association between parental imprisonment and delinquency and crime among offspring is partly due to the trauma of separation and other adolescent risk factors that result from parental absence (e.g., low parental supervision) (Murray & Farrington, 2008).

Family structure

Beginning with early twentieth century studies of the effects of broken homes on delinquency (e.g., Breckinridge & Abbott, 1912), researchers have investigated whether youth from two-parent families are at decreased risk of delinquency relative to those living in other family situations (e.g., single parent or step-parent families). A meta-analysis conducted two decades ago indicated that there was a modest association between living with fewer than two parents and delinquency (effect size: 0.10– 0.15). However, much of this effect may have been due to the way broken homes and delinquency were measured and by the sampling methods used in these studies (Wells & Rankin, 1991). Subsequent research has shown, though, that adolescents from single-father families or those who live with neither parent are at an especially high risk of delinquency, drug use, and other problematic behaviors (Hoffmann & Johnson, 1998). The risk of delinquency also tends to increase with more frequent family structure transitions, such as when a parent repeatedly marries and separates (Petts, 2009). Moreover, living with cohabiting parents increases the likelihood of delinquency relative to living with two married parents or single parents (Apel & Kaukinen, 2008).

Nevertheless, family structure alone may not be a sufficient predictor of adolescent problem behaviors. Several studies have shown that conflict in the home or poor parent–child attachment affects the association between family structure and delinquency. In fact, adolescents from two-parent, high-conflict families, or with married parents who engage in antisocial behaviors, are more prone to delinquency than those living in single-parent families (Amato & Cheadle, 2008). Thus, family processes appear to be more important predictors of adolescent misconduct than family structure alone.

Reciprocal Effects of Parenting and Delinquency

Although a majority of studies impose a strict temporal order that runs from parenting factors to subsequent delinquency, it is not surprising that delinquent behavior also has consequences for parenting practices (Gault-Sherman, 2012). Studies have shown that factors such as parental supervision, disciplinary practices, and parent–child attachment both affect and are affected by delinquency (Thornberry & Krohn, 2001). For example, parents of youth who get involved in delinquency often respond by increasing their level of monitoring. Some parents may also attempt to use more severe forms of discipline in an attempt to control an unruly child, even though this rarely works since it may begin a spiral of behaviors and controls that only increase problems in the family (Patterson, Reid, & Dishion, 1992). Moreover, parent–child attachments may be damaged when youth get involved in delinquent behavior.

What Mechanisms and Models Explain how Parenting Affects Delinquency?

The discussion thus far has been limited to a risk-factor approach, even though single aspects of parenting are unlikely to place an adolescent at uniform risk of delinquency. It is therefore important to describe some models that have been utilized to explain the association between parenting and delinquency. This section provides a brief discussion of some of the more commonly used models.

Attachment theory

One of the earliest attempts by behavioral scientists to account for the association between parenting and child and adolescent conduct involved attachment theory. This model focuses on the early emotional bond that is created between parents – mainly mothers – and young children. If mothers are able to form this bond early in children's lives, then children are expected to develop normally, with little risk of problem behaviors later in life. If this emotional bond does not develop well, then children are at risk of emotional and behavioral problems throughout life. John Bowlby (1969), a proponent of this theory, believed that mother–infant bonds were a biological necessity based in human evolution; they served to protect infants from harm and formed the basis for all subsequent bonds that youth would experience.

Attachment theory has had a strong, though often indirect, influence on other approaches to understanding parenting and delinquency. For instance, the parenting styles of Baumrind were based indirectly on attachment theory since the combination of parent–child affection – a key emotional bond – and offering the child clear and reasonable guidance, direction, and supervision should increase the attachment between parents and adolescents. Similarly, parental rejection is clearly at odds with the development of adequate attachment with one's child, and has been shown to lead to problematic behaviors later in life (Raine *et al.*, 1994). However, attachment theory may not offer a complete picture of how parenting and other relationships, such as with peers or siblings, affects delinquency. Nor does it take into account genetic influences on behavior that may affect the level of attachment that ensues within a family unit.

Control theories

The sociological analog to attachment theory is social bonding theory. Due mainly to Travis Hirschi's (1969) research on delinquency, this model focuses on attachments that form in the family and in schools, involvement in conventional activities, commitments that adolescents make, and beliefs they have about the norms of society. When parents invest in their children by developing warm and affectionate attachments and socialize them to believe in society's moral order, they create conditions that reduce the likelihood of delinquent behavior. Moreover, Hirschi (1983) endorsed the idea that parental monitoring and appropriate, consistent discipline from an early age is perhaps the most effective method for preventing future delinquent and criminal conduct.

Hirschi, along with Michael Gottfredson, later developed the idea that social bonding theory could be retargeted and made more parsimonious by invoking the concept of self-control: "the differential tendency of people to avoid criminal acts whatever the circumstances in which they find themselves" (Gottfredson & Hirschi, 1990, p. 89). Individuals with high self-control tend to have good social skills, are apt at delaying gratification, and have at least a modicum of empathy. Those low in self-control are impulsive, self-centered, and insensitive. Since the nature of most delinquent and criminal acts is to seek immediate gratification or the achievement of short-sighted goals, those low in self-control are more likely to engage in them. Gottfredson and Hirschi argued that the source of low self-control is the failure of parents to monitor and appropriately punish inappropriate behavior early in life. Those children not corrected for these behaviors do not develop adequate self-control, thus placing them at risk for later delinquency. And once low self-control takes hold of a child, it is difficult, if not impossible, to modify later in life. Moreover, the intergenerational transmission of criminal behavior can be explained by parents with low self-control failing to socialize their children to develop self-control.

Social learning theories

Learning theories address the experiences that people have throughout their lives. The most consequential learning may occur early in the life-course, yet it can also occur at any time during one's life. Although there are several learning theories that might be used to explain the association between parenting and delinquency, this section discusses two of the more prominent: Ronald Akers's social learning model, and Gerald Patterson's coercion model.

Akers's (1998) model focuses on norms, values, and attitudes that people are socialized to accept; the reinforcement of these that occur as people have relevant experiences or interact with others; the observation and imitation of others' behaviors; and direct associations one has with others. Because parents are among the most important associations in children's lives, most of their early learning occurs in the home. If parents inculcate conventional values and norms, and if they provide examples of law-abiding behaviors, then delinquency becomes less likely. However, if they furnish examples of illicit behaviors, if they fail to teach children to obey the law, and if they do not reinforce appropriate activities, then delinquency becomes more likely. Thus, parents who are neglectful, rejecting, physically abusive, or commit antisocial acts will teach their offspring that these are appropriate ways to interact with others.

Gerald Patterson's coercion theory addresses primarily early socialization experiences, not unlike those mentioned by self-control theorists. The most important aspects are how parents socialize their children to use or avoid coercive interaction styles. Coercive interaction involves using harsh, hostile verbal or physical cues in an attempt to get cooperation from another, such as when a parent employs harsh language to make a child to behave in a certain way. This is in contrast to using warmth and reasoning to get a child to cooperate. For example, in some families, parents yell or use physical means to get children to obey. They may use psychological control rather than authoritative means to discipline children. They tend to be lax in monitoring children's behaviors. Consequently, their children learn that aggression, coercion, and manipulation are appropriate interaction styles. Parents and children who engage in coercive and manipulative interactions with one another are unlikely to get along, so attachment suffers. Youth so disposed usually carry this interaction style outside the home into their relations with peers, teachers, and others. Thus, a cycle of problematic behaviors and interactions is perpetuated that increases the risk of delinquency during adolescence (Patterson *et al.*, 1992).

Genetic-based explanations

As the ability to study the human genome has developed, the number of studies concerning whether delinquency is caused in some way by genetic risk factors has grown. Some of this research has also addressed whether there are genetic influences on parenting. The consensus that has emerged from this body of research is that genetic factors affect some of the physiological and psychological processes that are implicated in parenting and delinquency. For example, a review of genetic studies of family relations showed that from 18–35% of the variability in the following parenting and family characteristics is accounted for by shared genetic influences: cohesion, conflict, expressiveness, parental warmth, and control efforts. Marital quality also has a substantial genetic component (Kendler & Baker, 2007). Moreover, meta-analyses have revealed that up to a third of the variability in antisocial behaviors, including delinquency, is accounted for genetic influences (Rhee & Waldman, 2002).

Some researchers argue that the links between parenting and delinquency are explained mainly by genetic influences. They contend that parenting practices are largely a reaction to the confluence of genetically influenced behaviors of children and their parents (Wright, Beaver, Delisi, & Vaughn, 2008). Thus, the association between parenting and adolescent behavior is due to a selection process. Suppose, for instance, that a child demonstrates substantial impulsiveness/low self-control or callousness, traits that have a genetic origin and are linked to antisocial behavior. In this situation, positive parenting may be impaired, affectionate parent–child relations difficult to maintain, and family stress amplified. If parents share one of these traits, then parenting becomes only more difficult. This is simply one scenario among many of how genetically based traits might account for the presumed association between parenting and delinquency.

However, researchers have suggested that the more important issue is how the family and parenting environment interacts with genetic influences to affect delinquency and other behaviors. Although it is conceivable that genetic characteristics completely account for the link between parenting and delinquency, recent studies indicate that environmental influences are not inconsequential. For instance, a recent study determined that variations of a particular receptor gene led to different risks of aggression depending on the parenting style that individuals experienced during childhood. Those who experienced parental hostility, verbal or physical abuse, or a lack of prosocial communication displayed more aggression when this receptor gene had the particular variant. However, those who experienced more positive parenting and had the variant actually displayed less aggression than those without the variant (Simons *et al.*, 2013).

Moreover, the key mechanism through which these genetic variations lead to delinquent outcomes is likely due to their effects on neurochemicals such as dopamine, monoamine oxidase (MAO), and gamma-amino butyric acid (GABA). These appear to interact with parenting characteristics (e.g., attachments, parental hostility) to predict delinquency (Simons *et al.*, 2013). A model that has been developed to explain these results is the differential vulnerability hypothesis. It suggests that certain genetic variants make some individuals more sensitive to their environment, such that if they experience untoward conditions their risk of delinquency increases. However, if they experience positive conditions, such as a good home environment, then their risk of delinquency decreases (Beaver & Belsky, 2012). This research implies that certain genetic variants do not lead directly to delinquent or antisocial behaviors; rather, they magnify how youth respond to negative or positive environments, including how they are treated by their parents.

Community and macro-level explanations

It is evident that parenting can be made more or less difficult by the social environment within which it takes place. Parental stress, for instance, is higher in neighborhoods where there is substantial interpersonal conflict or violence (Deater-Deckard, 2004). Similarly, families living in conflict-ridden or impoverished neighborhoods have more problems within the home, less parental monitoring, and an increased likelihood of erratic or harsh discipline (McLoyd *et al.*, 2009).

These macro-level influences point toward the need to consider not only the direct effects of parenting on delinquency, but also the contextual effects (Hoffmann, 2003). Parenting does not occur in isolation from its broader social context. Instead, it is the result of a whole host of background factors, including the conditions of the neighborhood within which it occurs. This is not to say that the macro-social context explains how parenting factors affect delinquency. But it does suggest that research needs to consider, for example, how living in an impoverished or violent neighborhood influences parenting, thus indirectly affecting the risk of delinquency. Moreover, some research has shown that certain neighborhood characteristics moderate the effects of parenting on delinquency. For example, one study found that the association between harsh or inconsistent parenting and youth problem behaviors is stronger in impoverished neighborhoods than in other neighborhoods (Brody *et al.*, 2003).

The Future of Research on Parenting and Delinquency

Even though the topic of parenting and delinquency has generated hundreds of studies over the past two or three decades, there is still much to learn. In this concluding section, I address three issues that seem most critical to our understanding of how parents influence their children's behaviors.

First, as noted earlier, parenting and child behaviors do not occur in isolation from other factors. Nor are particular aspects of parenting independent. Yet, most studies of parenting and delinquency use methods that fail to consider either the dependence of parenting factors on one another, or the context within which parenting takes place. As an example of the first issue, consider that a large majority of studies, including meta-analyses, attempt to isolate the effects of, say, parent–child attachment by using some type of regression model. Suppose we include measures of parent–child attachment and parental monitoring in a regression model designed to predict delinquent behavior. The resulting coefficients simply gauge the effects of attachment on delinquency regardless of the level of monitoring (or in the language of statistics, we have *adjusted* for the effects of monitoring). The same phenomenon occurs when examining family stress, parent antisocial behavior, family structure, parental rejection, and other factors in the same regression model.

However, it is unlikely that these parenting factors are independent predictors of delinquency. Rather, there is likely a complex set of interactive effects that influence subsequent behaviors. Baumrind's (1967) parenting styles model offers one view of how parenting factors interact. By examining cross-levels of praise/affection and supervision/control, she has addressed how parenting factors are dependent. What is needed is a broader and more complex view of the interrelationships among the myriad characteristics of parenting. As one example, consider that supervision and consistent discipline are more difficult when only a single parent is present.

Similarly, parenting does not occur in isolation from the environment within which it takes place or from other institutions, such as schools, that are concerned with child and adolescent development. The case of the neighborhood environment was discussed earlier. Yet other environments are implicated as well. Consider, for example, that recent studies suggest that high-quality schools – especially those where there are good relations among students and teachers, and students feel safe and secure – can partially compensate for a poor family environment (e.g., Hoffmann & Dufur, 2008).

Second, although several studies have examined reciprocal associations between a few parenting factors (e.g., attachment) and delinquency (Gault-Sherman, 2012), more work is needed. This is because reciprocal associations also occur among other aspects of parenting. Take child disclosure, for example. As the affectionate bonds between parents and offspring increase, it is likely that an adolescent will feel more comfortable disclosing her whereabouts to her parents. But, if this leads to reprimands due to what parents perceive as bad behavior, then attachment may suffer and future disclosure is reduced. This process is made more probable if the bad behavior includes delinquency.

If we are to develop a good understanding of reciprocal effects, it is important to have a model that accommodates them. A promising model for studying these effects is Terence P. Thornberry's interactional theory. This theory contends that delinquency is not the end result of a chain of variables, but rather is embedded within causal loops that include variables such as parent–child attachment (Thornberry & Krohn, 2001). By further elaborating interactional theory to include other aspects of parenting, we may better understand how delinquency is part of a complex series of associations with parenting and other family influences.

Third, without doubt research on genetic influences on delinquency has illuminated and, in some cases, cast doubt on whether parenting directly affects delinquency. Nevertheless, more work on the complex interactions among genetically based processes, parenting behaviors, and delinquent conduct is needed. As mentioned earlier, it is possible that genetic influences largely account for the association between parenting and delinquency. However, recent research has provided support for the differential vulnerability hypothesis (Beaver & Belsky, 2012), which, as described earlier, argues that there is a positive association between certain genetic variants and delinquency in risky environments, whereas the association is negative in low-risk environments. Risky environments include disadvantaged neighborhoods where parenting is more difficult. Yet, parenting is relatively easier in low-risk environments, which tend to offer better social support and institutions that promote conventional behaviors. Thus the likelihood of delinquency and antisocial behaviors is actually diminished. This suggests a need for additional research on genetics, parenting, and the social context within which they interact (Maccoby, 2000).

Conclusions

The substantial literature on parenting and delinquency has provided a fascinating set of findings. We know that inconsistent and overly harsh discipline, physical abuse, neglectful or rejecting parenting, lack of supervision, cold or hostile family relations, and parental antisocial behaviors place adolescents at heightened risk of delinquency and other ill-advised outcomes. But we do not yet fully understand why this is the case. Is it simply that bad people make bad parents and bad parents create bad children? Is the ultimate source of bad people making bad parents found in the genetics of the human body and the physiological processes that they influence? Or is bad parenting mainly a consequence of socialization experiences and the environmental context within which they occur. After all, it seems evident that the development of parenting skills is based on family, school, and neighborhood experiences, and what one observes in friends' homes and in the media.

The likely answer is that the link between parenting and delinquency involves some complex interplay among all these experiences and conditions. Thus, what is needed is more research that addresses the myriad influences that affect parenting, child and adolescent behaviors, and their reciprocal relationships. Large-scale studies that follow parents and children throughout the life-course and that consider physiological, interpersonal, and contextual characteristics are challenging, but may be the only way to fully comprehend the ways in which parenting affects delinquency and other behaviors.

References

Akers, R.L. (1998). *Social Learning and Social Structure*. Boston: Northeastern University Press.

Amato, P.R., & Cheadle, J.E. (2008). Parental divorce, marital conflict and children's behavior problems. *Social Forces, 86*, 1139–1161.

Apel, R., & Kaukinen, C. (2008). On the relationship between family structure and antisocial behavior: Parental cohabitation and blended households. *Criminology, 46*, 35–70.

Archard, D., & Benatar, D. (eds.) (2010). *Procreation and Parenthood*. New York: Oxford University Press.

Barnes, G., Hoffman, J.H., Welte, J.W., Farrell, M., & Dintsche, B.A. (2006). Effects of parental monitoring and peer deviance on substance use and delinquency. *Journal of Marriage and Family, 68*, 1084–1104.

Bartkowski, J.P., & Wilcox, W.B. (2000). Conservative protestant child discipline: The case of parental yelling. *Social Forces, 79*, 265–290.

Baumrind, D. (1967). Child care practices anteceding three patterns of preschool behavior. *Genetic Psychology Monographs, 75*, 43–88.

Bean, R.A., Barber, B.K., & Crane, D.R. (2006). Parental support, behavioral control, and psychological control among African American youth. *Journal of Family Issues, 27*, 1335–1355.

Beaver, K.M., & Belsky, J. (2012). Gene-environment interaction and the intergenerational transmission of parenting. *Psychiatric Quarterly, 83*, 29–40.

Bijleveld, C.J.H., & Wijkman, M. (2009). Intergenerational continuity in convictions: A five-generation study. *Criminal Behaviour and Mental Health, 19*, 142–155.

Bowlby, J. (1969). *Attachment: Attachment and Loss, Volume 1*. New York: Basic Books.

Bradley, K. (2013). Images of childhood in classic antiquity. In P.S. Fass (Ed.), *Routledge History of Childhood in the Western World* (pp. 17–38). Florence, KY: Taylor and Francis.

Breckinridge, S.P., & Abbott, E. (1912). *The Delinquent Child and the Home*. New York: Russell Sage.

Brody, G.H., Murry, V.M., Ge, X., Kim, S.Y., Simons, R.L., Gibbons, F.X., Gerrard, M., & Conger, R.D. (2003). Neighborhood disadvantage moderates associations of parenting and older sibling problem attitudes and behavior with conduct disorders in African American children. *Journal of Consulting and Clinical Psychology, 71*, 211–223.

Chrysostom, Saint John. (407 CE [1986]). *On Marriage and Family Life*. Translated by C.P. Roth, & D. Anderson. Crestwood, NJ: St. Vladimir's Seminary Press.

Conger, R.D., Patterson, G.R., & Ge, X. (1995). It takes two to replicate: A mediational model for the impact of parents' stress on adolescent adjustment. *Child Development, 66*, 80–97.

Deater-Deckard, K. (2004). *Parenting Stress*. New Haven, CT: Yale University Press.

Demuth, S., & Brown, S.L. (2004). Family structure, family processes, and adolescent delinquency. *Journal of Research in Crime and Delinquency, 41*, 58–81.

Derzon, J.H. (2010). The correspondence of family features with problem, aggressive, criminal, and violent behavior: A meta-analysis. *Journal of Experimental Criminology, 6*, 263–292.

Evans, S.Z., Simons, L.G., & Simons, R.L. (2012). The effect of corporal punishment and verbal abuse on delinquency: Mediating mechanisms. *Journal of Youth and Adolescence, 41*, 1095–1110.

Fagan, A.A., Van Horn, M.J., Antaramian, S., & Hawkins, J.D. (2011). How do families matter? Age and gender differences in family influences on delinquency and drug use. *Youth Violence and Juvenile Justice, 9*, 150–170.

Fagan, A.A., Van Horn, M.J., Hawkins, J.D., & Jaki, T. (2013). Differential effects of parental controls on adolescent substance use: For whom is the family most important? *Journal of Quantitative Criminology, 29*, 347–368. doi:10.1007/s10940-012-9183-9.

Farrington, D.P. (2011). Families and crime. In J.Q. Wilson, & J. Petersilia (Eds.), *Crime and Public Policy* (pp. 130–157). New York: Oxford University Press.

Farrington, D.P., Coid, J.W., & Murray, J. (2009). Family factors in the intergenerational transmission of offending. *Criminal Behaviour and Mental Health, 19*, 109–124.

Farrington, D.P., Loeber, R., Yin, Y., & Anderson, S.J. (2002). Are within-individual causes of delinquency the same as between-individual causes? *Criminal Behaviour and Mental Health, 12*, 53–68.

Gault-Sherman, M. (2012). It's a two-way street: The bidirectional relationship between parenting and delinquency. *Journal of Youth and Adolescence, 41*, 121–145.

Gershoff, E.T. (2002). Corporal punishment by parents and associated child behaviors and experiences: A meta-analytic and theoretical review. *Psychological Bulletin, 128*, 539–579.

Glueck, S., & Glueck, E. (1950). *Unraveling Juvenile Delinquency*. New York: Commonwealth Fund.

Goring, C. (1913). *The English Convict: A Statistical Study*. London: His Majesty's Stationery Service.

Gottfredson, M.R., & Hirschi, T. (1990). *A General Theory of Crime*. Stanford, CA: Stanford University Press.

Grant, J. (2013). Parent–child relations in Western Europe and North America, 1500–present. In P.S. Fass (Ed.), *Routledge History of Childhood in the Western World* (pp. 103–124). Florence, KY: Taylor and Francis.

Hirschi, T. (1969). *Causes of Delinquency*. Berkeley, CA: University of California Press.

Hirschi, T. (1983). Crime and the family. In J.Q. Wilson (Ed.), *Crime and Public Policy* (pp. 53–68). San Francisco: Institute for Contemporary Studies.

Hoeve, M., Blokland, A., Dubas, J.S., Loeber, R., Gerris, J.R.M., & van der Laan, P.H. (2008). Trajectories of delinquency and parenting styles. *Journal of Abnormal Child Psychology, 36*, 223–235.

Hoeve, M., Dubas, J.S., Eichelsheim, V.I., van der Laan, P.H., Smeenk, W., & Gerris, J.R.M. (2009). The relationship between parenting and delinquency: A meta-analysis. *Journal of Abnormal Child Psychology, 37*, 749–775.

Hoffmann, J.P. (2003). A contextual analysis of differential association, social control, and strain theories of delinquency. *Social Forces, 81*, 753–785.

Hoffmann, J.P., & Dufur, M.J. (2008). Family and school capital effects on delinquency: Substitutes or complements? *Sociological Perspectives, 51*, 29–62.

Hoffmann, J.P., & Johnson, R.A. (1998). A national portrait of family structure and adolescent drug use. *Journal of Marriage and the Family, 60*, 633–645.

Horn, C.B., & Martens, J.W. (2009). *Let the Little Children Come To Me: Childhood and Children in Early Christianity*. Washington, DC: Catholic University of America Press.

Jackson, D.B., & Hay, C. (2013). The conditional impact of official labeling on subsequent delinquency. *Journal of Research in Crime and Delinquency, 50*, 300–322.

Keijsers, L., Branje, S., Hawk, S., Schwartz, S.J., Frijns, T., Koot, H., van Lier, P., & Meeus, W. (2012). Forbidden friends as forbidden fruit: Parental supervision of friendships, contact with deviant peers, and adolescent delinquency. *Child Development, 83,* 651–666.

Kendler, K.S., & Baker, J.H. (2007). Genetic influences on measures of the environment: A systematic review. *Psychological Medicine, 37,* 615–626.

Locke, J. (1693). *Some Thoughts Concerning Education.* London: A. & F. Churchill.

Loeber, R., & Stouthamer-Loeber, M. (1986). Family factors as correlates and predictors of juvenile conduct problems and delinquency. *Crime and Justice: A Review of Research, 7,* 29–149.

Loukas, A., Paulos, S.K., & Robinson, S. (2005). Early adolescent social and overt aggression: Examining the roles of social anxiety and maternal psychological control. *Journal of Youth and Adolescence, 34,* 335–345.

Maccoby, E.E. (2000). Parenting and its effects on children: On reading and misreading behavior genetics. *Annual Review of Psychology, 51,* 1–27.

Maughn, B., & Gardner, F. (2010). Families and parenting. In D. Smith (Ed.), *A New Response to Youth Crime* (pp. 247–286). Oxfordshire, UK: Willan.

McCord, J. (1991). Family relationships, juvenile delinquency, and adult crime. *Criminology, 29,* 397–417.

McLoyd, V.C., Kaplan, R., Purtell, K.M., Bagley, E., Hardaway, C.R., & Smalls, C. (2009). Poverty and socioeconomic disadvantage in adolescence. In R.M. Lerner, & L. Steinberg (Eds.), *Handbook of Adolescent Psychology* (pp. 444–492). New York: John Wiley & Sons, Ltd.

Murray, J., & Farrington, D.P. (2008). Effects of parental imprisonment on offending. *Crime and Justice: A Review of Research, 37,* 133–206.

Ozment, S. (1983). *When Fathers Ruled: Family Life in Reformation Europe.* Cambridge, MA: Harvard University Press.

Patterson, G.R., Reid, J.B., & Dishion, T.J. (1992). *Antisocial Boys.* Eugene, OR: Castalia.

Petts, R.J. (2009). Family and religious characteristics' influences on delinquency trajectories from adolescence to young adulthood. *American Sociological Review, 74,* 465–483.

Plutarch. (110 CE [1927]). The education of children. In *Moralia, Volume 1* (pp. 5–70). Translated by F.C. Babbitt. New York: Loeb Classical Library.

Raine, A., Brennan, P., & Mednick, S.A. (1994). Birth complications combined with early maternal rejection at age 1 year predispose to violent crime at age 18 years. *Archives of General Psychiatry, 51,* 984–988.

Rhee, S.H., & Waldman, I.D. (2002). Genetic and environmental influences on antisocial behavior. *Psychological Bulletin, 128,* 490–529.

Rousseau, J.J. (1762 [1979]). *Emile, or On Education.* Translated by A. Bloom. New York: Basic Books.

Sampson, R.J., & Laub, J.H. (1994). Urban poverty and the family context of delinquency. *Child Development, 65,* 523–540.

Schaffer, M., Clark, S., & Jeglic, E.L. (2009). The role of empathy and parenting style in the development of antisocial behaviors. *Crime & Delinquency, 55,* 586–599.

Simons, L.G., & Conger, R.D. (2007). Linking mother–father differences in parenting to a typology of family parenting styles and adolescent outcomes. *Journal of Family Issues, 28,* 212–241.

Simons, R.L., Simons, L.G., Lei, M.-K., Beach, S.R.H., Brody, G.H., Gibbons, F.X., & Philibert, R.A. (2013). Genetic moderation of the impact of parenting on hostility toward romantic partners. *Journal of Marriage and Family, 75,* 325–341.

Smetana, J.G. (2008). 'It's 10 o'clock: Do you know where your children are?' Recent advances in understanding parental monitoring and adolescents' information management. *Child Development Perspectives, 2,* 19–25.

Smith, C.A., & Farrington, D.P. (2004). Continuities in antisocial behavior and parenting across three generations. *Journal of Child Psychology and Psychiatry, 45,* 230–247.

Steinberg, L. (2005). Psychological control: Style or substance? *New Directions for Child and Adolescent Development, 108,* 71–78.

Thornberry, T.P., & Krohn, M.D. (2001). The development of delinquency: An interactional perspective. In S.O. White (Ed.), *Handbook of Youth and Justice* (pp. 289–305). New York: Plenum Press.

Trentacosta, C.J., & Shaw, D.S. (2008). Maternal predictors of rejecting parenting and early adolescent antisocial behavior. *Journal of Abnormal Child Psychology, 36,* 247–259.

Wells, L.E., & Rankin, J.H. (1991). Families and delinquency: A meta-analysis of the impact of broken homes. *Social Problems, 38,* 71–93.

Wright, J.P., Beaver, K., Delisi, M., & Vaughn, M. (2008). Evidence of negligible parenting influences on self-control, delinquent peers, and delinquency in a sample of twins. *Justice Quarterly, 25,* 544–569.

13

School Effects on Delinquency and School-Based Prevention

Wayne N. Welsh and Courtney Harding

Introduction

This chapter will investigate school effects on delinquency within a multilevel framework (e.g., individual, family, school, community, and social structural explanations) that identifies major theoretical explanations, research evidence, and evidence-based practices for prevention and intervention. We make five major arguments: (1) despite considerable advances in multilevel research and methods, relatively few studies examine more than one level of analysis and fewer still examine cross-level interactions; (2) few studies combine analyses of both the physical and social environments of schools; (3) few studies incorporate measures of implementation quality and fidelity in their analyses; (4) the existing evidence base of "what works" (and what doesn't) still suffers from serious gaps; and (5) the overall quality of program implementation in schools (when assessed at all) is often weak, piecemeal, or inconsistent. In spite of these deficiencies, the field of school-based prevention has become increasingly attentive to evidence-based practice. We offer several recommendations to help further develop a coherent agenda for future theory, research and practice in this area.

Theoretical Perspectives

Individual-level influences

Schools provide a central venue for facilitating, or failing to encourage, social bonding. Those with poor academic or interpersonal skills may experience failure and alienation in school. They may not become attached to school

The Handbook of Juvenile Delinquency and Juvenile Justice, First Edition. Edited by Marvin D. Krohn and Jodi Lane.
© 2015 John Wiley & Sons, Inc. Published 2015 by John Wiley & Sons, Inc.

because their social interactions have been unrewarding. They may not become committed to educational goals because they view them as unrealistic. They may not get involved in conventional social activities either because meaningful activities are lacking or they are denied access. They may not believe in conventional rules because they do not perceive present or future rewards for compliance. Relationships between school bonding and delinquency have been supported by research (Cernkovich & Giordano, 1992; Krohn & Massey, 1980; Thornberry, Lizotte, Krohn, Farnsworth, & Jang, 1991).

Social bonding also occurs through family and peers. Farrington and Welsh (2007) noted a consistent link between low family socio-economic status and anti-social behavior, but this relationship is largely mediated by family socialization practices (e.g., parent management skills). While association with delinquent peers consistently predicts delinquent behavior, the probability of committing offenses with others decreases steadily with age. As Thornberry, Krohn, Lizotte, Smith, and Tobin (2003) noted, there appear to be reciprocal effects between delinquent peers and delinquent behavior. Associating with delinquent peers tends to increase rather than cause individual offending (facilitation), but delinquents are also more likely to be rejected by their peers and seek out gang membership (selection), further reducing their opportunities for non-delinquent peer associations. Structural disadvantage tends to reduce prosocial bonds, and both of these factors lead to an increased involvement in delinquency, as well as higher levels of stress, all of which increase the likelihood of joining a youth gang. Family bonding was not as significant as school performance and peers in predicting delinquency over time.

Classroom-level influences

Two classroom factors consistently associated with delinquency are a high amount of punishment and low amount of praise given by teachers in class (Johnson, 2009). In one study, positive classroom interactions significantly predicted less violent offending, but not property offending (Sprott, 2004). A stronger academic focus in the classroom significantly predicted less property offending, but not violent offending. Similarly, in schools with a greater perceived number of teachers with positive teaching behavior, there was significantly less disruptive behavior and intentional damage of property (Mooji, 1998).

In contrast, in schools with a greater number of strict teachers there was significantly more disruptive behavior, violent victimization, and intentional damage of property. In schools with a greater number of teachers reporting discipline problems, there was a significant increase in disruptive behavior, pre-meditated physical violence and intentional damage to property. Several classroom-based interventions have been found to reduce problem behaviors, but to a greater extent for boys than girls, and to a greater extent when outcome measures are based on teacher ratings as opposed to peer or parent ratings of problem behaviors (Ialongo *et al.*, 1999).

School climate

Schools have their own characteristic "personalities", just as individuals do (Welsh, 2000). School climate includes factors such as communication patterns, norms about what is appropriate behavior and how things should be done, role relationships and role perceptions, patterns of influence and accommodation, and rewards and sanctions. In a study of 5,203 middle school students, Welsh (2003) explored the effects of school climate (e.g., clarity and fairness of rules) and individual student characteristics (e.g., age, sex, race, and dimensions of bonding) on two different measures of school disorder: students' self-reported offending and less serious misconduct at school (Welsh, 2003). Using hierarchical linear modeling (HLM) analytical techniques, schools varied significantly on both measures of disorder, but school climate variables explained a larger percentage of variance in misconduct than offending (10% vs. 2%). The strongest predictors of both offending and misconduct were peer associations, belief in rules, and school effort. Older, non-white, and male students displayed higher levels of both offending and misconduct.

In a nationally representative study of 254 US secondary schools (Gottfredson, Gottfredson, Payne, & Gottfredson, 2005), researchers examined relationships among numerous indicators of school climate and disorder (e.g., self-reported victimization and delinquency). School climate explained a substantial percentage of the variance in school disorder, even when controlling for the effects of community characteristics and school student composition. Schools where students perceived greater fairness and clarity of rules had lower rates of delinquent behavior and student victimization, although rule fairness and clarity did not influence teacher victimization. Schools with a more positive psychosocial climate overall had lower teacher victimization, but this more general measure of school climate did not influence student victimization or delinquent behavior.

A sense of community in which an extended network of caring adults interacts regularly with students, and shares norms and expectations about their students, is generally related to lower levels of problem behavior. Communal school organization refers to supportive relationships between and among teachers, administrators, and students; a common set of goals and norms; and a sense of collaboration and involvement. Communally organized schools tend to experience less disorder, and the relationship between communal school organization and school disorder is partially mediated by student bonding (Payne, Gottfredson, & Gottfredson, 2003).

Routine activities

In a review of 25 studies, Johnson (2009) explored how a school's physical as well as social environment may impact students' behaviors. Principles of Crime Prevention Through Environmental Design (CPTED) helped guide the analysis. CPTED categorizes the possible impact of the environment into four mechanisms: (1) space design; (2) space use and circulation patterns; (3) territorial features; and (4) physical deterioration. In general, school violence rates were more strongly associated with aspects of the school's social rather than the physical environment. Lower rates of school violence were associated with five factors: (1) positive relationships with teachers; (2) student awareness of school rules and perceptions of fairness; (3) student perceptions of "ownership" of their school (stronger predictor than academic values and ability); (4) positive classroom and school environments focused on student comprehension; and (5) lower perceived physical deterioration and presence of school safety interventions aimed at improving the school physical environment.

In a Kentucky study (Wilcox, Augustine, & Clayton, 2006), improved territoriality and improved surveillance were related to better perceptions of safety for both students and teachers. Three other studies found that school deterioration (defined as litter, graffiti, and disrepair) was related to higher levels of teacher and student victimization as well as perceptions of school violence, but a fourth study found no relationship (Johnson, 2009). However, few studies have measured both social and physical environment, and only five studies assessed any aspects of the physical environment at all (Johnson, 2009). There is a need for more research on the school physical environment and its potential influence on violence, as well as examination of potential interactions between the physical and social environment.

Community influences

Although higher levels of crime, poverty, and unemployment in the community surrounding a school are often associated with higher levels of school victimization, the exact causal mechanisms are not entirely clear. Research has uncovered complex links between poverty and crime, and between social disorganization and violence (Sampson & Lauritsen, 1993). Community characteristics related to violence include concentrated poverty; high residential mobility and population turnover; family disruption; high density in housing and population; weak local social organization, such as low density of friends and acquaintances; few social resources; weak intergenerational ties in families and communities; weak control of street-corner groups; low participation in community events and activities; and opportunities associated with violence. Although such relationships are complex, it can safely be said that community influences combine with poverty and with one another to influence crime rates (Sampson, Raudenbush, & Earls, 1997).

Multilevel approaches

Although community characteristics predict delinquency and victimization, many school-based studies fail to account for crucial distinctions between characteristics of the community *surrounding* the school and characteristics of the communities where students actually *live*. In the modern era of bussing and student mobility, this distinction is crucial. In a study of 7,000 middle-school students and 400 teachers, researchers examined multilevel predictors (individual, neighborhood, and school characteristics) of school violence (Welsh, 2000, 2001, 2003; Welsh, Greene, & Jenkins, 1999; Welsh, Stokes, & Greene, 2000). Significant predictors of school disorder were found at the community level (poverty), the school level (fairness of rules, respect for students), and the individual level (belief in conventional rules, positive peer associations, age, race, sex). However, researchers also distinguished between local vs. imported (students attending school from other parts of the city) community characteristics. In general, local community variables explained school disorder slightly better than imported community characteristics, but neither provided strong explanations by themselves. School climate (e.g., attendance, turnover) strongly mediated the effects of community variables (poverty, residential stability, and community crime rates) on school disorder (as measured by school incident and dismissal rates). Poverty retained a significant but indirect effect through its influence on school climate. A school, then, is neither blessed nor doomed entirely on the basis of where it is located, nor on the basis of its student demographics.

A nationally representative sample of 254 public, non-alternative, secondary schools (National Study of Delinquency Prevention in Schools) was used to examine relationships among communal school organization, student bonding, and school disorder (Payne *et al.*, 2003). Schools that were more communally organized had lower levels of school disorder, although the effects were small and statistically significant only for student delinquency, but not for student or teacher victimization. Levels of student bonding mediated the relationship between communal school organization and student delinquency, but not the relationship between communal school organization and teacher victimization. Relatively small but significant portions of variance in student delinquency and victimization were attributable to differences between schools as opposed to individuals (Gottfredson *et al.*, 2005). Schools in areas of high residential crowding and concentrated poverty, and schools composed of higher proportions of African-American students and teachers, experienced higher levels of school disorder.

Using data collected from 7,407 students (6th and 8th Grades) and 1,792 teachers in Chicago, Kirk (2009) investigated the independent and interactive influence of five types of social control: parental supervision, student–teacher trust, school collective efficacy, parent–teacher trust, and neighborhood collective efficacy. Sixty-eight schools were nested in 67 neighborhoods. Dependent measures included suspensions and juvenile arrests. Findings suggested that social controls within schools were loosely coupled with social controls in neighborhoods and families. It was not the case that neighborhoods characterized by concentrated poverty and low collective efficacy necessarily contained dangerous schools or unstable families. Rather, different types of social controls may have operated *jointly* to reduce the likelihood of suspension and arrest. However, school-based and family-based informal social controls additively combined to reduce the likelihood of suspension and arrest. Neighborhood collective efficacy also interacted with school-based controls to influence suspensions and arrests. For suspensions, *compensatory* relations existed between collective efficacy in schools and their surrounding neighborhoods; the influence of school collective efficacy on suspension was relatively greater in neighborhoods that were low on collective efficacy. For arrest, an *accentuating* rather than a compensatory effect was observed between neighborhood collective efficacy and student–teacher trust; low neighborhood collective efficacy and low school-based social controls combined to substantially increase the likelihood of arrest. A multicontextual approach is thus warranted to understand the etiology of delinquency (Kirk, 2009).

School-Based Prevention Programs

School-based delinquency prevention broadly refers to strategies that take place in a school building, or under the authority of school personnel, designed to reduce or prevent the occurrence of problem behavior (Lawrence, 2006; Wilson, Gottfredson, & Najaka, 2001). One meta-analysis integrated results from 165 experimental or quasi-experimental studies of school-based prevention interventions (Wilson *et al.*, 2001). Outcomes of interest were alcohol and drug use, dropout and non-attendance, delinquency, and other conduct problems. Strategies were partitioned into environmentally and individually focused, and then categorized by the presence of 11 treatment components or activities. Interventions with an *environmental* focus may alter the organizational structure of the school, increase the safety of the school building, improve teacher classroom management, or adjust the disciplinary practices used by administrators (Wilson *et al.*, 2001). *Individually focused* strategies consist mostly of psychosocial programs that utilize individual counseling, behavior modification, skills-based learning, and the like.

School-based prevention strategies were generally effective for reducing alcohol and drug use, dropout and non-attendance, and other conduct problems. For delinquency, mean effect sizes across all program types were positive but had a 95% confidence interval that included zero. Three out of four environmental approaches were found to be effective for reducing delinquency: school and discipline management (0.16); classroom or instructional management (0.19); and reorganization of grades or classes (0.34). Establishing norms or expectations for behavior was the only environmentally focused intervention strategy that did *not* achieve a statistically significant effect size. Conversely, only one of the seven individually focused interventions had a significant and positive effect on reducing delinquency. This was an instructional approach to self-control or social competency *with* cognitive–behavioral or behavioral instructional methods (0.10). Without the cognitive–behavioral component, self-control and competency instruction had a null to negative effect size.

Another way to categorize school-based delinquency prevention efforts is in terms of their reach and focus (Greenberg, 2010). In a series of meta-analyses, Wilson & Lipsey (2005, 2007) grouped interventions into the following formats (i.e., reach): *universal; selected/indicated; comprehensive/multimodal programs;* and *special schools or classes.* These groupings were based on a general format as well as treatment modality within each format (i.e., focus).

Universal programs are delivered to an entire classroom of students, or an entire population of a school. Such programs often aim to improve resilience, coping and other social skills. Schools may be selected to deliver a particular program if it is located in a high-risk neighborhood, for example; but students receive programming simply by virtue of attending a particular classroom or school. Receipt of services is not based upon individual risk level or problem behavior. Universal strategies are the most commonly used in practice, and are often relatively inexpensive to implement (Greenberg, 2010; Hahn *et al.*, 2007). Universal interventions can have a variety of foci, including teachers' classroom management skills and communal school organization. Curricula that teach students new skills have received the most empirical attention (Greenberg, 2010; Hahn *et al.*, 2007). These programs often focus upon improving the ability to interact with others and on developing self-control and healthy values to resist delinquent behavior in the future (Greenberg, 2010; Hahn *et al.*, 2007). A majority of skills-based programs fall under the term "social and emotional learning" (Elias *et al.*, 1997; Elias, Tobias, & Friedlander, 2000). In their first meta-analysis, Wilson and Lipsey (2005) reported an overall mean effect size of 0.18 for universal interventions in schools ($n = 61$). In their most recent update (Wilson & Lipsey, 2007), 16 new programs were added ($n = 77$). The weighted mean effect size for universal programs increased to 0.21 (Wilson & Lipsey, 2007).

Common treatment modalities include cognitively-oriented programs, social skills programs, behavioral strategies, and counseling or talk therapy (Wilson & Lipsey, 2005). The most common modality was cognitively-oriented approaches, which also had the largest mean effect size (0.33). Social skills programs were a close second, with an overall mean effect size of 0.30. The mean effect size for counseling was 0.16, but only one program was included in this category, making this conclusion tentative (Wilson & Lipsey, 2005). Behavioral programs could not be examined using objective measures; but had an overall mean effect size of 0.16 using student and teacher self-report measures.

Younger students in kindergarten and elementary school, and students of low socio-economic status (regardless of grade level), benefited the most from universal strategies (Wilson & Lipsey, 2005). Despite treatment modality, studies with no implementation problems produced higher effect sizes than those with implementation issues (Wilson & Lipsey, 2005). Deciding on an appropriate universal strategy should depend upon school grade as well as risk level, the authors recommend, with cognitively-oriented approaches the most optimal for high-risk students, and social skills programs generally effective across risk levels.

Similarly, Hahn and colleagues (2007) found strong evidence that all intervention strategies in this format (e.g., informational, cognitive/affective, social skills building) consistently produced some reduction in violent behavior among school-aged children. Program effects were consistent at all grade levels. Hahn *et al.* (2007) confirmed that universal interventions can be effective at reducing various forms of violent behavior among high-risk school environments defined by low socio-economic status and high crime rates, as well as within schools that present none of these characteristics. There was no association between program effectiveness and either frequency, duration, or total exposure (Hahn *et al.*, 2007).

One example of an effective universal intervention is the Good Behavior Game (GBG), assessed as a "promising" program by Blueprints for Healthy Youth Development (2013). This intervention is delivered to all children in a particular classroom despite individual risk level. While the GBG can be administered to low-risk populations of early elementary school children, the strongest results have been found for children demonstrating early high-risk behavior. Primarily utilizing behavioral modification techniques, GBG is a classroom management strategy designed to improve classroom behavior while also preventing future criminality among elementary school-aged children. Teachers are taught ways to define tasks, set rules, and appropriately discipline students. Groups or "teams" of individually responsible students receive checkmarks for bad behavior on the board throughout the game. By the end of the exercise, teams that have not exceeded a set number of checkmarks are rewarded, while those in the other category receive no rewards. Students are encouraged to continuously monitor their own behavior, be accountable to their group, and conform to pro-social expectations. The GBG has consistently demonstrated beneficial effects for children on both a short-term and long-term basis. Students participating in the GBG were less aggressive and shy at the end of Grade 1 compared with control groups; and males at the highest levels of aggression in Grade 1 decreased their levels of aggression by Grade 6 (Blueprints for Healthy Youth Development, 2013).

In spite of overall positive effects, universal interventions have some limitations. First, they are often low-dosage. Programs may not deliver enough services for high-risk students who may require a higher dosage (Greenberg, 2010). Second, universal programs necessitate the participation of an entire school system. Given budget constraints and the pressures placed on school districts to improve academic performance, it may be difficult to convince an entire school district to implement a program with a non-academic focus.

Selected/indicated programs are delivered to particular groups of students who have been selected for participation because they exhibit characteristics that place them at an elevated risk for future delinquent behavior (Greenberg, 2010). Nearly all of the selected/indicated programs included in the Wilson and Lipsey (2005) meta-analysis were "pull-out" programs delivered to students outside of the primary classroom in either small groups or one-on-one. While the terms *selected* and *indicated* are often used interchangeably to describe strategies under the "targeted interventions" umbrella (Wilson & Lipsey, 2005, 2007), these are distinct approaches. Students can be chosen because they have already begun exhibiting high levels of aggression, depression or other evidence of maladjustment (indicated programs); or because of an experience that puts them at a higher risk for problem behavior in the future (selected programs). Selected and indicated interventions, like universal programs, can often be characterized as social and emotional learning or SEL (Greenberg, 2010). SEL skills are taught and reinforced in special group settings with an emphasis on skill learning and maintenance.

Wilson and Lipsey (2005, 2007) reported an overall mean effect size of 0.29 for programs in the selected/indicated format. Differences in mean effect sizes across treatment modalities (social skills training; counseling; cognitively-oriented approaches; behavioral programs implemented in small groups; and peer mediation) were small and statistically non-significant (Wilson & Lipsey, 2005). Similarly, there were no significant differences across different types of personnel who delivered the services or across different session formats (i.e., one-on-one vs. group) (Wilson & Lipsey, 2005). Selected/indicated programs were more effective for those exhibiting a higher risk for problem behavior (Wilson & Lipsey, 2005). Studies characterized by better implementation generally produced higher mean effect sizes than those reporting implementation issues. Selected/indicated programs were also more likely to be evaluated using random assignment compared with evaluations of universal interventions (Wilson & Lipsey, 2005).

One example of an effective selected/indicated program is the Incredible Years. The Incredible Years is a set of three comprehensive and developmentally-based curricula for parents, teachers and children to prevent or reduce behavior and emotional problems in young children (Blueprints for Healthy Youth Development, 2013). This program has been evaluated as both a "selected" strategy for high-risk children in preschool, and an "indicated" strategy for children in higher grades who have already exhibited conduct problems. The Incredible Years has been replicated and evaluated across the United States and in other countries including Wales, Norway, England, and Canada. Evidence demonstrates effectiveness at reducing aggressive behavior and long-term criminal involvement, but also improvements in family functioning, parenting skills, cooperation with teachers, and pro-social interactions.

Special schools or classes are delivered in schools or classrooms outside of the mainstream school environment. An academic curriculum is provided in addition to programming that targets social skills and/or aggressive behavior (Wilson & Lipsey, 2005). Typically such programs serve youth with serious behavioral or academic difficulties that resulted in their placement (Wilson & Lipsey, 2005). In their first meta-analysis, Wilson and Lipsey (2005) examined 37 programs within this format. The weighted mean post-test effect size was 0.07, and did not reach statistical significance. In 2007, the mean aggressive/disruptive behavior effect size for programs in this category was 0.11, with a p-value less than 0.10 (Wilson & Lipsey, 2007). Moderators of effect size included method of group assignment, level of risk of students, and (once again) quality of program implementation (Wilson & Lipsey, 2005, 2007).

Comprehensive/multimodal programs refer to the inclusion of multiple treatment elements and formats within the same intervention (Wilson and Lipsey, 2005, 2007). Most comprehensive programs utilized three or more formats or modalities simultaneously, while universal and selected/indicated generally used one only, and at most two or three. These strategies utilize classroom-based and pull-out components (removing targeted children from their primary classrooms for specialized programming). In addition to student-focused learning, these programs may also incorporate parent training, family involvement, capacity building among administrators, or teacher training. Comprehensive/multimodal programs were found to be surprisingly ineffective, with a non-significant mean effect size of 0.06 across 17 different programs. While some comprehensive programs were more or less effective than others in the group, a majority did demonstrate effect sizes greater than zero (Wilson & Lipsey, 2005). In an updated 2007 analysis, 21 programs were included in this category (Wilson & Lipsey, 2007). The overall mean effect size decreased to 0.05 and was not statistically significant. The authors advised that identifying which program components contributed to the success of some approaches over others would be of great benefit to practitioners.

Many agree that any school-based prevention strategy that is delivered in isolation of other developmental services is unlikely to have a substantial effect on delinquent behavior (Wilson *et al.*, 2001; Wilson & Lipsey, 2005). When programs are partitioned into categories for analysis, rarely are effect sizes large for single program components, even if they are statistically significant for a given category. In practice, multiple interventions are often implemented in the same school building and it becomes difficult to parse out which program components produce effective results (Wilson *et al.*, 2001).

What is Evidence-Based Practice?

Various organizations have developed systems to inform those seeking evidence-based practices for delinquency prevention (e.g., Blueprints for Healthy Youth Development, 2013; Coalition for Evidence-Based Policy, 2013; Office of Justice Programs, 2013; OJJDP, 2013; Penn State EPISCenter, 2013). No database deals exclusively with school-based programming, but all include some interventions that take place within the school. While many of these efforts involve ongoing reviews of evidence for program effectiveness, sources differ considerably in the criteria applied for inclusion in their review system. Outcomes of interest and target populations also vary substantially. It is thus deceptively simple to say that programs should be based on evidence because there is often considerable disagreement about how evidence should be gathered, sorted, and assessed (Gandhi *et al.*, 2007). There is little overlap between databases, with very few validated program models appearing in three or more databases and few that are ranked equally in each. For these reasons, there is no uniform listing of school-based programs effective at reducing delinquency.

Many consider the Blueprints ranking system as one of the most rigorous and reliable (Greenwood, 2006). Programs may be ranked as either "model" or "promising" depending upon the extent of high-quality supporting evidence available. In the Blueprints system, program effectiveness is based upon an initial screening review and then a final review by an advisory board of six experts in the field of violence prevention. Four standards for proven effectiveness include: an experimental or quasi-experimental design with random assignment or matched control group; evidence of a statistically significant deterrent effect on delinquency, drug use, and/ or violence; replication in at least one additional site with demonstrated effects; and evidence that the deterrent effect was sustained for at least one year following treatment. As of March 2013, more than 1,100 programs had been reviewed; only eight (less than 1% of all programs assessed) met the strict scientific standards of program effectiveness (model); and only 36 (about 3%) attained the less rigorous "promising" rating (Blueprints for Healthy Youth Development, 2013).

Model programs include the Brief Alcohol Screening and Intervention for College Students (BASICS), Functional Family Therapy (FFT), LifeSkills Training (LST), Multidimensional Treatment Foster Care (MTFC), Multisystemic Therapy (MST), Nurse-Family Partnership, Project towards No Drug Abuse, and Promoting Alternative Thinking Strategies (PATHS). PATHS is a multiyear, school-based pre- vention model for elementary school youths designed to promote emotional and social competence). LST is a three-year primary prevention program that provides general life skills and social resistance skills training to junior high and middle school students to increase knowledge and improve attitudes about drug use, and Project Towards No Drug Abuse is a drug-abuse prevention program that targets heterogeneous samples of high school youth aged 14–19.

Perhaps just as important is an awareness of which programs have demonstrated *no effect* for school-aged children. Many programs are imitations of evidence-based programs with critical components altered or removed. As Greenwood (2006) argued, some schools choose elements of their delinquency prevention efforts "like a diner at a buffet table", adding and subtracting components without any explicit or empirical basis for doing so. Not all programs are appropriate for all schools and all student populations, but few program components have been examined or validated as effective when used in isolation. Most studies are unable to definitively identify *which* elements of a particular program rendered it successful, and it is premature for schools and program administrators in general to begin parsing out components of interest instead of exactly replicating one or more of the few rigorous, evidence- based programs available.

Greenwood (2006) summarized a series of delinquency prevention approaches shown to be ineffective in multiple settings, many of which apply to schools. Primary prevention approaches demonstrating *no effect* on delinquency include: peer-led pro- grams (e.g., peer-led counseling, mediation); providing alternative recreation and leisure-time activities for disadvantaged youth; social competency training *without* using a proven cognitive–behavioral approach; and student drug-testing. "Notoriously ineffective" secondary prevention programs include efforts to shift peer-group norms by bringing at-risk youth (e.g., gang members) together for an intervention. These approaches have not only been shown to be ineffective, but may even make matters worse. Another failed secondary prevention strategy is "Scared Straight" and similar programs that aim to increase the deterrent effects of arrest and imprisonment by exposing at-risk youth to shocking information and scenarios (e.g., being yelled at and insulted by prisoners; being shown dead bodies in a morgue).

The largest category of ineffective strategies consists of tertiary prevention programs designed to deal with the most serious delinquent youth (Greenwood, 2006). Such programs include many residential programs, the boot camp model, certain approaches to individual counseling, milieu therapy, social casework, waivers to adult court, behavioral token programs, early release from incarceration to probation or parole, a number of vocational-focused programs, and wilderness challenge programs. It is important to note that negative peer associations have consistently been demonstrated to facilitate criminal and delinquent behavior among members of these groups (Gottfredson, 2001; Thornberry *et al.*, 2003). Another problem is that many ineffective programs persist despite evidence they are *not* working. One example is the Drug Abuse Resistance Education (DARE) program. Understanding why failed approaches persist may tell us a lot about the conflicting demands of those who control funding and other pivotal program decisions, as well as about the impact of public relations and public image on the persistence of ineffective approaches (Greenwood, 2006).

Agenda for Future Theory, Research and Practice

There are serious weaknesses in the quality of implementation of many school-based delinquency prevention programs. The National Study of Delinquency Prevention in Schools conducted a survey during the 1997 and 1998 school years to collect information about programs and practices intended to improve school safety (Gottfredson & Gottfredson, 2002; Gottfredson *et al.*, 2004). The study used a national probability sample of public, private, and Catholic schools, stratified by location (urban, suburban, and rural) and level (elementary, middle, and high). Principals were asked to identify activities their schools had in place to prevent or reduce delinquency, drug use, or other problem behaviors. Responses about 3,691 prevention activities in 848 schools were obtained. The median number of different prevention activities named was 14.

Direct services to students, families, or staff included group instruction, provision of instructional materials, and interventions aimed at preventing problem behavior, promoting school orderliness, and counseling students or their families. Schools used very few of these methods of influencing student behavior, and interventions such as community service, peer mediation, and student courts were used rarely compared with more punitive responses to misconduct. *Organizational and environmental arrangements* refer to use of architectural and structural arrangements to prevent problem behavior and promote school safety. Urban schools were more likely than schools in other locations to use gates, fences, walls, and barricades, and to physically block off sections of the building. *Discipline or safety management activities* included rules about dangerous behavior and the possession of weapons. Virtually all principals reported that they communicated such rules and most schools reported that they applied severe consequences when rules were broken. Most schools were likely to suspend or expel a student for possession of a gun, knife, alcohol, or other drugs. Suspension or expulsion for physical fighting, possession of tobacco, and use of profane or abusive language was also common.

For each activity for which a research base (e.g., prevention curriculum, classroom management) or a basis of informed professional opinion (e.g., counseling) was available, researchers developed "best practices" scales to assess program content and methods. Indicators of program *intensity* included level of use by school personnel, frequency of operation, duration, number of sessions, frequency of student participation, ratio of providers to students in the school, and proportion of students involved in the activity. Indicators of *fidelity* included organizational capacity (school amenability to program implementation, turnover in implementing staff), organizational support (amount of training in activity/program, quality of training in activity/program, supervision or monitoring of implementation of program), and program structure (e.g., standardization, local responsibility, amount of provider's job related to the program, whether the activity was a regular, required activity in the school). Scales were scored by calculating the proportion of the identified best practices with respect to content or methods that were used in a particular activity or program.

Results indicated an overall low quality of implementation in the typical school. Programs tended to have far fewer sessions and much shorter durations than suggested by research as optimal. The typical prevention activity used 71% of the identified best practices with respect to content and only 50% of the best practices with respect to methods. Although somewhat subjective, ratings of program quality based on best practices were unimpressive. For example, only 10% of the nation's schools reported using what researchers considered to be minimally adequate discipline practices. The majority of schools either did not use available methods of influencing behavior or did not apply consistent disciplinary responses.

In spite of much discussion in recent years about evidence-based practice, it is clear that different organizations and different pundits still have very different views about what constitutes "effective" practice or even what constitutes convincing evidence (whether favorable or unfavorable). Diverse schemes for defining and categorizing different types of programs make it difficult to compare findings across different studies, meta-analyses, and systematic reviews. School districts often select programs or program components without any rational or explicit basis for doing so, and often implement programs with little regard for fidelity to the original program model (Farrington & Welsh, 2007; Greenwood, 2006). Even more alarming, many programs are never evaluated and many have been shown to be ineffective or iatrogenic. Yet they remain.

As mentioned previously, Crimesolutions.gov (Office of Justice Programs, 2013) periodically updates a list of programs on their website that have been evaluated and have demonstrated *no effect* on the outcome of delinquency. At the current time, 27 of the 250 total programs (11%) in the database are on this list, but many more remain to be assessed.

It is encouraging that three school-based intervention strategies (LST, PATHS, and Project Towards No Drug Abuse) have received enough favorable empirical support to find themselves on the very short list of Model programs in arguably the most rigorous database available (Greenwood, 2006). This can be taken in part as demonstration of the relative effectiveness of school-based programming when compared with strategies delivered exclusively in other formats or settings. However, a large proportion of school-based intervention programs and components, like delinquency prevention strategies in general, persist despite a complete dearth of evidence for their effectiveness (Gottfredson & Gottfredson, 2002).

The vast majority of programs used by schools to address delinquency have not been evaluated at all. The implications of this finding include more than simply a need for more evaluation research on school-based interventions – although that is also imperative. The widespread use of non-evaluated programs and components suggests that implementing true evidence-based practice is not of paramount importance to public officials (Greenwood, 2006). The general lack of consensus about evidence-based practices in the delinquency prevention field argues for the importance of developing a culture of accountability among program officials and administrators (Greenwood, 2006). Without evidence-based practices on which to rely, a "culture of creativity" has proliferated, heralding novelty and discrediting replication. Because evaluation research has not kept up with program implementation, practitioners have not been forced to rely on research findings when choosing a "good" program. As a result, there are no expectations for programs to report on their effectiveness, or to show evidence other than anecdotes that they are achieving their program goals. A culture of accountability would maintain integrity and honesty among competing programs and researchers; and demanding suitable evaluation of effects from each program would allow objective judgments and comparisons across different strategies and efforts. Presenting prompt and reliable evidentiary support should be mandatory for any delinquency prevention effort.

A professional culture that emphasizes protective rather than risk factors has gained increasing support. Positive Youth Development (PYD) is an alternative way of thinking about the transition from adolescence to adulthood (Butts, Bazemore, & Meroe, 2010). The PYD framework suggests that all youth can thrive when given an appropriate combination of pro-social relationships and support during this sensitive period of development. PYD advocates for a strength-based focus on not only the programs administered to youth, but on measuring outcomes of program success and effectiveness (Butts *et al.*, 2010).

Positive Youth Justice (PYJ) applies PYD ideals to the treatment of youth and young adults who have either made contact with the criminal justice system or present an elevated risk for delinquent and maladaptive behavior in the future (Butts *et al.*, 2010). PYJ asserts that delinquency, problem behavior, and even serious adult offending can be prevented through programs that target the protective factors and strengths that youth possess. Instead of assessing risk and attempting to make these negative indicators "less bad," programs may be able to significantly reduce problem behavior and risk for future delinquency by building existing strengths and helping youth to discover new ones. Educational attainment, pro-social interactions, creative pursuits, healthy recreation, future planning and similar achievements are emphasized through programs that hope to help youth resist unhealthy and problematic behavior via the acquisition of life-relevant strengths and competencies.

Catalano *et al.* (2004) completed a systematic review of programs in use that attempt to achieve objectives in line with the ideals of PYD. From an initial list of 161 potential programs, a total of 25 were identified that satisfied the following criteria: incorporated PYD constructs into a universal or selective approach; had evaluations with strong experimental designs and an acceptable standard of proof; provided adequate methodological detail for analysis; and produced evidence of significant effects on at least one important behavioral outcome. Twenty-two of these programs demonstrated evidence of a significant reduction in delinquent behavior including alcohol and drug use, school misbehavior and aggression. In spite of encouraging results so far, Catalano *et al.* (2004) emphasized that few studies measure behavioral outcomes over time, often only surveying youth who complete a particular program. Once again, greater consensus on relevant outcome measures and more rigorous methodologies are still needed.

Conclusion

Further research should continue to disentangle the interactive influences of individual-, school-, and community-level variables on behavior, and inform the development of effective strategies for delinquency prevention. Although school and community factors play a significant role in shaping delinquency, individual level factors appear to offer stronger explanations of serious delinquency (Gottfredson *et al.*, 2005; Welsh *et al.*, 1999). School climate factors seem to better explain the more common but less serious forms of misconduct in schools (Welsh, 2001, 2003). Close scrutiny of school climate should be included in any school-based program designed to reduce violence, however. Efforts to change individuals, in the absence of attention to school policies that may be contributing to high levels of disorder, are likely to be counterproductive. School-based strategies should also address physical and environmental factors as well as social factors.

While a number of prevention and intervention approaches including universal and selected/indicated programs have been shown to be effective, there is still disagreement about appropriate standards to classify and assess such programs, and many programs remain unevaluated or persist despite negative evidence. One of the most glaring findings in the literature is the overall weakness of program implementation and lack of attention to program fidelity.

Many interventions fall far short of their goals because of poor planning, poor implementation, and poor evaluation (Welsh & Harris, 2012). We have not yet discovered a perfect formula for what schools should do to reduce delinquency, but considerable knowledge exists to help guide future efforts. In order to improve the effectiveness of school-based delinquency prevention policies and programs, however, we need a better understanding of the methods and processes by which interventions are developed, adopted, implemented, evaluated and managed. Progress in this area will require greater cooperation between school officials, students, parents, community-based groups, human services and other agencies. Most desperately needed, in our opinion, are not new programs but better ones (Welsh & Harris, 2012).

References

Blueprints for Healthy Youth Development. (2013). *Blueprints programs*. Retrieved from http://www.blueprintsprograms.com/allPrograms.php

Butts, J.A., Bazemore, G., & Meroe, A.S. (2010). *Positive Youth Justice: Framing Justice Interventions using the Concepts of Positive Youth Development*. Washington, DC: Coalition for Juvenile Justice. Retrieved from http://www.juvjustice.org/media/resources/public/resource_390.pdf

Catalano, R.F., Berglund, M.L., Ryan, J.A.M., Lonczak, H.S., & Hawkins, J.D. (2004). Positive youth development in the United States: Research findings on evaluations of positive youth development programs. *Annals of the American Academy of Political and Social Science, 591*, 98–124.

Cernkovich, S.A., & Giordano, P.C. (1992). School bonding, race, and delinquency. *Criminology, 30*, 261–291.

Coalition for Evidence-Based Policy. (2013). *Coalition for Evidence Based Policy: A nonprofit, nonpartisan organization*. Retrieved from http://coalition4evidence.org/

Elias, M.J., Tobias, S.E., & Friedlander, B.S. (2000). *Emotionally Intelligent Parenting: How to Raise a Self-Disciplined, Responsible, Socially Skilled child*. New York: Random House/ Three Rivers Press.

Elias, M.J., Zins, J.E., Weissberg, R.P., Frey, K.S., Greenberg, M.T., Haynes, N.M., *et al.* (1997). *Promoting Social and Emotional Learning: Guidelines for Educators*. Alexandria, VA: Association for Supervision and Curriculum Development.

Farrington, D.P., & Welsh, B.C. (2007). *Saving Children from a Life of Crime: Early Risk Factors and Effective Interventions*. New York: Oxford University Press.

Gandhi, A.G., Murphy-Graham, E., Petrosino, A., Chrismer, S.S., & Weiss, C.H. (2007). The devil is in the details: Examining the evidence for "proven" school-based drug abuse prevention programs. *Evaluation Review, 31*, 43–74.

Gottfredson, D.C. (2001). *Schools and Delinquency*. New York: Cambridge University Press.

Gottfredson, D.C., & Gottfredson, G.D. (2002). Quality of school-based prevention programs: Results from a national survey. *Journal of Research in Crime and Delinquency, 39*, 3–35.

Gottfredson, G.D., Gottfredson, D.C., Czeh, E.R., Cantor, D., Crosse, S.B., & Hantaan, I. (2004). *Toward safe and orderly schools – the National Study of Delinquency Prevention in Schools (NCJ 205005)*. Washington, DC: US Department of Justice, Office of Justice Programs, National Institute of Justice.

Gottfredson, G.D., Gottfredson, D.C., Payne, A.A., & Gottfredson, N.C. (2005). School climate predictors of school disorder: Results from a national study of delinquency prevention in schools. *Journal of Research in Crime and Delinquency, 42*, 412–444.

Greenberg, M.T. (2010). School-based prevention: current status and future challenges. *Effective Education, 2*(1), 27–52.

Greenwood, P.W. (2006). *Changing Lives: Delinquency Prevention as Crime-Control Policy*. Chicago: University of Chicago Press.

Hahn, R., Fuqua-Whitley, D., Wethington, H., Lowy, J., Crosby, A., Fullilove, M., *et al.* (2007). Effectiveness of universal school-based programs to prevent violent and aggressive behavior: A systematic review. *American Journal of Preventive Medicine, 33* (2 Suppl.), S114–129.

Ialongo, N.S., Wethamer, L., Kellam, S.G., Brown, C.H., Wang, S., & Lin, Y. (1999). Proximal impact of two first-grade preventive interventions on the early risk behaviors for later substance abuse, depression, and antisocial behavior. *American Journal of Community Psychology, 27*, 599–641.

Johnson, S.L. (2009). Improving the school environment to reduce school violence: a review of the literature. *Journal of School Health, 79*(10), 451–465.

Kirk, D.S. (2009). Unraveling the contextual effects on student suspension and juvenile arrest: The independent and interdependent influences of school, neighborhood, and family social controls. *Criminology, 47*, 479–517.

Krohn, M., & Massey, J. (1980). Social control and delinquent behavior: An examination of the elements of the social bond. *Sociological Quarterly, 21*, 529–543.

Lawrence, R.A. (2006). *School Crime and Juvenile Justice* (2nd Ed.). New York: Oxford University Press.

Mooji, T. (1998). Pupil-class determinants of aggressive and victim behavior in pupils. *British Journal of Educational Psychology, 68*, 373–385.

Office of Justice Programs. (2013). *CrimeSolutions.gov. Reliable research, real results.* Retrieved from http://www.crimesolutions.gov/

OJJDP. (2013). *The Office of Juvenile Justice and Delinquency Prevention's Model Programs Guide (MPG).* Retrieved from http://www.ojjdp.gov/mpg/

Payne, A.A., Gottfredson, D.C., & Gottfredson, G.D. (2003). Schools as communities: The relationships among communal school organization, student bonding, and school disorder. *Criminology, 41*, 749–778.

Penn State EPISCenter. (2013). *Evidence-Based Programs.* Retrieved from http://www.episcenter.psu.edu/ebp

Sampson, R.J., & Lauritsen, J.L. (1993). Violent victimization and offending: Individual, situational, and community-level risk factors. In A.J. Reiss, Jr., & J.A. Roth (Eds.), *Understanding and Preventing Violence: Social Influences* (Vol. 3) (pp. 1–115). Washington, DC: National Academy Press.

Sampson, R.J., Raudenbush, S.W., & Earls, F. (1997). Neighborhoods and violent crime: A multilevel study of collective efficacy. *Science, 277*, 918–924.

Sprott, J.B. (2004). The development of early delinquency: Can classroom and school climates make a difference? *Canadian Journal of Criminology and Criminal Justice [La Revue canadienne de criminologie et de justice pénale], 46*(5), 553–572.

Thornberry, T.P., Krohn, M.D., Lizotte, A.J., Smith, C.A., & Tobin, K. (2003). *Gangs and Delinquency in Developmental Perspective.* New York: Cambridge University Press.

Thornberry, T., Lizotte, A., Krohn, M., Farnsworth, M., & Jang, S. (1991). Testing interactional theory: An examination of reciprocal causal relationships among family, school, and delinquency. *Journal of Criminal Law and Criminology, 82*, 3–35.

Welsh, W.N. (2000). The effects of school climate on school disorder. *Annals of the American Academy of Political and Social Science, 567*, 88–107.

Welsh, W.N. (2001). Effects of student and school factors on five measures of school disorder. *Justice Quarterly, 18*, 401–437.

Welsh, W.N. (2003). Individual and institutional predictors of school disorder. *Youth Violence and Juvenile Justice, 1*, 346–368.

Welsh, W.N., Greene, J.R., & Jenkins, P.H. (1999). School disorder: The influence of individual, institutional and community factors. *Criminology, 37*, 73–115.

Welsh, W.N., & Harris, P.W. (2012). *Criminal Justice Policy and Planning* (4th Ed.). Waltham, MA: Elsevier/Anderson.

Welsh, W.N., Stokes, R., & Greene, J.R. (2000). A macro-level model of school disorder. *Journal of Research in Crime and Delinquency, 37*, 243–283.

Wilcox P., Augustine, M.C., & Clayton, R.R. (2006). Physical environment and crime and misconduct in Kentucky schools. *Journal of Primary Prevention, 27*, 293–313.

Wilson, D.B., Gottfredson, D.C., & Najaka, S.S. (2001). School-based prevention of problem behaviors: a meta-analysis. *Journal of Quantitative Criminology, 17*(3), 247–272.

Wilson, S.J., & Lipsey, M.W. (2005). *The Effectiveness of School-based Violence Prevention Programs for Reducing Disruptive and Aggressive Behavior (NCJ 211376)*. Washington, DC: US Department of Justice, National Institute of Justice.

Wilson, S.J., & Lipsey, M.W. (2007). School-based interventions for aggressive and disruptive behavior: update of a meta-analysis. *American Journal of Preventive Medicine, 33*(2), S130–S143.

14

Fleas and Feathers: The Role of Peers in the Study of Juvenile Delinquency

John M. Eassey and Molly Buchanan

Fleas and feathers. Two relatively innocuous, seemingly unrelated terms; yet, when used in the context of criminological peer research, these two words are paramount in the long-lived debate of the role of peers in the etiology of delinquency. With over eight decades of empirical support (e.g. Burt & Klump, 2013; Thrasher, 1927), associating with delinquent peers has consistently emerged as one of the strongest correlates of juvenile delinquency and crime (Akers, 1998). With early studies of peer influence utilizing observational (Thrasher, 1927), official (Shaw & McKay, 1931), and self-report (Short, 1957) data, along with the subsequent myriad of empirical literature elaborating and redefining the peer–delinquency relationship, one conclusion remains constant: "peers matter".

Despite the exploration of various causal models for delinquent peer associations and delinquency (Warr, 2002), a specific combination of predictors has yet to emerge as the sole explanation for the peer–delinquency link. Along the same lines, sizable empirical evidence suggesting that associations with deviant peers increases the likelihood of deviant behavior, while alternative findings point to *positive* peer influences during adolescence (Brown, Bakken, Ameringer, & Mahon, 2008). As such, it is difficult to understate the importance of peer relationships with respect to deviant behavior, normative development, and future outcomes throughout one's life course, but still, the question is raised: "*how* do peers matter?".

Because detailing the entire spectrum of peer–delinquency research is beyond the scope of this chapter, the following pages address some of the ways in which peers matter by outlining key criminological findings as well as future directions for delinquency research. Initial chapter sections synopsize the long-lived peer–delinquency debate, with particular focus on the theoretical underpinnings at the

The Handbook of Juvenile Delinquency and Juvenile Justice, First Edition. Edited by Marvin D. Krohn and Jodi Lane.
© 2015 John Wiley & Sons, Inc. Published 2015 by John Wiley & Sons, Inc.

heart of the controversy. Next, an overview of adolescent development, with special attention paid to peer influences, provides the developmental framework central to subsequent discussions of extant research. Further exploration into current peer–delinquency research reveals prior limitations, growing complexities, and novel advancements. Finally, a summary of the influence of peers within the juvenile justice system is provided. The chapter concludes with directions for future research.

Peers in Criminology

Since Short and colleagues' (1957; Nye, Short, & Olson, 1958) pioneering research on self-report methodologies, deviant peer association is one of, if not the strongest correlate of juvenile delinquency currently known to criminological scholars. Given the robust relationship between peer associations and deviant behavior, it is not surprising that numerous criminological theories have specified peers as an integral component in the etiology of crime and deviance (e.g., Burgess & Akers, 1966; Hirschi, 1969; Osgood, Wilson, O'Malley, Bachman, & Johnston, 1996; Sutherland, 1947). Further, propositional statements related to the peer–delinquency relationship have also been incorporated into many integrated (e.g., Elliott, Huizinga, & Ageton, 1985;) and life-course theories of crime and delinquency (e.g., Moffitt, 1993). However, the propositions derived from other theories offer competing explanatory hypotheses for the relationship, resulting in considerable contention around its appropriate interpretation.

For example, many scholars (e.g., Akers, 1998) attribute a causal influence to peers. Following from differential association and social learning premises, youths learn to be deviant by imitating the deviance of their peers, all the while gaining favorable attitudes toward deviance via differential reinforcement processes. This, in turn, increases the likelihood of future deviance (Akers, 1998). Furthermore, Sutherland (1947) notes that associations that "occur earlier (priority), last longer and occupy more of one's time (duration), take place most often (frequency), and involve others with whom one has more important or closer relationships (intensity) will have the greatest impact on behavior", indicating that it would not be appropriate to treat all associations as equally important.

The impact of delinquent peer associations on delinquency onset and further deviant socialization has been supported by both cross-sectional and longitudinal studies (e.g., Matsueda & Anderson, 1998; Warr, 2002). On the other hand, proponents of the social control tradition have alternatively asserted that the peer–deviance correlation is simply a consequence of youths' preferences to associate with others similar to themselves (e.g., Glueck & Glueck, 1950). Therefore, theories derived from the social control tradition consider the peer deviance relationship to be either the result of self-selection into delinquent peer groups or spurious with respect to a third variable (e.g., self-control). This concept of self-selection, or attraction of peers due to similarities, has also received its fair share of empirical support (e.g., Beaver *et al.*, 2009; Granic & Patterson, 2006; Quinton, Pickles, Maughan, & Rutter, 1993).

Describing his social control theory, Hirschi (1969) argued that deviant youths are less able to form meaningful, quality friendship ties and, as a result, are less bonded to conventional society. Without being able to form conventional bonds, deviant youths have no choice but to associate with one another. Hirschi also asserts that it is unlikely for deviant youths to influence one another because, compared to conventional youths, friendship ties between delinquent youths are more likely to be "cold and brittle". Contrary to this assertion, however, researchers have found especially close relationships among peers involved in delinquent and drug-using behaviors, perhaps even more intimate than non-delinquent peer relationships, directly refuting Hirschi's "cold and brittle" claim (e.g., Giordano, Cernkovich, & Pugh, 1986). For instance, Giordano and colleagues (1986) found that conforming *and* delinquent youths are just as likely to report close, trusting, and stable friendships.

A third interpretation, often adopted by life-course and developmental theorists, (e.g., Thornberry, 1987) views selection and socialization as complementary. As such, these variables are viewed as reciprocally interrelated over time. For instance, interactional theory (Thornberry & Krohn, 2005) posits that psychosocial risk factors and weakened social bonds initially lead youths into deviant behavior, thereby increasing the probability of deviant peer associations. Once formed, these deviant peer ties provide additional opportunities and support for deviance, further amplifying deviant behavior. In turn, deviant behavior is theorized to persist as youths become increasingly enmeshed in deviant peer groups, further weakening their conventional bonds to society. This phenomenon has been found to be especially prominent for youths who begin offending at an early age or commit particularly serious offenses (Thornberry & Krohn, 2005).

Although it has yet to be determined whether one interpretation will eventually prove superior, what *is* clear from decades of prior research is that peers cannot be ignored, and misspecification can occur if examining deviance without consideration of peers. Likewise, prior research has established that peer influence is a multifaceted phenomenon with both direct and indirect relationships to delinquency. Furthermore, the processes by which youths establish friendships and peer groups are similarly complex, yet have received relatively less scholarly attention compared to the impact of delinquent peer associations. Together, the processes by which youths come to have ties with delinquent peers and the potential impact of such ties must be considered in order to understand the influence of peers on delinquency.

The intricacies of peer–delinquency research are further explored in the remaining sections of this chapter. The developmental and life-course perspective (Elder, 1985) has been used to organize the extant literature, since friendships and peer groups are characterized by stability and change and conditioned by local life circumstances and life-course transitions. Moreover, the developmental and life-course perspective provides a logical framework for interweaving the various facets of peer–delinquency research, as the perspective emphasizes developmental trajectories and transitions consistent with the dynamics of peer group formation and influence during adolescence. Accordingly, we begin with a discussion of peers in the context of adolescent development and friendship acquisition.

Peers in Adolescent Development

"Adolescence" is a vague term, with no universal age of onset or completed maturity, but is generally understood as "a phase in development between childhood and adulthood beginning at puberty, typically about 12 or 13 and ending in the late teens or early 20s" (National Research Council, 2013, p.18). This developmental phase is of particular importance in peer–delinquency research, as adolescence marks a period where increased deviance is common and considered age-normative (Farrington, 1986). Additionally, deviant behaviors that may have isolated youths, or made them less popular during childhood, suddenly become more acceptable or even "cool" during adolescence (Burt, 2009). For some, the timing of this newfound acceptance of deviant behavior is key to successfully navigating adolescence (National Research Council, 2013).

Notwithstanding the importance of peers during this phase of the life course, developmental psychologists suggest that adult support and autonomy-promoting activities are instrumental for successful adolescent psychosocial development (Chung, Little, & Steinberg, 2005). With respect to delinquent behavior, the relative influence of each of these factors is decidedly age-graded in nature (Dick *et al.*, 2009). For example, parents are primarily responsible for socializing and providing for their children during infancy, childhood, and even into early adolescence, typically guiding them into preferred activities, as well as preferred peer groups (Parke, Burks, Carson, Neville, & Boyum, 1994). However, such authority typically begins to wane as youths continue into early- to mid-adolescence, and spend considerably more time in the company of peers and friends (Csikszentmihalyi & Larson, 1984). Parental figures become more or less relegated to monitoring youths' self-chosen peer groups and activities (National Research Council, 2013; Parke *et al.*, 1994; Warr, 2002).

This progression from parents to peers is considered integral to healthy adolescent development, as peer groups provide feedback about social norms, opportunities to experiment with self-identities and social roles, and allow budding adolescents the chance to develop social skills (Brown *et al.*, 2008). Correspondingly, the significance that youths attach to their relationships with friends becomes as important, if not more, as their relationships with parental figures (Warr, 1993). Interestingly, adolescents' identity formation processes often include experimentation with risky behavior that occurs within larger peer groups, with the willingness of youths to explore risks further amplified by the mere presence of said peers (Gardner & Steinberg, 2005). Therefore, notwithstanding the many positive influences peers can have on emotional and social development, peers can also exert many negative influences, including the development of and involvement in deviant behavior (Brown *et al.*, 2008).

Although most youths age out of adolescent antisocial behaviors by being better able to self-regulate and less susceptible to peer pressure (Steinberg & Monahan, 2007), it has been noted that the types of peers one has cultivated during adolescence can have an enduring impact on future outcomes. For instance, precocious transitions into adult roles (e.g., early parenthood; prematurely exiting school) become more likely for youths who associate with deviant peers (Krohn, Lizotte, & Perez, 1997). Likewise, delinquent peer associations during adolescence significantly increase the likelihood that youths will continue to commit crimes into emerging adulthood, as well as put youths at increased risk for adulthood antisocial personality diagnoses (Simonoff *et al.*, 2004). Given peers' integral influence during adolescent development, it is also important to recognize that "most adolescents do not belong to a single, densely knit, isolated friendship clique, but instead, are affiliated with many loosely bounded friendship groups with varying degrees of cohesion and permeability" (Haynie, 2001, p. 1014). Social networks present a useful way to organize the various ties between youths and their peers to better understand how friendships are formed and how they impact behavior.

Social Network and Friendship Formation

In formal terms, a network is a set of "nodes", linked together through some type of relationship. When applied to social relationships, nodes typically represent a person, while linkages represent friendship ties with other people. Although the application of social networks to the study of delinquency is not a recent innovation (see Krohn, 1986), a revitalized interest in social networks has resulted in a recent influx of studies utilizing the many benefits of social network-type data. For instance, prior studies on the influence of peer associations often limited their foci to the actions or beliefs of peers (Pratt *et al.*, 2010), typically asking respondents which proportion of their peers engaged in specific behaviors. Often, this method neglects other important facets of peer relationships, such as friendship quality and time spent together, while also assuming respondents could accurately assess peers' behaviors (for exceptions see Giordano *et al.*, 1986; Haynie, 2001, 2002; Krohn, Massey, & Zielinski, 1988; Krohn & Thornberry, 1993; Osgood *et al.*, 1996).

By exploring the peer–delinquency relationship from the direction of social networks, scholars are better able to delve into the complex nuances of peer relationships by addressing the specific links between youths and the contexts in which these links occur. Through design, scholars explicitly acknowledge the probability that youths are not only differentially affected by members of their network, but are also affected by their social positions within their network. Therefore, by directly surveying respondents' peers, studies utilizing social network data can also examine the structural patterns of friendship ties (i.e., the network-level influences) that have been found to influence behavior, independent of the particular peers comprising the network (Haynie, 2001).

Peers and friendships

Youths often attach different levels of importance to members of their social networks. This is perhaps best illustrated by the fact that, out of all the peers in their
network, youths typically have one or two close friends whom they consider their
"best friends". Recently, scholars have taken care to distinguish the numerous dimensions of friendships, including the types and frequency of interactions, the intimacy
of relationships, as well as characteristics and values shared by friends (Weerman &
Smeenk, 2005). In doing so, scholars have classified different types of friendships by
their varying significance and relative network positions, introducing such labels as
best friends, regular friends, acquaintances, close friends, distal friends/peers, and
friends of friends, to the literature.

Although social learning theory would suggest that best friends are the most
important sources of delinquent behavior, it has been noted that narrowly focusing
on the closest, most intimate friendships is inappropriate (Payne & Cornwell, 2007).
Even while more distal or less important relationships may be less intense than other
types of friendships, comparisons of regular friends and best friends suggest that
regular friends may be *as* influential as close friends (Giordano, 1995). There are a
number of reasons why this may be the case. For instance, youths often affiliate with
many different peers on varying levels and across numerous contexts (e.g., school,
athletic teams, jobs, afterschool activities), meaning that regular friends simply out-
number best friends (Rees & Pogarsky, 2011). Further, youths likely spend more
time with their best friends across several different contexts, which, based on network theory, suggests that youths will be less likely to engage in delinquent behavior
when in the company of their best friends as a result (Krohn, 1986). Similarly, youths
may be more likely to hide their delinquent behaviors from close friends in order to
avoid being perceived in a negative light.

Studies comparing the relative importance of friendships have found that,
despite the differential values that youths may place on their relationships, both
best friends and regular friends appear to equally impact delinquent behavior.
Payne and Cornwell (2007) found that the effect of peers indirectly linked to
youths by shared, direct friendship ties (i.e., friends of friends) is relatively
weaker than the corresponding effect of direct ties, yet the indirect ties are still
significantly related to involvement in delinquent behavior. Rees and Pogarsky
(2011) report similar patterns, finding comparable influences of best friends and
regular friends; however, when there was less behavioral concordance between
best friends and regular friends, the influence of best friends tended to be
weaker.

Overall, the differential value youths place on their friendships might suggest that
only specific peers, such as best friends, are relevant to delinquency research.
However, it appears that including only segments of youths' social networks risks
oversimplifying clearly nuanced relationships. Although the best friend–regular
friend distinctions are not commonly made in peer research, they are important for
understanding how youths' social networks impact delinquency. This notion is

revisited later in this chapter in the section considering methodological concerns of peer–delinquency research.

Structural characteristics

Social network methodology can be used to disaggregate friendship ties into the contexts around which they are formed, thereby alleviating the need to treat youths' peer networks as single, homogenous groups. This disaggregation property is important, as social networks are posited to promote conformity of behaviors deemed necessary to maintain network existence, as well as minimize the probability of behaviors threatening its existence (Krohn, 1986). Further, the more contexts youths share with the same peers, that is, the multiplexity of their contexts, has been found to be directly related to the probability they will engage in delinquent behavior (Krohn *et al.*, 1988). As previously mentioned, youths may have friendships centered around several different contexts (e.g., school, work, extracurricular activities, delinquency) and, in order to determine whether delinquent behavior will be promoted or constrained, the contexts, as well as the specific peers present, should be known.

The specific patterns of friendship ties have also been found to influence deviant behavior. For instance, in her study of social networks using data from the National Longitudinal Study of Adolescent Health, Haynie (2001) found that the impact of delinquent peers was stronger in networks that are dense, where youths occupy central positions among peers and are frequently nominated as someone's friend. Additional studies using European samples also identify the importance of network structural characteristics. Delinquency tends to be more prevalent in networks where strong ties exist among members, while severity of delinquent behavior is related to popularity, where youths who engaged in minor delinquency experience more popularity, especially among females, than non-delinquent or seriously delinquent youths (Weerman & Bijleveld 2007). Such findings are consistent with the proposition that delinquency makes youths appear "cool" during adolescence.

Network position

As mentioned above, not all youths belong to a single social network, as some youths belong to multiple networks while others may be completely isolated from peers. Youths who fall into either of these categories are exposed to unique social conditions that may also correlate with delinquency. Youths who bridge gaps between otherwise disjointed networks (i.e., only one tie connects them to a particular network) are often referred to as "liaisons" (Granovetter, 1973). Although liaisons are considered weakly connected to any single network, due to being linked to any group only by a single route, they are exposed to the norms and contexts of multiple groups and therefore may be more at risk for delinquent behavior than youths in fewer networks (Valente, Gallaher, & Mouttapa, 2004).

Whereas liaisons are tied to multiple peer groups, completely isolated youths, or "isolates", lack ties to any group. It is not clear what impact such peer isolation may have on emotional and social development, as being an isolate raises divergent hypotheses about the likelihood of delinquency from socialization and social control theories (Kreager, 2004), as well as many conflicting empirical results (Gifford-Smith & Brownell, 2003). For instance, Patterson (1982) hypothesized an interactional relationship where experiencing rejection furthers one's deviance, while Haynie (2002) found that isolates were no more or less likely to engage in delinquency than youths properly enmeshed in one or more social networks.

Kreager (2004) suggested that there are at least two types of social isolates – those who have trouble with their peers and those who are figuratively invisible to others. He finds that peer-troubled isolates are more likely to engage in property crime and join gangs. Invisible isolates are more likely to be minorities and have relatively stronger parental attachments, suggesting that isolation from peers may not necessarily be detrimental in terms of delinquent involvement.

Network formation

Given the importance of delinquent peer associations, contrasted with the potential consequences of being alienated from all peers, it is surprising that more research on peer acquisition has not been performed (Warr, 2005). Research generally supports the idea that homophily plays an important role in friendship formation, where youths typically form friendships with those whom they share something in common (Cairns & Cairns, 1994). It has been suggested that this preference for similarity extends to involvement in delinquency (Gottfredson & Hirschi, 1990). On the other hand, Warr (2005, p. 81) pointed out that:

> … as central as homophily is to understanding human relations (Cairns & Cairns, 1994), it begs the larger question. Unless one assumes that adolescents engage in delinquency before they acquire delinquent friends – and the evidence suggests otherwise (Elliott & Menard, 1996) – then homophily has little to say about how adolescents acquire delinquent peers in the first place.

However, even if it is true that friendships do not form on the basis of shared preferences for delinquent behavior, it is still plausible that youths are brought together on the basis of characteristics that eventually lead to delinquency, suggesting support for homophily.

Considerable research has attempted to determine the extent to which adolescents form friendships on the basis of shared delinquent tendencies, and if so, what impact those tendencies have on friendship quality (e.g., Baerveldt, Van Rossem, de Verman, & Weerman, 2004). For instance, Haynie's (2002) findings indicate that most social networks were more often composed of a mix of delinquent and nondelinquent youths, and that the proportion of delinquent peers in one's network is inversely related to network density. With respect to friendship quality, Dishion (1990), and later Pabon, Rodriquez, and Gurin (1992), found less emotional closeness and intimacy between youths who have more delinquent friends compared to those with fewer. On the other hand, more recent research examining the structural characteristics of peer networks found that background characteristics, and attitudinal and behavioral covariates, rather than delinquency *per se*, attenuated the differences in cohesion, stability, and popularity in networks with greater proportions of delinquent youths (Kreager, Rulison, & Moody, 2011). Although not entirely consistent, evidence suggests that delinquent groups differ little from non-delinquent groups with respect to the quality of ties, and that preferences for delinquent activities are not strong determinants of friendship formation (Krohn & Thornberry, 1993; Krohn *et al.*, 1988).

Additionally, friendships and other types of relationships are primarily formed with those with whom we share close proximity and have regular, consistent contact, otherwise known as propinquity (Warr, 2002). In the case of peer–delinquency research, propinquity suggests youths' routine activities, where they live, and where they go to school – among other considerations (e.g., popularity, attractiveness) – can impact peer group formation. Flowing from the principle of propinquity and developmental and life-course criminology's emphasis on transitions, peer associations are expected to change when youths' local life circumstances change (see Warr, 1998). For instance, graduating from high school and moving away to college or becoming employed, and thereby reducing time for socializing, often has direct consequences for when and with whom socializing occurs; however, less empirical attention has been paid to the behavioral impact of changes in peer associations as a result of these life-course transitions.

Taken together, propinquity and homophily suggest mechanisms by which friendships are formed, and that these mechanisms go beyond basic personality preferences or similarities in behavior (Brown, Lohr, & Trujuillo, 1990). They also suggest ways in which delinquent involvement may be affected by changes in friendships due to life-course transitions. The following section delves deeper into this phenomenon, pointing to the role of peers as co-offenders and the various aspects this role encompasses.

Peers and Co-offenders

It is well documented that during adolescence deviant behavior is predominately group behavior (Reiss, 1986; Warr, 2002). Not until emerging adulthood does solo offending become common (Reiss & Farrington, 1991), hence tying the study of the co-offenders and co-offending with the study of peers, as youths' peers represent their available pool of co-offenders. This section outlines empirically established aspects of co-offending relationships.

Perhaps the most established feature of group offending is the number of youths who are typically involved in a single incident (Warr, 2002), with most group offenses generally committed by two to four youths (Gold, 1970). While some offenses, such as assault, are more likely to be committed alone, the most frequently committed offenses are perpetrated in groups (Erickson, 1971). Further, it appears that group size is inversely related to age; that is, groups of four are more common in late childhood and early adolescence, while triads and dyads become more common during late adolescence (Reiss, 1986). Offending frequency has also been found to vary with peer group size. In particular, high-frequency offenders often have larger pools of co-offenders who also tend to offend at high frequencies, while low-frequency offenders tend to have smaller pools of potential co-offenders (Reiss, 1986).

These results suggest that as youths' co-offenders vary, so do their specific criminal opportunities and group preferences, ultimately changing the types of offenses youths are likely to commit (Farrington, 2005). Shaw and McKay (1931) demonstrated evidence of such change and variation in their case study of Sidney. Over his career, Sidney associated with three distinct groups of peers and, as he progressed from one group to the next, the types of offenses he committed accorded more closely to those committed by his current peer group rather than previous peer groups.

Warr (1996) further elaborated on this phenomenon, suggesting that specialization in offending is a within-peer-group characteristic and that diversity in offending reflects differing offense preferences across co-offending groups. Therefore, individuals demonstrate offense versatility as they associate with different groups. Transitions from delinquent to non-delinquent peer groups have also been found to precipitate desistance. For instance, Warr (1993) examined offending patterns over time in conjunction with patterns of delinquent peer association, finding a close resemblance to the age–crime trend, with the increasing delinquent peer associations during early adolescence peaking during mid to late adolescence, only to quickly decline thereafter. Similarly, Warr (1998) found that the well-established relationship between marriage and desistance is attributable to reductions in the amount of contact with peers.

Peers and Opportunity

Where and with whom youths spend their time is also centrally related to the particular opportunities for crime and deviance they will encounter. It is argued that peers provide opportunities for deviant behavior, as being in the company of one's peers makes deviance an easier and more rewarding endeavor (Osgood *et al.*, 1996). Further, youths tend to be more sensitive to proximal external influences (e.g., peer pressure), and are therefore more likely to conform their behavior to that of their peers when in their presence (Gardner & Steinberg, 2005). However, the amount of time spent with peers generally increases for all youths, suggesting it is not the amount of time *per se* that is related to deviant behavior (Warr, 2005). More important than the amount of time is the amount of time spent in particular types of activities that occur in the company of peers (Felson, 2002). Activities that are unsupervised and unstructured (i.e., those situations that do not restrict ways in which time can be used, such as at school in a classroom), such as driving around for fun, getting together with friends informally, going to parties, and spend evenings out for recreation, have been found to be directly related to deviant behavior, including violence and substance use (Haynie & Osgood, 2005; Hirschi, 1969; Krohn & Thornberry, 1993). While it is true that time spent informally socializing with peers carries no direct connotation of deviance, Osgood and Anderson (2004, p. 521) assert that "the presence of peers will make deviant acts easier and more rewarding, the absence of authority figures will reduce the potential for social control responses, and the lack of structure will leave time available for deviance". Therefore situations with all three of these qualities – the presence of peers, lack of supervision, and little restrictions on how time should be spent – are most conducive to deviant behavior (Osgood, Anderson, & Shaffer, 2005). Without the situational motivation provided by the presence of peers, it is less likely that unstructured activities, such as watching television, reading, and spending time alone, will result in deviant behavior (Hawdon, 1999). Further, the relationship between time use and delinquency has been found to be independent of peer delinquency (Haynie & Osgood, 2005).

Peer Research: Methodological Issues

Several methodological issues have historically plagued the study of peer relationships, especially as they relate to deviance. Chief among them was the inability to determine the temporal ordering among variables, making it impossible to explore the validity of socialization and selection hypotheses. The increased prevalence of longitudinal data in criminology has largely remedied this problem; however, with a few exceptions, longitudinal data have yet to be applied to the examination of social networks beyond a single follow-up observation. Extended observations over longer periods capture richer views of adolescent associations and are necessary for answering questions on how social network dynamics and changes in social networks impact criminal careers.

Similarly, the use of self-report surveys, asking youths to report the behavior of their peers in addition to their own, is often criticized as a possible source of bias (Jussim & Osgood, 1989), as youths cannot know for certain the entirety of another's behavior. Seemingly affirming these criticisms, studies utilizing social network data to compare direct and indirect measures of peer behavior typically find that indirect measurements tend to overestimate effects of delinquent peer associations on delinquency (Weerman & Smeenk, 2005; Boman, Ward, Gibson, & Leite, 2012). However, it is difficult to know whether the use of direct measurements is more accurate, as most currently available social network data place limits on friendship nominations, often requiring respondents to list only friends from their same grade or school. Such restrictions likely account for only a fraction of a youth's social network, and therefore may result in spuriously small estimates of the true effect of peer association based on the extent to which there is overlap between school networks and co-offending networks.

Secondly, many social network studies ask respondents to list their friends but provide no metric to indicate the importance of those friends (Rees & Pogarsky, 2011). As a result, it is not yet known whether youths' ties to nominated friends are comparable between respondents. Likewise, such studies do not consider the potential influence of more distal peers as was described earlier. Finally, wording variations of survey items that ask youths to nominate friends may elicit divergent responses (Jaccard, Blanton, & Dodge, 2005), raising issues of measurement reliability. Because these limitations speak directly to the appropriate measurement of peer delinquency, not addressing them threatens the validity of the entire body of research that relies on indirect measurements.

Peers in the Juvenile Justice System

Given the accumulation of empirical support for the peer–delinquency relationship, an auxiliary aspect of this research is the role of peers within the juvenile justice system. For youths adjudicated by the juvenile system, various punishments are available, some of which intentionally include further contributions from peers, while others focus on reducing peer interactions. Furthermore, research has shown that formal involvement in the juvenile justice system has short and long-term consequences for youths, significantly decreasing their likelihood of building prosocial peer bonds, as well as negatively impacting their chances of building positive relationships into adulthood (Laub & Sampson, 2001). Empirical support for adverse effects often highlights the potential detriments of congregating large groups of delinquent youths together for the purposes of intervention (e.g., lock-up, group therapy). Such gathering of youths seemingly increases exposure to delinquent peers, thereby increasing opportunities to learn additional delinquent behaviors. Referred to in the literature as "deviancy training" or the "contagion effect", scholars have identified conditions by which this phenomenon is more likely to occur (National Research Council, 2013). For deviancy training especially, these conditions include heightened susceptibility for younger offenders and offenders adjudicated for relatively minor infractions, intervention settings where minor or younger offenders are included among older, more serious offenders, and programs that inadequately supervise their wards (Dishion, Dodge, & Lansford, 2006).

Scott and Steinberg (2010) highlight the egregious yet common misstep of unsupervised interactions among peer groups comprised mainly, if not entirely, of, antisocial youths as a central challenge for juvenile justice interventions. Even still, more lax yet supervised intervention settings (e.g., group treatment sessions) have also been found to propagate deviant peer exposure, with youths' delinquent behaviors often shared and reinforced, especially among younger offenders (Weiss *et al.*, 2005). On the other hand, interventions particularly focused on reducing delinquent peer affiliations and actively involving youths in the treatment process show promise, having successfully reduced future delinquent outcomes (Curtis, Roman, & Borduin, 2004). Moreover, the extant literature suggests that best practices should limit and highly structure interactions with system-involved peers and increase interactions with prosocial peers, positing that smaller, community-based programs are best suited to provide such services (National Research Council, 2013).

Conclusion and Future Directions

Although research incorporating social network data has recently illuminated many aspects of the peer–delinquency relationship, a natural direction for future research is to expand data collection beyond schools in order to capture other social contexts. Much of the social network literature was born from a few prominent data sets that have limited friendship nominations to youths attending the same school, yet inquired about delinquent acts that occurred outside of the school context, underscoring the possibility that co-offenders may not attend the same school (for exception, see Kiesner, Kerr, & Stattin, 2004). Moreover, social network theory (Krohn, 1986) posits that networks are more likely to promote conforming behavior when members share a number of contexts, while potentially perpetuating delinquency if deviant contexts are common. Given that multiple contexts are infrequently considered, it is not yet clear what impact expanding contexts may have. However, results from school-based network studies which took note of the importance of "out-of-school" friends may be suggestive, as youths who report more out-of-school friends, or closer ties to their out-of-school friends, tend to be more delinquent (Baerveldt *et al.*, 2004; Kreager *et al.*, 2011; Krohn & Thornberry, 1993).

Another area of peer–delinquency research ripe for further exploration is the role of behavioral genetics in adolescent friendship formation and delinquency abstention. While sociological factors have historically been the focus of this line of research, behavioral genetics and the expertise of biosocial criminologists are being increasingly integrated into peer–delinquency literature (Caspi & Moffitt, 1993). As discussed at the outset of this chapter, adolescence is a developmental period fraught with many biological changes, new experiences and social adjustments. The relationships among these factors have gained recent scholarly attention. Genetic influences, in particular, on friendship formation would be considered an example of a gene–environment (GE) correlation whereby individuals actively seek out youths who are compatible with their genetic predispositions or are befriended by youths who respond positively to their genetically influenced traits and behaviors. With extant literature finding initial support for an indirect biological or genetic influence (e.g., see Cleveland, Wiebe, & Rowe, 2005), the magnitude of support has varied, leaving gaps for increasingly sophisticated designs and data analysis in the study of peer influence (Beaver & Wright, 2005).

Finally, although the preceding discussions present the relationship between peer associations, social networks, and versatility, opportunity, and co-offending, youths' social networks also have important consequences for other aspects of their criminal careers and offending trajectories, including initiation, frequency, and desistence, which were not dicussed here. Further, social networks formed during adolescence may also have important consequences later in life, as the friendships cultivated may directly impact youths' future social capital and subsequent, positive life-course transitions (Laub & Sampson, 1993). In sum, with the significance of peer relationships during adolescence and their potential impact on adulthood, along with advances in peer–delinquency research and avenues for alternative explanations, the quest to answer the question of "how do peers matter" continues to evolve, proving to be highly nuanced as new discoveries are made.

References

Akers, R.L. (1998). *Social Learning and Social Structure: A General Theory of Crime and Deviance*. Boston, MA: Northeastern University Press.

Baerveldt, C., Van Rossem, R., de Verman, M., & Weerman, F. (2004). Student's delinquency and correlates with strong and weaker ties: a study of students' networks in Dutch high schools. *Connections*, 26, 11–28.

Beaver, K.M., Schutt, J.E., Boutwell, B.B., Ratchford, M., Roberts, K., & Barnes, J.C. (2009). Genetic and environmental influences on levels of self-control and delinquent peer affiliation: Results from a longitudinal sample of adolescent twins. *Criminal Justice and Behavior*, 36(1), 41–60.

Beaver, K.M., & Wright, J.P. (2005). Biosocial development and delinquent involvement. *Youth Violence and Juvenile Justice*, 3(2), 168–192.

Boman IV, J.H., Ward, J.T., Gibson, C.L., & Leite, W.L. (2012). Can a perceptual peer deviance measure accurately measure a peer's self-reported deviance? *Journal of Criminal Justice*, 40(6), 463–471.

Brown, B.B., Bakken, J.P., Ameringer, S.W., & Mahon, S.D. (2008). A comprehensive conceptualization of the peer influence process in adolescence. In M.J. Prinstein, & K.A. Dodge (Eds.), *Understanding Peer Influence in Children and Adolescents* (pp. 17–44). New York: Guilford Press.

Brown, B.B., Lohr, M.J., & Trujillo, C. (1990). Multiple crowds and multiple life-styles: Adolescents' perceptions of peer-group academics. In R.E. Muus (Ed.), *Adolescent Behavior and Society: A Book of Readings*, 4th ed. (pp. 30–36). New York: McGraw-Hill.

Burgess, R., & Akers, R.C. (1966). A differential association–reinforcement theory of criminal behavior. *Social Problem*, 14, 336–383.

Burt, S.A. (2009). A mechanistic explanation of popularity: Genes, rule-breaking, and evocative gene-environment correlations. *Journal of Personality and Social Psychology*, 96, 783–794.

Burt, S.A., & Klump, K.L. (2013). Delinquent peer affiliation as an etiological moderator of childhood delinquency. *Psychological Medicine*, 43(8), 1269–1278.

Cairns, R.B., & Cairns, B.D. (1994). *Risks and Lifelines: Pathways of Youth in Our Time*. London: Harvester Wheatsheaf.

Caspi, A., & Moffitt, T.E. (1993). When do individual differences matter? A paradoxical theory of personality coherence. *Psychological Inquiry*, 4(4), 247–271.

Chung, H.L., Little, M., & Steinberg, L. (2005). The transition to adulthood for adolescence in the juvenile justice system: A developmental perspective. In W. Osgood, M. Foster, C. Flanagan, & G. Ruth (Eds.), *On Your Own Without a Net: The Transition to Adulthood for Vulnerable Populations* (pp. 68–91). Chicago, IL: University of Chicago Press.

Cleveland, H.H., Wiebe, R.P., & Rowe, D.C. (2005). Sources of exposure to smoking and drinking friends among adolescents: A behavioral-genetic evaluation. *Journal of Genetic Psychology, 166,* 153–169.

Csikszentmihalyi, M., & Larson, R. (1984). *Being Adolescent.* New York: Basic Books.

Curtis, N.M., Roman, K.R., & Borduin, C.M. (2004). Multisystemic treatment: A meta-analysis of outcome studies. *Journal of Family Psychology, 18,* 411–419.

Dick, D.M., Latendresse, S.J., Lansford, J.E., Budde, J.P., Goate, A., Dodge, K.A., Pettit, G.S., & Bates, J.E. (2009). The role of GABRA2 in trajectories of externalizing behavior across development and evidence of moderation by parental monitoring. *Archives of General Psychiatry, 66,* 649–657.

Dishion, T.J. (1990). The family ecology of boys' peer relations in middle childhood. *Child Development, 61,* 874–892.

Dishion, T.J., Dodge, K.A., & Lansford, J.E. (2006). Findings and recommendations: A blueprint to minimize deviant peer influence in youth interventions and programs. In K.A. Dodge, T.J. Dishion, & J.E. Lansford (Eds.), *Deviant Peer Influences in Programs for Youth: Problems and Solutions* (pp. 366–394). New York: Guilford Press.

Elder, G.H. (Ed.) (1985). *Life Course Dynamics: Trajectories and Transitions, 1968–1980.* Ithaca, NY: Cornell University Press.

Elliott, D.S., Huizinga, D., & Ageton, S.S. (1985). *Explaining Delinquency and Drug Use.* Beverly Hills, CA: Sage Publications.

Elliott, D.S., & Menard, S. (1996). Delinquent friends and delinquent behavior: temporal and developmental patterns. In D.J. Hawkins (Ed.), *Delinquency and Crime: Current Theories* (pp. 28–67). New York: Cambridge University Press.

Erickson, M.L. (1971). The group context of delinquent behavior. *Social Problems, 19,* 114–129.

Farrington, D.P. (1986). Age and crime. In M. Tonry, & N. Morris (eds.) *Crime and Justice: An Annual Review of Research* (pp. 189–250). Chicago, IL: University of Chicago Press.

Farrington, D.P. (2005). The integrated cognitive antisocial potential (ICAP) theory. *Integrated Developmental and Life-course Theories of Offending, 14,* 73–92.

Felson, M. (2002). *Crime and Everyday Life: Insights and Implications for Society.* Thousand Oaks, CA: Pine Forge Press.

Gardner, M., & Steinberg, L. (2005). Peer influence on risk taking, risk preference, and risky decision making in adolescence and adulthood: An experimental study. *Developmental Psychology, 41* (4), 625–635.

Gifford-Smith, M.E., & Brownell, C.A. (2003). Childhood peer relationships: Social acceptance, friendships, and peer networks. *Journal of School Psychology, 41* (4), 235–284.

Giordano, P. (1995). A wider circle of friends in adolescence. *American Journal of Sociology, 101* (3), 661–697.

Giordano, P.C., Cernkovich, S.A., & Pugh, M.D. (1986). Friendships and delinquency. *American Journal of Sociology, 91,* 1170–1202.

Glueck, S., & Glueck, E. (1950). *Unraveling Juvenile Delinquency.* Cambridge, MA: Harvard University Press.

Gold, M. (1970). *Delinquent Behavior in an American City*. Belmont, CA: Brooks/Cole Publishing Company.

Gottfredson, M.R., & Hirschi, T. (1990). *A General Theory of Crime*. Stanford, CA: Stanford University Press.

Granic, I., & Patterson, G.R. (2006). Towards a comprehensive model of antisocial development: A dynamic systems approach. *Psychological Bulletin, 113*, 101–131.

Granovetter, M.S. (1973) The strength of weak ties. *American Journal of Sociology, 78*, 1360–1380.

Hawdon, J.E. (1999). Daily routines and crime using routine activities as measures of Hirschi's involvement. *Youth & Society, 30(4)*, 395–415.

Haynie, D.L. (2001). Delinquent peers revisited: Does network structure matter? *American Journal of Sociology, 106*, 1013–1057.

Haynie, D.L. (2002). Friendship networks and delinquency: The relative nature of peer delinquency. *Journal of Quantitative Criminology, 18*, 99–134.

Haynie, D.L., & Osgood, D.W. (2005). Reconsidering peers and delinquency: How do peers matter? *Social Forces, 84(2)*, 1109–1130.

Hirschi, T. (1969). *Causes of Delinquency*. Berkeley, CA: University of California Press

Jaccard, J., Blanton, H., & Dodge, T. (2005). Peer influences on risk behavior: An analysis of the effects of a close friend. *Developmental Psychology, 41* (1), 135–147.

Jussim, L., & Osgood, D.W. (1989). Influence and similarity among friends: An integrative model applied to incarcerated adolescents. *Social Psychology Quarterly, 52*, 98–112.

Kiesner, J., Kerr, M., & Stattin, H. (2004). "Very important persons" in adolescence: going beyond in-school, single friendships in the study of peer homophily. *Journal of Adolescence, 27*(5), 545–560.

Kreager, D.A. (2004). Strangers in the halls: Isolation and delinquency in school networks. *Social Forces, 83*, 351–390.

Kreager, D.A., Rulison, K., & Moody, J. (2011). Delinquency and the structure of adolescent peer groups. *Criminology, 49*(1), 95–127.

Krohn, M.D. (1986). The web of conformity: A network approach to the explanation of delinquent behavior. *Social Problems, 33*, 601–613.

Krohn, M.D., Lizotte, A.J., & Perez, C.M. (1997). The interrelationship between substance use and precocious transitions to adult statuses. *Journal of Health and Social Behavior, 87–103*.

Krohn, M.D., Massey, J., & Zielinski, M. (1988). Role overlap, network multiplexity, and adolescent deviant behavior. *Social Psychology Quarterly, 51*(4), 346–356.

Krohn, M., & Thornberry, T. (1993). Network theory: A model for understanding drug abuse among African-American and Hispanic youth. In M.R. De La Rosa, & A. Juan- Luis Recio (Eds.), *Drug Abuse Among Minority Youth: Advances in Research and Methodology*. NIDA Research Monograph 130, US Department of Health and Human Services.

Laub, J.H., & Sampson, R.J. (1993). Turning points in the life course: Why change matters to the study of crime. *Criminology, 313*, 301–325.

Laub, J.H., & Sampson, R.J. (2001). Understanding desistance from crime. *Crime and Justice, 1–69*.

Matsueda, R.L., & Anderson, K. (1998). The dynamics of delinquent peers and delinquent behavior. *Criminology, 36*, 269–308.

McGloin, J.M., & Piquero, A. (2010). On the relationship between co-offending network redundancy and offending versatility. *Journal of Research on Crime and Delinquency, 47*, 63–90.

Moffitt, T.E. (1993). Adolescence-limited and life-course-persistent antisocial behavior: A developmental taxonomy. *Psychological Review, 100*, 674–701.

National Research Council. (2013). *Reforming Juvenile Justice: A Developmental Approach.* Committee on Assessing Juvenile Justice Reform, R.J. Bonnie, R.L. Johnson, B.M. Chemers, & J.A. Schuck (Eds.), Committee on Law and Justice, Division of Behavioral and Social Sciences and Education. Washington, DC: National Academies Press.

Nye, F.I., Short, J.F., & Olson, V.J. (1958) Socioeconomic status and delinquent behavior. In F.I. Nye (Ed.), *Family Relationships and Delinquent Behavior* (pp. 23–33). New York: John Wiley & Sons, Ltd.

Osgood, D.W., & Anderson, A.L. (2004). Unstructured socializing and rates of delinquency. *Criminology, 42* (3), 519–550.

Osgood, D.W., Anderson, A.L. & Shaffer, J.N. (2005). Unstructured Leisure in the After-School Hours. In J.L. Mahoney, R.W. Larson, & J.S. Eccles (Eds.) *Organized Activities as Contexts of Development: Extracurricular Activities, After-School and Community Programs* (pp. 45–64). Mahwah, NJ: Lawrence Erlbaum.

Osgood, D.W., Wilson, J.K., O'Malley, P.M., Bachman, J.G., & Johnston, L.D. (1996). Routine activities and individual deviant behavior. *American Sociological Review, 61*, 635–655.

Pabon, E., Rodriguez, O., & Gurin, G. (1992). Clarifying peer relations and delinquency. *Youth & Society, 24*, 149–165.

Parke, R.D., Burks, V., Carson, J., Neville, B., & Boyum, L. (1994). Family-peer relationships: A tripartite model. In R.D. Parke, & S. Kellam (Eds.), *Exploring Family Relationships with Other Social Contexts* (pp. 115–140). Hillsdale, NJ: Lawrence Erlbaum Associates.

Patterson, G.R. (1982). *Coercive Family Process.* Eugene, OR: Castalia.

Payne, D.C., & Cornwell, B. (2007). Reconsidering peer influences on delinquency: Do less proximate contacts matter? *Journal of Quantitative Criminology, 23*, 127–149.

Pratt, T.P., Cullen, F.T., Sellers, C.S., Winfree, T.J., Madensen, T.D., Daigle, L.E., Fearn, N.E., & Gau, J.M. (2010). The empirical status of social learning theory: A meta-analysis. *Justice Quarterly, 27*(6), 765–802.

Quinton, D., Pickles, A., Maughan, B., & Rutter, M. (1993). Partners, peers, and pathways: Assortive pairing and continuities in conduct disorder. *Development and Psychopathology, 5*, 763–783.

Rees, C., & Pogarsky, G. (2011). One bad apple may not spoil the whole bunch: Best friends and adolescent delinquency. *Journal of Quantitative Criminology, 27*, 197–233.

Reiss Jr, A.J., (1986). Co-offender influences on criminal careers. In A. Blumstein, J. Cohen, J. Roth, & C. Visher (Eds.), *Criminal Careers and Career Criminals* (pp. 121–160). Washington, DC: National Academy Press.

Reiss Jr, A.J., & Farrington, D.P. (1991). Advancing knowledge about co-offending: Results from a prospective longitudinal survey of London males. *Journal of Criminal Law & Criminology, 82*, 360–395.

Scott, E.S., & Steinberg, L.D. (2010). *Rethinking Juvenile Justice.* Cambridge, MA: Harvard University Press.

Shaw, C.R., & McKay, H.D. (1931). *Report on the Causes of Crime: Volume 2. Social Factors in Juvenile Delinquency.* Washington, DC: National Commission on Law Observance and Enforcement.

Short, J.F., Jr. (1957). Differential association and delinquency. *Social Problems, 5*, 233–239.

Simonoff, E., Elander, J., Holmshow, J., Pickles, A., Murray, R., & Rutter, M. (2004). Predictor of antisocial personality: Continuities from childhood to adult life. *British Journal of Psychiatry, 184,* 118–127.

Steinberg, L., & Monahan, K.C. (2007). Age differences in resistance to peer influence. *Developmental Psychology, 43* (6), 1531–1543.

Sutherland, E.H. (1947). *Principles of Criminology,* 4th ed. Philadelphia, PA: Lippincott.

Thornberry, T. (1987). Toward an interactional theory of delinquency. *Criminology, 25,* 863–891.

Thornberry, T.P., & Krohn, M.D. (2005). Applying interactional theory to the explanation of continuity and change in antisocial behavior. In D.P. Farrington (Ed.), *Integrated Developmental and Life-course Theories of Offending* (pp. 183–209). New Brunswick, NJ: Transaction.

Thrasher, F.M. (1927). *The Gang.* Chicago: University of Chicago Press.

Valente, T., Gallaher, P., & Mouttapa, M. (2004). Using social networks to understand and prevent substance use: A transdisciplinary perspective. *Substance Use & Misuse, 39,* 1685–1712.

Warr, M. (1993). Parents, deers, and delinquency. *Social Forces, 72,* 247–264.

Warr, M. (1996). Organization and instigation in delinquent groups. *Criminology, 34,* 11–37.

Warr, M. (1998). Life-course transitions and desistance from crime. *Criminology, 36,* 183–216.

Warr, M. (2002). *Companions in Crime: The Social Aspects of Criminal Conduct.* Cambridge: Cambridge University Press.

Warr, M. (2005). Making delinquent friends: Adult supervision and children's affiliations. *Criminology, 43,* 77–106.

Weerman, F.M., & Bijleveld, C.C. (2007). Birds of different feathers: school networks of serious delinquent, minor delinquent and non-delinquent boys and girls. *European Journal of Criminology, 4,* 357–383.

Weerman, F., & Smeenk, W.H. (2005). Peer similarity in delinquency for different types of friends: a comparison using two measurement models. *Criminology, 43,* 499–524.

Weiss, B., Caron, A., Ball, S., Tapp, J., Johnson, M., & Weisz, J.R. (2005). Iatrogenic effects of group treatment for antisocial youth. *Journal of Consulting and Clinical Psychology, 73,* 1036–1044.

15

Neighborhoods and Delinquent Behavior

Susan McNeeley and Pamela Wilcox

The influence of neighborhoods on delinquency has been an enduring part of American criminology. Nonetheless, there is no single unifying theory of neighborhood effects. Instead, multiple perspectives exist. Competing perspectives highlight diverse mechanisms operating at the neighborhood level to produce delinquency, including three processes that will be the focus of this review: (1) weak institutional control, (2) general strain, and (3) cultural prescription. We first review the origins of theory supporting these three neighborhood-level mechanisms, we describe important contemporary revisions to these original theoretical statements, and we take stock of each theoretical perspective by providing an overview of empirical support from recent literature. In short, the first part of the chapter focuses on what we currently know regarding neighborhood's role in delinquency. Then we shift focus and describe several unresolved issues with respect to neighborhood-level influence, thus presenting an agenda for future research on the neighborhood–delinquency relationship.

Neighborhoods and Delinquency: From Past to Present

The Chicago School and the social ecology of juvenile delinquency

Delinquency theories related to neighborhood effects are based, in part, on the concentric zone theory that was established during the formative years of American criminology (Park, Burgess, & McKenzie, 1925). This theory maintains that the competition for scarce resources – especially land – leads to spatial differentiation of

The Handbook of Juvenile Delinquency and Juvenile Justice, First Edition. Edited by Marvin D. Krohn and Jodi Lane.

urban areas into zones. The "zone of transition", or the area surrounding the central business district, contains the manufacturing industry available in the city as well as low-priced housing available for rent. The subsequent outer zones are residential, with the quality (and therefore the price) of housing increasing with distance from the city center. In a process known as "invasion and succession", the central business district undergoes expansion, and residents and businesses move away from the center of the city into more desirable areas in the outer zones. This results in high residential turnover in the zone of transition, as it is mainly occupied by immigrants or other poor workers who move to better parts of the city when they are able to do so. According to this theory, undesirable outcomes – such as unemployment or crime – are likely to be clustered in the transitional zone.

In their classic work, *Juvenile Delinquency and Urban Areas*, Clifford Shaw and Henry McKay (1942) mapped the home addresses of juvenile delinquents in Chicago in order to determine the spatial distribution of crime. In line with concentric zone theory, the results of their study demonstrated a concentration of juvenile offenders in certain parts of the city, especially in the inner city. High-delinquency neighborhoods were characterized by distinct social ecological characteristics, including high rates of poverty, ethnic heterogeneity, and residential instability. Importantly, communities with these characteristics had high rates of juvenile delinquents regardless of the ethnic group or groups that resided in the area, thus emphasizing that delinquency was influenced by neighborhood conditions.

Shaw and McKay also attempted to explain *how* the aforementioned neighborhood characteristics affected delinquency. They argued that the neighborhood disadvantage indicated by poverty, heterogeneity, and instability created delinquency in three ways: by weakening informal social control; by causing residents to experience strain due to poverty and relative deprivation; and by creating and maintaining criminogenic subcultures. Hence, Shaw and McKay's theory of delinquency was a "mixed model" in that it offered multiple explanations for the relationship between social ecological characteristics of neighborhoods and their rates of delinquency. In her seminal work, *Social Sources of Delinquency* (1978), Ruth Kornhauser criticized Shaw and McKay's mixed-model approach to delinquency and suggested a reformulation of the theory into what has become known as the systemic model of social disorganization. Drawing upon Kornhauser's appraisal, the systemic model removes two of the original causal mechanisms discussed by Shaw and McKay – cultural transmission and strain – and focuses exclusively on the role of community social systems that prevent crime through informal social control. Thus, Kornhauser reinvented Shaw and McKay's theory into a "pure" community-level control theory of delinquency, whereby neighborhood-level poverty, heterogeneity, and mobility increased rates of crime via weakened systemic control. Due partly to Kornhauser's work, the three intervening mechanisms originally offered by Shaw and McKay have thus developed as three distinct theoretical traditions regarding neighborhood effects on crime and delinquency. Each of these theories will be discussed in separate sections below, with attention given to the historical development and empirical support associated with each tradition.

Social disorganization theory: weak community-based control

As indicated above, Shaw and McKay suggested that one explanation for the correlation between delinquency and indicators of neighborhood disadvantage, including low socio-economic status, ethnic heterogeneity, and residential instability, was the effect of these factors on social systems within the neighborhood. For instance, high population turnover was presumed to result in changes in characteristics of the population (e.g., class, race/ethnicity), which devitalized community organizations, leaving little social support for residents of the community. In addition, residential instability was thought to weaken the social networks between residents and reduce residents' concern about the community. With residents planning to move quickly, the establishment of relational ties and community attachment was simply unlikely. Ethnic heterogeneity was also presumed to undermine social networks and community cohesion, as cultural differences acted as barriers against forming social relationships.

Shaw and McKay suggested that the weak social systems in disadvantaged communities prevented residents from maintaining order within the neighborhood. Simply put, the lack of strong social networks and neighborhood institutions compromised effective supervision of juveniles, which allowed youth to begin and maintain criminal careers. Weak systemic control thus fostered high rates of crime and deviance in transitional communities. Because the social characteristics behind weak control occurred persistently in the same areas (the zone of transition), Shaw and McKay observed stability in high-crime areas over time.

Despite their discussion of the importance of weak neighborhood systems of control, Shaw and McKay did not actually measure this process quantitatively. Initial tests of the mechanism of neighborhood-based systemic control came years after their path-breaking work. These tests were often conducted using a small number of neighborhoods, but findings looked promising nonetheless. For instance, a classic study by Maccoby, Johnson, and Church (1958) compared a high-delinquency area with a low-delinquency neighborhood in Cambridge, Massachusetts. They found that the low-delinquency neighborhood had higher community integration in terms of (1) neighbors knowing one another by name, (2) willingness for neighbors to borrow items from one another, (3) perceived common interests among neighbors, and (4) shared positive sentiments about the neighborhood. In addition, Simcha-Fagan and Schwartz's (1986) study of 12 New York City neighborhoods revealed that residents' participation in community organizations was an important predictor of self-reported and officially recorded delinquency.

Most scholars consider the first rigorous test of the full systemic model of social disorganization as Robert Sampson and W. Byron Groves' study, published in 1989. Using data from the British Crime Survey (BCS), Sampson and Groves found that the effects of poverty, ethnic heterogeneity, residential instability, and female-headed households on victimization were substantially mediated by sparse friendship networks, unsupervised teenage peer groups, and low organization participation. These findings supported the systemic model's assumption that neighborhood characteristics affect crime (particularly measured as victimization rates) through their impact on social networks within the community. These results were replicated using later waves of BCS data, adding additional support for the systemic model (Lowenkamp, Cullen, & Pratt, 2003).

Despite significant support for the systemic model, a number of other studies have found that social ties within communities do not always affect crime rates in expected ways. For example, research indicates that social ties among neighbors do not have to be strong to reduce crime; weak ties may have preventative capacity as well (see Bellair, 1997). Further, not all types of social ties appear to affect crime. Wilcox Rountree and Warner (1999), for instance, found that social ties among women in the community reduced crime, while social ties among male residents were not as important in differentiating between high- and low-crime areas. Other work indicates that, rather than reducing crime, strong social ties may actually inhibit informal social control in certain situations. For example, Patillo's (1998) ethnographic study of black middle-class communities in Chicago demonstrated that criminal networks are often highly integrated into the community and may perform important tasks within the neighborhood (see also Warner & Wilcox Rountree, 1997). Due to this familiarity with the neighborhood's criminal element, community members are often unable to effectively disrupt criminal activity.

In short, while the systemic model of social disorganization theory received initial empirical support, numerous studies have since revealed only modest or conditional support. This situation has led to recent refinement to the theory, including attention to the concept of "collective efficacy" in lieu of "systemic ties". Sampson, Raudenbush, and Earls (1997) presented the concept of collective efficacy, which includes two components: (1) the community's level of mutual trust and cohesion (which is only *partly* related to social ties, as trust can occur without strong relational networks); and (2) residents' willingness to intervene for the collective good (i.e., in order to stop undesirable behavior). Rather than assuming that crime is more effectively controlled when social ties are strong (per the systemic model), collective efficacy theory focuses more explicitly on the extent to which community members can and would collectively activate control in situations involving delinquency. Collective efficacy is expected to be lower in disadvantaged neighborhoods due to the effects that racial and economic isolation and residential instability have on feelings of powerlessness, causing residents of disadvantaged neighborhoods to be unlikely to feel that they can unite to solve problems in their communities.

In addition to introducing collective efficacy theory as a revision to the idea of systemic control, Sampson and colleagues (1997) tested the theory through analysis of 343 neighborhood clusters in Chicago. They found that collective efficacy was a significant predictor of violent crime rates; it also mediated much of the effect of neighborhood socio-economic characteristics on crime. Other research on the effect of collective efficacy demonstrates that communities with high levels of collective efficacy experience lower rates of crime and victimization incidents (Browning & Dietz, 2004; Morenoff, Sampson, & Raudenbush, 2001; Pratt & Cullen, 2005).

Finally, limited research has also shown support for the effects of collective efficacy on self-reported delinquent behavior (Kirk, 2009; Wikstrom, 2011).

Strain theory

Another possible explanation for the concentration of delinquency within disadvantaged communities is the experience of strain – or the frustration felt as a result of an inability to achieve traditional measures of success. As already mentioned, Shaw and McKay (1942) argued that residents of disadvantaged neighborhoods were susceptible to experiencing poverty-related strain. It was posited by Shaw and McKay that residents of such neighborhoods would turn to crime due to the lack of opportunities to achieve legitimate success. Therefore, differences in crime rates across neighborhoods could be due to the abundance of individuals experiencing strain within disadvantaged communities.

Though incorporated into Shaw and McKay's explanation of delinquency, strain theory actually began with the work of Robert Merton (1938), who argued that the "American dream" of achieving financial success is valued more greatly than are the means used to succeed. Because some segments of the population are unable to meet this goal legitimately, individuals begin to place even less value on the legitimate means of obtaining success. This can result in delinquency; individuals respond by rejecting traditional means of success in favor of illegitimate opportunities that are more readily available to them, such as crime.

This idea was later extended in strain-subculture models, put forth by scholars such as Albert Cohen (1955) and Richard Cloward and Lloyd Ohlin (1960) to explain delinquency in the context of juvenile gangs. According to Cohen, working- and lower-class boys had difficulty achieving success in the traditional (i.e., middle-class) sense, thus resulting in problems of adjustment and status frustration. Cohen suggested that there was a collective response to the status frustration experienced by disadvantaged boys. The strained youth rejected middle-class values and established a subculture with goals and values that were the antithesis of middle-class culture, thus creating gangs of boys that favored deviant values. Cloward and Ohlin (1960) also indicated that strained working- and lower-class youth turned to subcultures for the alleviation of status frustration. However, Cloward and Ohlin (1960) noted the presence of distinct types of subcultures. They observed that some gangs provided members with alternative (illegal) means to financial success (i.e., criminal gangs). Others gangs emphasized violence as a means of status enhancement (i.e., conflict gangs), and still others downplayed the search for status altogether and emphasized societal withdrawal through drug use (i.e., retreatist gangs). According to Cloward and Ohlin, strained youths' access to criminal, conflict, or retreatist gangs depended on neighborhood organization. Long-standing, interwoven networks of adult and juvenile criminals within some disadvantaged neighborhoods supported the existence of criminal gangs that could provide illegitimate opportunities for financial success to frustrated juveniles. Other neighborhoods could not support such networks, and thus offered strained youth little opportunity for financial success, legitimately or illegitimately. Such neighborhoods often offered conflict and retreatist gangs instead.

Although ideas about strain from Merton, Shaw and McKay, Cohen, and Cloward and Ohlin served as an early foundation for the strain theoretical tradition, most contemporary strain models of delinquency rely upon a version of the theory referred to as *general strain theory* (GST). GST extends the work of early strain theorists by describing sources of strain beyond blocked success goals (especially financial success), and it more clearly identifies factors that lead those who experience strain to engage in crime.

GST, posited by Robert Agnew (1992), identifies three types of strain. In addition to blocked goals, criminogenic strain can be caused by either a removal of positive stimuli or the presence of negative or aversive stimuli. An individual will experience strain after the removal (or threat of removal) of positive stimuli; this strain can encourage the individual to turn to criminal behavior in order to prevent the loss of valued items, retrieve the items, seek revenge for the loss, or express negative emotions after the loss. The presence of negative stimuli can also lead to criminality as the strained individual attempts to escape from or terminate a negative experience, seek revenge or express frustration, or cope with emotions that arise as a result of negative stimuli.

GST also identifies a range of factors that would mediate between strain and delinquent behavior. Agnew suggests that many variables posited by other criminological theories affect crime indirectly by influencing those individuals who experience strain. These variables include low self-control, previous learning conducive to criminal behavior, antisocial associates, and internalization of attitudes favorable to crime. Agnew also focuses on emotions, specifically anger, theorizing that strain accompanied by anger is likely to cause crime.

Agnew (1999) later presented *a macro-level strain theory (MST)* in which general strain is applied to neighborhood-level crime rates in several ways. First, strain theory expects crime rates to vary across neighborhoods due to the selection and retention of individuals who are experiencing strain, which creates a compositional effect. Individuals who are under economic strain are likely to move into disadvantaged neighborhoods and are likely to lack opportunities to move out of such neighborhoods. Second, neighborhood disadvantage contributes to financial strain, increasing delinquency among residents. In disadvantaged communities, individuals are likely to value certain goals, most notably monetary success, status or respect, and non-discriminatory treatment. However, in these communities, legitimate opportunities to achieve these goals are not readily available. This failure to achieve goals leads some people to turn to delinquency. Similarly, feelings of relative deprivation – which may lead to crime – are more likely to be experienced in disadvantaged communities, as they are often located near more affluent areas.

Additionally, Agnew argues that certain neighborhood characteristics function as strain-inducing negative stimuli. Specifically, disadvantaged neighborhoods are likely to contain individuals undergoing economic deprivation and family disruption, which are negative experiences that qualify as strain. Agnew also argues that community rates of crime and disorder affect strain, further contributing to delinquency. Community crime can cause strain directly; victimization can be a serious source of strain that has been linked to later delinquency. The effect can also be indirect; community crime rates cause outmigration of economically stable residents, which leads to a concentration of residents who experience strain and therefore are at risk for delinquency. Similarly, signs of incivilities – such as litter, graffiti, abandoned buildings, and the presence of gangs – can be negative for residents of these communities, creating strain that may lead to delinquent behavior.

In addition to *creating strain*, Agnew suggested that neighborhood characteristics may *condition the likelihood of responding to strain* with delinquency. For example, residents of disadvantaged communities spend more time with each other in public and are more likely to be interested in the personal affairs of other residents due to the devaluing of other markers of moral character, such as educational attainment. Because of the public nature of these communities, one's aversive experiences are likely to be known to others, which increases the frustration associated with these experiences and necessitates a response to the problem that is public or known to others. Another characteristic that conditions the response to strain is collective efficacy. Because disadvantaged neighborhoods tend to have lower levels of collective efficacy, residents are less able to legitimately cope with problems as a community, increasing the necessity of turning to delinquency to deal with strain. Similarly, the weak social networks characteristic of some disadvantaged communities leads to a lack of social support, which is important for channeling strain through prosocial avenues. Finally, these neighborhoods contain more opportunities for crime than do more affluent communities. Community members are more inclined to allow justification for delinquent behavior, and the presence of criminal peers in the neighborhood may facilitate the use of delinquency in order to cope with strain.

Studies testing Agnew's MST have provided mixed support. Wareham *et al.* (2005) conducted a multi-level study of high school students clustered within neighborhoods to test Agnew's argument that community characteristics contribute to individual-level strain. In their research, adverse neighborhood conditions were only likely to contribute to strain in less disadvantaged neighborhoods. Using a sample of adults, Warner and Fowler (2003) examined the relationships between neighborhood disadvantage and stability, community levels of strain, and violent crime rates in 66 neighborhoods in two cities. In accordance with Agnew's predictions, neighborhood disadvantage and residential stability affected community levels of strain. In turn, the amount of strain experienced in the community was related to higher rates of violence.

Scholars have also tested Agnew's arguments regarding whether neighborhood characteristics condition the effect of strain on delinquency. As Agnew predicted, strain is more likely to lead to delinquent behavior in certain communities than in others. Hoffman (2003) tested this idea by examining the interaction between individual monetary strain and neighborhood characteristics, such as urbanicity. In that study, monetary strain was only a significant predictor of juvenile delinquency in urban communities, supporting Agnew's theory regarding the differential effects of strain across neighborhoods. Similarly, some research indicates that stressful life events are more consequential in communities with high rates of male unemployment. For example, Warner and Fowler (2003) showed that community-level strain is likely to lead to violence in neighborhoods with low levels of social support, but not those with high levels of social support (but see Wareham *et al.*, 2005).

Subcultural theory

Recall that Shaw and McKay argued that criminal subgroups holding oppositional values would emerge in disadvantaged communities, with adults encouraging youths to adopt deviant values and teaching them the techniques necessary to engage in certain forms of delinquency. Case studies tracing the development of youths' delinquent careers (e.g., Shaw, 1930) showed that juveniles were often drawn into crime through association with older youths (such as siblings or friends). In turn, they later became delinquent "role models" for younger adolescents. This allowed for the maintenance of a "criminal tradition" within the neighborhood. Consistent with the life histories emerging from Shaw and McKay's studies, a number of early criminological theorists believed that criminal participation stemmed in part from adherence to oppositional subcultures that prized involvement in violence or delinquency rather than traditional measures of success or respect. According to these early subcultural theories, groups that held oppositional values viewed such behavior as appropriate or ideal rather than deviant.

For example, according to Cohen's (1955) strain-subculture theory, juveniles adopted oppositional values in response to a perception that they were unable to obtain social status according to the "middle-class measuring rod", which emphasizes academic achievement, delayed gratification, and financial success. Cohen argued that youth who did not "measure up" rejected traditional goals and turned to deviant subcultural values in a process known as reaction formation. This process relieved frustration over the inability to achieve success according to mainstream values, as social status was able to be attained using another set of (subcultural) rules. According to Cloward and Ohlin (1960), this process of turning to deviant subcultures in response to strain occurred disproportionately in disadvantaged neighborhoods, as such communities allow few legitimate opportunities but often offer illegitimate means of obtaining financial goals by way of established criminal networks. Cloward and Ohlin suggested that, in neighborhoods without a strong criminal tradition, youth may respond to their frustration by forming gangs that promote violence as positive achievement or by engaging in self-destructive forms of deviance, such as drug use.

Other early subculture theorists maintained that criminogenic values were a product of lower-class culture itself. For example, Walter B. Miller's lower-class culture theory (1958) suggested that urban delinquency arises due to "focal concerns" held by inner-city groups. According to Miller, the focal concerns held by lower-class groups include trouble, toughness, smartness (referring not to knowledge of a particular field but rather to the ability to outsmart or "dupe" others), luck, and autonomy. These goals manifest in an emphasis placed on physical prowess, the excitement that is characteristic of street life, and freedom from authority, including that held by parents, teachers, and employers. Following this theory, delinquent gangs offer a number of benefits for lower-class youth, including (1) a sense of "belonging" that they may lack due to the disorganized nature of their communities, and (2) the opportunity to gain desirable reputations within the community by demonstrating the characteristics – such as toughness and smartness – that are emphasized in lower-class culture.

The early subcultural theories described above have largely fallen out of favor, yet cultural influence remains an important part of understanding neighborhood effects in modern-day criminology. Important contemporary work on the influence of neighborhood culture includes Elijah Anderson's *Code of the Street*. Published in 1999, this impactful work explores, first, the effect of structural characteristics on culture. According to Anderson, the lack of upward mobility and the isolation from social and legal institutions in disadvantaged neighborhoods has caused some residents to reject traditional methods of achieving success, resolving conflict, and maintaining order. Instead, they turn to the code of the street, which encourages aggressive and violent behavior as a strategy for obtaining success and exerting social control within the community.

Following the street code, respect – which is necessary to demonstrate one's dominance and status – becomes the predominant capital in these neighborhoods. Ultimately, Anderson argues that the campaign for respect leads to violence in disadvantaged neighborhoods. Respect is important for mainstream society as well; however, traditional methods of obtaining respect – such as earning money legitimately, forming and providing for a family, and joining local organizations – are withheld from individuals living in communities marked by concentrated disadvantage. Therefore, some members of impoverished communities reject these indicators of status and seek new strategies for earning respect and prestige from the code of the street, which prescribes violence and sexual prowess as means of obtaining respect. Because respect is so highly valued, it is vital that one does not lose it by failing to respond appropriately to perceived slights. According to the code of the street, an individual must respond to any insult or expression of disrespect in order to maintain his or her status. Failure to deal aggressively with anyone who behaves disrespectfully may label one as a "chump" and show others that he is an easy target for future victimization. Therefore, the code of the street encourages violence and aggression as prescribed methods of dealing with insults or disrespect in order to maintain one's reputation as being tough and not to be messed with.

To date, much of the research on the effects of a "code of the street" has been done at the individual level. This research has shown that individual beliefs related to the code of the street, specifically pertaining to the use of violence as a source of respect, are a significant predictor of violent behavior and aggression in children and adolescents (e.g., Brezina, Agnew, Cullen, & Wright, 2004; Stewart & Simons, 2006).

Further, such attitudes partially mediate the effect of socio-economic characteristics on violent delinquency. In addition to affecting violent behavior, values in line with the street code have been found to be associated with other forms of delinquency, including gun-carrying, drug dealing, and substance use (Allen & Lo, 2010; McGrath, Marcum, & Copes 2012).

Limited work on the contextual influence of street code on crime has found that neighborhood-level subculture is a significant predictor of offending, above and beyond the effects of individual-level violent values. For example, Stewart and Simons (2010) found that neighborhood subculture had an independent effect on violent delinquency after controlling for other community and individual factors.

Looking to the Future: An Agenda for Neighborhood Studies

Each of the three theoretical traditions reviewed above has been invaluable in helping to understand how neighborhoods influence delinquency. As suggested by our review, each tradition has undergone theoretical refinement over the years. In short, we have come a long way since the foundational work of Shaw and McKay, Merton, Cohen, Cloward and Ohlin, and Miller. We now speak of neighborhood influence in terms of Sampson *et al*.'s (1997) collective efficacy theory, Agnew's (1999) macro-level strain theory, and Anderson's (1999) code of the street thesis. Each of these contemporary perspectives has spawned empirical tests that have yielded supportive results. However, new challenges to these theoretical traditions continually surface, and the current generation of delinquency researchers will need to tackle these dilemmas in order to keep the traditions fresh and relevant. While the challenges facing delinquency research in the social disorganization, strain, and subcultural traditions are numerous, we choose to focus here on three issues that affect each tradition: (1) the challenge in defining "neighborhood" and in accounting for multiple, embedded, and overlapping contextual forms; (2) the need to address the new face of immigration and its changing impact on neighborhood processes related to delinquency; and (3) the need to unpack developmental versus situational effects of neighborhoods.

What is "neighborhood?"

A consistent thorn in the side of neighborhood-level theorists has been the issue of defining and operationalizing "neighborhood" – the very unit of social life at which crime-causing processes purportedly operate. Despite the long history of theory and research on neighborhood processes in delinquency, this fundamental issue is still described as the "bedeviling challenge faced by all studies of neighborhood effects" (Hipp & Boessen, 2013, p. 287).

Many neighborhood theorists, either implicitly or explicitly, embrace a conceptualization of neighborhood similar to that offered recently by Sampson (2012); that is, a neighborhood is "a geographical section of a larger community or region (e.g., city) that usually contains residents or institutions and has socially distinctive characteristics" (p. 56). A typical approach to operationalizing this conceptualization of neighborhood – and the approach used by many studies cited throughout this chapter – is to use census tracts, clusters of tracts, or areas similar to clusters of tracts (i.e., zip codes, or political districts). While such "administrative units" seem rather arbitrary on the surface, these units are also theoretically relevant; they are typically created with geographic features (e.g., streets, parks) and "social distinctiveness" in mind. Nonetheless, criticism of this sort of conceptualization and operationalization of "neighborhood" influence has come from several distinct fronts.

First, a subset of criminologists have led a charge to focus on micro-geographic, sub-neighborhood units of analysis for the study of processes such as social disorganization (e.g., Taylor, 1998; Weisburd, Groff, & Yang, 2012). Advocates of this micro-spatial approach point to discernible *within-neighborhood* clusters of crime, suggesting the importance of *immediate* settings for understanding crime (e.g., Sherman, Gartin, & Buerger 1989). These "crime and place" scholars suggest that focusing on neighborhoods (such as those defined by census tracts or clusters of tracts) "can lead the researcher to miss variability within those larger units that is important to understanding the development of crime" (Weisburd *et al.*, 2012, p. 23). Simply put, neighborhoods such as those conceptualized by Sampson (2012) are considered "too big" a unit of analysis, and sub-neighborhood "places", such as street segments or specific addresses, are deemed more appropriate. According to crime and place scholars, units such as blocks or street segments are more clearly defined and easily recognized, and they represent a key behavioral setting for many of the processes key to neighborhood theories, including informal social control and public displays of street codes.

Second, aided by advances in software that allow for the mapping of relational networks, another group of "social networks scholars" have increasingly called for "neighborhood" to be defined in terms of relational ties rather than non-overlapping geographic boundaries (Hipp, Faris, & Boessen, 2012). Third, other research has shown that geographic areas in spatial proximity to one another appear interdependent when it comes to crime. In other words, it is not just the characteristics of a particular "neighborhood" (however operationalized) that affects its rate of crime. Due to processes of concentrated disadvantage and spatial diffusion, the characteristics of a neighborhood's neighbors matter as well (Morenoff, Sampson, & Raudenbush, 2001; Sampson, 2012; Wilson, 1987). In this sense, the *broader* contexts in which neighborhoods are situated are also important units.

Collectively, these various works – including crime and place research, social networks research, and research on spatially proximal neighborhood effects – have created a complex picture. It is a picture in which "neighborhoods" consist of multiple embedded and/or overlapping interdependent contexts (see also Kirk, 2009). As Sampson (2012, p. 55) summarizes, "neighborhoods are both chosen and allocated; defined by outsiders and insiders alike, often in contradistinction to each other; they are both symbolically and structurally determined; large and small;

overlapping or blurred in perceptual boundaries; relational; and ever changing in composition." Future work could shed greater light on neighborhood effects by abandoning the "bedeviling" search for a single, optimal definition of neighborhood and embracing instead a view of embedded and overlapping neighborhood forms.

New immigrant communities

An important update of early work on neighborhoods and delinquency is the recent evidence regarding the effect of immigrant populations on community rates of crime. Early theory and research on neighborhoods and delinquency, including Shaw and McKay's study of Chicago neighborhoods, generally found that immigrant communities suffered from higher crime rates than other communities. However, more recent research demonstrates a negative relationship between proportions of immigrants and crime rates; these studies show that communities with higher proportions of immigrants have lower rates of crime. According to recent reviews, there are several theoretical explanations for this (Kubrin, 2013; McNeeley & Wilcox, 2013). First, most immigrants are not criminally motivated; they generally relocate to the US for prosocial reasons. Second, the police may focus on these areas to a greater extent than other communities due to the general public's belief that immigrant communities are criminogenic. Third, immigrant neighborhoods should have low crime rates because they are socially organized. In the early twentieth century, when Shaw and McKay's study was conducted, immigrants tended to settle in disorganized areas for short periods of time. Now, it is more common for immigrants to settle permanently in areas already inhabited by members of their ethnic group, which allows recent immigrants to obtain resources more easily (Logan, Zhang, & Alba, 2002; Portes, 1997).

As suggested by Kubrin (2013) and McNeeley and Wilcox (2013), several limitations of the current research on immigrant communities make it difficult to fully understand the relationship between immigration and crime. First, most of the existing studies have simply established correlations between the presence of immigrants in a community and crime. Because researchers generally do not test the intervening mechanisms through which immigration is expected to affect crime, the precise reasons that immigrant communities experience lower rates of crime than other communities is not clear. Therefore, more research explicitly measuring possible explanations of the effect of immigration on crime is needed. Second, most studies test for relationships at one point in time rather than conducting longitudinal analyses. Therefore, differences in crime rates between immigrant communities and other communities are not necessarily attributable to the presence of immigrants. Third, few studies have examined the possibility that there are nuanced effects of immigration on crime; for example, some studies suggest that immigration has differential effects on white, black, and Latino crime rates.

An important step for future research on the relationship between neighborhood-level effects of immigration on delinquency is the inclusion of communities in new immigrant destinations. The spatial concentration of immigrants within the US has changed considerably in the last few decades (Singer, 2004). While immigrants traditionally settled in major cities (generally in the Northeast), there have been recent increases in the immigrant populations residing in smaller cities and rural areas in the South and Midwest. However, the majority of research on immigration and crime has focused on traditional migrant poles in large cities such as New York and Chicago. It is possible that immigration influences crime differently in non-traditional immigrant locations. There is a need for research on the effect of immigration in smaller areas (as opposed to major cities) and in regions, such as the Midwest and South, in which immigrant communities have been established relatively recently. Because these areas are less accustomed to high levels of immigrants and do not have established enclaves to provide resources to recent immigrants, communities within these new immigrant destinations may be more likely to experience negative consequences due to immigration.

Neighborhood effects: developmental or situational?

Currently, there is debate in all three major theoretical traditions reviewed herein as to whether neighborhood influences on delinquency – including disorganization-related, strain-related, or subcultural influences – are *developmental* or *situational* in nature. We explore this debate for each perspective, beginning with the social disorganization tradition.

A developmental social disorganization theory would predict that weak neighborhood systemic control or weak collective efficacy influences the behavior of youth in an enduring way, such that it affects their involvement in delinquency *in any location*, including places outside the confines of the community. On the other hand, a situational social disorganization theory would predict that weak systemic control (or weak collective efficacy) only affects rates of delinquent events that occur *within the community*, regardless of whether the events are committed by neighborhood residents or by youth from other areas.

If neighborhoods exhibit developmental effects, this suggests that neighborhoods influence their residents' underlying motivations to offend. For instance, weak community-based control inhibits successful socialization of youth, thereby creating individuals with weak social bonds and an inclination towards criminality. In contrast, if neighborhoods exhibit situational effects, this suggests that some neighborhoods provide opportunistic settings for the successful commission of delinquency. For example, weak community-based control inhibits adequate supervision of youth and "management" of public space.

This distinction between developmental and situational effects is thus tied to the division between theories of criminality and theories of crime events (see, e.g., Clarke & Cornish, 1985). Is social disorganization theory a theory of criminality or one of crime events? Historically, it has been treated as one of delinquent offending, or criminality. After all, Shaw and McKay's famous work linked neighborhood conditions to rates of individual juvenile offending behavior, not community-specific rates of crime events; their maps of "delinquency" plotted home addresses of known delinquents rather than locations of crime incidents. However, contemporary tests of social disorganization theory often implicitly allow for situational effects by testing the theory through examination of the effects of neighborhood ties or collective efficacy on incident rates of crime or victimization. In fact, though disorganization scholars have not set out to differentiate developmental and situational effects, the contemporary literature seems more supportive of situational effects. Specifically, there is plenty of evidence that systemic ties and/or collective efficacy influence neighborhood rates of violent events (e.g., Bellair, 1997; Morenoff *et al.*, 2001; Sampson & Groves, 1989; Sampson *et al.*, 1997; Velez, 2001; Warner & Wilcox Rountree 1997), but the effects on individual rates of offending among neighborhood youth is less apparent (e.g., Sampson & Groves, 1989; Sampson, Morenoff, & Raudenbush, 2005; see also Sampson, 2006, for review). It is worth noting that social disorganization can potentially affect *both* criminality and opportunity for crime events (Bursik, 1988; Felson, 1994). However, a clear picture of whether it does indeed affect both has remained elusive to date.

Work in the macro-level general strain tradition has been similarly unclear as to whether the effects of living in highly disadvantaged and violent neighborhood contexts produce enduring, cumulative strain or situational strain. The same debate also affects the subcultural tradition. Are "street" behaviors actually valued by members of some communities, and thus likely to be displayed wherever their activities take them? Or are they situationally useful in public spaces within disadvantaged neighborhoods, and thus "performed" in these specific settings but not valued (i.e., internalized)? Developmental approaches would view street behavior as reflective of neighborhood values that motivate delinquency. In contrast, situational approaches would suggest that street behavior is an adaptive tool used to achieve goals or provide self-protection in particularly deprived contexts. Such situational behavioral adaptations are presumed to be rooted in neighborhood-level shared cognitions that include moral and legal cynicism. In other words, the collective does not reject mainstream values, but it views them as not particularly useful for their lives, and thus tolerates deviance (Sampson & Bean, 2006; Sampson & Jeglum-Bartusch, 1998; Sampson & Wilson, 1995).

Most contemporary work is more supportive of the idea that street codes and street behavior are situational, but evidence remains preliminary. For instance, although Anderson (1999) depicts the code of the street as an oppositional subculture, he clearly states that the subculture originates from the extreme disadvantage and social isolation facing many contemporary inner-city neighborhoods (see also Sampson & Jeglum-Bartusch, 1998). Furthermore, Anderson describes that the majority of families in inner-city neighborhoods are "decent", meaning that they believe in and generally abide by traditional middle-class values rather than the values underlying the code of the street. However, even though decent families do not value the behaviors allowed under the code of the street, they teach their children the code so that they can protect themselves and survive on the street. Anderson explains that juveniles from these families engage in "code switching", in which they behave according to the code when necessary to avoid conflict. Code switching, then, suggests that behaving in accordance with the code of the street does not necessarily indicate a person's attitudes, as a developmental approach would suggest. Rather, code switching suggests that decent youth perform street culture when the situation dictates that it is wise to do so.

Beyond Anderson's work, research has shown that violence is more likely to occur in public situations, especially when these situations involve the use of drugs or alcohol. Luckenbill's (1977) analysis of official data shows that homicides often occur in the presence of bystanders, with the witnesses becoming an active part of the transaction between the offender and victim, often encouraging the offender's actions. Similarly, Griffiths, Yule, and Gartner (2011) found that trivial issues were more likely to evolve into violent incidents when a large number of bystanders were present at the incident. As suggested by Copes and Hochstetler's qualitative work (2003), failure to follow the street code's prescription for violence in public can severely damage one's masculine reputation and result in a loss of respect.

Despite the fact that contemporary theory and research favors the idea that street behavior is a performance of ecologically situated norms, rather than reflective of internalized subcultural values, both processes might still be relevant. What might start as situationally adaptive shared cognitions about delinquency can become enduring effects. Sampson (2012, pp. 365–377) recently summarized this position:

> But perceptions take on a new life and cohere into a cumulative texture when refracted through social interactions, practices, and collective reputations... Unlike interchangeable tools or contradictory scripts that individuals easily access and then discard, shared understandings and norms imply a greater coherence that has staying power across a wide spectrum of life.

Therefore, in all three traditions – social disorganization, strain, and subcultural theory – there is a recognition of the distinction between developmental and situational influences. There is preliminary evidence to support one over the other (usually situational), but there is also recognition that both types of effects can occur. Nonetheless, few studies explicitly aim to distinguish and arbitrate between the two, and thus conclusions are still tentative at best. We encourage future work within each tradition to unpack these differential effects, as the issue has clear implications for neighborhood-based prevention. If neighborhood processes affect the enduring behavior of residents but not necessarily the occurrence of local crime events, then prevention needs to tackle the underlying macro-level sources of disorganization, strain, and street codes – including amelioration of poverty, strengthening institutions, and so on. In contrast, if neighborhood processes affect the rate of delinquent events within the community (but not the behavior of its juvenile residents once their activities take them beyond the neighborhood), then opportunity reduction at specific problem places is a more appropriate approach to prevention (e.g., Eck & Guerette, 2012; Smith & Clarke, 2012).

Conclusion

There is a rich history in criminology of looking to neighborhood contexts for understanding the etiology of juvenile delinquency. Disadvantaged neighborhoods are particularly vulnerable to high rates of delinquency for a variety of reasons. Past literature suggests that chief among these reasons are three key processes: (1) disadvantaged neighborhoods offer weak community-based social control; (2) disadvantaged neighborhoods produce strain among residents while also offering few legitimate ways to respond to strain; and (3) disadvantaged neighborhoods foster the emergence of norms that tolerate, if not prescribe, delinquency. These mechanisms represent the traditions of social disorganization theory, strain theory, and subcultural theory, respectively. All of these theories have undergone substantial revision since their inception in the early part of the twentieth century, and the current-day versions of each of these theories have received preliminary empirical support. Despite the knowledge that each of these mechanisms is important, theoretical refinement is continually in order. In particular, we think that, moving forward, these theoretical perspectives need to: (1) better account for multiple, embedded, and overlapping "neighborhood" contexts; (2) address the impact of twenty-first century immigration on neighborhood processes related to delinquency; and (3) unpack developmental versus situational effects of neighborhoods.

References

Agnew, R.S. (1992). Foundation for a general strain theory of crime and delinquency. *Criminology, 30*(1), 47–87.

Agnew, R. (1999). A general strain theory of community differences in crime rates. *Journal of Research in Crime and Delinquency, 36*(2), 123–155.

Allen, A.N., & Lo, C.C. (2010). Drugs, guns, and disadvantaged youths: Co-occurring behavior and the code of the street. *Crime and Delinquency, 1–22*. doi:10.1177/0011128709359652.

Anderson, E. (1999). *Code of the Street: Decency, Violence, and the Moral Life of the Inner City.* New York: W.W. Norton and Company.

Bellair, P. (1997). Social interaction and community crime: Examining the importance of neighbor networks. *Criminology, 35*(4), 677–703.

Brezina, T., Agnew, R., Cullen, F.T., & Wright, J.P. (2004). The code of the street: A quantitative assessment of Elijah Anderson's subculture of violence thesis and its contribution to youth violence research. *Youth Violence and Juvenile Justice, 2*(4), 303–328.

Browning, C.R., & Dietz, R.D. (2004). The paradox of social organization: Networks, collective efficacy, and violent crime in urban neighborhoods. *Social Forces, 83*(2), 503–534.

Bursik, R.J., Jr. (1988). Social disorganization and theories of crime and delinquency: Problems and prospects. *Criminology, 26*(4), 519–551.

Clarke, R.V., & Cornish, D. (1985). Modeling offender's decisions: A framework for research and policy. In M. Tonry, & N. Morris (Eds.), *Crime and Justice: An Annual Review of Research, Vol. 6* (pp. 147–185). Chicago: University of Chicago Press.

Cloward, R.A., & Ohlin, L.E. (1960). *Delinquency and Opportunity: A Theory of Gangs*. New York: Free Press.

Cohen, A.K. (1955) *Delinquent Boys: The Culture of the Gang*. New York: Free Press.

Copes, H., & Hochstetler, A. (2003). Situational construction of masculinity among male street thieves. *Journal of Contemporary Ethnography, 32*(3), 279–304.

Eck, J.E., & Guerette, R.T. (2012). Place-based crime prevention: Theory, evidence, and policy. In B.C. Welsh, & D.P. Farrington (Eds.), *The Oxford Handbook of Crime Prevention* (pp. 354–383). New York: Oxford University Press.

Felson, M. (1994). *Crime and Everyday Life: Insight and Implications for Society*. Thousand Oaks, CA: Pine Forge Press.

Griffiths, E., Yule, C., & Gartner, R. (2011). Fighting over trivial things: Explaining the issue of contention in violent altercations. *Criminology, 49*(1), 61–94.

Hipp, J.R., & Boessen, A. (2013). Egohoods as waves washing across the city: A new measure of "neighborhoods." *Criminology, 51*(2), 287–327.

Hipp, J.R., Faris, R.W., & Boessen, A. (2012). Measuring "neighborhood": Considering network neighborhoods. *Social Networks, 34*(1), 128–140.

Hoffman, J.P. (2003). A contextual analysis of differential association, social control, and strain theories of delinquency. *Social Forces, 81*(3), 753–785.

Kirk, D.S. (2009). Unraveling the contextual effects on student suspension and juvenile arrest: The independent and interdependent influences of school, neighborhood, and family social controls. *Criminology, 47*(2), 479–517.

Kornhauser, R. (1978). *Social Sources of Delinquency*. Chicago: University of Chicago Press.

Kubrin, C.E. (2013). Immigration and crime. In F.T. Cullen, & P. Wilcox (Eds.), *The Oxford Handbook of Criminological Theory* (pp. 440–455). New York: Oxford University Press.

Logan, J.R., Zhang, W., & Alba, R.D. (2002). Immigrant enclaves and ethnic communities in New York and Los Angeles. *American Sociological Review, 67*(2), 299–322.

Lowenkamp, C.T., Cullen, F.T., & Pratt, T.C. (2003) Replicating Sampson and Groves's test of social disorganization theory: Revisiting a criminological classic. *Journal of Research in Crime and Delinquency, 40*, 351–373.

Luckenbill, D.F. (1977). Criminal homicide as a situated transaction. *Social Problems, 25*(2), 176–186.

Maccoby, E.E., Johnson, J.P., & Church, R.M. (1958). Community integration and the social sources control of juvenile delinquency. *Journal of Social Issues, 14*(3), 38–51.

McGrath, S.A., Marcum, C.D., & Copes, H. (2012). The effects of experienced, vicarious, and anticipated strain on violence and drug use among inmates. *American Journal of Criminal Justice, 37*(1), 60–75.

McNeeley, S., & Wilcox, P. (2013). Immigrant neighborhoods. In J. Ross (Ed.), *Encyclopedia of Street Crime in America* (pp. 207–211). Thousand Oaks, CA: Sage.

Merton, R.K. (1938). Social structure and anomie. *American Sociological Review, 3*(5), 672–682.

Miller, W.B. (1958). Lower class culture as a generating milieu of gang delinquency. *Journal of Social Issues, 14*(3), 5–19.

Morenoff, J.D., Sampson, R.J., & Raudenbush, S.W. (2001). Neighborhood inequality, collective efficacy, and the spatial dynamics of urban violence. *Criminology, 39*(3), 517–560.

Park, R.E., Burgess, E.W., & McKenzie, R.D. (1925). *The City*. Chicago: University of Chicago Press.

Patillo, M.E. (1998). Sweet mothers and gangbangers: Managing crime in a middle class neighborhood. *Social Forces, 76*(3), 747–774.

Portes, A. (1997). Immigration theory for a new century: Some problems and opportunities. *International Migration Review, 31*(4), 799–825.

Pratt, T.C., & Cullen, F.T. (2005). Assessing macro-level predictors and theories of crime: A meta-analysis. In M. Tonry (Ed.), *Crime and Justice: A Review of Research, Vol. 32* (pp. 373–450). Chicago: University of Chicago Press.

Sampson, R.J. (2006). Collective efficacy theory: Lessons learned and directions for future research. In F.T. Cullen, J. P. Wright, & K.R. Blevins (Eds.), *Taking Stock: The Status of Criminological Theory – Advances in Criminological Theory, Vol. 15.* New Brunswick, NJ: Transaction.

Sampson, R.J. (2012). *Great American City: Chicago and the Enduring Neighborhood Effect.* Chicago: University of Chicago Press.

Sampson, R. J., & Bean, L. (2006). Cultural mechanisms and killing fields: A revised theory of community-level racial inequality. In R.D. Peterson, L.J. Krivo, & J. Hagan (Eds.), *The Many Colors of Crime* (pp. 8–36). New York: New York University Press.

Sampson, R.J., & Groves, W.B. (1989). Community structure and crime: Testing social-disorganization theory. *American Journal of Sociology, 94*(4), 774–802.

Sampson, R.J., & Jeglum-Bartusch, D. (1998). Legal cynicism and (subcultural?) tolerance of deviance: The neighborhood context of racial differences. *Law and Society Review, 32*(4), 777–804.

Sampson, R.J., Morenoff, J.D., & Raudenbush, S.W. (2005). Social anatomy of racial and ethnic disparities in violence. *American Journal of Public Health, 95*(2), 224–232.

Sampson, R.J., Raudenbush, S.W., & Earls, F. (1997). Neighborhoods and violent crime: A multilevel study of collective efficacy. *Science, 277*(5328), 916–924.

Sampson, R.J., & Wilson, W.J. (1995). Toward a theory of race, crime and urban inequality. In J. Hagan, & R.D. Peterson (Eds.), *Crime and Inequality* (pp. 37–54). Stanford, CA: Stanford University Press.

Shaw, C.R. (1930). *The Jack Roller: A Delinquent Boy's Own Story.* Chicago: University of Chicago Press.

Shaw, C.R., & McKay, H.D. (1942). *Juvenile Delinquency and Urban Areas: A Study of Rates of Delinquency in Relation to Differential Characteristics of Local Communities in American Cities.* Chicago: University of Chicago Press.

Sherman, L.W., Gartin, P.R., & Buerger, M.E. (1989). Hot spots of predatory crime: Routine activities and the criminology of place. *Criminology, 27*(1), 27–55.

Simcha-Fagan, O., & Schwartz, J.E. (1986). Neighborhoods and delinquency: An assessment of contextual effects. *Criminology, 24*(4), 667–704.

Singer, A. (2004). *The Rise of New Immigrant Gateways.* Washington, DC: Brookings Institution.

Smith, M.J., & Clarke, R.V. (2012). Situational crime prevention: Classifying techniques using "good enough" theory. In B.C. Welsh, & D.P. Farrington (Eds.), *The Oxford Handbook of Crime Prevention* (pp. 291–315). New York: Oxford University Press.

Stewart, E.A., & Simons, R.L. (2006). Structure and culture in African-American adolescent violence: A partial test of the code of the street thesis. *Justice Quarterly, 23*(1), 1–33.

Stewart, E.A., & Simons, R.L. (2010). Race, code of the street, and violent delinquency: A multilevel investigation of neighborhood street culture and individual norms of violence. *Criminology, 48*(2), 569–605.

Taylor, R.B. (1998). Crime and small-scale place: What we know, what we can prevent, and what else we need to know. In *Crime and Place: Plenary Papers of the 1997 Conference on Criminal Justice Research and Evaluation*. Washington, DC: NIJ.

Velez, M.B. (2001). The role of public social control in urban neighborhoods: A multilevel analysis of victimization risk. *Criminology, 39*(4), 837–864.

Wareham, J., Cochran, J.K., Dembo, R., & Sellers, C.S. (2005). Community, strain, and delinquency: A test of a multi-level model of general strain theory. *Western Criminology Review, 6*(1), 117–133.

Warner, B.D., & Fowler, S.K. (2003). Strain and violence: Testing a general strain theory model of community violence. *Journal of Criminal Justice, 31*(6), 511–521.

Warner, B.D., & Wilcox Rountree, P. (1997). Local social ties in a community and crime model: Questioning the systemic nature of informal social control. *Social Problems, 44* (4), 520–536.

Weisburd, D., Groff, E.R., & Yang, S.-M. (2012). *The Criminology of Place: Street Segments and Our Understanding of the Crime Problem*. New York: Oxford University Press.

Wikstrom, P.O. (2011). Social sources of crime propensity: A study of the collective efficacy of families, schools, and neighborhoods. In T. Bliesener, A. Beelmann, & M. Stemmler (Eds.), *Antisocial Behavior and Crime: Contributions of Developmental and Evaluation Research to Prevention and Intervention* (pp. 109–122). Cambridge, MA: Hogrefe Publishing.

Wilcox Rountree, P., & Warner, B.D. (1999). Social ties and crime: Is the relationship gendered? *Criminology, 37*(4), 789–814.

Wilson, W.J. (1987). *The Truly Disadvantaged: The Inner City, the Underclass, and Public Policy*. Chicago: University of Chicago Press.

Part III
Explaining Delinquency

16

General Strain Theory and Delinquency

Robert Agnew

General strain theory (GST) states that certain strains or stressors increase the likelihood of delinquency, particularly among certain people (Agnew, 1992, 2007). The first section of this chapter provides an overview of GST, describing those strains most likely to result in delinquency, why these strains increase delinquency, and the characteristics of people most likely to respond to them with delinquency. The overview concludes with a discussion of the research on GST, noting areas in need of further research. The second section applies GST to the explanation of adolescent offending. It is argued that the changes associated with adolescence increase both the exposure to criminogenic strains and the likelihood of coping with them through crime, thereby accounting for the adolescent peak in offending. The third section briefly explores the policy implications of GST, particularly for adolescent offenders.

An Overview of GST

Strains are defined as events and conditions that are disliked (Agnew, 1992, 2007). Strains may involve the inability to achieve valued goals, such as the goals of money, status, autonomy, and thrills and excitement. Strains may involve the loss of positively valued stimuli, such as money, material possessions, and romantic partners. And strains may involve the presentation of negative stimuli, such as verbal and physical abuse. Objective strains are events and conditions disliked by most people in a given group, while subjective strains are events and conditions disliked by the particular people experiencing them. People sometimes differ in their subjective

The Handbook of Juvenile Delinquency and Juvenile Justice, First Edition. Edited by Marvin D. Krohn and Jodi Lane.

reaction to the same objective strain. Some adolescents, for example, are devastated by low grades, while others care little about such grades.

Criminogenic strains

Certain strains are more likely than others to lead to crime and delinquency (Agnew, 2001, 2007). These criminogenic strains are high in magnitude; that is, they are severe (e.g., a serious assault versus a minor insult), frequent, of long duration, and expected to continue into the future. They are also high in centrality, threatening the core goals, needs, values, activities, and/or identities of the individual. Further, criminogenic strains are seen as unjust. Unjust strains usually involve voluntary and intentional acts that violate relevant justice norms, with such norms described in the research on distributive, procedural, and interactional justice. For example, the norm of distributive justice is violated when an individual receives a punishment that is much more severe than that given to people who commit similar offenses. The norm of procedural justice is violated when an individual is punished without having a chance to tell her version of events. In addition, criminogenic strains are associated with low social control. For example, parental abuse is associated with a weak bond to parents. By contrast, the strain associated with studying long hours is associated with a strong commitment to school. Finally, criminogenic strains create some pressure or incentive for criminal coping. Such strains are easily resolved through crime (e.g., the need for money is easily resolved through theft). Also, such strains may involve exposure to others who model crime or teach beliefs favorable to crime (e.g., an abusive parent models violence).

Drawing on these criteria, GST predicts that the following strains will increase delinquency:

- Parental rejection, in which parents show little love or affection for their children, provide little support to them, and often display hostility toward them.
- Supervision/discipline that is erratic, excessive, and/or harsh (use of humiliation, insults, threats, screaming, and/or physical punishments).
- Child abuse and neglect.
- Negative secondary school experiences, including low grades, negative relations with teachers (e.g., teachers treat the juvenile unfairly, belittle or humiliate the juvenile), and the experience of school as boring and a waste of time.
- Peer abuse, which includes insults, ridicule, gossip, threats, attempts to coerce, and physical assaults.
- The failure to achieve selected goals, including thrills/excitement, high levels of autonomy, masculine status, and much money in a short period of time.
- Criminal victimization.
- Residence in economically deprived communities, which is associated with exposure to a host of strains, including victimization, family and school problems, and peer abuse.

- Homelessness.
- Discrimination based on characteristics such as race/ethnicity, gender, sexual orientation, and religion.

Why these strains increase delinquency

These strains increase the likelihood of delinquency for several reasons (Agnew, 1992, 2001, 2007). They lead to negative emotions, such as anger and frustration, which create pressure for corrective action. Juveniles feel bad and want to do something about it. Crime is one possible response. Crime may allow adolescents to end or reduce their strain. For example, adolescents may steal the money they desire or run away from abusive parents. Crime may allow for revenge against the source of strain or related targets. So adolescents may assault the peers who bully them. And crime may allow for the alleviation of negative emotions, as when adolescents use drugs to feel better. These strains may also lead to crime by reducing social control. Parental abuse, for example, reduces the juvenile's bond to parents. Negative school experiences reduce commitment to school. Further, these strains may foster association with delinquent peers and beliefs favorable to crime. Adolescents who have been victimized, for example, may join gangs for protection and come to believe that violence is a justifiable response to provocations. In fact, strain theory provides the leading explanation for the formation of criminal subcultures, which approve, justify, or excuse certain crimes (Agnew & Kaufman, 2010; Cohen, 1955). Finally, the chronic exposure to these strains contributes to traits conducive to crime, such as low self-control and irritability (Agnew, 1997, 2007; Agnew, Brezina, Wright, & Cullen, 2002; Bernard, 1990; Colvin, 2000). Chronic strain, for example, taxes coping resources and leads individuals to become especially sensitive to further strains – a key component of irritability.

Factors influencing the likelihood of delinquent coping

Not all individuals cope with these strains through delinquency, however. In fact, individuals most often cope through legal means. A juvenile being bullied by peers, for example, may try to avoid the peers, negotiate with them, report them to parents or other authorities, cognitively minimize the severity of their bullying, not think about the bullying, seek comfort from friends, and/or listen to music to feel better (see Agnew, 2007, forthcoming). Several factors influence the likelihood of delinquent coping, with these factors affecting the ability to engage in legal and delinquent coping, the costs and benefits of legal and delinquent coping, and the disposition for delinquent coping.

Delinquent coping is more likely among those with:

- Poor conventional coping skills and resources, including poor problem-solving and social skills, low socio-economic status (SES), low self-efficacy, low self-control, and high irritability. For example, adolescents from low-SES families have more trouble legally coping with poor school performance. Their parents more often lack the resources to provide them with academic assistance, negotiate with teachers, hire tutors and other experts, or enroll them in private schools that provide more academic support. Those low in self-control have more difficulty restraining themselves when provoked by others.

- Criminal skills and resources, including large physical size and strength, fighting ability, and criminal self-efficacy – or the belief that one can successfully engage in crime (see Agnew, 2007; Brezina and Topalli, 2012). Felson (1996), for example, found that bigger people were more likely to assault others than smaller people.

- Low levels of conventional social support from others such as family members, friends, and teachers. Such support may involve advice on how to cope, emotional comfort, and direct assistance in coping. For example, research suggests that "resilient youth" are able to avoid serious involvement in crime, despite the troubled families and communities in which they reside, partly because of the social support they receive from others, such as teachers, coaches, and religious figures (Rutter, Giller, & Hagell, 1988).

- Low social control, including direct control by parents, teachers, neighbors, and police; attachment to conventional others, such as parents and teachers; commitment to conventional activities, such as school and religion; and beliefs condemning crime. For example, juveniles who do not care about their parents should be more likely to run away from home when family problems arise.

- Delinquent friends, who often model and reinforce delinquent coping. For example, delinquent peers frequently pressure youth into responding to insults and other provocations with violence (Anderson, 1999).

- Beliefs favorable to delinquent coping. For example, the "code of the street" described by Anderson (1999) states that violence is a justifiable or excusable response to a range of slights, including minor slights such as being stared at.

- Greater exposure to situations where the costs of delinquency are low and the benefits are high, including situations where "capable guardians" are absent and attractive targets for crime are present (Agnew & Brezina, 2012). For example, adolescents who regularly visit shopping malls should be more likely to respond to monetary strain with theft.

The research on general strain theory

GST has most often been used to explain individual differences in delinquency, and the theory has received much support here (for overviews, see Agnew, 2007; Agnew and Scheuerman, 2010). The criminogenic strains listed above increase the likelihood of delinquency, with some being among the most important predictors of delinquency. Recent research, for example, suggests that victimization has a relatively large effect on delinquency (Agnew, 2007). And after being neglected by criminologists for many years, research indicates that racial discrimination likewise has a substantial effect on offending (Unnever & Gabbidon, 2011). Further, these strains increase delinquency partly through their effect on negative emotions, with most research focusing on anger. These strains also reduce social control, lead to beliefs favorable to delinquency, increase association with delinquent peers, and contribute to traits conducive to delinquency – such as irritability.

The research on those variables said to condition the effect of strains on delinquency, however, has produced mixed results (see Agnew, 2007, 2013, for overviews). For example, some studies indicate that juveniles who associate with delinquent peers are more likely to respond to strains with delinquency, while other studies do not. These mixed results may reflect the difficulty of detecting conditioning effects in survey research (Agnew, 2013). Also, they may be due to the fact that conditioning variables are usually considered in isolation from one another. That is, researchers usually examine the effect of one conditioning variable, with other variables controlled. It may be that delinquent coping is unlikely unless individuals possess several factors conducive to such coping (Agnew, 2013; Mazerolle & Maahs, 2000).

More recently, GST has been used to explain group differences in offending, including gender, age, race/ethnicity, class, and community differences (e.g., Agnew, 1997, 1999, 2007; Broidy & Agnew, 1997; De Coster & Zito, 2010; Kaufman, Rebellon, Thaxton, & Agnew, 2008; Unnever & Gabbidon, 2011; Warner & Fowler, 2003). It is argued that such differences are due to group differences in the exposure to criminogenic strains and in the likelihood of criminal coping. For example, Broidy and Agnew (1997) argued that while females may experience more strains than males, males are more likely to experience crimonogenic strains, such as negative school experiences and victimization. Further, males are more likely to cope with strains through crime. Among other things, this is because males are lower in self-control and higher in negative emotionality; lower in certain forms of social control, such as direct control; more likely to associate with delinquent peers and hold beliefs favorable to crime; and more likely to encounter opportunities for crime.

GST has also been used to explain patterns of offending over the life course, including "adolescence-limited" and "life-course persistent" offending (Agnew, 1997, 2007; Slocum, 2010). The manner in which GST explains adolescence-limited offending, which drives most juvenile delinquency, is discussed below. Life-course persistent offenders offend at high rates from childhood well into the adult years, with their offending including both minor and serious crimes. Drawing on the work of Moffitt (1993), Thornberry (1987), and others, GST explains such offending in two major ways (Agnew, 1997; Slocum, 2010). Many life-course persistent offenders develop traits such as negative emotionality and low constraint early in life. Such individuals are more likely to experience objective strains, to interpret these strains as high in magnitude and unjust, and to cope with them in a criminal manner over the course of their lives. Such individuals might be described as "mean" and "out of control". As such, they often evoke negative reactions from others, such as parents, teachers, and employers. They are also sorted into aversive environments. For example, conventional peers reject them and they come to associate with delinquent peers, who often mistreat one another and are treated negatively by others. These individuals are also more likely to react to strain or negative treatment with crime.

This crime, in turn, contributes to continued negative treatment. And the negative treatment they experience helps maintain the traits of negative emotionality and low constraint. Some individuals, however, engage in life-course persistent offending even though they did not possess the traits of low constraint and negative emotionality in childhood. Such individuals are part of the urban underclass, and their deep poverty increases the likelihood that they will experience strains involving family, school, peers, and others. Such individuals are also less able to cope with such strains in a legal manner. These effects, in turn, make it difficult to escape from poverty and lead to a pattern of high strain and criminal coping over the life course.

Most recently, GST has been used to explain offending in a range of countries outside the US (Agnew, 2007). It has been applied to particular types of crime and deviance, including bullying (e.g., Hay, Meldrum, & Mann, 2010), school violence (e.g., Levin and Madfis, 2009), suicidal behavior (Sigfusdottir, Asgeirsdottir, Gudjonsson, & Sigurdsson, 2008), and eating disorders (e.g., Piquero, Fox, Piquero, Capowich, & Mazerolle, 2010). It has been used to understand the relationship between natural disasters and crime (e.g., Robertson, Stein, & Schaefer-Rohleder, 2010). It has also been applied to issues in the criminal justice system, such as police deviance (Gibson, Swatt, & Jolicoeur, 2001) and the prediction of recidivism among ex-inmates (Listwan, Sullivan, Agnew, Cullen, & Colvin, 2013). GST, in sum, has moved well beyond the early research that focused on explaining individual differences in general levels of offending.

Research needs

There are now a few hundred studies examining GST, but several major gaps in the research remain (for overviews, see Agnew, 2007; Agnew & Scheuerman, 2010). While research suggests that most of the above strains increase delinquency, there is a need for more research on the effect of certain strains, such as discrimination and the inability to achieve valued goals. Researchers need to better measure strains, including their actual and perceived magnitude and their perceived injustice (e.g., Rebellon, Manasse, Van Gundy, & Cohn, 2012). Much research now employs gross measures of strain: often checklists that simply indicate whether particular strains have been experienced. Researchers should explore how the timing and clustering of strains affect crime. Some data suggest that crime is more likely when several strains are experienced at the same time, thereby overwhelming legal coping resources and generating strong negative emotions (Slocum, Simpson, & Smith, 2005).

Researchers need to devote more attention to the intervening mechanisms between strain and crime (see Agnew, 2007). Most research has examined whether trait anger mediates the effect of strain. Researchers should examine a range of negative emotions in addition to anger, such as frustration, humiliation, depression, and fear. They should ideally employ state as well as trait measures of emotion. They should also explore whether different strains lead to different emotions, and whether different emotions are conducive to different types of crime (Agnew, 2007; Ganem, 2010).

For example, strains seen as unjust may be most conducive to anger, and those seen as uncontrollable to depression. Anger may be especially conducive to aggression, while depression may be conducive to drug use. Further, researchers should devote more attention to the other intervening mechanisms between strain and crime, including social control, beliefs regarding crime, association with delinquent peers, and traits such as low constraint and negative emotionality (e.g., Agnew *et al.*, 2002).

Also needed is research that explores a broader range of conditioning variables, such as religion, gang membership, and bio-psychological factors (see Agnew, 2013). Researchers should examine conditioning effects with surveys that oversample on extreme cases, and with methods such as experiments and vignette studies. Researchers should examine the effect of several conditioning variables in combination, as noted above. And researchers should draw on recent research in the larger stress and coping literature, and examine the process of delinquent coping over time (see Agnew, 2013). Coping is often an extended process, with a range of strategies being employed over time, and more detailed examinations of this process may shed important light on the factors that prompt delinquent coping – as well as the factors that prompt legal coping even in the face of severe strains.

More research is also needed on the ability of GST to explain group differences in offending, and offending among special subgroups. There has been a fair bit of research on gender, but little on race/ethnicity, age, class, and communities, and much of the research only considers a limited range of strains and conditioning variables. Further, GST should be expanded to better incorporate the rapidly growing research on bio-psychological factors and crime (e.g., Walsh, 2000). There is little doubt that such factors influence the exposure and reaction to strains, and that bio-psychological factors are themselves affected by strains. Finally, research should examine how macro-level factors influence the nature of, exposure to, and reaction to strains. GST is compatible with several macro-level theories of crime, particularly conflict theories, which describe how some groups oppress others in an effort to maintain or enhance their privileged position. This oppression typically involves discrimination, since the members of certain groups are treated in a negative manner at least partly because of their group status. And this discriminatory treatment involves many of the strains listed above, such as economic deprivation and victimization, and it may indirectly lead to other strains, such as family problems (see Agnew, 2011). So while the core argument of GST has much support, that certain strains increase crime partly through their effect of negative emotions, many aspects of GST are still in need of testing and further development.

Using GST to Explain the Adolescent Peak in Offending

Yet another area in need of research involves the ability of GST to explain the adolescent peak in offending, one of the best established and most important facts about crime. Certain crimes, particularly interpersonal acts of theft and violence, tend to peak during the adolescent years, especially in developed societies (Agnew,

2003). This adolescent peak in offending is most characteristic of the "adolescence-limited" offenders described by Moffitt (1993), who make up the large share of offenders. But it also characterizes the life-course persistent offenders to some degree, as they offend at somewhat higher rates during the adolescent years. As suggested above, GST explains this peak in offending by arguing that adolescents are more likely than children and adults to experience criminogenic strains and to cope with them through crime. And there is limited support for this argument. Many criminogenic strains are more common among adolescents, such as criminal victimization, parental conflict, and negative school experiences. Likewise, adolescents experience higher levels of emotional distress than children and adults. Further, some evidence suggests that adolescents are more inclined to criminal coping (Agnew, 1997, 2003, 2007). But these arguments do not address the larger questions of why the exposure to criminogenic strains and the likelihood of criminal coping increase during adolescence. This section draws on the literature on adolescence and certain prior work on GST to address these questions, and in doing so, point to additional areas in need of research (Agnew, 1985, 1997, 2003, 2007).

Adolescents experience an increase in strain and the likelihood of criminal coping largely because of the unique social position they occupy, especially in developed countries. As adolescents prepare for adulthood, they leave the small, protected world of childhood. In particular, they are no longer closely supervised by parents, support from parents and other adults declines, and they enter larger, more diverse secondary schools. More is expected of them, with an increase in academic and social demands. Also they come to desire the privileges associated with adulthood, including money, status, and the freedom to engage in activities such as drinking and sexual relations. Unfortunately, they are not always able to cope effectively with the larger, more demanding world they encounter and they are often unable to legally satisfy their new desires. The result is an increase in both strain and criminal coping. But as adolescents become adults, their social world contracts as they form families of their own and get jobs. They have more control over this world, being better able to select and shape their social environments. They have the skills and resources to cope more effectively with problems that arise, and they obtain the privileges of adulthood – all of which reduce strain and criminal coping. I next elaborate further on these points.

Less supervision of adolescents by parents, teachers, and other authority figures

The lives of children are closely regulated by parents, teachers, and other authority figures, who largely determine what children do, when they do it, and who they do it with. Children are usually under the direct observation of an authority figure or one is nearby, listening for "signs of trouble". And if trouble does occur, the figure quickly intervenes – sanctioning misbehavior or providing assistance. This supervision declines as children age, with a dramatic decline occurring during the transition from childhood to adolescence (Agnew, 2003).

Parents provide more freedom to adolescents, including the freedom to select their associates and, beyond school, to select and schedule their activities. Direct monitoring by parents declines, with adolescents often having the freedom to go off on their own after school, on weekends, and sometimes in the evening. This freedom is enhanced in developed nations. Adolescents have few chores to keep them at home and they often possess the resources to escape from home, including cars, public transportation, and money to finance social activities away from home (e.g., shopping and entertainment). As a result, the time spent with parents declines by about half as juveniles move from childhood to adolescence (Agnew, 2003).

This drop in supervision is not as great at school, with secondary school students being subject to strict rules, special monitoring efforts (e.g., metal detectors, school police), and often harsh sanctions, including mandatory expulsion for certain offenses. Nevertheless, the level of supervision declines somewhat. Secondary schools are generally much larger than elementary schools and students change classes several times a day, making it more difficult for school officials to monitor students. Monitoring is often low at certain times, such as during lunch periods and class changes. Secondary-school students more often possess the knowledge and skills to escape monitoring, as described by Chambliss (1973). Beyond that, school officials are less likely to intervene when problems such as academic difficulties arise, in part because they expect adolescents to cope on their own.

By contrast, the transition from adolescence to adulthood is marked by an increase in supervision – although this increase occurs in a context of responsibility rather than dependence. Most adults form families and get jobs, and so find that their lives are heavily regulated by work and family responsibilities. That is, work and family obligations consume almost all of their time and largely dictate what they do, when they do it, and who they do it with. Related to this, they spend more time in environments where they are under the observation of other adults, such as spouses, co-workers, and employers, who would quickly notice if they fail to fulfill their responsibilities, calling them to task or offering assistance if there is a problem. Further, adults who violate the law are subject to the generally harsher sanctions of the adult justice system.

The reduced supervision of adolescents is usually said to affect delinquency for reasons related to control, routine activities, and social learning theories (Agnew, 2003; Agnew & Brezina, 2012; Felson, 2002). Adolescents are subject to less direct control, so they can commit delinquent acts with a reduced risk of detection and sanction. They are more likely to encounter opportunities for crime, with opportunities defined as situations where attractive targets are present and capable guardians are absent. For example, adolescents often spend much time at shopping malls, unsupervised by parents and exposed to a range of attractive merchandise. Poorly supervised adolescents are freer to associate with delinquent peers, who teach them to engage in delinquency.

But this reduction in supervision also has major implications for the exposure to strain (Agnew, 2003; Agnew, Rebellon, & Thaxton, 2000). Adults supervise children to prevent them from experiencing harm (i.e., strain), as well as to control their behavior. Supervision is partly intended to ensure that children avoid settings where they might be harmed, people who might harm them, and activities that might result in harm. Parents, for example, prohibit their children from spending time on the street because they view this as a dangerous setting (see Anderson, 1999). Parents prevent their children from associating with "bad kids" partly because they believe these kids might harm their children or involve them in dangerous activities. Further, authority figures supervise so that they might intervene when children are threatened with harm. For example, teachers are quick to help children to resolve disputes in a peaceful manner, so that they do not escalate into violence. So when the supervision by authority figures declines in adolescence, exposure to strain likely increases.

An expansion in the size and diversity of the adolescent's social world

As juveniles move from childhood to adolescence, they spend more time interacting with a larger and more diverse set of peers, often in unsupervised settings (Agnew, 1997, 2003; Osgood, Wilson, O'Malley, Bachman, & Johnston, 1996; Warr, 2002). These changes occur partly because of the reduction in supervision just noted. Adolescents have more time to associate with peers away from parents, more freedom to select peers, and more access to settings where diverse peers congregate, such as clubs and malls. Beyond that, the secondary schools that adolescents attend are generally larger and more diverse than their elementary schools. Also, adolescents change classes several times a day, dramatically increasing the number of peers they regularly encounter. And romantic involvements become common, as do mixed-sex peer groups.

The transition from adolescence to adulthood, however, involves a contraction and change in the nature of the individual's social world. Adults leave the peer-oriented world of school and typically form families of their own and get jobs. The demands and attachments associated with family and work lead to a dramatic reduction in the time spent with peers. Further, adults have much more control over who they associate with, usually confining their activities to a small group of friends similar to themselves. Relatedly, adults experience much lower turnover in friends, romantic partners, and coworkers.

The larger and more diverse social world of adolescents increases the exposure to strains for several reasons. Adolescents spend more time interacting with more peers, so there are more opportunities for mistreatment. These peers have fewer constraints against and more motivation for mistreatment. They are often weakly bonded to the adolescent; in fact, they may not even know the adolescent. Interaction often occurs in unsupervised settings. These peers may hold somewhat different norms and values than the adolescent, since they are often from different groups and communities. This increases the likelihood of disputes. Adolescents may view certain of these peers as members of out-groups, which may also increase the likelihood of disputes. Osgood *et al.* (1996) found that time spent with peers in unsupervised settings is one of the strongest correlates of delinquency. While there are several reasons for this, the increased likelihood of mistreatment or strain in such settings may be an important factor.

Increased association with delinquent peers

Adolescents not only spend more time interacting with more peers, but are also much more likely to interact with delinquent peers (Warr, 2002). Adolescents, in fact, are several times more likely than children and adults to report that their friends engage in criminal acts. There are several reasons why adolescents and their friends are more likely to be delinquent, including the decline in supervision mentioned above and the increase in strain discussed in this chapter (see also Agnew, 2003; Warr, 2002). Also, as individuals and their friends become more delinquent, a vicious cycle that leads to *further* delinquency is set in motion (Thornberry, 1987). The reason for this is most often described in terms of social learning theory. Friends model delinquency for one another, differentially reinforce delinquency, and teach beliefs favorable to delinquency. But whatever the reasons for the increased association with delinquent peers, the increase has the effect of exposing adolescents to more strains.

Delinquent peers, by definition, are more likely to mistreat or create strain for others. In this area, data suggest that they more often get into verbal and physical conflicts with one another (Giordano, Cernkovich, & Pugh, 1986). Also, delinquent peers may foster other strains, including problems with parents, school, and police. For example, research suggests that involvement in delinquent gangs increases the likelihood of victimization, arrest, school dropout, and employment problems (e.g., Krohn, Ward, Thornberry, Lizotte, & Chu, 2011).

Increased demands on adolescents

Adolescents are subject to increased demands as they prepare to assume adult family and work roles (Agnew, 1997, 2003). They are expected to devote more time and effort to educational pursuits. As such, they are given more work at school, graded in a more rigorous manner, and subject to a more competitive environment, including normative grading and public evaluations of their work. Many adolescents have trouble meeting these demands, resulting in an increase in school strain, including poor grades, dissatisfaction with school, and negative relations with teachers.

The social demands on adolescents also increase. They are expected to establish romantic relationships with others, something at which they have little experience. Popularity with peers becomes a central concern, reflecting the increased role that peers play in the lives of adolescents. (Adolescents spend about twice as much time with peers as with parents and other adults, excluding time spent in the classroom.) Interaction with peers, however, is governed by a more complex and subtle set of social cues than is the case with children. Further, interacting with a larger and more diverse set of peers regularly challenges the role-taking and social skills of adolescents. Consequently, interpersonal strains become more likely. As Greenberg (1977) pointed out, popularity with peers often requires money, so that adolescents can finance social activities and purchase such status-conferring items as fashionable clothes and cars. Many adolescents, however, lack legal access to sufficient funds, again increasing strain.

The desire for and denial of adult privileges

Adolescents come to desire many of the privileges of adulthood, such as increased respect and status, including masculine status for males; money; and autonomy – which involves the right to engage in such "adult" activities such as staying out late, consuming alcohol, and sexual relations (Agnew, 1997, 2003; Greenberg, 1977; Moffitt, 1993). Adolescents desire such privileges because they are physically and sexually mature; they are starting to assume certain adult responsibilities, so feel entitled to adult privileges; they see that certain of their peers have these privileges; and these privileges are generally viewed and experienced as desirable.

Most adolescents, however, are denied such privileges by parents, teachers, and others (Greenberg, 1977). They are sometimes treated like children. They frequently lack legitimate sources of income. They are often denied autonomy by parents and especially school officials. While they are given significantly more freedom than children, they are still subject to a range of rules at school and expected to behave in a docile or submissive manner. The result is much strain, with adolescents unable to achieve many of their key goals. Children, by contrast, have less desire for such goals, while adults are better able to legally achieve these goals (Agnew, 1997).

Traits that increase the exposure to objective and subjective strains

Adolescents possess several traits that increase the objective and subjective strains they experience (Agnew, 1997, 2003). Compared with children and/or adults, they are more impulsive, risk-seeking, aware of their environment, sensitive to mistreatment, inclined to blame others for their problems, and prone to strong emotional reactions. These differences partly stem from the fact that the adolescent's brain is still developing, particularly those areas concerned with self-control and emotional regulation.

As a result of such traits, adolescents are more likely to upset others and evoke negative reactions from them. Parents, for example, may sometimes respond to the risky and impulsive acts of their children with harsh, even abusive discipline. Adolescents are more likely to sort themselves into environments where the likelihood of mistreatment is high. For example, adolescents are more often attracted to the risky activities of delinquent peers. Similarly, adolescents are more likely to get involved in risky situations, with such situations frequently involving unsupervised activities with peers in the presence of alcohol and drugs. Finally, adolescents are more likely to perceive the objective strains they experience as high in magnitude and unjust; that is, they are more prone to subjective as well as objective strains.

For example, adolescents are more likely to become upset over seemingly minor slights and provocations than are adults.

An increased likelihood of delinquent coping

Adolescents are not only more likely to experience strains than children and adults, but are also more likely to cope with strains in a criminal manner. There are several reasons for this. Adolescents lack the coping skills and resources of adults (Agnew, 1985, 1990, 1997, 2003). As juveniles make the transition from childhood to adolescence, they are more often expected to cope with problems on their own. But unlike adults, adolescents have little experience at coping, and many lack the social and problem-solving skills necessary to successfully resolve certain strains in a legal manner. Also, adolescents are less likely to possess the resources that facilitate legal coping, including money, status, and power. As a result, they are often compelled to remain in environments that are quite stressful, including family, school, and neighborhood. There is often little they can do to legally reduce the mistreatment they receive from family members, peers, teachers, neighbors, and police. The one resource that adolescents do have in abundance is physical strength, but this resource is more conducive to aggressive than to legal coping (Agnew, 1990). Adults, by contrast, are better able to convince or pressure others to change their behavior if they are being mistreated. And, if this fails, they are more often in a position to leave the stressful environment, by divorcing spouses, changing jobs, or moving to a new neighborhood.

Adolescents are also lower in conventional social support than children and adults (Agnew, 1997, 2003). While children lack the skills and resources for effective coping, they receive much social support from parents and other adults, who frequently cope on their behalf. This support declines sharply during adolescence. Adults expect adolescents to more often cope on their own. Meanwhile, adults are less aware of the strains encountered by adolescents, due to their reduced monitoring of adolescents and the fact that adolescents are reluctant to share problems with them. Adolescents may turn to friends for support, but such support is not as effective at coping with strains as is the support of parents and other adults (Agnew, 1997, 2003). So adolescents are in a difficult state; they lack the social support of children on the one hand, and the coping skills and resources of adults on the other.

In addition, adolescents live in a very public world, both at school and beyond. The strains they experience often occur before an audience of peers or become known to peers. This increases the likelihood of delinquent coping for several reasons (Agnew, 1997). It is more difficult for adolescents to minimize or cognitively reinterpret the strains they experience, since their peers remind them of these strains, sometimes exaggerating their severity. Adolescents feel under more pressure to respond to many strains in ways that will allow them to maintain a positive reputation or save face. This often involves an aggressive response to insults and other provocations, and their peers often encourage an aggressive response, particularly when there is some acceptance of the "code of the street" (Anderson, 1999).

Further, adolescents have less social control (Agnew, 2003). As noted above, they are lower in direct control than children and adults. Also, the emotional bonds of juveniles to parents and teachers often weaken as they make the transition to adolescence, since adolescents are less dependent on and more often in conflict with these others. Adults, however, typically form strong bonds to their partners and children. Further, adolescents have less commitment to conventional activities, since their school performance and satisfaction generally decline. Adults, by contrast, often form strong commitments to their work and investments in their communities.

Finally, adolescents are more disposed to criminal coping. This disposition to criminal coping partly derives from the traits of adolescents, such as low self-control and negative emotionality. It also derives from their increased association with delinquent peers, who model, differentially reinforce, and present beliefs favorable to criminal coping. For example, peers sometimes place great stress on responding to disrespectful treatment with violence (Anderson, 1999).

Needed research

In sum, there is good reason to believe that adolescents are more likely than children and adults to experience criminogenic strains and to cope with them through crime. More research, however, is needed on the extent to which differences in the exposure and reaction to strains explain the adolescent peak in offending; that is, research that better examines exposure to criminogenic strains over the life course, the subjective reaction to such strains, and standing on those factors that influence likelihood of criminal coping. Beyond that, research is needed on the extent to which the life changes associated with adolescence, such as the decline in supervision and the increase in association with delinquent peers, influence the exposure to strains and the likelihood of criminal coping.

The Policy Implications of General Strain Theory

The major policy implication of GST is straightforward: reduce the exposure of adolescents to criminogenic strains (Agnew, 2007, 2010). Many of the more successful delinquency rehabilitation and prevention programs do just that, although they are not explicitly based on GST. These programs reduce exposure to strains such as child abuse, harsh/erratic parental discipline, parental rejection, negative school experiences, bullying, victimization, homelessness, and discrimination (for overviews, see Agnew, 2010; Agnew & Brezina, 2012; Farrington & Welsh, 2007). Parent-training programs, for example, teach parents how to better discipline their children, avoiding the use of harsh and erratic sanctions. They also attempt to reduce the stressors faced by parents, since these stressors contribute to bad parenting. New techniques of classroom instruction and management attempt to bolster student grades and improve relations between teachers and students. Anti-bullying programs reduce bullying in schools by having school officials and others publicize the negative consequences of bullying, better monitor students, and consistently intervene when bullying occurs.

The exposure to criminogenic strains can also be reduced in other, less obvious ways. Strains can be altered so as to make them less conducive to crime. The magnitude of strains can be reduced by lowering their degree, frequency, duration, and/or centrality. For example, adolescents can be taught to place less absolute and/or relative emphasis on goals such as masculine status. The perceived injustice of strains can also be reduced. The restorative justice approach, for example, reduces the perceived injustice of sanctions by giving offenders more voice in the proceedings, thereby increasing levels of procedural justice. We might also increase the level of social control associated with certain strains. For example, those who receive very low grades or severe sanctions at school might be targeted for mentoring and other special programs, with the aim of maintaining or increasing their bond to school.

Programs can also help juveniles better avoid or escape from strains. Social skills and problem-solving programs, for example, often teach juveniles that certain behaviors are likely to elicit negative reactions from others, such as peers, teachers, and police. And juveniles are taught more appropriate behaviors. For example, they are taught how to respond when stopped by the police or, more generally, how to be assertive without being aggressive. We also might make it easier for juveniles to legally escape from environments where they are negatively treated. For example, we might make it easier for juveniles to change classes in order to escape negative treatment by teachers or other students.

But despite these efforts, it is impossible to eliminate exposure to all criminogenic strains. So other programs try to teach juveniles how to better cope with strains, including programs that teach anger-management, problem-solving, and social skills. Related to this, some programs try to increase the social support available to adolescents, with mentoring programs being an example. Some schools and communities have developed programs where individuals such as former gang members monitor and try to resolve disputes in a non-violent manner, including disputes between gangs. Still other programs try to increase levels of social control and reduce the disposition for criminal coping. While all such programs have demonstrated some success in reducing delinquency, research is needed in order to estimate the extent to which the impact of these programs is explained by their effect on strains and coping.

Conclusion

There is much evidence that certain strains increase the likelihood of juvenile offending, partly through their impact on negative emotions such as anger. More research is needed in several areas, however, including research on why some individuals are more likely than others to cope with strains through delinquency, and the extent to which GST can explain the adolescent peak in offending.

References

Agnew, R. (1985). A revised strain theory of delinquency. *Social Forces*, 64(1), 151–167.

Agnew, R. (1990). Adolescent resources and delinquency. *Criminology*, 28(4), 535–566.

Agnew, R. (1992). Foundation for a general strain theory of crime and delinquency. *Criminology*, 30(1), 47–87.

Agnew, R. (1997). Stability and change in crime over the life course. In T.P. Thornberry (Ed.), *Developmental Theories of Crime and Delinquency* (pp. 101–132). New Brunswick, NJ: Transaction.

Agnew, R. (1999). A general strain theory of community differences in crime rates. *Journal of Research in Crime and Delinquency*, 36(2), 123–155.

Agnew, R. (2001). Building on the foundation of general strain theory: Specifying the types of strain most likely to lead to crime and delinquency. *Journal of Research in Crime and Delinquency*, 38(4), 319–361.

Agnew, R. (2003). An integrated theory of the adolescent peak in offending. *Youth & Society*, 34(3), 263–299.

Agnew, R. (2007). *Pressured Into Crime: An Overview of General Strain Theory*. New York: Oxford University Press.

Agnew, R. (2010). Controlling crime: Recommendations from general strain theory. In H.D. Barlow, & S.L. Decker (Eds.), *Criminology and Public Policy* (pp. 25–44). Philadelphia: Temple University Press.

Agnew, R. (2011). *Toward a Unified Criminology*. New York: New York University Press.

Agnew, R. (2013). When criminal coping is likely: An extension of general strain theory. *Deviant Behavior*, 34(8), 653–670.

Agnew, R., & Brezina, T. (2012). *Juvenile Delinquency: Causes and Control*. New York: Oxford University Press.

Agnew, R., Brezina, T., Wright, J.P., & Cullen, F.T. (2002). Strain, personality traits, and delinquency: Extending general strain theory. *Criminology*, 40(1), 43–72.

Agnew, R., & Kaufman, J.M. (Eds.) (2010). *Anomie, Strain and Subcultural Theories of Crime*. Farnham: Ashgate.

Agnew, R., Rebellon, C., & Thaxton, S. (2000). A general strain theory approach to families and crime. In G.L. Fox, & M.L. Benson (Eds.), *Families, Crime and Criminal Justice* (pp. 113–138). Amsterdam: JAI.

Agnew, R., & Scheuerman, H. (2010). Strain theories. *Oxford Bibliographies, Criminology*. Retrieved from http://www.oxfordbibliographies.com/view/document/obo-9780195396607/obo-9780195396607-0005.xml

Anderson, E. (1999) *The Code of the Street*. New York: W.W. Norton.

Bernard, T.J. (1990) Angry aggression among the "truly disadvantaged." *Criminology*, 29(1), 73–96.

Brezina, T., & Topalli, V. (2012). Criminal self-efficacy: Exploring the correlates and consequences of a "successful criminal" identity. *Criminal Justice and Behavior*, 39(8), 1042–1062.

Broidy, L.M., & Agnew, R. (1997). Gender and crime: A general strain theory perspective. *Journal of Research in Crime and Delinquency*, 38(3), 362–386.

Chambliss, W.J. (1973). The saints and the roughnecks. *Society*, 11(1), 24–31.

Cohen, A.K. (1955). *Delinquent Boys*. Glencoe, IL: Free Press.

Colvin, M. (2000). *Crime & Coercion*. New York: St. Martin's Press.

De Coster, S., & Zito, R.C. (2010). Gender and general strain theory: The gendering of emotional experiences and expressions. *Journal of Contemporary Criminal Justice, 26*(2), 224–245.

Farrington, D.P., & Welsh, B.C. (2007). *Saving Children from a Life of Crime*. New York: Oxford University Press.

Felson, M. (2002). *Crime and Everyday Life*. Thousand Oaks, CA: Sage.

Felson, R. (1996). Big people hit little people. *Criminology, 34*(3), 433–452.

Ganem, Natasha M. (2010). The role of negative emotion in general strain theory. *Journal of Contemporary Criminal Justice, 26*(2), 167–185.

Gibson, C.L., Swatt, M.L., & Jolicoeur, J.R. (2001). Assessing the generality of general strain theory: The relationship among occupational stress experienced by male police officers and domestic forms of violence. *Journal of Crime and Justice, 24*(2), 29–57.

Giordano, P.G., Cernkovich, S.A., & Pugh, M.D. (1986). Friendships and delinquency. *American Journal of Sociology, 91*(5), 1170–1202.

Greenberg, D.F. (1977). Delinquency and the age structure of society. *Contemporary Crises, 1*, 189–223.

Hay, C., Meldrum, R., & Mann, K. (2010). Traditional bullying, cyber bullying, and deviance: A general strain theory approach. *Journal of Contemporary Criminal Justice, 26*(2), 130–147.

Kaufman, J.M., Rebellon, C.J., Thaxton, S., & Agnew, R. (2008). A general strain theory of racial differences in criminal offending. *Australian and New Zealand Journal of Criminology, 41*(3), 421–437.

Krohn, M.D., Ward, J., Thornberry, T.P., Lizotte, A.J., & Chu, R. (2011). The cascading effects of adolescent gang involvement across the life course. *Criminology, 49*(4), 999–1028.

Levin, J., & Madfis, E. (2009). Mass murder at school and cumulative strain. *American Behavioral Scientist, 52*(9), 1227–1245.

Listwan, S.J., Sullivan, C.J., Agnew, R., Cullen, F.T., & Colvin, M. (2013). The pains of imprisonment revisited: The impact of strain on inmate recidivism. *Justice Quarterly, 30*(1), 144–168.

Mazerolle, P., & Maahs, J. (2000). General strain theory and delinquency: An alternative examination of conditioning influences. *Justice Quarterly, 17*(2), 323–343.

Moffitt, T.E. (1993). Adolescence-limited and life-course persistent antisocial behavior: A developmental taxonomy. *Psychological Review, 100*(4), 674–701.

Osgood, W.D., Wilson, J.K., O'Malley, P.M., Bachman, J.G., & Johnston, L.D. (1996). Routine activities and individual deviant behavior. *American Sociological Review, 61*(4), 635–655.

Piquero, N.L., Fox, K., Piquero, A.R., Capowich, G., & Mazerolle, P. (2010). Gender, general strain theory, negative emotions, and disordered eating. *Journal of Youth and Adolescence, 39*(4), 380–392.

Rebellon, C.J., Manasse, M.E., Van Gundy, K.T., & Cohn, E.S. (2012). Perceived injustice and delinquency: A test of general strain theory. *Journal of Criminal Justice, 40*(3), 230–237.

Robertson, A.R., Stein, J.A., & Schaefer-Rohleder, L. (2010). Effects of hurricane Katrina and other adverse life events on adolescent female offenders. *Journal of Research in Crime and Delinquency, 47*(4), 469–495.

Rutter, M., Giller, H., & Hagell, A. (1988). *Antisocial Behavior by Young People*. Cambridge: Cambridge University Press.

Sigfusdottir, I.D., Asgeirsdottir, B.B., Gudjonsson, G.H., & Sigurdsson, J.F. (2008). A model of sexual abuse's effects on suicidal behavior and delinquency. *Journal of Youth and Adolescence, 37*(6), 699–712.

Slocum, L.A. (2010). General strain theory and continuity in offending over time: Assessing and extending GST explanations of persistence. *Journal of Contemporary Criminal Justice, 26*(2), 204–223.

Slocum, L.A, Simpson, S.S., & Smith, D.A. (2005). Strained lives and crime: Examining intra-individual variation in strain and offending in a sample of incarcerated women. *Criminology, 43*(4), 1067–1110.

Thornberry, T.P. (1987). Toward an interactional theory of delinquency. *Criminology, 25*(4), 863–891.

Unnever, J.D., & Gabbidon, S.L. (2011). *A Theory of African American Offending*. New York: Routledge.

Walsh, A. (2000). Behavioral genetics and anomie/strain theory. *Criminology, 38*(4), 1075–1108.

Warner, B.D., & Fowler, S.K. (2003). Strain and violence: Testing a general strain theory model of community violence. *Journal of Criminal Justice, 31*(6), 511–521.

Warr, M. (2002) *Companions in Crime*. Cambridge: Cambridge University Press.

17

Social Learning Theory and Delinquent Behavior: Past, Present, and Future Investigations

L. Thomas Winfree, Jr.

Introduction

The variant of social learning theory (SLT) first proposed nearly 50 years ago by Burgess and Akers (1966) and subsequently refined by Akers (1973, 1977, 1985, 1998) is best viewed as a general theory of crime and deviance. That is, social learning is not simply a theory of juvenile delinquency, adult criminality or any other specific form of rule-breaking. Akers intended for it to serve as a general theory that explained the sociological, social psychological and, more recently, social structural forces behind a broad range of miscreant and aberrant behaviors. Indeed, Akers (1973, 1985) provided examples of how this merger of Sutherland's differential association theory (DAT) with principles of operant conditioning can be applied to collective and individual behaviors such as illicit drug use, drinking and alcohol behavior, sexual deviance, white-collar crime, professional crime, organized crime, domestic and family violence, suicide, and mental illness. The absence of a group context for the latter three clearly fixes Akers' theory in the realm of a general theory and not simply a behavior-specific theory.

The current chapter has five specific goals. First, we review the basic tenets of SLT, to include conceptual and operational definitions of key constructs, as well as an elaboration of social psychological processes that are at work. Second, we examine empirical tests of Akers' SLT, beginning with the first full test of the theory (Akers, Krohn, Lanza-Kaduce, & Radosevich, 1979) and culminating in what a recent meta-analysis revealed about nearly 30 years of SLT-related research (Pratt et al., 2010). Third, we review how well the theory explains youthful misbehavior outside of the dominant middle-class culture of the US. This topical area includes cross-cultural,

The Handbook of Juvenile Delinquency and Juvenile Justice, First Edition. Edited by Marvin D. Krohn and Jodi Lane.
© 2015 John Wiley & Sons, Inc. Published 2015 by John Wiley & Sons, Inc.

international/global and cross-national comparative analyses, most of which have occurred in the past 20 years. Fourth, beginning in the 1990s and continuing to the present, Akers' SLT has been tested against or fused with a range of other theories. Akers himself has participated in this intellectual enterprise, expanding social learning theory to include social structural elements (Akers, 1998). Moreover, SLT has played a role in the elaboration of victim–perpetrator overlap. Fifth, we examine new conceptual and empirical directions that challenge the efficacy of SLT. What will be made clear at the chapter's conclusion is that while the theory may not have been intended by Akers to serve as a focal theory of juvenile delinquency, no matter the range of conduct included under that term, criminologists have employed it repeatedly in the study of individual and collective delinquency.[1]

Social Learning Theory: The Basics

Burgess and Akers (1966) extended Sutherland's DAT, restating the latter's nine propositions –reducing them to seven – in the language of operant conditioning and calling it differential association-reinforcement theory. In essence, Burgess and Akers used operant conditioning to explain how any learned content becomes part of an individual's social psychological makeup, an element missing from Sutherland's formulation. For some sociologists, Akers' use of psychological behaviorism's operant conditioning, with its roots in the work of Skinner and Bandura (Sellers, Winfree, & Akers, 2012), meant that SLT was less sociological and more psychological, and as a consequence generally less interesting to them (Adams, 1973).[2]

As articulated by Akers (1985, pp. 52, 55), the theory has four component parts. First, *differential association* refers to direct social interaction with members of a primary group and less concrete but no less important identifications with more distal groups, the latter also serving as sources of learning. These are not simply peer associations, but rather the sum total of all social influences including family, school teachers and other public officials, neighbors, and religious figures. *Imitation* occurs when an individual copies the behavior of others, perhaps not completely understanding why the behavior is important or in what ways or even when it might be rewarding to the actor. Imitation is the most basic form of learning, essentially a case of monkey-see monkey-do. *Definitions* serve as guideposts for behavior, good and bad, rewarding and punishing. The final element, *differential reinforcement*, exists in both social and nonsocial forms; such reinforcements are anticipatory or prospective in nature, suggesting to the actor whether the behavior guided by those definitions is likely to be rewarded or punished, even if that reward is only physiological in nature. In essence, Akers took Sutherland's DAT and provided a detailed explanation of the mechanisms by which certain definitions become an integral part of a person's decision-making processes. Sutherland's rather vague "principle of differential association", which stated that delinquency ensues when the definitions favoring criminal conduct overwhelmed those definitions favoring lawful conduct, was recast in an operant conditioning framework. People, Sutherland (1947: 8) believed, turned to crime "because of contacts with criminal patterns and also because of isolation from anticriminal patterns". It remained for Akers to specify that differential reinforcements provided the discriminative stimuli that stood at the core of which definitions were to dominate a person's decisions to engage in deviant behavior, including delinquency. Such definitions contained unique normative meanings, which, as Akers (1985) noted, reinforced rule-breaking conduct by specifying which actions are right and which ones are wrong, condemning some and approving others. In the event that those definitions approving a specific behavior are in excess, then the individual "would be willing to commit the act and violate the law" (Akers, 1985: 54).

Testing Social Learning Theory

In 1979, Akers and associates published what many criminologists consider to be the first and most complete extant test of SLT. Using a multi-state sample of male and female Midwestern students in Grades 7 through 12, they tested the efficacy of a full SLT model to predict marijuana and alcohol use. Definitions included a neutralization scale, a combined law-abiding and law-violating scale, and the respondent's own positive and negative definitions of use. Differential association measured not only how many of the respondent's peers used the drugs in question, but the construct also included measures of the approving/disapproving attitudes of significant adults and peers whose opinions, what the authors called "norm qualities", were valued by the respondents. In terms of differential reinforcements, the researchers distinguished between those that included social and non-social reinforcements and those consisting of only social reinforcements. They tied imitation to the respondent's observations of substance use by "admired" models. The model worked better to predict marijuana use than alcohol consumption; moreover, imitation yielded the weakest insights into either form of drug use, followed by the reinforcement measures; the variables purporting to measure differential association consistently performed the best. While not without its analytical critics (cf., Lanza-Kaduce, Akers, Krohn, & Radosevich, 1982; Stafford & Ekland-Olson, 1982; Strickland, 1982), Akers and associates' study remains the benchmark against which all other tests of SLT must be compared.

Following Akers and associates' work, there were literally dozens of tests throughout the 1980s, 1990s, and early 2000s, most of which mimicked their study in several important ways. First, subsequent tests tended to focus on adolescent use of status-offending and illegal drugs, including cigarettes and alcohol in the former category, and marijuana and other controlled substances in the latter (Akers & Cochran, 1985; Hwang & Akers, 2006; Krohn, Skinner, Massey, & Akers, 1985; Lee, Akers, & Borg, 2004). Given this focus on cigarettes, alcohol, and illicit drugs, some criminologists discounted the theory as only having ties to minor forms of delinquency and status offending, and not serious delinquency or criminality (Curran & Renzetti, 1994, p. 196), although research published in the late 1990s and early 2000s, much of it reviewed later in this chapter, was to contradict this claim.

Second, many tests of SLT involved cross-sectional data collected from school-based studies of adolescents and young adults in college, which were often availability or purposive samples and not generally representative ones (e.g., Akers & Lee, 1996; Holt, Burruss, & Bossler, 2010; Jennings, Park, Tomsich, Gover, & Akers, 2011; Lanza-Kaduce & Klug, 1986; Lee *et al.*, 2004; Morris & Higgins, 2010; Sellers, Cochran, & Winfree, 2003; Sellers, Winfree, & Griffiths, 1993). Since the turn of the millennium, SLT-related studies have been based on more representative samples, such as the National Youth Survey (NYS), the National Longitudinal Survey of Youth (NLSY), the National Household Survey of Drug Use and Health, and the National Longitudinal Study of Adolescent Health (Add Health) (Bellair & McNulty, 2009; Haynie, Silver, & Teasdale, 2006; Hochstetler, Copes, & DeLisi, 2002; Jennings, Higgins, Akers, Khey, & Dobrow, 2013; Preston & Goodfellow, 2006; Rebellon, 2006). Longitudinal studies of social learning, some of which included variables drawn from other theories and employed samples that were nationally representative, have further cemented SLT's viability as an explanation for a range of behaviors across time (Bellair & McNulty, 2009; Carson, 2013; Higgins, Jennings, Marcum, Ricketts, & Mahoney, 2011; Hochstetler *et al.*, 2002; Maldonado-Molina, Jennings, Tobler, Piquero, & Canino, 2010; Sellers & Winfree, 1990; Winfree, 1985).

Akers and associates' (1979) first comprehensive test included variables drawn from every major element of the theory. However, subsequent tests rarely included measures of all four parts of SLT, but nearly all included at least differential associations, followed less often by definitions and even less often by imitation and either social or non-social reinforcements (Akers & Sellers, 2013). A recent trend involves studies of SLT's reinforcement constructs, focusing largely on the non-social reinforcements (Higgins, Jennings, Marcum, Ricketts, & Mahoney, 2011; Rebellon, 2006; Stevens, May, Rice, & Jarjoura, 2011), which have traditionally been ignored (Pratt *et al.*, 2010). This latter body of work suggests that differential reinforcements play a central role in the creation of discriminative stimuli, particularly when the non-social reinforcers have strong physiological results (Stevens *et al.*, 2011).

These summary observations could certainly be challenged as speculative. Less provisional are the conclusions of a recent meta-analysis about the first 30 years of SLT testing. Specifically, Pratt *et al.* (2010) were able to locate 133 studies in refereed journals all published between 1974, the year after Akers expounded the fully developed SLT in *Deviant Behavior*, and 2003, the year in which Akers and Jensen published the theory's last major theoretical and empirical statement in *Social Learning Theory and the Explanation of Crime*. This meta-analysis reproduced the results first reported by Akers *et al.* (1979); the findings for differential associations and definitions were, as a rule, quite strong, while those reported for the impact of differential reinforcements and imitation were far more modest (Pratt *et al.*, 2010). Moreover, as Akers and Sellers (2013, p. 90) reported, whenever SLT is tested head-to-head with other theories, using the same data and analytical techniques, it generally receives greater support than the others; and as importantly, whenever SLT variables are included in either combined or integrated theoretical models, the SLT-derived variables have the greatest main and net effects. Akers' variant of SLT remains one of the most tested and respected of all criminological theories (Cooper, Walsh, & Ellis, 2010; Ellis & Walsh, 1999).

Pushing the Boundaries of SLT: Cross-Cultural, Global and Comparative Studies of SLT

In perhaps SLT's first specifically cross-cultural application, Winfree, Theis, and Griffiths (1981) explored the insights provided by social learning and social control theories into the illicit drug use of a convenience sample of Caucasian and native American middle and high-school students. While no one variable dominated the analyses, those derived from SLT performed best and as predicted. Consistent with Akers *et al.*'s (1979) earlier test, Winfree *et al.* (1981) reported that the models worked best when predicting an illegal drug (marijuana), rather than a status-offending one (alcohol). SLT performed reasonably well for both ethnic groups, but there were interesting divergences from this generalization. For example, Winfree, Griffiths, and Sellers (1989) noted that variables drawn from the four SLT components made uniformly significant contributions in the equations predicting marijuana use for both ethnic groups; however, for the alcohol use models, parental definitions were unimportant for both ethnic groups, while peer definitions were unimportant for American Indians alone (see also Sellers *et al.*, 1993).

Over the past decade, other researchers have examined the extent to which SLT can be applied either in a unique cultural setting – that is, a nation other than the US – or two or more nations, although the latter type of study is even rarer than the former, which itself is not all that common. For instance, Hwang and Akers (2006), employing a representative and random sample of high-school students living in Pusan, South Korea, found that, in spite of strong parental oversight and influence in this family-centric culture, peer associations, more so than factors related to social bonding theory, played a significant role in the use of a wide range of drugs. Wang and Jensen (2003) used SLT to explore delinquency in a second Asian nation, this time Taiwan. Examining the responses of junior high-school students, they found general support for SLT. While observing that in Taiwanese culture grandparents are both a unique source of social control and serve as powerful socializing agents, Wang and Jensen (2003, p. 80) concluded the following: "Youth attending school in urban industrial settings in a global world system are likely to be subject to similar pressures, pulls and problems in Asian and Western Societies."

Researchers have not entirely ignored other North American nations. For example, Gallupe and Bouchard (2013), employing a convenience sample of Canadian high-school students, found support for a situational and group contextualized version of social learning. They argued for a unique "behavioral contagion" explanation for when and where adolescents are likely to use controlled substances: if there is considerable peer support for drug use in specific criminogenic situations, which in their analyses were teen parties, then drug use followed in that place and at that time. Miller, Jennings, Alvarez-Rivera, and Miller (2008) provided the first examination of SLT's ties to controlled substance use by Hispanic youth, in this case a convenience sample of public and private high-school students in two comparable Puerto Rican municipalities. They found that, as predicted, deviance-supporting peer and personal definitions had consistently strong ties to cigarette smoking, alcohol use, and marijuana use; however, the predictions were uniformly better for the students enrolled in the private as opposed to the public schools.

Truly comparative studies of the youthful misconduct of children residing in different nations, where the same (or very similar) measures are employed, can provide rigorous tests of any theory's fundamentals. As the experiences of the Eurogang Project – a network of over 100 scholars and practitioners in the US and nearly 20 European nations – have taught us, the task of simply agreeing on basic definitions is often very difficult, let alone deciding which theories to include (Klein, Kerner, Maxson, & Weitekamp, 2001). Eurogang members Esbensen and Weerman (2005), using data from the National Evaluation of Gang Resistance Education and Training and a national survey of school children in the Netherlands, found that theoretical constructs drawn from social learning, self-control, and social control theories worked equally well to predict gang membership and troublesome conduct in both nations. Winfree (2012) examined comparable groups of public school children in Germany and Bosnia-Herzegovina, youth that claimed membership in one of three types of groups (i.e., non-delinquent social groups, non-gang delinquent groups, and delinquent youth gangs). While he found support for SLT-derived variables, Winfree reported that the nation-specific scale analyses of the SLT items and predictive models that included SLT measures yielded slightly different results, suggesting that while the general explanatory power of SLT is high in comparative studies, future research should consider the cultural context in which such variables operate. Specifically, it is possible that measures using behavioral and cultural referents that have meaning in one culture may be less applicable in others, causing a reduction in such a scale's ability to measure accurately the intended construct (see also Tittle, Antonaccio, & Botchkovar, 2012).

The Second International Self-Report Delinquency Study (ISRD-2) included responses from nearly 70,000 children in grades 7 to 9 living in 30 countries (Junger-Tas *et al.*, 2012). Posick (2013), using a large subsample of the ISRD-2, examined how well social learning, social control, and strain theories explained the overlap between offending and victimization, maintaining that the theories should tell us more about offending than victimization. This is exactly what Posick found for SLT and self-control variables, but not for family bonding and negative life events. More importantly, the variables drawn from these criminological traditions worked well across the ISRD-2's 30 nations. Posick noted the inclusion of what he called a clustering variable, which aggregated the student responses into six international regional groupings (i.e., Anglo-Saxon, Northern Europe, Western Europe, Mediterranean, Latin American, and Post-Socialist nations) to account for common socio-cultural influences.

These efforts to apply SLT in other cultures have clear implications for other comparative studies. First, it is possible to compare the efficacy of delinquency theories cross-culturally even within a single dominant culture, as long as there are clearly delineated ethnic subgroups, ones that have steadfastly maintained their own unique and distinct cultural differences. Second, while single-nation studies are useful starting points, truly comparative analyses are needed, such as those endorsed by both the Eurogang Project and the consortium behind the ISRD-2. Finally, while it is essential to have consistency in the conceptual and operational definitions of key measures across multiple theories, researchers must exert caution when constructing "universal" measures, as this may prove to be an elusive goal, especially when the various nations' geo-political and cultural forces are quite different.

Expansions and Extensions of Social Learning Theory

Changes to first-iteration criminological theories are not unusual. Sometimes these changes are for conceptual clarity or to provide more direct ties to the empirical world. At other times, the original theory is linked to or even merged with another theory, one which did not exist when the first theory was formulated or such connections were not considered appropriate at the time. Indeed, SLT is itself an extension of Sutherland's DAT, although Akers' has contended that the two are synonymous (Sellers *et al.*, 2012). SLT too has been the object of expansions and extensions, two of which warrant our attention. The first is Akers' social structure social learning theory (SSSL), an expansion of SLT that provided a missing piece to his original formulation: what is the origin of the learning structures? The second is an extension of SLT into the area of victimization studies, as SLT has been proposed as a theory of both victimizers and victims.

Social structure social learning theory

More than a decade ago, Akers (1998) expanded SLT into social structure social learning theory, or SSSL, which differs from SLT in several important aspects. As Akers described it (1998, p. 322):

> [the theory's] main proposition is that variations in the social structure, culture, and locations of individuals and groups in the social system explain variations in crime rates, principally through their influence on differences among individuals on the social learning variables – mainly, differential association, differential reinforcement, imitation, definitions favorable and unfavorable and other discriminative stimuli for crime.

While Akers has previously detailed the social psychological elements of learning theory, the structural features remain ambiguous, including *differential social organization* (e.g., an area's population size and density, age, gender, and racial distributions and proportions, and general attributes related to regional cultural, geographical features, and cultural variability); *differential location in the social structure* (e.g., ascribed and achieved individual attributes, including race, gender, marital status, age, and socio-economic status); *social structure's criminogenic elements* (e.g., anomie, class oppression and patriarchical condition within the social groups where the individuals have membership); and *differential social location within social structure* (e.g., the individual's position within various reference groups where they have membership, including families, peer and friendship groups, leisure groups, collegial groups, and work groups, all of which can serve as the source of normative or deviant patterning of behavior)(Akers, 1998, p. 331). In simplified processual terms, Akers (1998, p. 342) argued that the social structure influenced the social psychological process leading to criminal behavior, which in the aggregate determined the crime rate.

Early critics of SSSL focused on the theory's general failure to signify the "relative theoretical importance of the structural covariates" (Akers, 1999, p. 481; see also Krohn, 1999; Morash, 1999; Sampson, 1999). Partial tests of the theory, most of which included only incomplete measures of the structural elements, began to appear in short order (Akers & Sellers, 2013). For example, the work of Lee *et al.* (2004), which returned to the question of adolescent drug use and employed the same Boys Town data as did Akers *et al.* (1979) in their seminal piece, included measures of differential location in the social structure, differential social location in reference groups, and differential social organization, three of SSSL's four dimensions. Even with this restricted model and what the authors acknowledged as weak indicators of the structural parts of SSSL, the sequential equation model analyses provided general support for Akers' extended theory. Haynie *et al.* (2006), in a study of violent peer networks, also reported strong support for SSSL's contentions about the impact of differential social organization, as did other youth violence studies that used similar analytical strategies (Bellair, Roscigno, & Velez, 2003; Gibson, Poles, & Akers, 2010). Finally, Bellair *et al.* (2003) observed that the influences of neighborhood were almost entirely mediated through the effects of the social learning process (see also Bellair & McNulty, 2009). What is not yet clear from the extant SSL research is the exact role played by the learning process, situated as it is between the structural features of one's environment and his or her delinquency (Lanza-Kaduce & Capece, 2003; see also Akers & Sellers, 2013, pp. 99–100). Specifically, we do not fully understand whether learning's effects are mediating – whereby learning accounts for the relationship between the structural features and delinquency – or moderating – whereby learning determines the strength or direction of the influence of structural features; essentially the former explain how or why such external factors work, while the latter specify when they will occur (Baron & Kenny, 1986, p. 1176).

Theory of violence perpetration or victimization (or both)

The correlation between being an offender and being a victim intrigues criminologists (Dobrin, 2001; Mustaine & Tewksbury, 2000). This relationship has various names, but is generally referred to as the "victim–perpetrator overlap". Clues as to this overlap can be found in studies that link SLT to interpersonal violence, including dating violence (Boeringer, Shehan, & Akers, 1991; Sellers *et al.*, 2003; Tontodonato & Crew, 1992), repetitive intimate partner violence (Cochran, Sellers, Wiesbrock, & Palacios, 2011), intergenerational transmission of battering among intimate partners (Sellers, Cochran, & Branch, 2005), and stalking (Fox, Nobles, & Akers, 2011). In each case, the learning variables performed much as we would expect: interpersonal violence between individuals who have pre-existing relationships or even partnerships has clear links to the learning process. This body of research suggests that pro-violence attitudes precede the conduct and are capable of transmission from one generation to the next. However, as Wareham, Boots, and Chavez (2009) revealed in their study of adult male batterers, SLT variables were not, as a rule, dependent upon measures of intergenerational transmission (i.e., family-of-origin violence measures). These works on the ties of SLT to adult and late adolescent intimate partner violence are significant in that they lay down the empirical and conceptual framework for the perpetration–victimization overlap studies, but generally lack a focus on the problems of juveniles.

A more recent series of studies has used criminological theories, including SLT, to provide insights into the observed linkage between being a victim and being a perpetrator. Interestingly, several of these studies have made use of somewhat unusual types of data – specifically intra-national ethnic groups, single nation studies outside the US, and comparative studies – and many of them have focused on the overlap issue as it impacts the lives of juveniles. For example, Miller's (2012) study of a homogenous subsample of Hispanic adolescent participants in the Project on Human Development in Chicago Neighborhoods found this overlap, and further revealed that foreign-born Hispanics are both less likely to be delinquent or the victims of violent crime; moreover, differential associations, her sole SLT variable, dominated self-control in predicting delinquency and victimization. In another study of a subcultural group embedded in a dominant culture, Maldonado-Molina *et al.* (2010) assessed this overlap within a Bronx-based subsample of Puerto Rican youth from the longitudinal Boricua Youth Study, and found that being both a victim and a perpetrator persists over time. However, the inclusion of risk factors, including peer influences, parental relationships, and school environment did not reduce the direct ties between being a victim and being a perpetrator. Deviant peers may provide the social context for learning to be delinquent, but may not provide much protection against being a victim (Schreck, Fisher, & Miller 2004). This is a case, Maldonado-Molina and associates maintained, of theorizing not keeping pace with the overlap phenomenon's empirical studies, resulting in an incomplete understanding of which forces are at work and how they operate.

Studies of the possible role of SLT in explaining the overlap outside the US are also instructive. Earlier we reviewed Posick's (2013) victim–perpetrator study using data from the ISRD-2, in which he found that the overlap was indeed present within the multinational sample and that the theoretical variables, including ones drawn from SLT, performed largely as expected. Looking at dating violence and perpetration among South Korean college students, Jennings *et al.* (2011), consistent with a growing body of international studies on this topic, also found this overlap. Like Maldonado-Molina and associates, they too found that even after controlling for variables measuring the influence of demographic, SLT, and self-control factors, a strong and significant correlation remained between dating violence offending and victimization.

Present and Future Applications of Social Learning

Lacking a criminological crystal ball, this section of the chapter owes much to a body of preliminary conceptual work that links SLT to two divergent paths. One path suggests that in order to achieve a complete understanding of learning as a process, we must consider the confluence of learning, gender, and the human brain. The other body of work pushes us in the direction of non-traditional dependent variables, ones outside the range normally examined in the study of juvenile delinquency. In this latter section, then, we explore SLT's links to macro- and micro-level forms of violence. Collectively, these divergent theoretical and empirical paths suggest the vitality and utility of SLT for the broader criminological enterprise.

Biological and gender influences on social learning theory

By the first decade of the twenty-first century, morphological studies of the brains of boys and girls began to suggest that significant differences exist in how information is processed by each sex, and these differences start early in human physiological development (Eliot, 2009; see also Wood, Heitmiller, Andreasen, & Nopoulos, 2008a; Wood, Murko, & Nopoulos, 2008b). That the brains of boys and girls, men and women are different is beyond dispute (Zaidi, 2010). Males and females are equal in intelligence, but persons of the opposite sex and similar intelligence process information and solve problems differently. It appears that the brains of young girls develop differently than those of boys of the same age, particularly in the area of social perception. Moreover, by the teenage years, boys' brains begin to "catch up" to those of girls, particularly in those areas of the brain that are critical for cognition.

Exactly what these observations mean for behavior has been the subject of much debate, research and theorizing. For example, these studies do not suggest that behavior, particularly in late adolescence and early adulthood, is "hardwired" in the womb (and sex-linked). Rather, the relationships between biological sex, "femininity" and behavior are complex and, contend the researchers, just as likely to be the products of social learning (Eliot, 2009).

One way in which these differences may manifest themselves is in the processes associated with social learning, especially if those differences change in gender-specific ways throughout the early life course. While disagreement exists on this point (Miller *et al.*, 2008), Sellers and Blackwell (2012) direct us to the putative need for gender-specific learning styles – and the absence of gender theorizing by

SLT advocates. They speculated that what we need are tests of SLT that make use of gender-linked differences in brain morphology and hormonal variability. As Sellers and Blackwell observed, even given the same or very similar learning environments, the outcomes – what is learned and what becomes part of one's behavior – may be just as different for boys and girls as is their brain morphology. Even the act of imitation may manifest itself differently in boys and girls, as different gender-based value systems come into play, suggestive of an additional cognitive component. Finally, Sellers and Blackwell (2012) speculated that just as Akers borrowed from behaviorism to create SLT, the integration of gender considerations into current variants of SLT may require further borrowing from cognitive psychology.

New dependent variables: applying SLT to individual and collective violence

One of the early criticisms of SLT was that researchers limited themselves to the study of relatively minor forms of youthful misconduct, including cigarette smoking and the consumption of alcohol. The focus on these activities, and related status offending, has given way to a wider range of conduct over the past three decades, including student cheating, mainly at the college level (Lanza-Kaduce & Klug, 1986); serious theft crimes, including the theft of video content, technology and related "cyber crimes", again largely by college students (Higgins, 2006; Holt *et al.*, 2010; Morris & Higgins, 2010); dating violence, also extracted from college-age samples (Tontodonato & Crew, 1992; Wareham *et al.*, 2009) or institutionalized youth (Stevens *et al.*, 2011); and gang behavior, including drive-by shootings, gang fights, and assaultive crime (Taylor, Peterson, Esbensen, & Freng, 2007; Winfree, 2012; Winfree, Vigil-Bäckström, & Mays, 1994).

In a particularly innovative and controversial move, Akers tied SLT to suicide in a chapter of 1973's *Deviant Behavior* entitled "A Social Learning Analysis of the Suicidal Process". Like Durkheim before him, who famously described in *Suicide* (1897) how a phenomenon viewed as a highly individualistic act could have social roots, Akers argued that both successful and unsuccessful suicides could be framed in social learning terms. More recently, Akers and Silverman (2004) described how SLT, especially given the expanded social structural elements of SSSL, might provide valuable insights into terror bombings. They observed that definitions and motivations are instrumental in the recruitment and deployment of terrorists, as such discriminative stimuli not only contain what are often virulently negative in-group norms and attitudes towards out-groups, but they also work against any norms that may constrain acts of terror.

Winfree and Akins (2008) extended this argument into suicide bombings, noting the conceptual linkages between "learning to be a suicide bomber" and SLT. Moreover, they suggested an additional technique of neutralization, one that may have applicability beyond suicide bombers. Specifically, Winfree and Akins

(2008, p. 152) observed that relatives of suicide bombers can gain special status in their communities, wherein being the next-of-kin is viewed positively, much like the neutralization technique of an appeal to a higher authority.

The examination of non-traditional dependent variables has taken SLT in several new directions, although the linkages to delinquency may not have been immediately apparent. Consider that juveniles are often the victims of both homicide and suicide; moreover, programs intended to reduce these events may well take advantage of SLT's linkages to other prevention and treatment measures (Akers & Sellers, 2013, pp. 100–109). Similarly, terrorism and suicide bombings include child perpetrators, suggesting a possible path for scholars interested in both empirical studies and preventative activities (Bloom, 2012). The employment of children as soldiers is another related topic, one that has gained considerable cachet over the past two decades (Coalition to Stop the Use of Child Soldiers, 2008). Taken together, these works suggest that SLT may have utility for both micro- and macro-level explanations of suicide, homicide, and terrorist attacks, and they collectively represent some of the theory's most unusual and intriguing empirical and conceptual applications.

Summary

The goals set for this chapter were, like those of each of the other contributions to this volume, rather daunting. Rather than give fully expository responses to the chapter's five goals, each of which could have been a fully developed chapter in its own right, we provided instead guideposts and benchmarks of the distance and direction traveled by SLT since its first formal statement in 1966. As promulgated by Akers, SLT is a general theory that should be able to yield insights into a wide range of behaviors, which has certainly been the case. Initial concerns about SLT being mainly a theory of minor forms of delinquency or only group-context acts have proven to be unfounded. Serious offending, individual acts and cross-cultural comparisons have found their way into the mix.

Finally, we acknowledge that this review far from exhausts all possible topics. For example, in the area of theoretical extensions, Akers himself has participated in a merger of self-control with social learning (Jennings *et al.*, 2013). Indeed, side-by-side tests of self-control and social learning theory, as well as claims that one mediates the effects of the other, could fill an entire chapter (cf. Burruss, Bossler, & Holt, 2013; Higgins, 2006; McGloin & Shermer, 2009; Yarbrough, Jones, Sullivan, Sellers, & Cochran, 2012). Instead, in this chapter we reviewed more than 40 years of work that elaborates on SLT, wherein we focused primarily on past trends, current studies, and future avenues of research that may hold promise for an even more in-depth understanding of the processes behind learning to become non-normative, no matter the age of the individual involved. This is, after all, the goal first set more than 65 years ago by Sutherland and restated a generation later by Akers. In this regard if no other, we have achieved our goals.

Notes

1 Defining delinquency's age parameters is made difficult by the tendency for researchers to include a rather broad range of ages for the "juveniles" in their samples, including pre-adolescents under the age of 10 and young adults up to the age 25 (Mays & Winfree, 2012, pp. 3–7). We will note when a study's sample includes persons above the age of 17.

2 Akers (2011) observed that when Burgess and he first presented their theory in 1966, Sutherland's student Donald Cressey was in the audience. Cressey, Akers noted, was "very encouraging and expressed the opinion that, had Sutherland lived, he would have approved of our efforts" (p. 362). Note too that Akers eschews the Skinnerian notions of operant conditioning, suggesting instead that SLT owes far more to Bandura's (2001) social cognitive theory (Akers & Sellers, 2013, p. 81)

References

Adams, L.R. (1973). The adequacy of differential association theory. *Journal of Research in Crime and Delinquency*, *11*, 1–18.

Akers, R.L. (1973). *Deviant Behavior: A Social Learning Approach*. Belmont, CA: Wadsworth Publishing Co.

Akers, R.L. (1977). *Deviant Behavior: A Social Learning Approach*, 2nd ed. Belmont, CA: Wadsworth Publishing Co.

Akers, R.L. (1985). *Deviant Behavior: A Social Learning Approach*, 3rd ed. Belmont, CA: Wadsworth Publishing Co.

Akers, R.L. (1998). *Social Learning and Social Structure: A General Theory of Crime and Deviance*. Boston: Northeastern University Press.

Akers, R.L. (1999). Social learning and social structure: Reply to Sampson, Morash, and Krohn. *Theoretical Criminology*, *3*, 477–493.

Akers, R.L. (2011). The origins of me and of social learning theory: Personal and professional recollections and reflections. In F.T. Cullen, C.L. Jonson, A.J. Myer, & F. Adler (Eds.), *The Origins of American Criminology* (pp. 347–366). New Brunswick, NJ: Transaction.

Akers, R.L., & Cochran, J.K. (1985). Adolescent marijuana use: A test of three theories of deviant behavior. *Deviant Behavior*, *6*, 323–346.

Akers, R.L., & Jensen, G.F. (Eds.) (2003). *Social Learning and the Explanation of Crime*. New Brunswick, NJ: Transaction.

Akers, R.L., Krohn, M.D., Lanza-Kaduce, L., & Radosevich, M. (1979). Social learning and deviant behavior: A specific test of a general theory. *American Sociological Review*, *44*, 448–462.

Akers, R.L., & Lee, G. (1996). A longitudinal test of social learning theory: Adolescent smoking. *Journal of Drug Issues*, *26* (2), 317–343.

Akers, R.L., & Sellers, C.S. (2013). *Criminological Theories: Introduction, Evaluation, and Application*. New York: Oxford University Press.

Akers, R.L., & Silverman, A. (2004). Toward a social learning model of violence and terrorism. In M.A. Zahn, H.H. Brownstein, & S.L. Jackson (Eds.), *Violence: From Theory to Research* (pp. 19–35). Cincinnati, OH: Lexis-Nexis-Anderson Publishing.

Bandura, A. (2001). Social cognitive theory: An agentive perspective. *Annual Review of Psychology*, *52*, 1–26.

Baron, R.M., & Kenny, D.A. (1986). The moderator-mediator distinction in social psychological research: Conceptual, strategic, and statistical considerations. *Journal of Personality and Social Psychology, 51*, 1173–1182.

Bellair, P., & McNulty, T.L. (2009). Gang membership, drug selling, and violence in neighborhood context. *Justice Quarterly, 26*, 644–669.

Bellair, P., Roscigno, V.J., & Velez, M.A. (2003). Occupational structure, social learning, and adolescent violence. In R.L. Akers, & G.F. Jensen (Eds.), *Social Learning and the Explanation of Crime* (pp. 197–226). New Brunswick, NJ: Transaction.

Bloom, M. (2012). Analysis: Women and children constitute the new faces of terror. CNN, August 6. Retrieved from http://security.blogs.cnn.com/2012/08/06/analysis-women-and-children-constitute-the-new-faces-of-terror/

Boeringer, S.B., Shehan, C.L., & Akers, R.L. (1991). Social contexts and social learning theory in sexual coercion and aggression: Assessing the contribution of fraternity membership. *Family Relations, 40* (1), 58–64.

Burgess, R.L., & Akers, R.L. (1966). A differential association reinforcement theory of criminal behavior. *Social Problems, 14*, 128–147.

Burruss, G.W., Bossler, A.M., & Holt, T.J. (2013). Assessing the mediation of a fuller social learning model on low self-control's influence on software piracy. *Crime and Delinquency, 59*(8), 1157–1184.

Carson, D.C. (2013). Perceptions of prosocial and delinquent peer behavior and the effect on delinquent attitudes: A longitudinal study. *Journal of Criminal Justice, 41*, 151–161.

Coalition to Stop the Use of Child Soldiers. (2008). *Child Soldiers: Global Report 2008.* London: Bell and Bain.

Cochran, J.K., Sellers, C.S., Wiesbrock, V., & Palacios, W.R. (2011). Repetitive intimate partner victimization: An exploratory application of social learning theory. *Deviant Behavior, 32*, 790–817.

Cooper, J.A., Walsh, A., & Ellis, L. (2010). Is criminology moving toward a paradigm shift? Evidence from a survey of the American Society of Criminology. *Journal of Criminal Justice Education, 21*, 332–347.

Curran, D.J., & Renzetti, C.M. (1994). *Theories of Crime.* Boston: Allyn and Bacon.

Dobrin, A. (2001). The risk of offending on homicide victimization: a case control study. *Journal of Research in Crime and Delinquency, 38*, 154–173.

Durkheim, E. (1897/1951) *Suicide: A Study in Sociology.* Glencoe, IL: Free Press.

Eliot, L. (2009). Girl brain, boy brain? *Scientific American*, September 8. Retrieved from http://www.scientificamerican.com/article.cfm?id=girl-brain-boy-brain

Ellis, L., & Walsh, A. (1999). Criminologists' opinions about causes and theories of crime and delinquency. *The Criminologist, 24*(4), 4–6.

Esbensen, F.-A., & Weerman, F. (2005). Youth gangs and troublesome youth groups in the United States and the Netherlands. *A cross-national comparison. European Journal of Criminology, 2*, 5–37.

Fox, K.A., Nobles, M.R., & Akers, R.L. (2011). Is stalking a learned phenomenon? An empirical test of social learning theory. *Journal of Criminal Justice, 39*, 39–47.

Gallupe, O., & Bouchard, M. (2013). Adolescent parties and substance use: A situational approach to peer influence. *Journal of Criminal Justice, 41*, 162–171.

Gibson, C.L., Poles, T.B., & Akers, R.L. (2010). A partial test of social structure social learning: Neighborhood disadvantage, differential association with delinquent peers, and delinquency. In M. DeLisi, & K.M. Beaver (Eds.), *Criminological Theory: A Life-Course Approach* (pp. 133–148). London: Jones and Bartlett Publishers.

Haynie, D.L., Silver, E., & Teasdale, B. (2006). Neighborhood characteristics, peer networks, and adolescent violence. *Journal of Quantitative Criminology, 22,* 47–169.

Higgins, G.E. (2006). Gender differences in software piracy: The mediating role of self-control theory and social learning theory. *Journal of Economic Crime Management, 4*(1), 1–30.

Higgins, G.E., Jennings, W.G., Marcum, C.D., Ricketts, M.L., & Mahoney, M. (2011). Developmental trajectories of nonsocial reinforcement and offending in adolescence and young adulthood: An exploratory study of an understudied part of social learning theory. *Journal of Criminal Justice, 39,* 60–66.

Hochstetler, A., Copes, H., & DeLisi, M. (2002). Differential association in group and solo offending. *Journal of Criminal Justice, 30,* 559–566.

Holt, T.J., Burruss, G.W., & Bossler, A.M. (2010). Social learning and cyber-deviance: Examining the importance of a full social learning model in the virtual world. *Journal of Crime & Justice, 33*(2), 31–61.

Hwang, S., & Akers, R.L. (2006). Parental and peer influences on adolescent drug use in Korea. *Asian Criminology, 1,* 51–69.

Jennings, W.G., Higgins, G.E., Akers, R.L., Khey, D.H., & Dobrow, J. (2013). Examining the influence of delinquent peer association on the stability of self-control in late childhood and early adolescence: Toward an integrated theoretical model. *Deviant Behavior, 34*(5), 407–422.

Jennings, W.G., Park, M., Tomsich, E.A., Gover, A.R., & Akers, R.L. (2011). Assessing the overlap in dating violence perpetration and victimization among South Korean college students: The influence of social learning and self-control. *American Journal of Criminal Justice, 36,* 188–206.

Junger-Tas, J., Marshall, I.H., Enzmann, D., Killias, M., Steketee, M., & Gruszcznska, B. (2012). *The Many Faces of Youth Crime: Contrasting Theoretical Perspectives on Juvenile Delinquency across Countries and Cultures.* New York: Springer.

Klein, M.W., Kerner, H.-J., Maxson, C.L., & Weitekamp, E. (2001). *The Eurogang Paradox: Street Gangs and Youth Groups in the U.S. and Europe.* Amsterdam: Kluwer Press.

Krohn, M.D. (1999). Social learning theory: Continuing development of perspective. *Theoretical Criminology, 3*(4), 462–476.

Krohn, M.D., Skinner, W.F., Massey, J.L., & Akers, R.L. (1985). Social learning theory and adolescent cigarette smoking: A longitudinal study. *Social Problems, 32,* 455–473.

Lanza-Kaduce, L., Akers, R.L., Krohn, M.D., & Radosevich. M. (1982). Conceptual and analytical models in testing social learning theory: Reply. *American Sociological Review, 47*(1), 169–173.

Lanza-Kaduce, L., & Capece, M. (2003). A specific test of an integrated general theory. In R.L. Akers, & G.F. Jensen (Eds.), *Social Learning and the Explanation of Crime* (pp. 179–196). New Brunswick, NJ: Transaction.

Lanza-Kaduce, L., & Klug, M. (1986). Learning to cheat: The interaction of moral-development and social learning theories. *Deviant Behavior, 7*(3), 243–259.

Lee, G., Akers, R.L., & Borg, M.J. (2004). Social learning and structural factors in adolescent substance use. *Western Criminology Review, 5*(1), 17–34.

Maldonado-Molina, M.M., Jennings, W.G., Tobler, A.L., Piquero, A.R., & Canino, G. (2010). Assessing the victim-offender overlap among Puerto Rican youth. *Journal of Criminal Justice, 38,* 1191–1201.

Mays, G.L., & Winfree, Jr., L.T. (2012). *Juvenile Justice,* 3rd ed. New York: Wolters Kluwer.

McGloin, J.M., & Shermer, L.O.N. (2009). Self-control and deviant peer network structure. *Journal of Research in Crime and Delinquency, 46*(1), 35–72.

Miller, H.V. (2012). Correlates of delinquency and victimization in a sample of Hispanic youth. *International Criminal Justice Review, 22*(2), 153–170.

Miller, H.V., Jennings, W.G., Alvarez-Rivera, L.L., & Miller, J.M. (2008). Explaining substance use among Puerto Rican adolescents: A partial test of social learning theory. *Journal of Drug Issues, 28*, 261–283.

Morash, M. (1999). A consideration of gender in relation to social learning and social structure: A general theory of crime and deviance. *Theoretical Criminology, 3*(4), 451–462.

Morris, R.G., & Higgins, G.E. (2010). Criminological theory in the digital age: The case of social learning theory and digital piracy. *Journal of Criminal Justice, 38*, 470–480.

Mustaine, E.E., & Tewksbury R. (2000). Comparing the lifestyles of victims, offenders, and victim-offenders: a routine activity assessment of similarities and differences for criminal incident participants. *Sociological Focus, 33*, 339–362.

Posick, C. (2013). The overlap between offending and victimization among adolescents: Results from the Second International Self-Report Delinquency Study. *Journal of Contemporary Criminal Justice, 29*, 106–124.

Pratt, T., Cullen, F.T., Sellers, C.S., Winfree, Jr., L.T., Madensen, T.D., Daigle, L.E., Fearn, N.F., & Gau, J.M. (2010). The empirical status of social learning theory: A meta-analysis. *Justice Quarterly, 27*, 765–802.

Preston, P., & Goodfellow, M. (2006). Cohort comparisons: Social learning explanations for alcohol used among adolescents and older adults. *Addictive Behaviors, 31*, 2268–2283.

Rebellon, C.J. (2006). Do adolescents engage in delinquency to attract the social attention of peers? An extension and longitudinal test of social reinforcement theory. *Journal of Research in Crime and Delinquency, 43*(4), 387–411.

Sampson, R.J. (1999). Techniques of research neutralization. *Theoretical Criminology, 3*(4), 438–451.

Schreck, C.J., Fisher, B.S., & Miller, J.M. (2004). The social context of violence victimization: A study of the delinquent peer effect. *Justice Quarterly, 21*, 23–47.

Sellers, C.S., & Blackwell, B.S. (2012). *Integrating gender into social learning theory.* Unpublished paper presented at the American Society of Criminology, Chicago, IL.

Sellers, C.S., Cochran, J.K., & Branch, K.A. (2005). Social learning theory and partner violence: A research note. *Deviant Behavior, 26*(4), 379–395.

Sellers, C.S., Cochran, J.K., & Winfree, Jr., L.T. (2003) Social learning theory and courtship violence: An empirical test. In R.L. Akers, & G.F. Jensen (Eds.), *Social Learning and the Explanation of Crime* (pp. 109–129). New Brunswick, NJ: Transaction.

Sellers, C.S., & Winfree, Jr., L.T. (1990). Differential associations and definitions: A panel study of youthful drinking behavior. *International Journal of the Addictions, 25*(7), 755–771.

Sellers, C.S., Winfree, Jr., L.T., & Akers, R.L. (2012). *Social Learning Theories of Crime.* Burlington, VT: Ashgate.

Sellers, C.S., Winfree, Jr., L.T., & Griffiths, C.T. (1993). Legal attitudes, permissive norm qualities, and substance use: A comparison of American Indian and non-Indian youths. *Journal of Drug Issues, 23*, 493–513.

Stafford, M.C., & Ekland-Olson, S. (1982). On social learning and deviant behavior: A reappraisal of the findings. *American Sociological Review, 47*, 167–169.

Stevens, J., May, D., Rice, N., & Jarjoura, G.R. (2011). Nonsocial versus social reinforcers: Contrasting theoretical perspectives on repetitive serious delinquency and drug use. *Youth Violence and Juvenile Justice, 9*, 295–312.

Strickland, D.E. (1982). Social learning and deviant behavior: A specific test of a general theory: A comment and critique. *American Sociological Review, 47*, 162–167.

Sutherland, E.H. (1947). *Principles of Criminology*. Philadelphia: Lippincott.

Taylor, T.J., Peterson, D., Esbensen, F.-A., & Freng, A. (2007). Gang membership as a risk factor for adolescent violent victimization. *Journal of Research in Crime and Delinquency, 44*, 351–380.

Tittle, C.R., Antonaccio, D., & Botchkovar, E. (2012). Social learning, reinforcement and crime: Evidence from three European cities. *Social Forces, 90*, 863–890.

Tontodonato, P., & Crew, B.K. (1992). Dating violence, social learning theory, and gender: A multivariate analysis. *Violence and Victims, 7*, 3–14.

Wang, S.-N., & Jensen, G.F. (2003). Explaining delinquency in Taiwan: A test of social learning theory. In R.L. Akers, & G.F. Jensen (Eds.), *Social Learning and the Explanation of Crime* (pp. 65–83). New Brunswick, NJ: Transaction.

Wareham, J., Boots, D.P., & Chavez, J.M. (2009). A test of social learning and intergenerational transmission among batterers. *Journal of Criminal Justice, 27*, 163–173.

Winfree, Jr., L.T. (1985). Peers, parents and adolescent drug use in a rural school district: a two-wave panel study. *Journal of Youth and Adolescence, 14*(6), 499–512.

Winfree, Jr., L.T. (2012). A comparative theoretical examination of troublesome youth in Germany and Bosnia-Herzegovina. *Journal of Comparative Criminal Justice, 28*, 406–425.

Winfree, Jr, L.T., & Akins, J.K. (2008) Extending the boundaries of social structure/social learning theory: The case of suicide bombers in Gaza. *International Journal of Crime, Criminal Justice, and Law, 3*(1), 145–158.

Winfree, Jr., L.T., Griffiths, C.T., & Sellers, C.S. (1989). Social learning theory, drug use, and American Indian youth: A cross-cultural test. *Justice Quarterly, 6*, 501–523.

Winfree, Jr., L.T., Theis, H.E., & Griffiths, C.T. (1981). Drug use in rural America: A cross-cultural examination of complementary social deviance theories. *Youth and Society, 12*(4), 465–489.

Winfree, Jr., L.T., Vigil-Bäckström, T., & Mays, G.L. (1994). Social learning theory, self-reported delinquency, and youth gangs: A new twist on a general theory of crime and delinquency. *Youth and Society, 26*(2), 147–177.

Wood, J.L., Heitmiller, D., Andreasen, N.C., & Nopoulos, P. (2008a). Morphology of the ventral frontal cortex: Relationship to femininity and social cognition. *Cerebral Cortex, 18*(3), 534–540.

Wood, J.L., Murko, V., & Nopoulos, P. (2008b). Ventral frontal cortex in children: Morphology, social cognition and femininity/masculinity. *Social Cognitive and Affective Neuroscience, 3*(2), 168–176.

Yarbrough, A., Jones, S., Sullivan, C., Sellers, C., & Cochran, C. (2012). Social learning and self-control: Assessing the moderating potential of criminal propensity. *International Journal of Offender Therapy and Comparative Criminology, 56*(2), 191–202.

Zaidi, Z.F. (2010). Gender differences in human brain: A review. *The Open Anatomy Journal, 2*, 37–55.

18

Social Control and Self-Control

Erich Goode

Why do social norms exist? Why do certain acts come to be defined as wrong, or deviant? Why and how are these norms enforced? What form does enforcement take? Why do violations of certain norms attract especially harsh sanctions, while others elicit milder punishments? Is sanctioning even-handed, impartial, and equitable, or do certain violators attract harsher sanctions than others, even for the same offenses? What would happen to society if all of us could do anything we wanted, without any normative constraints whatsoever? Does social control actually diminish the incidence of wrongdoing? Or generate and reinforce it? Is it possible that punishment decreases deviance among most wrongdoers, but reinforces it among others? Does being constrained by conventional values, peers, activities, and institutions vary among members of the society, and if so, can sociologists use this dimension as an explanation for deviance? Are these constraints in one's immediate present, or are past constraints (say, parental interventions in childhood wrong-doing) relevant to contemporary deviant behavior? Why, in short, do societies establish and enforce systems of social control? How does social control operate? And what consequences does the exercise of social control have on the occurrence and incidence of deviant behavior?

Sociologists agree that an understanding of social control, or efforts to ensure conformity to the norms, is essential to understanding how society functions. But as essential as *some* form of social control is to the survival and functioning of every society on earth, sociologists disagree as to the nature of the multiple processes by which violations and violators are sanctioned, and what the consequences of these sanctioning processes are. In the study of deviance, crime, and juvenile delinquency, the terms *social control* and *self-control* bear two meanings. They refer both to an institution, process, or condition; and to a particular theory, the name of which is *based* on that institution, process, or condition. Most who emphasize social control

The Handbook of Juvenile Delinquency and Juvenile Justice, First Edition. Edited by Marvin D. Krohn and Jodi Lane.

as a process or institution are *constructionists*; that is, they mainly investigate how rules are devised and enforced, and how violations are reacted to. In contrast, most of the sociologists and criminologists who adopt or argue for social control and self-control *theory* are positivists or *explanatory social scientists* who seek to understand the cause or causes of unconventional and illegal behavior. And as both a condition or trait, and an explanation, sociologists and criminologists who make use of self-control are likewise explanatory social scientists. When they refer to the term as a process, institution, or condition, sociologists and criminologists define *social control* as the efforts of members of collectivities to induce others to act in a socially approved manner and to refrain from acting in a disapproved manner. It includes all the institutions, mechanisms, and processes by which collectivities set, promulgate, and enforce laws, rules, and norms, by punishing those who violate normative expectations and rewarding members who conform to them. (Social scientists almost always investigate *negative* sanctions, rarely positive ones.) The stated or manifest goal of practitioners of social control is to ensure conformity to, and prevent deviation from, prescribed behavior; taken together, it represents all of society's efforts to proscribe wrongful behavior. As understood in this sense, social control can be positive or negative, formal or informal, internal or external, generic (applying to everyone in a given society) or status-specific (applying only to occupants of certain positions or members of certain groups or collectivities). Social control may very well be the most crucial and fundamental concept in the study of deviance.

In contrast, *control theory* and *social control theory* refer to explanations that attempt to account for wrongdoing. They argue that deviance is the natural, normal state of affairs; in the absence of controls, most of us would violate norms and break the law. But why don't we? What inhibits or prevents most of us from deviating, control theory argues, are our ties to conventionality or conformity. On the obverse side of the equation, control theorists argue that deviance, crime, and delinquency are the products of *weak* or *absent* social controls. The controls take the form of bonds to conventional society – attachments to individuals, involvement in activities, belief in values. The weaker these bonds are, the greater the likelihood of deviating.

Self-control is an individual quality, trait, or characteristic. As it is understood among sociologists of deviance, it refers to the ability of the individual "to exercise self-restraint when tempted to engage in deviance". Contrastingly, individuals who lack self-control "tend to act before thinking, prefer immediate over delayed rewards, like risky activities, have high activity levels, have trouble controlling their anger, and have little ambition or motivation" (Agnew, 2011, p, 117). *Self-control theory* attempts to explain deviance by explaining the origin of the *absence* of self-control, which is weak or absent parenting. Both social control and self-control theory are unique among explanations of deviance, crime, and delinquency. Instead of asking why people violate the norms, they ask why *don't* most of us do so. Their answer is that the explanation that accounts for deviating from the norms can be found in the *absence* or *weakness* of controls, whether in the form of current social bonds (control theory) or in the form of ineffective past parenting (self-control theory). These theories take for granted what traditional theories regard as problematic, and vice versa.

Social Control and the Social Order

All societies distinguish acceptable from unacceptable behavior. Now and throughout human history, all societies everywhere have set and enforced norms – rules about what their members should and should not do. Throughout the annals of time and among the world's many nations and societies, the behavior that the rules and norms prescribe, and the behavior that they punish and attempt to prohibit, differ radically, as do the nature and severity of the punishments for violating them. However, *rules and norms themselves are universal*. All societies set rules; some members of all societies violate some of those rules; and a significant number of the members of all societies attempt to enforce these rules by punishing or otherwise attempting to control the violators. There is not now and there has never been any country, society, or collectivity where "anything goes". If any such once existed, it could not long survive, for protectionist rules are, in all likelihood, the cornerstone of human survival. Functional sociologists have long assumed that the function of social control is to ensure and preserve the social order; a society that cannot maintain at least a minimum level of social order will eventually disintegrated into chaos, disorder, and brutality. In short, social control serves the social order.

"How is social order possible?" is the central question of functionalist sociologists. Even a casual historical and anthropological scan though time and around the globe currently tells us that in certain places at certain times, social control and the social order have utterly and completely collapsed. The map of the world is littered with failed states, where entire cities are hollow, burned-out shells, and armed thugs with automatic weapons patrol the countryside and through ravaged, destroyed neighborhoods and villages, ruling the huddled, terrified population with repression, exploitation, and violent, arbitrary brutality. Clearly in such places the traditional social order has collapsed, replaced with chaos and social derangement. World history is likewise littered with the dry bones of destroyed, collapsed, abandoned societies; the ongoing, functioning, contemporary ones we live in and see around us are the consequence of many thousands of years of a severe, deadly weeding-out process. In the past, many peoples or their leaders have made foolish or disastrous choices, or their populations have faced unimaginably harsh circumstances, or were conquered, destroyed, or absorbed by larger, more powerful societies – many of which themselves failed – or their culture did not prepare them to cope adequately with drastically changing circumstances. Fortunately, the majority of places around the globe are not like that, and we can learn from both failures and successes. Hence, say the functionalists, the necessity of social control: to preserve the ongoing social order.

In his masterwork, *Leviathan* (published in 1651), Thomas Hobbes (1588–1679), theorized about social control; his recognition of the problems and dilemmas that social control raises is insightful, but his solution to them seems inadequate. The natural passion of humans, explained Hobbes, seeks satisfaction of their self-interested desires. Moreover, this natural desire is infinite, without boundary or measure and, in the absence of constraint, our methods of obtaining what we desire would likewise be infinite. Without ruling constraint, where everyone is granted license to do anything he or she desires, humanity would face the reckless passion and untrammelled desires of our fellow humans, which would plunge us all into a "state of nature", forced to experience the "continual fear and danger of violent death". Under such a condition, said Hobbes, no industry would exist, nor any agriculture, navigation, commerce, education, or culture, no knowledge of the reckoning of time, the infinite rewards of art or literature, in fact, nothing we recognize as organized society. Consequently, the lives of all of us would be "solitary, poor, nasty, brutish, and short" – a "condition of war of everyone against everyone". And yet, at least in today's Western world, relatively few of us engage in a life-and-death struggle against our fellows; most of us do not live lives that are solitary, poor, nasty, brutish, or short. The majority of contemporary humans are members of a society, and recipients of a culture, that truly forms us and fashions our essential humanity, and ensures for us a measure of our physical safety. Thus, the question is, given Hobbes' premises, why *don't* most of us live under the condition of brutality he postulated? His answer is that we must agree to a kind of *social contract*: we give up our reckless attempt to obtain everything we lust for, knowing that if all of us actively sought our most extreme passions, none of us would get *anything* we wanted. We cede some quantum of control to organized society so that we will be able to receive a *smaller* measure of what we fantasize we could – but in fact *cannot* – have. We allow the ruling powers to have control over our basest passions and curtail our most fanciful aspirations because that is the only way we can stay alive, live with some measure of safety, and enjoy the fruits of our civilization.

Hobbes raised an extremely important issue, perhaps the most significant and foundational issue for this or any time: can organized society work? And if so, how? His answer is that what makes society is *social control through the social contract*. But Hobbes stumbled when he devised a solution to this quandary – that is, the specific institution to which we must hand over our freedom. To begin with, he erred in assuming that fear of punishment, *or* of hurling society into a bestial state of nature, are principally what motivates most of us, most of the time, to treat our fellow humans reasonably well.

It is clear that Hobbes ignored the process of internalization: the socialization process that instills in us the notion that following the norms is good, right, and proper, rather than merely instrumentally useful. Moreover, his notion of the entity to which the ordinary citizen must relinquish his or her freedom was the *sovereign* – that is, the English throne. It was in fact a solution that distinctly lacked prescience or foresight. Within a century plus a couple of decades beyond the publication of *Leviathan*, kings and queens would be overthrown, would lose their heads, and the public on two continents would institute democracies to replace these soon-to-be precarious monarchs; many more such insurrections would follow. Despite Hobbes' insightfulness in locating perhaps the most crucial, pressing, and vexing intellectual problem in all social and political philosophy, he utterly lacked vision on the matter of how to solve it – how a viable system of social control could be established to avoid social derangement. Yes, social control is essential for the survival of a society, but no, it cannot – and *should* not – be achieved by means of the exercise of power exerted by the throne. Royalties no longer function as sovereigns, kings and queens have been deposed or assigned ritualistic, ceremonial offices, and monarchies are the shattered, sand-covered wrecks that Shelly described in his poem *Ozymandias*. Many sociologists likewise commit a related fallacy by *affirming the consequent* of social control. To be plain about it, *social control is a process, not an outcome*; some sociologists find it difficult to analytically uncouple social control from social order. To Talcott Parsons, "social control mechanisms" are "those processes in the social system which tend to counteract the deviant tendencies". Taken as a whole, social control represents "a re-equilibrating mechanism" (1951, p. 297, 206). Similarly, Albert Cohen defined social control as "social processes tending to prevent or reduce deviance" (1966, p. 39). But is social control successful? In counterpoint to these consequentialists, Jack Gibbs complained that too many sociologists regard social control as "anything that contributes to social order". Instead, he raised a pertinent question: "*Does* social control contribute to social order?" (my emphasis). His conclusion, "if by definition social control contributes to social order, then questions about the *empirical* relationship between the two are precluded" (1981, p. 45), remains relevant. Social control may be especially harshly applied in crumbling or disintegrating societies in a failing effort to restore an old social order that is being replaced by a very different one – witness the persecution of witches during the early modern era (Ben-Yehuda, 1985, pp. 23–73; Jensen, 2007). If the relationship between social control and social order, and hence the very survival of a society, were direct and straightforward, the institutionalization of particular forms of social control would hardly be problematic; their investigation would merely reveal variations on a theme. Instead, what we find is vastly more variation in the outcomes of the application of social control. Not only is the relationship between social control and social order an empirical question, it is surprising how *few* norms are designed to condemn, punish, or protect a society or its members from injurious or predatory actions, such as murder, rape, robbery, or serious assault. Most norms attempt to discourage behavior that neither directly harms anyone nor threatens the society with chaos and disintegration. Most norms are intended to make a statement about what is considered – by some, many, or most members of a society – to be right, good, and proper. They embody certain principles of moral correctness, separate and independent of what they do for the society's physical survival. No one would be injured nor would society be threatened with disintegration if some of us were to wear our clothes backwards, eat with our hands, or insult others without restraint. But if any of us were to engage in these acts, others would react with derision, criticism, or disdain. Clearly, protecting the society from actions that are so harmful as to threaten our and the society's survival is not the sole purpose of social control. Many, and in all likelihood most, norms address the *symbolic* order; their enforcement represents a version of moral correctness, an ethos, a way of life that is *an end in itself.* We are expected to do certain things because they are *right,* because *that's the way things are done.* Violations of this ethos threaten or undermine righteousness itself. Even if deviant behavior causes no overt physical harm, audiences who exercise social control insist that the social and moral order and a decent way of life must be protected from subversion and aberration. Hence, the *social order* that social control protects is as much symbolic and cultural as physical and material.

Formal and Informal Social Control

The most important distinction among types of social control is that between *formal* and *informal* social control. In-between, we find what might be referred to as "semiformal" social control. "Informal" social control takes place in interpersonal interactions between and among people who are acting on their own, in an unofficial capacity. Reactions such as a frown or a smile, criticism or praise, shunning or being warm toward someone, are ways we have of exercising *informal* social control. They serve to remind others that their behavior upsets or annoys us. Since most people seek the approval of persons about whom they care, they tend to adjust their behavior to avoid the disapproval of significant others by discontinuing the offensive behavior or at least hiding it from public view. However, in large, complex societies, especially with a substantial volume of contact between and among strangers, informal social control is usually no longer sufficient to bring about conformity to the norms. In such societies, it becomes easy to ignore the disapproval of others if you do not care enough about them to be concerned about how they feel about you. So, *formal* social control becomes necessary. "Formal social control" is made up of efforts to bring about conformity to the law by agents of the criminal justice system: the police, the courts, and prisons. In principle, agents of formal social control act not as individuals with their own personal feelings about whether behavior is wrong or right, but as occupants of specific statuses in a specific bureaucratic organization, that is, the criminal justice system. The sanctions they apply to wrongdoers flow from their offices or positions, not from their personal relationship with the rule-violator. It is the job or function of such agents to act, when transgressions occur, to bring about conformity to the formal code, that is, the law. Both formal and informal social control may operate at the same time, or sequentially. A drug dealer may simultaneously be arrested by the police *and* shunned by his neighbors. A child molester may serve a 10-year sentence for his crime and, during his imprisonment, be taunted, shamed, and beaten by his fellow convicts and, after he is released, be condemned and humiliated by members of the community in which he lives. Somewhere in between informal social control, which is based on personal and interpersonal reactions between and among interacting parties, and the formal social control of the criminal justice system – the police, the courts, and the correctional institutions – we find "semiformal" social control. Here we have a huge territory of non-criminal, non-penal bureaucratic institutions of social control which attempt to deal with the troublesome behavior of persons under their authority. If a person's behavior becomes extremely troublesome to others, an array of agencies, bureaucracies, and organizations are likely to attempt to handle or control that person, to punish or bring him or her into line with the rules. Persons deemed difficult or problematic by others come under "the purview of professional controllers" (Hawkins & Tiedeman, 1975, p. 111). These "professional controllers" do not have the power of arrest or incarceration, but they can make recommendations to agents of the criminal justice system that may have a bearing on arrest and incarceration. Such agents include social workers, psychiatrists, truant officers, and representatives, functionaries, and officers of mental hospitals, civil courts, the Internal Revenue Service and other official tax agencies, social welfare offices, unemployment offices, departments of motor vehicles, and the educational system. The influence of formal and "semiformal" control on the lives of virtually all of us is enormous, especially if we run foul of them; but *most of the time* that social control is exercised, it is informal. Most of the time that deviant behavior is sanctioned, the actor is punished or condemned interpersonally, by individuals, not formally by representatives of a bureaucratic organization. Relatively speaking, formal social control tends to be much less common and more fitfully applied. The vast majority of rule-breaking behavior – such as making unwanted sexual passes at parties, breaking wind at the dinner table, insulting one's peers – is *ignored* by the apparatus of formal and semiformal social control. Informal social control is the foundation of social life.

Controlology or the New Sociology of Social Control

All constructionist theorists of deviance are interested in the dynamics of social control. The perspective that gives social control a central place and views social control as almost exclusively oppressive, centralized, and state-sponsored, is referred to as "controlology" or the "new sociology of social control". The spiritual father of the school of thought known as the new sociology of social control is Michel Foucault. For the controlologist, the field of deviance is about a "struggle over whose rules prevail" (Marshall, Douglas, & McDonnell, 2007, p. 71); above all, social control emanates from the exercise of power. This emphasis has been the foundation stone of the field at least since Howard Becker's *Outsiders* (1963). In *Discipline and Punish* (1979), Foucault elaborated the idea of enlightened but repressive social control. Historically, the centerpiece of social control was torture and execution. Its goal was the mutilation or destruction of the offender's (or supposed offender's) body. Traditional means of punishment were fitful and sporadic rather than continual and ongoing. Public confessions, torture, and execution created spectacle but, increasingly, they were ineffective. Eventually, crowds came not to be seized by the terror of the scaffold but instead began protesting the injustice of harsh punishment. In the end, public executions produced disorder and mob violence, not fear and compliance. The traditional prison was used almost exclusively to detain suspected offenders before trial or execution. It was only during the second half of the eighteenth century that the modern prison became a location specifically for the incarceration and punishment of the offender. The new prison, Foucault believed, revealed the special character of the new age. Jeremy Bentham (1748–1832), British philosopher, reformer, and utilitarian, came up with a plan for the modern prison. It was designed so that a small number of guards could observe a large number of inmates. He called this arrangement the *panopticon*. Foucault believed that the central thrust of the history of Western society was the evolution away from traditional society where the many observed the few (as was true in spectacles such as execution) to modern society, where the few observe the many (as in the modern prison, with its panopticon).

According to Foucault, Bentham's panopticon was typical, characteristic, or *paradigmatic* of modern society in general. The panoptic principle, Foucault believed, had become generalized and imitated throughout the entire society. We live, he said, in a society in which state and state-like agents are bent on observing and controlling its citizens in a wide range of contexts. In a very real sense, Foucault believed modern society had become one gigantic, monstrous panopticon. Foucault's argument was more literary and philosophical formulation than sociological. To describe historical changes, Foucault used clever analogies and metaphors that may or may not fit empirically. He took *thought* and *discourse* as concretely realized behavior, as indicative of the way things are: in a sense, as even more "real" than actions. In fact, modern prisons are not even remotely like Bentham's panopticon. In real-life prisons, surveillance and control require a substantial ratio of guards to prisoners. As a general rule, Foucault took consequences, including unintended consequences, as if they were a direct outcome of the motives of the powerful actors on the scene. He ignored all countervailing forces that operate to control the exercise of power. In his scheme, there is no political opposition. He nearly always presents the control potential of the powers that be as the reality. And, for all its claims to being a political understanding of modern society, *Discipline and Punish* presents a "strangely apolitical" analysis of the exercise of power (Garland, 1990, p. 170). There is no "motive to power" – only more power, more discipline, and more control. Why and for what purpose the power is wielded is never fully explained. Foucault wrote as if a society without the exercise of power is possible; he seemed to be against power *per se* (pp. 173–174). He never presented an alternative system, one that could operate through the humane, enlightened exercise of hegemonic government institutions. In fact, to Foucault, in the context of modern society, "humane" and "enlightened" mean only one thing: insidious attempts at greater and more effective control, that is to say, *repression*.

The school of controlology made the following major points. First, *social control is problematic; it should not be taken for granted*. By that, controlologists mean it does not emerge "naturally" and spontaneously by the "invisible hand" of society but is "consciously fashioned by the visible hand of definable organizations, groups, and classes" (Scull, 1988, p. 686). We cannot assume, as the functionalists seemed to have done, that society will be wise enough to preserve institutions and practices that serve the whole in the best possible way by sanctioning what is harmful and encouraging what is beneficial. Social control, as it is practiced, is not a product of a broad, widely shared social "need" or the workings of basic "functional prerequisites", to use functionalist terminology. Instead, the controlologists say, social control is imposed by specific and powerful social entities, for their own benefit, and at the expense of those individuals and groups who are controlled.

Second, *social control is typically coercive, repressive, and far from benign*. Agents of social control typically try to make control seem benevolent, or at least enlightened, but this is a façade; control appears as a "velvet glove" rather than an "iron fist". Traditional criminologists have looked upon social control generally, and the criminal justice system specifically, as society's natural, inevitable, and beneficial means of self-protection against harmful behavior. As viewed by controlologists, social control takes on a more sinister coloration; its purpose: to repress and contain troublesome populations. Hence, the purpose of psychiatry is not to heal but to control; the purpose of the welfare system is not to provide a safety net for the poor but to control; the purpose of education is not to teach but to control; the purpose of the mass media is not to inform or entertain but to control – or rather, the mass media entertain *in order to* control. And when segments of the population under institutional control are perceived as no longer threatening, they are dumped out of the system.

Third, *social control is coterminous with state or state-like control*. The government is made up of a virtual alphabet soup of agencies of social control, including the DEA (the Drug Enforcement Agency), the ATF (Bureau of Alcohol, Tobacco, and Firearms), the FDA (Food and Drug Administration), NIDA (the National Institute on Drug Abuse), NIMH (the National Institute of Mental Health), the INS (the Immigration and Naturalization Service), and so on, all of which have one aim: to monitor and control the behavior of troublesome populations. In addition, a number of organizations, agencies, and institutions are performing the function of social control *on behalf of* or *in the service of* the state. These include private social welfare agencies, psychiatrists and psychiatric agencies, professional organizations such as the American Medical Association, hospitals, clinics, mental health organizations, treatment facilities, educational institutions, and so on. It is the contention of controlologists that state control is increasingly being assumed by civil society. Troublesome populations can now be controlled on a wide range of fronts by a wide range of agencies. The same clients are circulated and recirculated between and among them. Even institutions that would appear to have little or nothing to do with the control of deviance as such, such as the mass media, are involved in social control through shaping public opinion about deviants.

Fourth, *the social control apparatus is unified and coherent*. The subsystems "fit together" into interrelated, functionally equivalent parts. Interlocking agencies and overarching institutions that work together to control troublesome populations may be referred to as the phenomenon of *transcarceration* (Lowman, Menzies, & Palys, 1987) – institutions of incarceration and control that reach across institutional boundaries. Foucault referred to this "transcarceral" system as the "carceral archipelago" (1979, p. 298), a reference to Aleksandr Solzhenetisyn's description of the Soviet prison camps, *The Gulag Archipelago*. The carceral archipelago transported the punitive approach "from the penal institution to the entire social body"

(Foucault, 1979, p. 298). Controlologists point to a "peno-juridical, mental health, welfare and tutelage complex" in which "power structures can be examined only by appreciating cross-institutional arrangements and dynamics" (Lowman *et al.*, 1987, p. 9). In other words, more or less all the organized entities in society have become a massive network dedicated to the surveillance and punishment of deviance. One must be impressed with the variety and range of people-processing institutions and agencies in modern society, many of them designed to deal with or handle the behavior of troublesome individuals and groups. No one can doubt that some of the functionaries who work for these agencies are often uncaring and insensitive. Especially in the inner cities, these agencies are overwhelmed by the sheer volume of clients, and the community is shortchanged. But most of these problems stem not from too much control but too few resources. Modern society is unprecedented in the number, variety, and near-ubiquity of organizations, agencies, and institutions that perform state-like functions that operate in place of and on behalf of the government. Social control is certainly one of their functions; how could this not be true? If people who make use of their services engage in unruly, troublesome, disruptive behavior, representatives of these agencies will predictably attempt to control that behavior. In most cases, from the client's perspective, that may not even be their main function. Such service and welfare service institutions are neither primarily nor exclusively agencies of social control. Clients themselves seek out the services of these organizations, institutions, and agencies and are more likely to see them as a shield to protect them than a net to catch them. Controlology or the new sociology of social control is not interested in social control *per se.* It is interested in how the state and its allied organizations and institutions control, or attempt to control, deviant behavior. In fact, the perspective's advocates are not really interested in deviant behavior either; they are interested more or less exclusively in the populations whom the elites consider troublesome and against whom the elites take action. What this perspective turns out to be is an exaggerated caricature of labeling theory, but with social control equated with formal (or semiformal) social control. It turns out to be an extremely narrow view of both deviance and social control.

Social Control Theory

Control theory is a major paradigm in the fields of deviance behavior and criminology. It is a very different approach from controlology – in fact, in most important respects, its perspective is very nearly its opposite. Control theorists see their perspective as a critique of and a replacement for both anomie theory and the subcultural or learning approaches. While most theories ask, "Why do they do it?" – that is, what processes *encourage* deviant behavior – control theory turns the question around and asks, "Why *don't* they do it?" In other words, control theory assumes that engaging in deviance is not problematic, that, *if left to our own devices*, all of us would deviate from the rules of society. Control theorists believe that deviance is *inherently attractive*. Under most circumstances, we are encouraged to break the rules; deviance-making processes are strong and obvious and commonsensical. Why *shouldn't* we lie and steal, if they are what get us what we want? *Why not* hang out on street-corners and get drunk and throw bottles through windows – it's so much fun! This approach takes for granted the allure of deviance, crime, and delinquency. What has to be explained, control theorists argue, is why most people *don't* engage in deviance, why are they discouraged from engaging in delinquent behavior, why are they dissuaded or deterred from breaking the law and engaging in a life of crime. Practically all the other theories of wrongdoing argue that deviance, crime, and delinquency are *positively motivated*; control theories argue the opposite – that wrongdoing results from *weak restraints and controls*. Most of us do not engage in deviant or criminal acts because of strong bonds with or ties to conventional, mainstream social institutions. If these bonds are weak or broken, we will be released from society's rules and will be free to deviate. It is not so much deviants' ties to an unconventional group or subculture that attracts them to deviant behavior, but their *lack* of ties with the conforming, law-abiding culture; this frees them to engage in deviance (Hirschi, 1969; Reckless, 1958; Reiss, 1951; Toby, 1957). What causes deviant behavior, these theorists say, is the *ineffectiveness* or *absence* of social control.

Researchers find three distinctly different *types* of social control: *direct control*; *stake in conformity*; and *internal* controls, or beliefs regarding wrongdoing. These types help explain *individual differences* in rates of offending, as well as *group differences over the life course*. Direct control refers to all those actions that agents take, and which act, to ensure that individuals refrain from engaging in deviance "out of fear that they will be caught and sanctioned" (Agnew, 2011, p. 115). They include the cop on the corner, the parent hovering over his or her child, the teacher watching students taking an exam. However, individuals vary with respect to the *effectiveness* of sanctioning because they vary with respect to their *stake in conformity*. In short, some people have less to lose if they are caught and punished. Some such "stakes" include plans for college, accomplishments, emotional attachments to others, material possessions, reputation; they may be jeopardized by being exposed as a thief, a cheat, a liar, a brawler, a substance abuser. It seems almost intuitively obvious that deviance is more likely among individuals who have little to lose if they are caught (p. 116). And lastly, social control may be internalized at a relatively early age. Children whose parents closely monitor and consistently sanction them tend to continue to believe that deviance is wrong and should not be committed; those whose parents are ineffective as agents of social control are more likely to be amoral toward offending and do not believe that deviant acts are wrong. For the most part, researchers have verified most propositions of social control theory, although as with many such perspectives, the causal arrow is not always clear. Control theory would predict that, to the extent that a person has a *stake in conformity*, he or she will tend not to break the law and risk losing that stake; to the extent that a person lacks that stake in conformity, he or she will be willing to violate the law. Thus, jobs, especially satisfying, high-paying jobs, may act as something of a deterrent to crime. Attending college, likewise, represents a stake or investment that many students are not willing to risk losing. Being married and having a family, too, will discourage criminal behavior to the extent that arrest may undermine their stability. Everyone knows that *some* crime is committed by the employed, college students, and married persons with a family. But control theory would predict that there are *major differences* in the crime rates of the employed versus the unemployed, college students versus their non-college age peers, and married parents versus the unmarried. To the extent that a society or a neighborhood is able to invest its citizens or residents with a stake worth protecting, it will have lower rates of crime; to the extent that it is unable to invest that stake in its citizens or residents, its crime rate will be correspondingly higher. Home ownership, for instance, can act as a deterrent to crime, as can organizational and community involvement. A society with many citizens who have nothing to lose is a society with a high crime rate. Control theory does not state that individuals with strong ties to conventional society are absolutely *insulated* from deviance, that they will *never* engage in *any* deviant or criminal action, regardless of how mildly unconventional it is. It does, however, assert that both deviance and social control are matters of degree: The more attached we are to conventional society, the lower the likelihood of engaging in behavior that violates its values and norms. A strong bond to conventionality does not insulate us from mildly deviant behavior, but it does make it less likely.

This theory works a great deal better for some behaviors than others. Control theory sees many deviant, criminal, and delinquent activities as natural, recreational, and requiring no special explanation. But what about more seriously aggressive and violent behavior, such as murder, robbery, and rape? Are they part of the same constellation of acts that, if left to our own devices and in the absence of simple societal controls, we would naturally gravitate toward and engage in? It is difficult to envision that the same logic applies. In fact, there may be a very good reason why the vast majority of the research applying control theory has been self-report surveys of relatively minor delinquencies among youths: it works best for them. Hirschi's 1969 study found few class differences in rates of delinquency, and there is a good reason why. The most important crimes, those that criminologists are most interested in (murder, robbery, and rape) tend to be relatively rare. The least important crimes are sufficiently common to make a self-report possible. The less common the behavior, the more difficult it is to study by means of self-report surveys, since so few of the sample will have engaged in them, especially within a recent time-frame. In spite of this restriction, control theory represents one of the more powerful and insightful approaches we have to explain crime, deviance, and especially delinquency.

The General Theory of Crime: Self-Control Theory

In 1990, Michael Gottfredson and Travis Hirschi published an explication of what they refer to as *a general theory of crime*, that is, force or fraud in pursuit of self-interest (p. 15). The field of criminology refers to it as self-control theory, and it shares with social control theory the idea that deviance is self-evident and inherently attractive. The authors claimed that their theory applies to any and all crimes, regardless of type: white collar and corporate crime, embezzlement, murder, robbery, rape, the illegal sale of drugs, underage drinking, burglary, shoplifting – indeed, any and all illegal actions. In fact, in their view, their theory is even more general than that, since it is an explanation of actions that may not even be against the law or entail inflicting force or fraud against a victim. More properly, it is a general theory of deviance and includes, in addition to crime itself, a variety and range of self-indulgent actions (such as smoking, getting high or drunk, and, one might suppose, even being a couch potato), and reckless behavior that has a substantial likelihood of resulting in self-harm or harm to others (such as driving dangerously fast, riding a motorcycle, and, especially for women, engaging in unprotected sex, sex with multiple partners, and sex with strangers). Their theory, they argue, stresses both the factors present in the immediate or "proximate" situation of the criminal action that determine or influence its *enactment* (which they refer to as "crime"), *and* those background or distal or "distant" factors that determine or influence the *tendency* or *propensity* to commit crime (which they term *criminality*). The origin of crime, Gottfredson and Hirschi say, is *low self-control*, which in turn results from inadequate, ineffective, and inconsistent socialization by parents early in childhood. Parents who raise offspring who eventually engage in delinquent and criminal behavior lack affection for them, fail to monitor their behavior, fail to recognize when they commit deviant acts, and fail to control their wrongdoing.

What makes crime especially attractive to people who lack self-control? We can characterize criminal acts, Gottfredson and Hirschi say, by the fact that they provide *immediate* and *easy* or *simple* gratification of desires (1990, p. 89). "They provide money without work, sex without courtship, revenge without court delays" (p. 89). People who lack self-control "tend to lack diligence, tenacity, or persistence in a course of action" (p. 89). In addition, criminal acts are "*exciting, risky, or thrilling*"; crime provides, in the typical case, "*few or meager long-term benefits*"; it requires "*little skill or planning*"; and often results in "*pain or discomfort for the victim*" (p. 89; the emphasis is theirs). As a result of the last of these characteristics, people with low self-control, and hence frequent enactors of criminal behavior, tend to be "self-centered, indifferent, or insensitive to the suffering and needs of others" (p. 89), although they may also "discover the immediate and easy rewards of charm and generosity" (p. 90). Since crime entails "the pursuit of immediate pleasure", it follows that "people lacking in self-control will also tend to pursue immediate pleasures that are *not* criminal: they will tend to smoke, drink, use drugs, gamble, have children out of wedlock, and engage in illicit sex" (1990, p. 90). Some crimes entail not so much pleasure but an attempt at relief from irritation or discomfort, such as physically abusing a crying child or beating up an annoying stranger in a bar. People with low self-control have little tolerance for frustration and little skill at dealing with difficult circumstances verbally or by applying complex, difficult-to-master solutions. "In short, people who lack self-control will tend to be impulsive, insensitive, physical (as opposed to mental), risk-taking, short-sighted, and nonverbal, and they will therefore tend to engage in criminal and analogous acts" (p. 90).

Their general theory of crime, Gottfredson and Hirschi argue, is both consistent with the facts of criminal behavior and contradicts the bulk of mainstream criminological theories. The authors are not modest either about the reach of their theory or its devastating implications for competing explanations. They insist that their general theory of crime *cannot* be reconciled with other theories; instead, they insist, it must of necessity *annihilate* them. In fact, Gottfredson and Hirschi abandon even Hirschi's own social control theory, formulated more than 40 years ago. The *social* controls that Hirschi saw previously as central, he and his co-author now view as secondary to the *internal* controls they argue are developed in childhood. They set aside current life circumstances such as marriage, employment, and home-ownership – so crucial to control theory – as having little or no independent impact on crime. After all, how can someone with low self-control maintain a marriage, keep a job, or buy a house? Criminals lack emotional and psychic wherewithal – the self-control – to do what has to be done in order even to be *subject* to external or social controls. It is self-control that determines social control, not the other way around, Hirschi and Gottfredson argue.

The problem with the theories of crime that are now dominant in criminology, Gottfredson and Hirschi claim, is that they are inconsistent with the evidence. Strain or anomie theory "predicts that offenders will have high long-term aspirations and low long-term expectations", but that turns out to be false; "people committing criminal acts tend to have lower aspirations than others", while, among offenders, "expectations for future success tend to be unrealistically high" (1990, p. 162). In anomie theory, crime is a long-term, indirect solution to current life circumstances, whereas, in reality, Gottfredson and Hirschi say, crime is an impulsive act that provides short-term, usually skimpy rewards. Criminals lack the skills, diligence, and persistence necessary for the deviant "adaptations" spelled out by anomie theory. Strain does not explain the incidence or rate of criminal behavior as a whole, since most crime is petty, impulsive, and immediate. Likewise, the many varieties of learning theory should be rejected as being manifestly falsified by the facts, Gottfredson and Hirschi argue. All such theories make the assumption that deviants engage in deviance as a result of a positive learning experience, that is, *they learn the value* of engaging in deviance and crime. In fact, one does *not* learn to engage in crime, since no learning is required. Criminal acts are simple, commonsensical, immediate, concrete, and result in immediate gratification. Neither the motivation nor the skill to commit crime is problematic; everybody has such motivation and skill. What causes such behavior is not the *presence* of something – learning – but the *absence* of something – self-control.

According to their ideas, learning theories simply fail utterly and completely to explain criminal, deviant, and delinquent behavior. More generally, they reject the idea that crime is *social* behavior (in fact, it is more accurate to refer to it as *asocial* in nature), that it is *learned* behavior ("when in fact no learning is required"), that the tendency to commit it can be an *inherited* trait (when it is clearly acquired through childhood experiences), that it is *economic* behavior (when, in fact, "it is uneconomical behavior outside the labor force"). They reject all other explanations of criminal behavior except their own (1990, p. 75); only a lack of self-control is truly consistent with the facts of crime. Gottfredson and Hirschi reject any effort to integrate their own theory with the explanations they critique, with two exceptions. Not all persons who exhibit low self-control commit crime; low self-control merely *predisposes* someone to commit crime. What determines which persons who are predisposed to commit crime will actually do so? In a word, opportunity. Hence, any explanation that focuses on the *patterning* and *distribution* of criminal opportunities, although incomplete, is consistent with the facts, Gottfredson and Hirschi argue. Their approach is an attempt to revitalize classical, free-will, or rational choice theory as half the crime equation.

The contemporary version of the classic approach to crime, referred to as opportunity theory, the routine activity approach, or rational choice theory, argues that crime can take place to the extent that a *motivated offender* has access to a "suitable target" (such as money and valuables) that lacks a "capable guardian". Routine activity theorists emphasize the factors of *proximity*, *accessibility*, and *reward*. They *assume* or *take for granted* a motivated offender – the criminal – since there will always be an abundant supply of them to go around; instead, they focus on the necessary preconditions for the commission of the crime (Felson, 1994). Gottfredson and Hirschi abandon routine activity's assumption that crime is the most rational means to acquire property, however, since they argue that most crimes do not net the offender much in the way of goods or cash. Nonetheless, they say, opportunity is a crucial element in the crime equation. (Not in *criminality*, or the individual *propensity* to commit crime, but in *crime*, in the likelihood that criminal *actions* will take place.) While incomplete, Gottfredson and Hirschi say, a theory that focuses on opportunity is consistent with self-control theory. Moreover, they say, both are necessary for a complete explanation of criminal behavior. In addition, they argue, social disorganization theory is both consistent with classical theory and consistent with the facts of crime; the inability of a disorganized community to monitor the behavior of its residents (Bursik & Grasmick, 1993) complements, and is parallel to, parental incompetence. Social disorganization theory is a form of control theory "writ large" (Agnew, 2011).

As might be expected, self-control theory has met with mixed reactions. Strain theorists argue that social strain and anomie are indeed significant causal precursors to criminal behavior. For instance, the aggression and anger that many criminals exhibit when committing their crimes is far more than a lack of self-restraint; only strain theory explains them, according to that theory's advocates (Agnew, 1995). Some learning theorists argue that a lack of self-control is a basic component or element of the deviant learning process (Akers, 1991) – hence, they say, learning theory *subsumes*, or swallows up, self-control theory. Certainly the reductionistic, either/or logic that Gottfredson and Hirschi display in their theorizing has led some observers to believe that these researchers may have missed crucial subtleties in characterizing and explaining human behavior. Some critics have taken Gottfredson and Hirschi to task for selectively reading the data, focusing on those that seem to confirm their theory and ignoring those that would damage it. Chances are, contrary to its claims, bits and pieces of the theory will be incorporated into mainstream criminology and deviance theory, while its global, overall – and perhaps overblown – critiques of rival theories will be taken far less seriously. It is likely that Gottfredson and Hirschi have not offered a "general theory" of crime and deviance, but a plausible account of portions of the phenomenon they purport to explain (Goode, 2008).

References

Agnew, R. (1995). The contribution of social-psychological strain theory to the explanation of crime and delinquency. In F. Adler, & W.S. Laufer (Eds.), *The Legacy of Anomie Theory* (pp. 113–137). New Brunswick, NJ: Transaction.

Agnew, R. (2011). Control and social disorganization theory. In C.D. Bryant (Ed.), *The Routledge Handbook of Deviant Behavior* (pp. 114–120). New York: Routledge.

Akers, R.L. (1991). Self-control as a general theory of crime. *Journal of Quantitative Criminology, 7*(2), 201–211.

Becker, H.S. (1963). *Outsiders: Studies in the Sociology of Deviance*. Glencoe, IL: Free Press.

Ben-Yehuda, N. (1985). *Deviance and Moral Boundaries: Witchcraft, the Occult, Science Fiction, Deviant Sciences and Scientists*. Chicago: University of Chicago Press.

Bursik, R.J., Jr., & Grasmick, H.G. (1993). *Neighborhoods and Crime: The Dimensions of Effective Community Control*. New York: Lexington Books.

Cohen, A.K. (1966). *Deviance and Control*. Englewood Cliffs, NJ: Prentice-Hall.

Felson, M. (1994). *Crime and Everyday Life: Insights and Implications for Society*. Thousand Oaks, CA: Pine Forge Press.

Foucault, M. (1979). *Discipline and Punish: The Birth of the Prison* (trans. Alan Sheridan). New York: Vintage Books.

Garland, D. (1990). *Punishment and Modern Society: A Study in Social Theory*. Chicago: University of Chicago Press.

Gibbs, J.P. (1981). *Norms, Deviance, and Social Control*. Oxford: Elsevier.

Goode, E. (Ed.). (2008). *Out of Control: Assessing the General Theory of Crime*. Stanford, CA: Stanford University Press.

Gottfredson, M.R., & Hirschi, T. (1990). *A General Theory of Crime*. Stanford, CA: Stanford University Press.

Hawkins, R., & Tiedeman, G. (1975). *The Creation of Deviance: Interpersonal and Organization Determinants*. Columbus, OH: Charles E. Merrill.

Hirschi, T. (1969). *Causes of Delinquency*. Berkeley, CA: University of California Press.

Hobbes, T. (1651). *Leviathan, or the Matter, Forme, & Power of a Common-wealth Ecclesiastical and Civill*. London: Green Dragon, St Paul's Churchyard.

Jensen, G. (2007). *The Path of the Devil: Early Modern Witch Hunts*. Lanham, MD: Rowman & Littlefield.

Lowman, J., Menzies, R.J., & Palys, T.S. (Eds.) (1987). *Transcarceration: Essays in the Sociology of Social Control*. Aldershot: Gower.

Marshall, H., Douglas, K., & McDonnell, D. (2007). *Deviance and Social Control: Who Rules?* South Melbourne: Oxford University Press.

Parsons, T. (1951). *The Social System*. Glencoe, IL: Free Press.

Reckless, W.C. (1958). A new theory of crime and delinquency. *Federal Probation, 24*(1), 42–46.

Reiss, A.J., Jr. (1951). Delinquency as the failure of personal and social controls. *American Sociological Review, 16* (April), 196–207.

Scull, A. (1988). Deviance and social control. In N.J. Smelser (Ed.), *Handbook of Sociology* (pp. 667–693). Thousand Oaks, CA: Sage.

Toby, J. (1957). Social disorganization and stake in conformity: Complementary factors in the predatory behavior of hoodlums. *Journal of Criminal Law, Criminology, and Police Science, 48*(1), 17–19.

19

Theoretical Perspectives on Delinquent Development: Propensity, Plasticity, and Range

Arjan A.J. Blokland

Introduction

Why do some youths engage in delinquency, while others do not? Are all juvenile delinquents destined to grow up to be adult criminals? Or is change possible, even for those most criminally active? Questions like these have occupied the minds of criminologists practically since the birth of the discipline, and a plethora of theories – some growing popular, some remaining obscure – have been offered to explain who becomes delinquent, and why some juvenile delinquents go on to live an adult life of crime. As they incorporate the ever-increasing knowledge on risk factors for antisocial behavior, like a difficult temperament, adverse family circumstances, delinquent peers, and failed transitions to adult social roles, these theories increasingly feature common elements. The position these risk factors take in the theorized causal structure, however, can be radically different from one theory to the next, and as a result, so can the remedies and interventions suggested to prevent young people from engaging in crime and curb delinquent pathways before they develop into fully-fledged criminal careers.

This chapter presents an overview of some of the currently most influential developmental and life-course criminological (or DLC) theories. Other theories besides those mentioned here exist, and the interested reader is referred to other, sometimes more extensive, reviews that have been published elsewhere (e.g. Farrington, 2005a; Thornberry, 1997). To facilitate the current presentation, after discussing the rationale behind a life-course approach to juvenile delinquency, this

The Handbook of Juvenile Delinquency and Juvenile Justice, First Edition. Edited by Marvin D. Krohn and Jodi Lane.

chapter introduces and discusses three overarching concepts – *propensity*, *plasticity*, and *range* – that help in appreciating important differences between different developmental theories, and help to explain why these different theories give rise to different policies to combat juvenile delinquent development.

A life-course approach to juvenile delinquency

Juvenile delinquency has been high on the criminological research agenda for decades, for substantive reasons as well as for reasons more prosaic. Substantively, juvenile delinquency was a common and very visible problem in the rapidly urbanizing environment of many Western industrialized countries in the early twentieth century. The juvenile period was also seen as developmentally distinct, and qualitatively different from adulthood, in terms of both susceptibility and flexibility of behavior. Lastly, juvenile delinquency was viewed as the gateway to adult offending. Criminological studies at the time therefore set out to explain why some juveniles became delinquent, while others did not (Farrington, 2005b), implicitly equating participation with persistence in offending. A more mundane reason for primarily studying juvenile delinquents was – and still remains – juveniles' accessibility for research. Ever since the advent of large-scale self-report surveys in criminology, researchers have had students fill out lengthy questionnaires in the convenience of their classroom (Hagan & McCarthy, 1997). Students typically participate only once, and answer questions about whether they have ever, or have in some period directly prior to the study, engaged in different forms of delinquent behavior. These initial studies showed (minor) juvenile delinquency to be even more common than expected, which led to a further convergence of research attention to this age period.

The problem with the theories constructed to explain the results of these early cross-sectional studies was that these theories basically predicted too much crime. If juvenile delinquents all were bound for adult crime, with each new generation the adult offender population – and with it the adult crime rate – would have to increase. In reality, however, it seemed that adult crime was far less prevalent than juvenile delinquency. As data from longitudinal studies following the same group of individuals over time became increasingly available, the continuity in delinquency and crime that had followed from the gateway perception proved to a large extent to be a matter of perception (Robins, 1978). While the overwhelming majority of adult criminals asserted they had engaged in delinquent behavior already when they were juveniles, many juvenile delinquents did not go on to develop lengthy adult criminal careers. The Philadelphia birth cohort study is now famous for being the first study to show that the criminal careers of many youths were only short-lived, and that much of the delinquency eventually committed by this cohort could be attributed to a relatively small group of highly frequent and persistent offenders (Wolfgang, Figlio, & Sellin, 1972). Other longitudinal studies soon replicated this finding (e.g. Farrington, 1983; Shannon, 1988). Against the backdrop of this building evidence of both continuity and discontinuity in offending, present-day theories of juvenile and adolescent delinquency can no longer suffice by merely pinpointing the causes for participating in delinquent behavior. They also have to explain why many former delinquents go on to live conventional lives, while others develop prolonged adult criminal careers (Farrington, 2005b; Thornberry, 2005).

Driven by the rapidly expanding longitudinal knowledge base on the development of antisocial behavior, the number of developmental and life-course criminological theories steeply increased from the early 1990s onwards. As longitudinal research into the development of delinquency and crime commenced, developmental psychologists broadened its scope to the childhood years, stressing the importance of early risk factors in the development of chronic offending and the developmental links between childhood problem behavior and adolescent delinquency (e.g. Loeber *et al.*, 1993). On the other hand, as with time the respondents in the various ongoing longitudinal studies aged, the age span under study also moved beyond adolescence to include the early adult years (Farrington, 1995; Loeber *et al.*, 2001; Moffitt, Caspi, Harrington, & Milne, 2002). Some studies eventually even spanned almost the entire life course (Blokland, Nagin, & Nieuwbeerta, 2005; Farrington *et al.*, 2006; Sampson & Laub, 1993). This in turn forced theorists to look beyond explanations of offending that were particularly linked to features of the adolescent period, and to describe the causal processes they proposed as governing the development of offending in terms that would render them applicable for the much broader age range now under study.

From a life-course perspective, expanding the scope of life-course criminology makes all the more sense since it is hardly conceivable for developmental processes to adhere sheep-like to socially constructed life stages like "childhood" and "adolescence", or formal categorizations like the minimum age of legal responsibility, or the age of majority at which offenders transfer from juvenile to adult court. Those in the juvenile justice system working with juvenile delinquents thus might be confronted with social and behavioral problems that have their origins in early childhood, or even prenatally for that matter. By the same token, actions currently taken by law enforcement, prosecution, judges and juvenile probation officers in response to a juvenile's current delinquent behavior can resonate in that youth's life course for years to come. In many ways, adolescents are still "getting ready to launch" – both psychologically and socially – and those in the system should therefore be cognizant of the long-term beneficial as well as detrimental effects their actions can have in shaping youths' future developmental trajectories (Sullivan, Piquero, & Cullen, 2012).

Extant developmental and life-course theories of delinquency and crime no longer limit themselves to explaining who becomes delinquent, but also address questions regarding the onset of antisocial behavior, the maintenance of delinquency and crime over time, as well as factors related to desistance from offending. Transcending traditional life stages, these theories focus on both continuity and change in delinquent development over the entire life span. In the wake of the growing amount of empirical studies, numerous DLC theories have emerged, proposing different causal mechanisms, and predicting different developmental trajectories. Yet, despite theoretical differences, all DLC theories need to address issues of propensity, plasticity, and range, as these concepts are key to explaining behavioral development.

Antisocial propensity

The term *antisocial propensity* refers to the constellation of individual characteristics, like personality, temperament, and cognitive abilities, that influences a person's likelihood of engaging in delinquency and crime throughout his or her entire life span, and net of any outside influences. Individuals differ in important ways in the characteristics underlying antisocial propensity, and as a consequence there are also significant between-individual differences in the propensity towards antisocial behavior, putting some at higher risk of offending than others. Most DLC theories furthermore assume, either explicitly or implicitly, that a person's antisocial propensity remains relatively stable across the life course, continuously exerting its influence on a person's likelihood to offend. Some theorists view antisocial propensity as a one-dimensional construct, placing individuals on a single continuum from low to high, with those towards the high end being most likely to engage in delinquency and crime (Gottfredson & Hirschi, 1990). According to others, however, antisocial propensity is best seen as a multidimensional construct involving many different factors, with certain combinations of characteristics having such a profound effect on individual development that, rather than characterizing individuals in terms of high or low, it is justified to speak of qualitatively different types of offenders (Moffitt, 1993; Patterson & Yoerger, 1993). Whether conceptualized as a single factor or as different offender types, individual differences in antisocial propensity mean that some are more prone to delinquency and crime than others from the very start.

Developmental plasticity

In evolutionary biology, developmental plasticity is defined as a single genotype's ability to alter its developmental processes and phenotypic outcomes in response to different environmental conditions (Moczek *et al.*, 2011). In neuroscience, developmental plasticity refers to changes in the central nervous system caused by environmental interaction or learning experiences (Li, 2003). Similarly, in the current context, developmental plasticity refers to the extent to which a person's behavioral patterns are thought to be susceptible to outside influences, leading to changes in these behavioral patterns.[1] Most theorists attribute high levels of plasticity to human behavioral development, including the development of delinquency and crime. They warn that antisocial propensity, while important, is not to be interpreted as an all-decisive blueprint of later behavioral outcomes. What happens to a person during the life course may drastically alter his or her developmental pathway and thereby their chances to desist or persist in offending. Still, levels of developmental plasticity may be inversely related to antisocial propensity, with those on the high end of the antisocial continuum least likely to change their behavior in response to outside influences. Some also argue that developmental plasticity is limited to certain types of offenders (Moffitt, 1997). Theories that ascribe high levels of plasticity to criminal development focus on the nature and timing of outside factors most likely to curb developmental trajectories (Sampson & Laub, 1993). Certain outside events may decrease delinquency and crime, whereas others may actually lead to an increase in a person's offending. The effect of external factors may furthermore depend on the individual's calendar age or developmental stage. Finally, unlike antisocial propensity, the level of developmental plasticity – the strength and variety of outside influences on subsequent development – may change over the life course, again either as a result of age or as a consequence of a person's prior behavior.

Developmental range

Developmental range refers to the breadth of the potential spectrum of developmental outcomes, including delinquency and crime, that can realistically be expected given a person's starting point. Both antisocial propensity and developmental plasticity contribute to developmental range. If both antisocial propensity and developmental plasticity are low, chances for deviant adult outcomes are also low. In contrast, if antisocial propensity is high and developmental plasticity is low, deviant adult outcomes are likely. If, however, developmental plasticity is thought to be high, the developmental range increases and adult outcomes become increasingly unpredictable, regardless of the person's level of antisocial propensity. As some theories take antisocial propensity and developmental plasticity to be inversely related, developmental range may be lower for those with high antisocial propensity than for those low on antisocial propensity. In this view, deviant adult outcomes are always within range of those with low antisocial propensity, while non-deviant outcomes may be unattainable for those high on antisocial propensity (Moffitt, 1997). Like developmental plasticity, a person's developmental range may vary across the life course, either directly due to outside influences, or as a result of a person's calendar age or developmental stage.

Figure 19.1 provides a schematic view of the inter-relatedness of antisocial propensity, developmental plasticity, and developmental range across the life course. The top pane (A) depicts a theory that emphasizes antisocial propensity and assumes low developmental plasticity. In this theory the developmental range is narrow, and adult outcomes strongly depend on a person's level of antisocial propensity. The middle pane (B), on the other hand, depicts a theory that emphasizes developmental plasticity. Regardless of a person's level of antisocial propensity, there is a broad range of developmental outcomes. Finally, the bottom pane (C) depicts a theory that assumes developmental plasticity is inversely related to antisocial propensity. Plasticity for those low on antisocial propensity is high, resulting in a broad range of potential adult outcomes. Developmental plasticity for those high on antisocial propensity, on the other hand, is low, diminishing the range of possible outcomes, and increasing the likelihood of persistence in delinquency and crime over the life span. In reviewing DLC theories, these three archetypical models will facilitate comparisons between the different theories.

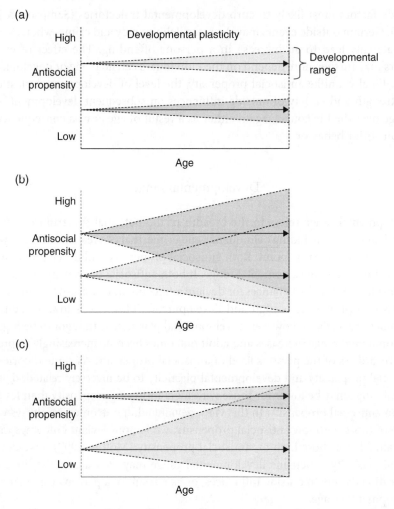

Figure 19.1   Schematic representation of the three developmental perspectives (see text for description).

Gottfredson and Hirschi's General Theory

In a highly influential book first published in 1990, Gottfredson and Hirschi proposed what they called the "General Theory" of crime. The "generality" of their theory lay in the fact that they claimed that it did not just explain delinquency and crime – behaviors as defined by law – but also conceptually similar behaviors, like truancy, binge drinking, and reckless driving, that may or may not be considered deviant, but are not necessarily legally penalized. What, according to Gottfredson and Hirschi, all these behaviors have in common is that while they are immediately beneficial, their potentially adverse consequences are most likely manifest only in the long run (Hirschi & Gottfredson, 1994). Whereas truanting, smoking pot or stealing from a department store can be socially, psychologically or financially rewarding, the potential long-term consequences of these behaviors – grade retention, (mental) health problems, being arrested – are far less desirable. According to the General Theory, people differ in the extent to which long-term consequences are salient in their behavioral decisions, and this explains why some are more likely to engage in delinquency and crime than others (Hirschi & Gottfredson, 1993). The General Theory refers to the ability to resist the temptations of the moment as "self-control". High levels of self-control thus translate to low levels of antisocial propensity and vice versa.

The General Theory traces the origins of self-control back to the child's family environment. To teach a child self-control, parents must (1) monitor their child's behavior, (2) recognize deviant behavior when it occurs, and (3) adequately punish such behavior, all within the context of an affectionate relationship with the child (Gottfredson & Hirschi, 1990, p. 97; Hirschi & Gottfredson, 2003). As parents – and later schools – differ in their ability or willingness to do these three things, significant between-individual differences in the degree of self-control will develop during the childhood years. Socialization reaches its zenith when the child is aged around 8–10. From that age onward the degree to which a person considers the long-term consequences of behavioral decisions becomes an enduring, trait-like tendency that affects future behavioral decisions without itself being affected by the outcomes of these decisions. This significant reduction in developmental plasticity from age 8–10 onwards is claimed to explain the stability in delinquency and crime over the life course as observed in many longitudinal studies (Gottfredson & Hirschi, 1995). While absolute levels of deviant behavior are likely to decline with age – a person at age 65 is less active than that same person at age 15 – between-person differences in delinquency and crime tend to persist. Those at the high end of the antisocial propensity continuum remain high, and those at the low end remain low, resulting in relatively stable between-person differences in delinquency and crime over the life course, despite the overall decline in the level of deviance with age.

Within the framework of the General Theory, after the formative childhood years outside influences are unable to alter a person's criminal trajectory or the likelihood of achieving certain adult outcomes. In fact, many outcomes, such as dropping out of school, taking a job, marrying, and moving from one community to the other, are viewed as resulting directly from a person's level of self-control (Gottfredson & Hirschi, 1990, p. 167). Stability in individual difference in self-control thus not only explains stability in criminal behavior over the life course, but also accounts for the association of delinquency and crime with other unfavorable adult outcomes, like academic failure, unemployment, and relational strife. In the absence of developmental plasticity during the adolescent and young adult years, adult developmental range is constricted and adult outcomes depend heavily on childhood antisocial propensity. As such, Gottfredson and Hirschi's General Theory closely resembles the type of theory depicted in the top pane of Figure 19.1.

Sampson and Laub's Age-graded Theory

Dissatisfied with its stability argument and the prominence given to between-individual differences in antisocial propensity in Gottfredson and Hirschi's General Theory, Sampson and Laub (1993) set out to develop their own views on delinquent development across the life course. Ironically, their theory of age-graded informal social control draws heavily on ideas first championed by Hirschi (1969), but which he seemed to have abandoned in his 1990 book.

In the Age-graded Theory, like in the General Theory, family processes are a crucial factor in delinquent development. Parents and caregivers who fail to supervise the child, have weak emotional attachment to the child or even reject the child, and discipline the child harshly or erratically, will increase the child's likelihood of engaging in delinquency and crime (Sampson & Laub, 1993, p. 65). Congenital characteristics, like irritability and temperament, may also contribute, but are hardly sufficient for explaining juvenile delinquency. Instead, both childhood problem behavior and juvenile delinquency are deemed highly malleable by external influences originating from the family and school environment. The Age-graded Theory diverges most sharply from the General Theory in its explanation of behavioral development after the age of 10. Whereas the General Theory claims developmental plasticity is drastically reduced – if not entirely absent – by the time the child enters adolescence, the Age-graded Theory states that high levels of plasticity are retained throughout life. With age, only the nature of the external factors capable of influencing development changes (Sampson & Laub, 1990).

According to the Age-graded Theory, the key factor to understanding delinquent development is informal social control: the inhibiting force that emerges from strong ties to age-appropriate social institutions.[2] For juveniles and adolescents, strong bonds to parents and school reduce the likelihood of engaging in delinquency. For adults, strong ties resulting from work, romantic relationships or parenthood similarly promote future norm-conforming behavior. At times when these ties are weakened or broken, crime and deviance tend to increase. Variability in informal social control is therefore linked to variability in criminal development, between persons as well as within persons over time. Changes in the level of informal social control (both positive and negative) are stated to result in part from chance events (e.g. being laid off from work, or meeting your soul-mate) that subsequently may constitute "turning points" in the criminal career. Good things sometimes happen to bad people, as well as bad things may happen to good people, and when they do they have the potential to alter the course of the person's criminal trajectory (Laub, Nagin, & Sampson, 1998). Antisocial propensity alone, therefore, does not readily predict adult outcomes, though it may set boundaries to the range of outcomes that can likely be attained (Laub & Sampson, 2003). Still, while it may be unrealistic to expect that adults with a high antisocial propensity may be wholly transformed by social institutions, adults, regardless of their antisocial propensity, will be inhibited from committing crime to the extent that they have social capital invested in work and family lives (Sampson & Laub, 1993, p. 141).

With age, increasing ties to institutions of social control may thus promote desistance even in those engaged in delinquency when they were younger. Yet the same processes leading to change in delinquency and crime may also give rise to behavioral continuity and persistence in criminal careers. To offer an alternative to trait-based explanations of criminal continuity, Sampson and Laub (1997) focused on the effects that delinquency and crime, and especially societal reactions to delinquency and crime, may have on the opportunities for behavioral change. Delinquency and crime may have deleterious consequences for future development, causing existing conventional bonds to be weakened or broken, and limiting the opportunities for forging new ties to conventional institutions. Rule-breaking and delinquent behavior may result in being expelled from school, as theft from the workplace leads to being fired. Official reactions to delinquency and crime, like an arrest, a conviction or a prison sentence, all "scar" a person's reputation in the eyes of friends and neighbors, and may cause potential employers to avoid hiring an ex-detainee (e.g., Pager, 2007). By weakening existing ties and knifing off future opportunities for conventional bonds, acting delinquent may indirectly reduce social control, thus perpetuating additional delinquency. Sampson and Laub (1997) referred to this downward spiral whereby delinquency and crime tend to diminish conventional prospects, and lack of conventional prospects fuels future crime as a process of cumulative disadvantage.

The Age-graded Theory thus attempts to explain both desistance and persistence in delinquency and crime. While behavioral change becomes less likely with age, for those involved in delinquent behavior at early ages, the funneling of opportunities and outcomes is the direct result of the presence of behavioral plasticity, rather than the absence of it. As the occurrence of important events and transitions that significantly increase or decrease levels of informal social control are mostly chance events, ranges of potential adult outcomes tend to overlap regardless of one's ranking in antisocial propensity. The associations between propensity, plasticity, and range within the Age-graded Theory are therefore represented by panel B of Figure 19.1.

Hawkins and Catalano's Social Developmental Model

Like in the Age-graded Theory, social bonds play an important role in the Social Developmental Model (Hawkins & Weis, 1985). Whereas the Age-graded Theory focuses on the presence or absence of conventional bonds inhibiting delinquency and crime, the Social Developmental Model explicitly recognizes a person's bonds may also extend to deviant others, groups and institutions, resulting in two socialization pathways: the pro-social pathway and the antisocial pathway.

The basic assumption of the Social Developmental Model is that both pro-social and antisocial behaviors are learned through social interaction (Catalano & Hawkins, 1996). What behaviors are learned depends upon the opportunities for learning, the degree to which a person engages in these opportunities, and the skills a person has for successfully engaging in these opportunities. Differential reinforcement of behaviors within different social settings will lead a child to adopt certain behaviors, and abandon others. Socialization simultaneously occurs in different settings, like the family, the school, the peer group, and the neighborhood. A child may learn pro-social behavior in the family setting, which provides opportunities to be sensitive to the needs of others, and rewards selfless behaviors. Concurrently, the child's peer group may provide opportunities to engage in delinquency and crime, rewarding antisocial behavior with tokens of appreciation and increased standing. Prolonged social interactions facilitate emotional attachment and feelings of mutual obligation, giving rise to social bonds. Depending upon the nature of the socializing unit, these bonds may facilitate pro-social or antisocial beliefs and either inhibit or increase the likelihood of continued delinquency and crime (Catalano, Kosterman, Hawkins, Newcomb, & Abbott, 1996).

Within the Social Developmental Model, antisocial propensity is linked to delinquent and criminal outcomes only through its influence on socialization processes (Catalano *et al.*, 2005). Individual characteristics that constitute antisocial propensity, like intelligence, impulsivity, and temperament, affect both the perceived opportunities for social interaction and the skills needed to successfully engage in these interactions. In turn, those who are relatively insensitive to punishments and rewards may find only those behaviors that result in peak emotional states gratifying and worthy of continuation (Catalano & Hawkins, 1996, p. 161). Antisocial opportunities may also become more attractive once children experience failure in engaging in pro-social interactions, and increasingly tend to seek the immediate rewards of antisocial behavior, like the excitement of breaking and entering, or the rush of substance use.

Though a high antisocial propensity may render individuals more prone to engaging on the antisocial pathway, according to the Social Developmental Model, development still remains open to outside influences. To the extent that contextual changes influence opportunities for learning, new behaviors may be reinforced and new bonds may be forged, potentially swinging the pendulum in a new developmental direction (Catalano *et al.*, 2005: 113). Events that decrease opportunities for antisocial interaction, like separation from an abusive parent or changing schools in response to being bullied, will tend to decrease antisocial involvement and rewards, and in turn stimulate pro-social experiences. Likewise, engaging in a romantic relationship with a conventional partner may increase opportunities for learning and consolidating pro-social behaviors. Events and transitions increasing opportunities for antisocial learning, like being hired by a fraudulent company, or decreasing opportunities for pro-social learning, like experiencing a divorce, may simultaneously weaken bonds to pro-social institutions and strengthen those to antisocial institutions, fostering future criminal involvement. Given that learning experiences may result in behaviors that conflict with obligations following from previously established bonds, the effect of contextual factors is likely to be gradual and to accumulate over time.

The Social Developmental Model does not distinguish between offender types. Rather, it assumes that individuals can either be high or low on pro-social and anti-social bonding, with those low on pro-social bonding and high on antisocial bonding most likely to persist in crime over time. Developmental plasticity may be somewhat lower for those who lack the skills to capitalize on pro-social learning opportunities, but behavioral change remains an option, even for those with strong antisocial ties. The Social Developmental Model therefore ranks alongside the Age-graded Theory and is best represented by panel B in Figure 19.1.

Moffitt's Dual Taxonomy

The Dual Taxonomy offered by Moffitt (1993) absorbs many elements of the theoretical models described above. It too focuses on family processes, peer influence, and adult role transitions. What sets the Dual Taxonomy apart is its claim that the offender population harbors different types of offenders whose criminal development is governed by different causal processes and distinct combinations of risk factors and protective factors (Moffitt, 2003).

For a small minority of youths, antisocial behavior originates from congenital factors, that in interaction with familial processes give rise to a developmental trajectory that starts at an early age, involves frequent delinquent and criminal behavior, and extends far into the adult years (Moffitt & Caspi, 2001). Newborns vary in activity level, temperament, impulse control, and cognitive abilities as a result of variation in neurological functioning. Highly active, easily irritated and slow-learning toddlers can be very demanding, even for the best of parents. Yet, as many of these characteristics are highly hereditable, difficult children disproportionately are born to parents that have less patience and are easily frustrated themselves, and are therefore likely to resort to ineffective parenting strategies in an attempt to curb their child's hyperactivity and repetitive tantrums. These failed parent–child interactions further exacerbate the child's behavioral problems, and by the time these children reach school-going age, they have developed an antisocial behavioral style that makes them clash with teachers, and causes age-mates to shun their company, further depriving them of opportunities for pro-social interaction (Moffitt, 1994).

As they grow older, negative interactions accumulate for these children, and their antisocial behavior becomes more and more entrenched in their behavioral repertoire to such a level that it gradually becomes immune to outside influence (Moffitt, 2003). From antisocial behavior in childhood, through delinquency during early adolescence, these youths quickly start engaging in increasingly serious types of criminal behavior, including interpersonal violence. Unrepelled by strong ties to conventional others and insensitive to temporal changes in levels of informal control resulting from chance encounters, these youths' criminal behavior tends to persist far into their adult years. In fact, when good things do happen to this type of offender, instead of having a dampening effect, the occasion is seized to broaden the scope of criminal behavior – such as employment giving opportunity for workplace crime, and marriage providing the opportunity for intimate partner violence (Moffitt, 1997). Hence, for a small minority of children, personal characteristics together with malfunctioning family processes combine into a level of antisocial propensity that severely limits their developmental plasticity and increasingly predestines them for adverse adult outcomes, including, but not limited to, a prolonged criminal career (Moffitt *et al.*, 2002).

The large majority of children however, do not suffer from neuropsychological deficits, or at least not to a level that sets off a downward spiral of failed pro-social interactions. Throughout early childhood up to early adolescence, these children do not show alarming levels of problematic behavior. Yet many of them start to engage in rule-breaking behavior and minor forms of delinquency during the adolescent period. By the end of adolescence however, these youths in turn desist from delinquency and crime and go on to live conventional lives. In the Dual Taxonomy, these youths are referred to as "adolescence-limited offenders", reflecting the temporal character of their antisocial behavior (Moffitt, 1993). Moffitt explains the onset of delinquency in this type of youth by a mix of ideas taken from strain and learning theories. In today's society, biological maturity and social maturity are increasingly delinked, and many adult privileges and responsibilities are denied to adolescents until several years after they reach physiological maturity. The strain resulting from a desire for expressing personal autonomy, in the face of still-limited opportunities for entering adult roles, motivates adolescents to look for innovative ways to meet their needs. In the adolescent peer context they are confronted with youths on the persistent antisocial pathway who seem to enjoy many of the liberties other adolescents as yet can only crave for. Persistent offenders become role models to previously unproblematic youths, who begin to mimic the antisocial behaviors of their persistently offending peers. While being practically indistinguishable in terms of offending frequency, the antisocial trajectories of both groups start to diverge again when with-age opportunities for engaging in conventional adult social roles present themselves. Previously unproblematic youths, while engaging in delinquency and crime during adolescence, are not as high on antisocial propensity as are life-course persistent youths, and therefore their behavior remains sensitive to outside influences (Moffitt, 2003). After the relatively role-free period of adolescence, youths on the adolescence-limited pathway finish their schooling, enter the labor market, engage in long-term romantic relationships, and start a family. With these ties their stake in conformity starts to increase, and consequentially rising levels of informal social control make them start to leave their delinquent ways behind. In a fine example of developmental plasticity, the delinquency and crime of those on the adolescence-limited trajectory most often vanishes as quickly as it emerged.

Ironically, the same openness for change that allows youths on the adolescence-limited pathway to readopt a law-abiding lifestyle also puts them at risk of developing a prolonged criminal career. Delinquent behavior during the adolescent period can have a deleterious effect on subsequent development, as some previously unproblematic youth can become ensnared by the consequences of their own deviance (Moffitt, 1997, p. 37). Truancy may result in school dropout, recreational substance use may grow into an addiction, and a criminal record may form an obstacle to entering the labor market. If adolescence-limited youths get caught in the downward spiral of cumulative disadvantage, it may be increasingly difficult for them to regain a stake in conformity, and a continued pattern of delinquency and crime may result. Whereas for life-course persistent offenders the range of developmental outcomes is severely limited from an early age onwards, outcomes for adolescence-limited youths thus in principle span the entire spectrum. Moffitt's Dual Taxonomy is reflected by panel C in Figure 19.1.

Thornberry's Interactional Theory

While recognizing its heuristic appeal, Interactional Theory does not support a clear-cut difference between offender types like that made by the Dual Taxonomy. Instead, Interactional Theory aims to reconcile findings that are generally offered as support of such distinctions, like the association of an early age of onset of antisocial behavior with an increased length of the criminal career, with that of the continuous distribution of these criminal career parameters usually found in empirical studies (Thornberry, 2005). Like most other life-course theories, Interactional Theory stresses developmental plasticity. However, even more so than the Dual Taxonomy and the Age-graded Theory, Interactional Theory emphasizes that the association between external factors and crime is not a one-way street but that there is constant interaction – hence Interactional Theory – between these two (Thornberry, 1987).

Interactional Theory uses a somewhat broader definition of antisocial propensity than other developmental theories, in stressing that like individual characteristics, some features of the social environment that children and adolescents are confronted with – like social class, poverty, or living in a bad neighborhood – also tend to be less liable to change (Thornberry, 1987). Despite upward and downward mobility, there is relative stability in these features across generations. As do stable individual characteristics, these stable structural variables give rise to initial variation in the causes presumed to underlie delinquency and crime. Interactional Theory, like the Age-graded Theory, views strong ties to age-appropriate social institutions as central in inhibiting antisocial behavior (Thornberry & Krohn, 2001). Children that grow up in poor, stressed, and conflict-ridden families, residing in disadvantaged neighborhoods offering few conventional opportunities, experience less conventional ties from the very start. Still, while a person's point of departure may greatly influence the course of his or her developmental trajectory, antisocial propensity does by no means equal "destiny", and criminal careers can differ in shape and form depending on outside influences occurring across the life span (Thornberry, 2005, p. 160).

According to Interactional Theory, delinquency and crime are more likely to occur when ties to conventional institutions are weakened or broken and social constraints over individual behavior are reduced. Sources of social constraint are considered to be age-graded. During childhood and early adolescent years, bonds to parents are most important, but with age bonds to peers and romantic partners become increasingly salient (Thornberry & Krohn, 2001). While weakened bonds set the stage, reinforcement of antisocial behavior is necessary for its maintenance and development over time. Like with social bonds, the sources of antisocial reinforcement are likely to differ with age, encompassing siblings, peers, coworkers, and marital partners. Key element to the Interactional Theory is that throughout development delinquency and crime are not merely regarded as outcomes, but are seen as an integral part of the developmental process (Thornberry, 1987). Lowered attachment to his or her parents may provide a youth the freedom to engage in delinquent behavior, yet this behaviour is likely to further strain the youth's relationship with his or her parents. Likewise, while peers may reinforce delinquency, delinquent behavior in turn can attract deviant peers and simultaneously result in the loss of pro-social friends, tipping the scale further and further in favor of continued antisocial behavior.

In Interactional Theory, processes of accumulation are not reserved to explain persistence in crime, like in the Age-graded Theory, nor to understand why some unproblematic youth go on to develop prolonged criminal careers, like in the Dual Taxonomy, but instead take center-stage in the explanation of crime and deviance. The longer a person continues to engage in delinquency and crime, through the perpetual deterioration of social ties, the more crime becomes its own cause (Thornberry & Krohn, 2005). On the other hand, pro-social behavior, through the strengthening of bonds and increasing investment in conventional lines of action, tends to set in motion a trajectory towards increased conformity. Over time both antisocial and pro-social trajectories generate a certain level of inertia (see also Blokland & Nieuwbeerta, 2010; Nagin & Paternoster, 1991). Interactional Theory therefore does not expect outside influences to result in sharp turning points, radically altering behavioral trajectories. While remaining susceptible to outside influence, changes in developmental direction are more likely to be gradual, as counterforces to current development, either social or antisocial, need time to gain momentum (Thornberry, 2005). The notion of inertia helps to clarify why relatively small differences in antisocial propensity can give rise to highly dissimilar adult outcomes. As with each cycle the consequences of both antisocial and pro-social behavior accumulate, a person's developmental range tends to decrease as he or she continues on the developmental path taken. Still, with its emphasis on the interactions between behavior and the social environment, Interactional Theory is best represented by panel B in Figure 19.1.

Farrington's Integrated Cognitive Antisocial Potential Theory

Summarizing decades of research on a cohort of working-class London boys, David Farrington recently advanced a theoretical framework to help organize existing knowledge on risk and protective factors for delinquent development. Central to this Integrated Cognitive Antisocial Potential (ICAP) theory is antisocial potential, or AP for short, which refers to the potential to commit antisocial acts, some of which are criminalized by law (Farrington, 2005c). Farrington's antisocial potential is different from antisocial propensity, as the term is used here, in that antisocial potential is intended to have less biological emphasis (Farrington, 2005c, p. 76). Furthermore, antisocial potential has both a long-term and a short-term component. Long-term AP is said to refer to between-individual differences in the likelihood to engage in delinquency and crime. While long-term AP is influenced by both childhood socialization and individual characteristics, it is also argued to depend upon antisocial models and life events, blurring the distinction between antisocial propensity and developmental plasticity made here. Given that Farrington concludes that between-individual differences in long-term AP tend to persist over time (Farrington, 2005d, p. 184), regardless of outside influences like becoming unemployed or getting married, both developmental plasticity and developmental range, however, appear limited within the ICAP framework.

Even those high on long-term AP, however, do not go about committing crime everywhere and always. In fact, even the most frequent offenders display norm-conforming behavior most of the time. According to the ICAP theory the commission of offences (in contrast to becoming an offender) is best explained by the interaction between the individual and his or her social environment (Farrington, 2005c). Short-term variations in psychological or physiological states, like being angry or drunk – labeled short-term energizers – may temporarily elevate a person's short-term AP. Situational features (e.g., a suitable target presenting itself) may also temporarily increase short-term AP. The higher short-term AP, the more likely an offence is committed by that offender, in that situation. Linking short-term AP to the commission of crime are cognitive choice processes, weighing the benefits and costs of committing the crime, the likelihood of those costs, and the availability of behavioral alternatives.

In the ICAP theory, long-term AP also adds to the equation, resulting in levels of short-term AP, though the causal mechanisms are as yet left unspecified. In principle, long-term AP may contribute to the prevalence of short-term energizing factors (such as being angry or drunk repeatedly), or make offenders seek out social environments where opportunities for delinquency and crime are more prevalent. Long-term AP may also impact upon the cognitive processes that link motivations and opportunities to the commission of crimes, for instance, by influencing the relative weight given to the immediate benefits and long-term costs of committing the crime.

The distinction between long-term and short-term AP allows for differentiating different types of offenders (Farrington, 2005c, p. 83). Those high on long-term AP may need little situational encouragement to act in a delinquent fashion, while for those low on long-term AP, short-term factors may be more crucial. Experiments by Farrington and Knight (1979) involving the opportunity to steal money from a lost letter indicated that the majority of passers-by can be lured into committing a crime if an ideal opportunity is presented.

At present, the ICAP theory is perhaps more an organizing scheme than a real theory, since it is largely silent on the precise causal mechanisms linking each of its proposed elements (Farrington, 2014). Yet, given the emphasis on rank order stability in long-term AP, and the potential influence of long-term AP on both the elements constituting short-term AP and the cognitive processes linking short-term AP to the commission of crimes, the ICAP theory seems best categorized as somewhere between panels A and B of Figure 19.1.

Implications for Policy

A life-course approach to juvenile delinquency, as sketched here on the basis of prominent theories on the development of delinquency and crime, has important consequences for practice and policy in juvenile justice.

All developmental theories reviewed here stress the importance of early childhood circumstances in the etiology of delinquency and crime, especially with regard to frequent and persistent patterns of offending. Even in the most rigid of conceptualizations of development, antisocial propensity is viewed as the product of the interaction between the child's individual and family characteristics, rendering the family a prominent target of intervention (Gottfredson & Hirschi, 1995). Newborns could be screened for the extent to which their behavior is extraordinarily taxing to their parents, and parents could be assessed on their child-rearing knowledge and skills, allowing the allocation of resources to those families who need it the most. To prevent stigmatization from being labeled as a "difficult child" or "unfit parent", general policies that make these services available for all income groups through perinatal healthcare, child pediatricians and preschool institutions should be considered. As antisocial propensity also entails the child's initial position with regard to structural factors, like poverty or neighborhood safety, policies aimed at reducing parents' financial and environmental strains also impact their children's likelihood of engaging in delinquency and crime (Catalano *et al.*, 2005).

According to Gottfredson and Hirschi's General Theory, the window of opportunity for successful interventions closes quickly after the age of 10. Within the framework of the General Theory, adolescents are not distinct from adults in terms of susceptibility to treatment, and expenditures specifically allocated to adolescent offenders' rehabilitation are a misuse. Similar conclusions seem to follow from Moffitt's Dual Taxonomy. By the time youths on the persistent pathway enter adolescence they already seem to have passed a point of no return at which the continued effects of individual characteristics combined with the cascading forces of negative environmental interactions seem to rule out behavioral change (Moffitt, 1997). According to these theories, much more is expected from reducing the opportunities for adolescents to offend, for instance through restricting the time adolescents spent unsupervised, or by taking a slice out of the youths' criminal career through incarceration (Gottfredson & Hirschi, 1995). According to the majority of developmental and life-course theories reviewed here, however, it is never too early, but also never too late to intervene in a youth's criminal trajectory (Loeber & Farrington, 1998). Despite individual and familial conditions predisposing some juveniles to delinquency more than others, behavioral development is highly flexible and continues to remain open to outside influences.

Within the life-course approach, the youth's delinquent trajectory is but one of the many trajectories that unfold with age to constitute his or her life course. Adversities encountered in any of these trajectories can influence the onset, maintenance, or desistance from delinquency and crime, often having the largest impact when occurring in tandem across domains (Thornberry, 2005). Accordingly, juvenile justice interventions should not be constricted to only the cause perceived most salient for the current delinquent behavior, but instead should employ a multifaceted approach, covering many life domains to increase effectiveness. While transitions to meaningful adult social roles seem important in desistance from delinquency and crime, as yet the causal mechanisms via which these transitions exert their effect still remain unclear. From the control perspective taken by both the Age-graded Theory and Interactional Theory, it follows that interventions should be primarily aimed at providing juvenile delinquents with a stake in conventional society (Laub & Sampson, 2001). Offering them an education or otherwise facilitating a successful entry into the labor market, for instance, is expected to yield more long-term benefits than mere detention. From the learning perspective taken by the Social Developmental Model, it follows that interventions should seek to increase pro-social reinforcements, while decreasing antisocial reinforcements (see also Warr, 2002). While the former could entail creating occasions where the youth's accomplishments are formally recognized, like a graduation ceremony, the latter could entail (temporary) relocating the adolescent from his or her prior neighborhood. Enhancing our insight into the exact workings of important life-course transitions and how they relate to delinquency and crime is pivotal for designing interventions that are able to effectively curb delinquent development.

Although most life-course theories contend that change is always an option, desistance is unlikely to happen overnight (Bushway, Piquero, Broidy, Cauffman, & Mazerolle, 2001). As pro-social opportunities present themselves, skills for materializing these opportunities need to be acquired, investments in these opportunities need to be made, conforming behavior needs to be reinforced, and cumulative forces driving towards persistence need to be counterbalanced. Furthermore, for many offenders, desisting from delinquency and crime is one thing, but to remain crime-free is another, requiring unremitting efforts as criminal opportunities and contacts continue to present themselves (Thornberry, 2005, p. 161). The ongoing process of desistance is therefore most likely to benefit from interventions that involve a considerable period of aftercare and provide an adequate response to temporary relapse. Given the gradual nature of desistance, evaluation studies into the effects of particular interventions also should consider a follow-up long enough for any beneficial effects to have gained momentum.

Developmental plasticity however, is a double-edged sword that should be wielded with care. While juvenile justice interventions can help to bring about desistance from delinquency and crime, by the same token they can also unintentionally increase rather than decrease the youth's likelihood of developing a prolonged criminal career. Formal interventions as potential triggers setting off a downward spiral of cumulative disadvantage figure prominently in both

Thornberry's (2005) Interactional Theory and Sampson and Laub's (1997) Age-graded Theory, as well as in Moffitt's (1997) account of adolescence-limited offenders becoming ensnared by the consequences of their deviance. A history of involvement with the juvenile justice system may block conventional educational and employment opportunities, thereby constricting adolescents' range of long-term outcomes. Given the importance of transitions to adult social roles and the stigma associated with a history of criminal justice involvement – information which is increasingly available to third parties through criminal record checks – policies that aim at extra-legal adjudications of juvenile delinquents, that seek to limit third-party access to juvenile records, or otherwise aim to preserve or even increase adolescents' conventional opportunities through, for example, training and schooling, are preferred in this respect.

Finally, though life-course theories champion the plasticity of human behavioral development, it is also important not to overestimate what can be reached through interventions. Antisocial propensity, and perhaps more importantly processes of cumulative advantage and disadvantage, may set limits to what can realistically be achieved. Especially for those youths experiencing strong adversities in many different domains, juvenile justice interventions may have a hard time trying to undo the snowballing effects of many years of antisocial development prior to entering the system. Recent research finds that juvenile delinquents, and especially those showing persistence in their criminal careers, are more likely than others to experience "life failure" in many conventional life-course domains, including housing, employment, and family life (Piquero, Farrington, Nagin, & Moffitt, 2010). As the criminal careers of the offenders in these studies are likely to have developed despite many opposing efforts, both formal and informal, the task set for the juvenile justice system is challenging to say the least. Life-course criminology, as represented by the theories reviewed in this chapter, seeks to offer us the tools to successfully meet this challenge.

Notes

1 The dichotomy between static (no plasticity) and dynamic (high plasticity) theories made by Paternoster *et al.* (1997) reflects the two extremes of the continuous range of developmental plasticity.
2 Though in later publications, Sampson and Laub (2005, p. 34; Laub & Sampson, 2003) seem to draw on a much wider range of theoretical mechanisms explaining desistance, including social support, routine activities, differential association, and identity transformation.

References

Blokland, A., Nagin, D., & Nieuwbeerta, P. (2005). Life span offending trajectories of a Dutch conviction cohort. *Criminology, 43*(4), 919–954.

Blokland, A., & Nieuwbeerta, P. (2010). Considering criminal continuity: testing for hetero-geneity and state dependence in the association of past to future offending. *Australian and New Zealand Journal of Criminology, 43*(3), 526–556.

Bushway, S.D., Piquero, A.R., Broidy, L.M., Cauffman, E.E., & Mazerolle, P. (2001). An empirical framework for studying desistance as a process. *Criminology, 39,* 491–515.

Catalano, R.F., & Hawkins, J.D. (1996). The social developmental model: a theory of anti-social behavior. In J.D. Hawkins (Ed.), *Delinquency and Crime: Current Theories* (pp. 149–197). Cambridge: Cambridge University Press.

Catalano, R.F., Kosterman, R., Hawkins, J.D., Newcomb, M.D., & Abbott, R.D. (1996). Modeling the etiology of adolescent substance use: a test of the social developmental model. *Journal of Drug Issues, 26*(2), 429–455.

Catalano, R.F., Park, J., Harachi, T.W., Haggerty, K.P., Abbott, R.D., & Hawkins, J.D. (2005). Mediating the effects of poverty, gender, individual characteristics, and external con-straints on antisocial behavior: a test of the social developmental model and implica-tions for developmental life-course theory. In D.P. Farrington (Ed.), *Integrated Developmental & Life-Course Theories of Offending* (pp. 93–123). New Brunswick, NJ: Transaction.

Farrington, D.P. (1983). Offending from 10 to 25 years of age. In S.E. Mednick (Ed.), *Prospective Studies of Crime and Delinquency* (pp. 17–37). Boston: Kluwer-Nijhoff.

Farrington, D.P. (1995). Development of offending and antisocial behaviour from childhood: Key findings from the Cambridge Study in Delinquent Development. *Journal of Child Psychology, 360*(6), 929–964.

Farrington, D.P. (Ed.) (2005a). *Integrated Developmental & Life-Course Theories of Offending.* New Brunswick, NJ: Transaction.

Farrington, D.P. (2005b). Introduction to integrated and life-course theories of offending. In D.P. Farrington (Ed.) *Integrated Developmental & Life-Course Theories of Offending* (pp. 1–14). New Brunswick, NJ: Transaction.

Farrington, D.P. (2005c). The Integrated Cognitive Antisocial Potential Theory. In D.P. Farrington (Ed.) *Integrated Developmental & Life-Course Theories of Offending* (pp. 73–92). New Brunswick, NJ: Transaction.

Farrington, D.P. (2005d). Childhood origins of antisocial behavior. *Clinical Psychology & Psychotherapy, 12*(3), 177–190.

Farrington, D.P. (2014). Integrated cognitive antisocial potential theory. In G.J.N. Bruinsma, & D. Weisburd (Eds.), *Encyclopedia of Criminology and Criminal Justice* (pp. 2552–2564).

Farrington, D.P., Coid, J.W., Harnett, L.M., Jolliffe, D., Soteriou, N., Turner, R.E., & West, D.J. (2006). *Criminal Careers up to Age 50 and Life Success up to Age 48: New Findings from the Cambridge Study in Delinquent Development.* London: Home Office.

Farrington, D.P., & Knight, B.J. (1979). Two non-reactive field experiments on stealing from a "lost" letter. *British Journal of Social and Clinical Psychology, 18,* 277–284.

Gottfredson, M.R., & Hirschi, T. (1990). *A General Theory of Crime.* Stanford: Stanford University Press.

Gottfredson, M.R., & Hirschi, T. (1995). National crime control policies. *Society, 32*(2), 30–36.

Hagan, J., & McCarthy, B. (1997). *Mean Streets. Youth Crime and Homelessness.* Cambridge: Cambridge University Press.

Hawkins, J.D., & Weis, J.G. (1985). The social development model: an integrated approach to delinquency prevention. *Journal of Primary Prevention, 6,* 73–97.

Hirschi, T. (1969). *Causes of Delinquency*. Berkeley, CA: University of California Press.

Hirschi, T., & Gottfredson, M.R. (1993). Commentary: Testing the General Theory of Crime. *Journal of Research in Crime and Delinquency, 30*, 47–54.

Hirschi, T., & Gottfredson, M.R. (1994). *The Generality of Deviance*. New Brunswick, NJ: Transaction.

Hirschi, T., & Gottfredson, M.R. (2003). Punishment of children from the perspective of control theory. In C.L. Britt, & M.R. Gottfredson (Eds.), *Control Theories of Crime and Delinquency* (pp. 151–160). New Brunswick, NJ: Transaction.

Laub, J., Nagin, D., & Sampson, R. (1998). Trajectories of change in criminal offending: good marriages and the desistance process. *American Sociological Review, 63*, 225–238.

Laub, J.H., & Sampson, R.J. (2001). Understanding desistance from crime. *Crime and Justice, 28*, 1–69.

Laub, J.H., & Sampson, R.J. (2003). *Shared Beginnings, Divergent Lives; Delinquent Boys to Age 70*. Cambridge, MA: Harvard University Press.

Li, S.C. (2003). Biocultural orchestration of developmental plasticity across levels: The interplay of biology and culture in shaping the mind and behavior across the life span. *Psychological Bulletin, 129*(2), 171–194.

Loeber, R., & Farrington, D.P. (1998). Never too early, never too late: risk factors and successful interventions for serious and violent juvenile offenders. *Studies in Crime and Crime Prevention, 7*, 7–30.

Loeber, R., Farrington, D.P., Stouthamer-Loeber, M., Moffitt, T.E., Caspi, A., & Lynam, D. (2001). Male mental health problems, psychopathy, and personality traits: Key findings from the first 14 years of the Pittsburgh Youth Study. *Clinical Child and Family Psychology Review, 4*(4), 273–297.

Loeber, R., Wung, P., Keenan, K., Stouthamer-Loeber, M., van Kammen, W.B., & Maughan, B. (1993). Developmental pathways in disruptive child behavior. *Development and Psychopathology, 5*, 101–132.

Moczek, A.P., Sultan, S., Foster, S., Ledón-Rettig, C., Dworkin, I., Nijhout, H.F., Abouheif, E., & Pfennig, D.W. (2011). The role of developmental plasticity in evolutionary innovation. *Proceedings of the Royal Society of Biological Sciences B, 278*. doi:10.1098/rspb.2011.0971

Moffitt, T.E. (1993). Life-course-persistent and adolescence-limited antisocial behavior: a developmental taxonomy. *Psychological Review, 100*, 674–701.

Moffitt, T.E. (1994). Natural histories of delinquency. In E. Weitekamp, & H.J. Kerner (Eds.), *Cross-national Longitudinal Research on Human Development and Criminal Behavior* (pp. 3–61). Dordrecht: Kluwer Academic Press.

Moffitt, T.E. (1997). Adolescence-limited and life-course-persistent offending: a complementary pair of developmental theories. In T.P. Thornberry (Ed.), *Developmental Theories of Crime and Delinquency* (pp. 11–54). New Brunswick, NJ: Transaction.

Moffitt, T.E. (2003). Life-course-persistent and adolescence-limited antisocial behavior: a 10-year research review and a research agenda. In B. Lahey, T.E. Moffitt, & C. Avshalom (Eds.), *Causes of Conduct Disorder and Juvenile Delinquency* (pp. 49–75). New York: Guilford Press.

Moffitt, T.E., & Caspi A. (2001). Childhood predictors differentiate life-course persistent and adolescent limited pathways, among males and females. *Development and Psychopathology, 13*, 355–375.

Moffitt, T.E., Caspi, A., Harrington, H., & Milne, B.J. (2002). Males on the life-course-persistent and adolescence-limited antisocial pathways: follow-up at age 26 years. *Development and Psychopathology, 14*(1), 179–207.

Nagin, D.S., & Paternoster, R. (1991). On the relationship of past to future participation in delinquency. *Criminology, 29*(2), 163–189.

Pager, D. (2007). *Marked: Race, Crime, and Finding Work in an Era of Mass Incarceration.* Chicago, IL: University of Chicago Press.

Paternoster, R., Dean, C.W., Piquero, A., Mazerolle, P., & Brame, R. (1997). Generality, continuity, and change in offending. *Journal of Quantitative Criminology, 13*(3), 231–266.

Patterson, G.R., & Yoerger, K. (1993). Developmental models for delinquent behavior. In S. Hodgins (Ed.), *Mental Disorder and Crime* (pp. 140–172). Newbury Park, CA: Sage.

Piquero, A.R., Farrington, D.P., Nagin, D.S., & Moffitt, T.E. (2010). Trajectories of offending and their relation to life failure in late middle age: findings from the Cambridge Study in Delinquent Development. *Journal of Research in Crime and Delinquency, 47*(2), 151–173.

Robins, L.N. (1978). Sturdy childhood predictors of adult antisocial behavior: replications from longitudinal studies. *Psychological Medicine, 8*, 611–622.

Sampson, R.J., & Laub, J.H. (1990). Crime and deviance over the life course: the salience of adult social bonds. *American Sociological Review, 55*, 609–627.

Sampson, R.J., & Laub, J.H. (1993). *Crime in the Making: Pathways and Turning Points through Life.* Cambridge, MA: Harvard University Press.

Sampson, R.J., & Laub, J.H. (1997). A life-course theory of cumulative disadvantage and the stability of delinquency. In T.P. Thornberry (Ed.), *Developmental Theories of Crime and Delinquency* (pp. 133–161). New Brunswick, NJ: Transaction.

Sampson, R.J., & Laub, J.H. (2005). A life-course view of the development of crime. *Annals of the American Academy of Political and Social Science, 602*, 12–45.

Shannon, L.W. (1988). *Criminal Career Continuity: Its Social Context.* New York: Human Sciences Press Inc.

Sullivan, C.J., Piquero, A.R., & Cullen, F.T. (2012). Like before, but better: the lessons of life-course criminology for contemporary juvenile justice. *Victims and Offenders, 7*, 450–471.

Thornberry, T.P. (1987). Toward an interactional theory of delinquency. *Criminology, 25*(4), 863–891.

Thornberry, T.P. (1997). *Developmental Theories of Crime and Delinquency.* New Brunswick, NJ: Transaction.

Thornberry, T.P. (2005). Explaining multiple patterns of offending across the life course and across generations. *Annals of the American Academy of Political and Social Science, 602*, 156–195.

Thornberry, T.P., & Krohn, M.D. (2001). The development of delinquency; an interactional perspective. In S.O. White (Ed.), *Handbook of Youth and Justice* (pp. 289–305). New York: Plenum.

Thornberry, T.P., & Krohn, M.D. (2005). Applying interactional theory to the explanation of continuity and change in antisocial behavior. In D.P. Farrington (Ed.), *Integrated Developmental & Life-Course Theories of Offending* (pp. 183–209). New Brunswick, NJ: Transaction.

Warr, M. (2002). *Companions in Crime; The Social Aspects of Criminal Conduct.* Cambridge: Cambridge University Press.

Wolfgang, M.E., Figlio R.M., & Sellin, T. (1972). *Delinquency in a Birth Cohort.* Chicago: University of Chicago Press.

20

Labeling Theory

Marvin D. Krohn and Giza Lopes

Criminals are made and not born.
President Lyndon B. Johnson, upon signing the Juvenile
Delinquency Prevention and Control Act of 1968

Introduction

At the core of the labeling perspective is the suggestion that humans are active participants in the construction and interpretation of social interaction. Based on that premise, the perspective has derived hypotheses concerning both what factors people take into consideration in identifying others as being deviant or criminal, and how those who are so labeled react to that label and the consequences thereof.

Early developments of the perspective date back to the 1920s (Tannenbaum, 1922; Thrasher, 1927) but it was not until Lemert's (1951) statement differentiating "primary" and "secondary" deviances that the perspective took shape. In the context of the critique of government and its agencies during the 1960s, the popularity of labeling theory reached its peak. Subsequent theoretical criticism and lack of convincing empirical support led to a questioning of the viability of the perspective, causing it to fall out of favor. With new developments in the theory and some empirical evidence to support its arguments, there has been renewed interest in the labeling perspective.

In this essay, we examine the roots and early development of the labeling perspective. We then assess the current state of both its theoretical development and empirical

The Handbook of Juvenile Delinquency and Juvenile Justice, First Edition. Edited by Marvin D. Krohn and Jodi Lane.

status. Finally, we discuss what future directions we see for the continuing development of theory and research on labeling.

Labeling's Theoretical Antecedents

While labeling theory enjoyed its scholarly peak in the 1960s and 1970s, its intellectual roots can be traced back to the early decades of the twentieth century. Notably, beginning in the 1920s, sociologists began to recognize the potentially negative consequences of officially ascribing criminal/delinquent labels to offenders. For instance, in his 1927 work on juvenile gangs in Chicago, Frederick Thrasher advanced the argument that gang members' search for status within the group includes not only assuming "a tough pose", committing "feats of daring or vandalism", but also "acquiring a court record" as a means of gaining prestige (1927, p. 333). Rather than "punishing or 'reforming' him", Thrasher argued, by processing a juvenile through the criminal justice system, "society is simply promoting his rise to power" and failing to "reach him through his vital social groups where an appeal can be made to his essential conception of himself" (1927, p. 334).

A few years earlier, Frank Tannenbaum (1922) had also expressed his views on the negative ramifications associated with official labeling. Once an offender is "stamped as a criminal" and imprisoned, he argued, his/her "every interest, every ambition, every hope, […] all his work and contacts" are cut away and the offender loses his/her original identity and is forced to reprocess it as to include a newly acquired criminal label (Tannenbaum, 1922, pp. 154–155).

Tannenbaum's emphasis on the "stamping" process through which an individual embraces a deviant identity was further developed in his classic study, *Crime and the Community* (1938).[1] There, focusing extensively on the criminal justice treatment of juveniles, he suggested that criminals are created by a societal reaction process to deviance, which separates an individual from conventional society and pushes him/her further into a deviant career:

> The first dramatization of the "evil" which separates the child out of his group for specialized treatment plays a greater role in making the criminal than perhaps any other experience. It cannot be too often emphasized that for the child the whole situation has become different. He now lives in a different world. He has been *tagged*. A new and hitherto non-existent environment has been precipitated out for him.
>
> The process of making the criminal, therefore, is a process of tagging, defining, identifying, segregating, describing, emphasizing, making conscious and self-conscious; it becomes a way of stimulating, suggesting, emphasizing, and evoking the very traits that are complained of. (Tannenbaum, 1938, pp. 19–20; our emphasis)

Tannenbaum's notion of "dramatization of evil" was developed against a much larger intellectual turning point that was concomitantly taking place within several disciplines directly or tangentially related to understanding deviance and crime, such as sociology, psychology, and philosophy. Specifically, deterministic explanations of human agency, including engagement in criminal activity, were gradually giving way to a more pragmatist view of behavior, which became known as "symbolic interactionism" (Blumer, 1937).

Based originally on the ideas of George H. Mead (1934), Charles H. Cooley (1902), W.I. Thomas (1923), among others, symbolic interaction theorists posit that reality is primarily a social construct, negotiated in interaction between individuals, during which meanings are created. It follows from this premise that "meaning" is a central mediating factor in human behavior: it determines how one conceives his or her sense of "self" and it orientates subsequent actions in which individuals engage.

A few of the early conceptualizations of symbolic interactionism were in consonance with the novel approach to deviance and crime, as articulated by early labelists. A relevant example is Cooley's notion of "reflected" or "looking-glass self" (1902). According to Cooley, individuals forge their sense of identity dialectically, through interpersonal interactions. One's "self", he states, is the result of "our imagination of how we *appear* to other persons; our imagination of how these others [...] *judge* our appearance; and the products of such imaginings, which are our *resultant* self-feelings" (1902, pp. 152–153).

While Cooley's focus when examining self-formation was on individuals' feelings, William Isaac Thomas (1923) turned his attention to individuals' adjusted responses to their constructed realities. In sum, Thomas argued that to understand one's behavior, it is imperative first to understand how he or she "defines the situation". The following excerpt from Tannenbaum's *Crime and the Community* elucidates the importance of Thomas' concept to labeling theorists:

> In the conflict between the young delinquent and the community there develop two definitions of the situation. In the beginning the definition of the situation by the young delinquent may be in the form of play, adventure, excitement, interest, mischief, fun. Breaking windows, annoying people, running around porches, climbing over roofs, stealing from pushcarts, playing truant – all are items of play, adventure, excitement. To the community, however, these activities may and often do take on the form of a nuisance, evil, delinquency, with the demand for control, admonition, chastisement, punishment, police court, truant school. This conflict over the situation gradually becomes redefined. [...] There is a gradual shift from the definition of the specific act as evil to a definition of the individual as evil, so that all his acts come to be looked upon with suspicion. (Tannenbaum, 1938, p. 14)

Symbolic interactionism ideas were crucial to the development of labeling theory, as they emphasize the importance of understanding behavior – such as deviance – as subjectively problematic, processually based, and symbolically driven.

Although original articulations of the labeling perspective, as discussed above, find their roots in the early decades of the twentieth century, it was only in 1951, with the publication of *Social Pathology: A Systematic Approach to the Theory of Sociopathic Behavior* by Edwin Lemert, that the theory made substantial epistemic strides. Written in an era of "red scares" and McCarthyism,[2] Lemert's book relies on the assumption that in order to understand *deviants*, one has to understand, first, society's *reactions to deviance*. In line with this thought, he later argued that "older sociology ...tended to rest heavily upon the idea that deviance leads to social control. I have come to believe that the reverse idea, i.e., social control leads to deviance, is equally tenable and the potentially richer premise for studying deviance in modern society" (1967, p. v). At the core of Lemert's "social reaction" theory was a two-pronged understanding of how deviance unfolds. "Primary deviance", he proposed, is an initial experimentation with norm-violating behavior that ultimately causes no long-term consequences for the offender because social reaction to the violation is either absent or mild. Primary deviance can occur for a variety of reasons (psychological, structural, or at random), and the violations are either rationalized or defined as socially acceptable by the individual. In other words, the deviant behavior is perceived by the actor as temporary, an aberration, and has "only marginal implications for the psychic structure of the individual" (Lemert, 1967, p. 17).[3]

"Secondary deviance", in turn, is a dynamic process through which an individual goes from *engaging in* deviance to *becoming* deviant. Precipitated by the response of others to the original norm-violating behavior, secondary deviance triggers a "self-fulfilling prophecy" (Merton, 1948) whereby the very behavior sanctioned is internalized by the offender as part of his/her identity who now, fully embracing that concept of him/herself, acts in accordance with the deviant label. In Lemert's words, if the primary deviant "acts are repetitive and have a high visibility, and if there is a severe societal reaction, which, through a process of self-identification is incorporated as a part of the 'me' of the individual, the probability is greatly increased that ...a process of reorganization based upon a new role will occur" (1951, p. 75). Even more significantly, Lemert posits that secondary deviance can bring with it a stabilization of the deviant behavior it involves:

> Objective evidences of this change in the offender's self-image will be found in the symbolic appurtenances of the new role, in clothes, speech, posture and mannerisms, which in some cases heighten social visibility, and which in some cases serve as symbolic cues to professionalization. (Lemert, 1951, p. 76)

In the 1960s, the labeling approach was further expanded to include the socially constructed nature of *deviance* itself. Epitomized by the work of Howard Becker in *Outsiders* (1963), and reflecting the anti-establishment sentiment of the decade, scholars began to look more closely at the conditions surrounding the creation of rules that institute what is considered "deviant" and what is not:

> Social groups create deviance by making the rules whose infraction constitutes deviance, and by applying those rules to particular people and labeling them as outsiders. From this point of view, deviance is not a quality of the act the person commits, but rather a consequence of the application by others of rules and sanctions to an "offender". The deviant is one to whom that label has been successfully applied; deviant behavior is behavior that people so label. (Becker, 1963, p. 9)

In discussing the process through which rules are defined and enforced, Becker proposed that only a few individuals, which he termed "moral entrepreneurs", have the power and legitimacy to determine which behaviors are "deviant". Generally, he argued, these moral entrepreneurs occupy higher social class positions, thereby affecting directly who will – and who will not – get labeled. Furthermore, he elaborated, "[t]he degree to which an act will be treated as deviant depends also on *who* commits the act" (1963, p. 12, our emphasis). In that sense, the decision to sanction certain behaviors is determined at least partly by the social characteristics of the offender (see also Paternoster & Iovanni, 1989).

These early articulations of the labeling perspective drew attention to the way in which the criminal justice system operates and processes individuals. Of particular importance was the perspective's influence on juvenile justice policy reform. We turn to that next.

Task Force Report on Juvenile Delinquency and Youth Crime

The publication in 1967 of the *Presidential Task Force Report on Juvenile Delinquency and Youth Crime* marked what might be the apex of the acceptance of the tenets of the labeling approach (President's Commission, 1967). The first chapter of the Report was an assessment of the state of juvenile justice with specific attention to the operation of the juvenile court. Overall, the Report was highly critical of the juvenile justice system confirming and, to some extent, documenting the oft-quoted statement by Chief Justice Abe Fortas in the *Kent v. United States* (1966) decision, that the juvenile received the worst of both worlds in that they were not accorded the rights of an adult while the system's charge to protect the child (*parens patriae*) was not being realized. A key passage in the Report's first chapter articulated the basic tenets of the labeling approach:

> Such a policy would avoid for many the long-lasting consequences of adjudication: curtailment of employment opportunity, quasi-criminal record, harm to personal reputation in the eyes of family and friends and public, reinforcement of antisocial tendencies… The juvenile will wear the label longer, while he is likely to outgrow the conduct that brought him the badge; one who acquires the status of a deviant in his youth faces the prospect of lifelong stigmatization. For a certain proportion of juvenile offenders the consequences appear to be cumulative. (p. 16)

The Report also contained a number of appendices, written by experts in the field, on various subjects relevant to either the juvenile justice system or juvenile delinquency. Wheeler, Cottrell, and Romasco (1967) addressed the prevention and control of juvenile delinquency, incorporating a section in which they raised the question of what the effect of labeling would be on youth. Their approach was a balanced one indicating that there was little actual research on the effects of involvement in the juvenile justice system, in support of either a deterrent or labeling effect.

However, they concluded that in the absence of evidence of the benefits of the juvenile justice system, "every effort should be made to avoid the use of a formal sanctioning system and particularly the official pronouncement of delinquency" because of the "potentially damaging effects of the labeling process" (p. 418). Their position was consistent with Lemert's assertion that:

> Court hearings, home investigations by social workers, arrests, clinical visits, segrega-tion within the school system and other formal dispositions of deviants under the aegis of public welfare or public protection in many instances are cause for dramatic redefi-nitions of the self and role of deviants which may not be desired. (Lemert, 1951, p. 78)

Within a few years, research began to accumulate. Much of this work either questioned labeling theory's tenets, or at least the views that were attributed to the perspective. This research, in addition to the reluctance of those scholars sympathetic to the labeling approach to articulate precise propositions, led to a vigorous debate throughout the next decade.

Critiques of the Theory

As Erich Goode (1975, p. 570) noted, by the early 1970s "the anti-labeling stance became almost as fashionable as labeling had been a decade earlier". There were a number of reasons for such criticisms. The labeling perspective was critiqued for its relativistic definition of deviance and the deviant, the impreciseness with which its concepts and propositions were stated, and, most importantly, for the failure to find convincing results supporting those propositions.

Labeling clearly attributes a significant role to the observer in identifying and defining behaviors as being deviant or not. Schur (1971, p. 14) acknowledged this when he stated that: "It is a central tenet of the labeling perspective that neither acts nor individuals are 'deviant' in the sense of immutable 'objective' reality without ref-erence to processes of social definition." However, labeling theorists do not discount that typically some act has been committed and that the act might be normatively defined as wrong or criminal (Lemert, 1974). Although some scholars may take the notion of a relative definition of deviance to an unfortunate extreme, what is impor-tant within the perspective is the examination of the nature of the social reaction to the behavior and its potential effect on the actor (Lemert, 1974; Schur, 1971).

The failure to provide a clear and consistent statement of a "labeling theory" (Gibbs, 1966; Gove, 1980) is more problematic than the relative definition of deviant behavior. Early labeling scholars themselves recognized that their approach was not stated in the traditional positivistic manner characteristic of the mainstream way of studying delinquency and crime (Becker, 1967; Schur, 1971). Some have suggested that the failure to state the theory in this way may have contributed to the imprecise way that labeling has been researched and the ambiguous results that have been found for some of the "propositions" derived from the perspective (Lemert, 1981;

Paternoster and Iovanni, 1989; Schur, 1971). Undoubtedly, the failure to provide a clear statement of what the perspective says and does not say has given rise to setting up of "straw men" in the form of overstatements of what the perspective predicts (Lemert, 1976). Indeed, in the absence of a clear statement, Lemert (1976, p. 244) suggested that "labeling theory seems to be largely an invention of its critics". As we will note below, more recent examinations of some of the implications of the labeling approach do provide more firm statements of the hypotheses that can be empirically examined.

It is fair to say that the labeling perspective probably would not have been declared dead or in decay (Gove, 1970; Manning, 1973) had the research regarding the two main concerns of the approach been more supportive. The labeling approach is concerned with how and why the label is attached to someone, focusing especially on the extra-legal attributes of those who are labeled, and how the experience of being labeled affects both the individual's self-concepts, other aspects of their lives (e.g., interpersonal interactions, life chances), and, of course, subsequent delinquent or criminal behavior. In the next section, we review selected prior research on these issues.

Applying the Label: The Label as the Dependent Variable

Based on the premise that the definition of deviance is, at least in part, a function of the interpretive reaction of the observer, labeling asks the question of what factors, other than the actual behavior, influence the identification of someone as a deviant or delinquent. From a labeling perspective, the expectation is that characteristics of the actor and victim will play some role in determining who gets labeled a delinquent. More specifically, the research exploring this expectation typically examines the influence of certain characteristics, such as race and social status of both the offender and victim, on decisions made within the juvenile justice system.

An early example of such research that illustrates the approach well is a study by Piliavin and Briar (1964) in which they examined what happened when police encountered juveniles on the street. They indicated that when the encounter involved a serious offense, the juvenile was almost always taken into custody. However, serious offenses only constituted about 10% of police–juvenile encounters. In cases involving more minor offenses, the decision to take into custody was importantly influenced by what Piliavin and Briar labeled "demeanor". Demeanor not only included behaviors that reflected hostile ("unco-operative") attitudes toward the police (resulting in increased likelihood of arrest), but also what the offender looked like in terms of both dress and race. Accordingly, the study found that youth who matched policemen's delinquent stereotype (i.e., those juveniles "who 'look tough' (…wear[ing] chinos, leather jackets, boots, etc.)") as well as those identified as "Negroes" were more likely to be arrested (Piliavin & Briar, 1964, p. 212). Piliavin and Briar also observed that the police reacted to certain styles of dress and the race of the offender partly because such characteristics cued the police to the type of individuals who, in the past, had given them problems.

There have been numerous subsequent studies of the impact of extra-legal characteristics on juvenile justice decision-making. Several summaries of the research literature on the effect of status characteristics point to the inconsistency of the results (Hagan, 1973; Hirschi, 1980; Paternoster & Iovanni, 1989; Petrosino, Turpin-Petrosino, & Guckenburg, 2013; Pratt, 1998; Tittle & Curran, 1988). It may be that the effect of status characteristics on decision-making depends on factors such as the geographical location of the study, the stage in the juvenile justice process (e.g., police intervention, courts), or other factors that differentiate these studies.

Liska and Tausig (1979) suggested that the labeling effect should be examined in terms of the cumulative effects across the stages in the juvenile justice system. That is, at any one stage in the process (e.g., the decision to arrest), there may only be a slight and statistically insignificant impact of status characteristics on the decision. In addition, at the next stage (e.g., the decision to prosecute), there may also be a slight but insignificant effect of status characteristics. Importantly, if one cumulates these effects across the different decision points in the process, the end result would be that status characteristics do make a difference. Walker *et al.* (2011) have argued that there is "contextual discrimination" in the sense that race-based decisions may occur in different geographical areas and at different stages of the criminal justice system.

Another avenue that the labeling approach has taken in regard to decision-making in the juvenile justice system is to examine the status characteristics of both the victim and the offender. Paternoster and Iovanni (1989) noted that it may not be the offender's race that matters, but rather the victim's race or the "racial disparity" between the victim and offender. There appears to be evidence of this in the adult court. For example, the death penalty is most likely to be implemented when there is a black offender and white victim (Paternoster, Braeme, Bacon, & Bright, 2008; Spohn, 1994). There is little research that examines the impact of victim–offender racial disparity in the juvenile justice system.

More recently, there has been discussion of racial profiling: the practice of police taking some action, not necessarily arrest, based on an individual's racial characteristics rather than a difference in the behaviors they exhibit. For example, there is evidence that black people are more likely to be stopped for traffic offenses, and when stopped, are likely to be given citations for a variety of violations. To some extent, the work of Piliavin and Briar (1964) anticipated the effect of racial profiling on attitudes towards the police exhibited by black juveniles. They suggested that the problematic demeanor of juveniles toward the police was the result of police deployment practices. Police patrolled areas disproportionally populated by black people, resulting in a perception among juveniles that they were being "hassled" by the police. This resulted in black juveniles expressing hostility toward the police, increasing the likelihood that the police would arrest them because of their demeanor.

The evidence in support of the hypothesis derived from labeling theory that extra-legal factors will play a role in decisions made by juvenile justice officials is equivocal; while some studies have found support for the hypothesis, others have not. At best, it appears that the support for the hypothesis is quite nuanced and may be contingent on a number of other factors, including the race of the victim.

Label as an Independent Variable

The hypothesis derived from labeling theory that has received the most attention is the prediction that societal reaction will have a deviance-enhancing – as opposed to a deviance-reducing – effect on the actor's subsequent behavior. Research exploring this hypothesis has examined two main pathways by which the predicted outcome could result. First, being labeled delinquent or deviant, particularly if it is a traumatic and public event ("dramatization of evil"), may result in the actors internalizing the appraisals others have of them, affecting a change in how they perceive themselves. Edwin Schur (1971) used the term "role engulfment" to describe the process by which labeled individuals get caught up in the delinquent role, thereby organizing their identities to conform to the label. Second, another pathway that may result in the exacerbation of delinquent behavior unfolds through opportunities that become limited once an individual is identified as deviant. Such limitations may include educational and employment opportunities, and the exclusion from conforming social networks.

Self-concept

The early literature on the impact of official intervention on the self-concept or identity of individuals has been unreliable and generally not particularly supportive of the hypothesized effect. In part, the inconsistency of the results may actually be compatible with the overarching premise of symbolic interactionism. Symbolic interactionism recognizes the individual's active participation in interpreting and responding to others. Thus, it is likely that some people may internalize the label, while others may interpret the situation differently and the label will not have an impact on their self-concept. Some early work on labeling found differences in the impact of official intervention on both self-concept and subsequent behavior by race (Ageton & Elliott, 1974; Harris, 1976). The impact may vary by the degree to which certain groups are inured to police intervening in their lives and the lives of their friends, families, and neighbors (Harris, 1976).

Drawing on labeling theory's tenets and other theoretical propositions, Matsueda (1992) has conceived an integrated framework that suggests that any impact of official intervention is a consequence of the reflected appraisals of others on the actor. Thus, he suggests it is important to take into consideration how friends, parents, and teachers view the actor in light of the application of a label. Using data from the National Youth Survey, Matsueda found that actors' reflected appraisals of themselves were determined by parental appraisals, and that subsequent delinquency was predicted by those reflected appraisals. Adams, Robertson, Gray-Ray, and Ray

(2003) also took into account how others perceived the actor as a result of the official intervention, and their results supported the main premise of the labeling approach.

It is also important to consider how the actor views those who are appraising him or her. Hirschfield (2008) found that, in neighborhoods where arrests have become common, arrests carry little stigma among 18–20 year old minority youths. He suggests that in those contexts the official labelers and the labels themselves have less legitimacy and, therefore, do not have an impact on reflected appraisals as they may have in other contexts where arrests are less common.

Life chances

The inconsistency in results when examining both the impact of extra-legal characteristics on the imposition of the label, and the impact of the label on some measure of self-concept, and subsequent delinquent behavior resulted in the labeling approach falling out of favor. As a result, some of the most acerbic critics suggested that the perspective was "dead" (Gove, 1980), while others declared it little more than the "sociology of the interesting" (Hagan, 1973). Paternoster and Iovanni (1989), in responding to a number of criticisms directed at labeling, emphasized the need to examine a number of possible mediating mechanisms between the imposition of the label and delinquent behavior, in addition to self-concept. They identified the work of Bruce Link (1982, 1987) in the field of mental health as an example of the type of theorizing and research that needed to be done in regard to delinquency and crime.

Link (1982) suggested that the focus of the impact of being identified as different or deviant should be on tangible and readily observable consequences of the label, such as educational and work-related outcomes. If being identified as suffering from some form of mental illness made it more difficult for one to obtain an education and acquire a job, Link hypothesized that stress would be increased, access to social supports decreased, and a process of self-devaluation would begin. The spiraling effect of the label could then lead, indirectly, to continuing, and perhaps increasing, mental distress.

Link has examined his theoretical model in a series of research articles. He has established that having been a mental patient is positively related to having a disadvantaged work status and is inversely related to income (Link, 1982). In a subsequent, modified statement of his theory, Link, Cullen, Struening, Shrout, and Dohrenwend (1989) included that the self-devaluation that occurs among former mental patients (Link, 1987) may then result not only in decreased educational and employment opportunities, but also in withdrawal from social networks. This body of research has found that official intervention increases stigma and decreases life chances such as employment and income, but the link between those outcomes and further mental illness has not been firmly established.

The impact of official intervention on life chances has clearly been recognized in the delinquency and crime literature. As early as 1962, the now classic Schwartz and

Skolnick study on the employment possibilities of ex-inmates established that stigmatization decreased the likelihood that employers would hire individuals with a criminal record. More recently, Sampson and Laub (1993) and Laub and Sampson (2003), supplementing the data originally collected by Glueck and Glueck (1950) beginning in 1939, examined the long-term implications of juvenile and criminal justice system intervention. Building on Merton's notion of the "Matthew Effect" (1988), they suggested that official intervention creates structural disadvantages that accumulate over time. Specifically, they state (Sampson & Laub, 1997, p. 147–148):

> Cumulative disadvantage is generated most explicitly by the negative structural consequences of criminal offending and official sanctions for life chances. The theory specifically suggests a "snowball" effect that adolescent delinquency and its negative consequences (e.g., arrest, official labeling, incarceration) increasingly "mortgage" one's future, especially later life chances molded by schooling and employment. …The theoretical perspective, in turn, points to a possible indirect effect of delinquency and official sanctioning in generating future crime.

Moreover, Sampson and Laub suggested that such intervention can represent a "turning point" in the lives of these men, decreasing the chances of a successful transition into adult statuses. In spite of the findings from these studies, until recently not many researchers have examined models consistent with Link's theoretical argument.

In a series of studies using the Rochester Youth Development Study (RYDS) data (see Thornberry, Krohn, Lizotte, Smith, & Tobin, 2003, for a description of the study), researchers have explored models consistent with Link's theory. The RYDS is a longitudinal panel study of high-risk youths. The sample included 1,000 youth who were enrolled in 7th and 8th grades in the Rochester (NY) school system. The study continued to collect data on these youths until they were approximately 31 years of age. In the first of these articles, Bernburg and Krohn (2003) examined the impact of police contact and arrest in early adolescence on educational attainment and unemployment in early adulthood. They found that those youth who experienced early intervention were less likely to graduate from high school and were more likely to be unemployed in early adulthood. Moreover, those who had less education and were unemployed were more likely to continue to commit illegal behaviors at the age of about 21.

Taking full advantage of additional years of RYDS data collection, Lopes *et al.* (2012) were able to extend the analysis to encompass the key years of emerging adulthood. Recognizing that Bernburg and Krohn were able to focus on outcomes only to the age of 21, when youths would not be expected to have completed their education or establish career-oriented jobs, Lopes *et al.* (2012) asked the question of whether the problematic outcomes of police intervention would still be evident at a time when people would, indeed, be expected to have finished schooling and be well on their way to establishing financial independence. Their findings provided mixed support for the theoretical model. While police intervention in adolescence did lead to lower educational attainment, a higher probability of unemployment, and a greater likelihood of being on welfare at age 29–31, it was only related to continuing drug use through young adult arrest, and was not directly or indirectly related to criminal behavior. Moreover, the impact of life chance variables did not significantly mediate the impact of arrest on drug use or criminal behavior.

Wiley and Esbensen (2013) recently explored the impact of police intervention using data from the Gang Resistance Evaluation and Training (GREAT) program. The subjects for the study were middle-school children in seven cities located across the US. The data spanned a period of four years. The most notable feature of their research is the use of propensity score matching, which takes into account the potential effect of selection factors, so more confidence can be attributed to findings regarding the relationship between police intervention and subsequent crime. They found that being stopped or arrested by the police increases delinquent behavior as well as deviant attitudes.

Using the same data and methodological approach, Wiley, Slocum, and Esbensen (2013) examined the mechanisms through which police contact potentially enhances offending. They found that compared with those with no contact, youth who were stopped or arrested by police reported higher levels of future delinquency, and that social bonds, deviant identity formation, and delinquent peers partially mediated the relationship between police contact and later offending.

The recent research reviewed above provides evidence to suggest that even rather minor intervention by law enforcement officials into the lives of juveniles can have problematic effects in areas that are important for one's life chances. There is also evidence to suggest that such intervention is indirectly related to subsequent crime and delinquency through indicators of educational attainment and employment. The impact of official intervention on life chances holds through to the age of 30 when education and employment trajectories should be well established. However, the link between life chances and continuing crime is not evident at that age, perhaps because by that time the tendency is for most offenders to desist. In the next section, we explore the impact of official intervention on social relationships such as peers and partners.

Social relationships

The labeling perspective also suggests that the stigma of being labeled a delinquent may affect social relationships. Youth who get into trouble with the law are not the type of friends with whom parents want their children to interact. Thus, isolation from "conforming" friends may increase the probability that labeled youth will be more likely to interact with deviant peers, which in turn would increase the probability of future delinquent behavior.

In the context of a study that also examined the impact of police contact on social bonds and deviant peer identity, Wiley and Esbensen (2013) examined the role of both isolation from conforming peers and association with delinquent peers on subsequent delinquent behavior. Isolation from conforming peers was not related to either police contact or to subsequent delinquent behavior. However, the probability of associating with delinquent peers was significantly increased by having contact with the police, and it partially mediated the effect of arrest on subsequent crime.

Bernburg, Krohn, and Rivera (2006) also examined the mediating role of having a delinquent social network. They predicted that, controlling for prior delinquent behavior, early intervention by the police (ages 14–15) would increase the likelihood of joining a delinquent gang. They found support for this hypothesis and, not surprisingly, also found that gang membership predicted an increase in delinquent behavior. Unfortunately, they did not examine whether isolation from conforming peers played a role in the process.

Schmidt, Lopes, Krohn, and Lizotte (2014) explored a related issue concerning the impact of labeling on social relationships. From a perspective consistent with that of labeling theory (King & South, 2011), they posited that individuals who have been labeled would not make attractive partners, and would experience more difficulties in their home lives if they did live with a partner. They examined the impact of having police contact at any time during the teenage years on whether individuals developed a relationship with a significant other and, if so, the effects, if any, on the quality of that relationship. Additionally, they proposed that the impact of the label would be indirect through education, employment, and financial disadvantage. That is, they suggested that those variables that were hypothesized to be explained by official intervention would make potential partners less attractive, or would create tensions that would increase conflict between the partners. They found overall support for the model. For instance, they found that police intervention during adolescence is associated with increases in financial hardship during young adulthood, which in turn decreases the odds of entering into a stable marriage by early 30s, and the extent to which those who have a romantic relationship feel their partner is supportive. In their study, early police intervention is also indirectly associated with a reduction in partner satisfaction and an increase in partner violence via young adult arrest.

The revitalization of the labeling perspective, with emphasis on the role that official intervention plays in decreasing life chances and increasing the probability of future delinquent or criminal behavior, shows much promise. Research has indicated that even relatively minor intrusions in youth's lives can have a detrimental effect on educational, employment, financial and relational outcomes. Research shows that the link between those outcomes and subsequent delinquent behavior also occurs in the short run. However, to date, most studies do not demonstrate a connection between detrimental life chances and subsequent delinquent behavior.

These promising findings suggest that, on the one hand, the labeling perspective should be pursued. On the other hand, research needs to be refined in order to take into consideration a number of questions that prior research has served to raise. In the final section of this chapter, we explore some of these future directions.

Future Directions

Recent research on treating the label as both a dependent and independent variable has provided sufficient support to suggest that the perspective should continue to be a lens through which the operation and effects of the juvenile and criminal justice systems be examined. The challenge of future labeling research will be to examine the basic tenets of the perspective in ways that recognize that the impact of intervention may vary depending on the context in which it occurs and the characteristics of the people whose lives are affected.

As suggested above, studies examining the impact of race and ethnic characteristics do not demonstrate strong effects on whether minority individuals experience more severe sanctions than people of other racial or ethnic origins, when focusing on any single decision point of the juvenile or criminal justice system. And yet it is evident that black males are much more likely to be incarcerated than any other demographic group. There may be a number of reasons for this, some which may be consistent with tenets of the labeling approach and some which may not. Research has suggested that black males may commit a different (and more serious) type of crime which is more likely to lead to arrest (Elliott & Ageton, 1980; Hindelang, Hirschi, & Weis, 1979). The likelihood that formal social control will be called upon in locations where informal social control is not as effective has also been suggested as a contributing factor. But these factors do not seem capable of accounting for the wide discrepancy in arrest and incarceration rates.

Recent work on racial profiling may provide a possible explanation. If law enforcement officials are being more vigilant in overseeing the behaviors of people with certain characteristics, then they are going to be more likely to observe offenses when they occur. Crime prevention strategies like "stop and frisk" programs, while effective deterrents to crime, lend themselves to being applied in a discriminatory manner. Police deployment strategies are also likely to make the offenses of people living in certain neighborhoods more evident than of residents of other communities. Future research on the implementation of official intervention needs to take into account the instructions that law enforcement officials are receiving in their training, and the attitudes which they either bring to their position or learn on the job, in order to understand the motivations for their behavior. In addition, the context in which they work may play a role in how they differentially dispense justice, so research accounting for group-level factors, as well as individual factors, is essential in examining whether extra-legal variables play a role in the labeling process.

Refocusing the labeling approach on the impact of official intervention on aspects of one's life chances has shown much promise. Early labeling has indirect effects on later life chances through peer relationships, educational attainment, and work status. Future research should continue to explore other indirect effects of official intervention on life-course outcomes. Incorporating Link's (1982) notion of "expectation of rejection" by labeled individuals into such models may also help account for why labeling has problematic outcomes. Link suggests that part of the explanation may be in the labeled person's recognition that he or she is ineffective or incapable of acquiring the necessary education or performing the job. In essence, the person self-selects out of what might be considered a life-course opportunity. While Link and associates (Link, Cullen, Frank, & Wozniak, 1987; Link, Struening, Neese-Todd, Asmussen, & Phelan, 2001) have examined this in terms of the mental illness label, such a model has not been applied to the impact of the juvenile or criminal justice systems.

Most importantly, future research on the impact of official intervention on those who are labeled must adhere to the admonition that has been repeated over the past 45 years (Bernburg & Krohn, 2003; Lemert, 1974; Paternoster & Iovanni, 1989) to examine how differences in characteristics, backgrounds and experiences of individuals can affect the way that official intervention influences their lives. When prior research has raised this issue, it has mainly focused on the racial characteristics of those who are labeled, suggesting that within some racial or ethnic groups official intervention is more common, so the impact muted. While this is certainly a possibility that is too often not pursued, there are other factors that might moderate the impact of official intervention.

The risk and protective factor approach (Rutter, 1987) to delinquent and criminal behavior may provide a model for future research in this area. By treating official intervention as a risk factor, there are a number of potential protective factors that might moderate the potentially negative effect. For example, a supportive home environment or a high academic aptitude might serve to lessen the impact of the label on future life chances, self-perceptions, and behaviors. Examining the interactive effects of these factors and official intervention upon outcomes may go a long way in understanding the labeling process.

Notes

1   Frank Tannenbaum wrote *Crime and the Community* as well as *Report on Penal Institutions* after serving one year behind bars for labor disturbances. The latter was considered "the standard textbook in the field" by contemporaneous scholars (Breit, 1951). Ironically, Tannenbaum was "slashed and robbed" in the elevator of his residence building by a 16-year-old drop-out and a "21-year-old laborer" (*New York Times*, 1966).

2   Beset by Cold War anxieties and by the prospects of nuclear war growing stronger, fears of communist infiltration and subversive activities reached boiling point in 1950 in the US. Known as "red scare" (in reference to the color of the Soviet Union flag), this post-World War II period of heightened public concern with radicalism is commonly referred to as "McCarthyism" after its main sponsor, Senator Joseph McCarthy. During this period, numerous official actions were taken to identify and punish "the enemy within our midst" (Lemert, 1951, p. 211).

3   Lemert offers an example of the process involved in the transition between primary and secondary deviations: "For one reason or another, let us say, excessive energy, [a] schoolboy engages in a classroom prank, and he is penalized for it by the teacher. Later, due to clumsiness, he creates another disturbance and again he is reprimanded. Then, as sometimes happens, the boy is blamed for something he did not do. When the

teacher uses the tag 'bad boy' or 'mischief maker' or other invidious terms, hostility and resentment are excited in the boy, and he may feel that he is blocked in playing the role expected of him. Thereafter, there may be a strong temptation to assume his role in the class as defined by the teacher, particularly when he discovers that there may be rewards and as well as penalties deriving from such a role" (1951, p. 73).

References

Adams, M.S., Robertson, C.T., Gray-Ray, P., & Ray, M.C. (2003). Labeling and delinquency. *Adolescence, 38*, 171–186.

Ageton, S.S., & Elliott, D.S. (1974). The effects of legal processing on delinquent orientations. *Social Problems, 22* (1), 87–100.

Becker, H.S. (1963). *Outsiders: Studies in the Sociology of Deviance*. New York: Free Press.

Becker, H.S. (1967). Whose side are we on? *Social Problems, 14*(3), 239–247.

Bernburg, J.G., & Krohn, M.D. (2003). Labeling, life chances, and adult crime: The direct and indirect effects of official intervention in adolescence on crime in early adulthood. *Criminology, 41*, 1287–1317.

Bernburg, J.G., Krohn, M.D., & Rivera, C.J. (2006). Official labeling, criminal embeddedness, and subsequent delinquency: A longitudinal test of labeling theory. *Journal of Research in Crime and Delinquency, 43*(1), 67–88.

Blumer, H. (1937/1969). Social psychology. In E.P. Schmidt (Ed.), *Man and Society: A Substantive Introduction to the Social Sciences* (pp. 144–198). New York: Prentice-Hall.

Breit, H. (1951). Talk with Frank Tannenbaum. New York Times, March 11. New York.

Cooley, C.H. (1902). *Human Nature and the Social Order*. Charles Scribner's Sons.

Elliott, D.S., & Ageton, S.S. (1980). Reconciling race and class differences in self-reported and official estimates of delinquency. *American Sociological Review, 45*, 95–110.

Gibbs, J.P. (1966). Conceptions of deviant behavior: The old and the new. *Pacific Sociological Review, 9*(1), 9–14.

Glueck, S., & Glueck, E. (1950). *Unraveling Juvenile Delinquency*. Cambridge, MA: Harvard University Press.

Goode, E. (1975). On behalf of labeling theory. *Social Problems, 22*(5), 570–583.

Gove, W.R. (1970). Societal reaction as an explanation of mental illness: An evaluation. *American Sociological Review, 35*(5), 873–884.

Gove, W. (1980). *The Labelling of Deviance*. Beverly Hills, CA: Sage.

Hagan, J. (1973). Labelling and deviance: A case study in the "Sociology of the Interesting." *Social Problems, 20*(4), 447–458.

Harris, A.R. (1976). Race, commitment to deviance, and spoiled identity. *American Sociological Review, 41*, 432–442.

Hindelang, M.J., Hirschi, T., & Weis, J.G. (1979). Correlates of delinquency: The illusion of discrepancy between self-report and official measures. *American Sociological Review, 44*, 995–1014.

Hirschfield, P.J. (2008). The declining significance of delinquent labels in disadvantaged urban communities. *Sociological Forum, 23*(3), 575–601.

Hirschi, T. (1980). Labelling theory and juvenile delinquency: An assessment of the evidence. In W. Gove (Ed.), *The Labelling of Deviance: Evaluating a Perspective*, 2nd ed. New York: John Wiley & Sons, Ltd.

Johnson, L.B. (1968). Remarks Upon Signing the Juvenile Delinquency Prevention and Control Act of 1968. Retrieved from http://www.presidency.ucsb.edu/ws/?pid=29054

Kent v. United States. (1966). 383 U.S. 541.

King, R.D., & South, S.J. (2011). Crime, race, and the transition to marriage. *Journal of Family Issues, 32*(1), 99–126.

Laub, J.H., & Sampson, R.J. (2003). *Shared Beginnings, Divergent Lives: Delinquent Boys to Age 70.* Cambridge, MA: Harvard University Press.

Lemert, E.M. (1951). *Social Pathology: A Systematic Approach to the Theory of Sociopathic Behavior.* New York: McGraw-Hill.

Lemert, E.M. (1967). *Human Deviance, Social Problems, and Social Control.* Englewoods Cliffs, NJ: Prentice-Hall.

Lemert, E.M. (1974). Beyond Mead: The societal reaction to deviance. *Social Problems, 21*(4), 457–468.

Lemert, E.M. (1976). Response to critics, feedback and choice. In L. Coser, & O. Larsen (Eds.), *The Uses of Controversy Sociology* (pp. 244–249). New York: MacMillan.

Lemert, E.M. (1981). Diversion in juvenile justice: what hath been wrought. *Journal of Research in Crime and Delinquency, 18*, 35–46.

Link, B.G. (1982). Mental patient status, work, and income: An examination of the effects of a psychiatric label. *American Sociological Review, 47*(2), 202–215.

Link, B.G. (1987). Understanding labeling effects in the area of mental disorders: An assessment of the effects of expectations of rejection. *American Sociological Review, 52*(1), 96–112.

Link, B.G., Cullen, F.T., Frank, J., & Wozniak, J.F. (1987). The social rejection of former mental patients: Understanding why labels matter. *American Journal of Sociology, 92*(6), 1461–1500.

Link, B.G., Cullen, F.T., Struening, E., Shrout, P.E., & Dohrenwend, B.P. (1989). A modified labeling theory approach to mental disorders: an empirical assessment. *American Sociological Review, 54*(3), 400–423.

Link, B.G., Struening, E.L., Neese-Todd, S., Asmussen, S., & Phelan, J.C. (2001). Stigma as a barrier to recovery: The consequences of stigma for the self-esteem of people with mental illnesses. *Psychiatric Services, 52*(12), 1621–1626.

Liska, A.E., & Tausig, M. (1979). Theoretical interpretations of social class and racial differentials in legal decision-making for juveniles. *Sociological Quarterly, 20*(2), 197–207.

Lopes, G., Krohn, M.D., Lizotte, A.J., Schmidt, N.M., Vásquez, B.E., & Bernburg, J.G. (2012). Labeling and cumulative disadvantage: The impact of formal police intervention on life chances and crime during emerging adulthood. *Crime & Delinquency, 58*(3), 456–488.

Manning, P.K. (1973). Labeling deviant behavior. *Contemporary Sociology, 2*(2), 123–128.

Matsueda, R.L. (1992). Reflected appraisal, parental labeling, and delinquency: Specifying a symbolic interactionist theory. *American Journal of Sociology, 97*, 1577–1611.

Mead, G.H. (1934). *Mind, Self, and Society from the Perspective of a Social Behaviorist* (edited by C.W. Morris). Chicago, IL: University of Chicago Press.

Merton, R.K. (1948). The self-fulfilling prophecy. *The Antioch Review, 8*(2), 193.

Merton, R.K. (1988). The Matthew effect in science, II. *ISIS, 79*, 606–623.

New York Times. (1966). *Slashed professor identifies suspects. New York Times*, June 29. New York.

Paternoster, R., & Iovanni, L. (1989). The labeling perspective and delinquency: An elaboration of the theory and assessment of the evidence. *Justice Quarterly, 6*, 359–394.

Paternoster, R., Braeme, R., Bacon, S., & Bright, S.B. (2008). *The Death Penalty: America's Experience with Capital Punishment*. New York: Oxford University Press.

Petrosino, A., Turpin-Petrosino, C., & Guckenburg, S. (2013). *Formal System Processing of Juveniles: Effects on Delinquency*. No. 9 of Crime Prevention Research Review. Washington, DC: US Department of Justice, Office of Community Oriented Policing Services.

Piliavin, I., & Briar, S. (1964). Police encounters with juveniles. *American Journal of Sociology, 70*(2), 206–214.

Pratt, T.C. (1998). Race and sentencing: A meta-analysis of conflicting empirical research results. *Journal of Criminal Justice, 26* (6), 513–523.

President's Commission on Law Enforcement and Administration of Justice (1967). *Task Force Report: Juvenile Delinquency and Youth Crime: Report on Juvenile Justice, and Consultants' Papers* (1st ed.). Washington, DC: US Government Printing Office.

Rutter, M. (1987). Psychosocial resilience and protective mechanisms. *American Journal of Orthopsychiatry, 57* (3), 316–331.

Sampson, R.J., & Laub, J.H. (1993). *Crime in the Making: Pathways and Turning Points Through Life*. Cambridge, MA: Harvard University Press.

Sampson, R.J., & Laub, J.H. (1997). A life-course theory of cumulative disadvantage and the stability of delinquency. In T.P. Thornberry (Ed.), *Developmental Theories of Crime and Delinquency* (pp. 133–162). New Brunswick, NJ: Transaction.

Schmidt, N.M., Lopes, G., Krohn, M.D., & Lizotte, A.J. (2014). Getting caught and getting hitched: An assessment of the relationship between police intervention, life chances, and romantic unions. *Justice Quarterly*. doi:10.1080/07418825.2013.865777

Schur, E.M. (1971). *Labeling Deviant Behavior; Its Sociological Implications*. New York: Harper & Row.

Schwartz, R.D., & Skolnick, J.H. (1962). Two studies of legal stigma. *Social Problems, 10*, 133–138.

Spohn, C. (1994). Crime and the social control of blacks: Offender/victim race and the sentencing of violent offenders. In G. Bridges, & M. Myers (Eds.), *Inequality, Crime, and Social Control* (pp. 249–268). Boulder, CO: Westview Press Inc.

Tannenbaum, F. (1922). *Wall Shadows: A Study in American Prisons*. New York: Knickerbocker Press.

Tannenbaum, F. (1938). *Crime and the Community*. New York: Columbia University Press.

Thomas, W.I. (1923). The unadjusted girl: With cases and standpoint for behavior analysis. *Criminal Sciences Monographs, 4*, 1–257.

Thornberry, T.P., Krohn, M.D., Lizotte, A.J., Smith, C.A., & Tobin, K. (2003). *Gangs and Delinquency in Developmental Perspective*. Cambridge: Cambridge University Press.

Thrasher, F.M. (1927). *The Gang: A Study of 1,313 Gangs in Chicago*. Chicago: University of Chicago Press.

Tittle, C.R., & Curran, D.A. (1988). Contingencies for dispositional disparities in juvenile justice. *Social Forces, 67*(1), 23–58.

Walker, S., Spohn, C., & DeLone, M. (2011). *The Color of Justice: Race, Ethnicity, and Crime in America*. Cengage Learning.

Wheeler, S., Cottrell, L.S. Jr., & Romasco, A. (1967). Prevention and control. In President's Commission on Law Enforcement and Administration of Justice, *Task Force Report: Juvenile Delinquency and Youth Crime: Report on Juvenile Justice, and Consultants' Papers*, 1st ed. (pp. 409–428). Washington, DC: US Government Printing Office.

Wiley, S.A., & Esbensen, F.-A. (2013). The effect of police contact: Does official intervention result in deviance amplification? *Crime & Delinquency*. doi:10.1177/0011128713492496

Wiley, S.A., Slocum, L.A., & Esbensen, F.-A. (2013). The unintended consequences of being stopped or arrested: An exploration of the labeling mechanisms through which police contact leads to subsequent delinquency. *Criminology, 51*(4), 927–966.

21

Routine Activities and Opportunity Theory

Nick Tilley and Aiden Sidebottom

According to www.quotegarden.com, there isn't much that opportunity doesn't do. Opportunity knocks, it flies by while we sit regretting the chances we lost and, most abstractly, opportunity is a bird that never perches. In this chapter we discuss an additional function of opportunity. Our aim is to demonstrate that opportunities cause crime; that this applies to juvenile crime; and to show what the implications of this are for crime prevention. This approach is not conventional criminology. Some advocates of opportunity theory consider its approach to be so different from that of the remainder of criminology that it no longer makes sense for it to be part of criminology at all. "Crime science" has been proposed as an alternative umbrella term to describe the work undertaken. It is clear that there is a family of closely related opportunity theories, which ask a distinctive set of questions (about crime events), tend to use a distinctive set of methods (emphasizing action research), look to different disciplines for their inspiration (notably engineering and the physical sciences), and use rather different criteria to distinguish better from worse work (prioritizing practical utility in reducing crime harms) compared with those of more traditional criminology. Whether this adds up to a new discipline or a new paradigm within criminology is rather moot. In practice, most scholars undertaking work within the opportunity framework publish their work in conventional criminology journals. Moreover, Frank Cullen's Sutherland address of the American Society of Criminology argues that opportunity theories are progressively coming into the mainstream of contemporary criminology (Cullen, 2011). It remains to be seen whether there is a rapprochement between traditional criminology and opportunity theories, or whether they go separate ways.

The Handbook of Juvenile Delinquency and Juvenile Justice, First Edition. Edited by Marvin D. Krohn and Jodi Lane.
© 2015 John Wiley & Sons, Inc. Published 2015 by John Wiley & Sons, Inc.

This chapter looks at the interface between opportunity approaches to crime and the more traditional perspectives that focus on what produces offenders. We begin with the proposition that opportunities cause crime. We then describe one of the most influential crime opportunity theories, namely the routine activities approach, as well as several allied theories of the same orientation. Next we turn to juvenile crime, which is the focus of this handbook, and explore how opportunity approaches make sense of juvenile involvement both in "terrestrial" and "virtual" crimes. We finish with ideas for future research.

On the Causal Role of Opportunities

Criminology has traditionally focused on why people become criminal. Why are certain individuals or groups disposed to become involved in crime whilst others are not so disposed? What underlying psychological, biological or social factors are at work, and in what combination? In contrast, this chapter focuses on criminological approaches that have flourished only since the mid-1970s. These largely take dispositions to commit crime for granted. They are concerned instead with the immediate situations in which criminal dispositions, from wherever they may derive, translate into criminal actions: what social and environmental conditions are conducive to the commission of crime and what makes people liable to commit crime in those conditions? The omnibus term used here to encompass this form of criminology is "situational", to emphasize those theories that use crime events as the unit of analysis, and which pay greater attention to the immediate situation in provoking or enabling the commission of specific crimes.[1]

That a situational perspective on crime causation did not surface until the 1970s should perhaps come as little surprise – it is not how we typically think of behavior. For some 50 years psychologists have known of the common tendency to attribute the behavior of others to dispositional factors and underplay the importance of situational causes. The so-called Fundamental Attribution Error (Ross & Nisbett, 1991) is a powerful and prevalent cognitive bias, and one that is frequently observed in lay and scholarly theories of crime causation. The term error should not be interpreted as meaning incorrect. In a criminological context, offender disposition and the factors underlying it undoubtedly *do* contribute to a fuller understanding of criminal behaviour. What the Fundamental Attribution Error emphasizes is the natural, everyday facility we have for coming up with dispositional explanations of criminal behaviour as against explanations that focus on situational determinants, a pattern that characterizes a large proportion of criminological theories.

A focus on the situational causes of behavior holds important implications for reducing undesirable behavior. The applied focus of traditional criminology lies in reducing criminal disposition. This is either in advance of criminal conduct, by identifying those liable to commit crime and intervening in ways that lessen their criminality, or after the event in the form of rehabilitation programs designed to alter offender motivations. The applied focus of situational criminology lies in identifying situations where crimes are commonplace and figuring out ways to change them so that crime is reduced.

Offenses need offenders, of course! And proponents of situational criminology deal with them and their dispositions to offend in varying ways. One is to take the position that offender disposition is simply a different topic for others to investigate. This was particularly prominent among the first wave of opportunity theories as they attempted to distinguish themselves from prevailing theories, and in doing so get a foothold in theoretical criminology. Another way is simply to note that dispositions vary and to recognize that this will affect openness to temptation or provocation on the one hand, and deterrence or dissuasion on the other. A third is to treat disposition as a consequence of the immediate situation, through feedback mechanisms in which those drawn into crime by the immediate situation have their dispositions reinforced when they are rewarded by their criminal acts. As the title of one paper advancing this line put it, "Opportunity makes the thief" (Felson & Clarke, 1998). This reflects broadly behaviorist thinking, where the consequences of past behavior shape future behavior. A fourth position is that crime is perfectly normal (much of what counts as predatory crime in human society is rife in nature), so a better question than "What makes people criminals?" is, "What prevents crimes from being committed?", and the answer to this question falls within the remit of situational criminology. A fifth is to try to understand in some detail the socio-psychological ways in which individuals interact with situations, generating patterns of crimes and patterns of criminal involvement. A sixth is to take some simplified model of the human being (normally a more or less rational, utility-maximizing decision-maker), and to work through the way situational contingencies will inform the choices made about crime commission.

Debate ensues as to the appropriate model of the offender in situational criminology (see Ekblom, 2007). Suffice to say that the above ways of construing the offender are not necessarily inconsistent with one another, and the same situational criminologist may switch from one to the other depending on the issue being discussed. In this chapter, we are satisfied to note the diverse ways in which the offender has been conceived, and to pitch our discussion at a level where the offender is treated simply as someone who may commit crime and whose criminality is strongly affected by the situations they encounter.

Given the focus on crime events rather than offender disposition, what can opportunity theories tell us specifically about subgroups that are especially prone to involvement in crime or vulnerability to victimization? Most particularly, given this volume's focus, how can opportunity theories help explain juvenile delinquency? We begin by outlining the main opportunity theories of crime before moving on to their application specifically to juvenile delinquency.

Routine activities

In a classic paper in 1979, Cohen and Felson devised *routine activities theory* to help explain the rise in crime rates in the US after the Second World War, notwithstanding improving social conditions, which most sociological theories at the time expected to result in reductions in crime. Their starting point is deceptively simple. They ask what is crucial for a direct contact predatory crime to occur. Their answer is that a "likely offender" must encounter a "suitable target" in the absence of a "capable guardian". In the absence of any one of these conditions – likely offender, suitable target, or capable guardian – a crime will not occur. This looks like a tautology: crime is by definition an event when likely offenders meet suitable targets and there is no one to intervene. As a tautology, on its own it would add nothing. However, looked at dynamically, changes in the supply, distribution, and movement of these three essential ingredients can help explain changes in both the rates and patterns of predatory crime. The substantive contribution of routine activities lies in accounts of the sources of supply, distribution, and movement of these ingredients and of changes in them over time.

The term "routine activities" refers to the rather prosaic features of everyday life that are emphasized as key influences on crime patterns. For example, post-war increases in participation in the paid labour market for working age women meant that more homes were left "unguarded" during the day, comprising an increased supply of burglary targets. Increasing affluence, improved transport (including cars and motorcycles), and reduced involvement in domestic chores meant that more young men went further afield as likely offenders. The proliferation of portable, small, anonymous, and high-value goods, such as handheld cameras, transistor radios, mobile phones, and laptop computers increased the supply of suitable targets for theft. Developments that are otherwise welcome can, thus, bring an unintended crime harvest by fostering increases in the supply of suitable targets, and/or decreases in the supply of capable guardians, and/or growth in the availability and mobility of likely offenders. What is novel about the routine activity approach is that it explains crime patterns and changes in them without recourse to factors affecting levels of disposition to commit crime, a focus which is the stock in trade of traditional criminology.

There have been developments in routine activities since 1979, both theoretically and when applied in the service of crime prevention. In terms of routine activity theory, for example, absence of "intimate handlers" has been added to the conditions needed for crime to occur (Felson, 1986). Whilst the capable guardian serves as an intermediary protecting the potential target, the intimate handler serves as an intermediary holding back the likely offender. To take a homely example, where predation may be at issue, a parent may act as an intimate handler, holding back an aggressive child who might be disposed to hit his sibling, while simultaneously acting as a capable guardian protecting the child who might be hit by his brother. Here, the same person plays both the intimate handler and capable guardian roles. This is not always the case. Teachers, parents and girl/boyfriends are archetypal intimate handlers. Police officers, park wardens and security staff are archetypal guardians, although citizens can also provide guardianship for one another.

The routine activities approach is also commonly used to better understand and respond to specific crime problems. This is often achieved through the use of John Eck's (2003) crime triangle, which usefully organizes the elements of routine activity theory to draw attention to those components of a presenting problem that warrant attention and might be modified so as to reduce the probability of crime occurring. It comprises two triangles, one inside the other. Each triangle has a different meaning. The inner triangle is a direct translation of the routine activity approach and signals what needs to co-occur for a crime to happen: one side indicates that a likely offender must be present with no-one there to control him or her, another that there must be a suitable victim or target with no-one to protect them, and the third that the place must be bereft of anyone with the responsibility and capacity to provide for the safety of those who are there. The outer triangle refers to those whose addition to the situation would reduce the likelihood that an offense will take place: either a handler to hold back the likely offender, or a guardian to protect the victim, or a place manager to provide security to those in an otherwise risky location (Tillyer & Eck, 2011).

Testing routine activity theory empirically poses some problems. The starting point appears almost vacuous, albeit that prior to Cohen and Felson no-one had stated what subsequently seems self-evident. There are also several ways in which concepts such as guardianship and exposure to likely offenders can be construed and measured. Focusing on the former, Reynald (2009) described how many standard measures of guardianship, such as the proportion of owner-occupied households in a given area, are imprecise and fail to determine whether home-owners are, say, *available* and *empowered* to act as guardians. Miethe and Meier (1994) similarly pointed out that guardianship can refer both to physical guard-ianship (such as household locks and bolts) and social guardianship (such as the togetherness of a community). Lemieux and Felson (2012) provided a related discussion on the challenges associated with accurately measuring exposure to crime risks. Notwithstanding issues of measurement and operationalization, the routine activity approach has furnished the basis for a fruitful research program where specific changes in the supply, distribution and movement of likely offenders, suitable targets, capable guardians and intimate handlers have been proposed as explanations for changes in particular crime patterns, which are open to empirical test. For example, reducing the suitability of cars as targets for crime by making them more difficult to steal has been found to produce substantial reductions in car theft (Farrell, Tseloni, & Tilley 2011). More recently, empirical assessments of the routine activities approach have been extended to the use of agent-based computer simulations to determine how crime patterns vary according to manipulation of offenders, targets and guardians (Birks, Townsley, & Stewart, 2012).

Crime pattern theory

Crime pattern theory has much in common with routine activities theory. It too emphasizes the importance of everyday life in shaping crime patterns, in particular spatial ones. It provides an explanation for how Cohen and Felson's requisite

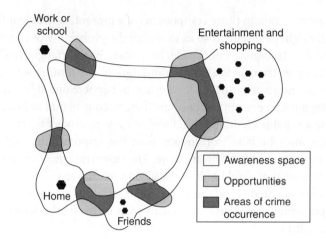

Figure 21.1   Crime pattern theory

elements of crime – offenders, targets and guardians – converge in time and space. According to crime pattern theory, crimes occur where there are opportunities within the offender's "awareness space" (Brantingham & Brantingham, 1981, 1984, 2008), and the offender's awareness space is a function of their routine activities. Offenders' routine activities are shaped in the same way as those of non-offenders: by the places they habitually visit and the routes between them, as illustrated in Figure 21.1. Our home, place(s) of work (or education) and where we spend our leisure time comprise the "nodes" between which we travel on a regular basis. We become familiar with the areas surrounding these nodes and the corridors between them. These corridors and the areas that border them comprise our awareness spaces. Within them potential offenders will know of available crime opportunities and be more comfortable with the known risks they face from committing crimes there. Geographical crime concentrations are therefore found in target-rich locations that are familiar to prospective offender populations, but where they expect the risks to themselves to be relatively low. These areas often comprise "edges" between well-protected areas where targets can be expected, but where the perceived chances of recognition and the detection of criminal activity are low.

Lifestyle theory

Lifestyle theory was proposed around the same time as the routine activity approach (Hindelang, Gottfredson, & Garofolo, 1978). It bears some resemblance to routine activity theory in that it emphasizes the association between vulnerability to victimization and patterns of everyday life (lifestyles that put some at high risk of encountering offenders). Many studies treat these approaches as one and the same, adopting what is commonly referred to as the lifestyle/routine activities perspective. Though widely practiced, the two approaches are subtly different. The difference lies in their emphasis. As Allen and Felson (2014) put it:

> [R]outine activity ideas emphasize the criminogenic effects of everyday routines, such as work, school and family life. In contrast, lifestyle theory gives more attention to personal lifestyle choices in leisure life. The two theories are not however completely distinct, since the former includes lifestyles and the latter includes work.

Situational crime prevention

The above theories share a common conviction – that crime is caused by more than the presence of a criminally disposed individual: necessary conditions are required for criminal disposition to translate into crime commission. It follows that removing or reducing criminogenic conditions can reduce crime, without the need to modify deviant motivations. This is the rationale for situational crime prevention. It comprises a menu of techniques (shown in Table 21.1) to reduce crimes by focusing on the near causes that permit or stimulate them. The underlying thinking emerges from the headings used to list different techniques, which work in different ways. Three of the techniques assume some (albeit "bounded") rational choice in the sense that they conceive of offenders as situated choice makers whose decisions are affected by the balance of expected effort, risks, and rewards (Clarke, 1997; Cornish & Clarke, 1986). This means that, other things being equal, crime is expected to drop (rise) when effort or risk rise (fall) and/or when reward falls (rises). One of the techniques assumes that prospective offenders are open at the margins to reminders of moral or legal rules relevant to behaviour they might otherwise engage in, such that crime will fall (rise) as the salience of rules proscribing it are reinforced (blunted). The last of the techniques assumes that prospective offenders may be drawn into crime they would otherwise not contemplate by the exigencies of the presenting situation. Hence relevant crimes will fall (rise) as provocations stimulating it are removed from (added to) the immediate situation in which the individual acts.

Situational crime prevention takes crime-commission to be open to the effects of immediate situations rather than being caused only by a set of dispositions that drive individuals to commit crimes whatever conditions they encounter. The image of all offenders as hell-bent on offending whatever the circumstances is rejected in favor of one where almost all are responsive to the presenting risks, efforts, rewards, provocations, and apparent permissibility of crime opportunities that are encountered. The least promising circumstances for situational crime prevention are presumably those where the offender is most emotionally or ideologically committed to the acts contemplated and hence least dissuadable. Yet even here there is convincing evidence that situational contingencies are important. The classic case is suicide, which of course is not a crime in most Western countries but is an unwanted act, and presumably requires a high level of emotional commitment. Even with this, rates have been found to be highly susceptible to changes in the situations furnishing

Table 21.1 The 25 techniques of situational crime prevention

Increase the effort	Increase the risks	Reduce the rewards	Reduce provocations	Remove the excuses
1. Target harden • immobilizers in cars • anti-robbery screens	6. Extend guardianship • Routine precautions: go out in groups at night • "Cocoon" neighborhood watch	11. Conceal targets • gender-neutral phone directories • off-street parking	16. Reduce frustrations and stress • efficient queuing • soothing lighting/music	21. Set rules • rental agreements • hotel registration
2. Control access • alley-gating • entry phones	7. Assist natural surveillance • improved street lighting • support whistleblowers	12. Remove targets • removable car radios • pre-paid public phone cards	17. Avoid disputes • fixed cab fares • reduce crowding in pubs	22. Post instructions • "No parking" • "Private property"
3. Screen exits • tickets needed for exit • electronic merchandise tags	8. Reduce anonymity • taxi driver IDs • school uniforms	13. Identify property • property marking • vehicle licensing	18. Reduce emotional arousal • controls on violent porn • prohibit paedophiles working with children	23. Alert conscience • roadside speed display signs • "Shoplifting is stealing"
4. Deflect offenders • street closures • separate bathrooms for women	9. Utilize place managers • CCTV for double-decker buses • Two clerks in liquor stores	14. Disrupt markets • monitor pawn brokers • licensed street vendors	19. Neutralize peer pressure • "idiots drink and drive" • "it's OK to say NO"	24. Assist compliance • litterbins • public lavatories
5. Control tools/weapons • toughened beer glasses • disabling stolen cell phones	10. Strengthen formal surveillance • security guards • CCTV in town centres	15. Deny benefits • ink merchandise tags • graffiti cleaning	20. Discourage imitation • rapid vandalism repair • V-chips in TVs	25. Control drugs and alcohol • breathalysers in pubs • alcohol-free events

Source: Tilley, N. (2009). *Crime Prevention.* Cullompton, Devon: Willan.

opportunities. In particular, the gradual switchover from toxic coal gas to non-toxic natural gas in British households in the 1960s was accompanied by a closely matched drop in overall suicide rates and suicides involving gassing, notwithstanding the many other possible ways of taking one's own life (see Clarke & Mayhew, 1988). Displacement to other suicide methods, a common criticism of situational crime prevention, was minor, as is often observed in formal assessments of crime displacement (Guerette & Bowers, 2009). Likewise, numbers of aircraft hijackings dropped dramatically with security improvements, making it much more difficult for would-be offenders (see Wilkinson, 1986, cited in Clarke, 1997). There is now overwhelming evidence from a variety of settings and for a diverse range of crime types to support the effectiveness of situational crime prevention (see Clarke, 1997; and http://www.popcenter.org/library/scp/pdf/bibliography.pdf).

Routine Activities, Opportunity and Juvenile Crime

Because the main focus of opportunity theories has been on crime events rather than on offenders, research in this tradition has paid relatively little attention specifically to juvenile offending, save to note that juvenile males comprise a group of likely offenders whose supply, distribution, and movement are liable to shape crime event patterns. The remainder of this chapter will, however, indicate ways in which juvenile offending has been and might further be understood through opportunity theory. We focus on three areas: the age-crime curve, routine activities and patterns of criminal involvement, and routine activities and cybercrime.

The age–crime curve

The age–crime curve describes one of criminology's best-established patterns. In differing jurisdictions and at different times, the same basic trajectory is found. Prevalence of participation in crime grows rapidly from around eight years of age, peaks in the mid-teens and then falls away, initially quite rapidly and then more gradually, until almost no-one in their 60s and older commits crime. The basic shape of the curve is the same for males and females, although the adolescent peak is much lower for females. Explanations for the age–crime curve abound (see Farrington, 1986). Such is the persistence of this pattern that any decent criminological theory must pass muster with respect to the age–crime curve. What, then, if anything, can opportunity theory contribute to understanding this general pattern or to understanding detailed variations of or changes in it?

An opportunity theory interpretation of the age–crime curve would focus on evolving routine activities as males and females age, and the changes that thereby occur in patterns of target encounter in the absence of either guardians or handlers. As adolescent males grow older they spend less time at home under the influence of the typical counter-crime intimate handling provided by family members, especially mothers. Spending more time away from home, they become more likely to encounter suitable targets for crime, some of which lack capable guardians. This provides a setting for potential crimes. Whether crimes are actually committed will depend on the presence and orientation of the intimate handlers with whom they are associating. If these are pro-crime (as they are liable to be in some youth gangs), then crime becomes more likely. If they are anti-crime, then crime becomes less likely. As boys grow out of adolescence, many will form intimate bonds with significant others who then become their new (normally anti-crime) intimate handlers. They are also liable to enter paid employment and form new families, which reduces their availability to offend. Hence crime drops as those who had offended during the period in which they associated with crime-promoting handlers become less available for criminal acts and more controlled by their new families of procreation. Although this account has clear affinities with differential association and social control theories, what it may add is a greater emphasis on the changing routine behaviors of individuals as they age, which affects the level and nature of their exposure to influence, temptation and opportunity.

Routine activities and patterns of criminal involvement

There have been changes in levels of crime and in juvenile criminality, which can also be explained using opportunity theories. The post-war expansion in the supply of suitable targets for theft was matched by a post-war increase in the leisure time available for young people to spend time with one another. More time for adolescents uncontrolled by intimate handlers, combined with an increase in the supply of goods for theft, led to a sustained increase in juvenile crime. For opportunity theories there is no need to invoke some change in the social climate, increasing the disposition of young people to commit crime. Rather, the situation changed to create a growth in opportunity, which makes sense of the crime increase. At a macro-level, social (e.g., less pressure to spend time with the family and therefore more for peer-group socializing), technological (e.g., more labour-saving devices, freeing youths from the need to help so much around the home), economic (e.g., more resources for recreation) and transport (e.g., affordable motorcycles) developments combined to increase the supply of young men who are liable to offend, whilst developments in technology and manufacturing provided a growing supply of suitable targets for crime (e.g., cars, computers, cameras, cell phones). To use Cohen and Felson's terminology, this provides a rich "chemistry" for crime. What is not explained so readily is why some but not other juveniles commit crime, and why some commit many crimes whilst some commit very few. For this a different criminology may be needed, one that is interested in distinctions between offending and non-offending subgroups, between early and late desisters (and non-desisters) from crime, and between prolific and occasional offenders.

Promising approaches relating to inter-group and interpersonal differences in juvenile criminal activity that draw something from opportunity theory are those that emphasize "turning points" (e.g., Homel, 2005; Laub & Sampson, 2003). Though not always framed in terms of opportunity theory, they can be read in ways that are highly sympathetic to it. That is, where there is some fracture in the routine activities of adolescents, they may be drawn into new ones that can challenge previous criminal or non-criminal behaviours by exposing those affected to fewer or more criminal opportunities. Parental divorce or remarriage, change of school, and change of address can all alter the routine activities of potential offenders and put them in contact with new patterns of opportunity. Looked at another way, this partly explains why juvenile (and adult) recidivism rates are high when offenders are released into the community and social groups with which they are already familiar and initially offended, an emerging literature known as the ecology of recidivism (see Tompson & Chainey, 2013).

In practice, most of the work on turning points and trajectories, and most of that which has examined the everyday lives of young people to try to understand why some but not others commit crime, have looked at mechanisms influencing disposition, rather than opportunity. Laub and Sampson (2003) invoked routine activities theory and in doing so mentioned opportunity: they referred to their finding that "persistent offenders… have rather chaotic and unstructured lives across multiple dimensions (such as living arrangements, work, and family)", noting that "Routine activities for these men were loaded with opportunities for crime and extensive associations with like-minded offenders... Thus situational variation, especially in lifestyle activities, needs to be taken into account when explaining continuity and change in criminal behaviour over the life course" (Laub & Sampson, 2003, p. 39). When looking at situations, most interest in near causes has focused on disposition rather than opportunity. Laub and Sampson (2003) noted thus the ways in which, for many persistent offenders, their situations made crime "normative", an expected everyday feature of their lives.

Situational action theory (SAT), as developed by Wikström (2009), comprises a major effort explicitly to build upon routine activities theory, combining it with self-control theory drawn from Gottfredson and Hirschi (1990) to produce an integrated account of crime causation that focuses on the interactions between personal and environmental factors. As he puts it: "According to SAT, acts of crime are an outcome of a perception–choice process guided by the interaction between a person's crime propensity and his or her exposure to criminogenic settings' (Wikström, 2009, p. 254). He adds that: "Acts of crime are regarded as moral action (action guided by what is the right or wrong thing to do in a particular circumstance)." These acts may be more or less "habitual" (automated) or "deliberate" (rational) depending on "familiarity with the setting". Wikström is primarily interested in *criminal involvement* and explains this though the interaction of *criminal propensity* (a product of capacity for self-control and morality) and exposure to *criminogenic features of the environment* that are encountered in a person's routine actions, the latter comprising features of the environment that foster criminality. What makes an environment criminogenic is the moral context (what the salient rules are and their enforcement), which will affect whether opportunities, temptations, provocations or frictions are responded to through criminal acts. Hence where a person whose morals tolerate or encourage crime, and/or who has low self-control, meets a local situation where moral rules condone crime or are unenforced, he or she is liable to respond to criminal opportunities, temptations, provocations, and frictions by offending. Other things being equal, more crime will be committed where there is greater exposure to criminogenic situations. Broader social factors shape rates of exposure to criminogenic situations.

Much of Wikström's work on SAT has focused on juveniles. He has pioneered painstaking, detailed research into the everyday lives of a sample of young people in Peterborough, UK, using space–time budgets to discover where they were and with whom every hour of the day, to try to capture variations in exposure to criminogenic settings (unsupervized in the company of delinquent peers in places with low levels of collective efficacy), and to assess whether this is associated with expected variations in criminal involvement. He also measures crime propensity, as he conceptualizes it, focusing on morality and self-control. He finds broad support for both hypotheses (Wikström & Butterworth, 2006).

Wikström attaches little if any causal importance to the supply of opportunities, notwithstanding his invocation of routine activities theory, which stresses the supply of suitable targets as one of the crucial conditions for crime. Wikström's main interest lies in explaining variations in acquiescence to opportunity and the role played in this by exposure to situations encouraging acquiescence. Informal and formal social control remains important, of course, and these do relate to "intimate handling" promoting or inhibiting crime and to "capable guardianship". Wikström's work has some affinities with situational crime prevention theory, in embracing provocation and absence-of-rule reminders as conditions that encourage or permit latent criminality (propensity) to be released. However, what Wikström's account neglects (or assumes to be causally irrelevant) are the opportunities for acting on released propensities, those features of situations that speak to risk, effort, and reward. Thus, whilst the writings of those interested in opportunity theory have shown rather little interest in understanding the genesis of offender propensity and the conditions under which it might be activated to take advantage of opportunities, this has been Wikström's major focus of attention. Wikström, in turn, in his SAT, has paid rather little attention to the independent causal role of opportunity in generating crime patterns.

Other studies have examined the relationship between the variations in patterns of routine activities of young people and their involvement in criminal activities. Miller (2013), for example, controlling for other factors associated with criminality, found an association between self-reported criminal activities and routine activities amongst a sample of over 3,000 15-year-olds in Edinburgh. What was especially interesting in this study was that particular types of crime were associated with particular routine activities. So going to youth clubs and playing sport was associated with fare evasion and assaults, whilst hanging out with local friends was associated with shop theft and vandalism, and nightlife activities were associated with assault and drug abuse. Involvement in different settings seemed to facilitate involvement in different crimes. Likewise, this time using police data from 1989 to 2002 in Seattle, Weisburd, Groff, and Morris (2011) found that in any given year, 50% of juvenile crime incidents were concentrated in just 1% of hot spots (street segments), and all juvenile crime fell within 3–5% of street segments, incidents being concentrated in public places where juveniles tend to congregate, such as malls, schools, youth centers, and restaurants.

A new synthesis may focus on the interaction between situationally released disposition (Wikström's propensity*setting) and situationally provided opportunities and their sources. This would cast situations not as mere stages on which crime occurs, but as settings that may prompt disposition whereby they provoke crime propensity, rather than simply release it. Temptations comprise one form of provocation, where those with no particular propensity to commit crime are drawn into it and where feedback from the outcome of the offense may reinforce propensity. For example, a long line to wait to pay for a train fare where there are no checks on payment leads to non-payment that is then rewarded financially, leading to further fare-dodging. This relationship has been demonstrated experimentally going back as far as Hartshorne and May's classic study (1928) that showed that children could be induced into cheating by changing the situation.

Routine activities and cybercrime

We mentioned at the beginning of this chapter that the routine activity approach was developed in response to the failure of the then prevailing sociological theories to adequately explain the patterns of crime in a changing post-war America. Consideration of the shifts in the supply, distribution and movement of offenders, targets and guardians as a function of everyday movement patterns proved more satisfactory. In doing so, it highlighted that crime is intimately related to social, economic and technological changes – changes that are not classically assumed to be root causes of crime and in many cases are sought-after developments, such as increasingly portable products and greater gender parity in the workplace.

The internet is arguably the most recent significant development with implications for the routine activities of offenders, targets, and guardians. It has altered the way we live, be it through how we make and interact with friends, bank, purchase products or watch television. For many it has become an essential part of their lives. Consistent with opportunity theory, it has also had a profound impact on crime, facilitating new opportunities for "old" crimes such as fraud, theft, and pornography, as well as generating novel "computer-focused crimes" such as hacking and phishing (see Furnell, 2002; Yar, 2005). This is particularly relevant to juveniles, who often are the most voracious internet consumers, particularly in relation to social networking sites.

Several studies have explored whether patterns of cybercrime can be explained from a routine activities perspective, taken here to refer to "computer-mediated activities which are either illegal or considered illicit by certain parties and which can be conducted through global electronic networks" (Thomas & Loader, 2000, p. 3). These studies typically attempt to adapt conventional measures of the routine activity approach and determine the association with risk of online victimization. For example, using self-report survey data from a sample of 974 college students, Reyns, Henson, and Fisher (2011) demonstrate that online exposure, greater proximity to motivated offenders, decreased guardianship and elevated target attractiveness, as measured therein, were all positively associated with risk of cyberstalking, consistent with expectation. Similarly, focusing on online harassment of a sample of Kentucky school children, Bossler, Holt, and May (2012) find broad support for the routine activity approach, particularly for their measure of offender proximity. While some researchers have argued that there are sufficient incongruities between terrestrial crime and online crime to suggest that a high-fidelity transplant of the routine activity approach for cybercrimes is unwise (see Yar, 2005), where quantitative studies are available the evidence does suggest that variations in the mix of offenders, targets, and guardians influence the levels and patterns of cybercrimes.

The above studies speak to just one way through which the routine activity approach can be applied to cybercrimes, focusing mainly on offender, target and guardian-related correlates of cyber victimization. A further way concerns the effect of the internet on individuals' routine activities, and by extension the supply and distribution of offenders, targets, and guardians.[2] There is mounting evidence pointing to a gradual shift away from outdoor activities among juveniles in industrialized countries, attributed in part to increased computer usage. A study comparing the performance of 10-year-old school children in England in 1998 with those from 2008 reported significant decreases in several measures of muscular fitness (Cohen *et al.*, 2011). Trembley and colleagues (2010) reported similar findings using nationally representative samples of 6- to 19-year-olds in Canada. Both studies ascribe the observed patterns to, amongst other things, increased "sedentariness". This is clearly a public health concern, yet it also holds implications for crime: if one assumes a standard level of crime, and if computer and specifically online activities are progressively replacing outdoor activities particularly for young people, a crime opportunity perspective would expect to see an increase in the levels of online crime and reductions in terrestrial crime. This is yet to be sufficiently explored. We think it should be. If true, it also has implications for the measurement of crime. We turn now to issues of method and measurement in relation to juvenile crime, routine activities and opportunity.

Issues of method, measurement, and future research

Van Dijk (2012) notes that the launch of crime victim surveys coincided with the initial formulations of crime opportunity theories, including routine activities. He goes on to claim that this is more than mere coincidence: the information obtained through victimization surveys affords a broader look at crime's causes beyond focusing solely on the offender. Detailed questions are asked about crimes experienced by victims and about the precautions taken to try to reduce risk. The crimes asked about relate to those to which respondents may be vulnerable. Patterns of everyday life affect the types of crimes that may be committed or suffered, and victimization surveys need to be sensitive to variations in vulnerability by place and time to understand variations in opportunity structure.

In relatively undeveloped rural Malawi, for example, theft of livestock is a significant issue that is not relevant in the same way to denizens of Manhattan! Patterns of everyday life are different in Malawi compared with New York. These lead to different likely offender distributions and movements, awareness spaces, and guardianship and intimate handler availability, producing distinct youth and other crime patterns (see Sidebottom, 2013). Likewise, the emergence of the internet has led to cyberspace as a novel location for crime, with novel crime opportunities through new types of risky space, new types of awareness space, new forms of crime, and new challenges for guardianship and handling. Whilst there is growing evidence that fears of displacement from situational crime prevention are largely misplaced (Guerette & Bowers, 2009), the new forms of everyday life create changed conditions that opportunity theory predicts will alter crime event patterns. The changed conditions may lead, as indicated earlier, to reduced opportunities for some forms of crimes by some people against some victims, whilst increasing opportunities for other crimes by other people against other victims. There is a rich agenda for future research here, adapting victimization surveys to reflect changing and varying conditions, the better to grasp what patterns of crime are changing and how these are facilitated by changed opportunity structures reflecting alterations in routine activities.

With regard specifically to youth and crime, Wikström's use of space–time budgets comprises an important innovation to better capture systematic and quantitative details of the everyday activities of young people, to determine who they are with, where they are, and at what times through the day and week (Wikström & Butterworth, 2006). This promises much more precise estimates of juvenile exposure to criminogenic settings. Alongside background data on the young people and data on their criminal activities, this offers an exciting area of future research to test and refine opportunity theories and to better understand interactions between opportunity and individual attributes. Other data sources may also be used more accurately to estimate movement patterns, such as anonymous cell phone data (see Song, Qu, Blumm, & Barabási, 2010).

Conclusions

"What causes crime" is arguably the most fundamental question in criminology. Different theories look to different sources of causation. Most are concerned with *criminality* and the presumed biological, social, and psychological factors that underpin it. In this chapter we presented a contrasting perspective, which uses *crime events* as the unit of analysis and which emphasizes the causal role of opportunities.

The routine activities approach is one of the most influential crime opportunity theories. It is fiendishly simple in reducing crime to three essential ingredients – offenders, targets, and guardians – but its apparent simplicity belies its impressive explanatory power, providing reliable explanations for macro-level changes in crime over time and micro-level variations in risk of victimization.

In focusing on crime events, researchers in the crime opportunity tradition tend to steer away from analyzing the offending patterns of particular population subgroups, such as juveniles. Yet as we have attempted to show in this chapter, many common youth offending patterns can be recast using an opportunity framework. We hope that in doing so, others will take up where we have left off to produce more fully worked up examples applying opportunity theory in the context of juvenile crime. We also see benefit in research that explores the interactions between opportunity and the individual, crossing the divide between the concerns of traditional criminology with the offender and those with crime event patterns focused on by the opportunity theories discussed in this chapter.

Notes

1   "Environmental" is also a commonly used term.
2   We thank Noemie Bouhana for making this point.

References

Allen, J., & Felson, M. (2014). Routine activity approach. In G. Bruinsma, & D. Weisburd (Eds.), *Encyclopaedia of Criminology and Criminal Justice*. New York: Springer.

Birks, D.J., Townsley, M., & Stewart, A. (2012). Generative models of crime: Using simulation to test criminological theory. *Criminology, 50*(1), 221–254.

Bossler, A.D., Holt, T.J., & May, D.C. (2012). Predicting online harassment: Victimization among a juvenile population. *Youth Society, 44*(4), 500–523.

Brantingham, P.J., & Brantingham, P.L. (1981). Notes on the geometry of crime. In P. Brantingham, & P. Brantingham (Eds.), *Environmental Criminology* (pp. 27–54). Beverly Hills, CA: Sage.

Brantingham, P., & Brantingham, P. (1984). *Patterns in Crime*. New York: Macmillan.

Brantingham, P.J., & Brantingham, P.L. (2008). Crime pattern theory. In R. Wortley, & L. Mazerolle (Eds.), *Environmental Criminology and Crime Analysis* (pp. 78–93). Cullompton, Devon: Willan.

Clarke, R. (1997). Introduction. In R. Clarke (Ed.), *Situational Crime Prevention: Successful Case Studies*. New York: Harrow and Heston.

Clarke, R., & Mayhew, P. (1988). The British gas suicide story and its criminological implications. In M. Tonry, & N. Morris (Eds.), *Crime and Justice*, Vol. 10 (pp. 79–116). Chicago: University of Chicago Press.

Cohen, D.D., Voss, C., Taylor, M.J.D., Delextrat, A., Ogunleye, A.A., & Sandercock, G.R.H. (2011). Ten-year secular changes in muscular fitness in English children, *Acta Paediatrica, 100* (10), e175–e177.

Cohen, L., & Felson, M. (1979). Social change and crime rate changes: A routine activity approach. *American Sociological Review, 44*, 588–608.

Cornish, D., & Clarke, R. (1986). Introduction. In D. Cornish, & R. Clarke (Eds.), *The Reasoning Criminal: Rational Choice Perspectives on Offending* (pp. 1–16). New York: Springer.

Cullen, F. (2011). Beyond adolescence-limited criminology: Choosing our future – The American Society of Criminology 2010 Sutherland Address. *Criminology, 49*(2), 287–330.

Eck, J.E. (2003). Police problems: The complexity of problem theory, research and evaluation. In J. Knutsson (Eds), *Problem-Oriented Policing: From Innovation to Mainstream* (pp. 79–113). Monsey, NY: Criminal Justice Press.

Ekblom, P. (2007). Making offenders richer. In G. Farrell, K. Bowers, S. Johnson, & M. Townsley (Eds.), *Imagination for Crime Prevention: Essays in Honour of Ken Pease* (pp. 41–57). Crime Prevention Studies 21. Monsey, NY: Criminal Justice Press/ Devon, UK: Willan Publishing.

Farrell, G., Tseloni, A., & Tilley, N. (2011). The effectiveness of vehicle security devices and their role in the crime drop. *Criminology and Criminal Justice, 11*(1), 21–35

Farrington, D.P. (1986). Age and crime. In M. Tonry, & N. Morris (Eds.), *Crime and Justice: An Annual Review of Research*, Vol. 7 (pp. 189–250). Chicago, IL: University of Chicago Press.

Felson, M. (1986). Routine activities, social controls, rational decisions, and criminal outcomes. In D. Cornish, & R.V.G. Clarke (Eds.), *The Reasoning Criminal* (pp. 119–128). New York: Springer-Verlag.

Felson, M., & Clarke, R. (1998). *Opportunity Makes the Thief. Police Research Series Paper 98*. London: Home Office.

Furnell, S. (2002). *Cybercrime: Vandalizing the Information Society*. Boston, MA: Addison-Wesley.

Gottfredson, M., & Hirschi, T. (1990). *A General Theory of Crime*. Stanford: Stanford University Press.

Guerette, R.T., & Bowers, K. (2009). Assessing the extent of crime displacement and diffusion of benefit: a systematic review of situational crime prevention evaluations. *Criminology, 47*(4), 1331–1368.

Hartshorne, H., & May, M. (1928). *Studies in the Nature of Character, Volume One, Studies in Deceit*. New York: Macmillan.

Hindelang, M., Gottfredson, M., & Garofolo, J. (1978). *Victims of Personal Crime: An Empirical Foundation for a Theory of Personal Victimization*. Cambridge, MA: Ballinger.

Homel, R. (2005). Developmental crime prevention. In N. Tilley (Ed.), *Handbook of Crime Prevention and Community Safety* (pp. 71–106). London: Routledge.

Laub, J., & Sampson, R. (2003). *Shared Beginnings, Divergent Lives: Delinquent Boys to Age 70*. Cambridge, MA: Harvard University Press.

Lemieux, A.M., & Felson, M. (2012). Risk of violent crime victimization during major daily activities. *Violence and Victims, 27* (5), 635–655.

Miethe, T.D., & Meier, R.F. (1994). *Crime and its Social Context: Toward an Integrated Theory of Offenders, Victims and Situations*. Albany, NY: State University of New York Press.

Miller, J. (2013). Individual offending, routine activities, and activity settings: Revisiting the routine activity theory of general deviance. *Journal of Research in Crime and Delinquency, 50*, 390–416.

Reynald, D.M. (2009). Guardianship in action: Developing a new tool for measurement. *Crime Prevention & Community Safety: An International Journal, 11*(1), 1–20.

Reyns, B.W., Henson, B., & Fisher, B.S. (2011). Being pursued online: Applying cyber lifestyle-routine activities theory to cyberstalking victimization. *Criminal Justice and Behavior, 38*(1), 1149–1169.

Ross, L., & Nisbett, R.E. (1991). *The Person and the Situation.* New York: McGraw-Hill.

Sidebottom, A. (2013). *Understanding and Preventing Crime in Malawi: An Opportunity Perspective* (unpublished PhD thesis). University College London.

Song, C., Qu, Z., Blumm, N., & Barabási, A-L. (2010). Limits of predictability in human mobility. *Science, 327*, 1018–1021.

Thomas, D., & Loader, B. (2000). Introduction: Cybercrime: Law enforcement, security and surveillance in the information age. In D. Thomas, & B. Loader (Eds.), *Cybercrime: Law Enforcement, Security and Surveillance in the Information Age* (pp. 1–14). London: Routledge.

Tilley, N. (2009). *Crime Prevention.* Cullompton, Devon: Willan.

Tillyer, M.S., & Eck, J.E. (2011). Getting a handle on crime: A further extension of routine activities theory. *Security Journal, 24*, 179–193.

Tompson, L., & Chainey, S. (2013). Integrating environmental considerations into prisoner risk assessments. *European Journal of Probation, 5*(2), 66–80.

Tremblay, M.S., Shields, M., Laviolette, M., Craig, C.L., Janssen, I., & Gorber, S.C. (2010). Fitness of Canadian children and youth: Results from the 2007–2009 Canadian Health Measures Survey. *Health Reports, 21*, 7–20.

van Dijk, J.J.M. (2012). Closing the Doors. *Stockholm Prizewinners Lecture 2012.* Retrieved from http://www.criminologysymposium.com/download/18.4dfe0028139b9a0cf4080001575/TUE13,+van+Dijk+Jan.pdf

Weisburd, D., Groff, E., & Morris, N. (2011). *Hot Spots of Juvenile Crime: Findings from Seattle. OJDP Juvenile Justice Bulletin.* Washington: US Department of Justice Office of Justice Programs Office of Juvenile Justice and Delinquency Prevention.

Wikström, P-O. (2009). Crime propensity, Criminogenic exposure and crime involvement in early to mid adolescence. *MschrKrim, 2/3*, 253–266.

Wikström, P-O., & Butterworth, D. (2006). *Adolescent Crime: Individual Differences and Lifestyles.* Cullompton, Devon: Willan.

Yar, M. (2005). The novelty of 'cyber crime': An assessment in light of routine activity theory. *European Journal of Criminology, 2*(4), 407–427.

Part IV

System Responses to Delinquency

Part IV

System Responses to Delinquency

22

Prenatal and Early Childhood Prevention of Antisocial Behavior

Lauretta M. Brennan and Daniel S. Shaw

Introduction

Overview of delinquency prevalence and consequences

Early-starting conduct problems (CP) that begin in childhood and persist throughout adolescence and adulthood, in the form of antisocial behavior, result in a substantial amount of harm to individual victims and to society. According to the US Department of Justice, in 2011 a violent crime occurred approximately every 26.2 seconds while a property crime occurred every 3.5 seconds (US Department of Justice Federal Bureau of Investigation, 2012). In addition to the serious consequences such behavior has on others, people who commit antisocial acts are often significantly impaired in psychological, social, and occupational domains (Bongers, Koot, van der Ende, & Verhulst, 2004). In fact, although it is estimated that approximately 1% of females and 3% of males in the population meet criteria for the clinical diagnosis of antisocial personality disorder, the prevalence of this disorder in clinical settings has been shown to be as high as 30%, with estimates even higher in substance-abusing and forensic populations (American Psychiatric Association, 2000). Moreover, research has shown that roughly 5% of individuals exhibit extreme persistent antisocial behavior that accounts for more than half of crimes committed (Loeber, 1982). It is known that individuals who engage in antisocial behavior as adults tend to be repeat offenders who have a long-standing history beginning with persistent CP in early childhood (Moffitt, 1993). Thus, efforts to intervene and prevent such chronic antisocial behavior have increasingly turned toward earlier ages.

The Handbook of Juvenile Delinquency and Juvenile Justice, First Edition. Edited by Marvin D. Krohn and Jodi Lane.

The importance of early identification of risk

For several reasons, researchers and interventionists have increasingly focused on preventing the development of CP and more serious forms of antisocial behavior by developing preventive interventions during the prenatal and early childhood periods (i.e., 0–3 years). First, age of onset of CP is a valuable way to identify subgroups of children who share similar causal mechanisms and show a common course to the development of their CP (Moffitt, 1993; Patterson, DeBaryshe, & Ramsey, 1989; Shaw, Bell, & Gilliom, 2000a). Research has consistently identified a subgroup of "early-starting" children, who demonstrate elevated levels of CP as early as toddlerhood and continue to do so throughout adolescence and adulthood, and show a more persistent and severe course, as well as more maladaptive outcomes, than children who do not show elevated rates of CP during early childhood (Aguilar, Sroufe, Egeland, & Carlson, 2000; NICHD Early Child Care Research Network, 2004). Moreover, children who have been found to *not* demonstrate high levels of CP before age 5 are unlikely to begin showing clinically elevated levels of externalizing behaviors at formal school entry (Shaw, Gilliom, & Giovannelli, 2000b; Shaw & Gross, 2008). Thus, many children at high risk for demonstrating persistent patterns of antisocial behavior can be identified during early childhood.

Second, children with early-starting and persistent CP have been found to be reliably characterized by a greater number of biological and contextual risk factors during very early childhood than those who show consistently low levels of CP or those with an adolescent onset (Aguilar *et al.*, 2000; Odgers *et al.*, 2008). Child variables measured before age 5 that have been linked with CP include measures of infant health such as birth weight (Horwood, Mogridge, & Darlow, 1998), aspects of temperament, such as negative emotionality and activity level (Caspi, Henry, McGee, Moffitt, & Silva, 1995), insecure or disorganized attachment (Munson, McMahon, & Spieker, 2001; Shaw, Owens, Vondra, Keenan, & Winslow, 1996), and self-regulation difficulties (Olson *et al.*, 2011). Similarly, numerous contextual factors during early childhood, ranging from low socio-economic status (NICHD Early Child Care Research Network, 2004) and family conflict (Odgers *et al.*, 2008), to parent mental health (Goodman *et al.*, 2011), and caregiving characterized by low sensitivity (Campbell *et al.*, 2010), have been shown to confer risk for early-starting and persistent CP. Accordingly, researchers have become increasingly capable of identifying profiles of children at high risk for antisocial behavior at younger and younger ages.

Third, child CP and parenting practices associated with its persistence appear to be more malleable during early than later childhood (Reid, 1993; Shaw & Gross, 2008). Specifically, prevention and intervention studies initiated prior to school entry have shown greater efficacy for treating children with clinically elevated rates of CP than for older children (Nowak & Heinrichs, 2008; Reid, 1993). The more positive outlook associated with early intervention is likely attributable to several factors, including the shorter duration of the child's CP (i.e., increased malleability), the decreased likelihood of incurring serious damage to parents' optimism for change, and the greater probability of children "growing" out of problem behavior in early versus later childhood. In sum, children who are at high risk of exhibiting a persistent course of CP and later antisocial behavior can be identified in the first few years of life, a period which is also optimal for intervention. Thus, numerous preventive intervention efforts have focused on very early childhood. The following chapter will review the current state of the field and offer recommendations for future refinement of early childhood intervention programs.

Theoretical Underpinnings and Associated Strategies of Early Intervention Programs

Several theories from the fields of developmental and social psychology have informed approaches to early intervention and prevention of child CP. A broad overview of theoretical and empirical bases for common intervention strategies is provided below. Although each theory is discussed separately, it is important to note that they are not mutually exclusive and, in practice, multiple theoretical perspectives have provided the basis for early intervention programs.

Social learning theory

Many parent-focused intervention programs are grounded in the principles of social learning theory (e.g., Parent Management Training, Kazdin, 1997; Family Check-Up, Dishion & Stormshak, 2007). Social learning theory posits that parent modeling plays a pivotal role in the development of child problem-solving and regulatory strategies (Bandura, 1977b). Patterson (1982) elaborated on the application of social learning principles to the development of CP in early childhood, suggesting that parents' use of harsh and aggressive behavior management techniques unwittingly reinforces child disruptive behavior, teaching children to use such conflict resolution strategies to deal with interpersonal difficulties with siblings in the home, and subsequently with both peers and adults outside of the home. Patterson also noted that by parents non-contingently reinforcing children's prosocial behavior, their attention to child disruptive behavior, albeit negative, was responsible for supporting children's use of disruptive behavior. Thus, at the heart of many theoretically based intervention programs is a focus on parent management strategies. Consistent with rapid developments in children's physical mobility and lack of cognitive appreciation for the consequences of their behavior (Shaw & Bell, 1993), social learning approaches have been initiated for children as young as age 2 (Shaw, Dishion, Supplee, Gardner, & Arnds, 2006). They focus on reducing negative parenting techniques such as hostility, harsh punishment, and coercion, and promoting positive parenting techniques such as sensitivity, positive reinforcement, and consistent limit-setting.

Attachment theory

Attachment theory has also played a significant role in guiding the development of early childhood CP intervention and prevention programs. Attachment theory emphasizes the role that warm, sensitive, and responsive caregiving plays in fostering a positive parent–child bond (Bowlby, 1990), which facilitates a child's internalization of behavioral and moral norms and increases his/her motivation to comply with parental requests (Belsky & Nezworski, 1987; Cicchetti, Toth, & Lynch, 1995). Such bonds are known to rapidly develop during infancy as children exclusively rely on caregivers for basic needs and form internal working models that guide their expectations of the world (Bowlby, 1990). Parental sensitivity and consistent responsiveness to the infant's needs are crucial for the formation of a secure attachment (De Wolff & van Ijzendoorn, 1997), which is thought to reflect the child's trust in his/her caregiver and in his/her own ability to influence the world (Bowlby, 1990). Several studies have documented associations between insecure or disorganized attachment classification during infancy and pre-school age CP, particularly within high-risk samples (Erickson, Sroufe, & Byron, 1985; Keller, Spieker, & Gilchrist, 2005; Shaw *et al.*, 1996). Accordingly, many attachment-based parenting intervention strategies have been developed for parents of infants and in some cases, young toddlers. These intervention approaches focus on promoting parental warmth, consistency, and sensitivity during the formative early childhood period (e.g., Van Zeijl *et al.*, 2006) to facilitate the development of a secure parent–child bond.

Human ecology and self-efficacy theories

From an ecological perspective (Bronfenbrenner, 1979, 1986), a child's development is influenced not only by how their parents care for them but also by characteristics of their families, social supports, neighborhoods, community resources, social policies, and the relationships among them. Empirical evidence has repeatedly shown that these contextual factors have direct influences on children but also can moderate the impact of how other factors (e.g., harsh parenting) are associated with risk for CP (Deater-Deckard & Dodge, 1997; Schonberg & Shaw, 2007). For example, in one review examining associations between risk factors for CP at different levels of socio-economic risk, family factors were often found to be more important for youth from disadvantaged backgrounds than for their more advantaged counterparts (Schonberg & Shaw, 2007).

Self-efficacy theory is a useful and related framework for understanding how caregivers make decisions that affect their child's development. This theory suggests that individuals' perceptions of whether they are capable of carrying out a given behavior and whether that behavior will lead to the desired outcome (i.e., self-efficacy) can influence their decision-making (Bandura, 1977a). For example, aspects of prenatal health are well-known determinants of child well-being

(Lobel *et al.*, 2008), and adverse perinatal health behaviors such as smoking have been linked with risk for later antisocial behavior in offspring (Wakschlag, Pickett, Cook Jr, Benowitz, & Leventhal, 2002).

Drawing on human ecology and self-efficacy theories, several early childhood interventions have been designed to target the broader context of a child's ecology by helping parents understand what is known about the influence of particular decisions on their own and their child's health, in conjunction with addressing parenting issues (Dishion *et al.*, 2008). Such programs frequently focus on the influence of parent socio-economic resources, mental health and social support, as well as other family dynamics (e.g., chaos versus structure of the home environment). Accordingly, these interventions facilitate family involvement with social supports and community resources while helping parents set attainable goals, meant to increase feelings of self-efficacy, promoting the parent's likelihood of tackling challenges in future.

Outline of Review

We continue this review by detailing inclusion criteria and then proceed to describe early childhood intervention programs and associated empirical support that has emerged for these programs. All results presented are statistically significant ($p < 0.05$), unless otherwise noted. We then provide a summary of the current state of the literature, discuss limitations of the review, and suggest future directions that would be important for the advancement of the current knowledge base and intervention dissemination.

Criteria for inclusion

Prior to delving into a review of the literature, it is important to describe the criteria used to select studies for inclusion in this review. First, because we are focusing on prenatal and very early childhood prevention of later antisocial behavior, the scope of this review is limited to studies initiated during the prenatal and early childhood period (i.e., between ages 0–3). Second, because the focus is on prevention of antisocial behavior, the review only includes interventions targeting the prevention of disruptive behavior problems or more serious forms of antisocial behavior, by either focusing on early forms (i.e., CP) or on known child or ecological risk factors directly related to antisocial behavior. Third, based on the existing theoretical knowledge base and corresponding empirical support for the development of antisocial behavior, only intervention programs that have a basis in theory are included. Fourth, in evaluation of program efficacy, a randomized controlled trial (RCT) is required. Finally, to ensure that intervention effectiveness extends beyond immediate intervention, only programs with at least one year of follow-up are reviewed.

Literature Review

Social learning interventions

A number of early and middle childhood interventions have emerged out of the social learning theory perspective. Many of these interventions use elements of parent management, an approach aimed at reducing negative parenting behaviors (e.g., harsh discipline) and promoting positive parenting behaviors (e.g., positive reinforcement). Data from RCTs have repeatedly shown that interventions targeting parent management strategies are efficacious at modifying parenting and, ultimately, reducing CP and antisocial behavior (e.g., Lundahl, Risser, & Lovejoy, 2006). Six social learning theory-oriented interventions targeting CP in children aged 0 to 3 that met inclusion criteria for this review were identified: Early Head Start, Early Start (New Zealand), Family Check-Up, Incredible Years Toddler Parent Program, Chicago Parent Program, and Triple P.

Early Head Start, a downward extension of the widely implemented Head Start pre-school program, targets low-income pregnant women, infants, and toddlers, as well as children eligible for disability services (Administration for Children, Youth and Families, 1994). Early Head Start offers home visitation, center-based services, or a combination of both until children are 3 years old. Results from a RCT of a diverse sample across 17 US sites including urban and rural locations ($n = 3,001$ families) demonstrated that at the end of intervention children showed modest benefits in multiple domains, including higher levels of cognitive and language skills ($d = 0.10–0.13$) and lower levels of parent-rated aggression ($d = 0.11$) than controls (Love et al., 2005). Modest benefits were also found on observed measures of parenting, including parent supportiveness and use of corporal punishment ($d = 0.11–0.15$), with parents who received a combination of home-based and center-based services showing the greatest improvements. Long-term follow-up results show that for the sample as a whole, benefits of the program largely dissipated by 5th Grade (Vogel, Yange, Moiduddin, Kisker, & Carlson, 2010). Only one group difference remained: children who received Early Head Start showed marginally higher levels of socio-emotional success, as measured by a composite index of parent and child report, compared with controls ($d = 0.10$). Only African-American children who participated in the program continued to show lower levels of parent-rated CP than control children ($d = 0.26$) at the 5th Grade follow-up (Vogel et al., 2010). Thus, evidence suggests that Early Head Start is a modestly promising approach for most low-income children, and somewhat more helpful for African-American children, who may have fewer alternative community resources available to them.

Another intervention, Early Start (New Zealand; Fergusson, Horwood, & Ridder, 2005), offers home visitation services by a family support worker to at-risk families with children under the age of 5 who meet at least two risk criteria (e.g., young maternal age, family violence). Services are offered at four levels based on a family's identified needs, varying in intensity from weekly home visitation (level one) to a maintenance visit every three months (level four). Results from a RCT of 443 predominantly white, low socio-economic status (SES) families randomly assigned to Early Start or control with a mean length of participation of 24 months showed that, at 36 months post-enrollment, parents enrolled in the program reported significantly higher levels of positive and non-punitive parenting than control parents, with small effect sizes ($d = 0.22$–0.27). In terms of reducing child CP, at 36 months post-enrollment there was only a trend level improvement found according to maternal report ($d = 0.19$; Fergusson, Grant, Horwood, & Ridder, 2005). However, a 9-year follow-up of this sample found continued benefits, including lower rates of parents' self-reported use of harsh punishment ($d = 0.29$) and parent, but not teacher, ratings of children's conduct and emotional problems ($d = 0.17$; Fergusson, Boden, & Horwood, 2013). In sum, Early Start appears to be associated with modest yet persistent improvements in both parenting and child problem behavior at home, but not child CP at school.

The Family Check-Up (FCU) is a parenting-focused home-visiting intervention targeting families with children at high risk for developing CP (Dishion & Stormshak, 2007). In two early-childhood RCTs (Dishion *et al.*, 2008; Shaw *et al.*, 2006), families were screened from Women, Infants, and Children Nutritional Supplement Centers (WICs) based on socio-economic (e.g., income), family (e.g., maternal depression) and child (e.g., early CP) risk. Parent consultants use data from annual ecological assessments to provide feedback to intervention families about child and family well-being using a motivational interviewing framework (Miller & Rollnick, 2002), which promotes motivation for change by creating dissonance for parents between the child's current status and the parents' aspirations for their child. Following the feedback, families have the option of engaging in individually-tailored follow-up intervention sessions that focus on parent management skills and factors that compromise parenting (Dishion *et al.*, 2008). In the first RCT with an urban, ethnically diverse sample of 120 2-year-old boys, intervention effects on both observed positive parenting (Gardner, Shaw, Dishion, Burton, & Supplee, 2007) and child CP ($d = 0.65$) were found 1–2 years after intervention (Shaw *et al.*, 2006). Another ongoing RCT includes 731 ethnically diverse, low-income boys and girls from three distinct US communities (i.e., urban, rural, and suburban), and has found intervention effects on both parent-reported CP from ages 2 to 4 (Dishion *et al.*, 2008) and both parent- and teacher-reported CP from ages 2 to 7.5 (Dishion *et al.*, 2014). Moreover, parents assigned to the FCU showed higher levels of observed positive parenting during interactions with their 3-year-olds than controls ($d = 0.33$), and these improvements were found to mediate intervention effects on child behavior at age 4 (Dishion *et al.*, 2008). Numerous collateral intervention effects for the FCU on factors that compromise parenting (e.g., maternal depression; Shaw, Connell, Dishion, Wilson, & Gardner, 2009) and child factors related to CP (e.g., academic achievement; Brennan et al., 2013) have also been identified. Thus, the FCU has demonstrated efficacy at improving parenting and reducing child CP, as well as other risk factors related to emerging CP, with follow-ups extending 2 to 5 years after intervention initiation.

The Incredible Years (IY) Training Series is a set of programs encompassing parent, child, and/or teacher-focused interventions delivered via weekly group sessions with a trained facilitator. Although IY began as a parent management program for treating preschoolers with disruptive behavior problems (Webster-Stratton, 1982), relatively recently the IY has initiated interventions directed at infants and toddlers. The IY Babies and Toddlers Parent Programs aim to help parents establish positive relationships with their children and utilize effective limit-setting and positive reinforcement techniques to manage the behavior of children under the age of 3. Whereas a great deal of research has evaluated the efficacy of the IY program on preschool and school-age children and shown consistently strong intervention effects on CP and parenting 1–2 years following intervention (i.e., ages 3–8; Reid, Webster-Stratton, & Hammond, 2003; Webster-Stratton, 1998), data suggest the IY parent program version for toddlers is also effective at improving parenting skills and reducing behavior problems (Gross *et al.*, 2003; McMenamy, Sheldrick, & Perrin, 2011). A RCT across 11 day-care centers serving predominantly low-income, minority toddlers demonstrated that parents assigned to the intervention showed more positive behaviors post-intervention and at 1 year follow-up than control parents ($d = 0.30$). In addition, intervention children in the "high-risk" behavior problems group (i.e., one standard deviation above the mean at baseline) showed significant reductions in teacher-rated problem behavior compared with controls, with 44% of intervention children but only 18% of control children moving into the "low-risk" range, with effects maintained at 1 year follow-up (Gross *et al.*, 2003). The IY Toddler Parent Program has demonstrated short-term across-informant efficacy at reducing problem behaviors in high-risk toddlers; however, more research is needed to determine whether the well-established benefits of the program for older children can be extended downward to infancy.

Adapted from the IY program, the Chicago Parent Program (CPP) is a 12-session parenting group intervention tailored to the needs of low-income African-American and Latino parents in Chicago, including the generation of videotapes modeling social learning parenting procedures (e.g., time-outs) carried out in ecologically valid contexts (e.g., laundromats, bathrooms of homes). Two RCTs have evaluated the effectiveness of the CPP on the behavior of 2- to 4-year-old children in day-care centers. In one study, pre-post intervention analyses showed that a greater percentage of children in the intervention group (50%) than in the control group (37.5%) moved from the clinical range to the non-clinical range on teacher-rated CP (Breitenstein *et al.*, 2007). Moreover, in a second trial of over 250 parents of 2- to 4-year-olds randomly assigned to the CPP or waiting-list control, findings showed that from baseline to 1 year follow-up, intervention parents were observed to issue fewer commands and use less corporal punishment with their children ($d = 0.24$–0.32). Similarly, children in the CPP showed greater reductions in observed aversive behavior (e.g., non-compliance) during interaction tasks than control children ($d = 0.44$; Gross *et al.*, 2009). Thus, the CPP has demonstrated small-to-medium effects on parenting behavior and negative child behaviors up to 1 year post-intervention.

The Triple P Positive Parenting Program is a flexibly delivered, multilevel parenting intervention promoting healthy social and emotional development of children through improved parenting quality. Similar to the development of the IY program for toddlers, Triple P was initially developed for older children and then adapted for toddlers and preschoolers. The program offers five levels of intervention for parents of children spanning from toddlerhood to adolescence. These include Universal Triple P (level 1), a broad communications-based approach (e.g., brochures, billboards), to intensive individual family support (level 5). The intervention is delivered via individual sessions, brief consultations in primary care, group sessions, and web-based programs, all tailored to a family's level of need (Sanders, 2012). As with other intervention programs in this review, numerous RCTs have demonstrated the effectiveness of Triple P in preschool and school-aged children (e.g., Sanders, Markie-Dadds, Tully, & Bor, 2000; Thomas & Zimmer-Gembeck, 2007), with meta-analyses demonstrating greater reductions in behavior problems for intervention than control children and medium effect sizes (e.g., $d = 0.49$) maintained at 6 months and 1 year follow-up (de Graaf, Speetjens, Smit, de Wolff, & Tavecchio, 2008). Data suggest the program is also effective when applied to parents of toddlers. For example, in a RCT of 126 mid-to-upper SES Australian parents who rated their 18- to 36-month-old children as having elevated CP, Morawska and Sanders (2006) demonstrated that children of parents who participated in a self-directed version of Triple P, whether or not they received weekly telephone consultations, showed greater decreases on mother-rated behavior problems than children whose parents were in the control group post-intervention and at 6 month follow-up ($d = 0.44$–0.68). Moreover, many evaluations of Triple P included children as young as 2, and a meta-analysis of moderation variables demonstrated stronger effects on all outcome measures for younger children (Nowak & Heinrichs, 2008). Thus, evidence suggests that Triple P is a promising approach for preventing CP in toddlers; however, more research with toddler-age samples and long-term follow-ups are needed.

Attachment-based interventions

Several programs targeting the prevention and intervention of behavior problems in very young children approach intervention with parents from an attachment perspective. Attachment-focused interventions have been repeatedly shown to be effective at increasing parental sensitivity and decreasing rates of attachment insecurity (Bakermans-Kranenburg, Van Ijzendoorn, & Juffer, 2003); however, the long-term benefit of these interventions on child CP is less clear. Three interventions addressing the prevention and/or treatment of early CP from this framework in children under the age of 3 met inclusion criteria for this review: Child and Family Interagency, Resource, Support, and Training (Child FIRST), Healthy Families America, and Video-feedback Intervention to Promote Positive Parenting and Sensitive Discipline (VIPP-SD).

Child FIRST is a home-visiting intervention available to pregnant women and families with children under the age of 6 who are identified as having emotional or behavioral concerns or at risk of experiencing negative outcomes. A comprehensive assessment establishes a family's level of need, and weekly home visits by a mental health clinician and care coordinator are initiated. The intervention is considered a dyadic approach aimed at strengthening the parent–child relationship through discussion of parent feelings/history, reflection, and reframing child behavior. In one RCT of 157 predominantly minority, urban mothers with children between 6 and 36 months of age, fewer mothers who received the intervention rated their children as showing clinically concerning levels of CP at the 12-month follow-up than mothers in the control group (17% vs. 29%, respectively; Lowell, Carter, Godoy, Paulicin, & Briggs-Gowan, 2011). The intervention was also found to have benefits on child language, maternal mental health, and service utilization at the 12-month follow-up.

Healthy Families America is another preventive intervention theoretically rooted in attachment theory that emphasizes the importance of relationship-based approaches for the prevention of negative child outcomes. Families are eligible to enroll in a local Healthy Families program either prenatally or within three months of their child's birth. Eligibility criteria are at the discretion of each site; families complete an initial assessment and eligible families are typically low-income and/or experiencing a significant family stressor (e.g., substance abuse, domestic violence). Weekly home visitation services by family support workers are then offered through the child's 3rd or 5th birthday, based on need. Numerous states have implemented a version of the Healthy Families project (Harding, Galano, Martin, Huntington, & Schellenbach, 2007). A review of eight RCTs and numerous quasi-experimental designs across 22 states demonstrated that the program's most consistent results are in the domain of parenting. For example, four out of six RCTs showed that families assigned to the intervention showed greater increases in observer-rated positive parent–child interaction at 1 and/or 2 years follow-up than control families (Harding *et al.*, 2007). Although many studies have shown positive impacts of Healthy Families America on child domains (e.g., lower rates of birth complications, higher cognitive development scores), there is less evidence for the program's effectiveness in preventing emerging CP (Harding *et al.*, 2007). One RCT across six sites of Healthy Families Alaska (*n* = 325), a predominantly Caucasian low-income sample, found that at the age 2 follow-up, more children whose parents were assigned to the intervention were rated by their mothers as in the "normal" range for CP than children of parents assigned to the control group (i.e., 82% vs. 77%, respectively; Caldera *et al.*, 2007) . However, only trend-level differences were found between group means on CP. Thus, Healthy Families America has been shown to be effective at improving child health and parenting outcomes. However, the program's long-term benefits on CP, more serious and later forms of antisocial behavior, are less clear.

The Video-feedback Intervention to promote Positive Parenting (VIPP) is an intervention for parents of infants that aims to buffer children from the development of CP and other negative outcomes by promoting parent sensitivity and reducing insecure parent–infant attachment (Van Zeijl *et al.*, 2006; Velderman *et al.*, 2006). In VIPP, parents and children are videotaped interacting in their home during daily situations (e.g., parent reading to the child), and trained home visitors provide feedback and reinforcement of the parents' use of sensitivity and other positive parenting skills (Velderman *et al.*, 2006). A modification to the program specifically targeting children at risk for the development of CP, Video-feedback Intervention to promote Positive Parenting and Sensitive Discipline (VIPP-SD), also focuses on the parent's use of sensitive discipline practices (Van Zeijl *et al.*, 2006). In one RCT of 77 first-time mothers in the Netherlands recruited based on their own insecure attachment representations, mothers received four VIPP home visits when children were between 7 and 10 months of age. A follow-up evaluation when children were 40 months old demonstrated that a smaller percentage of children whose mothers received the VIPP were in the clinical range on mother-rated CP than control group children (11% vs. 34%, respectively; Velderman *et al.*, 2006). Although VIPP was associated with improved maternal sensitivity at post-test, this result was not sustained at the 40-month follow-up. In a second RCT of 237 mid-to-upper SES Dutch mothers who rated their 1- to 3-year-old children as demonstrating elevated rates of CP, families received six home visit sessions of VIPP-SD. At a 1-year follow-up, mothers who received the VIPP-SD showed more observer-rated positive discipline practices than control mothers ($d = 0.34$). Moreover, the intervention was associated with greater reductions in levels of mother-rated child overactive behavior, but not child oppositional or aggressive behavior, among families experiencing high marital discord or high daily stress than for controls ($d = 0.35$; Van Zeijl *et al.*, 2006). In addition, at the 2-year follow-up, the VIPP-SD was associated with reductions in oppositional behavior for children with a particular genetic allele (i.e., 7-repeat version of the DRD4; Bakermans-Kranenburg, van Ijzendoorn, Pijlman, Mesman, & Juffer, 2008). Thus, there is evidence that VIPP is beneficial for the prevention of child CP for some children; however, these effects have not been reliably maintained for more than 1 year for the majority of children, perhaps due to the changing developmental challenges associated with infants moving into the "terrible twos" and concomitant increases in oppositional and aggressive behavior.

Human ecology/self-efficacy theory

In line with Bronfenbrenner's seminal theory on the moderating influence of context on child development (Bronfenbrenner, 1979, 1986), some interventions have emphasized the significance of parent health and economic-related decisions and behaviors for child outcomes. Although many approaches noted above incorporate some focus on family and child ecology into their models (e.g., Family Check-Up, Child FIRST), one program stands out for the centrality of its focus on family ecology and maternal decision-making for promoting positive child development. The Nurse–Family Partnership (NFP) offers first-time, low-income mothers and their children home visits by a registered nurse (or paraprofessional) beginning before the 28th week of gestation and concluding when the child turns 2 years old. Home visitors encourage and reinforce maternal behaviors that are consistent with program goals of improved health and economic self-sufficiency. Three RCTs of the NFP across distinct geographic locations (Memphis, TN, Denver, CO, and Elmira, NY) and diverse samples demonstrated a host of benefits associated with the NFP intervention on outcomes including maternal prenatal health (e.g., reductions in cigarette smoking; Olds, Henderson, Tatelbaum, & Chamberlin, 1986), child cognitive development and academic achievement up to 12 years' follow-up (Kitzman *et al.*, 2010; Olds *et al.*, 2004), and lower rates of verified child abuse by mothers who received the NFP up to 15 years post-intervention (Olds *et al.*, 1997). In many cases, benefits of the intervention were more robust for mothers rated as having low psychological resources (i.e., below the sample median on mental health, intelligence, and sense of control) at the study outset (Kitzman *et al.*, 2010; Olds *et al.*, 2004, 2007).

With respect to CP and more serious antisocial behavior, the program has produced somewhat inconsistent results across sites and development, with greater effects emerging at the age 15 and 19 follow-ups of the original, rural sample of predominantly white families than later cohorts of more ethnically diverse, urban youth (Eckenrode *et al.*, 2010). For example, in a RCT conducted in Memphis, TN, of predominantly African-American families, few benefits on parent or teacher reports of child CP were observed at the ages 6, 9, and 12-year follow-ups (Kitzman *et al.*, 2010; Olds *et al.*, 2004). In contrast, in the Elmira, NY, sample, youth whose mothers received the NFP showed reductions in self-reported arrests, convictions, and probation violations at age 15 and 19 relative to controls (Eckenrode *et al.*, 2010; Olds *et al.*, 1998). In sum, evidence suggests that NFP is an efficacious early-childhood approach for reducing later CP and antisocial behavior, particularly for families from rural, predominantly Caucasian samples. However, the generalizability of the NFP's effects to diverse samples is less clear.

Summary and Future Directions

Overall, the findings demonstrate that theoretically based approaches to prenatal and very early childhood prevention of CP and, in one case, more serious forms of antisocial behavior, produce small-to-medium effects on parenting and child behavior up to 1 to 2 years (e.g., Chicago Parent Program, VIPP), and in some cases more than 5 years later (e.g., Family Check-Up, Nurse–Family Partnership). Although the results are promising, there are a number of challenges. First, findings are largely inconsistent across measures, reporters, and subgroups of participants. Moreover, there are few interventions with long-term follow-up data available (only the NFP currently has data spanning to adolescence), and those with long-term data suggest that initial effects often fade, or are inconsistent, over time. For example, although the NFP showed effects on some measures of self-reported antisocial behavior in a predominantly Caucasian rural sample when youth were 15 years old, intervention effects in this sample were maintained only for females at the age 19 follow-up. In a predominantly African-American, urban sample, intervention effects were not evident at age 12 based on youth self-reports of antisocial behavior. Similarly, Early Head Start's initial effects on parent-rated aggression were not maintained 7 years after program completion for the majority of children; however, continued effects were found for parent-rated CP in African-American children. While many of the programs reviewed above show short-term intervention effects on CP, parenting, and related risk factors after the intervention ends, results from these studies also suggest that continued contact with families might be necessary to ensure such gains in child problem behavior, parenting, and related risk factors persist over time (Shaw, 2013).

Based on the diverse number of risk factors and pathways associated with the development of early-starting CP, it would follow that similar parenting issues and factors that compromise parenting quality would not be relevant for all families. Following the logic of the Family Check-Up model (Dishion & Stormshak, 2007) in which intervention is tailored to fit the risk profile of the individual family, it would behoove intervention programs to dedicate more time to the initial assessment of child CP and issues that might amplify or attenuate such concerns. Catering interventions to a family's specific assets and concerns (e.g., limit-setting, proactively anticipating contexts for child misbehavior, co-parenting, more accurately reading child cues, developing better emotion regulation skills) could result in a more focused and time-limited course of treatment compared with the 10–12 sessions typically conducted for most group-based models. Moreover, programs that maintain contact with families over time (versus those that provide intensive services ending in toddlerhood/preschool) show more consistent evidence of sustained effects into middle childhood (e.g., FCU, Early Start). Perhaps intensive early-childhood approaches that terminate prior to salient developmental transitions (e.g., the terrible twos, school entry) do less to prepare families for difficulties in managing child behavior than approaches that offer brief, ongoing support over time. Long-term follow-up studies that examine why some interventions are more beneficial in some subgroups and domains over time than others are needed.

In addition to modifying the content of preventive intervention programs, another burgeoning issue is identifying ways to increase the accessibility of early childhood programs for at-risk families. Despite low-income children's heightened risk for CP and higher rates of environmental risk factors linked to CP (e.g., harsh parenting, parental psychopathology, quality of day-care, neighborhood dangerousness), accessibility to and engagement in intervention programs is modest. Thus, to actually reduce levels of early-starting CP and prevent later antisocial behavior at the *population* level, identifying new platforms and methods to reach and engage low-income families with infants and toddlers should be a priority in the coming years (Shaw, 2013). Fortunately, there are existing examples of outreach programs, including IY in Head Start centers (Webster-Stratton, 1998) and FCU recruitment from WIC centers (Shaw *et al.*, 2006). In the next decade it is critical that prevention efforts be directed at using non-traditional settings (e.g., primary care, Head Start) for identifying at-risk children and families, and also further developing methods for engaging such families in these contexts.

References

Administration for Children, Youth and Families. (1994). *The Statement of the Advisory Committee on Services for Families With Infants and Toddlers.* Washington, DC: US Department of Health and Human Services.

Aguilar, B., Sroufe, L.A., Egeland, B., & Carlson, E. (2000). Distinguishing the early-onset/persistent and adolescence-onset antisocial behavior types: From birth to 16 years. *Development and Psychopathology, 12,* 109–132.

American Psychiatric Association. (2000). *Diagnostic and Statistical Manual of Mental Disorders* (4th ed.). Washington, DC: American Psychiatric Association.

Bakermans-Kranenburg, M.J., Van Ijzendoorn, M.H., & Juffer, F. (2003). Less is more: meta-analyses of sensitivity and attachment interventions in early childhood. *Psychological Bulletin, 129,* 195–215. doi: 10.1037/0033-2909.129.2.195

Bakermans-Kranenburg, M.J., van Ijzendoorn, M.H., Pijlman, F.T., Mesman, J., & Juffer, F. (2008). Experimental evidence for differential susceptibility: Dopamine D4 receptor polymorphism (DRD4 VNTR) moderates intervention effects on toddlers' externalizing behavior in a randomized controlled trial. *Developmental Psychology, 44,* 293–300. doi: 10.1037/0012-1649.44.1.293

Bandura, A. (1977a). Self-efficacy: toward a unifying theory of behavioral change. *Psychological Review, 84,* 191–215.

Bandura, A. (1977b). *Social Learning Theory.* Englewood Cliffs, NJ: Prentice-Hall.

Belsky, J., & Nezworski, T.M. (1987). *Clinical Implications of Attachment.* New York: Lawrence Erlbaum.

Bongers, I.L., Koot, H.M., van der Ende, J., & Verhulst, F.C. (2004). Developmental trajectories of externalizing behaviors in childhood and adolescence. *Child Development, 75,* 1523–1537. doi:10.1111/j.1467-8624.2004.00755.x

Bowlby, J. (1990). *A Secure Base: Parent-Child Attachment and Healthy Human Development*: New York: Basic Books.

Breitenstein, S.M., Gross, D., Ordaz, I., Julion, W., Garvey, C., & Ridge, A. (2007). Promoting mental health in early childhood programs serving families from low-income neighborhoods. *Journal of the American Psychiatric Nurses Association, 13,* 313–320. doi:10.1177/1078390307306996

Brennan, L.M., Shelleby, E.C., Shaw, D.S., Gardner, F., Dishion, T.J., & Wilson, M. (2013). Indirect effects of the Family Check-Up on school-age academic achievement through improvements in parenting in early childhood. *Journal of Educational Psychology, 105,* 762–773. doi:10.1037/a0032096

Bronfenbrenner, U. (1979). *The Ecology of Human Development: Experiments by Nature and Design.* Cambridge, MA: Harvard University Press.

Bronfenbrenner, U. (1986). Ecology of the family as a context for human development: Research perspectives. *Developmental Psychology, 22,* 723–742. doi:10.1037/0012-1649.22.6.723

Caldera, D., Burrell, L., Rodriguez, K., Crowne, S.S., Rohde, C., & Duggan, A. (2007). Impact of a statewide home visiting program on parenting and on child health and development. *Child Abuse & Neglect, 31,* 829–852. doi:dx.doi.org/10.1016/j.chiabu.2007.02.008

Campbell, S.B., Spieker, S., Vandergrift, N., Belsky, J., Burchinal, M., & NICHD Early Child Care Research Network. (2010). Predictors and sequelae of trajectories of physical aggression in school-age boys and girls. *Development and Psychopathology, 22,* 133–150. doi:10.1017/S0954579409990319

Caspi, A., Henry, B., McGee, R.O., Moffitt, T.E., & Silva, P.A. (1995). Temperamental origins of child and adolescent behavior problems: From age three to fifteen. *Child Development*, *66*, 55–68.

Cicchetti, D., Toth, S.L., & Lynch, M. (1995). Bowlby's dream comes full circle: The application of attachment theory to risk and psychopathology. *Advances in Clinical Child Psychology*, 1–75.

Deater-Deckard, K., & Dodge, K.A. (1997). Externalizing behavior problems and discipline revisited: Nonlinear effects and variation by culture, context, and gender. *Psychological Inquiry*, *8*, 161–175.

de Graaf, I., Speetjens, P., Smit, F., de Wolff, M., & Tavecchio, L. (2008). Effectiveness of The Triple P Positive Parenting Program on Behavioral Problems in Children: A Meta-Analysis. *Behavior Modification*, *32*, 714–735. doi:10.1177/0145445508317134

De Wolff, M.S., & van Ijzendoorn, M.H. (1997). Sensitivity and attachment: A meta-analysis on parental antecedents of infant attachment. *Child Development*, *68*, 571–591. doi:10.1111/j.1467-8624.1997.tb04218.x

Dishion, T., Brennan, L.M., Shaw, D.S., McEachern, A., Wilson, M.N., & Jo, B. (2014). Prevention of problem behavior through annual Family Check-Ups in early childhood: Intervention effects from the home to elementary school. *Journal of Abnormal Child Psychology*, *42*(3), 343–354. doi: 10.1007/s10802-013-9768-2

Dishion, T.J., Shaw, D.S., Connell, A.M., Gardner, F., Weaver, C., & Wilson, M. (2008). The Family Check-Up with high-risk indigent families: Preventing problem behavior by increasing parents' positive behavior support in early childhood. *Child Development*, *79*, 1395–1414. doi: 10.1111/j.1467-8624.2008.01195.x

Dishion, T.J., & Stormshak, E.A. (2007). *Intervening in Children's Lives: An Ecological, Family-centered Approach to Mental Health Care*. Washington, DC: American Psychological Association.

Eckenrode, J., Campa, M., Henderson Jr, C.R., Cole, P.M., Kitzman, H., …Olds, D.L. (2010). Long-term effects of prenatal and infancy nurse home visitation on the life course of youths: 19-year follow-up of a randomized trial. *Archives of Pediatrics and Adolescent Medicine*, *164*, 9–15. doi:10.1001/archpediatrics.2009.240

Erickson, M.F., Sroufe, L.A., & Byron, E. (1985). The relationship between quality of attachment and behavior problems in preschool in a high-risk sample. *Monographs of the Society for Research in Child Development*, *50*, 147–166. doi:10.2307/3333831

Fergusson, D.M., Boden, J.M., & Horwood, L.J. (2013). Nine-year follow-up of a home-visitation program: A randomized trial. *Pediatrics*, *131*, 297–303. doi:10.1542/peds.2012-1612

Fergusson, D., Horwood, J.L., & Ridder, E.M. (2005a) *Early Start Evaluation Report*. Christchurch, New Zealand: Christchurch School of Medicine and Health Sciences, Early Start Project Ltd.

Fergusson, D.M., Grant, H., Horwood, L.J., & Ridder, E.M. (2005b). Randomized trial of the Early Start Program of home visitation. *Pediatrics*, *116*, e803–e809. doi:10.1542/peds.2005-0948

Gardner, F., Shaw, D.S., Dishion, T.J., Burton, J., & Supplee, L. (2007). Randomized prevention trial for early conduct problems: Effects on proactive parenting and links to toddler disruptive behavior. *Journal of Family Psychology*, *21*, 398–406. doi: 10.1037/0893-3200.21.3.398

Goodman, S.H., Rouse, M.H., Connell, A.M., Broth, M.R., Hall, C.M., & Heyward, D. (2011). Maternal depression and child psychopathology: A meta-analytic review. *Clinical Child and Family Psychology Review*, *14*, 1–27. doi: 10.1007/s10567-010-0080-1

Gross, D., Fogg, L., Webster-Stratton, C., Garvey, C., Julion, W., & Grady, J. (2003). Parent training of toddlers in day care in low-income urban communities. *Journal of Consulting and Clinical Psychology, 71*, 261–277. doi: 10.1037/0022-006X.71.2.261

Gross, D., Garvey, C., Julion, W., Fogg, L., Tucker, S., & Mokros, H. (2009). Efficacy of the Chicago Parent Program with low-income African American and Latino parents of young children. *Prevention Science, 10*, 54–65. doi:10.1007/s11121-008-0116-7

Harding, K., Galano, J., Martin, J., Huntington, L., & Schellenbach, C.J. (2007). Healthy Families America® effectiveness. *Journal of Prevention & Intervention in the Community, 34*, 149–179. doi:10.1300/J005v34n01_08

Horwood, L.J., Mogridge, N., & Darlow, B.A. (1998). Cognitive, educational, and behavioural outcomes at 7 to 8 years in a national very low birthweight cohort. *Archives of Disease in Childhood – Fetal and Neonatal Edition, 79*, F12–F20. doi:10.1136/fn.79.1.F12

Kazdin, A.E. (1997). Parent Management Training: Evidence, outcomes, and issues. *Journal of the American Academy of Child and Adolescent Psychiatry, 36*, 1349–1356.

Keller, T.E., Spieker, S., & Gilchrist, L. (2005). Patterns of risk and trajectories of preschool problem behaviors: A person-oriented analysis of attachment in context. *Development and Psychopathology, 17*, 349–384. doi:10.1017/S0954579405050170

Kitzman, H.J., Olds, D.L., Cole, R.E., Hanks, C.A., Anson, E.A., Arcoleo, K.J., …Holmberg, J.R. (2010). Enduring effects of prenatal and infancy home visiting by nurses on children: Follow-up of a randomized trial among children at age 12 years. *Archives of Pediatrics and Adolescent Medicine, 164*, 412–418. doi:10.1001/archpediatrics.2010.76

Lobel, M., Cannella, D.L., Graham, J.E., DeVincent, C., Schneider, J., & Meyer, B.A. (2008). Pregnancy-specific stress, prenatal health behaviors, and birth outcomes. *Health Psychology, 27*, 604–615.

Loeber, R. (1982). The stability of antisocial and delinquent child behavior: A review. *Child Development*, 1431–1446.

Love, J.M., Kisker, E.E., Ross, C., Raikes, H., Constantine, J., Boller, K., …Brady-Smith, C. (2005). The effectiveness of Early Head Start for 3-year-old children and their parents: Lessons for policy and programs. *Developmental Psychology, 41*, 885–901. doi: 10.1037/0012-1649.41.6.885

Lowell, D.I., Carter, A.S., Godoy, L., Paulicin, B., & Briggs-Gowan, M.J. (2011). A randomized controlled trial of Child FIRST: A comprehensive home-based intervention translating research into early childhood practice. *Child Development, 82*, 193–208. doi:10.1111/j.1467-8624.2010.01550.x

Lundahl, B., Risser, H.J., & Lovejoy, M.C. (2006). A meta-analysis of parent training: Moderators and follow-up effects. *Clinical Psychology Review, 26*, 86–104. doi:dx.doi.org/10.1016/j.cpr.2005.07.004

McMenamy, J., Sheldrick, R.C., & Perrin, E.C. (2011). Early intervention in pediatrics offices for emerging disruptive behavior in toddlers. *Journal of Pediatric Health Care, 25*, 77–86. doi:dx.doi.org/10.1016/j.pedhc.2009.08.008

Miller, W.R., & Rollnick, S. (2002). *Motivational Interviewing: Preparing People for Change*, 2nd ed. New York: Guilford.

Moffitt, T.E. (1993). Adolescence-limited and life-course-persistent antisocial behavior: A developmental taxonomy. *Psychological Review, 100*, 674–701.

Morawska, A., & Sanders, M.R. (2006). Self-administered behavioral family intervention for parents of toddlers: Part I. *Efficacy. Journal of Consulting and Clinical Psychology, 74*, 10–19. doi: 10.1037/0022-006X.74.1.10

Munson, J.A., McMahon, R.J., & Spieker, S.J. (2001). Structure and variability in the developmental trajectory of children's externalizing problems: Impact of infant attachment, maternal depressive symptomatology, and child sex. *Development and Psychopathology, 13*, 277–296. doi:10.1017/S095457940100205X

NICHD Early Child Care Research Network. (2004). Trajectories of physical aggression from toddlerhood to middle childhood: Predictors, correlates, and outcomes. *Monographs of the Society for Research in Child Development, 69*, 1–143. doi:10.1111/j.0037-976X.2004.00312.x

Nowak, C., & Heinrichs, N. (2008). A comprehensive meta-analysis of Triple P-Positive Parenting Program using hierarchical linear modeling: Effectiveness and moderating variables. *Clinical Child and Family Psychology Review, 11*, 114–144. doi:10.1007/s10567-008-0033-0

Odgers, C.L., Moffitt, T.E., Broadbent, J.M., Dickson, N., Hancox, R.J., Harrington, H., …Caspi, A. (2008). Female and male antisocial trajectories: From childhood origins to adult outcomes. *Development and Psychopathology, 20*, 673–716. doi:10.1017/S0954579408000333

Olds, D.L., Eckenrode, J., Henderson, C.R., Kitzman, H., Powers, J., Cole, R., …Luckey, D. (1997). Long-term effects of home visitation on maternal life course and child abuse and neglect. *Journal of the American Medical Association, 278*, 637–643.

Olds, D.L., Henderson Jr, C.R., Cole, R., Eckenrode, J., Kitzman, H., Luckey, D.W., …Powers, J. (1998). Long-term effects of nurse home visitation on children's criminal and antisocial behavior: 15-year follow-up of a randomized controlled trial. *Journal of the American Medical Association, 280*, 1238–1244. doi:10.1001/jama.280.14.1238

Olds, D.L., Henderson, C.R., Tatelbaum, R., & Chamberlin, R. (1986). Improving the delivery of prenatal care and outcomes of pregnancy: A randomized trial of nurse home visitation. *Pediatrics, 77*, 16–28.

Olds, D.L., Kitzman, H., Cole, R., Robinson, J.A., Sidora, K., Luckey, D.W., …Holmberg, J. (2004). Effects of nurse home-visiting on maternal life course and child development: age 6 follow-up results of a randomized trial. *Pediatrics, 114*, 1550–1559.

Olds, D.L., Kitzman, H., Hanks, C., Cole, R., Anson, E., Sidora-Arcoleo, K., …Bondy, J. (2007). Effects of nurse home visiting on maternal and child functioning: Age-9 follow-up of a randomized trial. *Pediatrics, 120*, e832–e845. doi:10.1542/peds.2006-2111

Olson, S.L., Tardif, T.Z., Miller, A., Felt, B., Grabell, A.S., Kessler, D., …Hirabayashi, H. (2011). Inhibitory control and harsh discipline as predictors of externalizing problems in young children: A comparative study of US, Chinese, and Japanese preschoolers. *Journal of Abnormal Child Psychology, 39*, 1163–1175.

Patterson, G.R. (1982). *Coercive Family Process* (Vol. 3). Eugene, OR: Castalia Publishing Company.

Patterson, G., DeBaryshe, B., & Ramsey, E. (1989). A developmental perspective on antisocial behavior. *American Psychologist, 44*, 329–335. doi:10.1037/0003-066X.44.2.329

Reid, J. (1993). Prevention of conduct disorder before and after school entry: Relating interventions to developmental findings. *Development and Psychopathology, 5*, 243–262.

Reid, M.J., Webster-Stratton, C., & Hammond, M. (2003). Follow-up of children who received the Incredible Years intervention for oppositional-defiant disorder: Maintenance and prediction of 2-year outcome. *Behavior Therapy, 34*, 471–491. doi:dx.doi.org/10.1016/S0005-7894(03)80031-X

Sanders, M.R. (2012). Development, evaluation, and multinational dissemination of the Triple P-Positive Parenting Program. *Annual Review of Clinical Psychology, 8*, 345–379. doi:10.1146/annurev-clinpsy-032511-143104

Sanders, M.R., Markie-Dadds, C., Tully, L.A., & Bor, W. (2000). The Triple P-Positive Parenting Program: A comparison of enhanced, standard, and self-directed behavioral family intervention for parents of children with early onset conduct problems. *Journal of Consulting and Clinical Psychology, 68*, 624–640.

Schonberg, M.A., & Shaw, D.S. (2007). Do the predictors of child conduct problems vary by high- and low-levels of socioeconomic and neighborhood risk? *Clinical Child and Family Psychology Review, 10*, 101–136. doi:10.1007/s10567-007-0018-4

Shaw, D.S. (2013). Future directions for research on the development and prevention of early conduct problems. *Journal of Clinical Child and Adolescent Psychology, 42*, 418–428. doi: 10.1080/15374416.2013.777918

Shaw, D., & Bell, R. (1993). Developmental theories of parental contributors to antisocial behavior. *Journal of Abnormal Child Psychology, 21*, 493–518. doi:10.1007/bf00916316

Shaw, D.S., Bell, R.Q., & Gilliom, M. (2000a). A truly early starter model of antisocial behavior revisited. *Clinical Child and Family Psychology Review, 3*, 155–172.

Shaw, D.S., Connell, A., Dishion, T.J., Wilson, M.N., & Gardner, F. (2009). Improvements in maternal depression as a mediator of intervention effects on early childhood problem behavior. *Development and Psychopathology, 21*, 417–439.

Shaw, D.S., Dishion, T.J., Supplee, L.H., Gardner, F., & Arnds, K. (2006). Randomized trial of a family-centered approach to the prevention of early conduct problems: 2-year effects of the Family Check-Up in early childhood. *Journal of Consulting and Clinical Psychology, 74*, 1–9.

Shaw, D.S., Gilliom, M., & Giovannelli, J. (2000b). Aggressive behavior disorders. In C.H. Zeanah (Ed.), *Handbook of Infant Mental Health*, 2nd ed. (pp. 397–411). New York: Guilford.

Shaw, D.S., & Gross, H.E. (2008). What we have learned about early childhood and the development of delinquency. In A. Lieberman (Ed.), *The Long View of Crime: A Synthesis of Longitudinal Research* (pp. 79–127). New York: Springer.

Shaw, D.S., Owens, E.B., Vondra, J.I., Keenan, K., & Winslow, E.B. (1996). Early risk factors and pathways in the development of early disruptive behavior problems. *Development and Psychopathology, 8*, 679–699. doi:10.1017/S0954579400007367

Thomas, R., & Zimmer-Gembeck, M. (2007). Behavioral outcomes of Parent-Child Interaction Therapy and Triple P–Positive Parenting Program: A review and meta-analysis. *Journal of Abnormal Child Psychology, 35*, 475–495. doi:10.1007/s10802-007-9104-9

US Department of Justice Federal Bureau of Investigation. (2012). *Crime in the United States, 2011.* Retrieved from http://www.fbi.gov/about-us/cjis/ucr/crime-in-the-u.s/2011/crime-in-the-u.s.-2011/offenses-known-to-law-enforcement/standard-links/national-data

Van Zeijl, J., Mesman, J., Van Ijzendoorn, M.H., Bakermans-Kranenburg, M.J., Juffer, F., Stolk, M.N., …Alink, L.R. (2006). Attachment-based intervention for enhancing sensitive discipline in mothers of 1-to 3-year-old children at risk for externalizing behavior problems: a randomized controlled trial. *Journal of Consulting and Clinical Psychology, 74*, 994–1005.

Velderman, M.K., Bakermans-Kranenburg, M.J., Juffer, F., Van Ijzendoorn, M.H., Mangelsdorf, S.C., & Zevalkink, J. (2006). Preventing preschool externalizing behavior problems through video-feedback intervention in infancy. *Infant Mental Health Journal, 27*, 466–493. doi:10.1002/imhj.20104

Vogel, C.A., Yange, X., Moiduddin, E.M., Kisker, E.E., & Carlson, B.L. (2010) *Early Head Start Children in Grade 5: Long-Term Follow-Up of the Early Head Start Research and Evaluation Study Sample*. Washington, DC: Office of Planning, Research, and Evaluation, Administration for Children and Families, US Department of Health and Human Services.

Wakschlag, L.S., Pickett, K.E., Cook, Jr, E., Benowitz, N.L., & Leventhal, B.L. (2002). Maternal smoking during pregnancy and severe antisocial behavior in offspring: A review. *American Journal of Public Health*, 92, 966–974.

Webster-Stratton, C. (1982). Teaching mothers through videotape modeling to change their children's behavior. *Journal of Pediatric Psychology*, 7, 279–294.

Webster-Stratton, C. (1998). Preventing conduct problems in Head Start children: Strengthening parenting competencies. *Journal of Consulting and Clinical Psychology*, 66, 715–730.

23

School Prevention Programs

Steven P. Lab

The school has come to be seen as a prime actor in the development and prevention of delinquent/criminal behavior. This ascendance to prominence is reflected in research focusing on the correlates and causes of behavior, government and private reports linking schools and education to delinquency, and the advent of prevention programs intimately tied to schools and education. The ability to use school problems and concerns to predict possible problems later in life places school personnel in the midst of prevention. Schools are also prime locations for implementing prevention programs. Many interventions often deal with pre-delinquent youths and youths having problems in school.

Prevention programs may not always seem to be aimed at delinquency. The interventions are geared toward the specific problematic factors found in the schools. The present chapter will attempt to develop the role of schools as an agent of prevention through a three-step process. The focus is on primary and secondary schools. First, the chapter outlines the level of delinquent behavior in schools. Second, it is necessary to discuss the theoretical support for the role schools play in delinquency. Third, the specific aspects of the educational process that are important for discussing delinquency must be examined. Finally, the chapter will examine programs that have been established to intervene in the harmful aspects of school, with special attention paid to prevention programs demonstrating an impact on subsequent delinquency and in-school misbehavior.

The Handbook of Juvenile Delinquency and Juvenile Justice, First Edition. Edited by Marvin D. Krohn and Jodi Lane.
© 2015 John Wiley & Sons, Inc. Published 2015 by John Wiley & Sons, Inc.

Delinquent Behavior in Schools

Discussion of school prevention programs entails two related but distinct domains of delinquency and crime. The first is general crime and delinquency committed by individuals in society. The first is general crime and delinquency committed by individuals in society. Data on both crime and delinquency is available from official records (e.g. the UCR), self-report surveys, and victimization surveys (e.g. the NCVS). Official and victimization data are routinely reported in the media. The UCR reveals more than 10 million index crimes committed in 2010 (Federal Bureau of Investigation, 2011), while the NCVS shows almost 19 million victimizations (Truman, 2011). Beyond the levels of crime and delinquency in society, school prevention programs can address delinquency committed within the school setting.

Misbehavior also has an impact on others in the school, either directly as the target of an offense or indirectly through vicarious victimization. The US Departments of Justice and Education routinely collect data on crime and victimization in schools. In 2009–10 schools experienced almost 1.9 million crime incidents (a rate of 39.6 per 1,000 students), from 85.5% of schools (Robers, Zhang, Truman, & Snyder, 2012). Of these, 1.2 million (a rate of 25) were violent crime incidents. In light of media accounts of violent acts in schools (especially homicides), it is important to note that a good deal of in-school violence appears as threats and minor acts, including pushing and shoving, rather than serious violence. Indeed, homicides are rare at school (even with tragedies like Columbine and Sandy Hook), with only 15 during the 2008–9 school year while 7.7% of students reported being threatened or injured with a weapon at school (Robers *et al.*, 2012).

Students are not the only individuals victimized at schools. Teachers and staff are also victimized. During the 2007–8 school year, almost 290,000 teachers (7.5%) reported being threatened with injury by a student during school. Another 154,000 teachers (4.0%) were actually the victim of physical attack by a student at school (Robers *et al.*, 2012).

Bullying

A major topic of concern for many youths, parents and schools is the problem of bullying. The issue of bullying has received a great deal of attention over the past decade. This is partly due to the events at Columbine and other schools, where part of the blame/explanation for the behavior is attributed to past bullying. While most bullying does not lead to such levels of retaliatory violence, it clearly has an impact on the victim.

Bullying behavior can be classified into four types: verbal, physical, social and cyberbullying. Too often it is assumed that bullying is primarily verbal, such as teasing and name-calling. It is important to note that many forms of bullying involve physical confrontations that are actually criminal. Included here are hitting, shoving and punching. Starting rumors about someone or ostracizing him/her from participating in events are examples of social bullying. The final major form, cyberbullying, involves the use of the internet and other technologies to attack the victim. This can occur through posts on social media (such as MySpace and Facebook), texts, sexting, and unwanted internet contacts.

Information on the extent of bullying generally comes from survey data. According to the 2009 NCVS, 28% of students report being the victim of at least one form of bullying at school. The most common form of reported bullying is being made fun of, insulted or being called names (19% of respondents). Roughly one out of six are the subject of rumors and almost 10% are physically bullied. Cyberbullying, which is not restricted to the school setting, is reported by 6% of the students.

Responses to In-School Victimization

Victimization has the potential of eliciting a variety of student responses in school, many of which are debilitating or may lead the victim into criminal or delinquent behavior. One immediate response is fear. Robers *et al.* (2012) note that over 4% of students report being afraid at school. Data on avoidance behaviors due to fear among students aged 12–18 reveal that 5% of students report avoiding school or places at school. While less than 1% report staying home from school altogether due to fear, this still translates into more than 200,000 students. Almost 6% of students avoid specific places in school due to fear, including hallways, restrooms, and the cafeteria (Robers *et al.*, 2012). Other studies also show that a small but significant number of youth (10% or more) either stay at home or avoid certain places/events at school due to fear of assault or theft. Lab and Clark (1996), studying junior and senior high schools in one large Midwestern county, found that 16% rate their school as "unsafe" or "very unsafe". This fear of school leads students to avoiding school or taking what they see as protective actions.

Another student response to crime and fear is to carry weapons to school. Robers *et al.* (2012) report that almost 6% of youths carried a weapon in the past month at school. Lab and Clark (1996) reported that 24% of junior and senior high school students have carried a weapon to school for protection at least once over a six-month period. Studies focusing on inner-city schools report even higher levels of weapons in school.

For many youths, joining gangs is perceived as a way to garner protection and support in the face of threats. If a youth is victimized by gang members, joining a gang becomes a self-defense mechanism. It is natural for people to seek out support from those around them. Joining gangs as a response to victimization, however, is a double-edged sword. While the gang may supply some sense of protection, it typically demands participation in illegal behavior and conflict with other gangs and individuals. These demands often result in further victimization of the individual, rather than protection from victimization. Joining a gang can contribute to ongoing victimization, albeit as a member of a group and not just as an individual.

The level of misbehavior, victimization, fear, and safety responses by students in schools is a concern for various reasons. Many of the responses are more inappropriate than appropriate. The presence of weapons offers the possibility of more serious confrontations and problems, not to mention the illegality of bringing weapons to school. At the same time, misbehavior and victimization can be the result of factors and school practices that need to be addressed. Certainly, the schools do not exist in a vacuum. The failure to address these problems will simply add to the other deleterious aspects of schools.

Theoretical Views

Many theorists emphasize the importance of schools in developing behavior. Various writers point to blocked attainment and feelings of failure as a source of deviant behavior. Individuals faced with little or no chance of success in legitimate endeavors will turn to deviant sources of success and support. For juveniles who have not yet entered the adult world, the school becomes the setting for gauging success and failure. For example, a juvenile who is faced with failing grades while his friends are successful at their studies may be labeled as a failure by those same friends and/or teachers. The lack of success may push a youth to seek out others having the same difficulties. In an attempt to regain some feeling of status and success, failing youths may turn to deviant behavior (Agnew, 1992; Cohen, 1955).

The actual causal process relating schools and delinquency can take a variety of forms. One possible argument posits that diminished academic ability results in poor academic achievement. Failure in school can foster dislike for school attendance, a lack of concern for socially proscribed behavior, and eventual movement into delinquent behavior. Failure as a student may lead to failed aspirations and success expectations that, in turn, result in being excluded from more successful students and student activities. This exclusion invariably lowers a youth's self-image and feelings of worth, resulting in associating with other marginal youths or deviant behavior as a means of salvaging a positive self-image (Gold, 1978). This acts to counterbalance the negative feedback experienced in the school setting. Research in the early 1960s and 1970s supported the school failure–delinquency relationship (Gold & Mann, 1972; Hirschi, 1969; Polk & Hafferty, 1966; West & Farrington, 1973).

The relationship between educational achievement and delinquency is not a simple one. Various intervening variables enter into the formula. Most explanations involve student success and achievement. The ability of the student prior to entering school can affect academic success. One possible measure of ability is the IQ test. Another set of influences on achievement may be the format and workings of the school itself. Factors such as tracking, in-school indicators of success, and the quality of the teachers and resources can all affect student outcomes. Victimization in school may drive the student away from school. The following paragraphs attempt to outline the impact of various factors on student success.

IQ and delinquency

The role of intelligence in the etiology of deviant behavior has been a matter of debate for many years. The early IQ tests were used to screen entrants to the US in order to keep the mentally deficient out of the country. The so-called feeble-minded (those with low IQs) were viewed as a threat to the moral and intellectual life of the nation. It was assumed that these individuals would disproportionately contribute to the level of delinquency and criminal activity.

These early fears have found much support in later research. Hirschi and Hindelang (1977), in a review of the major research in the area, established that IQ is an important correlate of delinquency. A variety of studies substantiate that low IQ is positively correlated to higher levels of official and self-reported delinquency (e.g. Hirschi & Hindelang, 1977; Wolfgang, Figlio, & Sellin, 1972). The major question unanswered in most analyses is whether IQ is a direct causal factor or simply lays the groundwork for other factors. Hirschi and Hindelang (1977) argued that low IQ leads to a number of other events that, in turn, facilitate the acquisition of delinquent behavior. Among the intervening factors is school achievement, academic performance, and attitude toward school. The influence of IQ, therefore, appears only when IQ affects other school variables (Hirschi & Hindelang, 1977; Wolfgang *et al.*, 1972).

School practices and delinquency

Achievement in school emerges as the key element in the relationship between school and delinquency. The failure to succeed in school leads to frustration, withdrawal from the institution, and an increased potential for deviant behavior. A variety of school practices, however, can operate against success and school attachment, and lead to delinquency. Among these practices are tracking, poor instruction, irrelevant instruction, and methods of evaluation.

Tracking refers to the process of assigning students to different classes or groups based on the perceived needs of the student. The most common form of tracking appears in high school where students find themselves placed into "college preparatory" or "vocational" groups. The former indicates an expectation of going to and succeeding in college. The latter signifies a belief that college is beyond the abilities of the student. Schafer, Olexa, and Polk (1971) showed that students in the vocational track, regardless of their social class, prior grades or IQ score, responded with lower grades. In addition, these students typically participated in fewer activities and were more likely to drop out of school, misbehave, and commit delinquent acts. The reasons for the lower achievement lay in the expectation, by both teachers and students, that lower track students will not succeed, are not in the educational mainstream, and are not worth as much as college-bound students (Schafer *et al.*, 1971). Today, many school districts have specialized schools, including "vocational" schools that are, in essence, tracking that masquerades under a new name.

Many students are also faced with poor and/or irrelevant instruction. Views that lower-class and minority students are not college material often result in the assignment of less competent teachers to schools and classes serving these youths (Schafer *et al.*, 1971). In addition, these schools typically receive less financial support. As a result, the students develop a sense of failure, a lack of self-esteem, and may become dissatisfied and bitter towards the system. The practice of segregating some youths and implicitly labeling them as second class (particularly if they are in special classes within a larger school) can result in a self-fulfilling prophesy. They are expected to do worse and thus they live up (down?) to this expectation.

The irrelevance of instruction for some students grows out of the types of materials they are being taught, especially in the vocational education tracks (Wertleib, 1982). Schools are seldom able to keep up with the rapid changes and modifications in jobs and the workforce. The materials being taught in the school are outmoded before the youth has the opportunity to use the information. Vast changes in production and technology have established jobs for which many youths are unqualified, and have eliminated jobs that previously employed hundreds or thousands of people. Instruction becomes more irrelevant when students cannot find employment upon leaving school. Students often are trained in very specific tasks that they cannot use outside of the school. At the same time, they are not prepared to enter college, undertake further instruction, or secure other jobs.

The emphasis on testing invariably leads to feelings of failure. For the "A" student, grades are a reward for hard work and indicate positive achievement. The movement toward proficiency tests (mandated for promotion and graduation in many states) often results in resentment on the part of those students who do not pass the tests. The failing student may be held back or placed into special classes that segregate and label him. Slow and failing youths may be excluded from many of the extracurricular activities that can help make school a fun, enjoyable experience. Failing students may be humiliated in front of other students, may not be expected to achieve, and are often considered second-class citizens within an institution they are forced to attend (Schafer *et al.*, 1971).

Prevention Programs

A wide range of activities, programs, and educational strategies have emerged to address delinquency and crime both in and outside of schools. Prevention programs can focus on addressing general delinquency concerns, both in and out of the school setting. Other programs tend to target problems that appear mainly in the school itself. In many cases, the prevention efforts, regardless of the specific problem or location being addressed, have the potential to impact misbehavior in settings beyond the intended target location of problem. Prevention actions and programs can be loosely grouped into the following categories: early developmental prevention, physical security, police/guards in schools, elementary and high school programs, alternative schools, and other efforts. Many other suggested educational changes, such as the provision of relevant instruction and the use of flexible groupings that allow movement in and out of ability levels, have been proposed. Unfortunately, many of these have received only cursory attention and there is little research on their impact on crime/delinquency. This indicates that the impact of such changes on education in general, and delinquency in particular, is still unknown.

Early developmental prevention

Developmental prevention seeks to address crime and delinquency by identifying and eliminating factors that cause and promote misbehavior. Basically, there is a belief that individuals are conditioned through past experiences and forced to act in certain ways. Various developmental prevention programs seek to prepare young children, youths, and their families for success in school and beyond.

Parent training   Concern over the preparation and ability of parents to provide an appropriate environment for children is a major thrust in developmental preven-tion. These programs range from those targeting expectant mothers to those working with families of young children, to those addressing families with school-age chil-dren. Three recognized programs are examined below. These are the Elmira Prenatal/Early Infancy project, the Syracuse Family Development program, and the Incredible Years project.

The Elmira Prenatal/Early Infancy program targets the earliest stage of a child's development, specifically when the child is still in the womb. The centerpiece of the program is home visitation by nurses beginning during pregnancy and lasting through to the child's second birthday (Olds *et al.*, 1998). The target subjects are young, poor, first-time, and often unmarried mothers. Mothers were visited an average of 9 times during pregnancy and 23 times after birth (Olds *et al.*, 1998). The visiting nurses focus on three areas: health and health-related activities of the mother and child; learning how to provide appropriate care to the child; and social and personal skills development for the mothers. In addition, the nurses provide refer-rals and access to other assistance, and the project provides transportation for the mothers to access assistance. Evaluation of the program revealed a number of positive outcomes. First, maternal abuse and neglect were significantly reduced. Second, in a 15-year follow-up, the children reported significantly less running away, arrests, and substance abuse. Third, there were also fewer arrests of the program mothers (Olds *et al.*, 1998). The success of the project has led to its replication in other sites.

The Syracuse Family Development Research Project has many similar character-istics to the nurse home visitation program. Begun in 1969, the intervention targeted pregnant, young, single African-American mothers and worked with the families from birth to age 8. The project included home visitation by child development trainers, parent training in health, nutrition, and child-rearing, and individualized day-care for the children (Lally et al., 1988). The key element of the project was weekly visits to the subjects' homes. Children participating in the project have done better academically, demonstrate better self-control, and have fewer arrests than control youths.

Another program targeting parental training that has proven effective is the Incredible Years program. Whereas the above programs selected expectant mothers, the Incredible Years initially identified families for intervention that had youths displaying early conduct problems from age 4 to 8 (Webster-Stratton & Hammond, 1997). The program includes strong parent and child training components, as well as a teacher-training element for youths in school. Parents receive training in parenting skills, how to recognize and address their child's problem behaviors, how to set rules and use incentives, and other key components of child-rearing. The child component focuses on helping them recognize emotions, how to deal with anger, appropriate responses to problem situations, and educational skills. The teacher-training element deals with classroom management, providing skills to youths, handling problem youths and behaviors, and disciplinary practices. Evaluations reveal consistent positive results. Participating parents display more positive parenting skills and fewer coercive and punitive punishments. Children display fewer antisocial behaviors, better interpersonal skills, and better preparation for school (SAMHSA, 2012; Webster-Stratton, 2000; Webster-Stratton & Hammond, 1997). The strength of the program, its wide adoption and its consistent positive evaluations have led Substance Abuse and Mental Health Services Administration to list the Incredible Years on its National Registry of Evidence-based Programs and Practices.

Preschool programs   One suggestion for tackling school problems and antisocial behavior involves early preparation of children for school. Preschool programs are viewed as a means of establishing a level of competence that avoids early placement into differential ability tracks, building a positive attitude toward school, and providing basic social skills to youths who are not prepared to enter school. The expectation is that success in school will translate later to greater social success out of school, and lower delinquency and criminality.

Perhaps the best-known preschool program is Head Start. Head Start is meant to provide youths with positive early experiences and, in turn, successful long-term academic careers. The extent to which Head Start has succeeded in achieving its goals is questionable. It has not been evaluated in terms of its effect on later delinquency or criminality.

The most extensively studied preschool program is the Perry Preschool program. The program, begun in 1962, seeks to provide students with a positive introduction to education. This is accomplished by involving the children in the planning of activities, a low child:teacher ratio, enhanced reinforcement of student achievement, and frequent home visits with parents. Berrueta-Clement, Schweinhart, Barnett, Epstein, and Weikart (1984) claimed that the program sets in process a sequence of events that leads from program participation to higher academic performance, to enhanced educational commitment and scholastic achievement, to prosocial behavior. All study subjects are from low-income black families, typified by low parental education, unemployment, and single-parent households. All children are tracked throughout school and are periodically surveyed until age 19, with follow-up evaluations undertaken until age 40 (Berrueta-Clement *et al.*, 1984).

Evaluation of the Perry Preschool program presents some impressive claims. The program appears to significantly increase measures of academic performance, reduce the need for special education and remedial work, prompt more positive attitudes toward school, enhance the high school graduation rate, and result in lower unemployment after graduation from high school (Berrueta-Clement *et al.*, 1984). The program also claims that fewer experimental students are arrested as either adults or juveniles than are control students. Results to age 27 reveal that about half as many program participants are arrested compared with control group subjects. The frequency of their offenses is also about a quarter of that for control youths (Schweinhart, Barnes, & Weikart, 1993).

Physical security

The introduction of physical security measures is a common school response, especially in the wake of violent crimes and attacks at school. A typical call is for the installation of metal detectors, locks on doors, and sealed windows. Unfortunately, there is no evidence that such actions keep weapons out of schools (Hankin, Hertz, & Simon, 2011). More problematic is they do not keep offenders out of schools, since most offenders are themselves students. There has also been relatively little research on the impact of physical security devices in schools. Extrapolating from physical design research on communities, it should be evident that physical security is very limited in and of itself. It is only in concert with social interventions that physical security will have an impact.

Police/guards in schools

The use of police officers in schools has grown considerably since the early 1990s. Robers *et al.* (2012) note that almost 70% of schools have either security guards or police officers on the premises. Violent crime, drug violations, weapons violations, and bullying, as well as highly publicized shootings, have aroused concern and calls for increased police presence in schools. Over two-thirds of students report that their school has either a security guard or an assigned police officer (Robers *et al.*, 2012).

The presence of school resource officers (SROs) has become commonplace. A 2005 survey of almost 1,400 schools across the US found that 48% had SROs and 76% rely on public law enforcement (Travis & Coon, 2005). Most police in schools are involved in traditional police functions, including patrolling, making arrests, and providing security. At the same time, many police officers in schools, particularly those in an SRO capacity, provide mentoring and referrals, train teachers and parents, teach programs such as Drug Abuse Resistance Education (DARE), and chaperone school events (Travis & Coon, 2005).

The introduction of police to schools has not been without controversy. Some observers argue that SROs try to balance their roles as law enforcers and mentors/ instructors/problem-solvers. Others contend that the widespread introduction of police into the school setting criminalizes school discipline. At the same time as police have been introduced to school, there has been an introduction of zero tolerance policies whereby students are suspended or expelled for certain behaviors, such as bringing a weapon to school. Instead of seeing discipline problems as requiring solutions by teachers and principals, these practices treat students as quasi-criminals and mandate quasi-criminal justice solutions, and thereby label youths as criminals. Critics see this as part of a more general trend to ignore problems of poverty and deindustrialization (Hirschfield & Celinska, 2011).

Evaluations of effective school–police partnerships indicate that more is needed than simply placing police officers in schools (Brady, Blamer, & Phenix, 2007). Police officers cannot address problems of overcrowding, low attendance, large minority populations, and low funding. Parent cooperation is essential.

Elementary and high school programs

School atmosphere Altering the general school environment is one suggestion for addressing misconduct in schools. Opening up participation in decision-making (to both students and staff) allows everyone to take ownership of both the solutions and the successes of controlling problems. Denise Gottfredson (1986) reported on the effectiveness of Project PATHE (Positive Action Through Holistic Education) in Charleston, South Carolina. This project took a broad-based approach to the school environment by bringing teachers, administrators, students, parents, and agencies together in making decisions about education and the school. Underlying this approach is the idea that the various parties must see a stake in education and believe that education is important. The parties will care more about education if they have some say in the educational process. Project PATHE isolated a variety of factors including school pride, career-oriented programs, student team learning, and individual services as targets for change.

Pre- and post-program measures, as well as data from two non-equivalent comparison schools, were used in an evaluation of the program. The results offered mixed support. Experimental schools reported higher test scores and graduation rates than the control schools (Gottfredson, 1986). Attendance at school, however, did not seem to be affected by the program. Delinquency measures showed the greatest degree of disparity across and within schools. At the school level, there was some improvement in overall delinquency in the high school but no significant change for the middle schools. Changes in individual types of delinquency appeared in various schools. For example, drug use was reduced in one school but not in others. Some teachers reported lower levels of victimization in individual schools.

These results suggest that, while the program has no overall effect on the schools, improvements can be found in individual schools (Gottfredson, 1986). The qualified success of Project PATHE may be due to alterations in the school system and study design after the onset of the project. Changes in the school administration, the closing and consolidating of some schools, and the inability of some programs to be adequately implemented during the study suggest that the project would produce better results in a more stable setting (Gottfredson, 1986).

Lab and Clark (1996) also investigated the idea of altering the school environment through cooperative decision-making. Evaluating 44 junior and senior high schools, the authors note that order and control in a school is engendered most effectively by bringing students, staff, and administrators together. The traditional methods of administratively imposing strict control and harsh discipline on students is not productive (Lab & Clark, 1996). Schools with lower victimization and problem behaviors are those that work to develop a "normative" approach to discipline and control. This means that schools in which there is more agreement on discipline and control measures experience fewer problems than schools in which there is little agreement (Lab & Clark, 1996). Schools should strive, therefore, to build consensus through inclusion in the decision-making process.

The Charlotte School Safety Program attempted to address the issue of school safety by developing a cooperative problem-solving process that involved students, school staff, and police (Kenney & Watson, 1998). The program emphasized changing the school environment using techniques similar to those found in community-oriented policing. Problem identification and problem solving were key elements of the intervention, and an attempt was made to integrate these activities into the normal classroom curriculum. It was important to change the attitudes of the students and to turn the student body into an agent for positive change in the school (Kenney & Watson, 1998). The program was tested in the 11th Grade social studies classes of a single Charlotte high school during the 1994–95 school year. The problem-solving activities were addressed one to two days each week within small groups of 6 to 10 students.

An evaluation of the Charlotte program indicated positive changes in the target school compared with a matched control school. The evaluation used surveys of students at both schools, interviews with school staff, observations within the school, and inspections of student problem-solving worksheets. The first evidence of success was the ability of the students to identify and agree on problems in the school, and their ability to suggest and implement changes in school procedures. Kenney and Watson (1998) also noted significant reductions in students' fear of crime at school, reduced fighting, fewer threats against teachers, lower numbers of suspensions for violence, and fewer calls for police assistance. Teachers also reported fewer class disruptions and improved relations between students and faculty. The greatest concern with the evaluation was its reliance on a single school and work with only those students in 11th grade social studies. In general, the results of research on changing the school environment suggests the efforts bring about positive changes in the schools.

Skills training   Many social skills training initiatives appear in school settings and appear under various titles, including life skills training. These programs seek to teach children how to recognize problem situations and react in an appropriate manner. This is done by attempting to teach self-control, anger management, how to recognize feelings and emotions, building a positive self-image, identifying the needs and concerns of others, and problem-solving. In essence, the skills to be learned are how to interact with others in your environment without resorting to aggressive or antisocial methods. To a large extent, the training seeks to provide youths with the skills to combat peer pressure and aggression from other youths.

The Promoting Alternative Thinking Strategies (PATHS) program has been recognized as model program. PATHS is taught in regular classrooms and, ideally, is a five-year-long curriculum offered in elementary schools (Greenberg & Kusche, 1998). The curriculum is intended to reduce both behavioral and emotional problems, while building self control and problem-solving abilities. PATHS has undergone several evaluations utilizing experimental and control groups of regular students, as well as special-needs students. The results reveal improved problem-solving ability, reduced hyperactivity, increased planning activity, reduced self-reported conduct problems, less peer aggression, and reduced teacher reports of conduct problems. Greenberg and Kusche (1998) suggest that PATHS can be adopted for use with different populations and for implementation outside the school setting. Skills training is a component of many interventions. It is used in a variety of programs aimed at substance abuse.

Conflict management/resolution   Teaching students how to handle conflict and make proper choices when faced with difficult situations (such as peer pressure to use drugs or commit a crime) is a popular intervention that takes a variety of forms. Conflict management/resolution is a common program in schools. These programs appear under a variety of names, including dispute resolution, dispute mediation, conflict resolution, conflict management, and others. The basic goal of these programs is to avoid and/or resolve conflicts before they escalate into serious problems (such as physical confrontations). School programs typically include a strong teaching component in which kids learn that conflict is natural and that it can be managed through various processes. A key component in many programs is peer mediation, in which students are trained to assist one another in resolving disputes in such a way that all parties to the dispute accept the resolution. The growth of programs in the community, and the generally positive evaluations of those programs, have contributed to the establishment of school-based programs.

The Resolving Conflict Creatively Program (RCCP) in New York City included student mediation as a core component of the intervention. This program includes programming in the elementary, secondary, and special education curriculum, as well as a separate parent program (DeJong, 1993). The elementary curriculum consists of 12 lessons dealing with issues of communication, cooperation, feelings, diversity, peacemaking, and resolving conflicts. The entire curriculum (in primary and secondary schools) consists of 51 lessons and includes a heavy reliance on peer mediation and parental involvement. DeJong (1993) reported that students success-fully learn the lessons, are involved in fewer fights, and believe that they can handle problems better as a result of the program. The impact of the program increases with the number of lessons and the quality of the teacher training. Similarly, the Responding in Peaceful and Positive Ways (RIPP) program targets 6th graders, and includes lessons on appropriate responses to conflict situations and how students can avoid violence (Farrell & Meyer, 1997). Evaluations of the program show fewer discipline problems, fewer suspensions from school, and less fighting by students participating in the program. The growth of conflict management/resolution pro-grams in schools remains an important effort in many places, despite the fact that many programs have not undergone rigorous evaluations.

Peer pressure   The Gang Resistance Education and Training (G.R.E.A.T.) Program is a well-known program targeting peer pressure and the tendency for some youths to turn to gangs and gang behavior. Not unlike the Drug Abuse Resistance Education (DARE) program, G.R.E.A.T. is taught by local police officers in middle schools. The original curriculum, consisting of nine lessons, was expanded to 13 one-hour lessons and is presented in middle schools. The thrust of the program is to provide youths with the necessary skills for identifying high-risk situations and resisting the pressure of taking part in gangs and gang activity. Program curricula are also geared toward increasing self-esteem, changing attitudes, addressing peer pressure, and eliminating participation in violent behavior. A key component of G.R.E.A.T. is to teach non-violent conflict resolution techniques to the youths.

The G.R.E.A.T. program has undergone extensive evaluation. A national evaluation shows that participants are more positive about the police, are less positive about gangs, more often use refusal skills they have been taught, are better able to resist peer pressure, and are less involved in gangs (Esbensen *et al.*, 2011). At the same time, the evaluation fails to find a positive impact on delinquent activity.

Anti-bullying efforts   Bullying prevention has become a major initiative in many schools. The most notable program is that of Olweus (1995) and his colleagues. Developed in Norway, the model anti-bullying program is aimed at the entire school and relies on active student, teacher, and parent participation. The program attempts to raise awareness about the problem of bullying, establish rules and regulations governing the behavior and responses to offending, train staff on how to integrate discussions on bullying into the curriculum, requires meetings between parents and teachers, and between bullies and their victims. The program also works with the families of offenders to address the problems outside of school. Based on survey data gathered before the onset of the program and periodically over a two-year follow-up period, Olweus (1995) reported significant reductions in bullying, classroom dis-ruption, and general delinquency. Similar results have been reported in programs in the UK and the US. Based on these results, anti-bullying programs appear promising as a means to prevent both initial aggression and subsequent offending and antisocial behavior. The program is best suited for elementary schools, meaning that early intervention is preferable. The program also requires significant time, training, and effort on behalf of teachers and parents.

Alternative schools

Many school programs are targeted at specific groups of youths, rather than at the entire school. Such programs may seek to remove those having problems from the school or may set up individual classrooms or programs within the school. Alternative schools represent a major attempt to dispel the negative experiences of many problem youths. The basic idea behind alternative schools is the provision of a positive learning atmosphere, which increases feelings of success within an atmosphere of warmth and acceptance (Gold, 1978). The process involves recognizing the needs of the individual student and meeting those needs through interventions such as one-on-one instruction, unstructured grading practices, instruction tailored to the interests of the student, the development of close relationships between students and teachers, the involvement of the students in the instruction process, and advancement based on individual progress.

Although alternative education programs have become commonplace, few evaluations of these schools look at their effect on delinquent behavior, especially acts committed outside of the school. Cox (1999) considered the impact of an alternative school program for middle school students (grades 6–8). Youths attend the program for one semester and then return to their regular school. While at the alternative school, students participate in activities aimed at improving their academic performance and self-esteem, as well as lowering their delinquent behavior. The program evaluation compared students randomly assigned to the alternative school and a control group. The results show an immediate impact on self-esteem and grades. Unfortunately, there is no change in self-reported delinquency, and the positive changes disappear after the subjects return to their regular school. Cox (1999) speculated that a one-semester program may not be long enough to ensure long-term change. Students may need prolonged exposure to the alternative school format.

One meta-analysis suggested that alternative schools have little, if any, impact on delinquency. Cox, Davidson, and Bynum (1995) uncovered some evidence that alternative school programs increase school performance, improve attitudes toward school, and other similar outcomes. Unfortunately, they were unable to find any significant improvement in client delinquency. Compounding these results is the fact that the most methodologically rigorous studies show the least impact, particularly with later reintegration to regular schools. It would appear, therefore, that further study and experimentation with alternative schools is needed before making strong claims for its impact on subsequent delinquent behavior.

Other interventions

A wide range of other interventions are being used to alter youthful behavior in schools. The US Department of Education has initiated the Safe and Drug Free Schools program and the Safe Schools/Healthy Children initiative. These programs incorporate a wide range of interventions based on the wishes of the different school districts, who they include in the planning of programs (e.g., parents, police, etc.), and what programs they decide to implement. Various evaluations of these programs have focused primarily on measuring the extent of victimization and fear in schools, and process evaluations of the implementation of programs. Relatively little comprehensive outcome evaluation has been conducted.

Truancy reduction programs have received increased attention in recent years in many jurisdictions. Many of these efforts involve a combination of picking up truant youths and returning them to school (or taking them into custody) and holding parents accountable for their truant children. Two underlying issues drive most of these efforts. First, removing truants from the street eliminates any offenses those youths might have committed while out of school. The school provides supervision, thereby reducing the level of crime during the school day. Second, reducing truancy should lead to increased educational attainment and higher graduation rates. This should lead to greater chances of (meaningful) employment and fewer chances of turning to crime in the future. Most truancy reduction programs rely on process evaluations, which count the number of youths handled and the methods used to dispose of the cases.

Another common response has been to establish after-school programs for youths. The argument underlying these initiatives is that keeping youths busy and supervised after school mitigates the possibility of them getting into trouble. Indeed, there is clear evidence that youthful offending peaks in the late afternoon and early evening, particularly on school days (Office of Juvenile Justice and Delinquency Prevention, 1999). This argument also underlies the calls for midnight basketball leagues and similar initiatives. A secondary argument used to support many after-school programs reflects the belief that educationally-based programs can increase the academic achievement of participating youths. Interestingly, despite the great interest in these kinds of interventions, almost no evaluation has been conducted.

Summary

A great deal of additional research is needed on school-based prevention programs. While concerted efforts have gone into developing interventions and implementing the projects, relatively little time and effort has gone into assessing the impact of the initiatives on delinquency and youthful misconduct. Most of the evaluations are simple process studies that tell how the program was initiated, who was involved, how many meetings took place, and how much money was spent. What is needed now is to know how much delinquency was averted and to what extent the schools are safer places.

No magic bullet has been found. Schools take a wide range of approaches to preventing crime and addressing youthful misbehavior that may lead to later offending. Focusing attention on schools is an appropriate endeavor for several reasons. First, preventing in-school problems allows the schools to focus on their primary mission of educating youths. Second, teachers have both the training and experience needed to identify problem youths early. Third, the fact that youths are required to attend school means they are a "captive audience" for addressing how to act appropriately, deal with problem behavior, and prepare for future challenges outside of school. Schools need to identify the program that is right for their situation and problems. They also need to build support for the program from across the community, including students, teachers, staff, parents, and the outside community.

References

Agnew, R. (1992). Foundation for a General Strain Theory of crime and delinquency. *Criminology, 30,* 47–87.

Berrueta-Clement, J.R., Schweinhart, L.J., Barnett, W.S., Epstein, A.S., & Weikart, D.P. (1984). *Changed Lives: The Effects of the Perry Preschool Program on Youths Through Age 19.* Ypsilanti, MI: High/Scope Press.

Brady, K.P., Blamer, S., & Phenix, D. (2007). School–police partnership effectiveness in urban schools: An analysis of New York City's impact schools initiative. *Education and Urban Society, 39,* 455–478.

Cohen, A.K. (1955). *Delinquent Boys: The Culture of the Gang.* Glencoe, IL: Free Press.

Cox, S.M. (1999). An assessment of an alternative education program for at-risk delinquent youth. *Journal of Research in Crime and Delinquency, 36,* 323–336.

Cox, S.M., Davidson, W.S., & Bynum, T.S. (1995). A meta-analytic assessment of delinquency-related outcomes of alternative education programs. *Crime and Delinquency, 41,* 219–234.

DeJong, W. (1993). *Building the Peace: The Resolving Conflict Creatively Program (RCCP).* NIJ Program Focus. Washington, DC: Department of Justice.

Esbensen, F., Peterson, D., Taylor, T.J., Freng, A., Osgood, D.W., Carson, D.C., & Matsuda, K.N. (2011). Evaluation and evolution of the gang resistance education and training (G.R.E.A.T.) program. *Journal of School Violence, 10,* 53–70.

Farrell, A.D., & Meyer, A.L. (1997). The effectiveness of a school-based curriculum for reducing violence among urban sixth-grade students. *American Journal of Public Health, 87,* 979–988.

Federal Bureau of Investigation. (2011). *Crime in the United States, 2010.* Washington, DC: Department of Justice. Retrieved from http://www.fbi.gov/ucr

Gold, M. (1978). Scholastic experiences, self-esteem, and delinquent behavior: a theory for alternative schools. *Crime and Delinquency, 24,* 290–308.

Gold, M., & Mann, D. (1972). Delinquency as defense. *American Journal of Orthopsychiatry, 42,* 463–477.

Gottfredson, D.C. (1986). *An Assessment of a Delinquency Prevention Demonstration with Both Individual and Environmental Interventions.* Baltimore: Johns Hopkins University.

Greenberg, M.T., & Kusche, C. (1998). *Promoting Alternative Thinking Strategies (PATHS). Blueprints for Violence Prevention*. Boulder, CO: Institute of Behavioral Science.

Hankin, A., Hertz, M., & Simon, T. (2011). Impacts of metal detector use in schools: Insights from 15 years of research. *Journal of School Health, 81*, 100–106.

Hirschfield, P.J., & Celinska, K. (2011) Beyond fear: Sociological perspectives on the criminalization of school discipline. *Sociology Compass, 5*, 1–12.

Hirschi, T. (1969). *Causes of Delinquency*. Berkeley, CA: University of California Press.

Hirschi, T., & Hindelang, M. (1977). Intelligence and delinquency: a revisionist review. *American Sociological Review, 42*, 571–587.

Kenney, D.J., & Watson, T.S. (1998). *Crime in the Schools: Reducing Fear and Disorder with Student Problem Solving*. Washington, DC: Police Executive Research Forum.

Lab, S.P., & Clark, R.D. (1996). *Discipline, Control and School Crime: Identifying Effective Intervention Strategies. Final Report*. Washington, DC: National Institute of Justice.

Lally, J.R., Mangione, P.L., & Honig, A.S. (1988). The Syracuse University Family Development Research Program: Long-range impact on an early intervention with low-income children and their families. In D.R. Powell, & I.E. Sigel (Eds.), *Parent Education as Early Childhood Intervention: Emerging Direction in Theory, Research, and Practice. Annual Advances in Applied Developmental Psychology* (pp. 79–104). Norwood, NJ: Ablex Publishing Corporation.

Office of Juvenile Justice and Delinquency Prevention (1999). *Violence after School*. Washington, DC: Office of Juvenile Justice and Delinquency Prevention.

Olds, D., Henderson, C.R., Cole, R., Eckenrode, J., Kitzman, H., Luckey, D., …Powers, J. (1998). Long-term effects of nurse home visitation on children's criminal and antisocial behavior: 15 year follow-up of a randomized controlled trial. *Journal of the American Medical Association, 280*, 1238–1244.

Olweus, D. (1995). Bullying or peer abuse at school: Facts and intervention. *Current Directions in Psychological Science, 4*, 196–200.

Polk, K., & Hafferty, D. (1966). School culture, adolescent commitments, and delinquency. *Journal of Research in Crime and Delinquency, 4*, 82–96.

Robers, S., Zhang, J., Truman, J., & Snyder, T.D. (2012). *Indicators of School Crime and Safety, 2011*. Washington, DC: Bureau of Justice Statistics. Retrieved from http://nces.ed.gov/pubs2012/2012002.pdf

SAMHSA (2012). Incredible Years. Retrieved from http://www.nrepp.samhsa.gov/ViewIntervention.aspx?id=93#std174

Schafer, W.E., & Polk, K. (1967). Delinquency and the schools. In *President's Commission on Law Enforcement and the Administration of Justice. Task Force Report: Juvenile Delinquency and Youth Crime*. Washington, DC: US Government Printing Office.

Schweinhart, L.J., Barnes, H.V., & Weikart, D.P. (1993). *Significant Benefits*. Ypsilanti, MI: High/Scope Press.

Travis, L.F., & Coon, J.K. (2005). *The Role of Law Enforcement in Public School Safety: A National Survey*. Washington, DC: National Institute of Justice.

Truman, J.L. (2010). *Criminal Victimization, 2010*. Washington, DC: Bureau of Justice Statistics. Retrieved from http://www.bjs.gov/content/pub/pdf/cv10.pdf

Webster-Stratton, C. (2000). *The Incredible Years: Parent, teacher and child training series. Blueprints for Violence Prevention*. Boulder, CO: University of Colorado.

Webster-Stratton, C., & Hammond, M. (1997). Treating children with early-onset conduct problems: A comparison of child and parent training interventions. *Journal of Consulting and Clinical Psychology, 65,* 93–109.

Wertleib, E.L. (1982). Juvenile delinquency and the schools: a review of the literature. *Juvenile and Family Court Journal, 33,* 15–24.

West, D.J., & Farrington, D.P. (1973). *The Delinquent Way of Life.* New York: Crane Russack.

Wolfgang, M.E., Figlio, R.M., & Sellin, T. (1972). *Delinquency in a Birth Cohort.* Chicago, IL: University of Chicago Press.

24

Neighborhood-based Prevention of Juvenile Delinquency

Abigail A. Fagan and Andrea Lindsey

In recent years, numerous prevention programs have been found to reduce violence, delinquency, and drug use among youth (Sherman, Gottfredson, MacKenzie, Reuter, & Bushway, 1998; US Department of Health and Human Services, 2001). Such interventions have taken many forms, but have in common the goal of reducing risk factors – events, interactions, or conditions associated with an increased likelihood of delinquency – or increasing protective factors – experiences likely to reduce delinquency. By intervening in the processes leading to delinquency, such programs can help reduce the likelihood that youth will become law-breakers (Coie *et al.*, 1993).

While the accumulating number of effective preventive interventions is encouraging, it is also true that the impact of any one intervention is likely to be compromised if the community members and environments in which youth live do not support program goals and activities (Wagenaar & Perry, 1994). Community-based efforts can help to alter this larger environment, by changing features of the community that are related to crime, such as community norms and attitudes and informal actions by adult residents to control delinquency. Whereas individual prevention programs are typically delivered by one agency to a particular population (e.g., middle-school students or parents of children who have displayed behavioral problems), community-based efforts typically involve the coordinated delivery of multiple interventions by multiple agencies (Wandersman & Florin, 2003). The delivery of a set of coordinated activities not only increases the ability to affect multiple risk and protective factors, which should enhance the ability to reduce illegal behavior (Coie *et al.*, 1993), but also improves their ability to reach a majority of the community with services. By saturating the environment with prevention

The Handbook of Juvenile Delinquency and Juvenile Justice, First Edition. Edited by Marvin D. Krohn and Jodi Lane.
© 2015 John Wiley & Sons, Inc. Published 2015 by John Wiley & Sons, Inc.

strategies and messages, targeting multiple risk and protective factors faced in multiple contexts, and altering the larger community environment, community-based efforts have great potential to achieve significant, widespread, and long-lasting reductions in youth substance use, delinquency, and violence (David-Ferdon & Hammond, 2008).

Theoretical Basis for Neighborhood Interventions

Prevention strategies are thought to have the greatest likelihood of success when they are based on theoretical explanations of crime (Coie *et al.*, 1993). Theories outline the causes of crime and processes that increase or decrease the likelihood of illegal behavior. An intervention that is purposefully designed to target these mechanisms should have a better chance of preventing crime than a strategy with no theoretical basis.

Neighborhood-focused preventive activities have tended to be guided by two theoretical perspectives: social disorganization theory and routine activities theory. Social disorganization theory focuses on explaining the ways in which neighborhood context influences adolescent delinquency (Sampson, Raudenbush, & Earls, 1997; Shaw & McKay, 1942). According to empirical data, across time, cultures, and contexts, rates of youth delinquency are not equally distributed across communities; rather, delinquency is highest in communities with structural and social deficits (Shaw & McKay, 1942). In these neighborhoods, structural problems like poverty can increase the likelihood of criminal activities both directly and indirectly, by compromising the social processes that would otherwise protect against youth involvement in crime, such as cohesion between neighborhood residents and the ability of residents to informally control crime (Sampson *et al.*, 1997).

Neighborhood prevention strategies based upon social disorganization theory thus try to minimize or counteract the negative effects of neighborhood poverty and social problems. Because it is difficult to increase employment rates and income levels, more promising strategies may include efforts designed to change community norms regarding delinquency and to increase collaborative actions by residents to prevent delinquency. This chapter will review the effectiveness of these types of approaches in reducing youth crime.

According to routine activities theory (RAT) (Cohen & Felson, 1979), crime is most likely to occur in communities when three conditions are met: there is a motivated offender, a suitable target(s), and an absence of guardians. In this perspective, would-be offenders are thought to engage in rational decision-making processes prior to the commission of a crime. They are more likely to break the law when they perceive the benefits of doing so to be high (e.g., if there is an attractive target) and the consequences to be low (e.g., no visible guardians are present, so the chances of detection and punishment are low). The theory also presumes that most individuals are inherently predisposed to crime; it is the environmental circumstances that determine who will break the law at any given time.

A strength of RAT is that it offers clear and specific guidelines for how to prevent crime. The proposed methods for doing so focus on changing environmental opportunities for crime; thus, such efforts are usually referred to as "place-based" and "environmental" prevention (Lab, 2010). Examples include installing alarm systems in cars or homes, increasing street lighting, and using closed-circuit television (CCTV) to increase surveillance of city streets. The goal is to make targets as unappealing as possible, eliminate opportunities for crime, and increase guardianship and the risk of apprehension. Efforts do not focus on individuals, except by trying to influence one's perceptions of the relative costs and benefits of committing crime. Given this chapter's emphasis on *neighborhood-focused, youth delinquency prevention*, we will not extensively review place-based strategies, which usually focus on areas smaller than a neighborhood (e.g., homes, stores, or buses) and which often do not specifically target youth offending. However, we will discuss the "pulling levers" strategy (Braga & Weisburd, 2012), which is loosely based on RAT, given its goal of reducing illegal behavior in areas known to have a high density of motivated individuals, attractive targets, and absent guardians.

Review of the Literature

Although social disorganization and RAT theories are major criminological perspectives, few comprehensive reviews have examined the effectiveness of interventions based on these perspectives in preventing or reducing youth delinquency. The current chapter seeks to address this gap in the research by reviewing various neighborhood-based attempts to prevent adolescent delinquency. Our coverage is limited to interventions specifically aimed at *youth*. For the most part, we define this group as those aged 0–18 years, but interventions that focus on individuals up to age 25 are also considered. We further restrict our review to strategies that attempt to effect change at the community level – that is, interventions that seek to change environmental conditions and which rely on the active involvement of local residents to do so. The following sections thus discuss the ability of community-based, youth-focused, resident-driven efforts to prevent delinquency.

Changes in local laws and policies

Legal statutes and policies are posited to have direct and indirect effects on youth delinquency. Laws may be enacted to restrict access to illegal drugs or firearms, which make it more difficult for youth to use substances or weapons. They can also increase the costs and/or punishments of illegal behavior, which can deter delinquency if youth perceive these costs to be greater than the benefits of engaging in crime. Finally, by making explicit what is acceptable and unacceptable, laws can alter the normative culture of a community (i.e., residents' attitudes and beliefs regarding what is right and wrong), which in turn can shape youth behavior as posited by social disorganization theory.

The actual ability of legal statutes to reduce youth delinquency has been better established for substance use outcomes than for other types of illegal behaviors. For example, there is evidence that increases in the minimum drinking age (Wagenaar & Toomey, 2002) and monetary taxes on alcohol (Elder *et al.*, 2010) reduce drinking by teenagers. Evaluations of state policies restricting gun ownership (Loftin, McDowall, Wiersema, & Cottey, 1991) and imposing mandatory sentences for offenders convicted of gun-related crimes (McDowall, Loftin, & Wiersema, 1992) have demonstrated significant reductions in firearm-related homicides. However, these evaluations did not differentiate between youth- and adult-perpetrated crimes, thus leaving undetermined whether firearms policies reduce youth delinquency.

The above examples all refer to consequences stemming from the creation and enforcement of state or national laws, not local ordinances. As such, they technically fall outside the scope of this chapter. In contrast, juvenile curfew laws can be enacted at the local level. Typically, curfews restrict youth presence in designated areas of a community at particular times, with some variation across communities in the age(s) to whom these laws apply, the size of the geographical restrictions, and the days/times covered by the laws. A systematic review of ten studies evaluating the effectiveness of curfew laws in communities across the US demonstrated no overall evidence that they reduced juvenile delinquency (Adams, 2003). Most of these evaluations showed no effects at all, while some indicated increases in officially-reported youth crime following the establishment of curfew laws, and a few showed decreases in delinquency rates. Adams (2003) cautioned that evaluations of curfew laws have not been overly rigorous, and emphasized that additional research is needed to determine the effectiveness of curfew laws.

Adams (2003) did indicate the presence of strong public support for curfew laws, and other research has similarly emphasized that local residents often favor the passing of crime-related laws and policies. From a practical standpoint, legal statutes tend to be easier to enact compared with highly structured programs designed and tested by academic researchers, are less expensive to implement, and may be more cost-beneficial given their lower financial costs and greater potential to affect the entire population of youth in a community (given that laws apply to all residents). More research is needed to test the effectiveness of various laws intended to reduce youth crime, and policy-makers may need to think more creatively about how to design and implement such policies, using criminological theory as a guide. Sampson (2011), for example, has advocated the implementation of broad social policies that could affect youth crime as well as other outcomes. Examples of such interventions include staggering school closure times to reduce youth interactions with deviant peers in the absence of adult supervision, and creating mixed-income housing units to avoid the concentration of poverty and violence associated with low-income public housing.

Neighborhood relocation initiatives

One specific example of a creative and broader change effort with the potential to reduce youth crime is helping families move out of poor, dangerous neighborhoods. Recognizing the difficulties of changing neighborhood structural variables like concentrated poverty, but seeking to protect youth from the negative effects of these environments, the Moving to Opportunities initiative provided monetary incentives for families to relocate from highly disadvantaged neighborhoods to safer and higher income areas (Kling, Ludwig, & Katz, 2005). Families living in low-income housing communities in high-poverty areas of five cities (Baltimore, Boston, Chicago, Los Angeles, and New York) were targeted for the study. Approximately 4,600 families, mostly of minority (African-American and Hispanic) race/ethnicity, were then randomly assigned to experimental or control conditions. The former received housing vouchers to move to neighborhoods in which less than 10% of residents had incomes below the poverty level. Six years following the distribution of housing vouchers, when youth were an average age of 19 years old, females whose families were in the intervention group had significantly fewer lifetime arrests for violent and property offenses compared with those in the control group. Among males, no effects on lifetime arrests for violent offenses were found, and those in the intervention group had *more* arrests for property offenses compared with those in the control group (Kling *et al.*, 2005). In addition, the intervention showed reductions in marijuana and alcohol use among females, but not males (Kling, Liebman, & Katz, 2007). These results indicate mixed support for the benefits of helping families to relocate to higher income neighborhoods. For females, the project reduced delinquency; for males, it did not, and some negative outcomes were evidenced among this group, which demonstrates the importance not only of evaluating prevention efforts, but also investigating whether or not they have different effects for different individuals or groups.

Community mobilization using broad-based coalitions

Rather than focusing on structural variables that are difficult to change, other neighborhood-based efforts have sought to alter the social processes that can encourage or discourage youth delinquency, including cultural norms regarding appropriate and inappropriate behavior, social ties between residents, and informal attempts by residents to curb youth delinquency. The last characteristic, referred to as collective efficacy (Sampson *et al.*, 1997), is enhanced when neighborhood residents feel a sense of unity and cohesion, agree upon standards of behavior for adult and youth residents, and are willing to take action to prevent delinquency (e.g., by discouraging youth from skipping school and "hanging out" in the neighborhood).

An early attempt to improve neighborhood social conditions was the Chicago Area Project (CAP), initiated by Clifford Shaw in the early 1930s. This intervention involved the formation of broad-based groups of "natural leaders" (e.g., parents, youth, and adult representatives from local organizations) located in three of the highest-risk areas of Chicago. These coalitions were charged with taking ownership of neighborhood delinquency problems and collectively intervening to reduce youth crime. Importantly, groups were not given any formal instructions about how to intervene. The idea that local residents know what is best for their neighborhood, and that outsiders should not try to impose their own views on communities, provides the foundation for most coalition efforts. However, evaluations of the CAP and some other community mobilization efforts have shown that gathering community residents and asking them to "do their best" to solve crime has not led to desired reductions in delinquency (Bursik & Grasmick, 1993; Fagan & Hawkins, 2012).

These results seem contrary to the tenets of social disorganization theory, as having community stakeholders work collaboratively on actions intended to reduce delinquency should increase collective efficacy and, in turn, reduce crime. However, it is also true that members of the community are unlikely to have access to information regarding the causes or theoretical mechanisms leading to youth crime, nor will they be aware of strategies that have been developed, tested in scientific studies, and demonstrated as effective in reducing delinquency. As a result, coalitions often implement strategies that are easy or popular (e.g., providing afterschool recreational activities for youth or enhancing the physical environment of the community; Bursik & Grasmick, 1993), but which do not target or change the risk or protective factors associated with delinquency. To achieve desired reductions in delinquency, then, community coalitions need to know what works to prevent crime and be supported in their efforts to enact such strategies.

Fortunately, some community mobilization efforts do provide such assistance. To illustrate, the Communities That Care (CTC) prevention system provides structured, step-by-step guidance to community coalitions to help them become aware of and utilize effective delinquency prevention strategies (Hawkins & Catalano, 1992). Through a series of training workshops and ongoing technical assistance, CTC assists community members in: (1) gauging their readiness to engage in collaborative prevention efforts; (2) forming a representative and diverse coalition; (3) collecting and analyzing local data from students regarding their exposure to varied risk and protective factors; (4) selecting interventions that have been tested and shown to reduce risk factors, increase protective factors, and prevent or lower rates of delinquency; and (5) implementing individual-, school-, family- or community-focused interventions that address the specific needs of local youth and which reach as many youth as possible.

Through the completion of these steps, CTC helps foster collective efficacy. Coalition members reach consensus regarding the specific problems to be addressed in their community and agree that countering these problems requires the full and active participation of the community. Just as social disorganization theory recognizes that rates vary across communities, CTC emphasizes that communities differ in the types and levels of risk and protective factors faced by youth, and that different intervention strategies are needed in different communities. Thus, CTC does not mandate that coalitions choose particular interventions to implement. Rather, services are to be community-specific and tailored to the specific needs and circumstances of each community. This type of model is intuitively appealing to community members and should thus increase local support and collective action.

The effectiveness of the CTC system in producing community-wide reductions in youth substance use, delinquency, and violence has been shown in two studies. In a quasi-experimental study involving communities across Pennsylvania, greater reductions in self-reported rates of past-month smoking, drinking, binge drinking, and drug use were found for middle and high school students in cities implementing the CTC system, compared with those in communities not using the model (Feinberg, Greenberg, Osgood, Sartorius, & Bontempo, 2007). Reductions in other illegal behaviors (e.g., property and violent delinquency) favoring students in CTC communities were also found (Feinberg, Jones, Greenberg, Osgood, & Bontempo, 2010). In a randomized evaluation of CTC comparing 12 communities implementing CTC with 12 sites not using the model, the CTC intervention was shown to decrease juveniles' initiation of substance use and delinquency, and to reduce current substance use, delinquency, and violence (Hawkins *et al.*, 2008, 2012).

Evaluations of some other community coalition models have also demonstrated reductions in substance use and/or other types of delinquent behaviors. A review of this literature by the first author (Fagan & Hawkins, 2012) indicated that the specific interventions enacted by coalitions was less important to success than their ability to ensure that prevention efforts targeted risk and protective factors shown in criminological theories to lead to delinquency. Successful efforts tended to involve a coordinated array of programs and practices affecting multiple factors. Notably, the inclusion of school-based interventions appeared particularly likely to lead to success, perhaps because such interventions tend to target particularly influential risk factors (e.g., peer influences) and to reach a large segment of the population with services.

Community policing and neighborhood watch groups

Community policing and neighborhood watch groups can also be used to mobilize community members and seek improvements in collective efficacy. We cover these strategies only briefly, however, because they usually do not have an explicit goal of targeting youth delinquency. Community policing differs from the traditional focus of police activities on pure law *enforcement* and instead focuses on proactive, problem-solving attempts to address the root causes of crime (Lab, 2010). This approach relies on cooperation from community residents, who assist law enforcement officers in efforts to prevent and/or solve crime problems. Better relationships between officers and community members are also fostered through the posting of officers to particular neighborhoods, which allows them greater opportunities to get to know neighborhood residents and better understand local problems and potential resources to address them. Evaluations of community policing efforts have indicated mixed results. While there is evidence that agencies receiving funds for community policing make more arrests and have lower levels of crime (Lab, 2010; Zhao, Scheider, & Thurman, 2002), other reviews have not indicated crime reductions (Bursik & Grasmick, 1993; Weisburd & Eck, 2004). Also, we are not aware of any evaluations that have examined changes in youth crime in particular following the enactment of community policing efforts.

Neighborhood watch groups, like community coalitions, provide a forum for community members to work together to address identified problems and to build a sense of community among neighborhood residents (Lab, 2010). Activities of such groups vary across neighborhoods, but commonly include citizen patrols (e.g., having neighborhood volunteers walk the streets to patrol for crime) and altering the physical environment (e.g., creating more one-way and dead-end streets to make the neighborhood less accessible to strangers). The effectiveness of neighborhood watch groups in reducing crime has not been established, however (Lab, 2010; Sherman *et al.*, 1998). Similar to the results for community coalitions, it may be that neighborhood watch groups that do not alter the risk and protective factors associated with illegal behavior are less able to achieve reductions in delinquency.

The "pulling levers" and "hot spots" approaches to crime prevention

Like the prior strategies, the "pulling levers" crime prevention approach is based on social disorganization theory in that it relies on law enforcement officers and community members to work together to reduce crime. This strategy is also heavily influenced by routine activities theory and the belief that individuals will be deterred from crime when the perceived costs of doing so outweigh the benefits (Braga & Weisburd, 2012). In the pulling levers approach, police officers communicate to potential offenders that they will "pull all available legal levers" when crime occurs, especially violent offenses. That is, they increase the certainty of punishment by actively making arrests for low-level offenses, interfering with gang activities, and advocating to prosecutors for harsher sentences for offenders (Braga & Weisburd, 2012). Communicating that punishment will occur, and ensuring that actions are taken, are expected to deter potential offenders from committing crime.

While not all pulling levers approaches seek to reduce juvenile crime, two programs have prioritized delinquency prevention. Boston's *Operation Ceasefire* was spurred by city leaders' concerns regarding high rates of juvenile homicide and the recognition that much of this crime was committed by a small number of active youth gangs (Braga, Kennedy, Waring, & Piehl, 2001). Determined to reduce youth violence, *Operation Ceasefire* personnel used official forums and informal meetings with gang members to communicate that violent acts would "evoke an immediate and intense response" from law enforcement (Braga *et al.*, 2001, p. 200). These threats were backed up by police crackdowns aimed at disrupting gang activities. An evaluation of the initiative showed a 63% decrease in the monthly number of homicides that involved youth (those aged 24 and younger) following implementation of the program (Braga *et al.*, 2001). The success was credited not just to law enforcement efforts, but also to community members, who helped reinforce messages that violence was not acceptable (thereby changing community norms regarding crime), and offered social services to those at risk of committing violent crimes.

The success of *Operation Ceasefire* encouraged other cities to take similar steps to reduce crime. In Pittsburgh, the *One Vision One Life* program was begun by citizens concerned about violence and homicides, especially those involving youth, and community residents were active participants in this initiative. Project activities were coordinated by local community leaders, who were selected based on their knowledge of the neighborhoods targeted for the project and because they had prior experience with the criminal justice system as "victims, perpetrators, gang members, prisoners, or addicts" (Wilson, Chermak, & McGarrell, 2010). These individuals were trained in conflict resolution, mediation, and culturally sensitive outreach methods, then charged with gathering neighborhood-specific information that could be used to prevent violence, offering social services to at-risk youth (e.g., help finding a job or getting treatment services), and defusing disputes that might otherwise lead to violent altercations (Wilson *et al.*, 2010). While community coordinators used their discretion to identify high-risk individuals, they also sought input from other neighborhood residents and leaders to find potential clients, which gave all residents the opportunity to be involved in the program. Additionally, community coordinators tried to collaborate with local businesses, organizations, and residents so that the neighborhood could move towards a more unified set of values (Wilson *et al.*, 2010).

Despite its goals of increasing community collaboration and collective action, an evaluation of *One Vision One Life* showed no overall effect on official rates of violent crime (Wilson & Chermak, 2011). The authors speculated that the lack of success may have been due to poor implementation, as the activities of coordinators were not carefully monitored and may have lacked sufficient frequency to impact targeted outcomes. The evaluators further cautioned that strategies effective in one city (i.e., Boston) may not easily transfer to another city (i.e., Pittsburgh).

While the results of the One Vision program were disappointing, a meta-analysis that analyzed the combined impact of 11 programs utilizing the pulling levers framework (including the Pittsburgh and Boston initiatives) were more promising (Braga & Weisburd, 2012). Although there was variation in outcomes across programs, the overall effect was a reduction in crime rates. However, not all initiatives focused on youth crime, and the authors cautioned that more research and better evaluation procedures were needed to more firmly establish the effectiveness of this strategy.

An element incorporated into many of the pulling levers approaches that has been shown to be effective at reducing crime is "hot spots policing" (Braga, Papachristos, & Hureau, 2012). In this law enforcement strategy, crime data are analyzed to indicate areas of a community in which crime rates are particularly elevated. Law enforcement efforts, such as increased patrol, problem-oriented policing, and focused drug enforcement, are then concentrated on these specific areas (Braga *et al.*, 2012). While a promising strategy, hot spots policing focuses on offenders and victims of all ages, and its ability to affect youth crime in particular has not been established.

Summary of the literature

This review of community-based prevention strategies has indicated that such actions can take many different forms. This variety is considered a major strength of the approach, as strategies can be tailored to the particular needs of a community. A drawback, however, is that it is challenging to pinpoint the particular elements associated with success in reducing delinquency.

Based on the evidence reviewed, it appears that effectiveness of community-based prevention is enhanced when efforts seek to alter the risk and protective factors identified in criminological theory and established by empirical research to affect substance use and delinquency. When community members are made aware of this information and are well supported in their efforts to change these factors, they are more likely to see results. It is also desirable to implement strategies that change aspects of the community itself, including interactions between residents or between community stakeholders and law enforcement officers, and the beliefs and attitudes (i.e., norms) espoused by community members. However, efforts that focus only on adults – such as community policing strategies and neighborhood watch groups – are less effective than actions that simultaneously alter adult and youth residents, such as prevention activities coordinated by community coalitions.

This review has also indicated that there is much to be learned regarding the effectiveness of community-based prevention efforts. Some strategies have produced mixed evidence of success, some have not been well evaluated, and some have not been evaluated to determine effects on youth crime. In the following two sections, we identify challenges that may impede local efforts to successfully prevent youth crime, and we recommend additional actions needed to overcome some of these challenges and improve our understanding of how to impact youth delinquency using community-based approaches.

Challenges of Community-based Approaches

As summarized in Table 24.1, community-based prevention services have many advantages and offer much promise for preventing and reducing juvenile delinquency, but they are not easy to implement, evaluate, or sustain. The difficulties faced in engaging community members in collaborative prevention activities have been widely noted (Bursik & Grasmick, 1993). Even when coalition members share a concern or goal, such as reducing delinquency, it can be difficult to create and maintain a strong commitment to this cause, especially when relying on volunteers with limited time and resources. It is also challenging to ensure cohesion and collaboration among

Table 24.1   Challenges and benefits of neighborhood-based delinquency prevention approaches

Potential challenges	Potential benefits
Ensuring full and sustained engagement of community members	Increases collaboration between community members and research scientists
Ensuring that multiple interventions are implemented fully and with high quality	Targets community-level structural and social factors associated with youth delinquency
High financial and human costs given the increased scope of services	Increases collaboration and collective action across diverse community members
Lack of a natural "home" from which activities are coordinated and overseen	Ensures that services are coordinated across multiple agencies
Conducting high-quality evaluations of the effectiveness of the intervention	Fosters community ownership of prevention initiatives
• Recruiting multiple communities to participate	Addresses multiple risk and protective factors
• Measuring community-level processes which cannot be directly observed	Allows interventions to be tailored to the specific needs of the community
• Assessing the effectiveness of activities that vary across communities	Reaches a large proportion of the population in the community with services

coalition members who come from diverse backgrounds and who may have different skills, needs, and resources. Membership turnover is likely to occur, which further complicates the ability to maintain focus, commitment, and support. All of these problems may be exacerbated in urban areas where crime rates are highest and prevention efforts most needed (Bursik & Grasmick, 1993; Lab, 2010).

Even when strong coalitions exist, obstacles will arise when groups attempt to enact prevention services. Ensuring the adoption and high-quality implementation of a single prevention strategy is difficult, and problems are likely to be multiplied when adopting multiple programs, implemented in numerous settings by many service providers (Wandersman & Florin, 2003). Compared with single prevention programs, offering an array of services will also be costlier to implement, though it should be noted that coalitions can pool skills and resources across multiple agencies, which should produce economies of scale.

From a methodological standpoint, it can be difficult to evaluate the effectiveness of community-based delinquency prevention strategies, which may be why relatively few effective models exist. Because such interventions are enacted at a community level, well-designed evaluations require multiple communities, which can then be assigned to intervention and control conditions. As with any research project, recruiting subjects is time-consuming, and securing agreement from entire *communities* will likely be much more difficult than asking individuals to participate in a study. Compared with individual characteristics, it may be more challenging to measure and assess change in community-level processes and changes, particularly social conditions such as "collaboration" and "collective efficacy", which cannot be directly observed (Leventhal & Brooks-Gunn, 2000; Wandersman & Florin, 2003). Relatedly, many community-based interventions involve multiple strategies or components, some of which take different forms in different communities. While this flexibility may be appealing to community residents, it can be problematic for evaluators, who will struggle to identify the critical underlying processes and mechanisms that produce changes (Lab, 2010).

Recommendations for Research, Practice and Policy

In the final section of this chapter, we propose recommendations for researchers, policy-makers, and practitioners that will help advance our understanding of community-based delinquency prevention strategies and increase their use in communities.

Research scientists

Although challenging work, it is necessary that researchers strive to develop and evaluate additional models of community-based prevention. Compared with prevention programs in other domains (e.g., schools and families), there are relatively few models of effective community-level interventions. In practice, this means that communities wishing to address youth crime collectively have few science-based options for doing so. In the absence of model programs, community residents will be more likely to spend time and resources on strategies which may not lead to change, which in turn will lead to discouragement, frustration, and skepticism in the ability of science to solve real-world problems.

More effective community-based models are thus needed. Future evaluation efforts should not only assess the overall effectiveness of community-change efforts, but also identify the specific components of the interventions that are most closely linked with reductions in delinquency, so that we can improve our understanding of the ways in which community processes contribute to the development and prevention of juvenile delinquency. More specific information regarding a program's core components will also provide guidance to community members, helping them better understand which elements can and should be adapted or tailored to meet their local needs, and which principles must remain in place in order to ensure maximum effectiveness.

The benefits of "community-based participatory research" (CBPR) when designing and testing prevention models has been emphasized (Israel, Schultz, Parker, & Becker, 1998), and this type of approach is particularly relevant for community-based prevention models. CBPR calls for stronger relationships and true partnerships between researchers and community residents/practitioners. Both groups are asked to listen to and learn from one another, and to work collaboratively in creating and testing interventions (Bursik & Grasmick, 1993; Wandersman & Florin, 2003). While scientists can contribute valuable information regarding the known precursors of substance use and delinquency, and skills in designing evaluations to determine program effectiveness, community members provide much needed background and information regarding local culture and norms, politics, available resources, and decision-making processes, all of which are necessary for the successful adoption and implementation of new initiatives (Israel *et al.*, 1998).

One example of a community-based initiative that embraces the philosophy of academic/practitioner partnerships, as well as the need to enact strategies based on scientific information regarding the causes of crime, is the *Promise Neighborhoods* program (Komro, Flay, Biglan, & Consortium, 2011). This approach relies on partnerships between scientific experts, who compile information about effective interventions to reduce youth problem behaviors, and residents of high-poverty neighborhoods, who provide expert and insider information on the operations of their own communities. These groups collaborate to enact multiple, coordinated prevention strategies focused on improving the lives of high-risk children and their families. Such interventions include strategies and specific programs previously tested and shown to be effective in reducing risk factors, enhancing protective factors, and fostering healthy development, especially among low-income youth and families. These include, for example, interventions that provide support and information to new parents regarding effective child-rearing practices, high-quality early childhood educational opportunities, and social skills training to foster more positive peer relationships (Komro *et al.*, 2011).

Practitioners and local community members

Community-based prevention efforts will not succeed if a substantial proportion of community residents are unwilling to work together to reduce delinquency, or if their enthusiasm wanes quickly and collective action cannot be sustained. A potential solution to this problem is for communities to set aside financial resources to support a part- or full-time staff person to coordinate coalition activities, as advocated in the Communities That Care model (Hawkins & Catalano, 1992). Coordinators should have diverse skill sets, including the ability to facilitate meetings, encourage collaboration, foster joint decision-making, and delegate tasks, as well as high levels of enthusiasm for the mission, all of which are necessary for engendering support among coalition members. Additional leadership may be required, such as a coalition chairperson, who can assist in facilitating meetings, promoting a sense of ownership for coalition activities among members, providing meaningful opportunities for participation, and creating a climate of cohesion and joint decision-making.

Coalition staff may also serve as direct liaisons to academic researchers to foster community/researcher partnerships. In this role, they can learn more about the criminological theories underlying change efforts and the processes expected to influence delinquency. In turn, they can help monitor coalition activities to ensure that these critical elements are delivered and that implementation proceeds as planned.

Unlike school-based prevention programs, community-based models have no natural "home" in the community from which to conduct activities. Thus, it is recommended that communities identify early on an existing organization that can employ the coordinator, provide meeting space, and/or help to supervise prevention activities. Without such infrastructure, the coalition is likely to be short-lived.

Policy-makers

Our primary recommendation for policy-makers is to provide financial assistance to communities to encourage the use of effective community-based prevention strategies. The provision of resources is arguably more critical to the success of community-based initiatives than other types of strategies, given the lack of a natural home agency for these efforts. Fortunately, a variety of federally funded initiatives have been implemented or are planned for the future. We share some examples to indicate the scope of what is possible, and we encourage the continuation and expansion of these types of funding streams to support community-based prevention.

- In 2012, the **Bureau of Justice Assistance's (BJA)** *Project Safe Neighborhoods* program awarded 13 communities nearly US$4 million ($150,000 to $500,000 each) to enact neighborhood-based programs aimed at reducing gun crime and gang activities. Although not specifically focused on youth crime, this initiative called for the creation of local partnerships between community stakeholders and law enforcement to implement locally relevant and evidence-based policing strategies to combat violent crime.
- The **Center for Disease Control** has sponsored the creation of *Academic Centers for Excellence* (ACE) in communities identified at high risk for youth violence. The Center helps such communities implement multiple, coordinated prevention strategies that target factors related to youth violence. In 2010 and 2011, six ACE sites received approximately US$5.2 million. Also funded by the CDC, the *Striving To Reduce Youth Violence Everywhere* (STRYVE) initiative provides funding to community-based coalitions to implement comprehensive, evidence-based youth violence prevention strategies. In 2011, four local health departments received five-year grants totaling US$4.5 million.
- The **Office of Juvenile Justice and Delinquency Prevention's (OJJDP)** *Community-Based Violence Prevention Demonstration Program* is aimed at reducing violent crime. Although it does not specifically focus on youth violence, grantees must focus preventive interventions "on the high-risk activities

and behaviors of a small number of carefully selected members of the community who are likely to be involved in violent activities, specifically gun violence" – a group likely to include juveniles. A total of US$2.2 million was awarded to communities in 2011 and an additional US$6 million were awarded in 2012.

- The **Office of National Drug Control Policy's (ONDCP)** *Drug Free Communities* grants assist community coalitions in enacting programs aimed at preventing youth substance use. Since 1997, awards have been made to over 2,000 coalitions across the US. In 2012, 60 new communities received funding totaling US$ 7.9 million.
- The **Substance Use and Mental Health Services Administration (SAMHSA)** has awarded nearly every state funding to be used by local communities to prevent youth substance use. The *Strategic Prevention Framework State Incentive Grant (SPF SIG)* program requires that communities conduct needs assessments to identify locally-specific problems, develop strategic plans to address these issues, and implement evidence-based programs, policies, and practices to reduce risk factors and promote protective factors related to youth alcohol and drug use.

That so many community-based initiatives have already been funded by various federal agencies indicates that policy-makers do consider such efforts to be important. We hope that these programs are continued and even expanded in future years. Only by spreading the use of effective practices can substantial reductions be evidenced and healthy youth development fostered nationally.

References

Adams, K. (2003). The effectiveness of juvenile curfews at crime prevention. *Annals of the American Academy of Political and Social Science, 587,* 136–159.

Braga, A.A., Kennedy, D.M., Waring, E.J., & Piehl, A.M. (2001). Problem-oriented policing, deterrence, and youth violence: An evaluation of Boston's Operation Ceasefire. *Journal of Research in Crime and Delinquency, 38*(3), 195–225.

Braga, A.A., Papachristos, A.V., & Hureau, D. (2012). *Hot Spots Policing Effects on Crime. Campbell Systematic Reviews.* Oslo, Norway: The Campbell Collaboration.

Braga, A.A., & Weisburd, D.L. (2012). The effects of focused deterrence strategies on crime: A systematic review and meta-analysis of the empirical evidence. *Journal of Research in Crime and Delinquency, 49*(3), 323–358.

Bursik, R.J., & Grasmick, H.G. (1993). *Neighborhoods and Crime.* New York: Macmillan.

Cohen, L.E., & Felson, M. (1979). Social change and crime rate trends: A routine activity approach. *American Sociological Review, 44,* 588–608.

Coie, J.D., Watt, N.F., West, S.G., Hawkins, J.D., Asarnow, J.R., Marman, H.J., *et al.* (1993). The science of prevention: A conceptual framework and some directions for a national research program. *American Psychologist, 48*(10), 1013–1022.

David-Ferdon, C., & Hammond, W.R. (2008). Community mobilization to prevent youth violence and to create safer communities. *American Journal of Preventive Medicine, 34*(3S), S1–2.

Elder, R.W., Lawrence, B., Ferguson, A., Naimi, T.S., Brewer, R.D., Chattopadhyay, S., ... the Task Force on Community Preventive Services. (2010). The effectiveness of tax policy interventions for reducing excessive alcohol consumption and related harms. *American Journal of Preventive Medicine, 38*(2), 217–229.

Fagan, A.A., & Hawkins, J.D. (2012). Community-based substance use prevention. In B.C. Welsh, & D.F. Farrington (Eds.), *Oxford Handbook on Crime Prevention* (pp. 247–268). New York: Oxford University Press.

Feinberg, M.E., Greenberg, M.T., Osgood, D.W., Sartorius, J., & Bontempo, D. (2007). Effects of the Communities That Care model in Pennsylvania on youth risk and problem behaviors. *Prevention Science, 8*(4), 261–270.

Feinberg, M.E., Jones, D., Greenberg, M.T., Osgood, D.W., & Bontempo, D. (2010). Effects of the Communities That Care model in Pennsylvania on change in adolescent risk and problem behaviors. *Prevention Science, 11*, 163–171.

Hawkins, J.D., Brown, E.C., Oesterle, S., Arthur, M.W., Abbott, R.D., & Catalano, R.F. (2008). Early effects of Communities That Care on targeted risks and initiation of delinquent behavior and substance use. *Journal of Adolescent Health, 43*(1), 15–22.

Hawkins, J.D., & Catalano, R.F.J. (1992). *Communities that Care: Action for Drug Abuse Prevention*. San Francisco, CA: Jossey-Bass Publishers.

Hawkins, J.D., Oesterle, S., Brown, E.C., Monahan, K.C., Abbott, R.D., Arthur, M.W., & Catalano, R.F. (2012). Sustained decreases in risk exposure and youth problem behaviors after installation of the Communities That Care prevention system in a randomized trial. *Archives of Pediatrics and Adolescent Medicine, 166*(2), 141–148.

Israel, B.A., Schultz, A.J., Parker, E.A., & Becker, A.B. (1998). Review of community-based research: Assessing partnership approaches to improve public health. *American Review of Public Health, 19*, 173–202.

Kling, J.R., Liebman, J.B., & Katz, L.F. (2007). Experimental analysis of neighborhood effects. *Econometrica, 75*(1), 83–119.

Kling, J.R., Ludwig, J., & Katz, L.F. (2005). Neighborhood effects on crime for female and male youth: Evidence from a randomized housing voucher experiment. *Quarterly Journal of Economics, 120*, 87–130.

Komro, K., Flay, B.R., Biglan, A., & Consortium, P.N.R. (2011). Creating nurturing environments: A science-based framework for promoting child health and development within high-poverty neighborhoods. *Clinical Child and Family Psychology Review, 14*, 111–134.

Lab, S.P. (2010). *Crime Prevention: Approaches, Practices, and Evaluations*. New Providence, NJ: Anderson Publishing Company.

Leventhal, T., & Brooks-Gunn, J. (2000). The neighborhoods they live in: The effects of neighborhood residence on child and adolescent outcomes. *Psychological Bulletin, 126*(2), 309–337.

Loftin, C., McDowall, D., Wiersema, B., & Cottey, T.J. (1991). Effects of restrictive licensing of handguns on homicide and suicide in the District of Columbia. *New England Journal of Medicine, 325*, 1615–1620.

McDowall, D., Loftin, C., & Wiersema, B. (1992). A comparative study of the preventive effects of mandatory sentencing laws for gun crimes. *Journal of Criminal Law and Criminology 83*(2), 378–398.

Sampson, R.J. (2011). The community. In J.Q. Wilson, & J. Petersilia (Eds.), *Crime and Public Policy* (pp. 210–236). New York: Oxford University Press.

Sampson, R.J., Raudenbush, S.W., & Earls, F. (1997). Neighborhoods and violent crime: A multilevel study of collective efficacy. *Science, 277,* 918–924.

Shaw, C.R., & McKay, H.D. (1942). *Juvenile Delinquency and Urban Areas.* Chicago: University of Chicago Press.

Sherman, L.W., Gottfredson, D.C., MacKenzie, D., Reuter, P., & Bushway, S. (1998). *Preventing Crime: What Works, What Doesn't, What's Promising.* Washington, DC: National Institute of Justice.

US Department of Health and Human Services. (2001). *Youth Violence: A Report of the Surgeon General.* Rockville, MD: US Department of Health and Human Services, Centers for Disease Control and Prevention, National Center for Injury Prevention and Control; Substance Abuse and Mental Health Services Administration, Center for Mental Health Services; National Institutes of Health, National Institute of Mental Health.

Wagenaar, A.C., & Perry, C.L. (1994). Community strategies for the reduction of youth drinking: Theory and application. *Journal of Research on Adolescence, 4* (2), 319–345.

Wagenaar, A.C., & Toomey, T.L. (2002). Effects of minimum drinking age laws: Review and analyses of the literature from 1960 to 2000. *Journal of Studies on Alcohol, 14S,* 206–225.

Wandersman, A., & Florin, P. (2003). Community intervention and effective prevention. *American Psychologist, 58*(6–7), 441–448.

Weisburd, D.L., & Eck, J.E. (2004). What can police do to reduce crime, disorder, and fear? *Annals of the American Academy of Political and Social Science, 593,* 42–65.

Wilson, J.M., & Chermak, S. (2011). Community-driven violence reduction programs: Examining Pittsburgh's One Vision One Life. *Criminology and Public Policy, 10*(4), 993–1027.

Wilson, J.M., Chermak, S., & McGarrell, E.F. (2010). *Community-based violence prevention: An assessment of Pittsburgh's One Vision One Life program.* Washington, DC: National Institute of Justice.

Zhao, Z., Scheider, M.C., & Thurman, Q. (2002). Funding community policing to reduce crime: Have COPS grants made a difference? *Criminology and Public Policy, 2*(1), 7–32.

25

Policing Juvenile Delinquency

Reveka V. Shteynberg and Allison D. Redlich

Police officers are tasked with the dual responsibilities of protecting youth while also preventing, intervening, and investigating delinquent and criminal acts. As a result, police who deal with juveniles often experience a role conflict because acting as a law enforcer can be incongruent with protecting kids and helping them avoid trouble (Bazemore & Senjo, 1997). To that end, the present chapter will discuss the police–youth relationship as it relates to delinquency and crime. We will additionally examine perceptions of, and attitudes towards, police officers fulfilling multiple roles in connection with juvenile delinquency.

Although media primarily portrays "crime fighting" at the forefront of police work, most day-to-day police work involves order-maintenance and problem-solving (Hurst, Frank, & Browning, 2000). Police officers devote much of their time to providing services to juveniles and the community, aiming to reduce crime and delinquency through prevention and intervention methods. Although these methods can help reduce crime, police still must fulfill their role as law enforcers to maintain order and protect surrounding communities. To ensure appropriate identification and future prosecution of delinquents and criminals, police must proceed with a formal criminal investigation into specific criminal acts.

Police have many responsibilities in their roles to protect and serve, which we group into the following three discussions: (1) crime prevention; (2) crime intervention; and (3) crime investigation. Before delving into these three roles, we first discuss characteristics of juvenile delinquents and police practices.

The Handbook of Juvenile Delinquency and Juvenile Justice, First Edition. Edited by Marvin D. Krohn and Jodi Lane.
© 2015 John Wiley & Sons, Inc. Published 2015 by John Wiley & Sons, Inc.

Who are Juvenile Delinquents?

When addressing the question "Who are juvenile delinquents?", the answer can come in many forms, including descriptions of their demographic and crime characteristics, their developmental and legal capabilities, and how the public and police perceive them. Research on juvenile delinquency finds that minorities and economically disadvantaged males are overwhelmingly represented as suspected offenders in the criminal justice system. First, minority youth are significantly more likely to be arrested than non-minority juveniles, and report being stopped and harassed on a regular basis by police, more so than Caucasian youth (Cheurprakobkit, 2000). Specifically, minority youth are at increased risk of being police targets of abusive language and being detained, just to be told to "move on" (Gau & Brunson, 2010; Jackson, 2002; McAra & McVie, 2005). In addition, simply being from a disadvantaged neighborhood puts young black men at a higher risk of police suspicion of criminal activity (Whitehead & Lab, 2013).

Second, in comparison to males, females engage in much less crime and juvenile delinquency than males, although females are becoming increasingly more involved in the criminal justice system. According to the Federal Bureau of Investigation (2006), the arrests of girls increased whereas the arrests of boys decreased nationwide between 1980 and 2005. These arrest statistics can be interpreted in two possible ways: these increasing arrests indicate a real change in female behaviors but not male behaviors, and/or these arrests have increased as a result of changes in public attitudes, policy, and law enforcement toward female delinquency and violence (Zahn *et al.*, 2008). Interestingly, there is some support for an age–gender relationship for arrest; younger female suspects have been found more likely to be arrested than older females, a pattern which does not emerge for boys (Visher, 1983).

A third way to characterize juvenile delinquents is by the offenses they commit. According to the Uniform Crime Report (UCR), of 13.7 million annual arrests, 1.16 million are youths under the age of 18, not including neglect or traffic cases (Federal Bureau of Investigation, 2010). Although it may not appear so to the public, juvenile offenders commit far more status offenses (e.g., truancy, curfew law violations, and running away from home) than violent or serious criminal offenses (Federal Bureau of Investigation, 2010). For example, juveniles most often have their first police encounter for traffic-related offenses (e.g., speeding accidents and violations) (Durose, Smith, & Langan, 2007; Liederbach, 2007) and are more likely than adults to become targets of police force and to be arrested or issued citations (than warnings) during traffic stops (Engel, 2000). However, there is some evidence that arresting juveniles for minor offenses can lead to more delinquency compared with informal handling (Klein, 1986).

Finally, recent developmental research has painted a picture of juvenile delinquents as immature and impulsive decision-makers. Youths aged 13 to 18 – regardless of their delinquent status – often lack the judgmental maturity to make decisions that reflect their own preferences or to act in their own best interests rather than make coerced or peer-based decisions (Reppucci, 1999). Cauffman and Steinberg

(2000) found that adolescents aged 14 to 17 display less responsibility, temperance, and perspective than college students aged 18 to 21, young adults aged 22 to 27, or adults aged 28 to 49. Further, research on adolescent culpability establishes that youths' decision-making processes are highly susceptible to psychosocial influences and should therefore result in reduced criminal responsibility in the legal system (Modecki, 2008). And although individual variations exist, researchers argue that a categorical approach to handling of youths' diminished responsibility would be far more efficient and practical than an assessment of individual youths' maturity on a case-by-case basis (Steinberg & Scott, 2003). However, as we describe in the section on Perceptions of juvenile delinquents, the public holds many misperceptions of youthful offenders, perceptions that have greatly shaped policy.

Perceptions of juvenile delinquents

In the latter part of the twentieth century, crime was on the rise, and the public was led to believe that the rise was a result of an increase in violent young offenders. Younger suspects received more coverage in the media than their older counterparts (Pizarro, Chermak, & Gruenewald, 2007). Youth receiving the most media attention are usually the ones alleged to have committed crimes using the most "heinous modes" (e.g., involving guns or multiple victims) and involving the most extreme "motives" (e.g., child abuse and mental health issues). One response to the public's perception of a rise in juvenile crime was to label them as "super-predators", refer-ring to the most violent youth as a "new breed" of offenders. Specifically, Dilulio and colleagues wrote: "America is now home to thickening ranks of juvenile 'super-predators' – radically impulsive, brutally remorseless youngsters, including ever more pre-teenage boys, who murder, assault, rape, rob, burglarize, deal deadly drugs, join gun-toting gangs and create serious communal disorders" (Bennett, Dilulio, & Walters, 1996, p. 27).

However, predictions concerning juveniles as the most violent offenders were not realized. In fact, only 4% of juvenile arrests in 2009 were for violent offenses, whereas non-violent and status offenses accounted for 77.8%, or just over three-quarters, of all juvenile arrests. Moreover, according to the UCR, juvenile arrests have decreased by 8.9% from 2008 to 2009, and by 20.2% since 2000 for all crimes. In 2009, youths accounted for 14.1% of all arrests and 24.6% of property crime arrests (Federal Bureau of Investigation, 2010). Nonetheless, in 2003, 59% of US citizens believed violent juvenile offenders between 14 and 17 years of age should be treated the same as adults, while only 32% believed that they should be treated more leniently than adults in the criminal justice system (Maguire, 2003). The literature on juvenile jus-tice reflects two opposing ideologies about what juveniles are capable of as it relates to policing delinquency and crime. One the one hand, there is consensus that juve-niles who commit crimes are violating age norms and roles and should thus be treated more punitively by police and the legal system. On the other hand, there is the more recent recognition that youth are not fully mature, which in turn affects their capabilities in the legal system. By identifying the two opposing viewpoints of juveniles as that of violent and heinous "super-predators" versus that of immature adolescents with diminished responsibility and competence, police officers can exercise more informed discretion in crime-related matters and improve police–youth dynamics through more effective crime prevention, intervention, and investigation strategies.

Policing Delinquency

Police officers and law enforcement officers are the gatekeepers to the criminal justice system. Juvenile adjudication is based almost exclusively on police discretion to arrest and file charges against juvenile suspects that then make them defendants (Feld, 2013). Over time, police handling of juveniles has gone through several discrete phases. During the nineteenth and early twentieth centuries in the US, police often informally handled disputes involving youths by counseling them, returning them to their parents, or referring them to community resources or programs (Walker & Katz, 2005). These informal practices stemmed from the general public perception that youths were immature and were incapable of rational decision-making or malicious intent. Juvenile delinquency was believed to be a problem of poor parenting and growing up in disruptive homes (Myers, 2002).

The early to mid-twentieth century brought the Political Policing Era, which focused on handling youths through rehabilitation and treatment. Police often opted to use their discretion for more informal sanctions, unless it was to deter youths from committing additional offenses (Walker & Katz, 2005). Since arresting and treating a youth for a crime labels them as a "criminal" or "juvenile delinquent", police often wanted to avoid a self-fulfilling prophecy and chose to avoid formal sanctions when possible and deemed to be in the best interest of the youth. An emphasis on controlling and preventing juvenile crime came about during the Professional Policing Era in the late twentieth century. As noted in the "Who are Juvenile Delinquents?" section, the perception of a rise in juvenile crime increased public fear of these youths and switched the focus to youth crime prevention strategies (Walker, 1977). Specifically, police agencies created specialized youth crime prevention and intervention units and programs to handle youth-specific offenses (Fashola, 2002).

The current period of policing, sometimes referred to as the Community Era, combines an emphasis on youth crime prevention measures with using strict enforcement of law through formal sanctions (Myers, 2002). Regardless, police discretion remains mostly hidden and the decision to arrest includes the decision to hold or release youthful offenders (Whitehead & Lab, 2013). Since youth tend to be involved in less serious offenses, both urban and non-urban police typically opt to fulfill their roles as "gatekeepers" by resolving such matters informally without arrest (Gau & Brunson, 2010; Liederbach, 2007). This discretion is reflected in all three aspects of police–juvenile interactions: crime prevention, intervention, and investigation (Hurst *et al.*, 2000).

Preventing Juvenile Crime

Crime prevention is a results-oriented approach that focuses on reducing crime through preemptive measures. The crime prevention practices discussed in this section will focus on school-, family-, and community-based programs. Crime prevention programs, particularly programs that capture youth at a young age, have been shown to successfully prevent crime (Sherman *et al.*, 1998). Although crime prevention has previously been operationalized to include law enforcement and preventing crime at places through order-maintenance (Myers, 2002; Sherman *et al.*, 1998), we distinguish these practices as crime intervention and discuss them in the next section.

Police–youth crime prevention practices aim to reduce and prevent crime through interactive programs between youths, police, schools, families, and communities. School-based crime prevention practices include peer and group counseling and gang resistance, anti-bullying, and law-related education, and tend to focus on improving school discipline and social problem-solving skills (Sherman *et al.*, 1998). Family-based crime prevention practices involve education programs to improve family relationships, parent training for managing troublesome youths, and family violence prevention and intervention practices (Sherman *et al.*, 1998). Community-based crime prevention practices use community-based mentoring and after-school recreation programs to mobilize against crime by keeping juveniles off the streets (Sherman *et al.*, 1998).

Empirical studies suggest that unstructured socializing among youth increases the likelihood of their delinquency; youth who engage in highly structured school and positive social institutional activities are less likely to become involved in delinquent behaviors (Mahoney & Stattin, 2000). Police, tasked with crime prevention as part of their law enforcement duties, aim to increase future police–youth cooperation, interaction, and perceptions and attitudes, as well decrease and prevent delinquency and crime from a young age. Although many of these police–youth groups target individuals in different capacities, many of them have educational components. Some of the most widespread and well-known police–youth crime prevention programs include Drug Abuse Resistance Education (DARE), Gang Resistance Education and Training (GREAT), and the Police Athletic/Activities League, Inc. (PAL). DARE and GREAT are both educational programs and PAL is an after-school program. DARE focuses on school-based crime prevention, GREAT incorporates school-based crime prevention with family-based crime prevention, and PAL uses community-based crime prevention.

DARE was founded in 1983 in Los Angeles to teach youths the skills to avoid drugs, gangs, and violence. DARE views itself as a "police officer-led series of classroom lessons that teaches children from kindergarten through 12th Grade how to resist peer pressure and live productive drug and violence-free lives" (see www.dare.com). It typically ranges from a 10-week to a 17-week core curriculum and is now taught in 43 countries and in 75% of the school districts in the US (Ennett, Tobler, Ringwalt, & Flewelling, 1994; www.dare.com). Police officers undergo 80–120 hours of special training in the DARE curriculum, which includes classroom management practices, techniques for teaching, communication skills specific to youth, and child development. DARE is intended to benefit local communities by "humanizing" the police to youths, to open up lines of communication, and to ensure that youths see police officers in a "helping role" rather than just an "enforcement role". In addition, DARE is meant to create a dialogue between youths, parents, schools, and the police. Despite widespread usage of DARE programs, a recent meta-analysis of research evaluating its effectiveness has concluded that DARE is ineffective in deterring youth from using drugs (Ennett *et al.*, 1994; West & O'Neal, 2004). Rosenbaum (2007, p. 815) goes so far as to suggest "Just Say No to DARE" because of its lack of effectiveness.

The GREAT Program, developed in 1991 by the Phoenix Police Department, is a school-based classroom curriculum for middle-school students about gang and violence prevention. It is a 13-session long instructional program that focuses on crime prevention, taught by uniformed law enforcement officers (see www.great-online. org). Law enforcement officers undergo a comprehensive 60-hour training course that provides them with current gang trend information and teaches officers the structure and content of the GREAT curriculum (Carson, Esbenson, Taylor, & Peterson, 2008). Officers must undergo an additional two days of GREAT Families training to teach that component of the program. GREAT Families is a six-session long community policing effort geared towards parents/guardians and children aged 10 to 14 years. This family-based crime prevention curriculum promotes positive family relationships by providing tools for good parenting and communication skills (Carson *et al.*, 2008). In addition, the program tries to establish parents as positive role models for behavior change and to establish rules, limits, and discipline within families. They structure their curriculum by discussing family safety in the electronic age and trying to reduce bullying by developing personal character (Carson *et al.*, 2008).

Although students are taught about the impact of crime on the community and victims, as well as why and how to stay away from gang membership, the GREAT curriculum is less content- and methods-focused. Instead, the curriculum focuses on teaching social competency and conflict resolution skills, and how students have a responsibility to their school and neighborhood (Sherman *et al.*, 1998). The effects of the DARE and GREAT programs in reducing substance use and delinquency have been found to be short-lived and largely ineffective without continued education and skills training (Botvin, 1990; Sherman *et al.*, 1998). Nevertheless, these programs continue to be utilized in their current form as crime prevention programs across the US, though evaluations of these programs are still ongoing (Buckle & Walsh, 2013; Esbensen, Peterson, Taylor, & Osgood, 2012; Petrosino, Guckenburg, & Fronius, 2012).

Whereas DARE and GREAT are school-based educational programs that focus on crime prevention through transmitting content-based information and specific skill building, the PAL program, established in 1940, uses after-school recreation-based activities to develop positive youth attitudes toward police officers, and to prevent juvenile crime and violence (Anderson, Sabatelli, & Trachtenberg, 2007;

Ennett *et al.*, 1994; Myers, 2002). The PAL program gives youth aged 5 to 18 years a safe place to play sports, while under police supervision. Officers help with home-work, coach sports, and take youths to off-site events.

Currently, there are more than 400 PAL chapters in law enforcement agencies in over 700 cities and 1,700 facilities throughout the US (www.nationalpal.org). Research about PAL is sparse, especially when compared with research about DARE and GREAT, and almost exclusively focuses on assessments of Baltimore City PAL centers (Subhas & Chandra, 2004). Many Baltimore City PAL officers believe that youths, parents, and the community view the police more positively – as human beings rather than unapproachable authority figures – and thus respect laws that police officers enforce because of the PAL program. Despite having a good relation-ship with PAL officers and staff, Subhas and Chandra (2004) found that youths did not feel comfortable acknowledging their PAL involvement, which may be attributable to the influences of long-term police–youth relations in the community.

Overall, the DARE, GREAT, and PAL programs aim to provide youths with con-structive, informative, and social activities that reduce opportunities to engage in potentially dangerous and delinquent behavior. These programs also aim to facilitate and improve police–youth–community interactions. By improving these networks, police seek to increase cooperation among community members, lessen potential delinquent activities by youths, and gain leverage as law enforcers in the community.

Perceptions of crime prevention practices

Only a few studies exist on the perceptions of police-youth crime prevention programs. In general, crime prevention practices and programs are often viewed by the public as more efficient and cost-effective for reducing the economic and social costs of crime than law enforcement crime intervention practices (Roberts & Hastings, 2007). According to research on public preferences toward criminal justice spending priorities, respondents supported increased focus on and spending for youth prevention programs (Cohen, Rust, & Steen, 2006). Support for early crime prevention programs, which are designed to prevent and deter youth who are at a high risk for delinquency from engaging in criminal activities, is so strong that the public would rather give up potential tax rebates to spend more on these programs (Cohen *et al.*, 2006). This desire for more spending on youth crime prevention pro-grams reflects the public's views of the need for and effectiveness of police crime prevention programs.

Two studies to examine perceptions of youth crime prevention programs focused on the GREAT program. First, Peterson and Esbensen (2004) found that school administrators, teachers, and counselors viewed the program as effectively teaching youths the skills to avoid gang and delinquency involvement, cultivating their problem-solving skills, and improving their attitudes toward police officers. Second, Carson and colleagues (2008) found that GREAT officers believed the curriculum met the goals of the program, and that the decision-making and goal-setting lessons were the most effective. Despite these positive perceptions, school personnel were far less likely to agree that the program actually did reduce youths' participation in gangs. Peterson and Esbensen (2004) suggested that this may be a result of school person- nel's lack of deep familiarity with, and participation in, the implementation of the GREAT program, and recommended that a more comprehensive approach would have the greatest potential for reducing youth gang and delinquency involvement.

Intervening in Juvenile Crime

Police employ law enforcement and problem-solving strategies by reacting and responding to crimes during or after they happen, responding to citizens' calls to help intervene in criminal and delinquent acts, conducting investigations and visiting crime scenes, and finding and apprehending suspects. Police proactively maintain order through police patrols and crowd control. They fuse proactive and reactive approaches when they respond to victims of crimes and enforce laws against the perpetrators. In addition to policing criminal acts involving victims, the police must also intervene in non-criminal behaviors and enforce laws against victimless crimes, such as truancy, curfew violations, and running away (Sherman *et al.*, 1998).

As of 2006, 99% of police agencies incorporated training on juvenile issues and had implemented specialized units and bureaus for handling juveniles (Reaves, 2009). Police often use situational crime prevention by specifically blocking youths' crime opportunities at certain places (Sherman *et al.*, 1998). This involves increasing the presence of police officers at specific places at specific times that youths are likely to be engaging in delinquent behaviors (Sherman *et al.*, 1998).

Police are able to target and block opportunities to commit crimes by increasing the number of police officers engaging in random and directed patrols of youths, resulting in increased reactive and proactive detainments and arrests (Myers, 2002; Sherman *et al.*, 1998). Police–youth encounters are more often a result of police responses to dispatched 9-1-1 calls rather than police-initiated encounters (Myers, 2002). Police most often utilize their authority and discretion with youths to handle crime intervention matters informally. In doing so, police officers question juveniles, request that youths stop engaging in disorderly conduct and/or leave the area, or threaten youths with potential arrest and charges if they continue to pose problems (Myers, 2002). When problems persist, police can maintain order through increased enforcement of night curfew law violations and preempt youths from engaging in delinquency while loitering with minimal supervision (Sherman *et al.*, 1998).

Since youths spend most of their time in school, youth-specific order-maintenance practices are often connected to school issues. Specifically, police officers enforce truancy violations through daytime curfew laws. Police accomplish this by patrolling neighborhoods and seeking out truant and evasive youths (Sherman *et al.*, 1998).

Although police are doing a service to the community by ensuring that youths do not get into trouble while loitering without supervision, they are also preventing youths from engaging in delinquent and criminal acts when not in school. However, police are also aware that keeping youth off the streets is not a sure-fire remedy to prevent juvenile delinquency. For example, in 2003, one in eight students was in a school fight and one in three had their property stolen or damaged at school (Office of Juvenile Justice and Delinquency Prevention, 2006). To that end, police officers are also assigned to in-school patrols of youths.

In addition to having school-stationed police officers for order-maintenance purposes, the rise in school crime and the fear of youthful offenders has increased public sentiment for added security measures in schools (Jackson, 2002; Petrosino *et al.*, 2012). The shootings at Columbine High School were a high-profile event that mobilized an increase in police presence in schools (Addington, 2009). School resource officers (SROs), as part of the community-policing approach, serve as a deterrent to juvenile delinquency and offer a proactive approach to solving school violence and reducing negative school behavior such as bullying and gang-based activities (Addington, 2009; Cray & Weiler, 2011). Specifically, they are placed in schools for security reasons, to decrease violence and delinquency, and to improve relations between police, youths, and the community (Cray & Weiler, 2011).

SROs can offer guidance on the precautions that youths should take to protect themselves from potential harm at home and in their neighborhoods and communities (Jackson, 2002). They can also take on their law enforcement role to suppress drugs and acts of violence in schools to ensure a more successful educational program. SROs can also be good resources to other police and school personnel, and can refer youths to court when necessary (Jackson, 2002).

Like other police officers, SROs must meet multiple objectives without alienating youths and increasing delinquency (Jackson, 2002). SROs aim to improve the image of the police, inform youths about what the police do, make youths aware of potential dangers, inform youths about the legal system and the rights and duties they have as citizens, to help develop youths' sense of social responsibility, encourage information sharing between schools and law enforcement, and to foster crime prevention (Phillips & Cochrane, 1985). SRO objectives, which extend into programs such as DARE and GREAT, aim to improve citizens' perceptions of the police and develop a greater respect for law and order (Jackson, 2002). Ultimately, the police must capitalize on positive perceptions of police legitimacy to balance their dual role as protectors and law enforcers.

Perceptions of crime intervention practices

Police–citizen contact is the largest predictor of attitudes toward and satisfaction with juvenile policing (Durose, Schmitt, & Langan, 2005). Despite some citizens having feelings of animosity and victimization, so long as police are perceived to be acting fairly and justly, in general, citizens often hold neutral to positive feelings toward the police (Tyler & Folger, 1980). However, police often hold negative or cynical views of citizens. This paradox may be partially explained by the fact that police are far more likely to come into contact with citizens when they have broken the law (even if just traffic violations), been victimized, or witnessed a crime

(Whitehead & Lab, 2013). These are typically citizens – minority and younger citizens rather than older citizens – who may hold less positive or favorable views of the police or legal system in general (Whitehead & Lab, 2013).

Citizen attitude studies frequently overlook youths' opinions of police officers in favor of the opinions of adults over the age of 25 (Jackson, 2002). In a study of young rural socio-economically disadvantaged males, Jackson (2002) found that youths view the police as corrupt, harassing, and insensitive to community issues. Police presence in schools may pose a psychological threat to youths who may view SROs as a threat to their "freedom to move about, have open conversations, and experiment in legal activities that may be socially unacceptable to police and administrators" (Jackson, 2002, p. 647). As positive police contact with SROs increases, youths' perceptions of SROs generally increase as well (Jackson, 2002). However, another study of youths' perceptions of police in schools found that increased police–youth contact did not change youths' perceptions of the police in general (Hopkins, 1994). Although some youths viewed SROs positively, they did not view them as typical police officers and distinguished them from officers on the street, which may explain why SROs may not actually change youths' perceptions of the police (Hopkins, 1994).

Studies show that young males, particularly socially and socio-economically disadvantaged minorities, engage in a variety of evasive tactics to minimize contact with the police (Weitzer & Brunson, 2009). Youths often go out of their way to avoid approaching police officers to avoid looking like a "snitch", and also hide and flee from police officers to avoid involuntary contact (Weitzer & Brunson, 2009). When youths file formal complaints against officers, Weitzer and Brunson (2009) found that no appropriate action was taken or the youth were threatened with retribution. This disregard for youths' complaints reinforced teens' beliefs that police officers would not be held accountable for their problematic behaviors (Weitzer & Brunson, 2009). In general, youths view police officers less favorably than do older individuals, possibly because they have more negative contacts with police (Schafer, Huebner, & Bynum, 2003).

Youths who engage in more delinquent behaviors are also found to have less positive attitudes toward the police than youths who do not engage in such behaviors. This may be related to feelings of animosity toward police, prosecutors, and judges who label them as delinquent youths, thereby constructing the youth's own negative identity perceptions (Siegel, 2003). This can result in juveniles feeling victimized by police officers, other government actors, and public supporters and perpetrators of such labeling, which can further exacerbate the likelihood of negative interactions between police and juveniles, thus further reinforcing punitive policing of juveniles (Hurst *et al.*, 2000; Siegel, 2003).

Investigating Juvenile Crime

The criminal investigation of juveniles by law enforcement can take many shapes. However, to date, most of the research surrounding the police investigation of juveniles has focused on the interrogation process. This process and the research have centered on the pre-interrogation Miranda warning and the interrogation questioning itself (Redlich & Kassin, 2009). Other aspects of police investigation, such as crime scene processing, the location and processing of physical evidence, and interviewing of witnesses, would not be expected to differ when the suspected offender is a juvenile versus an adult.

In the landmark US Supreme Court decision, *Miranda v. Arizona* (1966), the court decided that all suspects must be made aware of the 5th Amendment rights against self-incrimination and their 14th Amendment rights to counsel. One year later, in *In re Gault* (1967), the Court extended these (and numerous other) rights to juvenile offenders. Today, "Miranda warnings" as they have come to be known are quite ubiquitous and heard often on the many crime-related television programs. The four basic components of the Miranda warning are: (1) you have the right to remain silent; (2) anything you say can and will be used against you in a court of law; (3) you have the right to an attorney; and (4) if you cannot afford an attorney, one will be provided to you free of charge (see, for example, Rogers, Harrison, Shuman, Sewell, & Hazelwood, 2007).

As determined by the Court in *Miranda*, suspects in custodial interrogation settings must be apprised of these rights before questioning can begin. Suspects have the choice to either waive their rights and speak to the police or invoke their rights. The choice must be made knowingly, intelligently, and voluntarily (Redlich, Silverman, & Steiner, 2003). Much of the research surrounding juveniles and the Miranda warning has focused on the knowing and intelligent portions (e.g., Redlich *et al.*, 2003; Rogers *et al.*, 2007); that is, do juvenile suspects understand and appreciate their rights? Some 40 years ago, Grisso (1981) conducted a landmark study comparing juveniles' and adults' understanding of their rights. He found that juveniles aged 14 years and younger were significantly less likely to provide a knowing and intelligent Miranda waiver decision in comparison with older juveniles and adults (see also Goldstein & Goldstein, 2010). Another telling aspect of these research studies is the demonstration that having the ability to paraphrase one's rights is not equivalent to having a functional understanding of them. Specifically, whereas some juveniles and adults were able to tell you in their own words the components of a Miranda warning, when asked to apply their rights in a variety of situations, it became clear that they lacked complete understanding (Grisso, 1981; Redlich *et al.*, 2003). Nonetheless, it is common practice for the police to simply read the Miranda warning (or have suspects read the warning themselves) and have suspects initial or verbally state their understanding (Leo, 2008). It is also common practice for the courts to accept these markers of understanding as evidence of a knowing and intelligent waiver (White, 2001).

Another indication that Miranda right waivers may not be done with full understanding stems from research on the reading comprehensibility and completeness of content. Research by Rogers and his colleagues (2007, 2008) demonstrated that Miranda warnings vary extensively in length and content and the reading grade level required to understand them. After locating 682 versions of Miranda warnings for juveniles and adults, the authors found that the warnings ranged from a

2nd-grade reading level to post-college. However, most offenders (juvenile and adult) have been found to read at the 6th-grade level or below (Haigler, Harlow, O'Connor, & Campbell, 1994). Rogers *et al.* (2007) also found that significant proportions of warnings were incomplete. For instance, only 32% of warnings were explicit that the right to counsel was free. The question then becomes: how can suspects knowing and intelligently waive their rights if the warnings themselves are incomplete and above their reading capacity?

The voluntariness prong of the Miranda waiver requirement has not been well-researched. However, the authority differential between juveniles and adults, generally, and law enforcement, specifically, is quite clear (e.g., Cialdini, 2008; Milgram, 1974). It is equally clear that juveniles tend to obey authority figures (Braine, Pomerantz, Lorber, & Krantz, 1991). Further, as discussed by Leo (2008), police downplay the significance of Miranda by claiming that it is a mere formality. This downplaying of the seriousness of the adversarial situation serves to increase the likelihood of suspects waiving their rights. Indeed, about 75% of adult and 90% of juvenile suspects waive their rights and submit to police interrogation (Redlich & Kassin, 2009).

If suspects waive their right to remain silent and agree to speak to the police, an interrogation will likely follow (Kassin *et al.*, 2010). By design, interrogations are guilt-presumptive in that the police only *interrogate* (as opposed to interview) persons believed to be involved in the crime (Kassin *et al.*, 2010). In addition, interrogations utilize psychologically manipulative techniques, such as feigning friendship, trickery and deceit, and isolation (Leo, 2008).

In most of the twentieth century, there was not much research attention paid to juvenile interrogations. Though there were some significant US Supreme Court cases on the topic (i.e., *Haley v. Ohio*, 1948; *Gallegos v. Colorado*, 1962), social scientists generally did not study juveniles' capabilities in the interrogation room. However, in the early twenty-first century, the increased identification of wrongful convictions and the subsequent recognition that juveniles appear to be at risk, especially for false confessions (see Redlich & Kassin, 2009), prompted researchers to do more studies. Today, more is known about juveniles in the interrogation room than before, but there is still much to be learned.

Knowledge about juvenile interrogation comes from studies of actual interrogations (Feld, 2013), laboratory research (Redlich & Goodman, 2003), perceptions and reports from law enforcement (Meyer & Reppucci, 2009), and police training manuals (Inbau, Reid, Buckley, & Jayne, 2013). Redlich and Kassin (2009) asked and answered four questions in regard to the interrogation of juveniles. First, are adolescents different to adults? As discussed above, the clear answer to this is "yes". In brief, adolescents are known to be less cognitively, socially, and emotionally mature than adults (Cauffman & Steinberg, 2000). This immaturity results in impulsive decision-making, suggestibility, obedience to authority, and many other aspects that can impede performance in the interrogation room. Second, are adolescents different from adults within interrogation settings? Again, the answer was determined by Redlich and Kassin (2009) to be "yes". In addition to lacking a full comprehension of Miranda warnings, juveniles have been found to be more apt to falsely confess and not appreciate the adversarial nature of interrogations (e.g., see Drizin & Leo, 2004; Redlich *et al.*, 2003).

Third, are adolescents interrogated differently from adults? Here, the answer is "no". Despite knowledge that youth and adults do not have the same capabilities generally or in interrogation settings, police do not appear to distinguish between them during the questioning process (see Feld, 2013; Inbau *et al.*, 2013). And fourth, Redlich and Kassin (2009) asked, "Why aren't children and adults interrogated differently?" The answer to this question is primarily dependent upon how the police perceive youthful offenders. As we discuss in the section on Perceptions of crime investigation practices, the police tend to view age as an aggravating factor rather than a mitigating one, especially when the crime is serious.

Perceptions of crime investigation practices

Although there is a dearth of research on perceptions of crime investigation practices with juveniles, the extant research suggests that police tend not to differentiate between juveniles and adults. For example, Meyer and Reppucci (2009) surveyed police officers about their perceptions of and practices with suspects of varying ages. In regard to comprehension of rights (level of agreement with statements: [children, youth, adults] understand their right to an attorney, to remain silent, the intent of a police interview, and Miranda rights), the authors found that police believed that youth (aged 14 to 17 years) and adults (18 years and older) did not differ in their comprehension levels, and that both groups were equally likely to understand their rights.

Further, Payne, Time, and Gainey (2006) surveyed police chiefs ($n = 97$) about their attitudes towards and perceptions of Miranda warnings. They found that the majority of police chiefs agreed or strongly agreed with the statements "Miranda warnings hinder voluntary confessions" (53%), "Courts are too cautious with regard to the Miranda warnings" (62%), and "Most offenders already know their rights" (66%). In regard to the latter statement, the authors note, "Police chiefs, in general, tended to think offenders already knew their rights. In fact, not one single police officer strongly disagreed with the statement" (p. 656). Although Payne *et al.* (2006) did not instruct their police chief participants to consider a specific age group when answering, the evidence to date suggests that police do not distinguish between juvenile and adult offenders, especially those suspected of serious crimes. Rather, police appear to equate crime seriousness with maturity and sophistication. As one officer put it, "The juveniles I interrogate aren't kids, they're monsters" (Owen-Kostelnik, Reppucci, & Meyer, 2006, p. 298).

Conclusion

Police interact with youth in many different roles and capacities. Police have to simultaneously act as both crime fighters and community protectors. In this chapter, we focused on the police's role in crime prevention, intervention, and investigation. We described the processes, as well how the police, youth, and public perceive them.

We found that: (1) police engage in crime prevention strategies, such as DARE, GREAT, and PAL programs, to teach youths decision-making and social skills, deter criminal activity, increase police legitimacy, and improve police–youth–community relations; (2) crime intervention strategies, specifically patrolling and targeting crime places, allow police officers to reactively and proactively maintain order and enforce laws against juvenile delinquency; and (3) police tend to employ the same interrogation strategies used with adults, and do not take into account the cognitive maturity or decision-making abilities of youths in the context of the crime investigation of juveniles.

Police officers can experience role conflicts when engaging in these different capacities with youths, which often fuels conflicting attitudes between the police and the public. The general public often holds neutral or positive attitudes toward the police – though minorities and socio-economically disadvantaged youths report feeling harassed by the police and tend to hold negative attitudes toward them. In contrast, police officers hold negative or cynical attitudes toward the public because their contact with citizens is mostly negative. By engaging in effective crime prevention programs, using appropriate crime intervention strategies, and ensuring appropriate crime investigation methods, police officers aim to improve attitudes and relationships between police officers, youths, and the public, which in turn, may result in the ultimate goal of crime reduction.

References

Addington, L.A. (2009). Cops and cameras public school security as a policy response to Columbine. *American Behavioral Scientist, 52*(10), 1426–1446.

Anderson, S.A., Sabatelli, R.M., & Trachtenberg, J. (2007). Community police and youth programs as a context for positive youth development. *Police Quarterly, 10*(1), 23–40.

Bazemore, G., & Senjo, S. (1997). Police encounters with juveniles revisited: An exploratory study of themes and styles in community policing. *Policing: An International Journal of Police Strategies & Management, 20*(1), 60–82.

Bennett, W.J., Dilulio, J.J., & Walters, J.P. (1996). *Body Count: Moral Poverty – and How to Win America's War Against Crime and Drugs*. New York: Simon & Schuster.

Botvin, G.J. (1990). Substance abuse prevention: Theory, practice, and effectiveness. In M. Tonry, & J.Q. Wilson (Eds.), *Drugs and Crime* (pp. 461–519). Chicago: University of Chicago Press.

Braine, L.G., Pomerantz, E., Lorber, D., & Krantz, D.H. (1991). Conflicts with authority: Children's feelings, actions, and justifications. *Developmental Psychology, 27*, 829–840.

Buckle, M.E., & Walsh, D.S. (2013). Teaching responsibility to gang-affiliated youths. *Journal of Physical Education, Recreation & Dance, 84*(2), 53–58.

Carson, C.C., Esbensen, F.A., Taylor, T.J., & Peterson, D. (2008). *National Evaluation of the Gang Resistance Education and Training (G.R.E.A.T.) Program: Results from Surveys and Interviews with G.R.E.A.T.-trained Officers*. Washington, DC: US Department of Justice, Office of Justice Programs, National Institute of Justice.

Cauffman, E., & Steinberg, L. (2000). (Im)maturity of judgment in adolescence: why adolescents may be less culpable than adults. *Behavioral Sciences and the Law, 18*(6), 741–760.

Cheurprakobkit, S. (2000). Police–citizen contact and police performance: Attitudinal differences between Hispanics and non-Hispanics. *Journal of Criminal Justice, 28*, 325–336.

Cialdini, R. (2008). *Influence: Science and Practice*. Boston, MA: Pearson.

Cohen, M.A., Rust, R.T., & Steen, S. (2006). Prevention, crime control or cash? Public preferences towards criminal justice spending priorities. *Justice Quarterly*, *23*(3), 317–335.

Cray, M., & Weiler, S.C. (2011). Policy to practice: A look at national and state implementation of school resource officer programs. *The Clearing House: A Journal of Educational Strategies, Issues and Ideas*, *84*(4), 164–170.

Drizin, S., & Leo, R. (2004). The problem of false confessions in the post-DNA world. *North Carolina Law Review*, *82*, 891–1007.

Durose, M.R., Schmitt, E.L., & Langan, P.A. (2005). *Contacts Between Police and the Public: Findings from the 2002 National Survey*. Washington, DC: US Department of Justice, Office of Justice Programs, Bureau of Justice Statistics.

Durose, M., Smith, E., & Langan, P. (2007). *Contacts Between Police and the Public*. Washington, DC: Bureau of Justice Statistics.

Engel, R.S. (2000). The effects of supervisory styles on patrol officer behavior. *Police Quarterly*, *3*(3), 262–293.

Ennett, S.T., Tobler, N.S., Ringwalt, C.L., & Flewelling, R.L. (1994). How effective is drug abuse resistance education? A meta-analysis of Project DARE outcome evaluations. *American Journal of Public Health*, *84*(9), 1394–1401.

Esbensen, F.A., Peterson, D., Taylor, T.J., & Osgood, D.W. (2012). Results from a multi-site evaluation of the GREAT program. *Justice Quarterly*, *29*(1), 125–151.

Fashola, O.S. (2002). *Building Effective After-School Programs*. Thousand Oaks, CA: Corwin Press, Inc.

Federal Bureau of Investigation. (2006). *Crime in the United States, 2005: Uniform Crime Reports*. Washington, DC: US Department of Justice, FBI.

Federal Bureau of Investigation. (2010). *Crime in the United States, 2009: Uniform Crime Reports*. Washington, DC: US Department of Justice, FBI.

Feld, B.C. (2013). *Kids, Cops, and Confessions: Inside the Interrogation Room*. New York: New York University Press.

Gallegos v. Colorado. (1962). 370 U.S. 49.

Gau, J.M., & Brunson, R.K. (2010). Procedural justice and order maintenance policing: A study of inner-city young men's perceptions of police legitimacy. *Justice Quarterly*, *27*(2), 255–279.

Goldstein, A.M., & Goldstein, N.E.S. (2010). *Evaluating Capacity to Waive Miranda Rights*. New York: Oxford University Press.

Grisso, T. (1981). *Juvenile's Waiver of Rights: Legal and Psychological Competence*. New York: Plenum.

Haigler, K.O., Harlow, C., O'Connor, P., & Campbell, A. (1994). *Literacy Behind Prison Walls: Profiles of the Prison Population from the National Adult Literacy Survey*, (NCES 94102). Washington, DC: US Department of Education.

Haley v. Ohio. (1948). 332 U.S. 596.

Hopkins, N. (1994). School pupils' perception of the police that visit schools: not all police are 'pigs'. *Journal of Community and Applied Social Psychology*, *4*, 189–207.

Hurst, Y.G., Frank, J., & Browning, S.L. (2000). The attitudes of juveniles toward the police: A comparison of black and white youth. *Policing: An International Journal of Police Strategies & Management*, *23*(1), 37–53.

Inbau, F.E., Reid, J.E., Buckley, J.P., & Jayne, B.C. (2013). *Criminal Interrogation and Confessions* (5th ed.). Burlington, MA: Jones & Bartlett Learning.

In re Gault. (1967). 387 U.S. 1.

Jackson, A. (2002). Police-school resource officers' and students' perception of the police and offending. *Policing: An International Journal of Police Strategies & Management, 25*(3), 631–650.

Kassin, S.M., Drizin, S., Grisso, T., Gudjonsson, G.H., Leo, R.A., & Redlich, A.D. (2010). Police-induced confessions: Risk factors and recommendations. *Law and Human Behavior, 34,* 3–38. doi:10.1007/s10979-009-9188-6.

Klein, M.W. (1986). Labeling theory and delinquency policy an experimental test. *Criminal Justice and Behavior, 13*(1), 47–79.

Leo, R.A. (2008). *Police Interrogation and American Justice.* Cambridge, MA: Harvard University Press.

Liederbach, J. (2007). Controlling suburban and small-town hoods: An examination of police encounters with juveniles. *Youth Violence and Juvenile Justice, 5*(2), 107–124.

Maguire, K. (2003). *Sourcebook of Criminal Justice Statistics: Table 2.48.* Retrieved from http://www.albany.edu/sourcebook/pdf/t248.pdf

Mahoney, J.L., & Stattin, H. (2000). Leisure activities and adolescent antisocial behavior: The role of structure and social context. *Journal of Adolescence, 23*(2), 113–127.

McAra, L., & McVie, S. (2005). The usual suspects? Street-life, young people and the police. *Criminal Justice, 5*(1), 5–36.

Meyer, J.R., & Reppucci, M.D. (2009). Police practices and perceptions regarding juvenile interrogation and interrogative suggestibility. *Behavioral Sciences and the Law, 25,* 757–780.

Milgram, S. (1974). *Obedience to Authority: An Experimental View.* New York: Harper Row.

Miranda v. Arizona. (1966). 384 U.S. 436.

Modecki, K.L. (2008). Addressing gaps in the maturity of judgment literature. *Law and Human Behavior, 32*(1), 78–91.

Myers, S.M. (2002). Police: Handling of juveniles. In J. Dressler (Ed.), *Encyclopedia of Crime & Justice* (pp. 1073–1083). New York: Macmillan Reference USA.

Office of Juvenile Justice and Delinquency Prevention. (2006). *Juvenile Offenders and Victims: A National Report.* Washington, DC: OJJDP.

Owen-Kostelnik, J., Reppucci, N.D., & Meyer, J.R. (2006). Testimony and interrogation of minors: Assumptions about maturity and morality. *American Psychologist, 61,* 286–304.

Payne, B.K., Time, V., & Gainey, R.R. (2006). Police chiefs' and students' attitudes about the Miranda warning. *Journal of Criminal Justice, 34,* 653–660.

Peterson, D., & Esbensen, F.A. (2004). The outlook is GREAT: What educators say about school-based prevention and the Gang Resistance Education and Training (GREAT) Program. *Evaluation Review, 28*(3), 218–245.

Petrosino, A., Guckenburg, S., & Fronius, T. (2012). 'Policing Schools' strategies: A review of the evaluation evidence. *Journal of Multidisciplinary Evaluation, 8*(17), 80–101.

Phillips, S.V., & Cochrane, R. (1985). *The role, functions and training of Police Community Liaison Officers.* Department of Psychology, University of Birmingham.

Pizarro, J., Chermak, S., & Gruenewald, J. (2007). Juvenile "super-predators" in the news: A comparison of adult and juvenile homicides. *Journal of Criminal Justice and Popular Culture, 14*(1), 84–111.

Reaves, B.A. (2009). *State and Local Law Enforcement Training Academies.* Washington, DC: Bureau of Justice Statistics.

Redlich, A.D., & Goodman, G.S. (2003). Taking responsibility for an act not committed: The influence of age and suggestibility. *Law and Human Behavior, 27,* 141–156.

Redlich, A.D., & Kassin, S.M. (2009). Police interrogation and false confessions: The inherent risk of youth. In B.L. Bottoms, G.S. Goodman, & C.J. Najdowski (Eds.), *Child Victims, Child Offenders: Psychology and Law* (pp. 275–294). New York: Guilford Press.

Redlich, A.D., Silverman, M., & Steiner, H. (2003). Factors affecting preadjudicative and adjudicative competence in juveniles and young adults. *Behavioral Sciences and the Law, 21*, 1–17.

Reppucci, N.D. (1999). Adolescent development and juvenile justice. *American Journal of Community Psychology, 27*(3), 307–326.

Roberts, J.V., & Hastings, R. (2007). Public opinion and crime prevention: a review of international findings. *IPC Review, 1*, 193–218.

Rogers, R., Harrison, K.S., Shuman, D.W., Sewell, K.W., & Hazelwood, L.L. (2007). An analysis of Miranda warnings and waivers: Comprehension and coverage. *Law and Human Behavior, 31*, 177–192.

Rogers, R., Hazelwood, L.L., Sewell, K.W., Shuman, D.W., & Blackwood, H.L. (2008). The comprehensibility and content of juvenile Miranda warnings. *Psychology, Public Policy, and Law, 14*, 63–87.

Rosenbaum, D.P. (2007). Just say no to DARE. *Criminology and Public Policy, 6*, 815–824.

Schafer, J.A., Huebner, B.M., & Bynum, T.S. (2003). Citizen perceptions of police services: Race, neighborhood context, and community policing. *Police Quarterly, 6*(4), 440–468.

Sherman, L.W., Gottfredson, D.C., MacKenzie, D.L., Eck, J., Reuter, P., & Bushway, S.D. (1998). *What Works, What Doesn't, What's Promising: A Report to the United States Congress.* Washington, DC: National Institute of Justice.

Siegel, L.J. (2003). *Criminology* (8th ed.). Belmont, CA: Wadsworth Thomson.

Steinberg, L., & Scott, E.S. (2003). Less guilty by reason of adolescence: Developmental immaturity, diminished responsibility, and the juvenile death penalty. *American Psychologist, 58*(12), 1009–1018.

Subhas, N., & Chandra, A. (2004). *Baltimore City Police Athletic League assessment study.* Retrieved from http://www.jhsph.edu/sebin/u/d/PAL_Report-long_version.pdf.

Tyler, T.R., & Folger, R. (1980). Distributional and procedural aspects of satisfaction with citizen-police encounters. *Basic and Applied Social Psychology, 1*(4), 281–292.

Visher, C.A. (1983). Gender, police arrest decisions and notions of chivalry. *Criminology, 21*, 5–28.

Walker, S. (1977). *A Critical History of Police Reform.* Lexington, MA: Lexington Books.

Walker, S., & Katz, C.M. (2005). *The Police in America: An Introduction* (5th ed.). New York: McGraw-Hill.

Weitzer, R., & Brunson, R.K. (2009). Strategic responses to the police among inner-city youth. *Sociological Quarterly, 50*(2), 235–256.

West, S.L., & O'Neal, K.K. (2004). Project DARE outcome effectiveness revisited. *American Journal of Public Health, 94*(6), 1027–1029.

White, W. (2001). *Miranda's* failure to restrain pernicious interrogation practices. *Michigan Law Review, 99*, 1211–1247.

Whitehead, J.T. & Lab, S.P. (2013). *Juvenile Justice: An Introduction* (7th ed.). Waltham, MA: Anderson Publishing.

Zahn, M.A., Brumbaugh, S., Steffensmeier, D., Feld, B.C., Morash, M., Chesney-Lind, M., ... Kruttschnitt, C. (2008). *Girls Study Group: Understanding and Responding to Girls' Delinquency.* Washington, DC: US Department of Justice, Office of Juvenile Justice and Delinquency Prevention.

26

Juvenile Diversion

James V. Ray and Kristina Childs

Juvenile diversion has become an extremely important, yet controversial, component of the juvenile justice system. This chapter provides an overview of various aspects of juvenile diversion. First, we discuss the conceptual issues surrounding diversion in order to arrive at a definition that will be used in the current chapter. Second, we review the emergence of diversion by discussing its theoretical underpinnings and the legislative reform that provided a push for alternative, non-punitive forms of dealing with juvenile offenders. Third, we highlight the heterogeneity in diversion programs and provide examples of programs used around the US today. Fourth, we discuss the empirical literature assessing the effectiveness of diversion. Finally, we suggest three future advancements in research and practice.

Defining Juvenile Diversion

Broadly speaking, the term *juvenile diversion* refers to minimizing the extent to which youthful offenders penetrate the juvenile justice system. However, juvenile diversion comes in many forms, with varying points of contact, implementation strategies, and goals, making identification of a universal definition a daunting task. This point was underscored by Lemert (1981) who stated that the term diversion has been "…applied very loosely and sometimes indiscriminately to such a wide variety of procedures and programs" (p. 36). Lemert highlighted two approaches to defining diversion which included (1) those that generally speak to informal, discretionary forms of diversion; and (2) more formalized means of diversion. The former mainly refers to counsel-and-release by the arresting or intake officer, whereby the youth is

The Handbook of Juvenile Delinquency and Juvenile Justice, First Edition. Edited by Marvin D. Krohn and Jodi Lane.
© 2015 John Wiley & Sons, Inc. Published 2015 by John Wiley & Sons, Inc.

released back to the community with no requirements, commitments, or sanctions, also referred to as "true diversion" (Whitehead & Lab, 2001). Chapin and Griffin (2005, p. 162), however, suggest that this "is not diversion in the sense it was originally intended". The latter refers to a more formalized means of diversion in which youth who are arrested enter into an agreement with the court, which discontinues formal processing, and may entail community service, restitution, or intervention. Thus, diversion can take on a variety of forms that hinge on a continuum of formality from completely halting system involvement upon arrest, to contractual agreement with sanctions. The common theme, however, is that diversion attempts to limit involvement with the juvenile justice system for youth who would have gone on to be formally charged. In the current chapter, we adopt a broad definition of diversion that describes any formal program designed to prevent or limit the extent to which juveniles are processed through the system, including counsel-and-release programs and those that occur prior to adjudication.

Emergence of Diversion

Some experts have argued that the creation of the juvenile justice system during the nineteenth century can be considered diversion because the goal was for the juvenile court to set aside the punitive sanctions of the adult court and focus specifically on rehabilitation and education (Models for Change Juvenile Diversion Workgroup, 2011). Just as a separate court system was created to prevent the negative effects of adult court involvement on juveniles during that time, diversion programs today are intended to save less serious offenders from the negative consequences of juvenile court involvement (Chapin & Griffin, 2005; c.f. Lemert, 1981). That is, diversion was (and still is) intended to limit stigma and negative life consequences that often resulted from juvenile justice involvement. Thus, two theoretical perspectives generally underscore the emergence of juvenile diversion. Social learning or peer contagion perspectives imply that juvenile court involvement leads to the adoption of attitudes favorable to crime and facilitates deviancy training (Dodge, Dishion, & Lansford, 2006). In other words, first-time, low-level offenders may adopt positive attitudes toward delinquency or learn new delinquent behaviors as a result of being exposed to more serious juvenile offenders through system involvement (Dodge *et al.*, 2006). In this sense, attempts by the juvenile justice system to correct behaviors of youth through secure placement may actually have iatrogenic effects, as relatively low-risk youth are exposed to high-risk, deviant peers (Cécile & Born, 2009).

Labeling theory is another perspective underpinning the development of juvenile diversion programs. Labeling theory suggests that formal responses to delinquency can stigmatize justice-involved youth, which can lead to the adoption of a delinquent self-identity (see Maddan & Marshal, 2009). Youth then become enmeshed in delinquent and criminal behavior, which, in turn, limits conventional opportunities. That is, the stigma resulting from official labeling will have negative consequences for positive life outcomes such as academic achievement and job attainment (Lemert,

1981). Therefore, diversion programs are implemented to reduce the labeling effect by routing youth out of the juvenile justice system and removing official labels.

While labeling and social learning perspectives continue as justification for diversion, shifting policies and political ideologies, along with fluctuations in trends in delinquency, also influenced the use of diversion. Formal pleas for diversion were born from recommendations by the President's Commission on Law Enforcement and Administration of Justice (1967) to identify responses to juvenile offending that limited official system involvement. These recommendations responded to several criticisms of the juvenile justice system, including a growing juvenile justice population and increasing juvenile crime rates (Cocozza *et al.*, 2005). Thus, despite increasingly punitive efforts, the juvenile justice system at the time was portrayed as ineffective at reducing crime. This call for reform resulted in a substantial growth in diversion programs and was supported by state and federal efforts to fund such programs (Lemert, 1981). Subsequently, however, the 1970s and 1980s saw a political shift toward conservatism which resulted in an attack on the juvenile justice system for being too lenient on offenders, and placed into question the practice of diversion. Additionally, many scholars believed that "nothing" worked, and that efforts to rehabilitate even low-level offenders should be abandoned and replaced with efforts rooted in deterrence (Roush, 1996).

The spike in juvenile crime rates during the mid-1980s to the early 1990s resulted in efforts to replace rehabilitative goals with a "get tough" mentality. Once again, opponents of diversion questioned the leniency of such programs in dealing with the juvenile crime threat. These positions were bolstered by media sensationalism and the threat of the juvenile "super-predator" (Pizarro, Chermak, & Gruenewald, 2007). As the juvenile population rose during the mid-1990s, the juvenile justice system saw subsequent overcrowding of detention facilities as well as increased recidivism among juvenile offenders, suggesting, once again, the ineffectiveness of the "get-tough" approach to juvenile crime. Scholars at the time began to call for efforts to revitalize the juvenile ideal of rehabilitation through diversion (Roush, 1996).

Statutes governing diversion

Currently, the majority of states have statutes that govern juvenile diversion procedures. In general, diversion statutes define various elements that should be applied to diversion programs within the state. These elements include the purpose of diversion, eligibility criteria for inclusion, conditions, contract requirements, confidentiality provisions, and outcome options related to completion of the program. There are also different labels for diversion specified in the statutes, including arbitration, deferral, consent decree, or adjustment. In some states, however, specific statutes focus on components of one particular diversion program such as civil citation or teen court. Based on a detailed review of diversion-focused state statutes, the Models for Change Juvenile Diversion Working Group (MFC Workgroup, 2011, p. 14) reported that most statutes "articulate a purpose, policy, goal, or objective for diverting youth from the formal court process".

Recent estimates suggest that approximately 25% of youth who enter the juvenile justice system are placed in a diversion program (Puzzanchera & Kang, 2008). Currently, states are continuing to reevaluate their approach to juvenile justice by seeking evidence-based practices that better serve youth at a lower cost, once again shifting towards a rehabilitative emphasis through the implementation of diversion programs while still holding youth accountable for their behaviors.

Overview of Diversion Programs

Heterogeneity in diversion

The primary goal of diversion seems to be reducing recidivism by limiting penetration into the system (Beck, Ramsey, Lipps, & Travis, 2006). Despite this commonality, however, the goals themselves can vary considerably across diversion programs. Thus, while there is a common theme across diversion programs of reducing youth involvement in the juvenile court, how programs go about achieving this end varies significantly across programs and jurisdictions. A diversion program can serve a multitude of purposes, including reducing recidivism, lowering costs of system processing, making youth accountable for their behavior, providing services to youth, and increasing successful outcomes for youth (MFC Workgroup, 2011). Nonetheless, having a clearly stated purpose is important for measuring the effectiveness of any given diversion program beyond recidivism, a point too often overlooked in research on diversion (MFC Workgroup, 2011).

Diversion programs also vary on the criteria used for deeming youth eligible (Cocozza *et al.*, 2005). Legally relevant factors, including a youth's criminal history and seriousness of the offense, are usually the first criteria considered. Diversion programs typically target first-time, low-level (e.g., status offenses, misdemeanors) offenders (Elrod & Ryder, 1999). However, some programs target specific types of offenses such as drug offenses or school-related offenses, or restrict inclusion due to violent or threatening behavior (e.g., Sullivan, Dollard, Sellers, & Mayo, 2010). Age of the offender may also be a consideration that is directly influenced by each state's jurisdiction of the juvenile court. For example, according to the Office of Juvenile Justice and Delinquency Prevention (OJJDP), the minimum age of juvenile court processing across states ranges from 6 to 10 while the maximum age for juvenile court processing ranges from 15 to 18 (OJJDP Statistical Briefing Book, 2013). However, diversion programs may specify an age range for eligibility (MFC Workgroup, 2011). Recently, programs have relied on assessment instruments to determine an offender's appropriateness for diversion, identify risk factors that may help to predict the likelihood of success, and determine the most appropriate program placement. Another important consideration deals with legal sufficiency. Legal sufficiency refers to the notion that youth are only eligible for diversion if the facts of the case are within the legal authority of the juvenile court and are sufficient to substantiate the offense. This ensures that only youth that would have otherwise gone on to be formally processed are eligible for diversion, which also helps to ensure that the right youth are being diverted (Snyder, 1996).

There is also heterogeneity across jurisdictions with regard to the point of contact within the juvenile justice system responsible for making diversionary decisions. First, there is variation in the stage of processing at which diversion may occur (Cocozza *et al.*, 2005). For instance, the decision to divert may occur at apprehension or in later stages of processing (e.g., intake, referral to the prosecutor's office, or adjudication hearing). Second, depending on when diversion occurs, the initial decision may fall on different justice system officials. The initial decision may be made by a law enforcement officer upon apprehension, or at later stages by an intake screener, the office of probation, the prosecutor, or the judge (Whitehead & Lab, 2001). Once a youth enters into diversion there is also variation across jurisdictions in the entities responsible for overseeing the youth's participation. Within the juvenile justice system, the parties responsible for overseeing diversion include but are not limited to juvenile probation, the district attorney's office, juvenile court, and law enforcement. In some cases, community-based agencies (e.g., mental health agencies) or juvenile justice agencies working in conjunction with community-based agencies will oversee diversion programs.

Diversion is typically posed as an agreement between the youth and the court, and requires that the youth fulfill his or her end of the bargain with the incentive being that the court will dismiss the charges and take no further action. The conditions of diversion can also vary greatly from program to program (e.g., Mears, Cochran, Greenman, Bhati, & Greenwald, 2011). Possible sanctions are directly linked to the goals of the particular diversion program, which, broadly speaking, depend on whether the program is rehabilitative or retributive. Nonetheless, diversion programs vary with regard to whether or not a contract is required, if and what types of sanctions are given, if and what treatment services will be provided, and the consequences of successful and unsuccessful completion. Counsel-and-release programs typically do not require a written contract. Most formal diversion programs do, however, require that the youth and guardian formally enter into diversion by signing a written contract. The contract clearly outlines the conditions of diversion (e.g., length of time, requirements, and incentives) and expresses the youth's knowledge and willingness of the conditions. Quite often the signing of the diversion contract requires the youth to admit guilt in order to participate in the program (MFC Workgroup, 2011).

Once a youth enters into a diversion agreement there are a variety of potential conditions that he or she must meet for successful completion (Mears *et al.*, 2011). These conditions are largely based on the goals of the particular diversion program in which the youth participates (Wilson & Hoge, 2013). If the purpose of the diversion program is to reduce recidivism, the conditions might require the youth to stay away from certain places or people (i.e., peers), agree to be monitored (i.e., case management), and stay out of trouble. If the focus is on accountability, the youth may be required to admit responsibility for the offense, resolve conflict with the victim and community (e.g., formal letter of apology, attend victim–offender mediation meetings), pay monetary restitution, or engage in community service. If the focus is on building skills and social support, there may be a mentorship component. If there is a rehabilitative focus, there may be some prescribed treatment services including drug abuse or mental health treatment programs. Since diversion programs often focus on more than one of these goals, a number of these sanctions may be specified as requirements through the written contract (e.g., community service and intervention). Successful completion of the program depends upon adherence to the contract's terms and usually results in the dismissal of charges; however, other incentives are also used (e.g., awards, praise, or reduction of requirements). Failure to adhere to the requirements of diversion most often results in proceeding with formal court processing, although in some cases the youth might be dismissed from the program without formal processing or program adjustments, or a referral might be made to a more intensive diversion program (e.g., increased monitoring or length of contract; MFC Workgroup, 2011).

Examples of juvenile diversion programs

The extensive heterogeneity regarding elements (e.g., goals, sanctions, and oversight) of diversion resulted in the development of several unique types of programs. In order to highlight this heterogeneity, a brief overview of some of the more common types of diversion programs used across the country is provided.

Youth courts are programs in which youth sentence their peers for minor delinquent or status offenses. According to the National Association of Youth Courts (NAYC), in 2010 there were over 1,050 youth court programs in operation in the US (NAYC, 2014). The goal of youth courts is to teach youth to respect the law, encourage civic responsibility, and promote prosocial behavior. The philosophy behind youth courts is that, by allowing peers to make sentencing decisions, positive peer pressure can positively influence first-time, non-serious offenders' behavior through accountability. Youth courts involve youth volunteers who serve as law enforcement officials, lawyers, and jurors and, together, these youth go through the judicial process. Most youth courts involve an official juvenile judge to oversee the process; however, some programs rely on peer juries or youth judges. Youth courts are often housed within existing juvenile or family courts or the prosecutor's office. According to NAYC, 93% of youth courts require the youth to admit guilt prior to participating in the program. Common sanctions include community service, a written apology, and participation as a "decision-maker" in additional youth court cases. Other sentencing options include curfew, educational workshops, restitution, jail tours, alcohol/drug assessment and counseling, mentorship, or drug testing. Upon successful completion of the program, 63% of courts dismiss the charges and 27% expunge the offender's record (NAYC, 2014). For example, in Kent County, Delaware, first-time offenders (misdemeanants) may be referred to youth court by the Deputy

Attorney General if the youth pleads guilty to the offense. With the exception of the judge, all participants are juveniles and they are responsible for determining the sanctions for the youth, which involve participation in the court as a juror, community service, letters of apology, and counseling (Garrison, 2001).

Civil citation programs are another form of diversion that allows law enforcement officers to make the decision to divert in the field. Civil citation programs typically target first-time, non-violent misdemeanor offenders and require a specified number of community service hours. For example, recently (2011), Florida passed a statute (F.S. 985.12) requiring all local jurisdictions to implement a civil citation program. After the officer writes the citation, offenders are required to meet with the local civil citation coordinator and sign a contract, which involves admitting guilt. The statute mandates that each youth receives a needs assessment, participates in no more than 50 hours of community service, maintains contact with the coordinator, and writes a letter of apology to the victim (Florida Department of Juvenile Justice, 2013). Other sanctions may include community-based treatment, restitution, drug testing, or school progress monitoring. Unsuccessful completion will result in the case being transferred to the prosecutor's office with a recommendation for further action (e.g., referral to a more intensive diversion program or formal processing). Successful completion requires no new arrests and completion of all sanctions listed in the contract. Once completed successfully, all charges are dropped. In 2013, a third of first-time, misdemeanor offenders in the state of Florida participated in a civil citation program.

Drug court programs are also commonly used as diversion services within the juvenile justice system. Juvenile drug court programs typically target first-time, misdemeanor drug offenders and focus on substance use education, skills building, and treatment. Drug courts often work closely with community-based agencies that specialize in substance abuse prevention and treatment. The components of drug court frequently involve case management, drug testing, and outpatient counseling. Participants are required to maintain sobriety, attend all scheduled meetings with case managers and counselors, and refrain from criminal activity. Typically, the length of drug court participation is much longer compared with other diversion programs because of the intensive treatment and monitoring components of the program. Due to the intense treatment component, non-compliance does not always lead to case failure. Instead, additional sanctions are added, focusing again on treatment and rehabilitation. Upon meeting all requirements and remaining drug-free for an extended period of time, the offender "graduates" from the program and all charges are dropped. For example, the Delaware Juvenile Drug Court Diversion Program focuses on first-time, misdemeanor drug offenders. The goal of the program is to prevent further criminal behavior through skills building. All participants receive case management services in addition to outpatient substance abuse services. To graduate from the program, youth are required to complete all treatment goals, report to the court on a monthly basis, and refrain from substance use and criminal activity. Once graduated, all charges are dismissed (see Miller, Scocas, & O'Connell, 1998 for an evaluation of this program).

The programs above provide examples of different diversion models used across the country. There are a large number of additional formalized diversion programs, including: neighborhood accountability boards (NAB), which rely on community members to determine the sanctions for the offender (Schiff, Bazemore, & Brown, 2011); victim–offender mediation programs that are based on the concept of restorative justice and bring the victim and offender together to determine the appropriate sanctions (Umbreit, Coates, & Vos, 2004); mentorship-focused programs that require youths to spend a specified number of hours with trained volunteers from the community (Smith, Wolf, Contrillon, Thomas, & Davidson, 2004); and specialty courts that focus on a specific risk factor such as violence, anger management, or mental health.

Net-widening

Net-widening, or widening the net, has been a long-standing criticism of diversion. Net-widening refers to increasing the jurisdiction of the juvenile justice system through the use of diversion programs. Opponents of diversion argue that it ensnares youth in the system who would have otherwise never been formally involved. That is, without the option of referral to diversion, first-time, low-level offenders, for example, would have been dealt with through counsel-and-release tactics by police. Relatedly, it has also been suggested that the option for police to divert such offenders has limited their discretion in handling youth without system involvement. By placing juveniles in formal diversion programs (rather than informally releasing them), the youths are subjected to undue surveillance and formal court involvement upon failure. This, in turn, results in placing an official label on youth who would never have been involved in the justice system otherwise (Binder & Geis, 1984). This potential for net-widening to occur, however, is reduced by the fact that the decision to place a youth in a formal diversion program should only occur if formal processing was likely on legal grounds (e.g., substantial evidence).

The concept of net-widening is important in two regards. First, if diversion acts to extend the jurisdiction of the juvenile justice system and formally involve youth who would have otherwise received zero sanctions, then it undermines one of its more salient goals of reduced justice system involvement. Secondly, net-widening raises the question as to whether diversion is reaching the intended population. That is, are diversion programs preventing at-risk youth from further penetration and future contact with the justice system, or are they focusing on those youth not at risk of becoming serious, habitual offenders (Bechard, Ireland, Berg, & Vogel, 2011)? Despite these potential implications, relatively little research exists examining this claim. Bechard *et al.* (2011) evaluated a California-based diversion program and examined whether or not it was reaching the intended population of juveniles. Their findings support the notion of net-widening and suggest that the intended at-risk population was not targeted. More specifically, they found that officially targeting broad crime categories implied that more serious types of offenses were the focus of diversion; however, once broken down to more specific crime types and examination of the circumstances, non-serious behaviors made up the majority of charges. Given the longstanding theoretical and philosophical debate regarding the capacity of diversion programs to net-widen (Binder & Geis, 1984; Decker, 1985), additional future research is needed to provide some empirical evidence to inform this debate.

Review of Research on Juvenile Diversion

The negative consequences (i.e., increased likelihood of recidivism) associated with traditional juvenile justice involvement have been documented for quite some time (Hengeller & Schoenwald, 2010; Petrosino, Turpin-Petrosino, & Guckenburg, 2010). This body of research has demonstrated the need for alternative, less punitive juvenile justice responses to formal court processing. In turn, there has been a proliferation of diversion programs followed by an abundance of research evaluating their effectiveness. Research in this area typically focused on outcomes of recidivism by comparing youth who were diverted to those who were formally processed. Although to a much lesser degree, research does also exist that examines the impact of diversion on other outcomes (e.g., educational attainment, psychosocial development, cost, and net-widening) that are also relevant for determining effectiveness (e.g., Schwalbe, Gearing, MacKenzie, Brewer, & Ibrahim, 2012).

A considerable amount of research has accumulated on the effectiveness of diversion in reducing recidivism compared with traditional juvenile justice involvement. Several meta-analytic studies synthesize this body of research and provide a comprehensive assessment of the effectiveness of these programs in reducing recidivism (Gensheimer, Mayer, Gottschalk, & Davidson, 1986; Lipsey, 2009; Petrosino *et al.*, 2010; Schwalbe *et al.*, 2012; Whitehead & Lab, 1989; Wilson & Hoge, 2013). In general, the findings of these meta-analyses are rather mixed. For example, Gensheimer *et al.* (1986) conducted the first meta-analysis of the extant research at that time based on a sample of 44 effect sizes. The findings from their study suggested that diversion programs were no more effective in reducing subsequent delinquency than traditional juvenile court processing. More recently, Lipsey (2009) compared the effectiveness of intervention strategies in reducing recidivism based on 548 unique samples. Consistent with Gensheimer *et al.*'s findings, these researchers found that diversion was no more successful in reducing recidivism than probation or incarceration strategies. A more recent meta-analysis by Schwalbe *et al.* (2012) included 45 studies that compared diversion to non-intervention (i.e., caution-and-release) and formal court processing, and found that diversion was no more effective than either of these two strategies in reducing recidivism.

Other meta-analyses have found that diversion is effective. Petrosino *et al.* (2010) found advantages of diversion over formal processing. They examined the effectiveness of formal juvenile court processing among a sample of 29 experiments and found that, on average, formal processing increased recidivism compared with diversion, regardless of the nature of the outcome measured (i.e., self-report, incidence, prevalence, severity). Wilson and Hoge's (2013) meta-analysis included 45 studies and initially found diversion to be more effective at reducing recidivism compared with traditional processing. However, once these scholars controlled for methodological factors (e.g., quality of study, published vs. unpublished) across the included studies, the positive effects for diversion were no longer significant.

In sum, the findings across these meta-analyses are equivocal in terms of the effectiveness of diversion over traditional processing in reducing recidivism. One potential explanation for this, however, could be differences in study goals and, perhaps more importantly, the methodological differences (e.g., study inclusion criteria, effect size calculation, and coding strategies) across these meta-analyses. For example, Lipsey (2009) and Schwalbe *et al.* (2012) included a variety of diversion programs including youth courts and drug courts; Wilson and Hoge (2013) excluded these types of programs. Additionally, across meta-analyses, the way that the sample studies measured recidivism (the dependent variable) varied in terms of length of time measured, source of information, and definition of recidivism (i.e., arrest, referral, conviction). Thus, none of the meta-analyses included a standard measure of recidivism. Variations in the measurement of recidivism alone can lead to very different results regarding effectiveness of diversion programs. It is also possible that heterogeneity across diversion program components (e.g., goals, eligibility criteria, program components) contributed to these inconsistent findings. Yet, most of these studies included an array of diversion programs including youth courts, drug courts, mediation programs, and general diversion programs (Lipsey, 2009; Petrosino *et al.*, 2010; Schwalbe *et al.*, 2012).

Although the existing body of research is not clear on whether or not diversion is effective, there is some preliminary evidence for specific elements of diversion that might work best. For instance, Whitehead and Lab (1989) conducted a meta-analysis of studies evaluating different juvenile justice interventions. While there was little evidence that any of these interventions were effective, they did find that compared with formal sanctions (i.e., institutionalization and probation/parole), non-system diversion (e.g., community-based agencies) and system diversion (i.e., diversion programs overseen by juvenile justice agencies) were most promising. Lipsey (2009) found that diversion programs implementing services with a "skill building" (e.g., cognitive–behavioral therapy, academic training, and social skills training) approach did significantly reduce recidivism. Schwalbe *et al.* (2012) broke diversion down into distinct intervention types and found that those utilizing family-based treatment approaches significantly reduced recidivism. Finally, in addition to examining several moderators, Wilson and Hoge (2013) also separately analyzed the recidivism-reducing effect of programs implementing some form of intervention and non-intervention (i.e., caution-and-release) programs. For all diversion types, they found that programs targeting youth prior to formal charge imposition compared with post-charge were more effective in reducing recidivism. Likewise, programs overseen by juvenile justice agencies were more effective in reducing recidivism than community-based programs. Their findings regarding analyses on programs with interventions suggested that programs targeting higher risk offenders, utilizing cognitive–behavioral therapy, and tailored to the specific learning style of the juvenile, are more effective at reducing recidivism.

Future Directions for Juvenile Diversion

Recently, the juvenile justice system placed an emphasis on developing practices informed by empirically driven research (i.e., evidence-based practices). This approach clearly extends to diversion and, as the above review suggests, there exist a number of studies attempting to identify what works best with diversion. Therefore, in the next few sections we offer three broad areas for future research to consider.

Identification of effective diversion strategies in reducing recidivism

The heterogeneity that characterizes diversion can be viewed in both a positive and negative light. On one hand, it is evidence of the flexibility that enables individual-ized and tailored interventions to meet the needs of the offender and the community. On the other hand, however, this heterogeneity also limits the interpretability and synthesis of the considerable amount of research on diversion. As a result, to date, findings from this body of research are rather inconsistent. Contributing to this shortcoming of the existing evidence base is the large variation in target populations, diversion services delivered, and the measurement of recidivism both across studies of individual programs and within meta-analytic studies. Therefore, future research should seek to disentangle the results of these studies as well as conduct studies that are more focused either on a specific type of diversion program or component, or limit studies to only the variables/components that all programs have in common. For example, over the past several decades, a number of studies evaluating the effectiveness of local youth court programs have been conducted. Therefore, studies that focus specifically on the overall effects (i.e., meta-analysis) of youth courts would provide a more targeted assessment of the overall effectiveness of this type of diversion program. Studies that focus on a specific diversion component, such as mentoring or community service, would also add to the evidence base regarding which services are most successful.

At the same time, there is a critical need for a standardized measure of recidivism. This issue is not unique to the evaluation of diversion programs, but is a central problem when attempting to compare the effectiveness of any juvenile justice program across samples of offenders, different types of services, individual studies, or jurisdictions. Certainly, this is a difficult task to accomplish. Given the large number of studies examining juvenile diversion, future researchers should attempt to replicate previous measures of recidivism and, in the case of future meta-analyses, include studies that rely on similar recidivism definitions (e.g., officially recorded arrest only, self-report only). More broadly, there is a need for influential organiza-tions such as the OJJDP or the National Council of Juvenile and Family Court Judges

(NCJFCJ) to develop recommendations of a standard measure of recidivism to be used in research and practice.

Not only does the extensive heterogeneity in diversion limit interpretability of findings; it also limits generalizability (Mears *et al.*, 2011). Among the numerous studies (even the more rigorous ones) that find an effect for diversion, it is not clear whether the effect stemmed from the program-specific elements or whether the effect was process-related (e.g., enthusiasm and support of community, quality of implementation, and poor alternatives). Mears *et al.* (2011) suggest that more research is needed that not only examines the program-specific effects, but also accounts for the contextual, social, and process-related factors that contribute to a program's success. Similarly, the MFC Juvenile Diversion Workgroup (2011), which developed a "roadmap" for development and implementation of diversion programming, suggests that agencies should "decide for themselves the proper answer to each step in light of their own community's circumstances" (p. 18). Thus, there is a clear need for research that identifies what elements and combinations of different programming work and for whom (Mears *et al.*, 2011).

Furthermore, it is also important to examine differences in effectiveness across subgroups of juvenile offenders. Empirical evidence has demonstrated variations in both the risk factors for delinquency and responsiveness to prevention and intervention services across a number of important characteristics such as gender, race/ethnicity, and age (Ogden & Hagen, 2009; Stein, Deberard, & Homan, 2012). Research also suggests that intervention programs that are specifically tailored to the risk and needs of particular subgroups of adolescents are the most successful in reducing antisocial behaviors. The reason for the effectiveness of tailored intervention programs stems from the acknowledgement that "…adolescents are a heterogeneous mosaic of subgroups of different ethnicities/cultures, behavioral risk characteristics, developmental levels, sexual preferences, and gender differences" (DiClemente *et al.*, 2008, p. 600). Therefore, in addition to understanding which specific diversion strategies are successful at reducing recidivism in general, research is needed to examine the effectiveness of these programs across important socio-demographic risk factors.

The evaluation of important juvenile diversion outcomes

Although reducing criminal behavior is most often the main goal of juvenile diversion programs, it is not the only goal. In fact, there are a number of additional outcomes that should be considered when evaluating the effectiveness of diversion. These outcomes include other relevant psychosocial outcomes, cost savings, and net-widening.

Although sparse, the available research does suggest a positive effect for diversion on positive life outcomes (e.g., education and occupation attainment; Bernburg & Krohn, 2003; Sweeten, 2006), monetary cost, family functioning (Hodges, Martin, Smith, & Cooper, 2011), and reducing secure confinement (Sullivan,

Veysey, Hamilton, & Grillo, 2007). However, these and a variety of other outcomes have been largely overlooked by research evaluating the effectiveness of diversion programs (Mears *et al.*, 2011; Schwalbe *et al.*, 2012). Given that a variety of goals drive diversion programs, research evaluating alternative outcomes can have strong implications for determining what truly is effective. For instance, concluding that diversion is no more effective in reducing delinquency compared with traditional processing is not necessarily evidence against it, particularly when diversion costs less and reducing cost is also a goal of diversion. Similarly, additional research regarding net-widening is also needed. Net-widening has the potential to substantially increase the cost of juvenile justice processing if a large number of youths are participating in services that they do not need. At the same time, the iatrogenic effects of participation in diversion are not well documented. If, in fact, net-widening has led to negative outcomes for youth who would not normally have been involved in the system, then the longer-term costs associated with these consequences (i.e., future criminal behavior, substance use) should also be considered.

In addition to cost, there are several other outcomes that could be examined to assess the effectiveness of diversion, including educational/job attainment, mental health, substance abuse, program adherence, and stigmatization (Hodges *et al.*, 2011; Sullivan *et al.*, 2010). For example, the influence of juvenile justice involvement on mental health and substance abuse has clear implications for subsequent offending, given the predominance of mental illness among this population (Cocozza & Skowyra, 2000). Interventions that do not address and may even further exacerbate such problems can have deleterious effects on the youth, and compound costs to society (Cocozza *et al.*, 2005). For instance, placing youth in secure facilities would detach them from the social support (e.g., family) that is often necessary to increase program adherence and individual functioning. Alternatively, without effective intervention, youth with mental health issues are at increased risk of future contact with the justice system (Sullivan *et al.*, 2007).

Even within the research on specialized diversion programs, recidivism remains as the hallmark for assessing effectiveness. However, research directly assessing the impact of diversion programs on important psychosocial outcomes that influence antisocial behavior, physical and mental health, and social stability across the life course also carries important implications related to effectiveness. This area of research can be informative in terms of identifying what types of treatment modalities work best in the long run. That is, research focusing solely on recidivism as an outcome assumes that reductions in recidivism are due to treatment effects on targeted areas. It may be that positive effects on recidivism are due to improvements in other aspects of functioning. An additional concern is that short-term reductions in recidivism may not be representative of the longer-term positive life outcomes. Despite its importance for informing the debate about what works best, research examining a broader scope of outcomes is lacking. Thus, there is a clear need for research that focuses on outcomes of diversion, and juvenile justice involvement more generally, other than recidivism.

The implementation and evaluation of screening and assessment instruments to make diversion decisions

There are two critical decision points regarding diversion. The first critical decision point is the initial processing decision. With concerns of bias and disproportionate minority contact (DMC), there is a need for objective procedures to guide the decision-making process throughout the juvenile justice system, such as the use of evidence-based screening and assessment instruments. This strongly applies to the initial decision to divert the offender or to refer to formal processing. The use of screening and assessment tools has the potential to limit bias and increase effectiveness regarding these decisions. The second critical decision point is matching the program components to clients' needs. According to the Risk-Needs-Responsivity (RNR) model, the most effective strategy for reducing delinquent behavior is to identify each individual's risk for future behavior (risk), assess the multidimensional needs of each individual (needs), and tailor services (responsivity) to the individual's risk and needs (Andrews, Bonta, & Hoge, 1990). The use of screening and assessment instruments throughout the juvenile justice system is based on the RNR principles. Although not covered here, there is a fair amount of research establishing the effectiveness of screening and assessment instruments in predicting future behavior, matching risk/needs to treatment, and reducing biased decision-making throughout various stages of the juvenile justice system (see Grisso, Vincent, & Seagrave, 2005, for a review).

Additionally, the general lack of evidence-based practices for identifying psychological, environmental, and substance abuse issues can lead to inappropriate and ineffective matching of juveniles to needs-based services, and in some cases may do more harm than good (Cocozza *et al.*, 2005). From a programmatic standpoint, the implementation of screening and assessment tools help guide the initial decision to divert, the selection of the appropriate diversion program, and the identification of youth who may be better off receiving services through community-based agencies. Such tools also enhance the ability to identify issues specific to each youth and to match youth to the appropriate interventions. From a larger policy standpoint, the information collected from these instruments could be used to monitor the risk/needs factors that are prevalent among low-level offenders in the community, and to allow stakeholders to continually monitor whether the services offered are able to meet the needs of the community. Finally, from an empirical standpoint, these instruments provide critical data on the characteristics of offenders that come into contact with the system and help to identify those most at-risk for delinquency, successful or unsuccessful program completion, and future criminal behavior.

Despite the potential for these tools to inform decision-making, their use during diversion decision-making has only recently started to receive attention. Therefore, more research is needed to address the appropriateness of specific instruments for assessing youth at the front-end of the system, as well as the effectiveness of assessing risk and needs across race, ethnicity, gender, and age. Research addressing these areas can help to create or validate existing screening/assessment instruments that are sensitive to the risks/needs of low-level, first-time offenders.

Conclusion

Although juvenile diversion programs have been used in jurisdictions across the country for quite some time, a number of unanswered questions remain regarding the occurrence of net-widening, as well as the effectiveness of diversion in reducing recidivism, cost-saving, and improving youth outcomes across other relevant domains. One potential reason for the lack of consistent information regarding diver sion program effectiveness is the variation in definitions of recidivism, program goals, eligibility criteria, and service components. Future studies on the effectiveness of these programs should strive to identify "what works" at the lowest cost. In addition, future research is needed on the benefits and utility of screening and assessment tools to reduce bias in the decision-making process, to determine whether diversion is appropriate, and to match clients' risks and needs to intervention.

In sum, the foundation of juvenile diversion is to provide non-punitive responses to misbehavior while reducing the likelihood of future criminal behavior and other negative life consequences. These goals align seamlessly with the broader ideals of the original juvenile justice system. Therefore, the adherence to and accomplishment of these goals is critical to ensuring that the juvenile justice system is operating as originally intended, by providing services that are in the best interests of the youth as well as the community.

References

Andrews, D.A., Bonta, J., & Hoge, R.D. (1990). Classification for effective rehabilitation: Rediscovering psychology. *Criminal Justice and Behavior, 17*, 19–52.

Bechard, S., Ireland, C., Berg, B., & Vogel, B. (2011). Arbitrary arbitration: Diverting juveniles into the justice system – a reexamination after 22 years. *International Journal of Offender Therapy and Comparative Criminology, 55*, 605–625.

Beck, V.S., Ramsey, R.J., Lipps, T.R., & Travis, L.F. (2006). Juvenile diversion: An outcome study of the Hamilton County, Ohio unofficial juvenile community courts. *Juvenile and Family Court Journal, 57*, 1–10.

Bernburg, J.G., & Krohn, M.D. (2003). Labeling, life chances, and adult crime: The direct and indirect effects of official intervention in adolescence on crime in early adulthood. *Criminology, 41*, 1287–1318.

Binder, A., & Geis, G. (1984). *Ad populum* argumentation in criminology: Juvenile diversion as rhetoric. *Crime and Delinquency, 30*, 624–647.

Cécile, M., & Born, M. (2009). Intervention in juvenile delinquency: Danger of iatrogenic effects?. *Children and Youth Services Review, 31*(12), 1217–1221.

Chapin, D.A., & Griffin, P.A. (2005). Juvenile diversion. In K. Heilbrun, N.E.S. Goldstein, & R.E. Redding (Eds.), *Juvenile Delinquency: Prevention, Assessment, and Intervention* (pp. 161–178). New York: Oxford University Press.

Coccozza, J.J., & Skowyra, K.R. (2000). Youth with mental health disorders: Issues and emerging responses. *Juvenile Justice, 7*, 3–13.

Cocozza, J.J., Veysey, B.M., Chapin, D.A., Dembo, R., Walters, W., & Farina, S. (2005). Diversion from the juvenile justice system: The Miami-Dade juvenile assessment center post-arrest diversion program. *Substance Use & Misuse, 40*, 935–951.

Decker, S.H. (1985). A systematic analysis of diversion: Net widening and beyond. *Journal of Criminal Justice, 13*, 207–216.

DiClemente, R.J., Crittenden, C.P., Rose, E., Sales, J.M., Wingood, G.M., Crosby, R.A., & Salazar, L.F. (2008). Psychosocial predictors of HIV-associated sexual behaviors and the efficacy of prevention interventions in adolescents at-risk for HIV infections: What works and what doesn't work? *Psychosomatic Medicine, 70*, 598–605.

Dodge, K.A., Dishion, T.J., & Lansford, J.E. (2006). *Deviant Peer Influences in Programs for Youth: Problems and Solutions.* New York: Guilford.

Elrod, P., & Ryder, R. (1999). *Juvenile Justice: A Social, Historical, and Legal Perspective.* Gaithersburg, MD: Aspen Publishers, Inc.

Florida Department of Juvenile Justice. (2013). Florida's statewide civil citation: Part of the community, part of the solution. Retrieved from http://www.djj.state.fl.us/partners/our-approach/florida-civil-citation

Garrison, A.H. (2001). An evaluation of a Delaware teen court. *Juvenile and Family Court Journal, 52*, 1–11.

Gensheimer, L.K., Mayer, J.P., Gottschalk, R., & Davidson, W.S. (1986). Diverting youth from the juvenile justice system: A meta-analysis of intervention efficacy. In S. Pater, & A. Goldstein (Eds.), *Youth Violence: Programs and Prospects* (pp. 39–57). Elmsford, NY: Pergamon Press.

Grisso, T., Vincent, G., & Seagrave, D. (2005). Mental health screening and assessment in juvenile justice. New York: Guilford Press.

Hengeller, S.W., & Schoenwald, S.K. (2010). Evidence-based interventions for juvenile offenders and juvenile justice polices that support them. *Social Policy Report, 25*, 1–20.

Hodges, K., Martin, L.A., Smith, C., & Cooper, S. (2011). Recidivism, costs, and psychosocial outcomes for a post-arrest juvenile diversion program. *Journal of Offender Rehabilitation, 50*, 447–465.

Lemert, E.M. (1981). Diversion in juvenile justice: What hath been wrought. *Journal of Research in Crime and Delinquency, 18*, 34–46.

Lipsey, M.W. (2009). The primary factors that characterize effective interventions with juvenile offenders: A meta-analytic review. *Victims and Offenders, 4*, 124–147.

Maddan, S., & Marshall, I. (2009). Labeling and symbolic interaction theories. In J. Miller (Ed.), *21st Century Criminology: A Reference Handbook* (pp. 253–262). Thousand Oaks, CA: SAGE.

Mears, D.P., Cochran, J.C, Greenman, S.J., Bhati, A.S., & Greenwald, M.A. (2011). Evidence on the effectiveness of juvenile court sanctions. *Journal of Criminal Justice, 39*, 509–520.

Miller, M.L., Scocas, E.A., & O'Connell, J.P. (1998). *Evaluation of the juvenile drug court diversion program.* National Criminal Justice Reference Services. Retrieved from https://www.ncjrs.gov/pdffiles1/Digitization/172247NCJRS.pdf.

Models for Change Juvenile Diversion Workgroup. (2011). *Juvenile Diversion Guidebook.* Retrieved on from http://www.modelsforchange.net/publications/301

National Association of Youth Courts. (2014). *Youth courts facts and statistics.* Retrieved from http://www.youthcourt.net/?page_id=24

Ogden, T., & Hagen, K.A. (2009). What works for whom? Gender differences in intake characteristics and treatment outcomes following multisystemic therapy. *Journal of Adolescence, 32*, 1425–1435.

OJJDP Statistical Briefing Book. (2013). *Jurisdictional Boundaries.* Retrieved from http://www.ojjdp.gov/ojstatbb/structure_process/qa04102.asp?qaDate=2012

Petrosino, A., Turpin-Petrosino, C., & Guckenburg, S. (2010). Formal system processing of juveniles: Effects on delinquency. *Campbell Systematic Reviews, 1.* Retrieved from http://www.campbellcollaboration.org/news_/formal_processing_reduce_juvenile_delinquency.php

Pizarro, J., Chermak, S.M., & Gruenewald, J.A. (2007). Juvenile 'superpredators' in the news: A comparison of adult and juvenile homicides. *Journal of Crime and Popular Culture, 14*, 84–111.

Puzzanchera, C., & Kang, W. (2008). *Juvenile court statistics databook.* Retrieved from http://ojjdp.gov/

Roush, D.W. (1996). *Desktop Guide to Good Juvenile Detention Practice.* Research Report. Washington, DC: US Department of Justice, Office of Justice Programs, Office of Juvenile Justice and Delinquency Prevention.

Schiff, M., Bazemore, G., & Brown, M. (2011). Neighborhood Accountability Boards: The strength of weak practices and prospects for a "community building" restorative model. *Journal of Law & Policy, 36*, 17–46.

Schwalbe, C.S., Gearing, R.E., MacKenzie, M.J., Brewer, K.B., & Ibrahim, R. (2012). A meta-analysis of experimental studies of diversion programs for juvenile offenders. *Clinical Psychology Review, 32*, 26–33.

Smith, E.P., Wolf, A.M., Contrillon, D.M., Thomas, O., & Davidson, W.S. (2004). The Adolescent Diversion Project: 25 years of research on an ecological model of intervention. *Journal of Prevention and Intervention in the Community, 27*, 29–47.

Snyder, H.N. (1996). The juvenile court and delinquency cases. *The Future of Children: The Juvenile Court, 6*, 53–63.

Stein, D.M., Deberard, S., & Homan, K. (2012). Predicting success and failure in juvenile drug treatment court: A meta-analytic review. *Journal of Substance Abuse Treatment, 44*, 159–168.

Sullivan, C.J., Dollard, N., Sellers, B., & Mayo, J. (2010). Rebalancing response to school-based offenses: A civil citation program. *Youth Violence and Juvenile Justice, 8*, 279–294.

Sullivan, C.J., Veysey, B.M., Hamilton, Z.K., & Grillo, M. (2007). Reducing out-of-community placement and recidivism: Diversion of delinquent youth with mental health and substance use problems from the justice system. *International Journal of Offender Therapy and Comparative Criminology, 51*, 555–577.

Sweeten, G. (2006). Who will graduate? Disruption of high school education by arrest and court involvement. *Justice Quarterly, 23*, 462–480.

Umbreit, M.S., Coates, R.B., & Vos, B. (2004). Victim-offender mediation: Three decades of practice and research. *Conflict Resolution Quarterly, 22*, 279–303.

Whitehead, J.T., & Lab, S.P. (1989). A meta-analysis of juvenile correctional treatment. *Journal of Research in Crime and Delinquency, 26*, 276–295.

Whitehead, J.T., & Lab, S.P. (2001). *Juvenile Justice: An Introduction.* Cincinnati, OH: Anderson Publication Co.

Wilson, H.A., & Hoge, R.D. (2013). The effect of youth diversion programs on recidivism: A meta-analytic review. *Criminal Justice and Behavior, 40*, 497–518.

27

Youth in the Juvenile Court and Adult Court

Michael J. Leiber and Jennifer H. Peck

Introduction

In this chapter we discuss a number of issues pertaining to the juvenile justice system. The extent to which youth commit crime as well as their presence in the juvenile and adult court is first introduced, followed by discussion of the disproportionate overrepresentation of minority youth in the juvenile justice system or what is also known as DMC. Second, the issue involving the representation of girls in the juvenile justice system is described, followed by how status offenses are treated in the juvenile court, as well as juvenile justice decision-making and treatment of these offenders. The overreliance on the use of secure detention and the transfer of youth from the juvenile court to the adult criminal court comprise the third and fourth concerns confronting juvenile justice policy. The final issue addressed surrounds the sentencing of juveniles to life without parole (LWOP). In addition, following a discussion of each issue is a concluding paragraph that is framed around policy initiatives and implementations.

Definitions and Presence of Youth in the Juvenile and Adult Court

One of the issues surrounding youth in the juvenile and adult court is the perception that serious juvenile offending is a significant problem in the US (Bernard & Kurlychek, 2010). Public perceptions of juvenile offending tend to focus on the context that youth disproportionately commit criminal acts, especially violent

The Handbook of Juvenile Delinquency and Juvenile Justice, First Edition. Edited by Marvin D. Krohn and Jodi Lane.

behavior. Concerns about youth violence emerged in the early 1990s when the public perception was that first-time juvenile offenders were qualitatively different than youthful offenders of years past, and that the lenient treatment of offenders by the juvenile justice system was perpetuating the high rates of juvenile crime (Zimring, 1998). The emergence of juvenile "super-predators" characterized by violence, impulsivity, and an absence of remorse were predicted to emerge by the early 2000s and would subsequently become high-rate, repeat offenders (Bennett, DiIulio, & Walters, 1996; Wilson & Petersilia, 2010).

The imagery of the rise of violent juvenile offending, especially juvenile homicide offending, resulted in legislative responses that shifted the role of the juvenile justice system from a rehabilitative effort to a more punitive, "get tough" system (Bernard & Kurlychek, 2010). Overall, changes were made to the purpose, processes, and dispositional outcomes of the juvenile court (Feld, 1999). Instead of a rehabilitative approach, the juvenile court shifted its primary purpose to protect the public from juvenile offenders. In terms of processing youthful offenders throughout the juvenile justice system, the experience would be more formal and mirror the adult system. There was also a shift in the nature of dispositional outcomes. Traditionally, the purpose of the disposition was to rehabilitate and provide treatment to youth who were brought to the juvenile court, yet the "get tough" movement resulted in dispositional outcomes that focused on protecting the community and taking into consideration victims of the offense (Bernard & Kurlychek, 2010).

According to Zimring (1998), the overall rise in homicides committed by juveniles throughout 1984–1994 resulted in longer sentences for juvenile offenders as well as the transfer of youth to the adult criminal justice system. While the early 1990s showed an increase in arrest rates for juvenile offenders, the middle-to-late 1990s saw a general decrease and stabilization of juvenile arrest rates, which mirrored the violent and overall arrest rates from the 1980s (Zimring, 1998). Concerning homicide, by 2002 arrests for murder by juveniles were even below the rates in the 1980s (Puzzanchera, Sladky, & Kang, 2012b). Therefore, these statistics are in disagreement with the public's imagery and legislative reform of the "violent juvenile offender", and the need to "get tough" on juvenile offending in the 1990s. The combination of official statistics (i.e., the Uniform Crime Reports) and self-report studies (e.g., Monitoring the Future) can provide the public with a more accurate insight into the distribution of crime committed by juveniles compared with media perceptions. Discussing the issue surrounding the imagery that juveniles disproportionately commit crimes compared with adults is important in reducing the stereotype that youth are violent predators who are overrepresented in the offending population.

The term *juvenile delinquency* refers to the participation in illegal behavior by an individual who falls under a statutory age limit. A specific delinquent act is any offense committed by a juvenile that, if it was committed by an adult, could result in criminal prosecution (Puzzanchera, Adams, & Hockenberry, 2012a). In the US there is no single juvenile justice system, and each state determines what age range qualifies for classification as a juvenile offender. In some states, a youth as young as

7 years old can be arrested for delinquent behavior. In other states, youth aged 16–18 are automatically processed as adults in the criminal justice system. For example, a youth who is 15 years old represents the "upper age of jurisdiction" in the states of Connecticut, New York, and North Carolina, and the upper age is 16 years old in Massachusetts, South Carolina, and Texas, among others (Puzzanchera *et al.*, 2012a).

In general, most states consider juveniles to be between the ages of 8–17. According to FBI arrest statistics, in 2010 over 1.6 million youth under the age of 18 were arrested for violent, property or other (e.g. vandalism, disorderly conduct) types of crimes (Puzzanchera *et al.*, 2012b). On average, throughout the 2000s juveniles represented over 25% of the general population. These youthful offenders were responsible for 15% of all (juvenile and adult) Part 1 violent crime arrests and 24% of property crime arrests. These statistics have remained stable or have been slightly decreasing since the early 1990s.

Furthermore, between 1998 and 2007, juvenile arrests for violent crime fell proportionately more (−14%) than adult arrests (−8%). The change in arrest rates for property crime was even more dramatic for juveniles than adults, with decreases of 33% and 2%, respectively (Puzzanchera *et al.*, 2012b). These arrest statistics conflict with the public perception that juveniles disproportionately engage in offending behavior compared with their representation in the general population, as technically they are underrepresented or almost equal to their overall representation in the US.

In order to understand the extent and presence of youth in the juvenile and criminal justice systems, it is important first to know offense-specific components of juvenile arrests. Arrest generally is a juvenile's first point of contact with the justice system. Juveniles represented approximately 5% of all arrests for Part 1 violent index crimes in 2009. Arrests for homicide included the smallest percentage (0.06%), while arrests for aggravated assault comprised the largest percentage (3%). Juvenile arrests for property crimes occurred more frequently, which mirrors the general trend when comparing arrests between property and violent offenses. For example, compared with all other Part 1 property crimes (burglary, motor vehicle theft, and arson), arrests for larceny-theft occurred the most frequently (17%). However, the majority of all juvenile arrests were for non-index offenses, including other assaults (12%), drug abuse violations (9%), disorderly conduct (9%), and curfew and loitering (6%) (Puzzanchera *et al.*, 2012b). Therefore, the specific arrest statistics from 2009 do not fully match the imagery of the violent juvenile offender, as arrests for the violent crimes of homicide and aggravated assault occur less often than other recorded types of offending behavior.

Out of the 1.6 million youth who were arrested in 2010, over 1.3 million of those juveniles were referred to the juvenile court (Sickmund, Sladky, & Kang, 2013). Table 27.1 presents the demographic characteristics by gender and race of all cases that were referred to the juvenile court in 2010. Of those cases that were referred to the juvenile court, youth were referred most often for property offenses, followed by public order, person, and then drug crimes.

Across all offense types, male and black juveniles were overrepresented in the juvenile court compared with their representation in the general population. Specific

Table 27.1 Demographic characteristics of cases handled by the juvenile court, 2010

	Male	Female	White	Black	Native American	Other[a]
Referral offense						
Person	240,631	106,186	198,920	139,127	4,808	3,962
	(70)[b]	(30)	(57)	(41)	(1)	(1)
Property	354,599	147,841	329,534	156,034	8,203	8,670
	(71)	(29)	(66)	(31)	(1)	(2)
Drugs	134,744	29,393	125,370	34,006	2,686	2,076
	(82)	(18)	(76)	(21)	(2)	(1)
Public order	256,688	98,069	222,587	121,896	5,445	4,828
	(72)	(28)	(63)	(34)	(2)	(1)
Detained	228,201	58,706	163,766	113,925	5,054	4,162
	(80)	(20)	(57)	(40)	(2)	(1)
Formally charged	564,297	168,875	441,890	267,543	12,655	11,084
	(77)	(23)	(60)	(37)	(2)	(1)
Adjudicated delinquent	337,072	91,085	266,182	146,839	8,752	6,383
	(79)	(21)	(62)	(35)	(2)	(1)
Probation	201,769	58,580	166,921	83,642	5,464	4,322
	(78)	(22)	(64)	(32)	(2)	(2)
Placed out of home	94,837	17,722	65,196	43,623	2,349	1,391
	(84)	(16)	(58)	(39)	(2)	(1)
Waived to adult court	5,506	458	3,122	2,654	140	48
	(92)	(8)	(52)	(45)	(2)	(1)

[a] Other includes Asian, Hawaiian, and Pacific Islander.
[b] Numbers in parentheses are percentages.
Data source: National Center for Juvenile Justice (2013). *National Juvenile Court Data Archive: Juvenile court case records 1985–2010* [machine-readable data files]. Pittsburgh, PA: NCJJ [producer].

issues about the role of race and gender within the juvenile and adult court will be discussed in more detail throughout the chapter, but it is important to introduce the general issue of males and minority group members being overrepresented throughout both court systems. More specifically, male and female youth under the age of 18 represented 51% and 49% of the overall juvenile population in 2010. While white youth made up 76% of the juvenile population, 17% was represented by black youth, and Native American and Other youth comprised 2% and 5% respectively. Over 70% of cases in each offense type were represented by males, while between 21% and 41% of all cases in each offense type were represented by black youth, with their largest overrepresentation being in person offenses. The largest representation of females across offense types was for person crimes (30%). Native American and Other youth are consistently equal to or underrepresented across each offense type compared with their representation in the overall juvenile population.

Gender and racial disparities are also evident in cases that resulted in preadjudicatory detention. Out of all of the cases that were detained, 80% were male, and 42%

were black youth. Disparities continued to occur as males represented 77% of all cases that resulted in formal charging, while black youth represented 37% of all cases that were formally charged. White youth are slightly more represented at the stage of adjudication compared with prior stages and proceedings (detention and formal charging). Whites represented 57% of all youth detained and 60% of those formally charged; they are the largest racial group to be adjudicated delinquent (62%). Recall though, that white youth represent 76% of the overall juvenile population, so they are still underrepresented throughout these stages compared with their overall representation. Once again, black youth are overrepresented at the adjudicatory stage, as they make up 35% of all youth who are adjudicated.

Data are provided yearly from the Office of Juvenile Justice and Delinquency Prevention (OJJDP) for three potential outcomes at judicial disposition: probation (community supervision), out of home placement (residential placement), and other (not described in table). Of those youth who were adjudicated delinquent (more than 438,000), over 260,000 juveniles received probation as a dispositional outcome, while approximately 112,000 youth were placed outside of the home. Females were more likely to receive probation (22%) compared with residential placement (16%), while black youth were more likely to receive the more severe outcome of out of home placement (39%) compared with community supervision (32%). Both Native American and Other youth were underrepresented at both dispositional outcomes, and had a similar likelihood of receiving either probation or out of home placement.

There are also a significant number of youth each year who are removed from the juvenile court and transferred/waived to the adult court for further proceedings. While the percentage of cases waved is relatively small (0.4%) compared with all cases that are initially referred to the juvenile court, approximately 5,900 juvenile cases were waived to adult court in 2010. Of those waived cases, male youth were over 11 times more likely to be waived compared with female youth. Disparities across racial groups were once again found, as minorities in general represented 48% of all waived cases, while black youth alone represented 45% of all youth waived. Overall, there is substantial evidence that gender and race disparities occur throughout all stages of juvenile justice proceedings, as males and black youth are consistently overrepresented throughout the juvenile justice system compared with their representation in the general juvenile population.

As introduced earlier, since the 1990s there has been a perception that youth violence is a severe problem in the US, and in order to reduce the occurrence of juvenile offending (and subsequent presence of youth in the juvenile and adult court), legislative reform occurred to "get tough" on youthful offenders. However, data have shown that juveniles do not disproportionately commit crime compared with their adult counterparts. While there was an increase in juvenile crime throughout the early 1990s, trends since then have declined and stabilized to reflect similar statistics from the 1980s. For the most part juveniles do not disproportionately engage in offending behavior. More specifically, as violent offenders, youth have been consistently below their representation in the general population. Depending on the year examined, juveniles have been slightly overrepresented as property offenders. There are additional issues surrounding the presence of youth in the juvenile and adult court systems. Some of these matters reflect potential race and gender biases, problems with the use of secure detention, concerns surrounding the transfer of youth to the adult court, and the debate surrounding juveniles who receive life sentences. The remainder of the chapter will focus on these specific issues.

Minority Overrepresentation in the Juvenile Justice System

As discussed, black youth are overrepresented in the juvenile justice system, especially at formal charging, out of home placement at judicial disposition, and placement in correctional institutions (Bishop & Leiber, 2011). Differential offending (i.e., minorities commit more, and more serious, delinquent acts compared with whites) and racial bias among juvenile justice decision-makers are the two main explanations for understanding the relationship between race/ethnicity and juvenile justice system proceedings (Leiber & Rodriguez, 2011).

While decisions to stop, release, refer, or arrest youth are contingent upon a variety of factors beyond the type of offense and its severity (e.g., patrolling patterns, style and structure of the police department, goals of the police department, socio-economic makeup of a community, where the youth lives), questions emerge concerning whether official arrest data reflect bias in police decision-making and procedures. Still, comparisons of arrest data with victimization and self-report data reveal race as an important correlate of crime (Pope & Snyder, 2003; Sampson & Lauritsen, 1997; Thornberry & Krohn, 2000). In most instances, minority youth, and in particular black youth, are involved in more offending and more serious offending compared with whites (Elliott, 1994; Hindelang, 1978). Although the racial differences are not as large as those reported in official arrest data, results from victimization data and self-report surveys lend some support to the differential offending explanation of minority overrepresentation in the juvenile justice system (Huizinga, Loeber, & Thornberry, 1994).

Racial and ethnic selection bias is a second explanation of minority overrepresentation in arrests and presence in the juvenile justice system. Up until the 1980s, people perceived that blatant, overt, or intentional racial bias and racism occurred against minorities. However, this was not necessarily true. A review of over 50 years of sentencing research concluded that from the time of the civil rights movement, there has been a transition from overt to covert racial bias. While overt discrimination was present throughout the 1930s to the mid-1960s (race was directly related to more harsh sentencing outcomes), sentencing decisions from the late 1960s to the early 1980s confirmed the effects of race were more implicit, subtle, or subconscious. Recent research has found the presence of unconscious negative race stereotypes that result in black youth being viewed as more blameworthy and culpable for their offenses; resulting in harsher outcomes in juvenile justice proceedings, while overt or conscious race bias had little impact. Subtle bias, however, is no less harmful than overt bias. Steen and colleagues found that probation officers adhered to a form of implicit racial bias by describing black offenders as actively making poor and destructive choices to maintain a criminal lifestyle (Steen, Bond, Bridges, & Kubrin, 2005). This thought process on part of the decision-makers was not extended to white youth.

From this overt to hidden transition, racism or racial bias has been discovered to operate indirectly or in interaction with other conditions (e.g., age, family situations). For example, age may seem race-neutral but can increase racial disparities at numerous decision-making stages (Leiber & Johnson, 2008). Within the juvenile justice system, age is considered a mitigating factor due to the belief that younger youth lack *mens rea* (intent) due to immaturity, inexperience, and inability to resist peer pressure. From this, older youth are seen as more responsible and handled more formally than younger youth, who receive a "youth discount". However, Leiber and Johnson (2008) found that white adolescents received a "youth discount" at the stage of intake, yet similarly situated black youth were referred to further proceedings. Therefore, the "youth discount" did not extend to black youth, regardless of the age criterion supported by the juvenile court. Another example of race effects that are masked by other conditions is the research by Bishop and Frazier (1996) who found that juvenile justice officials perceived single-parent minority families as more broken and dysfunctional than single-parent white homes. This perception resulted in minority youth subsequently being treated more harshly throughout juvenile court outcomes compared with white youth.

Overall, at least seven comprehensive reviews of existing literature report that legal (e.g., offense type, crime severity) and extra-legal factors (e.g., age, family structure) alone cannot account for racial differences in involvement in the juvenile justice system (Pope & Feyerherm, 1993). This conclusion lends support to the base premises of the race/ethnic selection bias perspective. Stated differently, race/ethnicity still matters in the court processing of juveniles. For example, Pope and Feyerherm (1993) discovered that roughly two-thirds of studies conducted from 1970 through 1988 found that minority youth, primarily black youth, experienced more severe outcomes relative to similarly situated white youth. A more recent literature review of over 150 studies on race and juvenile justice decision-making led Bishop and Leiber (2011) to a similar conclusion.

In conclusion, both differential offending and selection bias provide an understanding for the overrepresentation of minority youth in the juvenile justice system. In 1989, the disproportionate minority confinement mandate (DMC) was passed by Congress as part of the reauthorization of the Juvenile Justice and Delinquency Prevention Act (JJCPA) of 1974. In 2002, the JJDP Act was modified, shifting the emphasis from "disproportionate minority confinement" to "disproportionate minority contact", requiring the examination of possible minority youth overrepresentation throughout all decision points in the juvenile justice system, including referral and arrest. Throughout the history of the DMC initiative and continuing today, the underlying goal of the mandate is the equitable treatment of all youth within the juvenile justice system, regardless of race. Although there have been mixed views concerning the overall effectiveness of the mandate in reducing DMC (Leiber & Rodriguez, 2011), at a minimum, there has been greater sensitivity and awareness to the role(s) that differential offending and selection bias play in the overrepresentation of minority youth in the juvenile justice system.

Girls, Status Offenders, Juvenile Justice Decision-Making and Treatment

While the Juvenile Justice and Delinquency Prevention Act (JJDPA) of 1974, and its reauthorization in 1992 and again in 2002, dealt with the involvement and service needs of minorities, an additional focus was on females in the juvenile justice system. Before the passage of the JJDPA, female youth who were charged and placed in training schools for status offenses significantly outnumbered their male counterparts. Concerns were raised pertaining to the differential treatment of females compared with males for being involved in status offenses (e.g., running away, truancy, etc.) as well as among youth charged with delinquent offenses, and the JJDPA attempted to address these issues. One major goal of the JJDPA was also the deinstitutionalization of status offenders by requiring those charged with such behavior to be removed from juvenile detention and correctional facilities and dealt with in a less hostile manner. Currently, the presence of the status offender in the juvenile justice system has declined since the passage of the JJDPA.

Still, many have argued that while improvements have occurred in the response to girls relative to boys, problems still exist. For example, some have pointed out that the JJDPA has resulted in the encouragement of "bootstrapping" or upgrading status offenders to delinquents (Feld, 2009). Furthermore, a 1980 amendment to the JJDPA has allowed states to continue to confine status offenders if they violate a "valid court order" or are charged with contempt (Bishop & Frazier, 1992; Schwartz, 1989). In addition, youth may also be charged with a delinquent act (i.e. simple assault) instead of a status offense (i.e. incorrigibility), which leads to youth being labeled as delinquent rather than a status offender (Chesney-Lind & Belknap, 2004).

In terms of treatment within juvenile justice proceedings, some studies discover little to no disparate handling of female status offenders once factors such as prior record and family considerations are taken into account. At the same time, research also reports gender disparities among both status offenders and delinquents (Chesney-Lind, 1997). More specifically, when comparisons have been made that involve female status offenders relative to female delinquents, some prior research has found that the female status offender is responded to more severely than the female delinquent offender (Chesney-Lind, 1997).

To understand the treatment of females relative to males, the issue has been couched traditionally within the context of theoretical perspectives that focus on notions of chivalry and paternalism. Depending on the perspective, girls have been assumed to either receive more severe outcomes (the chivalry position) or more lenient outcomes (the paternalistic position) compared with boys (Bishop & Frazier,

1992; Chesney-Lind & Shelden, 2004; MacDonald & Chesney-Lind, 2001; Mallicoat, 2007). Although individual studies support the chivalry and paternalistic perspectives, some studies also have found that, when compared to males, female youth receive both more lenient and more severe outcomes depending on the stage of proceedings.

Some studies have argued that the inconsistencies in the gender bias literature may be explained by the confounding influence that race has on juvenile justice decision-making (Leiber, Brubaker, & Fox, 2009; Leiber & Peck, forthcoming). A similar point is echoed by Price and Sokoloff (2004), who suggest that girls receive lenient treatment within the juvenile justice system as a result of being considered weaker, innocent, and less responsible for their crimes, but this benefit generally is limited to white and heterosexual girls. Chesney-Lind (1997) also has posited that the deinstitutionalization of status offenses created a "two-track" juvenile justice system (one for white girls and one for minorities) where only black girls are labeled "deviant". Chesney-Lind (1997) believes that the racist legacy of excluding black girls from the chivalry perspective that is afforded to whites has been fundamental in maintaining interlocking systems of race and gender opposition. Likewise, some research has suggested that black females have not received preferential treatment (owed to their female status) for involvement in delinquency offenses, as they are the recipients of both sexism and racism. Gaarder, Rodriguez, and Zatz (2004) examined the perceptions of females held by juvenile court personnel through qualitative analysis, and discovered that attributes of delinquency and victimization assigned to females by court officials were often linked to racialized and gendered social constructions. The effects of such bias were particularly negative for Latinas, whose histories of victimization and delinquency were overlooked due to stereotypes regarding their sexuality invoked by officials.

Recently the intersectionality perspective has emerged as a framework to illustrate the presence of both gender and race bias. The perspective focuses on simultaneously being a female and/or a minority, instead of assuming that individuals across all situations have the same experiences. In other words, an individual's experiences vary by gender and race/ethnicity. The experiences of black girls in the juvenile justice system, for example, may be completely different than white females, whose experiences may also be unlike those of black males. Therefore, the intersectionality perspective recognizes the potential for multiple and intersecting inequalities in regard to court outcomes within a "race/gender/crime nexus" (Chesney-Lind, 2006, p. 10).

In addition to research on girls and their handling by and within the system, treatment services provided to females has been a growing subject of inquiry (Brubaker & Fox, 2010; Kempf-Leonard & Sample, 2000). Similar to boys in the system, girls who come into contact with the juvenile court come from problematic environments comprised of poverty, unemployment, high-crime neighborhoods, and unstable families (Chauhan, Reppucci, & Turkheimer, 2009; Chesney-Lind, Shelden, & Joe, 1996). Minority youth are much more likely to live in these environments, and as previously discussed, are overrepresented in the juvenile justice system. Research has shown significant differential service involvement by race and gender (Garland & Besinger, 1997), where minority and female adolescents consistently receive fewer treatment services (Kempf-Leonard & Sample, 2000).

Relative to boys, girls' issues are more often related to sexual assault and sexual risk that force them to run away from abusive relationships, contribute to serious mental health and substance abuse problems, and place them under the scrutiny of authority figures. These problematic situations typically subject them to punitive responses because of the violation of gender expectations. Although less is known about race differences among females, the literature indicates important research insights. For example, some studies report that black girls were more likely to be involved in more serious crimes such as unprovoked assault, possession of a weapon, and starting fist-fights, compared with other racial/ethnic females. Chauhan *et al.* (2009) also found that physical abuse by parents was related to violent behavior for white girls, whereas witnessing violence was associated with violent and delinquent behaviors for black girls. Overall, the limited research that exists emphasizes the importance of recognizing the intersection of race/ethnicity and girls' unique experiences. This is especially true within the contexts of their lives, shaping their problems and delinquent behavior in ways that are different from those of whites and males.

Issues Surrounding Secure Detention

Detention is one of the most frequently studied decision points throughout the juvenile justice system (Bishop & Leiber, 2011). Secure detention refers to holding youth in a juvenile detention facility after they are arrested and awaiting further court proceedings. Juveniles may be detained if the court has reason to believe that they will fail to appear at subsequent hearings, or may be held in "preventative detention" if they are predicted to commit future crimes. The justification for preventative detention is to protect the community from a juvenile's propensity to offend in the future.

In 2009, over 306,000 cases of youth aged 12–17 resulted in preadjudicatory detention, where male youth made up approximately 80% of those detained and female youth 20%. Across racial/ethnic groups, African-Americans were overrepresented in being held in secure detention (42%), compared with whites (55%), American Indians (1.6%), and Asians/Pacific Islanders (1.4%) (Bishop & Leiber, 2011). It has been argued that drug offenders and gang members are often targeted for presumptive detention (Orlando, 1999), while other research has found that over 30% of all youth who are held in secure detention are detained for status offenses, or technical violations while on probation (Austin, Johnson, & Weitzer, 2005).

The decision to detain youth is often linked to judgments by juvenile court officers based on family and school situations. For example, assessments about parental supervision, especially concerning youth who live in non-intact families compared with intact, are often predictive of detention. In addition, whether youth are enrolled and/or performing well in school, or are employed at the time of the referral, have also been predictive of detention outcomes (Leiber, 2013).

Empirical studies surrounding the effects of gender and race/ethnicity on detention outcomes report often that black youth are more likely that similarly situated whites to be held in pre-adjudication detention (Leiber & Fox, 2005). For example, some research has found that black males have the highest likelihood of being detained, followed by white males, then females in general (both white and black girls) (Guevara, Herz, & Spohn; 2006). Conflicting effects, however, have also been found in the detention literature. Black youth at times have been less likely to be detained compared with whites, including no racial differences in the likelihood of secure detention between white and American Indian youth.

Even though some states have tried to regulate the use of detention through risk assessment instruments and other screening criteria (Feyerherm, 2007), especially how the use of detention should be structured based on the use of standardized detention screening instruments, it has been argued that the standards and regulations in the application of detention are vague and subject to discretion (see Leiber & Boggess, 2012; Orlando, 1999). The utilization of standardized screening instruments has been a prominent strategy stressed by the Annie E. Casey Foundation (including the Juvenile Detention Alternatives Initiative), the MacArthur Foundation, and the Office of Juvenile Justice & Delinquency Prevention, to reduce the reliance on secure detention, and when it is employed, that there is greater consistency in the justification for its use (Annie E. Casey Foundation, 2009b). However, research has found that numerous jurisdictions do not use standardized screening instruments to arrive at detention decisions (Mulvey & Iselin, 2008). This is unfortunate because it has been argued that jurisdictions that do utilize detention screening instruments have been able to reduce the overall number of youth detained in facilities (Center on Juvenile and Criminal Justice, 2009).

Researchers have argued for the need for alternatives to secure detention, mostly due to issues with overcrowding in juvenile detention facilities, and the unproven effectiveness of detention. The unnecessary use of secure detention often has negative implications that further disadvantage youth, in that incarceration, even for a short period of time, has the potential to increase the risk of recidivism, subsequent incarceration, and hinder life chances in terms of education, marriage, and employment. Detaining juveniles further creates separation between the youth and potential positive influences such as family and school.

For example, cumulative disadvantage is a concept that is commonly tied with the use of secure detention. This disadvantage hinders youth, especially minority youth, because research has found that youth who are held in secure detention are more likely to receive disadvantaged outcomes throughout further juvenile court proceedings compared with youth who are not detained (Bishop & Leiber, 2011). For example, race differences in the use of secure detention can result in a cumulative mechanism for youth in general, as well as minority overrepresentation in subsequent stages of juvenile justice processing (e.g., adjudication, judicial disposition). Youth of color are severely overrepresented in secure detention compared with their representation in the overall population. In 2008, 69% of all youth detained were racial or ethnic minorities. Guevara and colleagues (2006) found that males and minority youth were more likely to be held in preadjudication detention compared with their gender and race counterparts. While minority males were more likely than white males to be detained, no race differences were reported between female youth. In addition, research by Rodriguez (2010) supports the argument that cumulative disadvantage exists for youth who are detained. Specifically, youth who were held in preadjudication detention in Arizona were more likely to be formally processed, more likely to be adjudicated, and more likely to receive a harsh sentence at judicial disposition (removal from the home), compared with youth who were not detained (Rodriguez, 2010). Harsh treatment at the stage of judicial disposition for youth who are detained has also been found in additional studies in that being detained is a strong predictor of severe treatment at judicial disposition.

In terms of policy implications regarding alternatives to secure detention, the Juvenile Detention Alternatives Initiative (JDAI) was formed in 1992 to support the Annie E. Casey Foundation's effort at detention reform. JDAI's main goals are to reduce the juvenile and adult justice systems' reliance on the secure confinement of youth, to improve public safety, to reduce racial disparities and bias in the use of secure detention, and to motivate overall juvenile justice reforms. For example, two of the objectives of secure detention are (1) to ensure that youth return for subsequent court hearings, and (2) to ensure public safety by making sure that youth do not commit crimes while awaiting court appearances (Mendel, 2009). JDAI has improved public safety while decreasing the number of youth held in detention prior to court hearings by setting up detention alternatives in the form of home confinement, evening reporting systems, and shelter care (Hsia & Beyer, 2000). This provides the youth with supervision, guarantees that the youth returns for court dates, and reduces the opportunity for the youth to reoffend. An example of this method of detention reform is executed in Cook County (Chicago), Illinois. Prior to the implementation of JDAI in Cook County, over 40% of all youth did not return to court for later hearings. After the implementation, 87% of all youth appeared before the court. In Multnomah (Orgeon) and Santa Cruz (California) counties (who also have implemented JDAI), over 90% of youth appear at court after being arrested (Annie E. Casey Foundation, 2009a).

With regard to reducing minority overrepresentation in secure detention, the JDAI has reduced the number of youth of color in detention. There have been reductions in the overall number of minorities detained; however, their overall representation in detention compared with the overall population may not have changed. For example, in 1996 in Cook County, minority youth represented 93% of all youth detained (658 of 710) when the JDAI was initiated (Annie E. Casey Foundation, 2009a). By 2006, the average daily population of youth being held in secure detention decreased from 710 to 426, but 411 of the 426 (96%) were minority youth. Due to the JDAI detention reforms, Cook County was detaining 247 fewer minority youth on a daily average, even though there was an 11% increase in the general minority population from 1996–2006. Multnomah County, however, reduced its overall minority overrepresentation in secure detention. Throughout the 1990s after the implementation of JDAI, the proportion of minority youth detained decreased from 73% to 50% (Annie E. Casey Foundation, 2009a).

Another example of detention reform is the detention diversion advocacy program (DDAP). DDAP has been recognized as a national model of evidence-based practice by the US Department of Justice, and its primary goal is to reduce overcrowding in secure detention, to ensure youth attend court hearings, and do not re-offend while awaiting case disposition (Austin *et al.*, 2005). This program specifically targets high-risk youth, and instead of placing them in secure detention, the program provides various services to address their multiple needs (Leiber & Rodriguez, 2011). Like the JDAI, this specific alternative to secure detention has the potential to reduce overcrowding, cut operating costs of juvenile detention centers, shield youth from possible stigmatization, and promote positive relationships between youth and their families, schools, and community.

Youth Transferred/Waived To Adult Court

Historically, juvenile court judges have had the ability to transfer youth from the juvenile court to the jurisdiction of the adult criminal justice system. The US Supreme Court, in the *Kent v. United States* (1966) decision, formalized judicial waiver hearings by mandating a hearing, access to counsel and probation reports, and written findings for the appellate court to review. In *Breed v. Jones* (1975) the Supreme Court required courts to determine jurisdictional control, juvenile or adult, before going to trial. The inclusion of the double jeopardy clause of the Fifth Amendment prevented youth from being tried twice for the same offense.

The waiver of youth to adult court expanded considerably starting in the 1980s and 1990s (Torbet *et al.*, 1996). Almost every state enacted policies to make it easier to transfer youth to adult court (e.g., lowering of the age for waiver to occur, offense-specific justifications for waiver to occur, prosecutorial discretion to exercise a direct file) (Torbet *et al.*, 1996). Many states also enacted reverse waiver procedures whereby a case begins in the adult system but later is transferred back to the juvenile justice system. In addition, states passed legislation known as "once an adult, always an adult" that involves the termination of a juvenile court's jurisdiction for future offenses. Overall, most states have one or more of these waivers to treat youth in the adult criminal justice system (Feld & Bishop, 2012).

As discussed earlier, this expansion and use of the waiver process was fostered by concerns over the rising juvenile crime rate, and in particular, violent crime (Feld, 1999; Singer, 1996). Accordingly, this method for handling youth represented efforts for greater accountability and punishment for offending behavior. The juvenile court was perceived as "soft" and failed to deliver on the rehabilitation of troubled youth (Fagan, 2010; Feld, 1999). Currently, it is estimated that 250,000 juveniles are processed in adult court (Feld & Bishop, 2012, p. 815). According to the Campaign for Youth Justice, each year judges waive roughly 7,500 cases, prosecutors direct-file approximately 27,000 juvenile offenders to the adult criminal justice system, and the remainder of the youth are accounted for by excluded offenses. The typical waived youth is aged 15 to 16 years old (Snyder & Sickmund, 2006). Research is somewhat mixed concerning what type of offender is responded to the most severely in the adult criminal court. For example, some research shows that juvenile waivers are often used for less serious offenders (i.e., property, drugs) than violent offenders; however, other studies have reported the opposite (Howell, 1996). The extent to which this finding is held to be true is conditioned by geography (see also Feld & Bishop, 2012: 818).

Research has shown that minority youth are disproportionately subject to waiver policies. Furthermore, black youth in the 1990s were 40% more likely to be waived to adult criminal court for a drug offense compared with white youth. Today, national data demonstrate that minority youth, especially black youth, are transferred to adult courts slightly in excess of their proportional representation in the youth population, as well as in the overall cases processed by the juvenile justice system.

Fagan and colleagues conducted two studies that focused specifically on the racial predictors of judicial transfer to adult court using multivariate statistical analyses. In the first study by Fagan and colleagues (1987), race was not a direct significant predictor of juvenile transfer in the multivariate analyses, but race indirectly affected the decision to waive a youth, as minority youth charged with a homicide offense were more likely than whites to be transferred. Kurlychek and Johnson (2004) compared the sentencing of juveniles in adult court to the sentences of young adults in adult court. They discovered that juvenile offenders (younger than 18 years old) were treated more severely than young adult offenders (aged 18 to 20) in adult court. Kurlychek and Johnson concluded that youth transferred to adult court were perceived as more dangerous and blameworthy, but this conclusion was not conditioned by race. Other studies have reported that whites were less likely to be incarcerated than blacks when sentences of juveniles in adult court were compared with those in the juvenile court (Kupchik, 2006). This differential treatment among whites and blacks was stronger in adult court than in juvenile court.

McNulty (1996) examined the likelihood of receiving incarceration or probation in adult court. Results indicated that blacks were three times more likely to be incarcerated than whites, while Hispanics were almost twice as likely to be incarcerated. Jordan and Freiburger (2010) focused specifically on race and the sentencing of youth in adult court in 19 of the nation's largest counties. They found that black youth were more likely than similarly situated white youth to be sentenced to both prison and jail instead of probation. Hispanic youth were also more likely to receive prison sentences over jail compared with whites. In addition, blacks with a prior record increased their chances of receiving a prison sentence over jail compared to whites. The authors argue that judges may view a prior record differently for blacks than for whites (Jordan & Freiburger, 2010). Blacks with a prior record may be viewed as more dangerous than similarly situated Whites.

Recidivism is another issue concerning the transfer of youth from the juvenile court to the adult criminal justice system: does waiver to adult court deter or enhance the likelihood of re-offending? The available evidence suggests the latter. Bishop, Frazier, Lanza-Kaduce, and Winner (1996), for example, matched youth transferred to adult court in the state of Florida to those retained in the juvenile court. It was discovered that offenders transferred to adult court had recidivated more times than youth handled as juveniles. This relationship existed across seven crime categories involving both misdemeanor and felony offenses. The main conclusion derived from the results is that the transfer of youth to adult court enhances, rather than minimizes, the likelihood of re-offending. Furthermore, those youth waived to adult court were significantly more likely to be re-arrested for involvement in violent offenses.

Furthermore, research by the UCLA School of Law Juvenile Justice Project (2010) analyzed all studies that have examined the recidivism of offenders retained in the juvenile court and those where jurisdiction was transferred to adult court. On the basis of the review, youth waived to adult court were found to be more likely to be re-arrested upon returning to the community, especially for violent crimes, and more quickly than youth in the juvenile justice system. One of the conclusions of the report was that the transfer process appears to result in more harm than good.

Concerning policy implications, research suggests that policy should focus on reforming the waiver process (i.e., making it more difficult to transfer youth to adult court). This reform is fundamental to the treatment of youthful offenders because minority youth are waived into adult court disproportionately, and also findings show that many of the youth transferred are involved in non-serious criminal behaviors, and that youth transferred to adult court are likely to recidivate (Bishop *et al.*, 1996). In addition, organizations and government entities should focus efforts on using alternative placements rather than adult jail for youth transferred to adult court.

Juvenile Offenders and Life without Parole

In the wake of the *Roper v. Simmons* (2005) and *Graham v. Florida* (2006) decisions, the death penalty was ruled unconstitutional for youth 17 years of age or younger and for non-homicide offenses. After those specific rulings, the most severe sentence for a convicted juvenile became serving life without parole (LWOP), which results in "natural life" in adult prison. Later, on June 25, 2012, the Supreme Court ruled in *Miller v. Alabama* that *mandatory* LWOP sentences for all children under the age of 18 convicted of homicide are unconstitutional.

Stated differently, the ruling in *Miller v. Alabama* decided that no-one who commits a crime prior to the age of 18 can be sentenced to LWOP without an examination of certain mitigating factors, which includes age. This ruling affects over 2,000 juvenile inmates who are currently serving mandatory LWOP sentences. However, the Court ruled that jurors could find that some juveniles who are "irreparably corrupted" or "irretrievably depraved" can still be given a LWOP sentence on the basis of the offense and individual consideration of the youth's life circumstances. Therefore, it is important to discuss the characteristics of juvenile lifers (i.e., youth serving LWOP sentences) and the implications for their life chances due to the rulings in *Miller v. Alabama*.

The research by Nellis (2012) describes results from a national survey of over 1,500 juvenile lifers. The results indicated some general trends across juveniles who were serving LWOP sentences. For example, most juvenile lifers experienced high levels of exposure to violence and social and economic disadvantage in their homes and communities. Almost 80% of respondents reported witnessing violence in their homes prior to the offense, and over 50% witnessed weekly violence throughout their neighborhood. Over 30% of respondents resided in public housing at some point throughout their lives, and 18% of juvenile lifers were not living with a family member just before being incarcerated. Some youth reported being homeless, living with friends, or residing in a detention facility, treatment center, or group home (Nellis, 2012). In addition, many juvenile lifers suffered high rates of abuse before incarceration. This is especially true for female juvenile lifers, where 79% and 77% of girls reported some form of physical and/or sexual abuse, respectively. Respondents from the national survey also reported numerous educational challenges, in that 40% were enrolled in special education classes at the time of the offense, and less than half of juvenile lifers were attending school.

Based on the results by Nellis (2012), 61.9% of juveniles who were serving LWOP sentences were not engaged in programming while incarcerated. However, this is not because a youth was not interested in rehabilitative programming – the unavailability of programming was due to state and/or prison policies. Many juvenile lifers also responded that they were attempting to positively alter their life chances through obtaining a high school diploma/GED and maintaining ties with family members while incarcerated.

The presence of racial disparities in LWOP sentences has consistently been a key finding in the research surrounding juvenile lifers (Leiber & Peck, 2013). It has been argued that the racial dynamics between offenders and victims may play a significant role in determining what offenders receive LWOP sentences, especially the race of the victim. Since 1976, black youth who are convicted of murdering a white person are more likely to be sentenced to life without parole compared with other offender/victim comparisons (Nellis, 2012). This is also true for black offenders in general, not just black juveniles who are convicted of murdering whites. For example, the proportion of black youth serving LWOP sentences for killing a white person is 43.4%, which is almost twice more than black youth who are arrested for the murder of a white person (23.2%) (Nellis, 2012). Furthermore, white youth who murder blacks are half as likely to receive a LWOP sentence (3.6%) compared with white youth who are arrested for the murder of a white person (6.4%).

It is important to note that all juveniles serving LWOP sentences were convicted of serious crimes, and the severity of the crimes cannot be dismissed. Nonetheless, policy recommendations for reform have been identified throughout the LWOP research. The recommendations focus on eliminating juvenile LWOP, reforming inmate housing, encouraging inmates to engage in rehabilitation programming, investing in prevention, and addressing racial disparities.

More specifically, the first reform suggestion is to eliminate juvenile LWOP, in that punishments would subsequently consider a juvenile's age, maturity, and potential for rehabilitation (Nellis, 2012) instead of a mandatory life sentence. The second suggestion is for juveniles who are transferred to adult court to be housed separately from adult offenders, or placed in juvenile detention centers until they are at least 21 years old before being transferred to adult prisons. The third suggestion is to increase the potential for lifers to engage in rehabilitative programming with the possibility that they may be released back into society at some point in time. The fourth suggestion posits that instead of spending resources on housing juvenile lifers, to shift resources to be directed at prevention and intervention programs (e.g. preschool programs and substance abuse treatment). The final suggestion focuses on reducing racial disparities in LWOP sentences. From this, policy reform has suggested a greater investment in prevention and early intervention strategies in high-risk communities with large minority populations (Nellis, 2012).

Conclusion

In this chapter we presented information on issues confronting the juvenile court. The concerns addressed were: (1) youth's involvement in delinquency and crime and their presence in the juvenile justice system; (2) the disproportionate overrepresentation of minority youth (DMC) in the juvenile and adult court; (3) the representation of female youth in the juvenile justice system, status offenses, and the treatment of these offenders; (4) the overreliance on the use of secure detention; (5) the transfer of youth from the juvenile court to the adult criminal court; and (6) the sentencing of juveniles to life without parole (LWOP). Policy initiatives were offered to inform the public and politicians of these issues, and methods offered to ensure greater equality for all youth.

References

Annie E. Casey Foundation. (2009a). *Detention Reform: An Effective Approach to Reduce Racial Disparities in Juvenile Justice.* Baltimore, MD: Annie E. Casey Foundation.

Annie E. Casey Foundation. (2009b). *Progress Report, Two Decades of JDAI: From Demonstration Project to National Standard.* Baltimore, MD: Annie E. Casey Foundation.

Austin, J., Johnson, K.D., & Weitzer, R.J. (2005). Alternatives to secure detention and confinement of juvenile offenders. *Juvenile Justice Bulletin* (September).

Bennett, W.J., DiIulio, J.J., & Walters, J.P. (1996). *Body Count: Moral Poverty – and How to Win America's War Against Crime and Drugs.* New York: Simon & Schuster.

Bernard, T.J., & Kurlychek, M.C. (2010). *The Cycle of Juvenile Justice.* New York: Oxford University Press.

Bishop, D.M., & Frazier, C.E. (1992). Gender bias in juvenile justice processing: Implications of the JJDP act. *Journal of Criminal Law & Criminology, 82,* 1162–1186.

Bishop, D., & Frazier, C. (1996). Race effects in juvenile justice decision-making: Findings of a statewide analysis. *Journal of Criminal Law and Criminology, 86,* 392–413.

Bishop, D.M., Frazier, C.E., Lanza-Kaduce, L., & Winner, L. (1996). The transfer of juveniles to criminal court: Does it make a difference? *Crime & Delinquency, 42*(2), 171–191.

Bishop, D., & Leiber, M. (2011). Race, ethnicity, and juvenile justice: Racial and ethnic differences in delinquency and justice system responses. In B. Feld, & D. Bishop (Eds.), *The Oxford Handbook of Juvenile Crime and Juvenile Justice* (pp. 445–484). New York: Oxford University Press.

Breed v. Jones. (1975). 421 S. Ct. 519.

Brubaker, S.J., & Fox, K.C. (2010). Urban African American girls at risk: An exploratory study of service needs and provision. *Youth Violence and Juvenile Justice, 8*, 250–265.

Center on Juvenile and Criminal Justice. (2009). *Reforming the Juvenile Justice System*. San Francisco: Center on Juvenile and Criminal Justice.

Chauhan, P., Reppucci, N.D., & Turkheimer, E.N. (2009). Racial differences in the associations of neighborhood disadvantage, exposure to violence, and criminal recidivism among female juvenile offenders. *Behavioral Sciences & the Law, 27*, 531–552.

Chesney-Lind, M. (1997). *The Female Offender*. Thousand Oaks, CA: Sage.

Chesney-Lind, M. (2006). Patriarchy, crime, and justice feminist criminology in an era of backlash. *Feminist Criminology, 1*, 6–26.

Chesney-Lind, M., & Belknap, M. (2004). Trends in delinquent girls' aggression and violent behavior. A review of the evidence. In M. Puytallaz, & P. Bierman (Eds.), *Aggression, Antisocial Behavior and Violence Among Girls: A Developmental Perspective* (pp. 203–222). New York: Guilford.

Chesney-Lind, M., & Shelden, R.G. (2004). *Girls, Delinquency, and Juvenile Justice* (3rd ed.). Belmont, CA: Wadsworth.

Chesney-Lind, M., Shelden, R.G., & Joe, K.A. (1996). Girls, delinquency, and gang membership. *Gangs in America, 2*, 185–204.

Elliott, D. (1994). Serious violent offenders: Onset, developmental course, and termination – The American Society of Criminology 1993 Presidential Address. *Criminology, 32*, 1–21.

Fagan, J. (2010). The contradictions of juvenile crime and punishment. *Daedalus (Summer), 139*, 43–61.

Fagan, J., Forst, M., & Vivona, T.S. (1987). Racial determinants of the judicial transfer decision: Prosecuting violent youth in criminal court. *Crime and Delinquency, 33*(2), 259–286.

Feld, B. (1999). *Bad Kids: Race and the Transformation of the Juvenile Court*. New York: Oxford University Press.

Feld, B. (2009). Violent girls or relabeled status offenders? An alternative interpretation of the data. *Crime and Delinquency, 55*, 241–265.

Feld, B., & Bishop, D.M. (2012). *The Oxford Handbook of Juvenile Crime and Juvenile Justice*. New York: Oxford University Press.

Feyerherm, W. (2007). *An Analysis of Detention Decision-Making in Three Iowa Counties*. Portland, OR: Portland State University.

Gaarder, E., Rodriguez, N., & Zatz, M.S. (2004). Criers, liars, and manipulators: Probation officers' views of girls. *Justice Quarterly, 21*, 547–578.

Garland, A.F., & Besinger, B.A. (1997). Racial/ethnic differences in court referred pathways to mental health services for children in foster care. *Children and Youth Services Review, 19*, 651–666.

Graham v. Florida. (2010). 130 S.Ct.

Guevara, L., Herz, D., & Spohn, C. (2006). Gender and juvenile justice decision making: What role does race play? *Feminist Criminology, 1*, 258–282.

Hindelang, M.J. (1978). Race and involvement in common law personal crimes. *American Sociological Review, 43*, 93–109.

Howell, J.C. (1996). Juvenile transfers to the criminal justice system: State of the art. *Law and Policy, 18*, 17–60.

Hsia, H., & Beyer, M. (2000). *System Change through State Challenge Activities: Approaches and Productions*. Bulletin. Washington, DC: US Department of Justice, Office of Justice Programs, Office of Juvenile Justice and Delinquency Prevention.

Huizinga, D., Loeber, R., & Thornberry, T.P. (1994). *Urban Delinquency and Substance Use: Initial Findings*. Washington, DC: US Department of Justice, Office of Justice Programs, Office of Juvenile Justice and Delinquency Prevention.

Jordan, K.L., & Freiburger, T.L. (2010). Examining the impact of race and ethnicity on the sentencing of juveniles in the adult court. *Criminal Justice Policy Review, 21*(2), 185–201.

Kempf-Leonard, K., & Sample, L.L. (2000). Disparity based on sex: Is gender-specific treatment warranted? *Justice Quarterly, 17*, 89–128.

Kent v. United States. (1966). 383 S. Ct. 541.

Kupchik, A. (2006). The decision to incarcerate in juvenile and criminal courts. *Criminal Justice Review, 31* (4), 309–336.

Kurlychek, M.C., & Johnson, B.D. (2004). Juvenile penalty: A comparison of juvenile and young adult sentencing outcomes in criminal court. *Criminology, 42*(2), 33.

Leiber, M.J. (2013). Race, pre-and postdetention, and juvenile justice decision making. *Crime & Delinquency, 59*, 396–418.

Leiber, M.J, & Boggess, L.N. (2012). Race, probation violations, and structured secure detention decision making in three jurisdictions. *Youth Violence and Juvenile Justice, 10*, 333–353.

Leiber, M.J., Brubaker, S.J., & Fox, K.C. (2009). A closer look at the individual and joint effects of gender and race on juvenile justice decision making. *Feminist Criminology, 4*, 333–358.

Leiber, M.J., & Fox, K.C. (2005). Race and the impact of detention on juvenile justice decision making. *Crime & Delinquency, 51*, 470–497.

Leiber, M., & Johnson, J. (2008). Being young and Black: What are their effects on juvenile justice decision making? *Crime & Delinquency, 54*, 560–581.

Leiber, M.J., & Peck, J. (2013). Race in juvenile justice and sentencing policy: An overview of research and policy recommendations. University of Minnesota Law School. *Law & Inequality: A Journal of Theory & Practice, Summer, 2*, 331–368.

Leiber, M.J., & Peck, J.H. (forthcoming). Race, gender, crime severity, and decision-making in the juvenile justice system. *Crime & Delinquency*. doi:10.1177/001112871244689

Leiber, M.J., & Rodriguez, N. (2011). The implementation of the disproportionate minority confinement/contact (DMC) mandate: A failure or success? *Race & Justice, 1*, 103–124.

MacDonald, J.M., & Chesney-Lind, M. (2001). Gender bias and juvenile justice revisited: A multiyear analysis. *Crime & Delinquency, 47*, 173–195.

Mallicoat, S. (2007). Gendered justice: Attributional differences between males and females in the juvenile courts. *Feminist Criminology, 2*, 4–30.

McNulty, E.W. (1996). the transfer of juvenile offenders to adult court: panacea or problem? *Law & Policy, 18*(1–2), 61–75.

Mendel, R. (2009). *Two Decades of JDAI: A Progress Report*. Baltimore, MD: Annie E. Casey Foundation.

Miller v. Alabama. (2012). 132 S. Ct. 2455.

Mulvey, E.P., & Iselin, A.R. (2008). Improving professional judgments of risk and amenability in juvenile justice. *Future of Children, 18*, 35–57.

Nellis, A. (2012). *The Lives of Juvenile Lifers: Findings from a National Survey*. Washington, DC: The Sentencing Project.

Orlando, F. (1999). *Controlling the Front Gates: Effective Admissions Policies and Practices*. Vol. 3 in *Pathways to Juvenile Detention Reform*. Baltimore, MD: Annie E. Casey Foundation.

Pope, C.E., & Feyerherm, W. (1993). *Minorities and the Juvenile Justice System*. Washington, DC: US Department of Justice, Office of Juvenile Justice and Delinquency Prevention.

Pope, C.E., & Snyder, H.N. (2003). *Race as a Factor in Juvenile Arrests*. Bulletin. Washington, DC: US Department of Justice, Office of Justice Programs, Office of Juvenile Justice and Delinquency Prevention.

Price, B.R., & Sokoloff, N.J. (2004). Criminal justice system and women: Offenders, prisoners, victims, and workers. *The Windsor Review of Legal & Social Issues, 17*, 29.

Puzzanchera, C., Adams, B., & Hockenberry, S. (2012a). *Juvenile Court Statistics 2009*. Pittsburgh, PA: National Center for Juvenile Justice.

Puzzanchera, C., Sladky, A., & Kang, W. (2012b). *Easy Access to FBI Arrest Statistics 1994–2009*. Retrieved from http://www.ojjdp.gov/ojstatbb/ezaucr/

Rodriguez, N. (2010). The cumulative effect of race and ethnicity in juvenile court outcomes and why preadjudication detention matters. *Journal of Research in Crime & Delinquency, 47*, 391–413.

Roper v. Simmons. (2005). 125 S. Ct. 1183.

Sampson, R.J., & Lauritsen, J.L. (1997). Racial and ethnic disparities in crime and criminal justice in the United States. *Crime and Justice*, 311–374.

Schwartz, I.M. (1989). *(In)justice for Juveniles: Rethinking the Best Interests of the Child*. Lexington, MA: Lexington Books.

Sickmund, M., Sladky, A., & Kang, W. (2013). *Easy Access to Juvenile Court Statistics: 1985–2010*. Retrieved from http://www.ojjdp.gov/ojstatbb/ezajcs/

Singer, S.I. (1996). *Recriminalizing Delinquency: Violent Juvenile Crime and Juvenile Justice Reform*. New York: Cambridge University Press.

Snyder, H.N., & Sickmund, M. (2006). *Juvenile Offender and Victims: 2006 National Report*. Washington, DC: US Department of Justice, Office of Juvenile Justice and Delinquency Prevention.

Steen, S., Bond, C., Bridges, G., & Kubrin, C. (2005). Explaining assessments of future risk: Race and attributions of juvenile offenders in presentence projects. In D. Hawkins, & K. Kempf-Leonard (Eds.), *Our Children, Their Children: Confronting Racial and Ethnic Differences in American Juvenile Justice* (pp. 23–82). The John D. and Catherine T. MacArthur Foundation, Research Network on Adolescent Development and Juvenile Justice. Chicago, IL: University of Chicago Press.

Thornberry, T.P., & Krohn, M.D. (2000). The self-report method for measuring delinquency and crime. *Criminal Justice, 4*, 33–83.

Torbet, P., Griffin P., Hurst, H., Montgomery, I., Szymanski, L., & Thomas, D. (1996). *State Responses to Serious and Violent Juvenile Crime: Research Report*. Washington, DC: Office of Juvenile Justice and Delinquency Prevention.

UCLA School of Law Juvenile Justice Project. (2010). *The Impact of Prosecuting Youth in the Adult Criminal Justice System: A Review of the Literature*. Los Angeles: UCLA School of Law.

Wilson, J.Q., & Petersilia, J. (2010). *Crime and Public Policy*. Oxford: Oxford University Press.

Zimring, F.E. (1998). *American Youth Violence*. New York: Oxford University Press.

28

Community-Based Sanctions and Juveniles: What Works, What Does Not, and What Looks Promising

Crystal A. Garcia

Over the last 25 years, American juvenile courts have become fairly creative at developing dispositions for youth in their jurisdictions. This adeptness was forced by two decades of increasing caseloads, shrinking budgets, and too few dispositional options. Though crime (both property and violent) rapidly increased from the early 1960s throughout the 1970s (Federal Bureau of Investigation, 2012), punishment options did not. Most county juvenile justice systems only had two basic dispositions to choose from: routine probation and commitment to state correctional institutions. The same probation/prison dichotomy was also a problem in the criminal courts (Petersilia, 1987). Sentencing options did not start to expand in the juvenile justice system until the very end of the 1970s and the beginning of the 1980s, when some jurisdictions began to test sentencing alternatives such as community service orders, probation camps, and intensive supervision probation (Morris & Tonry, 1990). These dispositional alternatives (like probation) are referred to as community-based sanctions (CBSs). CBSs are dispositions that take place in the community, outside the walls of correctional institutions. CBSs are critically important to the juvenile justice system as most youth that are adjudicated will fulfill their dispositions in the community.

While the major purpose of this chapter is to detail the more common CBSs typically seen in American juvenile courts, it is just as important to consider the extant research regarding the efficacy of these dispositions and the historical context in which they were developed. As such, the ensuing chapter includes a quick overview of the birth of today's most commonly used CBS, probation, a discussion of how routine probation works today, and an explanation for what led to the development of the other community-based dispositions. Following those topics, each of the more commonly used CBSs are described and a discussion is offered regarding their relative efficacy.

The Handbook of Juvenile Delinquency and Juvenile Justice, First Edition. Edited by Marvin D. Krohn and Jodi Lane.

The concluding portions of the chapter focus on two important concerns. First, many juvenile justice jurisdictions still have not implemented well-established, research-based treatment (i.e., evidence-based) programs for youth in their care. The various local and state agencies that are responsible for correcting juvenile delinquency and providing treatment to youth in need of services, must investigate the treatment, rehabilitation and "what works" literature, to determine what they can reasonably implement and provide such programs with all expediency. Identifying such programs is no longer an onerous task. An abundance of articles have been published in the juvenile justice, psychology and child welfare journals demonstrating the effectiveness of particular programs and treatment modalities. It is time that all agencies that work with at-risk and system-involved youth invest in programming that both "does justice" and offers them a real chance at improving the lives of kids, their families, and the communities in which they live. Several examples of evidence-based programs are detailed near the end of the chapter. Second, a few other treatment/programmatic approaches are introduced that address growing areas of concern for juvenile justice practitioners (e.g., the growing number of girls entering the system and the impact that past traumas have had on system-involved youth). For some readers these topics will be new, for others not, yet these approaches show promise and should at least be considered as we venture further into juvenile justice in the twenty-first century.

Probation is Born

While probation is not the oldest punishment in America,[1] it is likely the oldest of the CBSs still in use today. In early America, capital, corporal, and shame-inducing (e.g., stocks and pillory) punishments preceded the use of both imprisonment and probation (Rothman, 2011). Incarceration as a sentence (versus solely being used for pre-trial detention) began to pick up in popularity near the very end of the 1700s and at the beginning of the 1800s (Hirsch, 1992). For a generation or so, low-level offenders had no alternative to incarceration – none came about until the birth of probation.

In 1841, a Boston citizen and successful cobbler decided to attend a police court (Fields, 2012). That cobbler, John Augustus, had noticed that far too many people in his community were getting incarcerated for minor offenses – offenses he believed he could help them overcome. Augustus' purpose in attending court that day was to bail out an individual who had an "appetite for drink" (New York City Department of Probation, n.d.). Augustus had to convince the court that he would work closely with this gentleman to abstain from alcohol, find him shelter and a job. The court agreed that if Augustus' ward was successful, the gentleman would avoid prison (Augustus, 1852). This first probation case was successful and the individual was able to remain in the community.

This early success bolstered Augustus' efforts and led him to continue what was to become his life's work. Within two years of his first success, this "father of probation" decided to turn his efforts toward working with troubled youth. He began by taking in two very young girls and one young boy (ages 8 and 11) who were accused of stealing (Augustus, 1852). By 1846, the number of children under Augustus' supervision increased to 30 (Augustus, 1852, p. 42). He continued to volunteer in this capacity until his death in 1859 (Fields, 2012). Just over 20 years later, the State of Massachusetts passed the nation's first juvenile probation statute; however, it took another 13 years before a formal, statewide probation system was in place (Fields, 2012).

A separate juvenile court and probation department was first established in 1899 in Cook County, Illinois, four decades after Augustus' death. This new court provided guidance to wayward, neglected and troubled youth (American Bar Association, n.d.). The court's purpose was to provide rehabilitation rather than punishment. Other jurisdictions took notice, and by 1925 all but two states had juvenile courts. What all these courts had in common was their guiding philosophy, their approach to probation services, and the goal of turning wayward youth into productive citizens utilizing "treatment" that included warnings, probation, and training school confinement.

Modern Probation

Routine probation (RP) is a non-incarcerative disposition imposed by a judge that takes place in the community. As such, when given a disposition of probation, a juvenile is allowed to remain in the home (often in lieu of incarceration); in return, juveniles must agree to abide by certain conditions (e.g., curfews, mandatory school attendance, etc.) set forth by the court. The most important of these conditions is to submit to regular supervision by a probation officer. Failure to abide by such conditions can result in the imposition of additional conditions or even revocation of probation and loss of community status. Perhaps the best way to think of probation is to see it as a collection of strategies that include, at the very least, routine supervision levels (i.e., face-to-face meetings with a probation officer at least once a month), but quite often also include other intermediate sanctions, such as electronic monitoring and community service.

Probation has been (and continues to be), the most common disposition given to adjudicated youth. In particular, the proportion of juveniles that received a probation disposition has increased 16% since 1985. Furthermore, by 2010, the number of youth on probation in the US for a delinquent offense reached nearly a half a million (Puzzanchera & Hockenberry, 2013).

Given the size of routine probation (RP) caseloads, these juveniles receive little one-on-one attention and very little, if any, specialized treatment. This is not particularly surprising as the individuals placed on RP are considered at low risk of committing another offense. Nevertheless, RP that utilizes basic case management has not been found to reduce recidivism (Greenwood & Turner, 2012; Washington State Institute for Public Policy, 2013).

Community-based vs. Intermediate Sanctions

CBSs (also known as community corrections) can be thought of as any disposition that takes place outside correctional institutions. In other words, CBSs are punishments that are carried out in the community. They have become increasingly important to both the juvenile and criminal justice systems as states have grappled with crowded correctional institutions and empty coffers. During the "get tough" movement (1980 to 2010), the number of Americans incarcerated increased by 500% (The Sentencing Project, 2014, p. 2). At the same time, probation caseloads also grew unabated (DeMichele & Payne, 2007).

For the most part, modern American CBSs (with the exception of probation) are less than 50 years old. In fact, the majority of CBSs used today were not in place until the 1980s and 1990s. Prior to the development of modern CBSs, there were few sentencing options available to judges other than routine probation and incarceration in state correctional facilities (i.e., prisons for adults and training/ reforms schools for juveniles). This may not have seemed like a major problem at that time; however, as the US population grew and crime began to rise steadily after the Vietnam War, the paucity of correctional options became problematic. Justice practitioners were forced to develop other dispositions that offered more surveillance and control over offenders kept in the community than general probation could provide. In many instances, correctional administrators, policy-makers and at times academics joined together to create these alternatives for individuals that needed more formal social control than routine probation could provide, yet were not serious enough to require incarceration (Garcia, 1996). The need to solve this "prison–probation" dichotomy is what led to the "intermediate sanctions movement" (Morris & Tonry, 1990).

It is common for individuals to become confused about the differences between CBSs and intermediate sanctions (ISs). As such, it makes sense to clarify the vernacular. As previously mentioned, CBSs are all dispositions that are served in the community. ISs are any dispositions that fall on a continuum between routine probation and prison. Therefore, all ISs are CBSs with one exception: routine probation. Intermediate sanctions exist on a punishment continuum. This continuum is flexible and allows for punishment and treatment to be individualized according to the needs of the juvenile and the risk they pose to the community. Youth that pose a greater risk can be placed on an intermediate sanction that incorporates heavier surveillance and control measures.

The court can order a disposition that includes only one IS such as electronic monitoring, or they can "stack" other ISs onto a probation term (Petersilia, 2002). This offers a variety of treatment and service opportunities for the juvenile, while also allowing the court other mechanisms to supervise and control its wards.

The continuum referred to above is a graduated sanctions continuum, which can be envisioned as a staircase. The least restrictive response that the juvenile justice system can utilize is when a youth is counseled and released. That step is followed by minor increases in control. Intermediate sanctions begin after routine probation and continue exerting more control and providing more services, until all community options are exhausted. Should a young person not respond to the various ISs and treatment programs offered, or they commit a new, more serious offense, they will likely end up at the top of the correctional continuum. When this happens, they

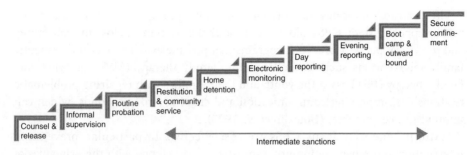

Figure 28.1   Example of a graduated sanctions continuum

often face a commitment to their state's department of correction (DOC). Figure 28.1 shows an example of a graduated sanctions continuum. On such a continuum, dispositions such as restitution and community service, home detention and electronic monitoring, day and/or evening reporting, and shock (e.g., boot camp) and outward bound programs should be thought of as ISs.

Advantages of CBS

There are several advantages gained by keeping youth in CBSs programs over incarcerating them in juvenile correctional institutions. First, regardless of one's attitude about U.S. incarceration practices, state juvenile justice systems simply do not have the capacity to incarcerate or detain the majority of young people who are funneled through the courts. Unlike incarceration, CBS dispositions like probation can absorb large numbers of young people that do not need to be incarcerated. As such, well-designed CBSs can alleviate overcrowding at correctional institutions (Palmer, 1992).

Second, CBSs also allow for the scalability of punishment and individualized treatment that is lacking in many youth service systems. By offering a CBS with other add-ons (e.g., probation plus electronic monitoring and random drug testing), juvenile justice agencies can increase supervision efforts and treatment participation (Garcia, 1996).

Third, these programs are also designed to reduce the physical and psychological trauma (i.e., pains of confinement) that can result from incarceration (Fagan & Kupchik, 2011). Moreover, by their very nature, CBSs also protect against the criminogenic effects of confinement, which can be especially detrimental to the very young and criminally unsophisticated (Fagan & Kupchik, 2011).

Fourth, many proponents argue that CBSs promote offender responsibility (Lucken, 1997). For example, juveniles sentenced to CBSs are often required to attend school, and if they cannot reenter school or have reached their state's school compulsory attendance age, they must be gainfully employed. When these young people work, they pay taxes, court-ordered restitution, and any child support they may owe if they are parents.

Fifth, research indicates that offenders attempting to "go straight" need a strong social support system. CBSs allow youth the chance to remain close to their family and pro-social peers. Moreover, programs that provide evidence-based therapeutic family interventions such as multisystemic family therapy (MST) or functional family therapy (FFT) assist the youth and their families with repairing problematic relationships, improving communication and creating stronger bonds, which can improve justice outcomes (Bourdin *et al.*, 1995).

Sixth, if done well, many CBSs are cost-effective. In particular, prevention, intervention and rehabilitation programs that are developed with the principles of effective correctional intervention (PECI)[2] in mind, and that offer the appropriate treatment dosage and have high program fidelity, reduce recidivism and save money (Marion, 2002). However, poorly designed community-based programs often lead to excessive technical violations, which inflate recidivism rates and seriously compound correctional costs (Petersilia, 1990).

Disadvantages of CBSs

Perhaps the greatest disadvantage of many CBSs is that they often lack strong theoretical foundations (Petersilia, 1990), particularly if their purpose is to reduce recidivism. That was definitely true in the midst of the IS movement in the 1990s, and unfortunately, it still true with many programs today. A good example of this problem is how some intensive supervision probation (ISP) programs are structured. In particular, ISPs are often designed to increase surveillance and control of high-risk juvenile offenders (i.e., to enhance public safety) and to swiftly revoke their community status should major violations occur (Garcia, 1996). At the same time, one of their major goals is to reduce recidivism. The surveillance aspect of these programs is grounded in specific deterrence (i.e., the threat of imprisonment will keep offenders from committing technical violations or new offenses). However, solely relying on deterrence theory in this scenario, without addressing offender criminogenic needs, is not likely to achieve recidivism reduction. For example, when deterrence-based programs are used with drug-involved offenders (which is common), and supervision levels are increased but no evidence-based substance abuse treatment is provided, it is very common for these offenders to continue their substance use, which results in their eventual incarceration (or re-incarceration).

Additionally, the overall mission and goals of many CBSs have been unclear, which ultimately has threatened their effectiveness and sustainability (Garcia, 1996; Petersilia, 1990). Is their mission to rehabilitate offenders? Or is it to increase public safety, or is it supposed to serve a retributive purpose? Further still, are these programs trying to reintegrate offenders? Or deter future crime? Mission and goal confusion make it difficult for line staff to do their job effectively. Moreover, the lack of clarity can make it difficult for adolescents participating in them to understand what they can expect of the program and to develop a trusting relationship with program staff and/or supervision officer.

As mentioned above, CBSs can increase correctional costs if the programs are poorly designed (Marion, 2002). When community-based sanctions do not include proper treatment and fail to address the criminogenic needs of clients, the programs are less likely to be successful (Petersilia & Turner, 1993). How this increases costs is interesting. For example, when a juvenile is placed on a CBS with a suspended commitment to the state correctional authority, and the young person fails on the CBS, their community status may be revoked. Upon revocation, the costs incurred dramatically increase because taxpayers are on the hook for the price of the original court proceedings (and possible detention), the CBS and subsequent supervision, the court costs associated with a revocation hearing, and then again for the time the young person is incarcerated.

Finally, there is always the possibility that some individuals are inappropriate for community supervision; such a placement creates a risk to public safety. Even though there are CBSs that are quite structured and incorporate high degrees of surveillance and control (e.g., intensive supervision probation with electronic monitoring), they will not stop a young person from perpetrating a crime if he or she is committed to doing so.

Judging the Effectiveness of Juvenile CBSs

There are numerous ways to determine whether various CBSs are effective at reducing recidivism and improving other pro-social behaviors. The most common way to understand whether a program or intervention is able to reduce recidivism is to conduct a program evaluation; however, the conclusions that can be drawn from one evaluation of one program are minimal. For example, the results from a single evaluation may not be generalizable for any number of reasons – for example, it did not use an experimental design, or the program revolved around a characteristic that was idiosyncratic to a particular jurisdiction, or the sample size was too small so that it could not provide enough power in the analysis to uncover any statistically significant differences that might actually exist. Fortunately, there have been several efforts to build knowledge about what works (in terms of program or treatment type) and why it works (i.e., which programmatic components are driving the program or treatment's success).

In the following section, four major efforts will be discussed that have focused on determining what works for juveniles in community settings. These efforts include: Blueprints for Healthy Youth Development (BHYD), the Washington State Institute for Public Policy (WSIPP), the Office of Juvenile Justice and Delinquency Prevention – Model Programs Guide (OJJDP–MPG), and other meta-analyses conducted on CBSs or programmatic components of CBSs (with special attention focused on those completed by Mark Lipsey).[3] After these efforts are detailed, some of the more commonly used non-residential and residential juvenile CBSs will be discussed. When possible, notations about the effectiveness of each program type or treatment modality will be included, as well as what group (BHYD, WSIPP, OJJDP-MPG, and meta-analyses) made that determination. See Greenwood (2010) and Greenwood and Turner (2012) for a thorough discussion of the effectiveness of juvenile CBSs and program components and the means by which their effectiveness was determined.

Blueprints for Healthy Youth Development (BHYD)

This knowledge base was originally developed as part of a national violence prevention initiative aimed at identifying programs that are effective for preventing or intervening successfully in the lives of at-risk and delinquent youth. Recently, the Blueprints effort expanded its focus from solely reporting on justice outcomes, to also including information on education, emotional well-being, physical health, and positive relationships outcomes (Blueprints for Healthy Youth Development, n.d.). The BHYD knowledge base is searchable and simple to use. It includes only programs that it has deemed to be effective or promising.

Washington State Institute for Public Policy (WSIPP)

According to Lee *et al.* (2012), the Washington State Institute for Public Policy developed an inventory of known juvenile treatment programs. After collecting all available program evaluations and determining those that utilized either experimental or quasi-experimental research designs, WSIPP conducted meta-analyses to determine which programs, treatment modalities or components of programs were found to be effective at reducing recidivism. What makes WISPP's knowledge base different from others is that it also includes cost–benefit calculations for most of the programs and treatment modalities it reviewed.

Office of Juvenile Justice and Delinquency Prevention – Model Programs Guide (OJJDP–MPG)

This program knowledge base contains information about evidence-based juvenile justice and youth prevention, intervention, and reentry programs. Each program in the knowledge base is coded for the following information: the type of program (e.g., intensive supervision, mentoring, cognitive behavioral, etc.); whether it is a prevention program, immediate intervention, intermediate sanction or reentry program; detailed program characteristics; and whether the program has been evaluated (Office of Juvenile Justice and Delinquency Prevention, n.d.). The details provided about the outcome evaluations include: whether the evaluation used an experimental, quasi-experimental or some other study design; how control groups were chosen; the data collected; the follow-up timeframe; the statistical testing conducted; and lastly, the evaluation findings. The knowledge base is searchable and simple to use. In large part, the knowledge base was designed to inform practitioners and policy-makers about what programs have been shown to be effective, what programs show promise and those that do not work.

Other Meta-analyses

Since the early 1990s, several juvenile justice experts have been conducting meta-analyses to understand whether particular types of programs or programmatic elements reduce juvenile offending. In other words, instead of making judgments regarding the efficacy of a program type by evaluating just one individual program (e.g., Family Functional Therapy of Indianapolis), the meta-analytic technique allows researchers to develop a more thorough assessment by gathering together all known functional family therapy program evaluations that utilize experimental or quasi-experimental designs that include – at the very least – measures of recidivism. Once done, this quantitative synthesis allows for the calculation of average impact (i.e., effect size) for that group of studies. Cullen and Jonson (2011, p. 301) further explain the meta-analytic technique:

> …each study is coded to determine the statistical relationship – the effect size – between the treatment intervention and recidivism. The researcher then computes what is analogous to a batting average across all studies, or what is known as an average effect size. This is a precise point estimate of the impact of treatment on recidivism. To make sense of the statistics, most analysts assume a base rate of recidivism of 50 percent for the control group. They then compute, based on the meta-analysis, what the recidivism rate would be for the treatment group.

When conducting a meta-analysis, one calculates the average effect size (i.e., the mean phi coefficient) for the treatment or program under study. As Cullen (2002) explained if one calculates a phi coefficient of 0.20 and, "… if one were to assume a base recidivism rate of 50 percent, the recidivism rate for the treatment group would be 40 percent and for the control group it would be 60 percent," (Cullen, 2002, p. 262).

While numerous meta-analyses have been conducted on correctional treatment approaches and programs over the last 20 years, one researcher – Mark Lipsey – is best known for conducting meta-analyses on juvenile justice programming (Greenwood & Turner, 2012). Therefore, much of what we know about what does and does not "work" in juvenile corrections comes from his accomplished career.

Non-residential CBSs/Intermediate Sanctions Utilized in Juvenile Justice

There are several type of CBSs/ISs in the juvenile and criminal justice systems. While nearly all CBSs take place entirely in community settings, a few are administered in residential settings located in the community. In this next section, non-residential CBSs will be detailed first. Residential intermediate sanctions will be discussed after that.

Monetary penalties

Monetary penalties are much less common for juveniles than adults for obvious reasons. Juveniles have limited financial resources, though the parents of juveniles are often ordered to pay basic court and correctional supervision fees. Beyond typical monetary fines and fees, restitution and community service orders are common for judges to levy against young offenders.

Restitution can be satisfied by paying the victim for the value of goods that were damaged or destroyed. If the crime was violent and/ or caused injury or death, several states have victim compensation funds to provide resources to victims to purchase things like counseling, assist with bills that cannot be paid due to lost wages if the victim could not work, or partially cover funeral expenses if a death occurred (Office for Victims of Crime, 2004). However, for young juvenile offenders, it can be difficult to find legitimate work that would enable them to fulfill their restitution orders. It is true that some juvenile offenders' families have resources and simply pay the restitution order in full; this is unfortunate as the stronger lesson is learned when the youth works for the funds to fulfill restitution. Some jurisdictions provide a means for youth to complete "symbolic restitution". Symbolic restitution allows offenders to complete community service hours whose monetary value is equivalent to the restitution order. In Greenwood and Turner's (2012) review of juvenile community sanctions, they reported that restitution reduced recidivism in juveniles.

Community service

In the US, community service was first used as a court-ordered sanction in the mid-1960s in California for adults with motor vehicle violations. By 1978, community service orders were utilized in juvenile court (Harris & Wing Lo, 2002). It is rare for a juvenile offender to be given a community service order (CSO) as a standalone sanction, rather it is more commonly a condition of diversion or probation. CSOs can also be used along with many other intermediate sanctions (Morris & Tonry, 1990; Petersilia, 1987).

Typically, when a juvenile receives a CSO the number of hours to be completed is indicated and the young person is placed in a project that is overseen by the probation department (Maloney, 2007). On the other hand, some jurisdictions use community service agencies (operated by both government and non-profit organizations). In these counties, a juvenile is referred to such agencies and they find appropriate projects for the individual (Maloney, 2007).

Not everyone agrees with the value of requiring service of youth when there is no "learning" tied to the activity, yet others argue that such orders are useful sanctions that require accountability (Degelman, Pereira, & Peterson, 2006). Some practitioners suggest that completing community service can be a very meaningful experience for juveniles as long as:

- the work they are given is worthwhile and has meaning;
- the juveniles doing the community service are seen as essential resources needed to complete the job;
- the projects given to these young people have "transferable competencies" and aid them in building skills useful for their future;
- it provides opportunities for recognition so that the youth can see their value and the community can see that these young people are valuable to the community; and
- the service focuses on disadvantaged populations such as children with special needs, animals in shelters, elderly shut-ins, and so on.

Maloney (2007) argued that this "restorative community service" model (which includes the elements above) is sorely needed in juvenile justice and can make community service meaningful in the eyes of these young people, hold them more accountable, and help them to build important competencies.

While it is rare to see full outcome evaluations on community service programs, the research does suggest that programs that focus heavily on skills-building do reduce recidivism (see Greenwood & Turner, 2012, for a discussion of Lipsey's work); therefore, if jurisdictions were to implement restorative community service like Maloney suggests, one might expect that these programs would stand up well to evaluation.

House arrest (HA)

In an earlier section of this chapter, a discussion was offered about the early roots of HA (also known as home confinement, home detention, or home supervision). This section of the chapter deals only with modern HA. This control-oriented punishment confines offenders (both juvenile and adult) in their homes, making their homes a mini prison. HA can be used preadjudication (meaning pretrial), as a stand-alone disposition, as a condition of probation, or as a way to assist juveniles in their transition back into society after a term of incarceration.

Juveniles on HA are not allowed to leave their home without prior approval from their supervision officer. The general exceptions to this rule are when juveniles attend school, treatment, or work. Additionally, some circumstances allow a juvenile on HA to leave their house (e.g., a doctor's appointment, church, wedding, funeral, etc.); however, whatever the reason, their supervision officer must give permission before the fact. Should the juvenile decide to go to an event without first garnering permission, they face the possibility of a violation of their house arrest conditions.

It is difficult to find information regarding the number of youth under HA in the United States. Quite often these youth are identified in juvenile statistics as being on probation. In fact, most of these individuals are given probation dispositions and terms of HA. For example, in states like California, youth on HA (referred to as home supervision) are placed on probation and the county probation department is the agency responsible for making sure these youth abide by their home supervision requirements and their various conditions of probation. It is also common (but not always the rule) that California youth are given a disposition of home supervision with electronic monitoring. When this happens, the youth could be counted as being on HA, probation and electronic monitoring (EM).

California began to refocus its energies away from its over-reliance on state correctional facilities to a reinvestment in county-based community corrections for juveniles beginning in 2002. When the state did this, the use of home supervision (with and without electronic monitoring) increased substantially, so that by 2009 close to 35,000 youth were under home supervision (Krisberg, Vuong, Hartney, & Marchionna, 2010).

HA can be a good alternative for some juvenile offenders; however, abiding by the strict curfew and rules associated with HA can be tough for a teenager – if they were particularly good at following rules, they likely would not be on house arrest. Nevertheless, it is fairly common for the judge or probation department to place an offender on house arrest for six, nine or even 12 months. The major purposes of HA are as follows: to confine and restrict the offender's movements, thereby reducing opportunities to commit crime; to save taxpayer dollars and correctional resources (i.e., local detention or state correctional beds); and to avoid the stigmatization of incarceration and pains of confinement experienced as a result of incarceration. Even though HA is able to achieve some of its goals, its biggest drawback as a punishment is that it works only if the person placed on HA decides to abide by the rules of their confinement. Furthermore, while HA can save resources, a meta-analysis conducted by Gendreau, Goggin, Cullen, and Andrews (2000) found that it was not particularly effective at reducing recidivism.

Electronic monitoring (EM)

EM is a correctional technology that can be used as a mechanism for pre-adjudication release, a stand-alone disposition, a condition of probation, or part of an aftercare plan.[4] Regardless of the way it is used, the purposes of EM remain the same: to control and monitor the offender's movements in order to maintain public safety; to save taxpayer dollars and correctional resources (i.e., local detention or state correctional beds); to avoid the stigmatization of incarceration and pains of confinement; and to increase the likelihood that offenders will participate in their treatment and appear at scheduled court hearings (Bales *et al.*, 2010; Maxfield & Baumer, 1991; Weibush, Wagner, Prestine, & Baird, 1992).

The technology underlying EM was first developed in the late 1970s, but an actual EM system did not become available for commercial use until late 1984 (Maxfield & Baumer, 1991). Not long after, the use of EM quickly spread to juvenile and adult courts across the country (DeMichele & Payne, 2009). Table 28.1 includes information about the number of EM units (both radio frequency systems (RFS) and global positioning satellite (GPS) systems) that were in use between 1999 and

Table 28.1   Use of electronic monitoring (EM) over time, 1999–2009

	Type of EM technology		*Total units used*	*% change year to year*
	No. of RFS units	*No. of GPS units*		
1999	75,000	230	75,230	n/a
2000	73,013	395	73,408	−2.4%
2001	73,647	647	74,294	1.2%
2002	75,398	1,276	76,674	3.2%
2003	79,181	2,394	81,575	6.3%
2004	82,643	5,000	87,643	7.4%
2005	85,863	10,250	96,113	9.6%
2006	90,643	20,046	110,689	15.1%
2007	96,191	37,299	133,490	12.4%
2008	102,747	62,121	164,868	23.5%
2009	108,912	91,329	200,241	21.4%

Source: DeMichele & Payne (2009). *Offender Supervision with Electronic Technology: Community Corrections Resource, 2ⁿᵈ Ed.*

2009 (DeMichele & Payne, 2009). By 2009, the number of individuals on either form of electronic monitoring reached 200,241, up 166% since 1999. These data include units used by both juveniles and adults. Unfortunately, the data in Table 28.1 are not disaggregated by age, and there is no national database of juveniles on electronic monitoring or any other CBS with the exception of routine probation. As such, there is no truly accurate way to determine the number of youth on electronic monitoring at a given time. It is possible to estimate a figure based on some general criteria. For instance, one could determine the number of juveniles that were arrested in 2009 by using the Federal Bureau of Investigation's Uniform Crime Report (UCR) data. After calculating what percentage that represents (14% was the actual figure), one could use that proportion as a proxy to determine the percentage of juveniles using electronic monitoring devices. As such, without another more plausible calculation, our estimate would be that 2,803 juveniles were on electronic monitoring in the US in 2009.

There are a few different EM technologies currently available. In general, how the technology works is that offenders wear ankle or wrist bracelets that communicate with either telephone landlines or with global positioning satellites. Like HA, this CBS allows youth to remain in the community and go to school or work. The more advanced EM with GPS systems allows supervision officers to program inclusion and exclusion zones (Baumer & Garcia, 2009). Inclusion zones delineate where an offender is allowed to be and exclusion zones demarcate where an offender is not allowed to go.

When it comes to EM with GPS, most individuals think of the importance of *exclusion* zones to compliance. Frankly, the real-time nature in which violation reports are generated as a result of an offender entering an exclusion zone can be critical to ensuring a previous victim's safety. For example, if an EM supervision officer learns that a juvenile entered an exclusion zone, the EM officer can request that a police cruiser be immediately dispatched to the location and intercept the youth. On the other hand, *inclusion* zones can also be extremely helpful as a case management tool. For instance, the EM officer can use the inclusion zones to "check up" on his probationer who is supposed to be at work, or in this example, in therapy at his doctor's office. If this probationer is at his therapist's office (in his inclusion zone), the officer knows that his client is in compliance with both his treatment requirements and the geographic boundaries that were set for him (Baumer & Garcia, 2009). Furthermore, the client understands that his location can be detected real-time, which might serve as an incentive to go to treatment when it is scheduled. Previous studies have indicated that offenders "do better" while on EM; part of that "doing better" includes higher participation and treatment completion (Maxfield & Baumer, 1991). One would like to believe that the offenders' greatest motivations for going to treatment are that they want to "turn their lives around" and they enjoy treatment; however, the more probable explanation is that they are motivated by the fact that they can leave their house when they go to treatment, and if they do not go to treatment, their supervision officer can see that they are not in compliance with their EM conditions.

In addition to the general benefits that exist for all CBSs (and the positive outcome with regard to treatment), EM also offers increased control (compared with other less strict forms of community supervision). Moreover, it is less costly than incarceration and protects youth from both the pains of confinement and the criminogenic effects of imprisonment. In fact, EM is a viable stand-alone disposition or add-on to a disposition of probation, for many non-violent offenders. In particular, youth who commit burglaries, motor vehicle thefts, or certain drug violations often receive dispositions of incarceration (i.e., short-term commitments to local detention, terms in juvenile camps or ranches, or even longer terms in state juvenile correctional facilities). Dispositions of incarceration are always costly and the jurisdiction ends up shouldering the financial burdens associated with that incarceration. The costs related to staffing, housing, clothing, feeding, providing medical treatment, and offering schooling can be quite high. Juvenile courts often order parents to pay a portion of the associated costs, but much of the time incarcerated youth come from families with limited resources. As such, the jurisdiction often does not recoup those costs related to state incarceration. Given that the juvenile's family must house, feed, clothe him and provide medical care, it is far less expensive to the system to supervise them on house arrest.

Another less obvious benefit of EM is that is protects youth from the pains of confinement and the criminogenic effects of incarceration (e.g., sexual and physical violence, loss of educational opportunities, and strained social supports). It is no secret that violence is an issue in custodial settings. Youth can be physically and/or sexually assaulted by peers and/or staff. Furthermore, they may suffer from depression and anxiety resulting from the incarceration, or as a result of the types of violence previously mentioned. Additionally, important bonds with members of a juvenile's social support system can be broken or damaged because of a period of state incarceration or an extended stay in detention. Conversely, a period of EM in lieu of incarceration can help protect against strained relationships because family and important pro-social others can spend time with the juvenile at their home.

Finally, EM can help preserve the progress that a young person has made towards their education; whereas incarceration can damage their progress in school. Juveniles who have yet to reach the state's compulsory education age are required to attend school while in detention. However, it is often difficult for many young people in juvenile hall to take the detention center school seriously when they know they will not be receiving any credits for the school work they do while there (Ziemba-Davis, Garcia, Kincaid, Gullans, & Myers, 2004). This author has witnessed instances where high school teachers learned of their student's incarceration and worked with the facility school to keep the students up to date on the material they missed at their home school. Such effort and cooperation are rare and are only viable if a juvenile's detention is short. Most detained youth do not benefit from this level of assistance. Furthermore, adding insult to injury, juveniles find it difficult to return to the school they attended prior to being arrested because local principals do not want "trouble-makers in their schools" (Ziemba-Davis *et al.*, 2004). What results is that many youth experience a "time out" in their education while detained pretrial or while completing their disposition in juvenile hall. Given the unequivocal link between academic success and education, any time a young person is away from credit-bearing schooling can have long-lasting negative effects (Maguin & Loeber, 1996).

One of the most common criticisms of EM is that it is discriminatory against the poor. In many jurisdictions in the country, EM is still provided via telephone landlines. Youths from poor families often cannot afford to have a landline installed; nor can they afford monthly telephone bills or rental fees for the EM equipment (Aalsma, Garcia, Haight, Jarjoura, & Ostermann, 2013). When EM is used as a detention alternative, it is very common for poor youth to be excluded from this way out of detention, which often negatively impacts their lives long-term. In particular, youth held in detention (preadjudication) are more likely to be adjudicated and receive more severe dispositions than youth that are released preadjudication, regardless of the reason for the detention (Aalsma *et al.*, 2013).

Finally, even after 25 years of evaluation, the findings for EM remain inconclusive. In particular, the early research was quite promising. In 1992, Weibush and colleagues conducted a randomized field experiment with 300 youth, examining the efficacy of EM compared with regular house arrest (preadjudication), and intensive supervision probation with EM versus intensive supervision without it (as a disposition). He found that youth on EM and house arrest performed pretty much the same – both with 4% recidivism or less. Weibush also conducted a separate random assignment study (of 288 youth) to determine whether EM would enhance ISP. Again, he found no difference in the performance between the two groups at a six-month follow-up (Weibush *et al.*, 1992).

In 2010, Bales and colleagues employed a quasi-experimental design to examine the impact of both GPS and RFS types of EM on offender behavior (i.e., revocation for a technical violation, revocation for a new offense, or absconding during placement on supervision) in Florida. They found that offenders on both RFS and GPS did better than those on community supervision (i.e., their risk of failure was reduced by 31%). Furthermore, the GPS offenders outperformed individuals on RFS by six percentage points. Finally, no major findings were found across age groups (juveniles and adult), though the positive impact of EM was less for violent offenders than for other offender types (Bales *et al.*, 2010).

Intensive supervision probation (ISP)

The aim of ISP is to increase the surveillance, control, and supervision of high-risk offenders who would have otherwise been incarcerated (Petersilia & Turner, 1993). There are no set program models, though a number of general program components are common in ISPs (Corbett, 2000). For example, ISP greatly increases required face-to face and collateral contacts – two to three face-to-face contacts each week compared with about one meeting per month with routine probation (Petersilia & Turner, 1993). Early on, OJJDP suggested that juvenile ISP caseloads be no larger than 25 youth per one ISP officer (Krisberg, Nuenfeldst, Weibush, & Rodriguez, 1994). Other aspects of ISP include random drug testing, usually some period of electronic monitoring, required school attendance (or work if the youth is no longer in school), community service, and participation in requisite treatment programs (Morris & Tonry, 1990).

   Benefits of ISP are identical to the various benefits of CBSs discussed previously, with just a few differences. First, juveniles on ISP meet with their supervision officers far more frequently than juveniles on other CBSs (e.g., electronic monitoring and routine probation). ISP officers also conduct numerous collateral contacts related to their juvenile clients each month. Collateral contacts are in-person or phone contacts with individuals (other than the offender) that can directly speak to how ISP participants are performing on various indicators. Such close contact between family members, teachers, coaches, etc., and the supervision officer may well help to build a positive, cohesive team focused on helping the juvenile to be successful.

   Another benefit of ISP is that the close contact between a juvenile and their supervision officer allows the officer to uncover whether their client is having trouble and can correct the behavior before an arrest is necessary. Finally, and perhaps most importantly, ISP offers the opportunity to marry treatment with surveillance, which is thought to be critical to recidivism reduction.

   One common criticism of ISP is that it is still not punitive enough (Petersilia & Turner, 1993). Other criticisms include that ISP is rarely implemented as designed, that it relies too heavily on surveillance, does not incorporate the proper treatment levels, lacks the requisite community-based treatment networks in offender neighborhoods, and is rarely funded at appropriate levels (Petersilia, 1990).

   Early research on juvenile ISP seemed promising. Specifically, the early studies found that intensive supervision was a viable alternative to juvenile incarceration; juveniles who participated in intensive supervision programs fared as well (in terms of recidivism) as those who had been in state correctional settings (Barton & Butts, 1988; Krisberg, Rodriguez, Bakke, Neuenfeldt, & Steele, 1989). Moreover, juvenile

ISP programs were found to be far less costly (approximately a third of the cost) than sending juveniles to correctional institutions. It might seem odd that the initial sentence in this paragraph states that the early findings seemed promising, but this author and others have long argued that if participants in alternatives to incarceration do as well as (i.e., no worse than) individuals who were incarcerated on recidivism measures, and the alternative was less costly, than the alternative should be seen as having a modicum of success. This is particularly true if public safety was not threatened, the alternative disposition (ISP) was fiscally sound, the juvenile was spared the pains of confinement, *and* was shielded from the criminogenic influences that exist in correctional settings.

Later ISP research also indicated that it did not reduce recidivism (Gendreau *et al.*, 2000; Lane, Turner, Fain, & Sehgal, 2005; Petersilia & Turner, 1993; Washington State Institute for Public Policy, 2013); yet when married with appropriate treatment, it could reduce recidivism by 10–15% (Petersilia & Turner, 1993). Furthermore, Petersilia argued that intensive supervision probation is not more effective, in part because it is not designed, implemented (i.e., low program fidelity), and funded adequately (Petersilia, 1990). This is not to say that ISP cannot be a successful CBS. ISP holds promise if the field would entertain a shift in paradigm from its focus on surveillance to a therapeutic-based approach that is supported by surveillance (Lipsey, 2009); utilize validated risk assessment instruments that sort offenders by risk to public safety; and deliver treatment programs that are evidence-based and address the juvenile's specific criminogenic needs (Petersilia, 2011). ISP programs that do this and incorporate the principles of effective correctional intervention would likely reduce recidivism and correctional costs, as well as serve as meaningful alternatives to incarceration.

Day reporting centers (DRCs)

DRCs are highly structured, community-based programs where clients spend most of their day in various activities (Parent, 1990). They were first developed in 1972 in the UK for minor offenders who were facing prison terms because of chronic low-level crimes (Mair, 1990). However, DRCs took longer to catch on in the US. In fact, it was not until 1986 that the first DRC was used in Massachusetts. A county sheriff developed this first DRC as a mechanism for early release from jail (Diggs, n.d.; Parent, 1990). Fairly soon after that, DRCs began popping up all over the country (Bulman, 2013).

Generally speaking, juvenile DRCs target high-risk or adjudicated youth between the ages of 12 and 17 (Parent, 1990). The beauty behind DRCs is that they provide supervision for youth when they are not in school (whether they have been kicked out, dropped out or reached the compulsory age of attendance). The delinquency literature has established that two of the biggest predictors of delinquency are inconsistent discipline and lax supervision (Jacob & Johnson, 1997). Supervision and accountability are typically integral parts of DRC programs. In particular, DRCs are designed to provide constant supervision (while the juveniles are at the center), and use behavioral contracts with participants that detail what the program rules are and what the consequences are for violations of those rules. These are important aspects of day reporting programs, particularly because individuals who are sent to them generally have shown themselves not to be particularly adept at following rules. According to David Diggs (n.d.), a long-time community corrections administrator, day reporting centers are well suited for the offender that needs closer supervision and treatment than routine probation can provide.

Typically, juveniles are ordered to report to the center during certain days and times (e.g., 8am to 7pm), participate in alternative schooling, vocational and job training, submit to random drug tests, and sometimes to wear electronic monitoring bracelets to provide an extra level of supervision for the times when they are not at the center (Cohen & Hinkle, 2000). DRCs also have functions other than super-vision and surveillance. Participants are often required to participate in individual or group counseling; they may complete a cognitive restructuring class, and take basic education courses (Bulman, 2013). Additionally, adjudicated youth that are required to participate in DRCs also receive assistance with family dynamics, sub-stance abuse, or other programs that address their dynamic[5] criminogenic needs (Lowencamp & Latessa, 2005).

Extrapolating from the "what works" and PECI literatures, DRCs that are:

- grounded in theory;
- highly structured and include the appropriate level of supervision;
- address as many dynamic criminogenic needs as possible (at least four);
- are individualized to address a youth's specific dynamic criminogenic needs (particularly if they have substance abuse issues or have suffered a major trauma in their lives);
- therapeutic in nature – offering cognitive–behavioral approaches to treatment, but respond to violations quickly with a graduated sanctions approach;
- focused on bringing the youths' family into their treatment plan; and
- inclusive of plans for them to transition back into their neighborhoods

are likely to be successful at reducing recidivism and improving a whole host of other important pro-social indicators (Andrews *et al.*, 1990, Cullen & Jonson, 2011; Lowencamp & Latessa, 2005; Lipsey, 1992, 2009). In fact, some DRC programs have been evaluated that do include a number of programmatic factors and treatment approaches that are mentioned above. Some of these programs have found positive (reduced recidivism) or promising results (participants did no worse on recidivism than control groups, or showed other important positive outcomes such as reduced drug use and increased likelihood of appearance at important court hearings). However, nearly all of these evaluations were conducted on adult day reporting and residential community corrections centers (Bulman, 2013; Diggs & Piper, 1994; Mair, 1990; Martin, Lurigio & Olson, 2003; McBride & Vanderwaal, 1997; Parent, 1990). One recent study did show that juvenile parolees participating in day reporting programs in New Jersey performed better than parolees that were supervised on intensive supervision (Bulman, 2013).

Restorative justice (RJ)

RJ is not a sanction; rather, it is a theory of justice, a purpose of punishment, and a process. There are various forms of RJ (e.g., victim–offender mediation, community court, sentencing circles); however, underlying them all is a theoretical framework that brings together the injured parties (i.e., the actual victim and the community) and the accused to determine the best way to ameliorate the harm caused by the criminal event (Bazemore, 1999). This approach does not excuse wrong-doing; rather, it acknowledges the need to restore the victim and society to the pre-crime state, while promoting reconciliation and offender accountability, and providing a voice to all involved (Bazemore, 1999). Thus, what makes RJ revolutionary in the Western world is that it acknowledges that the crime harms everyone (including the perpetrator) and that everyone (at least symbolically) should be included in determining how to right the wrong that occurred (Gavrielides, 2007).

Critics of RJ approaches suggest that they threaten public safety and trade punishment for feel-good policies. However, RJ approaches are more promising than any drawbacks they might present. In a 2005 meta-analysis, Latimer, Dowden, and Muise compared restorative justice programs to traditional non-restorative approaches for controlling criminal behavior. In addition to participant satisfaction measures, the authors also examined the impacts of restorative justice programs on restitution compliance and recidivism. They found that both victims and offenders involved in restorative justice programs were more satisfied with the process than victims and offenders who experience "justice as usual". Additionally, this study demonstrated that participants in restorative justice programs had higher compliance with restitution orders and also had lower recidivism rates than offenders receiving typical punishments (e.g., incarceration or probation).

In Greenwood's (2010) review, he explained that both the Lipsey meta-analyses and WSIPP efforts found restorative justice victim–offender mediation with restitution to be an effective approach for dealing with low-risk juvenile offenders. In particular, Greenwood claimed that Lipsey reported a 10% reduction and WSIPP an 8% reduction in recidivism. Moreover, WSIPP also reported that the program had a major cost benefit (see also Greenwood & Turner, 2012). Additionally, of the three RJ programs the OJJDP-MPG assessed, all were rated as promising programs.

Examples of Residential Intermediate Sanctions

As previously mentioned, residential intermediate sanctions (IS) are generally not located in state correctional facilities (e.g., residential community corrections center, county probation camps, etc.) (see Nieto, 2008). In fact, several states are attempting to create out-of-home placements that are not administered by the state, but by the counties. These alternatives may be located in rural areas, as is the case with probation camps and ranches (Nieto, 2008). Moreover, group homes and residential community corrections centers are often located in and around urban and suburban areas. What makes residential ISs different from non-residential ISs is the level of surveillance and control exerted over offenders.

Boot camps

The impetus for the development of correctional boot camps in the US was similar to that of other CBSs. They were born of rising juvenile crime rates, irrational fears over what was believed to be a coming onslaught of juvenile super-predators, predicted by John DiIulio and others (Bennett, DiIulio, & Walters, 1996), and a widespread belief that community correctional programs were a slap on the wrist. Many baby-boomer males remembered back to their military days and realized that their time in boot camp made them men (Stinchcomb & Terry, 2001). As such, there was a good amount of *common wisdom* involved in the development of boot camps and their widespread adoption during the 1990s. When boot camps were first implemented, the US was in the throes of "get tough" frenzy. And frankly, what is tougher than boot camp? The only sentences available to (non-waived) juveniles that were tougher were those that held adolescents in state training schools until their age of majority.

Boot camps are also referred to as shock incarceration because they "shock" program participants by incarcerating them for a short time (for 60, 90, or 180 days) in a prison setting that follows a military-like regiment. These institutions often require extensive physical training, group counseling, and educational classes, before releasing youth to serve the rest of their disposition on probation (Stinchcomb & Terry, 2001).

Knowledge about boot camps is extensive. There have been a number of outcome evaluations, some demonstration projects, replication studies and meta-analyses conducted to see whether boot camps reduce recidivism. What we know is that the military-style boot camp does very little to redirect criminal offenders from crime, particularly when little to no aftercare is put in place. As the authors of one study explained, the drill sergeants from the institution will be replaced on the street by drug dealers and criminals in the communities from which the participants came. Additionally, even when the research showed slight positive gains after boot camp participation, the gains were short-lived (Stinchcomb & Terry, 2001). It is interesting to note that millions of dollars were spent across the country to implement boot camps – even after there was convincing evidence that boot camps did not reduce recidivism. In fact, some instances resulted in higher recidivism post-participation (Andrews *et al.*, 1990; Cullen, Blevins, Trager, & Gendreau, 2005; Lipsey *et al.*, 2010; Mackenzie, 2006; Stinchcomb & Terry, 2001). In addition to these studies, WSIPP also found boot camps to be ineffective at reducing crime and costs (WSIPP, 2013).

Probation camps

As previously discussed, the "get tough" approach to punishment led juvenile justice practitioners to experiment with some interesting CBSs (e.g., probation camps) in the 1980s and 1990s. Perhaps the best-known juvenile probation camps and ranches are those developed and implemented in California. Probation departments first developed these camps as a means of housing somewhat serious juvenile offenders locally in the county, rather than sending them to (what was at the time known as) the California Youth Authority (CYA).

California has a total of 52 juvenile camps; 47 of these camps house males, and 5 females (Nieto, 2008). Some of these camps are basic probation camps, whereas others use boot camp models, others are ranches, and there is even one juvenile "fire camp". From 1999 to 2000 the number of youth in probation camps increased substantially as the use of juvenile halls decreased (Krisberg *et al.*, 2010). By 2007, a total of 4,229 youth were living in these camps in California (Nieto, 2008).

In his review of California juvenile probation campus and ranches, Nieto (2008, p. 14) explained:

> The camps and ranches provide juveniles with intense supervision, behavioral remediation, and an opportunity to earn a diploma or GED or learn a vocational skill. Juveniles can be ordered to attend a camp or ranch program for periods ranging from three months to a year.

These probation camps are usually located in rural (and sometimes remote) areas. Residents live in medium-sized to large dorms and are supervised by the probation staff around the clock, seven days a week. The physical setting is both locked and staff-secured (Watson, Bisesi, Tanamly, & Mai, 2003).

Camp Routh, California's only youth "fire camp", is located in Los Angeles County (Nieto, 2008). Residents of this camp are young men who were put on probation as juveniles, but turned 18 while under the jurisdiction of the juvenile court.[6] They were not successful on traditional probation and failed other intermediate sanctions. The camp can serve a maximum of 90 residents who stay there for between 6 and 12 months. While at this camp, the young men work with the California Forestry Department to learn how to fight wildfires (Nieto, 2008).

Few outcome evaluations seem to have been conducted on probation camps. A 2008 study by Nieto suggested that outcome evaluations of these programs would be very difficult as the data were not readily available for the programs. However, in 1984, Palmer and Wedge reviewed data from every juvenile probation camp in the State of California. They randomly sampled the records of 2,835 youth (both those that successfully completed the camp program and those that ended up being removed from the program), to see whether they recidivated during the two-year follow-up period. Palmer and Wedge argued that the camps helped probation departments achieve their goal of providing local alternatives to placement in the state correctional institutions while not causing any threat to public safety in the local communities (Palmer & Wedge, 1989a), but they did not produce major reductions in recidivism. Specifically, almost two-thirds (65%) of the youth that were sent to these camps were arrested during the 48 months after their release. A total of 16% of them committed a new, violent offense, and 29% ended up being committed to a state correctional institution (Palmer & Wedge, 1989b).

Reentry

Virtually all youth committed to state and privately operated juvenile correctional institutions will return to the community. While there is no national database that details the number of youth being released from these facilities, estimates suggest that approximately 100,000 will return home to their own communities each year (Snyder, 2004).

The term "reentry" refers to the coordination of services that are offered to juveniles ready to reintegrate into the community after a period of incarceration (OJJDP, n.d.). Model reentry programs should focus on coordinating case management, needs assessments, and the identification of rehabilitative programs and reintegrative services (Bouffard & Bergseth, 2008) in the communities that youth are reentering. Additionally, the literature suggests that prerelease planning should begin once a juvenile arrives at the correctional facility and initial diagnostics and assessments are complete (Altschuler & Armstrong, 1999). Moreover, reentry planning should continue throughout the community-based service phase.

Many state and local jurisdictions have developed their own reentry programs, though most have not undergone outcome evaluations. Two large-scale model reentry programs funded by federal agencies have been evaluated: the Intensive Aftercare Program (IAP) and the Serious and Violent Reentry Initiative (SVORI).

IAP is a reentry model that targets high-risk juvenile offenders to assist in their attempt to reintegrate successfully back into the community upon their release from a state correctional facility. The model itself is grounded in three criminological theories: strain, social learning, and social control. It is made up of three phases that are separate but also overlap. These phases include the planning and preparatory phase that takes place prior to release from the facility; the second phase incorporates the "structured transition that requires the participation of institutional and aftercare staff prior to and following community re-entry"; and work done over the long-term that incorporates treatment and services in the community which bolster social control and meaningful support networks (Altschuler & Armstrong, 1996, p. 15).

The IAP was first implemented and tested in four states (Altschuler & Armstrong, 1999). The evaluators found no significant differences between the experimental and control groups on recidivism measures during the one-year follow-up period (Weibush, Wagner, McNulty, Wand, & Le, 2005). As is common with field experiments in corrections, the demonstration projects were hurt by small sample sizes and program fidelity issues (Wiebush *et al.*, 2005). Nevertheless, the evaluators uncovered some promising gains. Specifically, they learned that some IAP youth actually received high levels of service both while incarcerated and while out during their aftercare period, and that:

> ...the small group of IAP youth in Colorado who consistently received high levels of treatment services recidivated significantly less than the control group. Although the between-group differences were not statistically significant in Nevada and Virginia, each of these sites experienced a similar trend toward lower recidivism. (Wiebush *et al.*, 2005, p. 81)

Additionally, Wiebush and colleagues found that the IAP program positively impacted the behavior of participating youth while incarcerated (in Nevada and Virginia), and directly impacted how long participants spent in the facilities in Colorado and Virginia, both of which are important positive outcomes (2005, p. 82).

The other large-scale reentry model that was evaluated was the Serious and Violent Reentry Initiative (SVORI). SVORI offers an approach to reentry for both juveniles and adults that relies on a federal–state–local collaboration (OJJDP, n.d.). According to Lattimore *et al.* (2004), the major goals of SVORI were to improve the self-sufficiency of returning offenders (through employment, housing, family, and community involvement); to improve their physical and mental health (with a special emphasis on sobriety and relapse prevention); and reduce recidivism and enable systemic change through multi-agency collaboration. Only one assessment of SVORI for juveniles was available at the time of this writing. That evaluation was detailed in the OJJDP-MPG, which suggested SVORI had no effect on recidivism (OJJDP, n.d.).

Other information related to juvenile aftercare and reentry

OJJDP-MPG identified another aftercare program, Operation New Hope, as promising. This aftercare program "...is a curriculum-based aftercare treatment program designed to assist chronic, high-risk juvenile offenders in their reintegration to the community after they are released from secure confinement" (OJJDP, n.d., para 1). Additionally, Greenwood and Turner, (2012) reported that WSIPP found very positive results after reviewing aftercare programs for juveniles who experienced mental illness and substance abuse problems in Washington State. The program demonstrated the ability to reduce recidivism and save money.

Much of the research done over the last 15 years on correctional programming (for males and females) that incorporates at least some incarceration time (whether that time was short-term confinement in a local detention center or longer confinement as a result of a commitment to a state correctional institution), suggests that well-designed reentry programming must be included as part of the correctional experience. In fact, now there is consensus in the field that reentry programming cannot be an afterthought and must be started while youth are still incarcerated (Altschuler & Armstrong, 1999). Furthermore, pre-release reentry programming and the continued provision of reentry services while correctional clients are working to become self-sustaining and independent are critical to successful transition.

Unfortunately, there is much less consensus about what constitutes best practice for juvenile reentry in general, let alone what might constitute best practice for particular subpopulations in the juvenile system. More clearly stated, we are not in a position to authoritatively claim what best practice may be for the reentry of majority and minority girls or LGBT youth. Furthermore, while we do know some about what constitutes quality reentry for boys (e.g., prerelease planning, mentoring, cognitive–behavioral therapy, functional family therapy, etc.), we need to further investigate whether that knowledge holds true for boys of color. The one thing that can be said with full confidence is that we know reentry services are important for these groups. As such, jurisdictions need to take stock of the knowledge they have about these particular subpopulations and determine whether there are particular modalities or culturally informed approaches that might be more effective for them.

Parting Thoughts: The future of Juvenile CBSs

First, a mild admonishment: local juvenile courts and correctional agencies have added, in part, to the very problem they are charged with reducing, namely juvenile crime. Obviously, resources are constrained and have been since the court's inception, but that does not diminish the responsibility that juvenile courts and community corrections departments share for perpetuating and supporting programs that are known to be ineffective (e.g., routine (supervision only) probation, surveillance/control-only ISP, boot camps, and "scared straight" programs), while ignoring those that we know are effective (family functional therapy, cognitive–behavioral treatment, restorative justice, etc.). Once more, according to the community corrections literature, participation in ineffective, deterrence-based programs such as boot camps actually increase recidivism. It is one thing for the general public not to know that these programs cause more problems than they fix; it is entirely another thing if practitioners do not know that fact, or know these facts and continue to use the programs anyway.

Enough evidence has been amassed to make the claim that all community corrections agencies and providers of aftercare programming should incorporate as many high-impact, evidence-based treatment approaches as possible. In what is left of this chapter, I discuss five approaches that have been designated as effective/ evidence-based but are *underused*, and three others that are *promising* and deserve further study.

Five underused effective approaches

There are five approaches to treatment/justice that have been evaluated, replicated, judged as effective, and remain *underused*. Perhaps the best known of these underused treatment technologies is cognitive–behavioral therapy (CBT). If one were to visit any decent-sized probation or community corrections agency in America and ask the staff if they had heard of CBT, most would say yes. Fewer, however, would be able to properly explain the theory behind it or how it translates into practice. Even fewer agencies would be able to describe what is involved in functional family therapy, multisystemic therapy, multidimensional treatment foster care, or restorative justice. In this section, each of these treatment approaches is described and their efficacy is addressed.

Cognitive-behavioral therapy (CBT)   CBT is a therapeutic approach that is problem-focused. CBT teaches individuals to identify and understand their problematic thoughts and beliefs and how they affect their behaviors (OJJDP, n.d.). In essence, CBT suggests that thoughts affect emotions, which in turn influence behaviors. If people can learn to change their thinking, they can change how they respond to various situations.

CBT can be used effectively in prevention, intervention, and aftercare programs (Lipsey, 1995, 2009). Why CBT is thought to be such a strong model is that it combines two very effective kinds of psychotherapy: *cognitive therapy* and *behavioral therapy* (OJJDP, n.d.). Furthermore, there is growing evidence from meta-analyses and program evaluations that cognitive–behavioral treatment lowers reoffending among both juveniles and adults (Cullen & Jonson, 2011; Greenwood & Turner, 2012; Lipsey *et al.*, 2010). Additionally OJJDP-MPG deemed CBT to be effective at reducing recidivism; whereas, WSIPP found CBT to reduce recidivism, but not to the same degree that it was found to impact recidivism in the other reviews (see Greenwood & Turner, 2012; Lipsey *et al.*, 2010; Washington State Institute for Public Policy, 2013). Interestingly, OJJDP-MPG labeled nearly all of the cognitive–behavioral based programs assessed in their review as very effective (OJJDP, n.d.).

Multisystemic therapy (MST)   MST is an intensive family and home-based therapeutic approach that uses behavioral techniques to work with youth that are having issues with substances, serious crime and violence both in the home and in school (OJJDP, n.d.). MST therapists have general therapy backgrounds but have also received training in the MST model. According to Henggeler (1997), MST therapists work with and across the various systems that impact the behavior of the youth (e.g., family, school, peers and neighborhood).

MST is effective according to numerous sources: Blueprints for Healthy Youth Development (n.d.), Washington State Institute for Public Policy (2013), and Lipsey *et al.* (2010). Moreover, according to the OJJDP-MPG, two of the MST programs it rated were designated as effective and three were considered promising.

Multidimensional treatment foster care (MTFC)   MTFC is targeted at adolescents that will be placed out of the home as a result of serious delinquency histories or because of a serious delinquent event. Foster parents take into their homes at-risk and delinquent youth and are trained in adolescent development and problem behaviors. MTFC parents provide consistent supervision, appropriate discipline, and the structure that all young people need. These foster care placements also create an environment that allow these youth to stabilize, exist in a normalized setting, work on academic and effective life skills, and develop healthy relationships with both peers and authority figures (Weibush et al., 2005). Washington State Institute for Public Policy (2013), OJJDP (n.d.), and Blueprints for Healthy Youth Development (n.d.) each determined that MTFC is effective in curbing the development of delinquency, youth violence, and other problem behaviors. Moreover, this same research indicated that it is also more cost-effective than congregate care placements that are aimed at preventing youth reoffending.

Functional family therapy (FFT)   FFT is a family-based prevention and intervention program that specifically targets high-risk youth aged 11–18 and their families (Sexton & Turner, 2010). FFT "…addresses complex and multidimensional problems through clinical practice that is flexibly structured and culturally sensitive" (OJJDP, n.d., para. 1). The program employs trained clinicians to work with the family to recognize factors (especially familial factors) that put youth at risk of abusing substances and participating in problem behaviors or violence (Alexander, Pugh, Parsons, & Sexton, 2000). The goal is to get the youth and family to concentrate on reducing those negative factors; to build on strengths that exist in the family; and to work towards increasing protective factors that reduce participation in delinquency and substance abuse (Alexander et al., 2000).

According to Greenwood and Turner (2012), FFT has been used for several decades, has been evaluated and replicated many times, and is effective at reducing recidivism for system-involved youth (Lipsey et al., 2010). Additionally, Blueprints for Healthy Youth Development (n.d.), Washington State Institute for Public Policy (2013), and OJJDP (n.d.) all conclude that this therapeutic approach is effective. Additionally, OJJDP (n.d.) claims that the FFT model is effectively a prevention program, an immediate intervention, and an intermediate sanction.

Restorative justice (RJ)   This treatment approach was discussed above under the non-residential CBSs section. While much of Europe is following Australia's lead by widely implementing RJ programs (Gavrielides, 2007), the US is slower to adopt it widely. However, given the evidence of its effectiveness, RJ should be more widely adopted in all areas of the juvenile justice system. Additionally, RJ programs offer a reasonable alternative to a number of zero-tolerance-based school discipline policies that have disproportionately impacted youth of color and exacerbated the school-to-prison pipeline.

Three approaches that deserve more attention

Finally, there are three treatment/programmatic areas that deserve far more attention at the local level than they have been given in practice: gender-responsive programming, trauma-informed care, and restorative community service. While two of the three (gender-responsive programming and trauma-informed care) have increasingly been written about in the academic community and implemented in a few places, none could currently be considered a mainstream treatment approach. It is time that juvenile justice agencies take a closer look at them, as could well hold real promise for changing the lives of system-involved youth.

Gender-responsive programming   The development of gender-responsive programming (GRP) came about as a response to the acknowledgement that girls and women were entering the juvenile and criminal justice systems at unprecedented rates in the mid-1990s (Chesney-Lind, Morash, & Stevens, 2008; Garcia & Lane, 2013; Snyder & Sickmund, 2006). As practitioners attempted to identify intervention and correctional programming that would reverse this course, it quickly became apparent that the programming that had been developed for male offenders rarely met the needs of girls and women (American Bar Association and the National Bar Association, 2001; Garcia & Lane, 2010). GRP (once referred to as gender-specific programming) focuses on providing treatment and programming that revolves around girls' particular psychological, social, and developmental needs (Garcia & Lane, 2013).

The development of GRP models is still in its infancy (Zahn, Day, Mihalic, & Tichavsky, 2009). Several programs have been put in place across the country and have undergone process and implementation evaluations, but far fewer have undergone extensive outcome evaluations. To be clear: some outcome evaluations exist, but relatively few have been conducted using a gold-standard experimental design. At this time, very few studies have utilized rigorous methods to study GRP, and those that have, have found little impact (Chesney-Lind *et al.*, 2008). Given the paucity of outcome evaluations and the reality that virtually no replication studies have taken place to test the veracity and generalizability of GRP, it is too early to make a judgment on the efficacy of particular gender-responsive program models. Therefore, more time, attention, and resources must be focused on developing evidence-based practice for girls' delinquency.

Until the field amasses a larger body of GRP research, it is important to share what the GRP experts believe should be included in programming designed for girls. What the gender-responsive literature suggests is that girls' programming needs are extensive and interventions must address the myriad problems that girls in the system present. Listed below are commonly cited programmatic and treatment needs identified in the GRP literature. (For a more detailed discussion of these needs, see Garcia & Lane, 2010, 2013; Chesney-Lind *et al.*, 2008).

- Programs must be offered in environments where girls feel safe, nurtured, respected, heard, and are treated with dignity.
- Programs should utilize culturally competent treatment models and allow for the girls to develop healthy bonds with treatment staff.
- Programs should address the serious trauma girls have experienced (e.g., abandonment, neglect, and emotional, physical and sexual abuse), as well as the

results of such traumas (e.g., depression, substance abuse, self-mutilation, and other psychological and personality disorders).

- Programs should (when possible) teach girls how to build trusting, healthy relationships with the service providers, family members and important others in their lives.
- Programs must also inform young women how to protect themselves from unwanted pregnancies, STDs, and domestic violence.
- Programs should instruct girls about body hygiene, nutrition, and how to develop and maintain healthy romantic relationships with significant others (whether they be heterosexual or same-sex partnerships).
- Programs also need to teach girls how to identify pro-social activities and to develop and foster positive peer networks.
- Finally, the programs and agencies that sponsor GRP should be certain to offer wrap-around services and aftercare assistance to optimize program success.

Trauma-informed care (TIC)   In the last several years, more and more attention is being paid to the important role that experiencing trauma plays in the way that we think, feel and act. Trauma-informed care: is a

> ...therapeutic approach for individuals exposed to trauma, and can operate on many levels. 'Trauma informed care' involves the provision of care that, borrowing from the field of cultural competence, is "trauma competent" (Hodas, 2006, p. 32).

A child can experience trauma if he or she is emotionally, physically and/or sexually abused; witnesses violence; is neglected; is homeless; or lives in violent surroundings. TIC begins by making sure the youth is physically safe and that the treatment is provided in an environment (and with staff) with which the child feels safe. TIC can be conducted in an in-patient setting, in the community, with youth that are under correctional supervision, or in a correctional institution. According to Hodas (2006), TIC is grounded in a public health approach to prevention, and as such can be conducted in groups or with an individual youth.

Treatment that is trauma-informed understands the need of the survivor to be respected and informed of the process, and to work collaboratively with the survivor, his or her family and trusted others in such a way that empowers the survivor. Lastly, TIC must appreciate the interrelatedness of trauma and the symptoms of trauma presenting (National Center for Trauma Informed Care, n.d.).

Why should we invest in TIC program models, pilot and evaluate them? Because according to Adams (2010, p. 1), "...between 75 and 93 percent of youth entering the juvenile justice system annually in this country are estimated to have experienced some degree of trauma." Yet much of this trauma is undiagnosed or untreated. As Hodas (2006) noted, childhood trauma has very real consequences both throughout childhood and adolescence but can continue long into adulthood. These consequences include mental health disorders (e.g., depression, anxiety, and personality disorders), physical health disorders (e.g., hypertension, headaches, obesity, sleep disturbances, and autoimmune diseases), and involvement in delinquency and crime. If policy-makers and practitioners are serious about trying to help youths and reduce juvenile crime, justice system workers and other service providers must become more adroit at identifying trauma when it is occurring and treat it then. Schools, pediatricians, law enforcement, and social services need to be trained to identify trauma and its effects and get these youth into TIC as quickly as possible. Short of this, the juvenile justice system will have to become a trauma informed system of care to improve outcomes for these youth and society as a whole. Finally, not many programs that utilize all of the major tenets of trauma-informed care with juveniles have been evaluated and replicated. Nevertheless, OJJDP-MPG suggests that those that appear to be heavily trauma-focused are either effective or promising.

Restorative community service (RCS)　　RCS was described in more detail in the section that reviewed the non-residential CBS – community service. Maloney (2007) argued that community service orders affect behavior in a more meaningful way if justice practitioners are more deliberate in the way that community service programs are devised. He argued that when young people see a purpose in their service, understand why the community needs it done, are treated like the useful resources that they are, and are given the opportunity to demonstrate accountability, they will and can build important competencies at the same time.

Conclusion

Given the balance of the empirical evidence, there is no excuse for juvenile prevention and correctional agencies to ignore the "what works" literature and continue investing scarce resources in programs that do not help (and sometimes hurt youth). Thus it is time that agencies stop using boot camps and "scared straight" style programs, outright. Additionally, if agencies continue to use routine probation, house arrest, intensive supervision probation, and probation camps (because they are desperate for alternatives to incarceration), they must redesign these correctional methods to include the principles of effective correctional intervention, and restructure them so that they become therapeutic approaches to corrections rather than surveillance-oriented approaches (see Lipsey et al., 2010). Further still, these same agencies should incorporate the high-impact treatment modalities that have been shown to be effective (i.e., restitution, restorative justice, CBT, FFT, MST, and MTFC) and those that show some promise but need further restructuring (i.e., day reporting centers, and both general community service and restorative community service). Finally, agencies that are interested in making meaningful changes for girls, and anyone who has survived significant trauma, should investigate, implement and evaluate gender-responsive programming and trauma-informed treatment models.

Notes

1   The first civilly authorized execution took place in 1609 in James City, Virginia. Captain George Kendall was thought to be spying for the Spanish. See Kronenwetter, M. (1993). *Capital Punishment: A Reference Handbook* (p. 71). Santa Barbara, CA: ABC-CLIO, Inc.

2   According to Smith, Gendreau, and Swartz (2009), there are three conditions that must be met for a rehabilitation program to be most effective. These ***principles of effective correctional intervention*** include the following tenets.

- The program must be delivered to high-risk offenders (this is referred to as the ***risk principle***).
- It must target criminogenic needs (the ***need principle***). There are two types of criminogenic needs – static and dynamic. Static needs cannot be changed; these are things like birth order or having criminal parents. Dynamic needs are factors that are associated with delinquency and can be impacted by correctional programming (i.e., choice of delinquent peers or motivation to change).
- Finally, it must employ cognitive–behavioral treatment programs (e.g., cognitive restructuring or social learning approaches) that specifically address the particular needs of the offender "while taking key offender characteristics into consideration when making decisions about the mode and style of service delivery". This is referred to as the ***responsivity principle*** (Smith, Gendreau, & Swartz, 2009, p. 153).

"Together these three conditions form the core of what is known as the principles of effective correctional intervention" (Smith, Gendreau, & Swartz, 2009, p. 153). For a complete discussion of the principles of effective correctional intervention, see Andrews and Bonta (2006) and Gendreau (1996).

3   Detailed discussions of Lipsey's meta-analyses of juvenile justice programs can be found by referring to the following sources: Lipsey (1992, 1995, 2009); Lipsey, Howell, Kelly, Chapman, and Carver (2010); Cullen & Jonson (2011); Greenwood (2010); and Greenwood & Turner (2012).

4   Aftercare is the juvenile equivalent of parole.

5   Criminogenic needs are attributes of an individual that are correlated with crime and recidivism. There are two categories of criminogenic needs: static and dynamic. Static needs are things that cannot be changed (i.e., prior criminal history and age at first arrest). Dynamic needs can be changed and include things like drug addiction, attitudes, and delinquent peers (Lowencamp & Latessa, 2005). Lowencamp and Latessa (2005, p. 15) stated: "…programs that target at least to four to six criminogenic needs can reduce recidivism by 30 percent."

6   The arm of juvenile court jurisdiction reaches until the age of 25 in California.

References

Aalsma, M., Garcia, C.A., Haight, K., Jarjoura, R.J., & Ostermann, L. (2013). *Assessing DMC in Indiana*. Indianapolis, IN: Indianapolis Criminal Justice Institute,

Adams, E.J. (2010). *Healing Invisible Wounds: Why Investing in Trauma-Informed Care for Children Makes Sense*. Washington, DC: Justice Policy Institute.

Alexander, J.F., Pugh, C., Parsons, B.V., & Sexton, T.L. (2000). Functional family therapy. In D.S. Elliott (Ed.), *Blueprints for Violence Prevention (Book 3)*, 2nd ed. Boulder, CO: Center for the Study and Prevention of Violence, Institute of Behavioral Science, University of Colorado.

Altschuler, D.M., & Armstrong, T.L. (1996). Aftercare not afterthought: Testing the IAP model. *Juvenile Justice, 3*(1), 15–22.

Altschuler, D.M., & Armstrong, T.L. (1999). *Reintegration, Supervised Release, and Intensive Aftercare.* Washington, DC: US Department of Justice, Office of Justice Programs, Office of Juvenile Justice and Delinquency Prevention.

American Bar Association (n.d.). *Part 1: The History of Juvenile Justice.* American Bar Association's Division for Public Education. Retrieved from http://www.americanbar. org/content/dam/aba/migrated/publiced/features/DYJpart1.authcheckdam.pdf

American Bar Association and the National Bar Association (2001). *Justice by Gender: The Lack of Appropriate Prevention, Diversion and Treatment Alternatives for Girls in the Justice System.* Retrieved from http://www.americanbar.org/content/dam/aba/ publishing/criminal_justice_section_newsletter/crimjust_juvjus_justicebygenderweb. authcheckdam.pdf

Andrews, D.A., & Bonta, J. (2006). *The Psychology of Criminal Conduct*, 4th ed. Cincinnati, OH: Anderson/ LexiNexis.

Andrews, D.A., Zinger, I., Hoge, R.D., Bonta, J., Gendreau, P., & Cullen, F.T. (1990). Does correctional treatment work? A clinically relevant and psychologically informed meta-analysis. *Criminology, 28*(3), 369–404.

Augustus, J. (1852). *John Augustus' Original Report of his Labors. Reprinted in 1939.* Montclair, NJ: Patterson Smith.

Bales, W.D., Mann, K., Blomberg, T.G., Gaes, G.G., Barrick, K., Dhungana, K., & McManus, B. (2010). *A Quantitative and Qualitative Assessment of Electronic Monitoring.* Tallahassee, FL: Florida State University, College of Criminology and Criminal Justice, Center for Criminology and Public Policy Research.

Barton, W.H., & Butts, J. (1988). *The Metro-County Intensive Supervision Experiment: Project Brief, Selected Results From a Five-Year Program Evaluation.* Ann Arbor: University of Michigan, Institute for Social Research.

Baumer, T., & Garcia, C.A. (2009). *25 years of ELMO: What do we know and where should we go?* Presented at the Annual Meeting of the American Society of Criminology, Philadelphia, PA.

Bazemore, G. (1999). Crime victims, restorative justice and the juvenile court: Exploring victim needs and involvement in the response to youth crime. *International Review of Victimology, 1*(6), 295–320.

Bennett, W.L., DiIulio Jr., J.J., & Walters, J.P. (1996). *Body Count: Moral Poverty and How to Win America's War against Crime and Drugs.* New York: Simon & Schuster.

Blueprints for Healthy Youth Development. (n.d.). About 'Blueprints for Healthy Youth Development'. Retrieved from http://www.blueprintsprograms.com/about.php

Bouffard, J.A., & Bergseth, K.J. (2008). The impact of reentry services on juvenile offenders' recidivism. *Youth Violence and Juvenile Justice, 6*(3), 295–318.

Bourdin, C.M., Mann, B.J., Cone, L.T., Henggeler, S.W., Fucci, B.R., Blaske, D.M., & Williams, R.A. (1995). Multisystemic treatment of serious juvenile offenders: Long-term prevention of criminality and violence. *Journal of Consulting and Clinical Psychology, 63*(4), 569–578.

Bulman, P. (2013). Day reporting centers in New Jersey: No evidence of reduced recidivism. *Corrections Today, 75*(2), 12.

Chesney-Lind, M., Morash, M., & Stevens, T. (2008). Girls' troubles, girls' delinquency, and gender responsive programming: A review. *Australian and New Zealand Journal of Criminology, 41*(1), 162–189.

Cohen, E., & Hinkle, M. (2000). Juvenile corrections in Indiana. *Annals of the American Society of Political and Social Science, 567*, 198–208.

Corbett, R.P. (2000). Juvenile probation on the eve of the next millennium. *APPA Perspectives, 24*, 22–30.

Cullen, F.T. (2002). Rehabilitation and treatment programs. In J.Q. Wilson, & J. Petersilia (Eds.), *Crime: Public Policies for Crime Control* (pp. 253–290). Oakland, CA: Institute for Contemporary Studies.

Cullen, F.T., Blevins, K.R., Trager, J.S., & Gendreau, P. (2005). The rise and fall of bootcamps: A case study in common-sense corrections. *Journal of Offender Rehabilitation, 40*(3), 53–70.

Cullen, F.T., & Jonson, C.L. (2011). Rehabilitation and treatment programs. In J.Q. Wilson, & J. Petersilia (Eds.), *Crime and Public Policy* (pp. 293–344). New York: Oxford University press.

Degelman, C., Pereira, C., & Peterson, S.B. (2006). *Introduction to Community Service Learning, Volume 12:1*. Los Angeles, CA: Service Learning Network, Constitutional Rights Foundation. Retrieved from http://www.crf-usa.org/service-learning-network/12-1-introducing-community-service-learning-article.html

DeMichele, M., & Payne, B.K. (2007). Probation and parole officers speak out – Caseload and workload allocation. *Federal Probation, 71*(3). Retrieved from http://www.uscourts.gov/uscourts/FederalCourts/PPS/Fedprob/2007-12/officersSpeakOut.html

DeMichele, M., & Payne, B.K. (2009). *Offender Supervision with Electronic Technology: Community Corrections Resource, 2nd ed.* Washington, DC: Office of Justice Programs, Bureau of Justice Assistance.

Diggs, D.W. (n.d.). *Day Reporting Centers as an Effective Correctional Sanction.* Retrieved from http://www.fdle.state.fl.us/content/getdoc/36d83075-990c-4c75-80c1-71227a823655/diggs.aspx

Diggs, D.W., & Pieper, S.L. (1994). Using day reporting centers as an effective alternative to jails. *Federal Probation, 58*, 1.

Fagan, J., & Kupchik, A. (2011). Juvenile incarceration and the pains of confinement. *Duke Forum for Law and Social Change, 3*(29), 29–61.

Federal Bureau of Investigation. (2012). *Crime in the United States, 2009.* Clarksburg, WV: Federal Bureau of Investigation.

Fields, C.B. (2012). Augustus, John. In S.M. Barton-Bellessa (Ed.), *Encyclopedia of Community Corrections* (pp. 17–18). Thousand Oaks, CA: SAGE.

Garcia, C.A. (1996). Measurement in community corrections: Intensive supervision revisited. *UMI Dissertation Services* (University Microforms No. 9700027).

Garcia, C.A., & Lane, J. (2010). Looking in the rear view mirror: What incarcerated women think girls need from the system. *Feminist Criminology, 5*(3), 227–243.

Garcia, C.A., & Lane, J. (2013). What a girl wants; what a girl needs: Findings from a gender-relevant focus group study. *Crime and Delinquency, 59*(4), 536–561.

Gavrielides, T. (2007). *Restorative Justice Theory and Practice: Addressing the Discrepancy.* Helsinki: European Institute for Crime Prevention and Control.

Gendreau, P. (1996). The principles of effective correctional intervention with offenders. In A.T. Harland (Ed.), *Choosing Correctional Interventions That Work: Defining the Demand and Evaluating the Supply* (pp. 177–130). Newbury Park, CA: Sage.

Gendreau, P., Goggin, C., Cullen, F.T., & Andrews, D.A. (2000). The effects of community sanctions and incarceration on recidivism. *Forum on Corrections Research, 12* (May), 10–13.

Greenwood, P.W. (2010). *Preventing and Reducing Youth Crime and Violence: Using Evidence-base Practices.* Sacramento: Governor's Office of Gang and Youth Violence Policy, State of California.

Greenwood, P.W., & Turner, S. (2012). Probation and other non-institutional treatment: The evidence is in. In B. Feld, & D. Bishop (Eds). *The Oxford Handbook of Juvenile Crime and Juvenile Justice* (pp. 723–747). New York: Oxford University Press.

Harris, R.J., & Wing Lo, T. (2002). Criminal justice: Its use in criminal justice. *International Journal of Offender Therapy and Comparative Criminology, 46*(4), 427–444.

Henggeler, S.W. (1997). *Juvenile Justice Bulletin – Treating Serious Antisocial Behavior in Youth: The MST Approach.* Washington, DC: US Department of Justice, Office of Juvenile Justice and Delinquency Prevention.

Hirsch, A.J. (1992), *The Rise of the Penitentiary: Prisons and Punishment in Early America,* New Haven, CT: Yale University Press.

Hodas, G.R. (2006). *Responding to Childhood Trauma: The Promise and Practice of Trauma Informed Care.* Pennsylvania Office of Mental Health and Substance Abuse Services. Retrieved from http://www.childrescuebill.org/VictimsOfAbuse/RespondingHodas.pdf

Jacob, T., & Johnson, S. (1997). Parenting influences on the development of alcohol abuse and dependence. *Alcohol Health and Research World, 21*(3), 204–209.

Krisberg, B., Nuenfeldst, D., Weibush, R., & Rodriguez, O. (1994). *Juvenile Intensive Supervision: Planning Guide.* Washington, DC: Office of Juvenile Justice and Delinquency Prevention, Office of Justice Programs.

Krisberg, B., Rodriguez, O., Bakke, A., Neuenfeldt, D., & Steele, P. (1989). *Demonstration of Postadjudication Nonresidential Intensive Supervision Programs: Assessment Report.* San Francisco: National Council on Crime and Delinquency.

Krisberg, B., Vuong, L., Hartney, C., & Marchionna, S. (2010). *New Era in California Juvenile: Justice: Downsizing the State Youth Corrections System.* Oakland, CA: National Council on Crime and Delinquency.

Lane, J., Turner, S., Fain, T., & Sehgal, A. (2005). Evaluating an experimental intensive juvenile probation program: Supervision and official outcomes. *Crime and Delinquency, 51*(1), 26–52.

Latimer, J., Dowden, C., & Muise, D. (2005). The effectiveness of restorative justice practices: a meta-analysis. *The Prison Journal, 85*(2), 127–144.

Lattimore, P/K., Brumbaugh, S., Visher, C., Lindquist, C., Winterfield, L., Salas, M., & Zweig, J. (2004). *National Portrait of SVORI: Serious Violent Offender Initiative.* Washington, DC: US Department of Justice, Office of Justice Programs, National Institute of Justice.

Lee, S., Aos, S., Drake, E., Pennucci, A., Miller, M., & Anderson, L. (2012). *Return on Investment: Evidence-based Options to Improve Statewide Outcomes (Document No. 12-04-1201).* Olympia, WA: State Institute for Public Policy.

Lipsey, M.W. (1992). Juvenile delinquency treatment: A meta-analytic inquiry into the variability of effects. In T.D. Cook, D.S. Harris Cooper, H. Cordray, L.V. Hartmann, R.J. Hedges, T.A. Light, & F. Mosteller (Eds.), *Meta Analysis for Explanation: A Casebook* (pp. 83–127). New York: Russell Sage.

Lipsey, M.W. (1995). What do we learn from 400 research studies on the effectiveness of treatment with juvenile delinquency? In J. McGuire (Ed.), *What Works: Reducing Reoffending* (pp. 63–78). Chichester: John Wiley & Sons, Ltd..

Lipsey, M.W. (2009). The primary factors that characterize effective interventions with juvenile offenders: A meta-analytic overview. *Victims and Offenders, 4*(4), 124–147.

Lipsey, M., Howell, J.C., Kelly, M.R., Chapman, G., & Carver, D. (2010). *Improving the Effectiveness of Juvenile Justice Programs: A New Perspective on Evidence-Based Practice.* Washington, DC: Center for Juvenile Justice Reform, Georgetown University.

Lowenkamp, C., & Latessa, E. (2005). Increasing the effectiveness of correctional programming through the risk principle: Identifying offenders for residential placement. *Criminology and Public Policy, 4*(2), 263–290.

Lucken, K. (1997). "Rehabilitating" treatment in community corrections. *Crime and Delinquency, 43*(3), 243–259.

MacKenzie, D.L. (2006). *What Works in Corrections: Reducing the Criminal Activities of Offenders and Delinquents.* New York: Cambridge University Press.

Maguin, E., & Loeber, R. (1996). Academic performance and delinquency. In M. Tonry (Ed.), *Crime and Justice, 20,* 145–264. Chicago, IL: University of Chicago Press.

Mair, G. (1990). Day centres in England and Wales. *IARCA Journal, 3,* 9.

Maloney, D. (2007). Restorative community service: Earning redemption, gaining skills, and proving worth. *Reclaiming Children and Youth, 15*(4), 214–219.

Marion, N. (2002). Effectiveness of community based correctional programs: A case study. *The Prison Journal, 82*(4), 478–497.

Martin, C., Lurigio, A., & Olson, D. (2003). An examination of rearrests and reincarcerations among discharged day reporting center clients. *Federal Probation, 67,* 24–30.

Maxfield, M.G., & Baumer, T.L. (1991). *Evaluation of Pretrial Home Detention with Electronic Monitoring: Brief Summary.* Washington, DC: US Department of Justice, Office of Justice Programs, National Institute of Justice.

McBride, D., & Vanderwaal, C. (1997). Day reporting centers as an alternative for drug using offenders. *Journal of Drug Issues, 27,* 379.

Morris, N., & Tonry, M. (1990). *Between Prison and Probation: Intermediate Punishments in a Rational Sentencing System.* New York: Oxford University Press.

National Center for Trauma Informed Care. (n.d.). *Trauma-Informed Care and Trauma Services.* Rockville, MD: Substance Abuse and Mental Health Services Administration. Retrieved from http://www.samhsa.gov/nctic/trauma.asp

New York City Department of Probation. (n.d.). *The History of Probation.* New York City Department of Probation. Retrieved from http://www.nyc.gov/html/prob/html/about/history.shtml

Nieto, M. (2008). *County Probation Camps and Ranches for Juvenile Offenders.* Sacramento, CA: California Research Bureau, California State Library.

Office for Victims of Crime (2004). *State crime victim compensation and assistance grants program.* OVC Fact Sheet. Washington, DC: Office of Justice Programs, Office for Victims of Crime. Retrieved from http://www.ovc.gov/publications/factshts/compandassist/welcome.html

Office of Juvenile Justice and Delinquency Prevention (n.d.). *OJJDP Model Programs Guide.* Washington, DC: US Department of Justice, Office of Juvenile Justice and Delinquency Prevention. Retrieved from http://www.ojjdp.gov/MPG/

Palmer, T. (1992). *The Reemergence of Correctional Intervention.* Newbury Park, CA: Sage.

Palmer, T., & Wedge, R. (1989a). *California Juvenile Probation Camps: Summary.* Sacramento, CA: State of California, Department of the Youth Authority.

Palmer, T. and Wedge, R. (1989b). California's juvenile probation camps: Findings and implications. *Crime & Delinquency, 35*(2), 234–253.

Parent, D. (1990). *Day Reporting Centers for Criminal Offenders: A Descriptive Analysis of Existing Programs.* Washington, DC: US Department of Justice.

Petersilia, J. (1987). *Expanding Options for Criminal Sentencing.* Santa Monica, CA: RAND.

Petersilia, J. (1990). Conditions that permit ISP programs to survive. *Crime and Delinquency, 36*(1), 126–145.

Petersilia, J. (2002). *Reforming Probation and Parole.* Lanham, MD: American Correctional Association.

Petersilia, J. (2011). Community corrections: Probation, parole and prisoner reentry. In J.Q. Wilson, & J. Petersilia (Eds.), *Crime and Public Policy* (pp. 499–531). New York: Oxford University Press.

Petersilia, J., & Turner, S. (1993). Intensive probation and parole. In M. Tonry (Ed.), *Crime and Justice: An Annual Review of Research* (pp. 281–335). Chicago, IL: University of Chicago Press.

Puzzanchera, C., & Hockenberry, S. (2013). *Juvenile Court Statistics 2010.* Pittsburgh, PA: National Center for Juvenile Justice.

Rothman, D.J. (2011). *The Discovery of the Asylum: Social Order and Disorder in the New Republic.* New Brunswick: Aldine Transactions.

Sexton, T.L., & Turner, C.W. (2010). The effectiveness of functional family therapy for youth with behavioral problems in a community practice setting. *Journal of Family Psychology, 24*(3), 339–348.

Smith, P., Gendreau, P., & Swartz, K. (2009). Validating the principles of effective intervention: A systematic review of the contributions of meta-analysis in the field of corrections. *Victims and Offenders, 4,* 148–169.

Snyder, H.N. (2004). An empirical portrait of the youth reentry population. *Youth Violence and Juvenile Justice, 2*(1), 35–55.

Snyder, H.N., & Sickmund, M. (2006). *Juvenile Offenders and Victims: 2006 National Report.* Washington, DC: Office of Justice Programs, Department of Justice, Office of Juvenile Justice Delinquency Prevention.

Stinchcomb, J.B., & Terry, III, W.C. (2001). Predicting the likelihood of rearrest among shock incarceration graduates: Moving beyond another nail in the boot camp coffin. *Crime and Delinquency, 47,* 221–242.

The Sentencing Project. (2014). *Fact Sheet: Trends in US Corrections.* Washington, DC: The Sentencing Project.

Washington State Institute for Public Policy. (2013). *June 2013 Inventory of Evidence-Based, Research-Based, and Promising Practices For Prevention and Intervention Services for Children and Juveniles in Child Welfare, Juvenile Justice, and Mental Health Systems.* Olympia, WA: Washington State Institute for Public Policy. Retrieved from http://www.wsipp.wa.gov/ReportFile/1374/Wsipp_Updated-Inventory-of-Evidence-Based-Research-Based-and-Promising-Practices_Inventory.pdf

Watson, D.W., Bisesi, L., Tanamly, S., & Mai, N. (2003). Comprehensive residential education, arts and substance abuse treatment. *Youth Violence and Juvenile Justice, 1*(4), 388–401.

Weibush, R.G., Wagner, D., McNulty, B., Wand, Y., & Le, T.N. (2005). *Implementation and Outcome Evaluation of the Intensive Aftercare Program: Final Report.* Washington, DC:

US Department of Justice, Office of Justice Programs, Office of Juvenile Justice and Delinquency Prevention.

Wiebush, R.G., Wagner, D., Prestine, R., & Baird, C. (1992). *The Impact of Electronic Monitoring on Juvenile Recidivism: Results of an Experimental Test in the Cuyahoga County Juvenile Court*. Madison, WI: National Council on Crime and Delinquency.

Zahn, M.A., Day, D., Mihalic, S., & Tichavsky, L. (2009). Determining what works for girls in the juvenile justice system: A summary of evaluation evidence. *Crime and Delinquency*, 55(2), 266–293.

Ziemba-Davis, M., Garcia, C.A., Kincaid, N.L., Gullans, K., & Myers, B. (2004). *What About Girls in Indiana's Juvenile Justice System?* Indianapolis, IN: Indiana Criminal Justice Institute.

29

Institutionalization and Treatment

Barry Glick

Past

History and description of the juvenile justice system

We can trace the first social sanctions for crimes against society, both property and personal, back to biblical times. The Old Testament is replete with social laws, for which violations led to immediate punishment that ranged from public humiliation to death. The Bible was specific to make the penalty fit the crime, and was especially intolerant of youth who were incorrigible and disobeyed their parents. (cf. Numbers 35:16–19; Deuteronomy 18:18–21; Leviticus 24:17–22).

In Greco-Roman times, citizens were banished from the city-states if they violated laws. In the Middle Ages, disputes were settled by family feuds, duels, and vigilantism. After the eleventh century, criminal law and punishment were used to maintain public order. Like in Roman times, the more harsh punishments, such as public whippings or death, were given to the poor, slaves, or others who were not part of the privileged class. During the Middle Ages, the public policy was harsh punishment for aggression against community, rather than deterrence.

Juveniles were treated similarly to adults throughout societies, when they behaved aggressively or violently. Usually they were incarcerated, either in criminal justice systems or mental hygiene systems. It was not until 1899 that the first family court was created in Cook County (Chicago, Illinois) to deal with aggressive and violent children and youth. However, by the early 1990s, within a mere century of operation, youth violence was so uncontrolled in our neighborhoods that policy-makers enacted legislation to resolve the youth social assaults on communities and citizen

The Handbook of Juvenile Delinquency and Juvenile Justice, First Edition. Edited by Marvin D. Krohn and Jodi Lane.

safety. Harsh laws to incarcerate young children, within adult systems, were enacted, and family courts were even dismantled, so that treatment and rehabilitation were no longer primary concerns of our society.

Family courts and juvenile systems quickly grew throughout the US, modeled after the Chicago juvenile court reformation. By the early 1920s and continuing until the end of World War II, state jurisdictions grew their institutional systems through a variety of training schools and reformatories to deal with delinquents incapable of living in their communities. By the mid-twentieth century, advocacy groups such as the American Law Institute and Civil Liberties Union successfully lobbied for states to form Youth Authorities to deal with the special needs of juveniles who were incorrigible and delinquent.

Thus, over the last century or so, the juvenile justice system has evolved from a rather informal structure motivated by church people to provide services to the unwanted and the destitute, to, in recent decades, a multi-billion dollar industry that employs thousands of people to provide services to juvenile delinquents, some of whom have committed the most heinous of crimes. For example, the juvenile justice system of the 1980s relied upon the public and private sectors in order to provide services to youth. These programs represented an array of community- and non-community-based residential facilities that were available to local family courts as they disposed of juvenile cases. The administrators of these programs and services were charged to rehabilitate youth placed in their care and return these youth to communities as productive, effective, and contributing citizens.

These conditions continued through the turn of the twenty-first century with many jurisdictions restructuring their juvenile justice systems. For example, the State of New York eliminated their Division for Youth, the premier agency that dealt with juvenile delinquency, providing both incarceration and prevention services, combining those functions with their Department of Social Services to create a new, larger agency: the Department of Children and Family Services. This newer agency concentrated on broader children and family services, reducing the juvenile justice system to a subdivision of the larger agency. The State of California similarly eliminated the California Youth Authority, transferring the entire system into their existing Department of Corrections Agency. Many other states also rolled youth services, which enjoyed independent agency status, under a broader umbrella agency, either Social Services or Corrections. These actions were often taken either as budget efficiencies or social policy, to reflect the attitudes of their constituencies.

For the last decade, the focus on youth services has been even further reduced because of other economic problems and social issues. Youth services, especially within the justice systems, has taken a back seat to global economic recession, terrorism, wars in the Persian Gulf, and other political priorities. Yet jurisdictions have been creative in managing their delinquent populations. Many have restructured their organizations, and most have sought to use those evidence-based programs that are proven to be effective and cost-efficient – partly because researchers and program evaluators acquired better science to prove program efficacy, and partly because diminishing fiscal resources required program practitioners to justify what they were doing. We shall now turn our attention to the history and development of those programs and services that comprise effective juvenile justice treatment interventions.

The History and Development of Juvenile Justice Treatment Programs

There is an African proverb that goes something like this: "We stand on the shoulders of our ancestors." It teaches us that we are where we are because of those who have come before us, and the contributions that we make are only possible because of the contributions made by our ancestors. Juvenile justice programs and interventions, too, are best understood when the historical roots upon which they are based are studied and fully comprehended. In that way, we can apply past knowledge to current experience, and extrapolate information to apply and synthesize new concepts and ideas. Indeed, as we explore the historical development of these programs, we will see their evolution into a class of services that have been well researched, is outcome based, and is fast approaching a science of human behavior change.

Custodialism vs. habilitation

We define *habilitation* as teaching that was never previously learned; and *rehabilitation* as an attempt to reinstate earlier learned qualities now in disuse (Glick & Gibbs, 2011). Martinson (1974) published his article "What works" in which he reviewed diverse efforts to alter deviant aggressive behaviors in juvenile offenders. His conclusion, "With few and isolated exceptions, the rehabilitative efforts that have been reported so far have had no appreciable effect of recidivism" (p. 40), was disastrous for the child-caring, juvenile justice, and criminal justice fields. After this publication in the 1970s, those who endorsed a treatment intervention for aggressive children and youth were hard pressed to provide support for their position, and were subject to budget reductions. Those who believed that aggression should be punished and not habilitated began to gain support for their position to punish harshly, leading to the incarceration of youth in adult systems throughout the last two decades of the twentieth century.

Palmer (1975) refuted Martinson and showed that Martinson's singularly negative conclusion rested upon what Goldstein & Stein (1976) has called the "one true light assumption". This assumption holds that specific treatments are sufficiently powerful to override substantial individual differences and aid heterogeneous groups of patients. Indeed, aggression is a very complex behavior that requires a multimodal intervention if changes in behavior and attitude are to occur.

Martinson's error was that he assessed heterogeneous samples without evaluating homogenous subsamples. When the latter was done, it was found that many treatment interventions do work. The fact remains that corrections research, as with most intervention research efforts, does suffer from methodological faults (i.e., lack of appropriate controls, inadequate samples in both size and randomness of selection, poorly conceived and inconsistently implemented interventions, inadequate or inappropriate outcome measures, insufficient attention to issues of internal and external validity, inappropriate statistical analyses). Nonetheless, custodialism as the intervention of choice is a poor decision. It is not prescriptive, humane, or cost-effective, nor does it lead to long-term changes in aggressive and criminal behavior. However, research and practical experience have shown that effective treatment interventions for youth have specific characteristics, and the following sections discuss them in detail.

Prescriptive programming

Research to date has shown that effective intervention is differential intervention. Differential interventions ensure that an array of services and programs are available to those children and adolescents involved in the juvenile justice system. Once programming is available and sufficient, *prescriptive programming* ensures that different children and adolescents will be responsive to different change methods. The central question that must be addressed in prescriptive programming for the juvenile justice system is: "Which types of youth, meeting with which types of change agents, for which types of interventions, will yield optimal outcomes?" This approach is counter to the "one true light assumption" underlying most interventions for youth. As such, until practitioners are able to conceptualize the merit of these philosophical underpinnings, effective and efficient programs are at a disadvantage.

The psychological schools of behavioral change

Until the 1970s, practitioners relied on one of three schools of psychology to engender behavioral change. These included: the School of Psychodynamic, Psychoanalytic Theories (addressing issues in the unconscious mind), the School of Human/Client-Centered Theories (using a warm, accepting approach), and the School of Behaviorism/Behavior Modification (providing reinforcements for desirable behavior). While each of these three intervention philosophies differ from the others in major respects, they significantly agree that clients have, somewhere within themselves, as yet unexpressed, the effective, satisfying, non-aggressive, or pro-social behaviors whose expression was among the goals of these interventions. All three of these psychotherapies assume the sought-after goal that behaviors lie within the client's repertoire, whether it is released by interpretation, therapeutic climate, or contingent rewards.

The Evolution of Predicting Aggression, Violence, and Criminal Behaviors

It was not until the beginning of the 1970s with the design of the microchip, which placed personal computers on the desktops of statisticians and researchers, that meaningful progress towards understanding the science of aggression, violence, and criminal behavior was better mastered. There are a number of individuals, "movers and shakers", as we call them, giants in their field, who have advanced our art and technology to the point where we understand the theory better, but are also able to apply our knowledge prescriptively to create better programs, services, and interventions for at-risk youth. These individuals have taken programs that have been reported in the literature, literally thousands of them, and applied a statistical technique called *meta-analysis* to their sample of studies. Meta-analysis is a technique that allows the researcher to compare multiple variables simultaneously, and to discern which are most important to a particular problem experienced by at-risk youth. Works by these scholars have been instrumental in improving policy and program development with regard to how to treat at-risk and delinquent youths.

Donald Andrews (Carleton University Group)

Don Andrews (Andrews & Bonta, 1994, 1998) and his research group have analyzed thousands of independent studies to explore the relationships that exist between certain variables and criminal behavior. He and his colleagues identified a series of factors, called "criminogenic factors", that are highly related with antisocial behaviors. These include:

- companions – those individuals with whom the offender associates, usually aggressive, violent, and antisocial;
- interpersonal relationships – the ability to form relationships;
- personal attitudes, values, beliefs supportive of crime;
- behavioral history – offenders usually have a history of antisocial, aggressive, and violent behavior;
- psychopathology;
- lower social class family of origin;
- personal temperament, aptitude, early behavioral history;
- early family conditions;
- school-based risk factors – very often labeled special education, learning disabled, developmentally delayed;
- personal educational/vocational/ socio-economic achievement.

As a result of these factors, certain programs may be designed to mitigate against these issues. Programs that seem to impact those criminogenic needs identified by Andrews and Bonta (1998, 1999) as part of their goals and outcomes include those that:

- Change antisocial attitudes.
- Reduce antisocial peer associations.
- Promote familial monitoring and supervision.
- Promote identification/association with anti-criminal role models.
- Change antisocial feelings.
- Increase self-control, self-management, and problem-solving skills.
- Replace the skills of lying, stealing, and aggression with more prosocial alternatives.
- Reduce chemical dependencies.

Paul Gendreau (New Brunswick University Group)

Gendreau (1996) has spent his career studying programs that work with offenders. He and his colleagues have identified certain program characteristics that should be present in order to effect change in aggressive and violent offenders. Essentially these programs impact upon offenders' criminogenic needs. These include:

- social learning strategies
- behavioral techniques
- cognitive methods
- educational
- family-based (structural, systemic).

According to this research group, programs that do not work with offenders, and do not impact their antisocial, aggressive, or violent nature, include:

- non-directive, client-centered counseling
- unstructured psychodynamic therapy
- programs that involve intense group interactions without regard to personal responsibility
- variations on themes of official punishment.

Mark Lipsey

Lipsey (1999) studied programs that were reported to be effective in the literature for offenders who were involved in treatment interventions to help with their anti-social and aggressive personalities. He found as a result of his meta-analysis that the best treatments:

- reduced recidivism by about 30% on average;
- were structured and focused;
- were those that had been defined as "appropriate" (clinically relevant), as defined by professional program staff or clinicians.

He also found that milieu therapy provided weak or no effects for treatment of serious juvenile offenders.

Edward Latessa (University of Cincinnati Group)

Latessa (2006), a protégé of Gendreau, and his research group use the instrument Gendreau developed (the Correctional Program Assessment Inventory) to study programs throughout the US and Canada. These researchers have found that programs that effectively impact criminal behavior, and reduce aggression, violence, and propensity to re-offend, have the following characteristics:

- the chief executive of the program was involved in the program's development and implementation;
- program staff were trained, supervised and supported in their work;
- the offender was involved with his/her own program planning and implementation;
- the program was evaluated and modified, based upon the new knowledge acquired; and
- the program was developed with integrity, according to how it was designed and developed.

Having reviewed the history and development of the juvenile justice system and the programs and treatment interventions which have been used, we are now ready to explore the current state of the juvenile justice systems, the basic models used to deliver services, and examples of programs and services that are considered effective and cost-efficient.

Present

Supreme Court decisions impact juvenile justice policy

While harsh penalties for juveniles were popular throughout the latter part of the twentieth century (i.e., death penalties for capital offenses, and life without parole for other felonies such as second-degree murder), these were mitigated during the first decade of the twenty-first century. Indeed, 24 states prohibited the execution of juveniles in the 1980s and 1990s. Those actions allowed the Supreme Court to review court cases during the early 2000s, modifying the harsh Juvenile Offender Laws in a series of rulings that significantly altered juvenile justice policies. For example, the Supreme Court ruled in *Roper v. Simmons* (2005) that it is unconstitutional to impose capital punishment for crimes committed while under the age of 18. Citing the Eighth Amendment to the US Constitution protecting against cruel and unusual punishment, the Supreme Court in a 5-4 decision overturned its prior ruling upholding such sentences for youthful offenders above the age of 16.

In 2010, the Supreme Court broadened its restrictions concerning youthful offenders and its interpretation of the Eighth Amendment when it ruled in *Graham v. Florida* (2010) that youthful offenders cannot be sentenced to life imprisonment without parole for non-homicide cases. Thus, it overturned 37 state statutes, although juvenile offenders were not serving life sentences without parole in all of them. The Supreme Court completed its revision of the harsh juvenile offender policies in its landmark case, *Miller v. Alabama* (2012) when it held that: "Mandatory life without parole for a juvenile precludes consideration of his chronological age and its hallmark features; among them failure to appreciate risks and consequences, impetuosity, and, immaturity" and was a violation of the Eighth Amendment constituting cruel and unusual punishment. Justice Kagan added: "It prevents taking into account the family and home environment that surrounds him – and from which he cannot usually extricate himself – no matter how brutal or dysfunctional."

Treating mental health needs of juveniles

The Office of Juvenile Justice and Delinquency Prevention (OJJDP) reports incidences of juvenile crime and characteristics in its annual *Statistical Briefing Book*. Consistently, of the two million youth arrested each year, between 1,300,000 and 1,400,000 of those arrested are found to have some mental health dysfunction. These data have been consistent from 2000–2012, and states have taken steps to deal with the mental health of the adjudicated juvenile delinquent. During the first decade of the twenty-first century more than 27 states have passed mental health legislation to deal with issues posed by juveniles within their systems.

Minnesota, Nevada, Texas, Idaho, North Dakota, and Oregon were among the first states to address the need for assessment and screening of juveniles who enter the justice system to determine their mental health status and treatment needs. North Dakota and Oregon expanded upon the initiatives of earlier statutes and policies by adding the assessment for drug and alcohol abuse among arrested youth. The following is a summary of the more critical actions taken by states, setting precedence for others to enact legislation and/or promulgate policy (National Conference of State Legislatures, 2012):

- 2001: The State of Arizona passed a law that required residential treatment if the court found that the juvenile had psychological and mental health needs. It further required that the court periodically review the progress of the treatment given.
- 2003: The State of Connecticut authorized the court to order a juvenile charged with cruelty to animals to undergo counseling or participation in an animal cruelty prevention and education program.
- 2005: The State of California provided education on mental health and developmental disability issues affecting juveniles in delinquency proceedings to judicial officers, and other public officers and entities that may be involved in the arrest,

evaluation, prosecution, defense, disposition, and post-disposition or placement phases of delinquency proceedings.

- 2009: The State of Montana provided children with mental health needs with in-state service alternatives to out-of-state placement. The statute also established reporting requirements regarding high-risk children with multi-agency service needs who were suffering from mental health disorders.
- 2010: The State of Tennessee required the state to pay for court-ordered mental health evaluations of juveniles who have been charged with commission of an offense that would be a felony if committed by an adult.
- 2011: The State of Iowa provided that if, prior to the adjudicatory or dispositional hearing, a child is committed with a mental illness and ordered into a residential facility, institution or hospital for in-patient treatment, the delinquency proceeding be suspended until the juvenile court terminates the order or the child is released for purposes of receiving outpatient treatment.

The state of the juvenile justice system in 2013 continues to move towards the rehabilitation/habilitation end of the spectrum, away from harsh punishment and incarceration. States have now adopted policies that endorse cognitive–behavioral interventions that are evidence-based, outcome-based, cost-effective and efficient. Further, most of the states in the US and provinces in Canada have shortened the length of stay in detention and institutions, require risk assessments that place youth in the least restrictive alternatives to incarceration, and reduced overcrowding in residential placements.

Treating females in juvenile systems

There has been a significant increase in females in the juvenile justice system. Females represent 15% of the population in the justice system and as much as 35% in some jurisdictions. Lawmakers have noticed the increase of females, and at least in five states (Connecticut, Florida, Hawaii, Minnesota, and Oregon) statutes have been enacted requiring gender-specific programs for females targeted to their prevention, rehabilitation, and mental health needs. In 2011, the State of New Mexico legislature enacted a law requiring their Department of Children, Youth and Families to develop a plan that would specifically respond to the needs of its female clients.

States have also begun to ensure that youth have proper aftercare services once their incarceration is complete, or when they return to their communities. After years of research and advocacy that cited aftercare programs and services as reducing recidivism, and a sound investment to prevent further involvement with the criminal justice systems, states have enacted legislation throughout the first decade of the twenty-first century to ensure aftercare services are relevant and available. These include, for example:

- A 2004 Maryland law requiring "step-down aftercare" to provide individualized rehabilitation and services to youths returning to their communities.

- Oklahoma (in 2004) and Virginia (in 2005) implemented regulations for mental health, substance abuse, and other therapeutic treatment services for juveniles who return to the community.
- In 2010, Illinois legislation required the Illinois Juvenile Justice Commission to develop recommendations regarding due process protections for youth during parole and parole revocation proceedings. The bill also clarifies that the Prisoner Review Board has options other than re-incarceration for juvenile parolees who may violate a condition of parole.
- In 2006, Indiana established a Juvenile Reentry Court.
- In 2007, Mississippi required that community-based services be provided for all youth leaving detention facilities.
- In 2008, Colorado legislation required use of an objective risk assessment to identify aftercare treatment and parole services for juveniles.
- In 2010, Ohio passed legislation that allowed representatives of faith-based organizations to provide reentry services to juveniles. In the same year, Connecticut established a community-based pilot program to provide reentry services for youth.

All of these are examples of jurisdictions investing in aftercare services as prevention to further reduce incarceration, and as a cost-effective measure to reduce recidivism (National Conference of State Legislatures, 2012).

System models of service: The John D. and Catherine T. MacArthur Foundation

It is impossible to discuss models of service used by juvenile justice systems, no less identify the more innovative ones, without referencing and highlighting the John D. and Catherine T. MacArthur Foundation and the phenomenal work they have accomplished. The MacArthur Foundation provides millions of dollars worldwide to a variety of programs that advance the good of humanity. Within the juvenile justice systems, the centerpiece of the MacArthur Foundation's efforts is their $130 million *Models of Change* Initiative to create a juvenile justice system that is fairer, more equitable, and developmentally appropriate for youth who enter these systems. The Foundation entered the Juvenile Justice arena in 1996 when it established the MacArthur Research Network on Adolescent Development and Juvenile Justice. This was in direct response to the harsh policies that treated youth as adults when they committed crimes in society. As a result of that Research Network, the Models of Change framework was developed and the following core principles were identified as the keystone upon which grants would be provided to jurisdictions to make significant contributions to juvenile justice policy:

- Fundamental fairness – all system participants (that is, all those who have a right to expect justice, including youth, families, victims, and communities) deserve fair treatment.

- Juvenile–adult differences – a juvenile justice system must account for the fact that youth are fundamentally and developmentally different from adults.
- Individual differences – juvenile justice decision-makers must acknowledge and respond to young peoples' differences from one another in terms of development, culture, gender, needs and strengths.
- Youth potential – youth have strengths and are capable of positive growth.
- Safety – communities and individuals deserve to be and to feel safe.
- Responsibilities – youth must be encouraged to accept responsibility for their actions and the consequences of those actions. Communities have an obligation to safeguard the welfare of children and youth, to support them when in need, and to help them to grow into adults. The juvenile justice system should reflect that it is a vital part of society's collective exercise of its responsibility toward youth (see http://www.modelsforchange.net/publications/154)

There was a rigorous application process that resulted in four states being selected as the initial core for the Models of Change project, all of which took into account political and fiscal commitment to change, support for change both inside and outside the juvenile justice system, and the likelihood that reforms would influence change in other locations. The four states – Pennsylvania, Illinois, Louisiana, and Maryland – were all chosen because they represented different geographic locations of the country, with different cultures, political structures, organizational needs, and system challenges. Up to $10 million were awarded to these jurisdictions to accomplish the six core areas of the grant and provide significant changes to their systems.

Pennsylvania concentrated on strengthening their aftercare system, reducing disproportionate minority contact with the juvenile justice system, and improving mental health services for juveniles in the juvenile justice system. Illinois focused on right-sizing the juvenile court's jurisdiction, expanding community alternatives to incarceration of juveniles in the juvenile justice institutions, and reducing minority contact with the juvenile justice system.

Louisiana was determined to expand alternatives to incarceration and formal processing, increase evidence-based programs, and reduce disproportionate minority contact within its system. Washington directed its efforts at expanding alternatives to secure confinement and formal adjudications, reducing ethnic and racial disparities, and improving the ways in which the juvenile justice system identifies and responds to the mental health needs of its youth. All of these issues were identified by the Research Network as priorities for Models of Change. Others include aftercare and juvenile indigent defense.

Finally, The MacArthur Foundation expanded its core project to include action networks, involving 12 additional states to concentrate on the following:

1. Disproportionate Minority Contact Action Network: Maryland, Wisconsin, Kansas, North Carolina.
2. Juvenile Indigent Defense Action Network: California, Florida, Massachusetts, New Jersey.

3. Mental Health/Juvenile Justice Action Network: Connecticut, Colorado, Ohio, Texas.

For more details about the Models of Change project, visit the MacArthur Foundation website at http://www.macfound.org

Alternative institutional models

Over the last 50 years, there have been several attempts by juvenile justice systems and agencies to reduce the number of youth placed deep within their institutional systems. Many jurisdictions attempted to reduce their youth residential populations by diverting institutional placements for those youth who posed less risk to public safety. Screening instruments such as the Youth Level of Security Inventory (Andrews & Bonta, 2003) were used to assess youth risk for less intrusive institutional placements. Many of those youth who traditionally were incarcerated far from their home communities were often placed in community-based group residences. Some jurisdictions, such as New York, reduced their institutional capacities by building smaller residential centers. Rather than placing youth in the larger traditional training schools and secure treatment centers, during the late 1980s and early 1990s New York built 30-bed residential centers that architecturally resembled Pizza Hut restaurants. Unfortunately, these system changes required greater budgets for personnel, since the staff to youth ratio was also dramatically increased. The New York State model was committed to prevention services, alternatives to incarceration, and increased aftercare services, which served as a basis for other states to emulate. However, economic downturn and recession caused New York and other states with similar juvenile justice initiatives to abandon their innovative youth policies.

The Missouri Model of juvenile justice   As referenced earlier in this chapter, Latessa, Gendreau and others have provided juvenile and adult criminal justice systems with a blueprint to ensure program success. Missouri applied many of these principles as they reinvented their own system. The underpinning of the Missouri Model is a well-articulated philosophical statement that details their core beliefs in treating and habilitating youth who enter their system. The Missouri Division of Youth Services believed that youth placed in their system desired to do well and succeed; that with the right kinds of interventions by concerned adults, all of their clients will make lasting behavioral changes and succeed; and that the mission of their department must be to provide appropriate programs and services, consistent with public safety, so that young people make the necessary changes to lead successful adult lives. Missouri also benefited from the experiences and program development of sister jurisdictions. Borrowing heavily from the programs and services from such states as New York, Florida, Connecticut and others, Missouri embellished upon these, combining them with their philosophical and legislative mandates to produce their program model.

The success of the Missouri Model and its replication across the US is based, in part, upon its youth development philosophical and theoretical principles. During a time when youth were treated as adults, and incarcerated in adult prisons, Missouri opted to view their delinquents as youth who were capable of positive change and who could be rehabilitated to return to their communities as constructive citizens. Beyond that, the Missouri DYS imposed principles for staff to embrace a positive, humane approach to deal with antisocial youth behaviors, requiring staff to amend their punitive, negative tactics for proven, outcome-based cognitive interventions. The Missouri Model is yet another example of how the justice system pendulum swings on a continuum from punishment to habilitation.

Effective and cost-efficient programs and services

Cognitive–behavioral programs have been used in the juvenile justice system for more than five decades. No longer are programs for youth at risk chosen and implemented on a trial and error, see-if-it-works basis; nor are programs used because they are the latest fad found while attending a professional conference. Rather, juvenile justice programs have evolved into a science, and those chosen to be implemented in most cases are well researched, outcome-based, cost-effective and efficient. While it is always a risk to identify and showcase programs as models to be replicated, we have opted to describe several programs at this juncture because they have been evaluated, found to be effective interventions, are outcome-based with proven results, and are cost-effective.

Cognitive self change: Dr John D. Bush (1977)   Cognitive self change is a cognitive–behavioral intervention that is based upon the principles of cognitive restructuring: those programs that attempt to change individuals' patterns of thinking. The intervention is designed to be neutral and objective when dealing with clients as they explore their thoughts, feelings, beliefs and attitudes. According to Bush (personal communication), cognitive self change is now touted as a skill that has four steps:

1. Learn to observe objectively one's own thoughts, feelings, attitudes, and beliefs.
2. Learn to recognize the thinking (thoughts, feelings, attitudes, and beliefs) that leads one to do antisocial behaviors.
3. Find new thinking that does not lead one to do antisocial behavior, and that helps an individual to feel good about themselves when they use new thinking.
4. Practice the new learning until one is proficient at it.

The group facilitator meets with clients two to three times a week and conducts group sessions to deal with issues that clients had during the previous week. Using a formal, structured technique, the Thinking Report, clients learn how to perform these four steps of cognitive self change, keeping it simple and non-judgmental.

Rites of Passage: G. Rosaline Preudhomme and Leonard G. Dunston (1989, 1996)   Rites of Passage (1989) is a program designed primarily for African-American youth. While rites of passage processes exist in most cultures, the rituals and ceremonies are specific to a particular culture. For this particular program, the Rites of Passage curriculum is targeted to develop both cultural and maturational growth in young African-Americans. It is anchored in the Seven Principles of the Nguzo Saba, which also serves as the foundation of the Kwanzaa holiday celebrated from December 26 through January 1. The Nguzo Saba principles are:

1. *Umoja*, which means unity; to strive for and maintain unity in the family, community, nation, and race.
2. *Kujichagulia*, which means self-determination; and obligates us to define ourselves, name ourselves, create for ourselves, and speak for ourselves.
3. *Ujima*, which means collective work and responsibility that is fundamental to maintaining the community, sharing each other's problems, and together solving issues.
4. *Nia*, which means purpose, giving our lives, our work, and our lives together meaning.
5. *Ujamaa*, which means cooperative economics, and is the basis to build businesses within the community and support them.
6. *Kuumba*, which means creativity, requiring every individual to strive to leave their community more beautiful and beneficial than we found it.
7. *Imani*, which means faith, and requires each of us to believe with all our heart in our people and the righteousness and victory of the struggle we face.

The program provides a series of clusters or lessons that are organized around the Seven Principles of the Nguzo Saba. Each cluster is designed to explore historical, social, cultural, and personal issues relevant to the individual and the principle being explored. There are five components within the curriculum: instruction, field trips, and artistic expression are all included in each of the lessons. The final two components, mentoring and community service, are implemented at the convenience of the mentor and the initiate (youth client) who completes the program.

The program is both labor- and time-intensive. It requires a great deal of coordination to ensure knowledge, relationships, content, and process are executed well. It requires staff and community volunteers to act as elders to the initiates and guide them through much of their experiences and exploration. It requires cooperation from family members and significant caregivers, including school personnel and friends, to guarantee successful completion of the program. However, the process leads to a celebration of mature growth, community development, and self-pride.

Problem-solving: Dr Juliana Taymans (1991, 1998)   Problem-solving is a cognitive–behavioral intervention providing youth with a potential mechanism to deal with conflict and stress. The curriculum teaches six skills of problem-solving so that a young person may better manage their emotional negative reactions to situations, and have a better chance to take pro-social thoughtful decisions rather than impulsive actions that lead to greater problems. Indeed, if done correctly, the youth often change their perception and attitudes toward stressful, negative situations from that of overwhelming and burdensome to manageable.

The six skills of problem-solving include:

1. Stop and think (identify that you are in a problem situation).
2. State the problem (what is happening that is bothering me?).
3. Set a goal and gather information (what information can help me solve this problem, and what do I want?).
4. Think of choices and consequences (what is my best choice?).
5. Make a plan (decide what to do, how to do it, with whom and when).
6. Do and evaluate (put the plan into action and identify whether the plan worked).

The program is 25 lessons and may be delivered two or more times per week. Co-facilitators are strongly advised to conduct group sessions with 8–10 youth in a class that can last 60 to 90 minutes.

Aggression Replacement Training®: Dr Barry Glick Aggression Replacement Training® (ART®) is a multi-modal cognitive–behavioral intervention for aggressive and violent adolescents. Developed by Goldstein and Glick (1987), the third edition of the book (Glick and Gibbs, 2011) builds on more than four decades of practical implementation, research and program evaluation to refine the program without compromising the original theoretical and philosophical foundations upon which it was designed.

ART® comprises three components; each in its own right is a well-established, well-evaluated intervention. The three components include:

- Social skills training (the behavioral component) – teaching pro-social skills using a four-step procedure: modeling, role-playing, performance feedback, and transfer training.
- Anger control training (the affective component) – teaching youth to manage their angry impulses by learning a set of concepts that include: triggers, cues, anger reducers, reminders, thinking ahead (long-term consequences), using a learned social skill to break the angry behavior cycle, and self-evaluation.
- Moral reasoning (the cognitive component) – using Kohlberg's Theory and process of Moral Development, youth enter into a group discussion of a moral problem situation for which there is no right or wrong answer. Through discussion, youth are provided to take perspectives other than their own, and through directed debate with others who are no more than one moral stage of development higher than they, learn to view their world in a more fair and equitable manner.

Youth attend one class each week in each of the three components for ten weeks. It is important that the youth attend all three classes each week in each of the components, for each component is carefully matched in both process and content such that each week builds on the previous. Groups of between 8 and 10 youth are involved with the ART® program for the ten weeks, with two group facilitators who manage the group.

Girls...Moving On: Dr Marilyn Van Dieten (1999)   There is a paucity of cognitive behavior interventions and programs that are gender-specific for girls. Girls... Moving On is one that has been especially designed and targeted for females in the juvenile justice system. Based upon research, developmental theory and female-specific needs, Girls...Moving on is a prescriptive program to meet the needs of females in the justice system.

Girls...Moving On comprises seven distinct and independent modules. The first and last modules are delivered individually, while modules 2–6 are administered to groups of between 8 and 10 youth. Each module consists of five sessions with approximately two hours of program content. The design of the program is organized such that after the first session, girls can enter the groups at the beginning of whatever module is being offered. The program is deliberately flexible so the facilitator may choose any module in any order (except the first and last).

There are 25 sessions that can be delivered up to five sessions per week (residential settings). There is an 18-session version for community youth. The modules are organized around a specific theme that can be offered in any order once the individual modules are completed. These include:

- Module 1: Looking Forward
- Module 2: Listening and Being Heard
- Module 3: Building Healthy Relationships
- Module 4: Expressing Emotions
- Module 5: Making Connections
- Module 6: Making Healthy Choices
- Module 7: Transitions

There is a facilitator's guide for each module with specific directions for each session, both content and process. The program is extensively used throughout Canada and the US. The Illinois Office of Court Administration was the first to adopt the program in the Greater Chicago area in 2006.

Future

Organizational and administrative issues

Managers and administrators of juvenile justice systems are charged with the responsibility to provide programs and services for youth placed in their custody that meet adolescent developmental needs, and at the same time provide opportunities to cognitively change delinquent and criminal thinking. The burden to take a young person who has committed a criminal act and return that individual to their community as a constructive, contributing member of society is daunting. Yet that is the expectation of the taxpayers, citizens and other stakeholders. There are several core areas that administrators must manage in order to fulfill their legal, ethical, and moral obligations to those who have placed young offenders in their custody. These include:

- Budget and finance – the logistics of preparing, implementing and managing the budget process, including allocation and appropriation of funds.
- Personnel – the recruitment, training, supervision and retention of a workforce to deliver programs and services to offenders competently, effectively, and efficiently.
- Program development – this is perhaps one of the most critical and challenging issues facing juvenile justice administrators. Programs have always been a critical part of well-organized institutions and juvenile justice systems. Over the past 40 years, programs have evolved into an array of sophisticated cognitive–behavioral interventions.
- Staff development – one of the most important tasks a juvenile justice administrator must manage, for it plays a vital role in the quality of services that are provided to youth at risk.
- Research, program development and planning – these activities have not been a high priority for juvenile systems until recently. Researchers such as Latessa (2006) have conducted extensive research on what works in juvenile justice systems; and Van Voorhis (2006) identified program evaluation paradigms to assess program efficacy and efficiencies.
- Quality assurance – this was introduced by Shewhart (1939) as he developed quality control strategies for manufacturing, although the earliest of these concepts were based upon the scientific method developed by Francis Bacon (1620). The scientific method can be written as hypothesis–experiment–evaluation, or Plan, Do, and Check – "evaluate". Shewhart applied these methods in his work. However, quality assurance systems were popularized when Deming (1986) formalized the lectures he gave throughout Japan in the 1950s.

Advocacy

As detailed earlier in this chapter, the rights of children and youth placed in child-care institutions were rarely protected prior the 1940s. Even less concern was given to those youth adjudicated as delinquent and removed from their communities. Many advocacy groups were organized to monitor the inhumane treatment of youth placed in juvenile institutions. These advocacy groups made recommendations for change, and lobbied governments to make changes in statutes and regulations. These early system-wide advocacy efforts had a great impact on jurisdictions and ultimately the institutions operated by them. While many youth benefited from these efforts, a great deal more still suffered from inept administrators, managers, supervisors and direct care staff. These organizations were often left to individual litigation on behalf of youth whose civil liberties were violated. Ultimately it was the court system that imposed changes on those juvenile systems resistant to fair and accessible treatment for its incarcerated youth.

It takes a proactive, visionary, well-organized executive to ensure that programs and services are delivered to at-risk youth in juvenile systems with integrity, effectively, and competently. Advocacy must be accomplished through third-party involvement. Most efforts are reactions to poor, abusive conditions within institutions, including but not limited to: overcrowding, lack of medical and mental health services, poor sanitation, physical and/or sexual abuse of clients, inadequate educational services, nonexistent counseling and psychotherapy, and little or no spiritual programs. It is critical that executives and administrators create opportunities to obtain objective information about their institutional operations. Toward that end, advocacy should be encouraged and fostered through deliberate management efforts. I recommend the following:

- create a local advisory community group to participate in monthly meetings at the institution or agency;
- allow visitors to inspect the physical plant at designated times;
- empower the advisory committee to consider unannounced inspections of programs and services;
- invite family court judges and community stakeholders to visit the institution;
- provide contact numbers to family members so they remain involved with their youth's case plan;
- direct staff to allow youth to contact supervisors and managers with issues and/or complaints;
- create message centers and drop-boxes for youth to submit comments and suggestions directly to the chief executive officer;
- ensure that all institutional executives and managers inspect and tour the facility daily, at least several times throughout the day.

Advocacy, if managed well, provides juvenile justice administrators the information and support to create organizational and system change. At the same time it can protect the agency from political, fiscal, and adversarial attacks, especially when new programs or additional resources are needed.

Practitioner skill sets needed to deliver programs and services

Every program is designed and developed by its author with clear and well-defined theoretical and philosophical foundations. Based on these, program principles are identified that dictate those strategies and procedures the program will use to meet the program's treatment goals and objectives. Another factor to consider is the policies and directives the agency or system has promulgated that direct program implementation. These often include such areas as staff competencies and minimum qualifications, right of treatment, protection of human rights of juveniles, standards for program delivery, and safety and security. A third factor to consider is the cost of delivery, which usually requires additional money and personnel resources. The program costs, however, must be compared to the cost-benefit that results from successful implementation.

These several factors, filtered by the needs of the youth, which are pre-eminent, serve to provide policy-makers, agency executives, program directors, and supervisors the pathway to select competent, skilled staff to implement programs. Beyond that, the juvenile justice field has the benefit of research and the experiences of program developers to identify those skill sets and qualities that staff should have and maintain. These include, but are not limited to the following. Staff should:

- be competently trained in the program they are expected to deliver
- be knowledgeable in group processes and be able to direct groups
- be able to manage youth behaviors and ensure a safe and secure group environment
- be able to stand in front of a group of youth comfortably and competently
- be flexible and able to change directions to meet youth needs
- like youth and not be intimidated by them
- be able to redirect group members from antisocial to prosocial actions
- enjoy teaching and sharing knowledge
- put ego aside to get the group tasks completed
- be able to deliver programs with fidelity and integrity as the program was designed and developed
- seek support and direction to ensure proper group and program procedures are followed.

Some Final Thoughts

The purpose of this chapter was to provide the reader with a comprehensive overview of the juvenile justice system, specific to the institutionalization and treatment of the youth placed within its custody. Toward that end we provided the history and development of the juvenile justice system, and the programs, services, and treatment interventions that it uses. We also provided examples and descriptions of model juvenile justice systems and model programs, specifically cognitive–behavioral interventions that have been shown to be cost-effective and efficient.

References

Andrews, D., &. Bonta, J. (1994). *The Psychology of Criminal Conduct*. Cincinnati, OH: Anderson.

Andrews, D., &. Bonta, J.(1998). *The Psychology of Criminal Conduct* (2nd ed.). Cincinnati, OH: Anderson.

Andrews, D., &. Bonta, J. (1999). *The Psychology of Criminal Conduct* (Revised ed.). Cincinnati, OH: Anderson.

Andrews, D., &. Bonta, J. (2003). *The Psychology of Criminal Conduct* (3rd ed.). Cincinnati, OH: Anderson.

Bacon, F. (1620). *Novum Organum.* Middlesex, England.

Bush, J.D. (1977). *Cognitive Self Change.* Longmont, CO: National Institute of Corrections.

Deming, W. (1986). *Out of Crises.* Cambridge, MA: MIT Press.

Federal Bureau of Investigation. (2001–2012). *Uniform Crime Statistics Report.* Washington, DC: US Justice Department.

Gendreau, P. (1996). Offender rehabilitation: What we know and what needs to be done. *Criminal Justice and Behavior, 23,* 144–161.

Glick, B., & Gibbs, J. (2011). *Aggression Replacement Training: A Comprehensive Intervention for Aggressive Adolescents* (3rd ed., Revised and Expanded). Champaign, IL: Research Press.

Goldstein, A., &. Glick, B. (1987). *Aggression Replacement Training: A Comprehensive Intervention for Aggressive Adolescents.* Champaign, IL: Research Press.

Goldstein, A., & Stein, N. (1976). *Prescriptive Psychotherapies.* New York: Pergamon Press.

Graham v. Florida. (2010). 560 U.S.

Latessa, E.J. (2006). Effectiveness of cognitive behavioral interventions for youthful offenders: Review of the research. In B. Glick (Ed.), *Cognitive Behavioral Interventions for At Risk Youth.* Kingston, NJ: Civic Research Institute .

Lipsey, M. (1999). Can intervention rehabilitate serious delinquents? *Annals of the American Academy of Political and Social Sciences, 564,* 142–166.

Martinson, R. (1974). What works? Questions and answers about prison reform. *The Public Interest, 35,* 22–54.

Miller v. Alabama. (2012). 567 U.S.

National Conference of State Legislatures. (2012). *Trends in Juvenile Justice State Legislation 2001–2011.* Washington, DC: National Conference of State Legislatures.

Palmer, T. (1975). Martinson revisited. *Journal of Research in Crime and Delinquency, 12,* 131–152.

Preudhomme, G.R., & Dunston, L. (1989). *Rites of Passage: A Program Model for the New York State Division for Youth.* New York: Division for Youth, Budget Proposal.

Preudhomme, G.R., & Dunston, L. (1996). *Ritual for the Transformation: A Rites of Passage Program Manual.* Charlotte, NC: Great Copies Plus.

Roper v. Simmons. (2005). 543 U.S. 551.

Shewhart, W. (1939). *Statistical Method from the View Point of Quality Control.* New York: Courier Dover Publications.

Van Dieten, M. (1999). *Moving On. A program for criminal justice involved women.* Unpublished manuscript.

Van Voorhis, P. (2006). Comprehensive evaluation of cognitive behavioral programs in corrections – Guidelines and approaches. In B. Glick (Ed.), *Cognitive Behavioral Interventions for At-Risk Youth* (pp. 10–16). Kingston, NJ: Civic Research Institute.

Part V

Special Issues in Juvenile Delinquency

30

Gang Trends, Trajectories, and Solutions

James C. Howell

Introduction: Defining Gangs

It is a curious thing that teenagers, juvenile services staff, and law enforcement are adept in recognizing gangs, yet criminologists are rarely in agreement on criteria for defining them. For one thing, developing a gang definition that captures the younger gangs, yet excludes law-violating youth groups and adult criminal organizations that are not considered youth gangs is challenging. To complicate matters, multiple terms are used interchangeably in describing gangs – *youth gang, street gang, criminal street gang,* and *drug gang* – and whether or not each of these terms refers to a common problem in practical applications is not always clear. Moreover, there is considerable variation in youth gangs. "No two gangs are alike, and they change constantly in membership, structure, and behavior; new gangs are formed and old ones fade away or merge with others" (Short & Hughes, 2009, p. 406). Defining gangs is also confounded by numerous misunderstandings about them, largely because they are at once shrouded in myths (some of which they create themselves in folklore), media exaggerations, popular misconceptions, and international intrigue often associated with them (Howell & Griffiths, 2015).

Youth gang is the preferred term for drawing attention to the younger gangs, from the latter years of childhood through late adolescence or young adulthood (18–24 years of age). Moore (1998) suggests that three characteristics distinguish the American youth street gang from other youth groups: self-definition, street socialization, and the potential to become quasi-institutionalized in a specific local community. *Self-definition* implies not only that group members define themselves as a gang, but that the group has a social structure and group-determined norms

The Handbook of Juvenile Delinquency and Juvenile Justice, First Edition. Edited by Marvin D. Krohn and Jodi Lane.

that are not controlled by adults in any way. *Street socialization* means that unsupervised young people are socialized by each other (and by older peers in some cases) far more effectively than by conventional socializing agents such as families and schools. In regard to *quasi-institutionalization,* gangs develop the capacity for self-maintenance, meaning that they recruit continuously, with places in the gang for younger members, and that they extend respect and solidarity toward older members.

The following is a practical definition that incorporates research-supported criteria for classifying a group as a youth gang (Bjerregaard, 2002; Howell, 2013; Howell & Griffiths, 2015):

- Five or more members.
- Members share an identity, often linked to a name and other symbols.
- Members view themselves as a gang and are recognized by others as a gang.
- The group has some permanence and a degree of organization.
- The group is involved in an elevated level of delinquent or criminal activity.

Many legal definitions of a gang specify only three or more members. A higher standard of five members is consistent with extensive research on delinquent groups which finds that typical sizes of these groups range from two to four members, and that the number of active participants tends to diminish in late childhood and early adolescence to triads and dyads in middle and late adolescence. In a multi-city sample of surveyed middle-school students, just 13% of respondents claiming to be active gang members said their gang had five or fewer members (Esbensen, Brick, Melde, Tusinski, & Taylor, 2008). Hence a standard of five members should winnow out most very small friendship groups or cliques that typically are involved only in general delinquency.

The requirement of a name helps distinguish actual gangs from the many other law-violating youth groups. Bjerregaard (2002) insists that this is the most potent criterion for defining gangs. Her position is buttressed by nationwide US student survey data showing that having a name is a main indicator of gang presence – one that 8 out of 10 US students use – along with spending time with other members of the gang (Howell & Lynch, 2000).

Viewing their group as a gang and being recognized by others as such provides individualized distinction to gang participation; that is, individual status in the gang that is set apart from everyday social cliques, in and out of which adolescents constantly drift. Hence, initiation into a gang carries with it personal commitment to the gang and opposition to conventional rules for behavior. If gang recognition is not incorporated in the definition, over-classification of youth as gang members is likely (Medina, Aldridge, Shute, & Ross, 2013).

There is little research basis for a specified period of gang existence to meet the "permanence" criterion. In the aforementioned multi-city sample of surveyed middle-school students, 25% of the youth said the gang to which they belonged had been in existence for 1 year or less, with all others specifying a longer period

(Esbensen *et al.*, 2008). Thus 6 to 9 months is a reasonable minimum standard for gang permanence. Several studies have pinpointed indicators of gang organization that suggest gang permanence, including rules, punishment for breaking the rules, symbols of membership, responsibilities to the gang, meetings, and leadership roles (Decker, Katz, & Webb, 2008).

Involvement in delinquent or criminal activity is a criterion found in most gang definitions. This indicator is supported by abundant research showing that crime rates are higher among gang members than other delinquent youth (Krohn & Thornberry, 2008; Thornberry, Krohn, Lizotte, Smith, & Tobin, 2003). Specifying involvement at an elevated level thus helps to distinguish youth gangs from ordinary delinquent groups.

For males and females, the gang joining process is similar, the increased level of involvement in serious crimes while gang-involved is compatible, and the detrimental short- and long-term effects of gang joining are quite similar for both genders (Petersen & Howell, 2013; Peterson, 2012). Thus the trends reported herein apply to females and males alike. However, the two genders display some distinctive risk factors and specific treatment needs that should be addressed within the prevention and treatment programs discussed later in this chapter (Petersen and Howell, 2013; Chesney-Lind, 2013).

National Trends in Reported Gang Presence, Participation, and Homicide

The most important feature of gang crime trends is that the key indicators recently have not followed the same pattern as overall crime reports in the US. Nationally, violent crime and property crime arrest rates have declined dramatically over the past decade (Federal Bureau of Investigation, 2013). Firearm homicides in 2011 were down by 39% from a high in 1993 (Planty & Truman, 2013). During the same period, the rate of violent crime victimization declined by 72% (Truman & Planty, 2012). Several indicators of youth gangs are examined here – the prevalence of gangs, the prevalence of individuals' gang involvement, the number of reported gangs, and the level of gang homicide – each of which suggests anything but a declining trend.

Gang problem prevalence trend: 1996–2011

Gang activity has not subsided in concert with the overall drop in violent and property crime in the US over the past decade. Youth gang problems in the US grew dramatically between the 1970s and the 1990s, with the prevalence of gangs reaching unprecedented levels in the mid-1990s (Miller, 2001). The size of gang problem localities also changed, with gang problems spreading to cities, towns, villages, and counties smaller in size than at any time in the past, as seen in the National Youth

Gang Survey (NYGS). By the mid-1990s, all 50 states and the District of Columbia, and 40% of local law enforcement agencies nationwide, reported youth gang problems in the NYGS (Egley & Howell, 2013; see Figure 30.1). Thereafter, a sharp decline was seen in the percentage of agencies reporting youth gang problems, which continued until 2001 (Egley & Howell, 2013). From that low point, the prevalence of gang activity nationwide increased steadily until 2007, though not quite to the mid-1990s peak, and then leveled off. In 2011, gangs were active in nearly a third (32%) of the responding jurisdictions in the NYGS. This estimate has remained fairly stable since 2005.

Over the past decade, annual estimates of the number of gang members reported by law enforcement agencies averaged around 750,000 nationally, with little change from year to year (Egley & Howell, 2013). However, estimates of the proportion of youth who join a gang are larger in surveys of young persons. In a national youth survey, nearly 1 in 12 youth said they belonged to a gang at some point during their teenage years (Snyder & Sickmund, 2006). In contrast with the downward trend in overall crime in the US, the estimated number of gangs increased 36% between 2002 and 2011 (Egley & Howell, 2013, p. 2).

Gang activity is now very prevalent in public schools and surrounding communities. In 2012, 16% of a national sample of students reported that gangs were present in their schools (Robers, Kemp, Truman, & Snyder, 2013). More broadly, 45% of high-school students and 35% of middle-school students say that there are gangs or students who consider themselves to be part of a gang in their schools (National

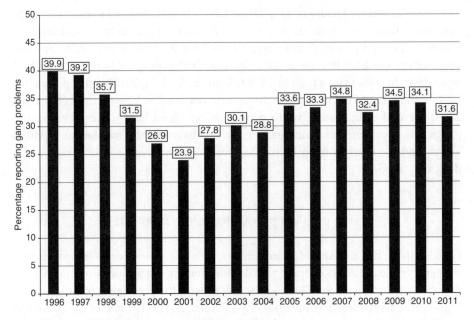

Figure 30.1 Percentage of law enforcement agencies reporting youth gang problems, 1996–2011. Data from Egley & Howell (2013)

Center on Addiction and Substance Abuse, 2010). Students are very adept in recognizing gangs. Gang presence at schools is correlated with criminal activity, particularly in metropolitan areas with populations between 100,000 and 1 million (Howell & Lynch, 2000).

Gang Trajectories: Individuals, Gangs, and Cities

Developmental criminology has introduced a life-course perspective in its focus on criminal careers that transcend adolescence and continue into adulthood. Pathways that extend over multiple life-course stages are called "trajectories", and trajectory modeling has been widely used in the classification of individuals according to their pattern of offending over time. A decade ago, researchers began to apply this group-based trajectory method to model the criminal histories of geographic areas, like street segments and census tracts, to capture trajectories across time and space (Griffiths & Chavez, 2004; Weisburd, Bushway, Lum, & Yang, 2004). We apply the life-course perspective loosely here as a framework for reviewing individuals' gang careers, gang formation and growth, and cities' gang problem histories.

Individual trajectories

The prevalence of juvenile delinquency increases in late childhood, peaks in middle to late adolescence, and then precipitously decreases during the transition from middle adolescence to early adulthood. This is known as the age–crime curve. Gang participation follows a similar age-linked trajectory. Joining is a gradual process. Children who are involved in delinquency, violence, and drug use at an early age are at higher risk for gang membership than other youngsters (Craig, Vitaro, Gagnon, & Tremblay, 2002; Hill, Howell, Hawkins, & Battin-Pearson, 1999; Lahey, Gordon, Loeber, Stouthamer-Loeber, & Farrington, 1999). More than a third of the child delinquents in Montreal and Rochester samples became involved in crimes of a more serious and violent nature during adolescence, including gang fights (Krohn, Thornberry, Rivera, & Le Blanc, 2001). A youth typically begins hanging out with gang members at age 11 or 12, and joins the gang between ages 12 and 15 (Craig *et al.*, 2002; Esbensen & Huizinga, 1993; Huff, 1996, 1998). This process normally takes six months to a year or two from the time of initial association. Gang association, however, does not presume gang joining. Two studies show that many youth who reported never having been in a gang said they had engaged in certain behaviors that suggested gang involvement: they had flashed gang signs, worn gang colors on purpose, hung out with gang members, consumed alcohol or drugs with gang members, or had gang members as friends (Curry, Decker, & Egley, 2002: Eitle, Gunkel, & Gundy, 2004).

The proportion of youth who are members of a gang at a particular point in time can vary from 3% upward in rural areas and in very large cities (Esbensen, Peterson,

Taylor, & Freng, 2010). Measured across the teenage years, up to 30% of youth may join a gang in high crime areas of very large cities (Thornberry, 1998). But gang involvement is a relatively short-term experience for most youth. Findings from longitudinal studies in Denver, Pittsburgh, Rochester, Seattle, and a multisite sample (GREAT) indicate that the trajectories of gang membership are relatively brief (Pyrooz, Sweeten, & Piquero, 2013). The majority of gang youth remained involved with gangs for only one year or less (48–69%) in the four representative samples. The length of active involvement decreased sharply from two (17–48%), to three (6–27%), or four or more (3–5%) years of gang membership. Nevertheless, up to 1 in 4 (27%) gang members remain active for at least three years in these samples, and multiyear and even intergenerational gang membership is far more common in cities with longstanding gang problems.

There is abundant evidence from a number of longitudinal studies that youth gangs facilitate or elicit sharply increased involvement in delinquency, violence, and drugs (Krohn & Thornberry, 2008). In comparison with non-members, both short-term and stable gang members (multiyear participation) have significantly higher rates of self-reported crime, carrying a weapon, and being arrested. In particular, delinquency associated with gang membership is concentrated in two offense combinations: (1) serious violence and drug-selling; and (2) serious violence, drug-selling, and serious theft (Gordon *et al.*, 2014). At somewhat older ages, drug-dealing and illegal peer gun ownership replace gang membership as the primary determinants of illegal gun-carrying (Lizotte, Krohn, Howell, Tobin, & Howard, 2000). In this circumstance, gang membership can catapult youth to lethal violence. Indeed, both homicide offenders and homicide victims often engage in drug dealing, and street conflicts coupled with gang membership further fuels victimization and retaliation (Loeber *et al.*, 2012).

Most gang members desist from gang fighting by their early 20s, but some adolescents desist by age 17, while others take longer (Bushway, Krohn, Lizotte, Phillips, & Schmidt, 2013). Stability in gang membership has a greater impact on the life course than short-term gang membership. Longer-term gang members are considered to be "embedded" in the gang. This concept refers to frequency of contact with the gang, position in the gang, importance of the gang to the individual, proportion of friends in the gang, and frequency of gang-involved assaults (Pyrooz *et al.*, 2013). Studies are accumulating showing that desistance is delayed among embedded members (Pyrooz *et al.*, 2013; Sweeten, Pyrooz, & Piquero, 2013). More embedded offenders are apt to remain active for a longer period of time. Indeed, in a sample of court-adjudicated youth (ages 14 to 17), gang members with low levels of embeddedness left the gang quickly, crossing a 50% percent threshold in six months after the baseline interview, whereas gang members with high levels of embeddedness did not show similar reductions for a year or more (Pyrooz *et al.*, 2013).

Despite the typically short-lived period of gang membership, participation normally occurs during a stage in the development of youth that is critical in determining the course of their lives – at a time when building-blocks for successful transitions to adulthood are laid. "Specifically, gang members are more likely to fail to graduate from high school, leave the parental home before finishing high school, father a child during their teenage years, and/or engage in early cohabitation" (Krohn, Ward, Thornberry, Lizotte, & Chu, 2011, p. 1016). These precocious transitions lead to economic hardship and family problems in early adulthood, often followed by arrests in adulthood and continued involvement in street crimes. In sum, the long-term research on gang-involved youth reveals that street gangs are a particularly "pernicious group" over the life-course, with "long-lasting effects not only on continuation of criminal behaviors but also, perhaps more importantly, on the opportunities for adult success in major conventional social roles as well" (p. 1015). In addition, research demonstrates a strong relationship between gang membership and violent victimization (Melde, Taylor, & Esbensen, 2009).

The consequences of gang membership also cascade into the next generation, as seen in the children of the Seattle sample of gang members that first was studied as adolescents in the 1990s (Hill *et al.*, 1999). Parental adolescent gang membership was significantly related to later development in their children. When compared to a matched sample of non-gang peers, those who joined a gang in adolescence reported poorer outcomes in multiple areas of adult functioning, including higher rates of self-reported crime, receipt of illegal income, incarceration, drug abuse or dependence, poor general health, welfare receipt, and lower rates of high school graduation (Gilman, Hill, and Hawkins, 2014). Negative consequences of joining a gang cascade not only into the adult life of the individual but into the next generation as well, laying a foundation to repeat the cycle. In the original study, parental adolescent gang membership was significantly related to later developmental problems of subjects' children, from ages 1 to 15 (Hill, Gilman, & Hawkins, 2011). Effects on offspring were prominent in personal–social delays (at 1 to 5 years of age), child misbehavior and low bonding (at 2 to 8 years), and externalizing (conduct and social problems) and internalizing (affective, anxiety) behaviors (at 6–15 years).

Gang trajectories

Youth gangs, too, have trajectories over time, though far less is known about gang histories than individual trajectories. Owing largely to the fact that most gang research has focused on members instead of the gangs themselves, few documented histories of modern-day gangs are available. But some research has documented the formation of embryonic gangs and processes that account for their growth and establishment. Interestingly, most new youth gangs do not survive. Nationwide, Howell and Egley (2005) found only 4% to 10% of gangs survive in small cities, towns, and rural areas. Even those gangs that do survive are constantly changing – consolidating, reorganizing, and splintering (Monti, 1993; Moore, 1991).

Virtually all youth gangs are home-grown. Gangs form where youth congregate, in schools and in neighborhoods. One example illustrates a typical process. A French study (Debarbieux & Baya, 2008) suggests that many embryo gangs may emerge from "difficult schools" that contain a small group of highly rebellious pupils. This group of students (4–5% of the student population) was responsible for most of the disorder and violence in 16 schools that were studied. In the most difficult schools, as many as 11% of all students were members, far more than proportions seen in schools with a good social climate and student support. Other research shows that being on the margins of the school norms slowly leads them to identify themselves as a group. Students who were experiencing problems at home and at school tended to associate with one another away from school. Fleisher (1998, p.119) added that "rejected boys and girls adopt the equivalent of distinctive school clothing and colors, the insignia of membership. Members learn group cheers, rhymes, and folklore, wear group clothing, engage in rites of passage and intensification, uphold communal values (like school children's loyalty to their school) and they give themselves a name." The final stage of gang formation is often group involvement in delinquency. Altogether, 20 cliques of the *Hoya Marvilla* Chicano gang were formed over a half-century period through systematic expansion methods (Moore, 1991). Many other Chicano gangs expanded in the same manner in Los Angeles and other cities, as have gangs comprised of all other race and ethnicities. In the present era, because of the integration of gang culture in the youth subculture, member recruitment occurs in a wide variety of settings and via electronic communications. Ongoing conflicts also serve to perpetuate gangs, to be sure, and the structure and capacity of a youth gang may also play a large role in the duration of association by its members (Melde, Diem, & Drake, 2012).

City gang problem trajectories

The three commonly-used gang magnitude indicators – number of gangs, gang members, and gang-related homicides – reveal that most gang activity is located in very large population centers. More than half (56%) of all gangs, 75% of gang members, and nearly 9 out of 10 gang-related homicides (87%) were located in metropolitan areas[1] in 2011(Egley & Howell, 2013). The explanation for this observation is straightforward: gang activity and serious gang crime remained highly concentrated in the most populated jurisdictions. In cities with populations greater than 100,000, more than a quarter of homicides are gang-related (Howell, Egley, Tita, & Griffiths, 2011). An assessment with a sample of the largest 45 cities (with populations of approximately 400,000 or greater) found that respondents (police, schools, health departments, and mayor's offices) identified gang violence as the major type of youth violence that needs to be addressed (Weiss, 2008). Specifically, 61% of the city representatives identified gang violence as the major type of youth violence affecting their city.

As expected, the number of gangs and their memberships vary directly with population sizes of gang problem areas (Egley, 2005):

• Rural counties and small cities, towns, and villages (with population below 50,000) typically have 6 or fewer gangs with a total of about 50 members.

- Cities with populations between 50,000 and 100,000 typically have up to 15 gangs, and a total of about 100 members.
- Cities with populations between 100,000 and 250,000 typically have up to 30 gangs, and a total of about 500 members.
- Cities with populations greater than 250,000 typically report more than 30 gangs and a total of 1,000 or more members.

Neighborhoods are said to have criminal trajectories in their own right (Griffiths & Chavez, 2004; Tita & Cohen, 2004). This line of research prompted Howell and colleagues (2011) to perform a trajectory analysis of cities' gang homicide patterns using the proportion of all homicides that are gang-related in 247 cities with populations in excess of 100,000 persons. Two distinct groups of these very large cities, together making up 70% of all large cities, consistently reported that between 20% and 40% of their homicides were gang-related from 1996 to 2009; and only one group, comprising less than a quarter of the cities, exhibited very few or no gang homicides in the study period. Three important observations can be made from this analysis. Overall, more than 7 out of 10 very large cities reported a consistently high level or increasing proportion of gang-related homicides over the 14-year period. Second, a remarkable degree of consistency in the rate of gang-related homicides across trajectory groups was observed. Third, none of the trajectory groups found in these cities displayed a pattern consistent with a decline in the prevalence of gang homicide. While it has been reasonably assumed that gang-related violence would follow the overall dramatic declines in violent crime nationally, these analyses provided overwhelming evidence to the contrary; that is, gang violence rates in very large cities have continued at exceptional levels over the past decade *despite* the remarkable overall crime drop, suggesting that gang violence in major cities should be a priority public safety concern.

But can the specific locations of gang violence be pinpointed? In 1996, at the height of gang violence in Chicago, Block's (2000) study showed that multiple-gang activity was observed in just 4.5% of the more than 25,000 grid squares citywide; however, "these squares accounted for 23.0% of the assaults and 44.3% of all drug-related incidents" (p. 379). Similarly, Tita, Cohen, and Engberg's (2005) study indicates that the location of gang set space in Pittsburgh is usually a very small geographic area, much smaller than neighborhoods or even census tracts. However, Block (2000) found that gangs do not necessarily need to be large to carry out a significant number of homicides. Many of these homicides were attributed to relatively new, smaller street gangs, predominantly Latino, and continuously fighting among themselves over limited turfs.

California researchers used data on between-gang violent crimes of members of 13 criminal street gangs in East Los Angles to map locations of violence (Brantingham, Tita, Short, & Reid, 2012). Overall, more than 1,000 violent crimes (assault with a deadly weapon, attempted homicide, and homicide) occurred in the relatively small study area in the three-year period 1999–2002. As expected, ongoing inter-gang conflicts predominantly clustered along the boundaries between gangs' respective "set spaces" (Tita, Riley, & Greenwood, 2005). Sets of two of the very early gangs in that area, the Chicano[2] Cuatro Flats and White Fence gangs – now nearly 80 years of age – accounted for much of the violence. Intergroup rivalries produce what Block and Block (1993) identify as "peaks and valleys" in homicides and other violence.

Clearly, cities with chronic gang activity have elevated rates of gang violence, and this violence is concentrated within very small neighborhood areas where multiple gangs interact.

> Gang violence rates have continued at exceptional levels over the past decade *despite* the remarkable overall crime drop. Gang violence that is rather commonplace in very large cities seems largely unaffected by, if not independent from, other crime trends – with the possible exceptions of drug trafficking and firearm possession. (Howell *et al.*, 2011, p. 13)

To be sure, interpersonal "beefs" and territorial disputes in adjacent set spaces account for the overwhelming majority of gang violence (Block & Block, 1993; Brantingham *et al.*, 2012). Papachristos's (2009) research suggests "that gangs are not groups of murderers per se, but rather embedded social networks in which violence ricochets back and forth … [and] what begins as a single murder soon generates a dozen more as it diffuses through these murder networks" (p. 76). These events become, in effect, "dominance contests" in which "violence spreads through a process of social contagion that is fueled by normative and behavioral precepts of the code of the street" (p. 81).

Programs and Control Strategies for the Three Trajectory Groups

This section reviews programs and strategies for modifying the trajectories of gang members, gangs, and gang problem cities. Very few effective gang programs and strategies are available within these three levels. Moreover, readers are cautioned that the outcomes of the best programs and strategies reported to date are somewhat modest.

Gang membership trajectories

Only one primary gang prevention program has been found to be effective in preventing gang-joining. The four-year follow-up on effects of the universal school-based Gang Resistance Education and Training (GREAT) program, a core middle school curriculum, showed that it reduced the odds of gang-joining by 24%, and also produced more favorable attitudes toward the police and less positive attitudes about gangs (Esbensen, Osgood, Peterson, Taylor, & Carson, 2013). The validity of these findings are attributable to the strength of the skill-based instruction, which incorporates skill development strategies employed in the evidence-based LifeSkills® training program (Dusenbury & Botvin, 1992), random assignment of classrooms in seven cities in separate states, and the high fidelity with which the GREAT curriculum was implemented.

The Montreal Preventive Treatment Program also demonstrated an impact on gang-joining, even though it was not developed specifically for the purpose of preventing youth from joining gangs. Rather, it was designed to prevent antisocial behavior among boys aged 7 to 9 who had previously displayed disruptive problem behavior in kindergarten. This program consists of a combination of parent training and childhood skill development. Tremblay, Masse, Pagani, and Vitaro's (1996) evaluation showed both short- and long-term gains, including less delinquency, less substance use, and less gang involvement at age 15.

Goldstein and Glick's Aggression Replacement Training (ART) proved effective with gang-involved youth in Brooklyn, New York (Glick and Gibbs, 2011). Also an evidence-based delinquency program (Drake, 2012), ART targets the most violent youth. The strength of ART comes mainly from its cognitive–behavioral therapeutic approach (CBT). Another application of CBT, the Aggressive Behavioral Control Program, targeted high-risk, high-need inmates who demonstrated low responsiveness to rehabilitative services; and the program was equally effective in reducing recidivism in the community with gang and non-gang inmates in a controlled study (Di Placido, Simon, Witte, Gu, & Wong, 2006). The program clients averaged about 25 years of age.

One program, the Comprehensive Gang Prevention, Intervention, and Suppression Model (commonly called the Comprehensive Gang Model), has demonstrated evidence of effectiveness in reducing gang-related violence of youth served in the program, while also promoting desistance from active gang membership. The main component of this model is a multidisciplinary intervention team with integrated street outreach work, ensuring coordinated delivery of needed services to targeted gang members and support in disengagement from gangs. When implemented with high fidelity (in Chicago, Illinois; Riverside, California; and Mesa, Arizona), there were moderate but statistically significant reductions in both gang violence (in three sites) and drug-related offenses (in two sites) in controlled studies (Spergel, 2007; Spergel, Wa, & Sosa, 2006). In addition, some evidence suggests that departure from gangs was hastened. "Some youth changed from leaders to core members or regular members, peripherals, or nonmembers (odds ratio = 2.0)" (Spergel *et al.*, 2006, p. 214). Reductions in youth's level of gang affiliation were associated with lower violence and drug arrests.

Gang trajectories

Very little success has been seen in efforts to truncate the trajectory of individual gangs with police suppression. Of course, the law enforcement objective is to eliminate them altogether. Almost without exception the gangs returned, usually in a morphed form. Historically, the major strategy with gang elimination in mind has been massive street "gang sweeps" by police and sheriff's agencies, but these have not proved successful (Klein, 2004). The single well-researched police and prosecutorial "takedown" of a gang is the Chicago Gangster Disciples gang (Papachristos, 2001). But following the successful federal prosecution of selected members of the Gangster Disciples, the remaining members aligned themselves with other criminal gangs.

The more modest goal of reducing the volume of crimes committed by members of particular gangs has seen more success: in the Chicago Gang Violence Reduction Program (Spergel, 2007), the Chicago Cure Violence program (Ransford, Kane, Metzger, Quintana, & Slutkin, 2010; Skogan, Hartnett, Bump, & Dubois, 2008; see also Howell and Young, 2013), and Operation Ceasefire (Braga & Weisburd, 2012). Interestingly, the Cure Violence program has a prevention strategy in which out- reach workers concentrate on changing the behavior and risky activities of a small number of selected members of the community who have a high chance of either "being shot" or "being a shooter" in the immediate future. The Tri-Agency Resource Gang Enforcement Team (TARGET) approach in Orange County, California, repre- sents a multiagency approach to targeting current gang members with control measures, while also targeting entire gangs with police suppression. The TARGET program produced a sharp increase in the incarceration of gang members and a cumulative 47% decrease in gang crime over a seven-year period (Kent, Donaldson, Wyrick, & Smith, 2000) and has been given credit for reducing the overall level of gang crime in a targeted hotspot to near zero (Wiebe, 1998).

City gang problem trajectories

No success has been seen in modifying the long-term trajectory of gang problem cities. Without a doubt, the most widely publicized gang suppression initiative is the Boston Operation Ceasefire, which targeted mainly gang members aged 15–21 and was credited with a 63% reduction in youth homicide (Braga, Kennedy, Waring, & Piehl, 2001; Piehl, Cooper, Braga, & Kennedy, 2003). Operation Ceasefire was based on an analysis of homicide among Boston's youth that determined that this violence was gang-centered, neighborhood-based, and concentrated in a small number of repeat-offending, gang-involved youth. Suppression tactics included "pulling levers" to impose costs on offenders related to their chronic offending by serving warrants, enforcing probation restrictions, and deploying federal enforcement powers. Braga and Pierce (2005) reported that serious gang problems returned and homicides increased after the successes attributed to the Boston Ceasefire project.

Subsequent replications of the Boston strategy that specifically targeted gang members reduced violence within targeted police reporting districts in the Boyle Heights community of East Los Angeles (Tita, Riley, & Greenwood, 2003, 2005), and citywide in Lowell, MA (Braga, McDevitt, & Pierce, 2006; Braga, Pierce, McDevitt, Bond, & Cronin, 2008).When implemented in the city of Lowell, this gang suppres- sion strategy significantly reduced serious assaultive gun violence incidents in a controlled study using seven comparison Massachusetts cities (Braga *et al.*, 2006,

2008). Several initiatives have more broadly targeted "hot" persons, gangs, places, and crimes under what are dubbed "smart policing" initiatives (Coldren, Huntoon, & Medaris, 2013), though the effectiveness of the particular strategies in suppressing gang violence is unknown.

Conclusion

Gang activity and its associated violence remains an important and significant component of the US crime problem. While it has been reasonably assumed that gang-related violence would follow the overall dramatic declines in violent crime nationally, gang violence rates have continued at exceptional levels over the past decade *despite* the remarkable overall crime drop. Gang activity and serious gang crime have remained highly concentrated in very large cities, with populations greater than 100,000 persons. Gang violence that is rather commonplace in these large cities seems largely unaffected by, if not independent from, other crime trends, with the possible exception of drug trafficking and firearm possession.

Participation in gangs changes the life-course of most youth, particularly those who remain active for multiple years. Thus, preventing youth from joining gangs and promoting desistance from gangs is of paramount importance. Much like individuals' criminal careers, gangs typically have developmental histories, with periods of growth and decline. In a similar fashion, cities also have gang problem histories. Very large cities – in which one in four homicides is gang-related – consistently have serious gang problems. Officials in the largest of these cities have identified gang violence as the major type of youth violence that needs to be addressed.

Few programs have proved particularly effective in altering any of the three gang trajectories described in this chapter. Findings from rigorously evaluated programs can be summarized as follows. Just one gang program has demonstrated effectiveness in preventing gang-joining, the GREAT program, although it is noteworthy that the Montreal Preventive Treatment Program also reduced gang-joining, even though it was not developed specifically for this purpose. Rather, it was designed to prevent delinquency among disruptive kindergartners.

Several programs have shown evidence of dampening down the level of criminal activity of gang members, and one of these programs (the Comprehensive Gang Model) has demonstrated effectiveness in multiple sites and also holds potential for truncating gang members' careers. The evidence shows that the most successful gang crime reduction initiatives are community-wide, have broad community involvement in planning and delivery, are multi-agency, utilize an intervention team, and provide integrated outreach support and services. However, successfully promoting termination from gang involvement on a widespread basis remains an elusive goal. Most youths eventually terminate gang membership without the benefit of outside intervention.

Very little success has been seen in efforts to truncate the trajectory of individual gangs, even with police suppression. The gangs typically re-emerge because they are homegrown: rooted in fractures in families, schools, social services, and communities. No evidence of significant alteration of the long-term trajectory of gang problem cities is available, though a few targeted gang suppression strategies – focused on high-rate violent offenders – have shown noteworthy short-term violent crime reductions in some cities, communities, and neighborhoods. Whether or not these reductions can be maintained over long periods of time remains to be seen.

Notes

1   In this analysis, cities with populations greater than 100,000 and suburban county sheriff and police departments.
2   Second-generation Mexican; also called Mexican-American.

References

Bjerregaard, B. (2002). Self-definitions of gang membership and involvement in delinquent activities. *Youth and Society, 34*, 31–54.

Block, C.R., & Block, R. (1993). *Street gang crime in Chicago. Research in Brief*. Washington, DC: US Department of Justice, National Institute of Justice.

Block, R. (2000). Gang activity and overall levels of crime: A new mapping tool for defining areas of gang activity using police records. *Journal of Quantitative Criminology, 16*, 369–383.

Braga, A.A., Kennedy, D.M., Waring, E.J., & Piehl, A.M. (2001). Problem-oriented policing, deterrence, and youth violence: an evaluation of Boston's Operation Ceasefire. *Journal of Research in Crime and Delinquency, 38*, 195–225.

Braga, A.A., McDevitt, J., & Pierce, G.L. (2006). Understanding and preventing gang violence: Problem analysis and response development in Lowell, Massachusetts. *Police Quarterly, 9*, 20–46.

Braga, A.A., & Pierce, G.L. (2005). Disrupting illegal firearms markets in Boston: The effects of Operation Ceasefire on the supply of new handguns to criminals. *Criminology and Public Policy, 4*, 717–748.

Braga, A.A., Pierce, G.L., McDevitt, J., Bond, B.J., & Cronin, S. (2008). The strategic prevention of gun violence among gang-involved offenders. *Justice Quarterly, 25*, 132–162.

Braga, A.A., & Weisburd, D.L. (2012). The effects of focused deterrence strategies on crime: A systematic review and meta-analysis of the empirical evidence. *Journal of Research in Crime and Delinquency, 49*, 323–358.

Brantingham, P.J., Tita, G., Short, M.B., & Reid, S. (2012). The ecology of gang territorial boundaries. *Criminology, 50*, 851–885.

Bushway, S.D., Krohn, M.D., Lizotte, A.J., Phillips, M.D., & Schmidt, N.M. (2013). Are risky youth less protectable as they age? The dynamics of protection during adolescence and young adulthood. *Justice Quarterly, 30*, 84–116.

Chesney-Lind, M. (2013). How can we prevent girls from joining gangs? In T.R. Simon, N.M. Ritter, & R.R. Mahendra (Eds.), *Changing Course: Preventing Gang Membership* (pp. 121–133). Washington, DC: US Department of Justice, US Department of Health and Human Services.

Coldren, J.R., Huntoon, A., & Medaris, M. (2013). Introducing smart policing: Foundations, principles, and practice. *Police Quarterly, 16*, 275–286.

Craig, W.M., Vitaro, F., Gagnon, C., & Tremblay, R.E. (2002). The road to gang membership: Characteristics of male gang and non-gang members from ages 10 to 14. *Social Development, 11*, 53–68.

Curry, G.D., Decker, S.H., & Egley, A. Jr. (2002). Gang involvement and delinquency in a middle school population. *Justice Quarterly, 19*, 275–292.

Debarbieux, E., & Baya, C. (2008). An interactive construction of gangs and ethnicity: The role of school segregation in France. In F. van Gemert, D. Peterson, & I.-L. Lien (Eds.), *Street Gangs, Migration and Ethnicity* (pp. 211–226). Portland, OR: Willan Publishing.

Decker, S.H., Katz, C.M., & Webb, V.J. (2008). Understanding the black box of gang organization: Implications for involvement in violent crime, drug sales, and violent victimization. *Crime and Delinquency, 54*, 153–172.

Di Placido, C., Simon, T.L., Witte, T.D., Gu, D., & Wong, S.C.P. (2006). Treatment of gang members can reduce recidivism and institutional misconduct. *Law and Human Behavior, 30*, 93–114.

Drake, E.K. (2012). Reducing crime and criminal justice costs: Washington State's evolving research approach. *Justice Research and Policy, 14*, 97–115.

Dusenbury, L., & Botvin, G.J. (1992). Competence enhancement and the development of positive life options. *Journal of Addictive Diseases, 11*, 29–45.

Egley, A., Jr. (2005). *Highlights of the 2002–2003 National Youth Gang Surveys (OJJDP Fact Sheet, June 2005–01)*. Washington, DC: US Department of Justice, Office of Juvenile Justice and Delinquency Prevention.

Egley, A., Jr., & Howell, J.C. (2013). *Highlights of the 2011 National Youth Gang Survey. OJJDP Fact Sheet (September)*. Washington, DC: Office of Juvenile Justice and Delinquency Prevention.

Eitle, D., Gunkel, S., & Gundy, K.V. (2004). Cumulative exposure to stressful life events and male gang membership. *Journal of Criminal Justice, 32*, 95–111.

Esbensen, F., Brick, B.T., Melde, C., Tusinski, K., & Taylor, T.J. (2008). The role of race and ethnicity in gang membership. In F.V. Genert, D. Peterson, & I. Lien (Eds.), *Street Gangs, Migration and Ethnicity* (pp. 117–139). Portland, OR: Willan.

Esbensen, F., & Huizinga, D. (1993). Gangs, drugs, and delinquency in a survey of urban youth. *Criminology, 31*, 565–589.

Esbensen, F., Osgood, D.W., Peterson, D., Taylor, T.J., & Carson, D.C. (2013). Short and long term outcome results from a multi-site evaluation of the G.R.E.A.T. program. *Criminology and Public Policy, 12*, 375–411.

Esbensen, F., Peterson, D., Taylor, T.J., & Freng, A. (2010). *Youth Violence: Sex and Race Differences in Offending, Victimization, and Gang Membership*. Philadelphia: Temple University Press.

Federal Bureau of Investigation. (2013). *Crime in the United States, 2012*. Washington, DC: US Department of Justice, Federal Bureau of Investigation.

Fleisher, M.S. (1998). *Dead End Kids: Gang Girls and the Boys They Know*. Madison: University of Wisconsin Press.

Gilman, A.B., Hill, K.G., & Hawkins, J.D. (2014). The long-term consequences of adolescent gang membership on adult functioning. *American Journal of Public Health, 104*, 938–945.

Glick, B., & Gibbs, R. (2011). *Aggression Replacement Training: A Comprehensive Intervention for Aggressive Youth* (3rd ed.). Champaign, IL: Research Press.

Gordon, R.A., Rowe, H.L., Pardini, D., Loeber, R., White, H.R., & Farrington, D. (2014). Serious delinquency and gang participation: Combining and specializing in drug selling, theft and violence. *Journal of Research on Adolescence, 24*, 235–251.

Griffiths, E., & Chavez, J.M. (2004). Communities, street guns and homicide trajectories in Chicago, 1980–1995: Merging methods for examining homicide trends across space and time. *Criminology, 42*, 941–975.

Hill, K.G., Gilman, A.B., & Hawkins, J.D. (2011). *The Consequences of Adolescent Gang Membership on Functioning in the Next Generation.* Paper presented at the Annual Meeting of the Society for Social Work Research, Tampa, FL, January.

Hill, K.G., Howell, J.C., Hawkins, J.D., & Battin-Pearson, S.R. (1999). Childhood risk factors for adolescent gang membership: Results from the Seattle Social Development Project. *Journal of Research in Crime and Delinquency, 36*, 300–322.

Howell, J.C. (2013). Why is gang membership prevention important? In T.R. Simon, N.M. Ritter, & R.R. Mahendra (Eds.), *Changing Course: Preventing Gang Membership* (pp. 7–18). Washington, DC: US Department of Justice, US Department of Health and Human Services, Centers for Disease Control and Prevention.

Howell, J.C., & Egley, A., Jr. (2005). *Gangs in Small Towns and Rural Counties. NYGC Bulletin No. 1.* Tallahassee, FL: National Youth Gang Center.

Howell, J.C., Egley, A. Jr., Tita, G., & Griffiths, E. (2011). *US Gang Problem Trends and Seriousness, 1996–2009. National Gang Center Bulletin.* Tallahassee, FL: Institute for Intergovernmental Research, National Gang Center.

Howell, J.C., & Griffiths, E. (2015). *Gangs in America's Communities* (2nd. ed.). Thousand Oaks, CA: Sage.

Howell, J.C., & Lynch, J. (2000). *Youth Gangs in Schools.* Juvenile Justice Bulletin, Youth Gang Series. Washington, DC: US Department of Justice, Office of Juvenile Justice and Delinquency Prevention.

Howell, J.C., & Young, M.A. (2013). What works to curb US street gang violence. *The Criminologist, 38*, 39–43.

Huff, C.R. (1996). The criminal behavior of gang members and non-gang at-risk youth. In C.R. Huff (Ed.), *Gangs in America* (2nd ed.) (pp. 75–102). Thousand Oaks, CA: Sage.

Huff, C.R. (1998). *Comparing the Criminal Behavior of Youth Gangs and At-Risk Youth. Research in Brief.* Washington, DC: US Department of Justice, Office of Justice Programs, National Institute of Justice.

Kent, D.R., Donaldson, S.I., Wyrick, P.A., & Smith, P.J. (2000). Evaluating criminal justice programs designed to reduce crime by targeting repeat gang offenders. *Evaluation and Program Planning, 23*, 115–124.

Klein, M.W. (2004). *Gang Cop: The Words and Ways of Officer Paco Domingo.* Walnut Creek, CA: Alta Mira Press.

Krohn, M.D., & Thornberry, T.P. (2008). Longitudinal perspectives on adolescent street gangs. In A. Liberman (Ed.), *The Long View of Crime: A Synthesis of Longitudinal Research* (pp. 128–160). New York: Springer.

Krohn, M.D., Thornberry, T.P., Rivera, C., & Le Blanc, M. (2001). Later careers of very young offenders. In R. Loeber, & D.P. Farrington (Eds.), *Child Delinquents: Development, Interventions, and Service Needs* (pp. 67–94). Thousand Oaks, CA: Sage.

Krohn, M.D., Ward, J.T., Thornberry, T.P., Lizotte, A., & Chu, R. (2011). The cascading effects of adolescent gang involvement across the life course. *Criminology, 49*, 991–1028.

Lahey, B.B., Gordon, R.A., Loeber, R., Stouthamer-Loeber, M., & Farrington, D.P. (1999). Boys who join gangs: A prospective study of predictors of first gang entry. *Journal of Abnormal Child Psychology, 27*, 261–276.

Lizotte, A.J., Krohn, M.D., Howell, J.C., Tobin, K., & Howard, G.J. (2000). Factors influencing gun carrying among young urban males over the adolescent–young adult life course. *Criminology, 38*, 811–834.

Loeber, R., Menting, B., Lynam, D.R., Moffitt, T.E., Stouthamer-Loeber, M., Stallings, R., Farrington, D.P., & Pardini, D. (2012). Findings from the Pittsburgh Youth Study: Cognitive impulsivity and intelligence as predictors of the age-crime curve. *Journal of the American Academy of Child and Adolescent Psychiatry, 51*, 1136–1149.

Medina, J., Aldridge, J., Shute, J., & Ross, A. (2013). Measuring gang membership in England and Wales: A latent class analysis with Eurogang survey questions. *European Journal of Criminology, 10*, 591–605.

Melde, C., Diem, C., & Drake, G. (2012). Identifying correlates of stable gang membership. *Journal of Contemporary Criminal Justice, 28*, 482–498.

Melde, C., Taylor, T.J., & Esbensen, F. (2009). "I got your back": An examination of the protective function of gang membership in adolescence. *Criminology, 47*, 565–594.

Miller, W.B. (2001). *The Growth of Youth Gang Problems in the United States: 1970–1998*. Washington, DC: Office of Juvenile Justice and Delinquency Prevention.

Monti, D.J. (1993). Gangs in more- and less-settled communities. In S. Cummings, & D.J. Monti (Eds.), *Gangs: The Origins and Impact of Contemporary Youth Gangs in the United States* (pp. 219–253). Albany: State University of New York Press.

Moore, J.W. (1991). *Going Down to the Barrio: Homeboys and Homegirls in Change*. Philadelphia: Temple University Press.

Moore, J.W. (1998). Understanding youth street gangs: Economic restructuring and the urban underclass. In M.W. Watts (Ed.), *Cross-cultural Perspectives on Youth and Violence* (pp. 65–78). Stamford, CT: JAI.

National Center on Addiction and Substance Abuse. (2010). *National Survey of American Attitudes on Substance Abuse XV: Teens and Parents, 2010*. New York: National Center on Addiction and Substance Abuse, Columbia University.

Papachristos, A.V. (2001). *A.D., After the Disciples: The Neighborhood Impact of Federal Gang Prosecution*. Peotone, IL: New Chicago Schools Press.

Papachristos, A.V. (2009). Murder by structure: Dominance relations and the social structure of gang homicide. *American Journal of Sociology, 115*, 74–128.

Petersen, R., & Howell, J.C. (2013). Program approaches for girls in gangs: Female specific or gender neutral? *Criminal Justice Review, 38*, 491–509.

Peterson, D. (2012). Girlfriends, gun-holders, and ghetto-rats? Moving beyond narrow views of girls in gangs. In S. Miller, L.D. Leve, & P.K. Kerig (Eds.), *Delinquent Girls: Contexts, Relationships, and Adaptation* (pp. 71–84). New York: Springer.

Piehl, A.M., Cooper, S.J., Braga, A.A., & Kennedy, D.M. (2003). Testing for structural breaks in the evaluation of programs. *Review of Economics and Statistics, 85*, 550–558.

Planty, M., & Truman, J.L. (2013). *Firearm Violence, 1993–2011 (NCJ 241730)*. Special Report. Washington, DC: US Department of Justice, Bureau of Justice Statistics.

Pyrooz, D.C., Sweeten, G., & Piquero, A.R. (2013). Continuity and change in gang membership and gang embeddedness. *Journal of Research in Crime and Delinquency, 50*, 239–271.

Ransford, C., Kane, C., Metzger, T., Quintana, E., & Slutkin, G. (2010). An examination of the role of CeaseFire, the Chicago police, Project Safe Neighborhoods, and displacement in the reduction in homicide in Chicago in 2004. In R.J. Chaskin (Ed.), *Youth Gangs and Community Intervention: Research, Practice, and Evidence* (pp. 76–108). New York: Columbia University Press.

Robers, S., Kemp, J., Truman, J., & Snyder, T.D. (2013). *Indicators of School Crime and Safety, 2012*. Washington, DC: US Department of Justice, National Center for Education Statistics, Bureau of Justice Statistics.

Short, J.F., Jr., & Hughes, L.A. (2009). Urban ethnography and research integrity: Empirical and theoretical dimensions. *Ethnography, 10*, 397–415.

Skogan, W.G., Hartnett, S.M., Bump, N., & Dubois, J. (2008). *Evaluation of CeaseFire-Chicago.* Final Report to the National Institute of Justice. Chicago, IL: Northwestern University. Retrieved from http://www.ncjrs.gov/pdffiles1/nij/grants/227181.pdf

Snyder, H.N., & Sickmund, M. (2006). *Juvenile Offenders and Victims: 2006 National Report.* Washington, DC: Office of Juvenile Justice and Delinquency Prevention.

Spergel, I.A. (2007). *Reducing Youth Gang Violence: The Little Village Gang Project in Chicago.* Lanham, MD: AltaMira Press.

Spergel, I.A., Wa, K.M., & Sosa, R.V. (2006). The comprehensive, community-wide, gang program model: Success and failure. In J.F. Short, & L.A. Hughes (Eds.), *Studying Youth Gangs* (pp. 203–224). Lanham, MD: AltaMira Press.

Sweeten, G., Pyrooz, D.C., & Piquero, A.R. (2013). Disengaging from gangs and desistance from crime. *Justice Quarterly, 30*, 469–500.

Thornberry, T.P. (1998). Membership in youth gangs and involvement in serious and violent offending. In R. Loeber, & D. P. Farrington (Eds.), *Serious and Violent Juvenile Offenders: Risk Factors and Successful Interventions* (pp. 147–166). Thousand Oaks, CA: Sage.

Thornberry, T.P., Krohn, M.D., Lizotte, A.J., Smith, C.A., & Tobin, K. (2003). *Gangs and Delinquency in Developmental Perspective.* New York: Cambridge University Press.

Tita, G.E., & Cohen, J. (2004). Measuring spatial diffusion of shots fired activity across city neighborhoods. In M.F. Goodchild, & D.G. Janelle (Eds.), *Spatially Integrated Social Science* (pp. 171–204). New York: Oxford University Press.

Tita, G.E., Cohen, J., & Engberg, J. (2005). An ecological study of the location of gang "set space." *Social Problems, 52*, 272–299.

Tita, G.E., Riley, K.J., & Greenwood, P. (2003). From Boston to Boyle Heights: The process and prospects of a "pulling levers" strategy in a Los Angeles barrio. In S.H. Decker (Ed.), *Policing Gangs and Youth Violence* (pp. 102–130). Belmont, CA: Wadsworth/Thompson Learning.

Tita, G.E., Riley, K.J., & Greenwood, P. (2005). *Reducing Gun Violence: Operation Ceasefire in Los Angeles.* Washington, DC: National Institute of Justice.

Tremblay, R.E., Masse, L., Pagani, L., & Vitaro, F. (1996). From childhood physical aggression to adolescent maladjustment: The Montreal Prevention Experiment. In R.D. Peters, & R.J. McMahon (Eds.), *Preventing Childhood Disorders, Substance Abuse, and Delinquency* (pp. 268–298). Thousand Oaks, CA: Sage.

Truman, J.L., & Planty, M. (2012). *Criminal Victimization, 2011*. Washington, DC: US Department of Justice, Office of Justice Programs, Bureau of Justice Statistics (NCJ 239437).

Weisburd, D., Bushway, S., Lum, C., & Yang, S. (2004). Trajectories of crime at places: A longitudinal study of street segments on the city of Seattle. *Criminology, 42*, 283–321.

Weiss, B. (2008). *An Assessment of Youth Violence Prevention Activities in USA Cities*. Los Angeles, CA: Southern California Injury Prevention Research Center, University of California at Los Angeles, School of Public Health.

Wiebe, D.J. (1998). *Targeting and Gang Crime: Assessing the Impacts of a Multi-Agency Suppression Strategy in Orange County, California*. University of California, Irvine, CA: Focused Research Group on Gangs.

31

A Look at the Street Gang Violence Situation in Europe

Elmar G.M. Weitekamp

In reviewing the developments on the European gang situation and looking at more information about the actual situation of street gangs and gang-like youth groups, one finds some interesting developments. First, one can no longer deny that European cities have street gangs or gang-like youth groups, who are according to Klein (1995) mainly speciality gangs and more compressed than the traditional American gangs. These street gangs have to be differentiated from motorcycle gangs, prison gangs, hooligans, right-wing groups and neo-Nazi gangs. Second, most Europeans seem to acknowledge the existence of youth groups, but do not consider them as street gangs. It appears to us that this is merely a matter of definition and takes attention away from the fact that we do indeed have street gangs in Europe.

We can rely on the history and background of the Eurogang program of research, which according to Esbensen and Maxson (2012, pp. 2–6) was founded and developed originally in Leuven, Belgium, and later the same year in San Diego. The first official Eurogang meeting took place in 1998 in Schmitten, Germany. Subsequent meetings took place in Oslo, Leuven, Egmond aan Zee, Straubing, Copenhagen, and Stockholm, among other cities. It was realized that the Eurogang group needed a solid definition of what a street gang is, reflecting the different opinions on what constitutes a gang and what does not. Malcolm Klein led this tremendous task group, and after some years of discussion and deliberations the Eurogang group came up with the following definition, according to Esbensen and Maxson (2012, p. 7): "A street gang/troublesome youth group is any durable, street oriented youth group whose involvement in illegal activity is part of its group identity." In examining the publications of the Eurogang research group with regard to the existence and the development of gangs, one has to come to the conclusion that most cities in

The Handbook of Juvenile Delinquency and Juvenile Justice, First Edition. Edited by Marvin D. Krohn and Jodi Lane.

Europe have their troublesome youth groups and gangs. European countries seem to be doing everything to create more gangs and to develop a serious gang problem which might eventually look as bad as the American gang situation, a situation most people cannot even imagine for Europe. Despite the denial that they exist, most European cities describe some common features, as follows:

- Gangs exist in deprived communities.
- Gangs often consist of minority or immigrant members of society, either by race, nationality or ethnicity.
- Gangs are predominantly male.
- Gang members are almost always alienated, marginalized youth who are socially excluded from society and whose opportunities are blocked.
- Gang members are usually young and typically adolescents or young adults.
- Gang members are involved in all sorts of criminal activities, with quite a range in the variation of delinquent and criminal behaviour.
- Gangs are stable over time and can exist for long periods of time.

Street gangs in German cities are mainly formed by young immigrant groups. After immigrating, these groups had to take over the responsibilities and educational tasks their parents and families were no longer able to provide. In addition, some European countries cut official resources and programs for juveniles and adolescents, and most importantly, crucial language training. This is one main reason that eventually leads youngsters to form and join gangs. Societies that shift more and more to "winner–loser" cultures make it very hard for young people to get a good education or jobs (James, 1995). They are often excluded from full-time, career-oriented work. Young immigrants in particular are the biggest losers, since they are usually the least integrated and often live in poorer and neglected neighbourhoods, which can serve as breeding grounds for street gangs. Recent developments in crime and, in particular, violent crimes, which are mainly group offenses, point in the direction of an increasing street gang problem, and therefore it is no surprise that we find in Germany, in both small towns as well as big cities, newspaper reports about crime by gangs or gang-like groups.

Kersten (2007) added, especially for Germany, the existence of right-wing gangs or extremist youth groups. Despite the fact that right-wing or extremist youth groups do not fit the strict definition of a troublesome youth group or gang as defined by the Eurogang research group, we want to include them in this review of street gangs in German cities since, in the recent past, countless research reports have indicated a varying degree of identification with extremist issues, xenophobia, and anti-Semitic attitudes among German youth. According to Kersten (2007), it is necessary to differentiate between attitudes, organizations, and displays of extremist behaviour if one wants to gain a deeper understanding of this development. Of importance is who takes part in which activities and at which times. Kersten (2007) concludes that because of Germany's particular sensitivity about its history and the German guilt factor, the provocative potential of any racist and anti-Semitic symbolism is extremely high and very attractive for rebellious youth and subcultures, and therefore used often by skinheads. Xenophobia and hate crimes, on the other hand, often depend upon situational factors. Weitekamp and Kerner (1996) concluded that the rise in right-wing violence by youth groups was, after reunification, as great in the old states as it is in the new states. The reality in Germany is that most of the perpetrators are not organized in military right-wing organizations. Rather, they are only directed by right-wing ideology and take part in the right-wing movement to express their frustration about the political and social situation in Germany.

Pfeiffer (1998), in his evaluation of juvenile crime and violence in ten countries in Europe, concluded that since the mid-1980s there has been a substantial increase in youth violence. He sees the main cause for this as the shift of European countries towards a "winner–loser culture" in which many disadvantaged youth appear to be the losers. Pfeiffer is basing his argument on the findings of James (1995), who argued that at least three major elements are part of the creation of such "winner–loser" cultures:

> It is abundantly clear from many studies… that inequality in incomes combined with false promises of equality of opportunity, American-style of welfare support for the disadvantaged and poor job-quality are major causes of violence developing and developed nations alike. From 1979 onwards in Britain, all three of these patterns were adopted as a deliberate government policy; the gap between rich and poor increased to pre-war levels, the amount and kind of state support for the disadvantaged was reduced dramatically; the quality of jobs available to young men decreased after union power to guarantee minimum wages and conditions of work was removed. These changes coincided with an unprecedented increase in violence against the persons since 1987. (James, 1995, p. 74)

Polk and Weitekamp (1999) talked in this context about youth abandonment. Young people experience economic abandonment and are caught in a dreadful developmental trap. Polk and Weitekamp (1999) further pointed out that, historically, virtually all young people, at high, middle and low points of the class structure, could look forward to a process of moving from childhood through schooling into adulthood with some combination of work and family roles. These prospects are not relevant any more, and the problem of abandonment is greater for those young people who leave school early and enter the labour force with little to offer in the way of qualifications, skills, or experience. Wilson (1996), in his work about the new urban poor, talked about a process in which work disappeared for this group of people. The lack of full-time work for this group leads to undesired consequences, such as a lack of money, and delays in becoming independent from parents, the establishment of sexual relationships, marriage, and the establishment of a family. These individuals become stuck in a social and economic "no man's land", one where a central feature of their existence is that normal supports for identity as man or woman are not available. Polk and Weitekamp (1999) call this a developmental trap that forces young people to engage in complicated and innovative ways to struggle with their central identities as males or females. This developmental trap is even worse for members of racial, national, or ethnic minority groups. Dubet and Lapeyronnie (1994) investigated the "winner–loser" hypothesis in France and found that a significant shift has occurred in social problems, including crime trends. They concluded that the social exclusion of marginal groups had become the key problem of the 1990s. Further, they considered the criminal acts by the marginalized youngsters to be an expression of their helplessness of being unable to live a normal life and their inability to gain access to society.

It is here where we can see the clear connection to violence and gangs. The situation of abandoned youngsters is such that issues of status and manhood arise and cry out for a solution. The lack of traditional pathways to define "who am I as a man" is, according to Polk and Weitekamp (1999) particularly relevant when comparing one's status with others for whom joining a gang may be appealing. The gang can change the rules of the game and can make the loser into a winner again.

There are many signs in European countries that we are on the way to creating more "winner–loser" cultures, which could serve as a fertile ground for the formation of gangs and increased violence as a way of contesting masculinity. Pfeiffer's (1998) research clearly indicates that Europe is experiencing a substantial increase in violence. In addition, Dünkel and Skepenat (1998) found that, for the State of Mecklenburg-Vorpommern, Germany, the increase in violent crimes is mainly caused by group offending. From group offending or offending within a group to the formation of gangs seems to be just one step away. This may be especially true if processes of youth abandonment are not countered by any meaningful social policy and the opening of legitimate pathways for the youngsters, in order to allow them to participate in society.

To demonstrate the "dangerous" situation, we use the example of the German Aussiedler (Russians who are descendants of Germans who have migrated back to Germany) The developments with the Aussiedler are fairly new ones starting around the mid-1990s. We are convinced that other European countries have similar problem groups, even though the Aussiedler exhibit some peculiarities. One of them is that the Aussiedler immediately get a German passport and are considered to be Germans when they immigrate to Germany. According to Reich, Weitekamp, and Kerner (1999), around two million immigrants from the former Soviet Union have come to Germany since 1988, peaking with close to 400,000 coming in 1990. Germany used substantial aid packages in order to integrate the Aussidler into German society. They received, among other aid, so-called integration aid, which is a kind of unemployment payment, for 312 days, and German language courses were paid for 12 months. However, new laws in 1993 reduced the amount of aid for the Aussiedler drastically. Integration aid is now only paid for 156 days and the language courses were also reduced by half. The so-called guarantee fund, which amounted in 1991 to 450 million German marks, was reduced by 65% and is now at the equivalent of 180 million marks per year. This reduction, in particular, hurts young people the most, since this fund provided re-education, job training programs, and social integration support programs. In addition to these financial restrictions, at the beginning of their stay in Germany, Aussiedlers lived in so-called "temporary special housing arrangements". While theoretically they are supposed to leave these special housing units as fast as possible, they stay longer. For example, in Tübingen, on average they remain in special housing units for two years (Stoll, 1999). These units are usually very cramped and the living arrangements are very poor, reminding us of a ghetto-like situation where sometimes hundreds of people live. In general, the people who live there have no privacy or common rooms that could be used for social activities. There are no facilities for young people, who are forced to hang out in the hallways or outside of the buildings.

The situation for the young Aussiedler is particularly difficult. While in Russia they were considered to be a minority group because of their German descent and labelled as German fascists. In Germany, even though having a German passport, they are labelled Russians and once again considered a minority. In addition to their minority status, they often have language problems, and difficulties in schools. The school and/or job education they received in Russia is worth nothing in their new country of residence, thus blocking the legal opportunities and serving to marginalize them even more. It is not surprising that these young people form and join gangs in order to find a place where they belong and identify themselves. Hanging out in groups was already very much part of their culture when they lived in the former Soviet Union, since it was often too dangerous to go and hang out alone. Here in Germany they perceive the German culture and environment as too dangerous, and these circumstances force them to hang out together and to form gangs. Stoll (1999) reported that in the "temporary special housing units" of Tuebingen the gangs can be considered as neo-traditional ones. The youngsters usually hang out in front of the housing unit and have a strong hierarchical order, determined by age and experience in the country of the "enemy". These housing units are often the only possibility to find friends, especially in rural areas. After the families move away, members of these gangs often come back and are admired because they display the status symbols they were able to obtain. These status symbols are cars, clothes, and other ways to indicate wealth. The older gang members recruit the younger ones from the newly arrived immigrants and use them for their illegal activities. The gang members are involved in all sorts of criminal activities, and a quick look in juvenile correctional facilities reveals that a disproportionately high number of Aussiedler youngsters are incarcerated. The group cohesion of the "Russian gangs" is particularly high, since, in their country of origin, they were used to treating any outsiders, especially the State, as the enemy, and regulated conflicts among themselves. In addition, the Aussiedler youngsters exhibit a very strong machismo culture and attitudes in which a high level of violence is considered to be normal (Reich et al., 1999).

This brief description of the situation of the Aussiedler in Germany clearly shows that Germany is on its way to creating a serious and long-lasting street gang problem. We assume that similar developments can be found throughout Europe and for different immigrant groups, since all European countries have serious problems related to minority groups. Minority group members live in poor housing, drop out of schools often because of language problems, have a poor education, are unskilled, often hold low-paying jobs, are socially excluded and marginalized, and often look for an identity. The Aussiedler in Germany are in a way even privileged compared with other minority groups since the State provides them with integration privileges that do not exist for other immigrants. If this group is forming gangs in order to cope with the circumstances of their new home country, the formation of gangs and gang activities seems to be an even more viable solution for other immigrant groups.

It looks to us that we in Europe have to open our eyes and tune our ears with regard to the existence of gangs and the emergence of a serious gang problem. We cannot deny the existence of street gangs in European cities, even though they do not seem to reflect the "worst American gang" scenario. Signs of emerging "winner–loser" cultures can be found in all European countries, and their influence on the use of violence to achieve one's aims cannot be denied. Franz von Liszt claimed at the end of the last century that "the best criminal policy is a good social policy", something which the European countries seem to have forgotten. This negligence can lead to serious problems, and with regard to gangs, we might be on a direct path to creating a very serious gang problem in Europe.

Assuming for the moment the possibility of actual increases in violent behaviour in these countries, the analysis will naturally shift to social factors that might provide some explanation or interpretation of why such trends are occurring. The available literature suggests three general dimensions that should be addressed in such an analysis:

(a) the degree to which the violence in the developed countries takes collective form, including the development of forms of youth gang violence;
(b) the emergent social class structure which snares some young people in a trap of economic deprivation and abandonment; and,
(c) ways of interpreting the overwhelmingly masculine character of youth violence (despite recent increases in female violence).

From these summary observations, it would appear that Europe is now moving into a new phase in terms of the way social life is organized for young people, especially those prone to engage in criminal activity, with that behaviour at times beginning to take distinctly collective form. It is also clear that within these emergent collective units, violence can be a central feature of the activities of the groups. Weitekamp (2001) reports that within ethnic groups such as the Aussiedler, the tentative evidence suggests exceptional levels of violence, and the centrality of violence for the maintenance of individual identity.

During youth, peer groups are especially attractive. Those groups or cliques take over functions of socialization, provide orientation and stabilize behaviour during a period of juvenile transition. This clique formation, however, is not purely a youth developmental phenomenon. On a societal level, processes existent that are not only beneficial for the attachment of juveniles to peer groups, but tend to promote the formation of delinquent, violent or drug-consuming gangs that feature deviant attitudes towards normative actions as a part of their group identity.

Research shows that particularly increased immigration numbers since the early 1990s, with associated processes of social exclusion and discrimination as well as a growing poverty of children and juveniles in Germany, have added to this trend (Förtig, 2002). With regard to social and material concerns, both factors contribute to experiences of deprivation and marginalization of juveniles. In their peer groups, young people are looking for ways to overcome their social, cultural and economic circumstances, and "try to handle the vital struggle for existence on the streets" (Thrasher, 1927). Finally, the increasing individualization in society leads to the fact that, in some social strata, no common shared orientations are present that would show alternative ways of gaining reputation, money, and happiness. If juveniles do not succeed in achieving accepted norms and values by socially recognized means, then deviant behaviour may be one alternative. Good examples for this are described by van Gemert and Weermann (2013) for the Netherlands, and Wilhelm Heitmeyer's disintegration theorem illustrates in detail these processes within the right-wing youth gangs in Germany (Heitmeyer, 1995).

From our analysis we can draw the following conclusions. First, underprivileged youths are for several reasons more likely to join delinquent youth groups. On the one hand, they have more risk factors that primarily force them to seek a sense of belonging and acknowledgement outside their families. They may tend to affiliate with peer groups at an earlier age than juveniles without this underprivileged background, and feel a greater challenge to maintain self-worth and self-esteem through delinquent acts. Other juvenile needs and values, especially of the male population, are power, strength, and respect, which they seem to achieve through violent acts. Additionally, members of delinquent youth groups are disproportionately involved in delinquent and violent acts and therefore responsible for a considerable amount of criminality.

So far the formation of troublesome or delinquent youth groups can be explained as a reaction to social segregation and disadvantages in several dimensions of life. It is basically an attempt to overcome their marginalized situation and to make themselves noticeable, or in other words, to move from the edges of society to be the focus of public attention.

It is a widespread phenomenon that the problems and causes of juvenile delinquency in the group context often remain unmentioned because the media are occupied with sensational reporting about gang offenses in such a way that the public gains the impression that vandalizing youth gangs make city centres or public places unpredictably dangerous. This leads to a lot of prejudice towards youths, which can further minimize, especially for underprivileged youths, their chances of participation in society.

In consequence, the task for social sciences will be to investigate not only delinquency, violence, or the differences of those respective groups of juveniles, but to keep an eye on the developmental process of those groups and the underlying factors, especially those that lead to a no-win situation. Society has to take care that juveniles get the sense of being the main persons who shape the future and that they are important for this enterprise. In order that juveniles do not become "lost", it is necessary to provide them with space for autonomous development on the one hand, and with a framework, orientation, and emotional backing on the other hand.

References

Dubet, F., & Lapeyronnie, D. (1994). *Im Aus der Vorstädte: der Zerfall der demokratischen Gesellschaft*. Stuttgart: Klett-Cotta Verlag.

Dünkel, F., & Skepenat, M. (1998). Jugendliche und Heranwachsende als Täter und Opfer von Gewalt. In H.-D. Schwind, E. Kube, & H.-H. Kühne (Eds.), *Essays in Honor of Hans-Joachim Schneider: Criminology at the Threshold of the 21st Century*. Berlin: Walter de Gryter.

Esbensen, F.-A., & Maxson, C.L. (Eds.) (2012). *Youth Gangs in International Perspective: Results from the Eurogang Program of Research*. New York: Springer Verlag.

Förtig, H. (2002). *Jugendbanden*. München: Herbert Utz Verlag

Heitmeyer, W. (1995). *Gewalt. Schattenseiten von Individualisierungsprozessen bei Jugendlichen aus unterschiedlichen Milieus*. Weinheim/München: Juventa.

James, O. (1995). *Juvenile Violence in a Winner-Loser Culture*. London: Free Association Books.

Kersten, J. (2007). Youth groupings, identity, and the political context: On the significance of extremist youth groupings in unified Germany. In J.M. Hagedorn (Ed.), *Gangs in the Global City: Alternatives to Traditional Criminology*. Urbana: University of Illinois Press.

Klein, M.W. (1995). *The American Street Gang: Its Nature, Prevalence, and Control*. New York: Oxford University Press.

Pfeiffer, C. (1998). Juvenile crime and violence in Europe. In M. Tonry (Ed.), *Crime and Justice: A Review of Research* (Vol. 23). Chicago: University of Chicago Press.

Polk, K., & Weitekamp, E.G.M. (1999). *Emerging Patterns of Youth Violence*. Paper presented at the American Society of Criminology Meeting in Toronto.

Reich, K., Weitekamp, E.G.M., & Kerner, H.-J. (1999). Jugendliche Aussiedler: Probleme und Chancen im Integrationsprozess. *Bewährungshilfe, 46*(4), 335–359.

Stoll, F. (1999). *Von Rußland nach Württemberg: Eine Studie zur Integration jugendlicher-Spätaussiedler* (unpublished Master's thesis). Faculty of Social and Behavioral Sciences, University of Tübingen.

Thrasher, F. (1927). *The Gang: A Study of 1314 Gangs*. Chicago: University of Chicago Press.

van Gemert, F., & Weermann, F. (2013). Youth groups and street gangs in the Netherlands. In *European Forum for Urban Security "EU Street Violence"* (pp. 203–227). Paris: EFUS.

Weitekamp, E.G.M. (2001). Gangs in Europe: Assessments at the Millenium. In M. Klein, H.-J. Kerner, C. Maxson, & E.G.M. Weitekamp (Eds.), *The Eurogang Paradox*. Dordrecht: Kluwer Academic Publishers.

Weitekamp, E.G.M., & Kerner, H.-J. (1996). *Right Wing Violence, Xenophobia, and Attitudes Towards Violence in Germany*. Paper presented at the Minerva Center for Youth Policy, University of Haifa, Haifa.

Wilson, W.J. (1996). *When Work Disappears: The World of the New Urban Poor*. New York: Vintage Books.

32

Weapon Carrying and Use Among Juveniles

Amanda D. Emmert and Alan J. Lizotte

Adolescent weapon carrying and use can be, and has been, explored in a number of manners. Below we discuss theories and research regarding youth's motivations for carrying weapons, the demographics of weapon carriers, and predictive, protective, and risk factors for juvenile weapon carrying. Through exploring the literature, we document areas in which scholars can expand with future research and potential implications for policy development. While scholars have brought a great deal of understanding to the topic of adolescent weapon carrying and use, we argue that more research is necessary to comprehend the behavior.

Motivation

The potential motivations for carrying weapons as an adolescent are plentiful. There are multiple points of view on why adolescents carry weapons, and it is our intent to discuss them in this chapter. While various researchers discuss correlates of weapon carrying as if they stand alone, this is likely an oversimplification of a complex social phenomenon that drives carrying and use by adolescents (Brennan & Moore, 2009). Weapon carrying is multifaceted, changing with time, age, and other factors. So, it is not surprising that the motivations that adolescents give for carrying weapons vary on many social dimensions, such as use and sale of drugs, age, and their friends carrying weapons (Lizotte, Krohn, Howell, Tobin, & Howard, 2000). This is important to keep in mind, as different camps initially presented the correlates discussed below as competing, and suggested distinct policy implications. We see the correlates as complementary rather than competing, and our

The Handbook of Juvenile Delinquency and Juvenile Justice, First Edition. Edited by Marvin D. Krohn and Jodi Lane.

suggestions for preventing weapon carrying and use are integrative. For example, there is a chicken-and-egg problem between obtaining weapons and committing crime with them that has important policy implications. Some researchers argue that weapons enable otherwise normal people to commit crime (weapons cause crime), while others suggest that criminals obtain weapons so that they can commit crime (weapons don't kill people, people do). Ironically, both arguments can be true, and neither side has substantiated their claims with research evaluating the temporal ordering of events.

Before discussing specific hypotheses of adolescent weapon carrying and use motivation, it is important to note that, with few exceptions, severe limitations exist in the research for each position. These include a lack of variety in weapon types explored, failure to include measures that would account for the presence of multiple motivations, inability to demonstrate temporal ordering, and failure to consider the influence of gender and age on motivation. Until future research overcomes these limitations, many of the correlates discussed below fail to be more than shots in the dark.

Fear and victimization

Fear-and-victimization or "fear and loathing" (Wright, Rossi, & Daly, 1983) is one proposed motivation for adolescent weapon carrying, suggesting that adolescents carry weapons because of an emotional fear of crime, a perceived risk of crime, or previous victimization experiences (Cao, Cullen, & Link, 1997). This suggests that individuals carry weapons for defensive purposes, assuming that doing so will reduce their fear, perceived risk, and victimization (Wilcox, May, & Roberts, 2006). And, this conclusion may be correct. Many adolescents who initially fear victimization will ultimately reach for a weapon, which reduces their fear of victimization (Aspy et al., 2004; Blumberg et al., 2009; Callahan & Rivera, 1992; DuRant, Beckford, & Kahn, 1996; DuRant, Getts, Cadenhead, & Woods, 1995; Sheley, McGee, & Wright, 1992). But, while this conclusion appeases some, others find little to no support for the fear and victimization hypothesis (Bailey, Flewelling, & Rosenbaum, 1997; Lane, Cunningham, & Ellen, 2004; Melde, Esbensen, & Taylor, 2009; Watkins, Huebner, & Decker, 2008; Webster, Gainer, & Champion, 1993; Wilcox et al., 2006).

Scholars have posed multiple explanations for the ambiguity in results. For example, it is difficult to establish causal order with the cross-sectional data used by many researchers. Furthermore, the causal ordering of these factors may differ by types of weapons: adolescents may believe guns have more protective efficacy than knives or other weapons. We cannot know if this is true because little if any research compares weapon type by efficacy of use.[1] In addition, inclusion of control variables is inconsistent across studies. Even the meaning of fear and perceived risk may be more distinct than one might expect. People may be fearful not so much for themselves but for their loved ones, while at the same time perceiving high risk. So, the measurement of these concepts are sometimes vague and clouded (Melde *et al.*, 2009; Warr, 2000; Wilcox *et al.*, 2006). As such, future research concerned specifically with the fear-and-victimization hypothesis should attempt to overcome these limitations to better inform policies.

Deviance and crime

Just because an adolescent obtains a weapon in response to fearing crime, does not mean that same adolescent is not motivated to commit crime with it. Adolescents intent on committing crime or behaving deviantly can, and do, find weapons to do so (Bjerregaard & Smith, 1993; Black & Ricardo, 1994; Callahan & Rivera, 1992; DuRant *et al.*, 1995, 1996; Sheley *et al.*, 1992; Valois, McKeown, Garrison, & Vincent, 1995; Vaughn *et al.*, 2012; Webster *et al.*, 1993). In fact, Blumberg *et al.* (2009) find that 3.8% of adolescents report their primary reason for carrying weapon is criminal use. Weapons can facilitate doing crime in a number of ways. Victims are more likely to cooperate when weapons are used, they serve as protection from both victims and other deviants, and weapons serve as an ace in the hole, guaranteeing the adolescent a feeling of confidence. In response, other adolescents feel the need to arm themselves, and an arms race begins. However, just like fear-and-victimization, research on this topic frequently does not establish temporal ordering, making it difficult to determine whether weapon carrying leads to criminal activity or criminal activity motivates weapon carrying.

Fighting   Fighting is just a special case of what we discuss above. A weapon can facilitate fighting, or result from past victimization in anticipation of future victimization. Bringing a weapon to a fight can improve the odds of coming out ahead, regardless of physical strength. As we stated above, at a minimum, possession of a weapon during a fight serves as a backup plan for an adolescent. If one starts losing, the weapon can be pulled to regain the advantage. Moreover, the mere presence of a weapon sends a message that the carrier is not someone to trifle with. So, it is not surprising that adolescents who participate in physical fighting also tend to carry weapons, if not use them (Callahan & Rivera, 1992; DuRant *et al.*, 1995, 1996; DuRant, Kahn, Beckford, & Woods, 1997; Kodjo, Auinger, & Ryan, 2003; Simon, Crosby, & Dahlberg, 1999; Webster *et al.*, 1993). One study finds that the link between physical fighting and weapon carrying is stronger for males than for females (DuRant *et al.*, 1995).[2]

Despite knowing that a relationship exists between physical fighting and adolescent weapon carrying, no one has established whether physical fighting leads to weapon carrying, weapon carrying leads to fighting, or whether the two manifest simultaneously. Without knowing more about the causal ordering of these behaviors, it is nearly impossible to make empirically based policy decisions or understand the connection between the two behaviors. But, once again it is certainly possible, if not highly probable, that each is true.

Substance use and selling   Similar to physical fighting, weapon carrying is particularly common among youths involved with illegal substance use and selling (Black & Ricardo, 1994; DuRant et al., 1996; DuRant, Krowchuk, Kreiter, Sinal, & Woods, 1999; Kodjo et al., 2003; Kulig, Valentine, Griffith, & Ruthazer, 1998; McKeganey & Norrie, 2000; Sheley, 1994; Vaughn et al., 2012). In one such study, Altschuler and Brounstein (1991) find that, in a sample of boys living in Washington DC, two-thirds of the juveniles who use or sell drugs report carrying concealed weapons. The type, amount, and number of different drugs adolescents either use or sell predict the crimes they participate in and the probability that they carry a weapon (Altschuler & Brounstein, 1991; Vaughn, Howard, & Harper-Chang, 2006). For example, Lizotte et al. (2000) report that high levels of drug use in early adolescence and high levels of drug sales in later adolescence and young adulthood are associated with increased likelihoods of gun carrying.

Selling and using illicit substances may impact the actual use of weapons. The "drug–gun diffusion hypothesis" reasons that adolescents active in illegal drug markets carry guns for self-protection from the dangerous environment and to resolve possible disputes (Blumstein, 1995a, 1995b). More precisely, weapons are necessary in drug trade to protect money collected from sales, to protect the dealer from robbery, to secure territory, and to protect that territory against "turf" invasions by competing drug sellers (Wilkinson & Fagan, 1996). Additionally, having taken on a normative role in the drug trade, weapons serve as a necessary status symbol or proof of authenticity (Wilkinson & Fagan, 1996). In arming themselves, adolescents involved in the drug market also pose a risk to adolescent drug buyers and peers with whom they interact. Ultimately, such behaviors lead to clients arming themselves against the crossfire. This perpetuates an "arms race" among local youths (Blumstein, 1995a), while increasing the probability of weapon use and weapon-related homicides among adolescents (Bennett & Holloway, 2004; Blumstein, 1995a).

While this is one possible explanation for the drug/weapon link among adolescents, complementary explanations exist. Frequent drug users may carry weapons for committing crimes, such as robberies, to generate the money necessary to buy drugs (Lizotte et al., 2000). Or, drug use may prevent juveniles from considering the consequences of weapon carrying, thus increasing the probability of weapon carrying by adolescent substance abusers (Kodjo et al., 2003).

Despite the breadth of literature regarding adolescents, substance use/selling, and weapon behaviors, research has focused more on guns than other weapon types. For example, research regarding the "drug–*gun* diffusion hypothesis" only considers the association between drugs and gun carrying. Ultimately, by focusing specifically on gun carrying, literature on the connection between substance activity and weapon carrying has a blind spot. Understanding the broader association of substance use, selling, and *weapons* would provide necessary knowledge on the issue at hand.

Peer carrying

Peer weapon carrying is a consistent indicator of adolescent weapon carrying (Bailey et al., 1997; Hemenway, Vriniotis, Johnson, Miller, & Azrael, 2011; Sheley et al., 1992; Williams, Mulhall, Reis, & DeVille, 2002). Similar to deviance or crime and weapon carrying, multiple explanations exist to explain how peer carrying influences adolescent weapon carrying. Some argue that perceived or actual peer carrying suggests to other adolescents that carrying is normative (Lizotte et al., 2000). If adolescents feel that carrying a weapon is an expected or acceptable behavior among their peers, they will likely follow suit. In a sense, weapon carrying can function as a fashion statement in some circles, conveying status, edginess, or participation in a certain crowd (Cook, Ludwig, Venkatesh, & Braga, 2007). However, the cool factor of carrying a weapon quickly translates to real danger.

Thus, another reason for "packing" a weapon is that peer carrying causes adolescents to perceive that they are at risk of victimization from their peers. Because of the frequency of interaction, the likelihood of being victimized by a peer is high. So, if peers carry, it is in adolescents' best interests to arm themselves. Concern can result from fear of direct victimization from a peer, or indirect victimization resulting from peers' carrying that draws danger (Lizotte et al., 2000). This is just another manifestation of the arms race we discuss above.

Of course, adolescents and their peers are likely to share contextual factors operating at the school, neighborhood, or community level. Thus, the same factors may influence adolescents and their peers to carry weapons. For example, rampant crime in a neighborhood may independently motivate youth to carry weapons. Or, adolescents who carry weapons may associate more with peers who carry (Bailey et al., 1997; Bauman, Botvin, Botvin, & Baker, 1992).

Additionally, in surveys where adolescents report their own carrying and their perception of peer carrying, correlations between the two may result from adolescents projecting their own behaviors on to others. In other words, adolescents may think their peers carry even when peers do not. Additionally, adolescents have a propensity for overestimating the percentage of their peers that participate in risky behaviors, including weapon carrying (Hemenway et al., 2011).[3] This suggests that survey results showing an association between perceived peer carrying and adolescent weapon carrying are likely biased by the adolescent's inability to estimate accurately the proportion of their peers who in fact carry weapons. Considered as a whole, juveniles are likely motivated to carry weapons based on potentially inaccurate or vastly inflated perceptions of peer weapon carrying, resulting from misunderstanding normative behaviors or the projection of their own behavior onto others.

Bearing in mind these revelations, an important policy consideration in combatting adolescent weapon carrying is to educate juveniles about the true likelihood of youth weapon carrying, and encourage them to approach an authority figure if they are concerned about others being armed, as opposed to carrying weapons themselves.

Gangs   Gangs are just an example of delinquent peer groups on steroids, with an axe to grind and a propensity for finding trouble (Thornberry, Krohn, Lizotte, Smith, & Tobin, 2003, p. 42). Gang members not only encourage antisocial behavior among members, but in a structural way they facilitate it. For example, gang members can help each other obtain weapons for individual use and they can share them. So, one weapon can be involved with many crimes for each of many individuals in the gang. In a sense, within gangs, there are more crimes than members of the gang, and more members than weapons. The interconnectedness of gang involvement and weapon carrying and use, particularly for guns, has been thoroughly explored (Bjerregaard & Lizotte, 1995; Decker & Van Winkle, 1996; Melde *et al.*, 2009; Sheley *et al.*, 1992; Thornberry *et al.*, 2003; Watkins *et al.*, 2008). Not surprisingly, all suggest that gang membership and weapon carrying by adolescents are highly associated. However, gang research overwhelmingly focuses on guns and not on other weapons.

Bearing in mind that adolescents' motivations for carrying firearms change over time, gang membership is the largest influence for carrying before the age of 16 (Lizotte *et al.*, 2000). And, when compared with adolescents who are not gang members, adolescent gang members are twice as likely to own guns and carry their guns outside the home (Bjerregaard & Lizotte, 1995). Similarly, juvenile arrestees who report gang involvement demonstrate three times higher odds of reporting gun ownership, carrying, and use (Watkins *et al.*, 2008). One reason for this development is the sharing of guns within gangs. As mentioned above, although there are more gang members than weapons, everyone in the gang has access to the "weapon cabinet" (Lizotte, Bonsell, McDowall, Thornberry, & Krohn, 2002; Thornberry *et al.*, 2003). Thus, a large proportion of juveniles involved in gangs report having carried at one point in time.

Weapon carrying by gang members is especially alarming when we realize the frequency with which gang members use their weapons. Adolescents who report participation in a gang are four times as likely to also report firing a gun in the past year compared with adolescent non-gang members (Watkins *et al.*, 2008). Two-thirds of active gang members who report carrying guns report having used their gun at least once (Decker & Van Winkle, 1996). While gang fights are the most commonly reported use, occasional use in drivebys, attacks on strangers, and other incidents are reported (Decker & Van Winkle, 1996). In other words, gangs most often use guns against other gangs.

Consensus suggests that the motivation for carrying weapons when in a gang results from members' perceived or actual need for protection (Decker & Van Winkle, 1996; Horowitz, 1990; Lizotte *et al.*, 2000; Sheley & Wright, 1993; Strodtbeck & Short, 1964; Wright, Sheley, & Smith, 1992). Often described as a gun diffusion process, gang members' perception or observation that their rivals or fellow gang members carry guns encourages weapon carrying by other gang youth, in order to prevent a perceived or actual disadvantage, and for protection against a dangerous environment. Once again, this fuels an arms race.

With the majority of literature discussing gangs and *guns*, future research can easily expand current understandings by exploring gangs' involvement with other weapon types. Additionally, future policy and initiatives may benefit from weapon interventions that focus specifically on gangs (Melde *et al.*, 2009).

Characteristics of Weapon Carriers

In order to implement policy, it is necessary to know precisely who carries specific types of weapons. It is not enough simply to know that adolescents carry out of fear, to commit crime, or to fit in with peers. Powerful policies should target specific populations. For this very reason, it is important to explore current understandings of demographic characteristics among adolescent weapon carriers. To accomplish this we focus on gender, age, race, and income.

Gender

Gender is often considered a decisive divider of weapon carriers. Many people, including scholars and politicians, assume that males participate in weapon behaviors more frequently than females. In survey snapshots, males do seem more likely to carry. For example, between 15% and 35.4% of males report carrying weapons, while only 5% to 19.3% of females carry weapons (Callahan & Rivera, 1992; DuRant *et al.*, 1995, 1997; Lewis *et al.*, 2007; Muula, Rudatsikira, & Siziya, 2008). More importantly, compared with females, males are more likely to do so both on and off school property (Aspy *et al.*, 2004; Bailey *et al.*, 1997; Blum *et al.*, 2000; Kodjo *et al.*, 2003). Overall, adolescent males hold more supportive beliefs about weapon carrying compared with females. This includes reporting a perceived need for a weapon that is 1.7 times higher than that reported by females (Lewis *et al.*, 2007; Penny, Walker, & Gudjonsson, 2011).

There are several reasons these snapshots could be wrong. First, the gender gap in weapon carrying is decreasing, possibly as a result of reductions in male violent offending (Lauritsen, Heimer, & Lynch, 2009; Penny *et al.*, 2011), gender equality demonstrated in female carrying and violent offending, or both. Second, Emmert and Lizotte (2014) find that weapon carrying differs based on gender and weapon type. More specifically, males and females are equally likely to report carrying guns at some point in time, while males are more likely than females to report carrying (Emmert & Lizotte, 2014). While Emmert and Lizotte's (2014) finding regarding guns is at odds with those finding a gender difference, methodological design differences between studies may explain the contradiction. For example, surveys that use cross-sections find that girls are less likely than boys to carry weapons (DuRant *et al.*, 1995; Muula *et al.*, 2008). However, if females move in and out of weapon carrying more quickly than males, they would appear to be less likely to carry. Longitudinal designs better capture the more intermittent nature of female carrying. Additionally, allowing adolescents to self-define weapon carrying broadens the research focus beyond a single weapon type. Finally, studies of weapon carrying overwhelming focus on carrying in schools (Brennan & Moore, 2009). Unfortunately, this focus could be limiting the scope through which we consider adolescent carrying behaviors. Since males and females might carry in different environments, it is important that future studies do not limit their attention to weapon carrying in schools.

Based on the discussion above, it is clear that any policy on adolescent weapon carrying needs to focus on both boys and girls. But our understanding that females and males carry different types of weapons allows for cutting-edge and targeted intervention policies. Meanwhile, future research can explore the continuity or intermittency of long-term weapon carrying by gender.

Age

The relationship between age and adolescent weapon carrying has received appropriate and in depth attention. Perhaps surprisingly, early adolescents, between ages 13 and 16, are the most frequent weapon carriers in the US (DuRant *et al.*, 1999). A number of factors may contribute to this phenomenon. First, young adolescents are smaller than their older peers, thus weapons serve as equalizers. Additionally, immaturity and an inability to think through the consequences of carrying weapons likely contribute to young adolescents demonstrating higher carrying frequencies. Such explanations are supported by the finding that, compared with adult arrestees, adolescent arrestees are more willing to carry and use firearms (Decker, Pennell, & Caldwell, 1997; Watkins *et al.*, 2008). However, it is interesting to note that within the juvenile age group, research demonstrates that as adolescents increase in age, so too does the frequency with which they carry weapons (Dukes, Stein, & Zane, 2010; Forrest, Zychowski, Stuhldreher, & Ryan, 2000; Lowry, Powell, Kann, Collins, & Kolbe, 1998). In other words, younger adolescents are more likely to carry weapons at some point, but as adolescents get older, they are more likely to carry weapons on a regular basis.

Despite the frequency with which older adolescents carry weapons, when participation in delinquent activity is controlled, age fails to predict weapon carrying (Barlas & Egan, 2006; Muula *et al.*, 2008). In other words, as adolescents get older their opportunities and frequencies of participating in delinquency increase, and weapon carrying is associated more with delinquent behavior than age.

Other research has found that age of initial delinquent behaviors predicts weapon carrying (Brennan, Shepherd, & Moore, 2010). As discussed above, participation in gangs before the age of 16 and drug dealing after 16 years old both predict firearm carrying (Lizotte *et al.*, 2000). Similarly, contact with police before the age of 14 doubles the likelihood of being arrested for a firearm related offense compared with offenders whose first contact with police occurs after the age of 14 (McCluskey, McCluskey, & Bynum, 2006).

In summary, we know that adolescents, specifically between the ages of 13 and 16 years old, are the most *likely* carriers of weapons, and that age of initial delinquent behavior can predict weapon carrying. Additionally, the *frequency* with which adolescents carry weapons increases with age. This suggests that programs and policies interested in reducing the frequency of juvenile weapon carrying will be most successful if focused on adolescents aged 15 and 16, while policies and initiatives attempting to prevent adolescents from ever carrying weapons might do best to focus on juveniles participating in delinquency between ages 11 and 13.

Race and income

Stereotypes of weapon carrying and use emphasize a race effect, primarily suggesting that blacks, and in some cases Hispanics, are more likely to carry or use weapons than non-Hispanic whites. However, while numerous studies have attempted to isolate a race effect on weapon carrying or use (Aspy *et al.*, 2004; Bjerregaard & Lizotte, 1995; Blum *et al.*, 2000; Cook & Ludwig, 2004; Lizotte *et al.*, 2000; Smith, Lizotte, Thornberry, & Krohn, 1997; Vanderschmidt, Lang, Knight-Williams, & Vanderschmidt, 1993; Watkins *et al.*, 2008), consensus has yet to be reached. Race may act as a risk marker – "a characteristic or condition that is associated with known risk factors but exert no causal influence of its own" – as opposed to being a causal factor of violent behavior (Centers for Disease Control and Prevention, 2001).

Similarly, income has an indirect effect on weapon carrying (Blum *et al.*, 2000; Kodjo *et al.*, 2003; Lizotte *et al.*, 2000). Income affects the financial and economic resources of families, and often reflects the economic resources of the community in which families live. As such, low family income and or neighborhood poverty both increase weapon carrying (Blum *et al.*, 2000; Kodjo *et al.*, 2003). Similarly, low family income and neighborhood poverty may reflect dangerous environments that beget armed responses.

Ultimately, race and income likely reflect other causal factors that lead more directly to adolescent weapon carrying, as opposed to demonstrating race or income effects. These may include peer, family, and neighborhood characteristics that are more appropriate for policy development.

Predicting and Protecting Factors

Beyond the demographic characteristics of adolescent weapon carriers and users, a more complex set of factors predict adolescent weapon carrying. While numerous measures successfully predict adolescent weapon behaviors, we will limit our discussion to family, maltreatment, and community involvement.

Family

Overwhelming consensus establishes that family can serve as a protective factor against adolescent weapon carrying. In fact, multiple aspects of family dynamics play an important role, including family structure, family or parental involvement and supervision, family communication, and the absence of family conflict. Taken as a whole, family factors serve as a powerful tool against adolescent weapon carrying.

As mentioned above, the mere structure of juveniles' families impacts their weapon carrying behaviors. Adolescents living in homes that include both natural parents are less likely to report carrying weapons (Bailey *et al.*, 1997; Orpinas, Murray, & Kelder, 1999). However, a study of gun-related violence in an inner-city environment did not find family structure to be a significant predictor of juvenile weapon carrying (Sheley *et al.*, 1992). This contradiction may result from methodological differences in weapon type, since Sheley *et al.* (1992) only studied guns, while Bailey *et al.* (1997) and Orpinas *et al.* (1999) considered all weapon types. Or, environment might dictate the differences observed, as Bailey *et al.* (1997) included a sample of urban, suburban, and rural adolescents, while Sheley *et al.* (1992) focused on urban youth. As such, it would be interesting for future research to explore whether weapon type or environment impact the influence of family structure on teen weapon behaviors. Additionally, we need more details about why family structure influences adolescent behaviors.

Beyond mere structure, family interactions and communication prove to be important in various forms. Adolescents who report that a parent is involved in their life or monitors their actions and behaviors – even those not related to delinquency or weapons – are less likely to carry weapons (Ferguson & Meehan, 2010; Orpinas *et al.*, 1999; Vaughn *et al.*, 2012). Proactively discussing delinquency or topics such as the dangers of tobacco, alcohol, and drugs proves to protect juveniles against weapon carrying as well (Vaughn *et al.*, 2012). In other words, adolescents who discuss prosocial behaviors with their families are less likely to carry weapons. Thus, action in the forms of both supervision and communication serve to reduce youth weapon behaviors.

In general, family communication reduces the likelihood of juveniles carrying weapons (Aspy *et al.*, 2004; Black & Ricardo, 1994). This relationship is evident again in the influence of parental approval on adolescent weapon carrying. Juveniles who report that their parents express pride or appreciation in something they have done are less likely to report carrying weapons (Vaughn *et al.*, 2012). Lack of adult support, along with the presence of family or parent–child conflict, whether it be verbal or physical in nature, predicts youth weapon carrying (Bailey *et al.*, 1997; Hemenway *et al.*, 2011; Orpinas *et al.*, 1999). More simply, adolescents who feel close to the people they live with or get along well with their family are less likely to carry weapons.

The finding that adolescent weapon carrying is linked to family characteristics is simply an extension of studies that find that family factors are connected to adolescent delinquency (Bailey *et al.*, 1997; Hirschi, 1969; Jessor & Jessor, 1977; Rankin, 1983). Such conclusions suggest that parents and families have a great deal of influence on adolescent weapon carrying. Thus, attempts to prevent juvenile weapon carrying should consider including mechanisms designed to strengthen parent–child relationships and improve healthy parental supervision of children and adolescents.

Maltreatment and exposure to violence

Research has established that maltreatment and exposure to violence predict adolescent weapon carrying, and pose strong policy implications. In general, childhood abuse is linked to delinquent behavior among adolescents (DuRant *et al.*, 1995; Hamilton, Falshaw, & Browne, 2002; Herrera & McCloskey, 2001; Stewart, Dennison, & Waterson, 2002; Stouthamer-Loeber, Wei, Homish, & Loeber, 2002). As a subset of delinquency, weapon carrying is associated with childhood maltreatment. Youths with histories of physical abuse are almost three times more likely to carry weapons than youths who report no physical abuse in their past (Lewis *et al.*, 2007). Juveniles who report sexual assault demonstrate even higher odds, being 4.4 times more likely than those without a sexual assault history to report carrying weapons (Lewis *et al.*, 2007). "The direct experience of abuse, coupled with a tendency to misperceive hostile intent (Dodge, Pettit, & Bates, 1997), may lead youth to identify an extreme measure (i.e., a weapon) as a viable option for self-protection, which may subsequently lead to weapon carrying or weapon use" (Lewis *et al.*, 2007, p. 265). Alternatively, abuse may push youth from the home, resulting in the potential for greater exposure to negative influences in the community, and vulnerability due to lack of positive role models.

More generally, simple exposure to violence predicts weapon carrying by adolescents (Hemenway *et al.*, 2011; Henrich, Brookmeyer, & Shahar, 2005; Kodjo *et al.*, 2003; Leeb, Barker, & Strine, 2007; Molnar, Miller, Azrael, & Buka, 2004). And, not only does witnessing violence predict weapon carrying; it also increases the likelihood that adolescents will commit weapon offenses at a later time.

To combat the influence of physical abuse, sexual abuse, and observed violence on juvenile weapon behaviors, policy-makers might pursue efforts to encourage or enhance therapy or counseling for children and adolescents following abusive experiences or witnessing violence. Additionally, strengthening policies that remove adolescents from abusive home situations might reduce a host of delinquent behaviors, including weapon carrying. More research looking for the nexus on how exactly this operates would inform better policy.

Community involvement

Getting youths involved in their communities has served as a longstanding solution to delinquency in the popular media. Novels and movies teem with stories of children saved from their own negative behaviors by participating in football, choir, and the like. However, when it comes to diverting adolescent weapon carrying, the influence of community involvement is unclear. In fact, contradictory findings exist for the influence of religion, sports, community groups, and extracurricular activities on youth weapon behaviors (see Aspy *et al.*, 2004; Jessor, van den Bos, Vanderryn, Costa, & Turbin, 1995). However, research suggests that adolescents who are positively involved in school are less likely to carry weapons. More specifically, getting good grades, having positive relationships with teachers and/or peers, happiness at school, and good school attendance all reduce the likelihood that juveniles will carry weapons on or off school grounds (Aspy *et al.*, 2004; Bailey *et al.*, 1997; Kodjo *et al.*, 2003).

Because engagement in community activities is such a popular technique for deterring and interrupting adolescent misbehaviors, it is imperative for future research to explore the influence of community engagement on adolescent weapon carrying. We recommend this research takes at least two forms. Since the literature currently fails to reach consensus on the impact of community activity (in the forms of religion, sports, community groups, and extracurricular activities) on weapon carrying, we would first recommend that future research establishes whether a relationship exists between adolescent involvement in community activities and weapon carrying. Second, in order to accurately inform policy, it is necessary to demonstrate that a causal relationship exists between community involvement and desistance from weapon carrying; thus we recommend research using longitudinal data to determine the time ordering of events. Armed with this information, policy-makers can better determine whether community activities serve as successful intervention methods for adolescent weapon carrying.

And, just as youths can become engaged in the community, communities should become involved with adolescents. It is possible, and even likely, that community intervention, in the form of teachers, social workers, coaches, parents, and criminal justice actors, working to resolve individual instances of adolescent weapon carrying, would serve to interrupt the behavior and de-escalate the arms race. It is imperative not only to institute community intervention techniques, but also to continue research to evaluate interruptive interventions by community members.

Summary

Having discussed the current state of research knowledge concerning adolescent weapon carrying motivations, demographics, and protective and risk factors, it is important to re-emphasize the policy implications that can be derived from those findings and the areas in which future research can expand. First, it is clear that very few studies explore adolescent weapon *use*. This is a substantial gap in the literature. Adolescent weapon use desperately needs attention. For example, we know that adolescents who carry guns participate in more crime (Lizotte *et al.*, 2002), but we do not know whether this applies to other weapons.

A second problem we see in the research literature is an overemphasis on adolescent weapon carrying in school. While incidents of mass school violence are horrific and receive a great deal of media attention, they are extremely rare. School-related violence accounted for less than 0.3% of US violent deaths between 2005 and 2009,[4] and homicides in schools accounted for approximately 1.3% of homicides of juveniles aged 5 to 18 from 1992 to 2009 (Robers, Zhang, & Truman, 2012). In fact, the rarity of school shootings and violence partially explains the overwhelming attention these incidents receive. Research regarding adolescent weapon carrying in schools could prove to be significant to policy if we could identify separate or specific protective or risk factors for carrying on and off school property. Such information would enable educators to employ intervention techniques against school weapon carrying. However, with the majority of research currently available focusing on school weapon carrying, comparative information regarding general adolescent weapon carrying is in short supply. As such, further research into general juvenile weapon carrying is necessary to the field of study.

Third, we emphasize three issues we discussed above: causal ordering, variety of weapon types, and gender. To substantiate causal explanations of adolescent weapon carrying and use, research *needs* to use longitudinal data and establish the time ordering of events. For example, does criminal behavior precede weapon carrying or follow it? Additionally, an overemphasis is often placed on guns and adolescents. Future research can vastly increase our current understanding of adolescents and weapons by broadening its scope to include the full arsenal of weapons that adolescents choose to carry. A single gender perspective on weapons similarly limits our understanding of adolescent weapon behaviors. Future literature should attempt to fill in the gaps of previous literature by studying female weapon carrying, or male *and* female weapon carrying.

Fourth, qualitative research could greatly expand current understandings of adolescent weapon carrying and use motivations. Ethnographic, mixed methods, or other qualitative pursuits can better explore how weapon carrying leads to delinquency, adolescent motivations for carrying, and other correlations observed with carrying, by asking and observing adolescents as they participate in carrying behaviors.

Finally, we recommend various policy implications throughout this chapter, but when reviewed as a whole, it is clear that drugs, violence, peers, family, and school all play a role in influencing weapon behaviors among adolescents. Policies and interventions focused on single influences will likely miss the bigger picture. As such, a holistic approach that attempts to change an adolescent's world through multiple avenues at once could be the most successful tactic to intervention.[5] Unfortunately, this approach is both underutilized and severely under-evaluated. We recommend that more practitioners use this intervention approach when confronting juvenile weapon carrying, and more scholars conduct research on the approach. Techniques for preventing and interrupting adolescent weapon carrying and use are vital to developing successful public policy.

Notes

1   Discussion does exist on the effectiveness of guns (see Kleck, 1991) and the interaction between weapon choice and intent to do harm, on level of injury by weapon type (see Wells & Horney, 2002).
2   Not to say that females do not participate in physical fights, just that participation in fights is not as likely to be linked with female weapon carrying.

3   In local samples where respondents know a large percentage of the local population, reports of peer weapon carrying may overlap as respondents all know a single peer who carries. This can result in overestimation of peer carrying.
4   Calculated based on data from the National Center for Education Statistics and National Violent Death Reporting System.
5   Similar proposals have been made for combatting general delinquency and gang membership (Thornberry *et al.*, 2003).

References

Altschuler, D.M., & Brounstein, P.J. (1991). Patterns of drug use, drug trafficking and other delinquency among inner city adolescent males in Washington, DC. *Criminology, 29*, 589–621.

Aspy, C.B., Oman, R.F., Vesely, S.K., McLeroy, K., Rodine, S., & Marshall, L. (2004). Adolescent violence: The protective effects of youth assets. *Journal of Counseling & Development, 82*(3), 268–276.

Bailey, S.L., Flewelling, R.L., & Rosenbaum, D.P. (1997). Characteristics of students who bring weapons to school. *Journal of Adolescent Health, 20*(5), 261–270.

Barlas, J., & Egan, V. (2006). Weapons carrying in British teenagers: The role of personality, delinquency, sensational interests, and mating effort. *Journal of Forensic Psychiatry & Psychology, 17*(1), 53–72.

Bauman, K.E., Botvin, G.J., Botvin, E.M., & Baker, E. (1992). Normative expectations and the behavior of significant others: An integration of traditions in research on adolescents' cigarette smoking. *Psychological Reports, 71*, 568–570.

Bennett, T., & Holloway, K. (2004). Possession and use of illegal guns among offenders in England and Wales. *Howard Journal of Criminal Justice, 43*(3), 237–252.

Bjerregaard, B., & Lizotte, A.J. (1995). Gun ownership and gang membership. *Journal of Criminal Law & Criminology, 86*(1), 37–58.

Bjerregaard, B., & Smith, C.A. (1993). Gender differences in gang participation, delinquency, and substance use. *Journal of Quantitative Criminology, 9*(4), 329–355.

Black, M.M., & Ricardo, I.B. (1994). Drug use, drug trafficking, and weapon carrying among low-income, African-American, early adolescent boys. *Pediatrics, 93*, 1065–1072.

Blum, R.W., Beuhring, T., Shew, M.L., Bearinger, L.H., Sieving, R.E., & Resnick, M.D. (2000). The effects of race/ethnicity, income, and family structure on adolescent risk behaviors. *American Journal of Public Health, 90*(12), 1879–1884.

Blumberg, E.J., Liles, S., Kelley, N.J., Hovell, M.F., Bousman, C.A., Shillington, A.M., Ji, M., *et al.* (2009). Predictors of weapon carrying in youth attending drop-in centers. *American Journal of Health Behavior, 33*(6), 745–758.

Blumstein, A. (1995a). Violence by young people: Why the deadly nexus? *National Institute of Justice Journal, August*, 1–9.

Blumstein, A. (1995b). Youth violence, guns, and the illicit-drug industry. *Journal of Criminal Law and Criminology, 86*, 10–36.

Brennan, I.R., & Moore, S.C. (2009). Weapons and violence: A review of theory and research. *Aggression and Violent Behavior, 14*(3), 215–225.

Brennan, I.R., Shepherd, J.P., & Moore, S.C. (2010). Aggression and attitudes to time and risk in weapon using violent offenders. *Psychiatry Research, 178*(3), 536–539.

Callahan, C.M., & Rivera, F.P. (1992). Urban high school youth and handguns. *Journal of the American Medical Association, 267,* 3038–3042.

Cao, L., Cullen, F.T., & Link, B.G. (1997). The social determinants of gun ownership: Self-protection in an urban environment. *Criminology, 35*(4), 629–658.

Centers for Disease Control and Prevention. (2001). *Youth Violence: A Report of the Surgeon General.* Washington, DC: Centers for Disease Control and Prevention.

Cook, P.J., & Ludwig, J. (2004). Does gun prevalence affect teen gun carrying after all? *Criminology, 42*(1), 27–54.

Cook, P.J., Ludwig, J., Venkatesh, S., & Braga, A.A. (2007). Underground gun markets. *The Economic Journal, 117,* F558–F588.

Decker, S.H., Pennell, S., & Caldwell, A. (1997). Illegal firearms: Access and use by arrestees. *National Institute of Justice in Brief, January,* 1–6.

Decker, S.H., & Van Winkle, B. (1996). *Life in the Gang.* New York: Cambridge University Press.

Dodge, K.A., Pettit, G.S., & Bates, J.E. (1997). How the experience of early physical abuse leads children to become chronically aggressive. In D. Cicchetti, & S.L. Toth (Eds.), *Developmental Perspectives on Trauma: Theory, Research, and Intervention* (pp. 263–288). Rochester, NY: University of Rochester Press.

Dukcs, R.L., Stein, J.A., & Zane, J.I. (2010). Gender differences in the relative impact of physical and relational bullying on adolescent injury and weapon carrying. *Journal of School Psychology, 48,* 511–532.

DuRant, R.H., Beckford, P.H., & Kahn, J. (1996). Weapon carrying on school property by high school students. *Journal of Adolescent Health, 18,* 124.

DuRant, R.H., Getts, A.G., Cadenhead, C., & Woods, E.R. (1995). The association between weapon carrying and the use of violence among adolescents living in and around public housing. *Journal of Adolescent Health, 17*(6), 376–380.

DuRant, R.H., Kahn, J., Beckford, P.H., & Woods, E.R. (1997). The association of weapon carrying and fighting on school property and other health risk and problem behaviors among high school students. *Archives Pediatric and Adolescent Medicine, 151*(4).

DuRant, R.H., Krowchuk, D.P., Kreiter, S., Sinal, S.H., & Woods, C.R. (1999). Weapon carrying on school property among middle school students. *Pediatrics & Adolescent Medicine, 153*(1), 21–26.

Emmert, A.D., & Lizotte, A.J. (2014). *Which comes first, weapons or crime? An examination of the causal order of weapon carrying and delinquency amon g adolescents.* Working paper. Albany, NY.

Ferguson, C.J., & Meehan, D.C. (2010). Saturday night's alright for fighting: antisocial traits, fighting, and weapons carrying in a large sample of youth. *Psychiatric Quarterly, 81*(4), 293–302.

Forrest, K.Y., Zychowski, A.K., Stuhldreher, W.L., & Ryan, W.J. (2000). Weapon-carrying in school: Prevalence and association with other violent behaviors. *American Journal of Health Studies, 16,* 133–140.

Hamilton, C.E., Falshaw, L., & Browne, K.D. (2002). The link between recurrent maltreatment and offending behaviour. *International Journal of Offender Therapy and Comparative Criminology, 46,* 75–94.

Hemenway, D., Vriniotis, M., Johnson, R.M., Miller, M.J., & Azrael, D. (2011). Gun carrying by high school students in Boston, MA: Does overestimation of peer gun carrying matter? *Journal of Adolescence, 34*(5), 997–1003.

Henrich, C.C., Brookmeyer, K.A., & Shahar, G. (2005). No weapon violence in adolescence: Parent and school connectedness as protective factors. *Journal of Adolescent Health, 37*(4), 306–312.

Herrera, V.M., & McCloskey, L.A. (2001). Gender differences in the risk for delinquency among youth exposed to family violence. *Child Abuse & Neglect, 25*, 1037–1051.

Hirschi, T. (1969). *Causes of Delinquency.* Berkeley, CA: University of California Press.

Horowitz, R. (1990). Sociological perspectives on gangs: Conflicting definitions and concepts. In C.R. Huff (Ed.), *Gangs in America.* Newbury Park, CA: Sage.

Jessor, R.J., van den Bos, J., Vanderryn, J., Costa, F.M., & Turbin, M.S. (1995). Protective factors in adolescent problem behavior: Moderator effects and developmental change. *Developmental Psychology, 31*, 923–933.

Jessor, R., & Jessor, S.L. (1977). *Problem Behavior and Psychosocial Development: A Longitudinal Study of Youth.* San Diego, CA: Academic Press.

Kleck, G. (1991). *Point Blank: Guns and Violence in America.* New York: Aldine De Gruyter.

Kodjo, C.M., Auinger, P., & Ryan, S.A. (2003). Demographic, intrinsic, and extrinsic factors associated with weapon carrying at school. *Archives of Pediatrics and Adolescent Medicine, 157*(1), 96–103.

Kulig, J., Valentine, J., Griffith, J., & Ruthazer, R. (1998). Predictive model of weapon carrying among urban high school students: Results and validation. *Journal of Adolescent Health, 22*(4), 312–319.

Lane, M.A., Cunningham, S.D., & Ellen, J.M. (2004). The intention of adolescents to carry a knife or gun: A study of low-income African American adolescents. *Journal of Adolescent Health, 34*(1), 72–78.

Lauritsen, J.L., Heimer, K., & Lynch, J.P. (2009). Trends in the gender gap in violent offending: New evidence from the National Crime Victimization Survey. *Criminology, 47*(2), 361–399.

Leeb, R.T., Barker, L.E., & Strine, T.W. (2007). The effect of childhood physical and sexual abuse on adolescent weapon carrying. *Journal of Adolescent Health, 40*, 551–558.

Lewis, T., Leeb, R.T., Kotch, J., Smith, J., Thompson, R., Black, M.M., Pelaez-Merrick, M., et al. (2007). Maltreatment history and weapon carrying among early adolescents. *Child Maltreatment, 12*(3), 259–268.

Lizotte, A.J., Bonsell, T.L., McDowall, D., Thornberry, T.P., & Krohn, M.D. (2002). Carrying guns and involvement in crime. In R.A. Silverman, T.P. Thornberry, B. Cohen, & B. Krisberg (Eds.), *Crime and Justice at the Millennium: Essays by and in Honor of Marvin E. Wolfgang* (pp. 145–158). Norwell, MA: Kluwer Academic Publishers.

Lizotte, A.J., Krohn, M.D., Howell, J.C., Tobin, K., & Howard, G.J. (2000). Factors influencing gun carrying among young urban males over the adolescent-young adult life course. *Criminology, 38*(3), 811–834.

Lowry, R., Powell, K.E., Kann, L., Collins, J.L., & Kolbe, L.J. (1998). Weapon carrying, physical fighting, and fight related injury among U.S. adolescents. *American Journal of Preventive Medicine, 14*, 122–129.

McCluskey, C.P., McCluskey, J.D., & Bynum, T.S. (2006). Early onset offending and later violent and gun outcomes in a contemporary youth cohort. *Journal of Criminal Justice, 34*(5), 531–541.

McKeganey, N., & Norrie, J. (2000). Association between illegal drugs and weapon carrying in young people in Scotland. *British Medical Journal, 320*(7240), 982–984.

Melde, C., Esbensen, F.F., & Taylor, T.J. (2009). "May piece be with you": A typological examination of the fear and victimization hypothesis of adolescent weapon carrying. *Justice Quarterly, 26*(2), 348–376.

Molnar, B.E., Miller, M.J., Azrael, D., & Buka, S.L. (2004). Neighborhood predictors of concealed firearm carrying among children and adolescents. *Archives of Pediatrics & Adolescent Medicine, 158*, 657–664.

Muula, A.S., Rudatsikira, E., & Siziya, S. (2008). Correlates of weapon carrying among high school students in the United States. *Annals of General Psychiatry, 7*, 8.

Orpinas, P., Murray, N., & Kelder, S. (1999). Parental influences on students' aggressive behaviors and weapon carrying. *Health Education & Behavior, 26*(6), 774–787.

Penny, H., Walker, J., & Gudjonsson, G.H. (2011). Development and preliminary validation of the Penny Beliefs Scale – Weapons (PBS-W). *Personality and Individual Differences, 51*(2), 102–106.

Rankin, J.H. (1983). The family context of delinquency. *Social Problems, 30*, 466–479.

Robers, S., Zhang, J., & Truman, J. (2012). *Indicators of School Crime and Safety: 2011*. Washington, DC: American Institutes for Research.

Sheley, J.F. (1994). Drugs and guns among inner-city high school students. *Journal of Drug Education, 24*, 303–321.

Sheley, J.F., McGee, Z.T., & Wright, J.D. (1992). Gun related violence in and around inner-city schools. *American Journal of Diseases of Children, 146*, 677–682.

Sheley, J.F., & Wright, J.D. (1993). Motivations for gun possession and carrying among serious juvenile offenders. *Behavioral Sciences and the Law, 11*, 375–388.

Simon, T.R., Crosby, A.E., & Dahlberg, L.L. (1999). Students who carry weapons to high school: Comparison with other weapon-carriers. *Journal of Adolescent Health, 24*(5), 340–348.

Smith, C.A., Lizotte, A.J., Thornberry, T.P., & Krohn, M.D. (1997). Resilience to delinquency. *The Prevention Researcher, 4*, 4–7.

Stewart, A., Dennison, S., & Waterson, E. (2002). Pathways from child maltreatment to juvenile offending. *Trends & Issues in Criminal Justice, 241*, 1–6.

Stouthamer-Loeber, M., Wei, E.H., Homish, D.L., & Loeber, R. (2002). Which family and demographic factors are related to both maltreatment and persistent serious juvenile delinquency? *Children's Services: Social Policy, Research, and Practice, 5*, 261–272.

Strodtbeck, F.L., & Short, J.F. (1964). An explanation of gang action. *Social Problems, 12*, 127–140.

Thornberry, T.P., Krohn, M.D., Lizotte, A.J., Smith, C.A., & Tobin, K. (2003). *Gang and Delinquency in Developmental Prespective*. New York: Cambridge University Press.

Valois, R.F., McKeown, R.E., Garrison, C.Z., & Vincent, M.L. (1995). Correlates of aggressive and violent behaviors among public high school adolescents. *Journal of Adolescent Health, 16*, 26–34.

Vanderschmidt, H.F., Lang, J.M., Knight-Williams, V., & Vanderschmidt, G.F. (1993). Risks among inner-city young teens: The prevalence of sexual activity, violence, drugs, and smoking. *Journal of Adolescent Health, 14*(4), 282–288.

Vaughn, M.G., Howard, M.O., & Harper-Chang, L. (2006). Do prior trauma and victimization predict weapon carrying among delinquent youth? *Youth Violence and Juvenile Justice, 4*(4), 314–327.

Vaughn, M.G., Perron, B.E., Abdon, A., Olate, R., Groom, R., & Wu, L. (2012). Correlates of handgun carrying among adolescents in the United States. *Journal of Interpersonal Violence, 27*(10), 2003–2021.

Warr, M. (2000). Fear of crime in the United States: Avenues for research and policy. In D. Duffee (Ed.), *Measurement and Analysis of Crime and Justice (Vol. 4)*. Washington, DC: US Department of Justice.

Watkins, A.M., Huebner, B.M., & Decker, S.H. (2008). Patterns of gun acquisition, carrying, and use among juvenile and adult arrestees: Evidence from a high crime city. *Justice Quarterly, 25*(4), 674–700.

Webster, D.W., Gainer, P.S., & Champion, H.R. (1993). Weapon carrying among inner-city junior high school students: Defensive behavior vs aggressive delinquency. *American Journal of Public Health, 83*(11), 1604–1608.

Wells, W., & Horney, J. (2002). Weapon effects and individual intent to do harm: Influences on the escalation of violence. *Criminology, 40*(2), 265–296.

Wilcox, P., May, D.C., & Roberts, S.D. (2006). Student weapon possession and the "fear and victimization hypothesis": Unraveling the temporal order. *Justice Quarterly, 23*(4), 502–529.

Wilkinson, D.L., & Fagan, J.A. (1996). The role of firearms in violence "scripts": The dynamics of gun events among adolescent males. *Law & Contemporary Problems, 59*(1), 55–89.

Williams, S.S., Mulhall, P.F., Reis, J.S., & DeVille, J.O. (2002). Adolescents carrying handguns and taking them to school: psychosocial correlates among public school students in Illinois. *Journal of Adolescence, 25*, 551–567.

Wright, J.D., Rossi, P.H., & Daly, K. (1983). *Under the Gun: Weapons, Crime, and Violence in America*. New York: Aldine.

Wright, J.D., Sheley, J.F., & Smith, M.D. (1992). Kids, guns, and killing fields. *Society, 30*, 84–89.

33

Youth Drug Trends and Societal Reactions

John M. Stogner and Bryan Lee Miller

Introduction

One of the greatest concerns facing America is the use of intoxicating substances by youth. Drug use among our nation's youth remains a major public health concern, as substance use and abuse drastically increases the risk of injury, violence, antisocial behavior, and the spread of infectious diseases (Centers for Disease Control and Prevention, 2013a). In addition to the negative health consequences of drug use and abuse, crimes associated with drug use, including drug dealing, trafficking, crimes of acquisition, and violence within the illicit drug markets, remain a great concern and result in a large number of arrests (OJJDP, 2013). The purpose of this chapter is to explore several of the most common explanations for youth drug use, review trends in various forms of substance use among adolescents, and evaluate the role of the juvenile justice system in dealing with the drug problem.

A Brief Introduction to Theories of Drug Use and Drug Data

Explanations of youth drug use can generally be categorized as psychological, biological, or criminological/sociological theories. Psychological theories of drug use and addiction often focus on the impact that reinforcement has on drug use, continuance, and dependence. Similar to any activity that is able to produce an enjoyable experience, drug experimentation and continued use is explained through positive reinforcement or, in other words, the desire to repeat pleasurable sensations (McAuliffe & Gordon, 1975).

The Handbook of Juvenile Delinquency and Juvenile Justice, First Edition. Edited by Marvin D. Krohn and Jodi Lane.
© 2015 John Wiley & Sons, Inc. Published 2015 by John Wiley & Sons, Inc.

Biological theories largely focus on physical mechanisms that, under certain environmental conditions, may influence whether an individual experiments with (or escalates use of) drugs. These theories often focus on how different genes or combinations of genes may interact with the environment to alter the likelihood or level of substance use. Further, they note that genetic factors may affect the way in which the body metabolizes various drugs, builds a tolerance, or experiences negative or pleasurable reactions to drug use.

In the field of criminology, three main theories developed to explain deviance more generally are often applied to drug use. Considered to be "core" criminological theories, Akers' (2009) social learning theory, Agnew's (1992) general strain theory, and Gottfredson and Hirschi's (1990) low self-control theory have each been repeatedly used to explain youth drug use (Cullen, Wright, & Blevins, 2008). Akers (2009) explains that drug use (and continuance or desistance) is connected to peer behaviors, favorable or unfavorable definitions of a behavior, and anticipated rewards and punishments. Agnew's (1992) general strain theory, on the other hand, argued that anger and other negative emotions are the products of stress that individuals may try to alleviate through drug use. Gottfredson and Hirschi (1990) argued that low self-control, or the inability to refrain from pleasurable acts that produce instant gratification, is the single factor that drives drug use and other negative behaviors.

Data on youth drug use falls into several broad categories. Official crime statistics that are collected by law enforcement are useful in determining the amount of arrests, dispositions, and treatment diversion for drug offenders, but are seldom able to capture the full extent of youth drug use. In order to better understand adolescent drug use, criminologists have mainly relied on self-report surveys, interviews, and ethnographies of drug users. In the US, national data on juvenile drug use primarily comes from several large-scale self-report surveys that are administered annually. These surveys employ complex methodological sampling techniques to produce nationally representative data that allows researchers to track youth drug trends over time. Most notably, Monitoring the Future (MTF), the National Survey on Drug Use and Health (NSDUH), and the Youth Risk Behavior Survey (YRBS) provide researchers with information about national trends in youth drug use.

Tobacco

While academics and policymakers often view tobacco as the most minor drug, or even fail to consider it a drug at all, it is typically one of the first substances used by juveniles and contributes to more deaths than all other psychoactive substances combined (Centers for Disease Control and Prevention, 2013b). Tobacco is administered in numerous ways, including pipes, cigars, cigarettes, chewing tobacco, and snuff. In the US, cigarette smoking is the most common form of tobacco consumption and is linked to nearly half a million deaths (Centers for Disease Control and Prevention, 2013b), US$96 billion of healthcare expenditure, and US$97 billion in lost productivity each year (Centers for Disease Control and Prevention, 2008).

Tobacco use and production is intricately woven into the history of the US, and it is therefore not surprising that reducing tobacco use is a complex and challenging task. Tobacco use in America pre-dates the formation of the United States, and restrictions on tobacco sales to minors were even established in some states prior to the Civil War (Hanson, Venturelli, & Fleckenstein, 2011). Despite restrictions, tobacco consumption rapidly increased following the invention of the cigarette-rolling machine in the late nineteenth century, which allowed the mass production of cheap cigarettes (Kluger, 2010). Use reached a precipice in the mid-1960s, at which time the Surgeon General released *Smoking and Health*, summarizing the known dangers of smoking (United States Surgeon General's Advisory Committee on Smoking, 1964). Use later began to plummet as a result of advertising restrictions, non-smokers rights movements, massive increases in federal taxes, and increased health consciousness (Brandt, 2007).

Juvenile cigarette usage began a rapid decline in the late 1990s. Whereas nearly 60% of high-school students had smoked cigarettes in 1996, only 27% of juveniles reported having smoked in 2012 (Johnston, O'Malley, Bachman, & Schulenberg, 2013). Daily juvenile smoking has similarly fallen from 16.9% to only 5.2%, and the prevalence of half-pack daily smokers is less than a quarter of what it was just 15 years ago. Smokeless tobacco prevalence among teenagers has also fallen from 26% in the mid-1990s to 13.5% today (Johnston *et al.*, 2013). These decreases have been attributed to heightened perceptions of risk and decreased approval of tobacco consumption among teens. While these numbers indicate that the attempt to curtail juvenile smoking has been highly successful, teen tobacco use still represents a significant concern. It is estimated that 4,000 adolescents try their first cigarette each day and a thousand of these youth become daily smokers (Centers for Disease Control and Prevention, 2013b). Multiple strategies continue to be employed to further reduce smoking generally, and specifically teen smoking, including bans on indoor smoking, increased cigarette taxes, health-related advertising campaigns, enhanced social stigmatization of tobacco, and population-based tobacco cessation programs (Fernander, Rescinow, Visnawath, & Pérez-Stable, 2011). Recent studies have suggested that these interventions have had a much greater impact on reducing tobacco use among middle and upper class youth, compared with the lower classes (Durkin, Biener, & Wakefield, 2009).

Alcohol

Due to its widespread use and pharmacological effects, alcohol use by juveniles perhaps represents a more expansive problem than all other psychoactive substances combined. Each year, 80,000 deaths in the US are linked to alcohol, and the economy bears an estimated burden of US$223.5 billion in alcohol-related damages (Centers for Disease Control and Prevention, 2013c). The acute effects of the drug increase the likelihood of injuries, physical altercations, violence, traffic accidents, and risky sexual behaviors, while long-term use is associated with hepatitis, cirrhosis, mouth cancer, cardiovascular issues, and problems with family and work. Adolescent use accounts for 5,000 deaths annually and is additionally problematic in that the majority of underage drinking occurs in the form of binge drinking (Centers for Disease Control and Prevention, 2013c). Further, adolescent drivers under the influence of alcohol present an even greater concern than adult drivers due to their limited experience behind the wheel.

Much like tobacco, alcohol has long been utilized by juveniles in the US despite regulations and restrictions. Following prohibition, most states instituted a minimum age of 21 for alcohol purchase. Many dropped the restriction to a lower age in the 1970s and later returned it to 21 in the early 1980s as a result of the National Minimum Drinking Age Act. Alcohol and binge drinking among adolescents in the US peaked during the years that many states had lower minimum drinking ages (Johnston et al., 2013), but as other drug use also peaked at this time, so readers should not infer that the lowered drinking age was solely responsible for alcohol's heightened use by juveniles.

Whereas over 40% of high-school seniors reported binge drinking in the last two weeks in the early 1980s, only 24% of seniors in 2012 reported the behavior, though 54.2% reported having been drunk and 69.4% had consumed alcohol at some point in their lifetime (Johnston et al., 2013). The reductions in binge drinking are associated with heightened perceptions of risks among teens and increased social disapproval. These findings from Monitoring the Future mirror those of both the NSDUH and the Youth Risk Behavior Survey. However, drunk driving remains a major issue; getting behind the wheel in the last month after drinking to the point of intoxication is still reported by 8% of adolescent drivers.

One of the reasons adolescents may choose to consume alcohol and binge drink may be linked to their perceptions of social norms and peer behaviors. Perkins and Berkowitz (1986) suggested that young people strongly overestimate the alcohol intake of their peers, and as a result increase their own use to a level consistent with their misperception. Extant research supports their hypotheses and suggests that a person's perceptions of others' behavior may be a stronger influence on their own behavior than their peers' actual behavior (Perkins, Haines, & Rice, 2005). As such, one potentially effective direction for intervention efforts is to combat the misperceptions of alcohol-related normative behaviors. Programs based on these assumptions are labeled "social norms campaigns" and attempt to alter perceived norms so that they are more consistent with actual social norms. It appears that social norms campaigns, at least in the short-run, can effectively reduce youthful alcohol consumption and driving under the influence (Haines & Spear, 1996).

Treatment for a juvenile's problematic alcohol use is often more challenging than that of an adult (Kinney, 2009). First, alcohol use is often a form of rebellion, and participation in a treatment program can be viewed as releasing the autonomy perceived to be gained through drinking. Second, juvenile alcohol use is affected by numerous factors outside of their own personal control. Family influences may have contributed to the problem, or the family may have excused, ignored, or covered up the problem (Kinney, 2009). To be effective, juvenile alcohol treatment often needs to affect the family environment as much as the individual, but changing an environment is more difficult than changing an individual's response. Overall, treatment and recovery options for juveniles are quite diverse, ranging from intensive in-patient programs to self-help groups, but most successful programs share a few common elements. These include a focus on patient responsibility, feedback about risk, personalized advice, empathy, improved self-efficacy, and multiple routes to recovery (Walters, Bennett, & Miller, 2000).

Marijuana

Marijuana is the illicit drug most widely used by youth in the US. Marijuana is a product of the cannabis plant, a complex organism that contains over 400 chemicals including 61 with psychoactive properties, collectively referred to as cannabinoids. The most potent and common cannabinoid is Tetrahydrocannabinol (THC), but other chemicals such as Cannabidiol (CBD) and Cannabinol (CBN) are contained within the cannabis plant. What is typically sold as marijuana in the US is the flowering tops (buds) of the female plants *Cannabis sativa* or *Cannabis indica,* and is primarily smoked either in hand-rolled joints, cigars, pipes, or water pipes (bongs). Although sometimes the leaves of the plant may contain psychoactive compounds and may be sold as marijuana, this has become less common. An even more potent form of cannabis is produced through a process of compressing or purifying the stalked resin glands of the female plant and is often referred to as "hashish" or simply "hash". Because marijuana is a very complex and unique substance, at different times it has been classified as a hallucinogen, sedative, depressant, narcotic, stimulant, and a psychomimetic (producing psychotic symptoms such as paranoid delusions). This difficulty in fitting marijuana into one of these categories has led most experts to put marijuana in a category by itself (Goode, 2011).

Marijuana use has its origins in the ancient medicine and religious practices in Central and South Asia. During the colonization period, the British denounced the use of marijuana. Although during this time period the strong fibers of the cannabis plant were largely used for rope, paper, and other goods, the use of marijuana for intoxication was not popular in North America before the twentieth century. In contrast, the Spanish were familiar with the smoking of cannabis and permitted slaves to plant it between rows of sugar cane in Central and South America. Natives of the region adopted cannabis into their medical and religious traditions, and use spread to the Caribbean and Mexico (Courtwright, 2001). Mexican immigrants introduced cannabis smoking into the US in the early 1900s, and it became popular among jazz musicians in the 1930s. The Marihuana Tax Act of 1937 effectively banned the use of marijuana. During the 1960s marijuana emerged again as a popular drug and was embraced by the "hippie" and youth subcultures.

Use among adolescents peaked in the 1970s, but has remained relatively stable since. In 1979, over half of 12th graders reported using marijuana in the last year, while this number dropped to a low of 22% in 1992, and has risen again to 34% in

2012 (Johnston *et al.*, 2013). In recent years, there have been slight increases in marijuana use among high-school students. Since 2009, past-month marijuana use among 12th graders has surpassed cigarette smoking. This may be related to teens' perception of marijuana's harmfulness, which has decreased in recent years. Only 20.6% of 12th graders see occasional marijuana use as harmful, which is the lowest level since 1983, while 44.1% see regular marijuana use as harmful, the lowest level since 1979 (Johnston *et al.*, 2013).

One thing that has changed in recent years is that the potency of marijuana has dramatically increased. A more recent trend in marijuana use among both adults and adolescents is the use of butane-extracted hash oil (BHO) often referred to as "shatter," "budder," "wax," or "taffy," which is produced by extracting the cannabinoids from the plant using a butane gas solvent. The result of this process is a concentrated resin (taking on different textures depending on the process) that can contain over 80% THC. To put this in context, the THC in wild cannabis is typically less than 1%, average marijuana sold on the streets in the US in recent years is about 3%, higher grades being about 4–8%, hashish has about 8–14%, and hash oil up to about 50% (Goode, 2011). Through a process referred to as "dabbing", the user dips a metal rod into the substance and then heats the dap using a heating devise such as a pipe, bong, vaporizer, or specially designed tool known as an "oil rig", and inhales the vapors produced. Users claim that a small amount of BHO (a dab) the size of a Tic-Tac can be compared with smoking an entire joint in one massive toke. Experienced marijuana users have compared dabbing to "getting high for the very first time. Your head spins, your eyes get fluttery, a few beads of sweat surface on your forehead and, suddenly, you're *cosmically* baked" (Breathes, 2013, p. 1). Many marijuana activists believe that dabbing may set back their cause, with the potent effects being more similar to that of hard drugs, new devices more closely resembling crack pipes than marijuana paraphernalia, and homemade BHO operations resulting in injuries from meth-lab-like explosions from amateur chemists working with volatile gases (Breathes, 2013).

Along with dabbing, recent changes in marijuana legislation such as the state-level legalization of marijuana use within Colorado and Washington, along with medical marijuana in 19 states and the District of Columbia, have allowed new innovations in the forms of marijuana products. A wide array of new products have become available at medical dispensaries, including edible marijuana products such as baked goods, candy bars, and breath sprays. These products have been criticized for containing high quantities of THC and may pose new dangers to users (Fitzgerald, Bronstein, & Newquist, 2013). Although most of these states prohibit minors from purchasing and engaging in the use of marijuana (even with legitimate medical reasons), increased legal access for adults to these substances and innovations in marijuana products have prompted many to worry about diversion to adolescents. This is particularly an area of concern with the first marijuana retail stores in Colorado opening in 2014.

Marijuana use is deeply embedded in youth culture and is often considered a "gateway drug" because it is typically an adolescent's first exposure to an illicit substance. Due to this status, a large plethora of criminological research has evaluated the various reasons why youth engage in marijuana use (Ulmer, Desmond, Jang, & Johnson, 2012; Tang & Orwin, 2009). Research suggests that among adolescents, peers play a vital role in the initiation of marijuana use (Coronges, Stacy, & Valente, 2011; Creemer *et al.*, 2010). Although marijuana does not have strong withdrawal symptoms, habitual marijuana use can become problematic especially for adolescents, because frequent use can affect cognitive processes during the development of the brain. As of 2009, there were over 100,000 youths between the age of 12 and 17 in treatment for habitual marijuana use (Treatment Episode Data Set, 2012). Additionally, one of the primary targets of drug education campaigns, including the Partnership for a Drug Free America, has been to focus on preventing youth marijuana use. Between 1998 and 2005, over US$1.4 billion was spent on anti-marijuana campaigns targeting teens (Dubey, 2012).

Stimulants

Unlike marijuana, recreationally used drugs in the stimulant category have a high potential for dependence. These substances lead users to feel energetic, alert, and euphoric, which can become strongly reinforcing. While there is some variability in their mechanisms of actions, speed of onset, duration, and potential for dependence, drugs in this category typically excite the sympathetic nervous system leading to changes associated with a "flight or fight" response: increased heartbeat and breathing rate, heightened alertness, restlessness, and decreased hunger. This category includes all forms of amphetamines, methamphetamine, and cocaine. As is the case with most drugs, substances in this category can be administered in multiple ways which affects the intensity and duration of their psychoactive effects. The most immediate, strongest, and most reinforcing effects follow inhalation or intravenous injection, though some users rely on insufflation or ingestion.

While cocaine was introduced and used in the US in the late 1800s, cocaine use became minimal after the Harrison Act of 1914 (Ashley, 1975). Similarly, amphetamines were first synthesized in 1887 but not heavily misused until World War II (Grinspoon & Heblom, 1975). Cocaine use reappeared in the 1960s, with use slowly escalating and then exploding in the late 1970s and early 1980s. Whereas only 1% had ever used cocaine in the 1960s, a quarter of the young adult population had tried cocaine by the mid-1980s (Musto, 1991). Though Monitoring the Future did not begin assessing use rates of high-school students until 1975, juvenile use seems to have followed a similar trend, topping out at 17.3% in 1985 (Johnston *et al.*, 2013). The cocaine boom included the spread of smoking crack-cocaine, but was not driven by it, as all forms of cocaine use increased during this timeframe and the initial increase preceded the widespread use of crack-cocaine (Hatsukami & Fischman, 1996; Johnston *et al.*, 2013). Illicit stimulant use dropped in the 1990s to near its present levels.

Presently, only 4.9% of high-school students report ever having used cocaine, and 2.1% report having used crack-cocaine (Johnston *et al.*, 2013). Amphetamine use is more common (12%), but methamphetamine has only been used by 1.7%. Frequent use by juveniles is uncommon, with no more than 0.3% reporting daily use of any of these drugs (Johnston *et al.*, 2013).

Stimulants are not linked to the typical model of addiction; that is, they are not associated with a strong physical dependence, and ceasing use does not typically yield strong withdrawal symptoms. However, they can lead to the development of an intense psychological dependence which is equally challenging to treat (Goode, 2011). Stimulant dependence does not seem to be as amenable to pharmacological therapies as other drugs, but levodopa, amantadine, and others may aid in the recovery process (Amato *et al.*, 2011). Recovery programs typically have high dropout rates (Agosti, Nunes, Stewart, & Quitkin, 1991) and therefore may be most efficient when backed by the threat of legal consequences. A variety of in-patient and out-patient treatment programs exist that largely focus on cognitive–behavioral therapy (Bahr, Masters, & Taylor, 2012). Research by Ahmadi and colleagues (2009) suggests that increasing self-efficacy and decreasing depressive symptoms may be the most crucial parts of any recovery program.

Heroin

Heroin is a very potent narcotic synthesized from the opium poppy, a flowering plant historically used for medicine, food (through its seeds), and ornamental purposes. As a form of medicine, it is used to treat severe pain, but is referred to as diamorphine as so not to be confused with the illicit form of the drug. Heroin, often known as "dope", "h", "horse", and "smack", like other opiates produces euphoric, analgesic (pain relief), and anxiolytic (anti-anxiety) effects. Heroin can be smoked (in a freebase form) and inhaled, but is best known for its users' intravenous injection of the drug, which imbues an extremely high risk for overdosing, dependency, and transmitting infectious diseases (most notably HIV/AIDS).

Opium use and cultivation of the poppy plant first emerged in central Europe in 1600 BC and spread into the eastern Mediterranean and the southeast (Merlin, 1984). The opium poppy became prominent in medicine for treating anxiety, fatigue, and pain. As Islam frowned upon alcohol, opium became popular as an alternative recreational substance (Courtwright, 2001). Opium use became widespread during the period of Colonization and became important to British trade, leading to two large-scale conflicts with China (referred to as the Opium Wars) in the mid-nineteenth century (Courtwright, 2001). In 1803, Friedrich Serturner, a German pharmacist, discovered the alkaloid morphine, and in 1874, C.R. Alder Wright first synthesized what is now known as heroin. However, it did not gain popularity until it was re-synthesized, marketed, and labeled as heroin (linking it to "heroic") by Bayer in 1897. International pressures, including a ban on opiates in US-controlled Philippines, led to the passage of the Harrison Narcotic Act of 1914, which prevented the non-medical use of opiates including heroin. Several groups at various times, including the Chinese Triads and the Sicilian Mafia, have controlled illicit heroin distribution. After major arrests in the 1970s, heroin distribution shifted to Southeast Asia, in what is known as the Golden Triangle. Recently, heroin in the US has largely come from Mexico, Colombia, and Afghanistan.

Heroin, largely because of its powerful effects and reputation as a "hard" drug, has always been more popular among adults than juveniles. The average age for first-time use of heroin is 22 years, and most users are adult (SAMHSA, 2006). In 1980, *Washington Post* writer Janet Cooke's vivid and Pulitzer Prize-winning description of an 8-year-old heroin addict's life increased concerns about heroin use among youths. Her story was later found to be completely fabricated and the award rescinded. Schneider's (2008) exploration of the post-World War II heroin panic suggests that the fear of drug pushers forcing heroin on adolescents was far greater than the reality. According to Monitoring the Future, heroin use among youths has remained relatively low, with less than 2% of 12th grade students reporting past-year heroin use in each year from 1975 through 2012 (Johnston, O'Malley, Bachman, & Schulenberg, 2011; Johnston *et al.*, 2013).

One of the biggest challenges with heroin and all opiates is that they have the potential for very strong physical dependencies and severe withdrawal symptoms. Because of the withdrawal symptoms, treatment for heroin is difficult and several programs employ the use of methadone (or buprenorphine) maintenance, a contro-versial treatment program that supplies heroin users with a weaker and longer-lasting opioid to prevent withdrawal symptoms. In the US there are over 1,000 methadone clinics (SAMHSA, 2006). Other harm reduction treatment programs popular in other countries have started to be embraced in the US, including needle exchange programs, and safe-use zones where users can administer heroin without fear of arrest. These programs often provide rehabilitation counselors and treatment information to help heroin users take the first steps into treatment. These sites may also include heroin testing kits to provide users with information about the purity of the substance. The goal of these programs is to reduce harms associated with the use of heroin, including the spread of infectious diseases that affect intravenous heroin users. Although these programs have been largely successful in parts of Europe and Canada, they remain controversial and are often met with resistance in the US as opponents argue that they enable drug use.

Pharmaceutical misuse

One category of recreational drugs whose use has appeared to escalate in recent decades is pharmaceuticals (Johnston *et al.*, 2013). While prescription medications are authorized tools of the legitimate healthcare industry, many products have the potential to be misused by individuals seeking to achieve euphoria, relax, increase alertness, or otherwise alter their body. Since pharmaceutical use has legally sanc-tioned purposes, it is appropriate to distinguish legitimate from problematic use. As such, the intake of any prescription medical product outside of the direction of a physician, including those with valid prescriptions taking more than recommended or altering a drug, is referred to as *pharmaceutical misuse*. Pharmaceutical misuse can be subdivided into the categories of instrumental and recreational misuse. Pharmaceutical misuse can be further divided based on drug type. McCabe, Boyd, and Teter (2009) discuss the major categories of pharmaceutical misuse as including analgesics, sedatives, and stimulants, but their taxonomy may benefit from adding a category for substances such as anabolic steroids and human growth hormone which are increasingly being taken to develop skeletal muscle and androgenic traits (van Amsterdam, Opperhuizen & Hartgens, 2010).

The recreational misuse of pharmaceuticals in America is far from a new phenomenon. In fact, many of the substances that are now referred to as "street drugs" were once frequently utilized by physicians and offered to juveniles and adults alike. For example, cocaine was used and championed by numerous physicians including Sigmund Freud (Musto, 1998), and ecstasy (MDMA) was first patented by Merck and later evaluated by Dow (Freudenmann, Oxler, & Bernschneider-Reif, 2006). Many of the substances used by previous generations of juveniles to get high were produced by pharmaceutical companies; however, the focus on pharmaceuticals as a single group of misused substances is a more recent phenomenon. One trait these pharmacologically diverse products share that makes their study as a group beneficial is that potential misusers often misinterpret the drugs' safety due to their use in legitimate medicine. The false sense of safety that adolescents perceive towards recreational pharmaceutical misuse is linked to the belief that products prescribed by a physician are generally safe (Schachter, 2012) and may have contributed to the recent increase in pharmaceutical misuse (Compton & Volkow, 2006).

Monitoring the Future reports that pharmaceuticals are now the third most widely used category of recreational drug behind marijuana and alcohol (Johnston *et al.*, 2013). Use among teens substantially increased between the mid-1990s and late 2000s, but has become more stable in recent years. Overall, 14.3% of students report pharmaceutical misuse in the last year, and 21.2% of high-school seniors report recreationally using a pharmaceutical at some point in their life (Johnston *et al.*, 2013). While these numbers appear quite high, it should be noted that even the most common pharmaceuticals are used by fewer than 5% in the last year (Adderall 4.4%, Vicadin 4.3%, OxyContin 2.9%).

Given that the US is prescribed and purchases more pharmaceuticals than any other country per capita (Kanavos, Ferrario, Vandoros, & Anderson, 2013), it is not surprising that pharmaceutical diversion to, and misuse by, teens is a significant problem. A number of states have instituted closer monitoring of prescribing practices by physicians and purchases by consumers through prescription drug monitoring programs (or PDMPs). Monitoring programs, however, may only indirectly affect the misuse by juveniles, who unlike adults do not obtain pharmaceuticals through "doctor shopping" and fraud. Adolescents instead report obtaining pharmaceuticals from family members, friends, or misuse drugs prescribed to them (Johnston, O'Malley, Bachman, & Schulenberg, 2012). Use of several drugs in this category can lead to dependence and necessitate treatment and counseling, similar to their illicit counterparts described in other sections.

Club drugs

What have been referred to as "club drugs" first became popular with teenagers in the 1980s and 1990s and are closely associated with the "rave" and electronic music subcultures. Including ecstasy (MDMA), GHB, and ketamine, club drugs gained their reputation as substances that could enhance dance parties. Raves emerged as large-scale dance parties centered around electronic music that would often continue through the night. Drugs have long been associated with dancing, with alcohol being the most common, but this new group of synthetic substances became popular among a more technologically advanced youth subculture.

In 1965 while working as a biochemist for Dow Chemicals, Alexander Shulgin synthesized and evaluated MDMA (3,4-methylenedioxy-N-methylamphetamine), a chemical relative of the stimulant MDA (3,4-methylenedioxyamphetamine). MDMA has been found to raise levels of serotonin, dopamine, and norepinephrine, increase empathy, and be useful in marriage counseling. Unlike other amphetamines, MDMA releases more serotonin than dopamine or norepinephrine, leading to an elevated mood with feelings of euphoria, intimacy, and closeness to others.

Often also categorized as club drugs is a subset of substances known for their sedative properties and use in drug-facilitated sexual assaults or "date rape". Known by the trade name Rohypnol or the street name roofies, flunitrazepam is a powerful sedative and used medically with those suffering from insomnia. GHB (4-hydroxybutanoic acid) also falls into this category and has been used as an anesthetic, sleeping aid, and hypnotic. GHB initially became popular among bodybuilders for its ability to elevate growth hormones, and was sold in health food stores. Unlike flunitrazepam, GHB produces euphoria, disinhibition, enhanced sensuality, and empathogenic states, and has been compared to alcohol and MDMA. In small amounts, GHB can act as a stimulant and enhance a partygoer's experience, prompting users to refer to it as "liquid ecstasy", "liquid X" and "liquid E."

Ketamine is often categorized as a club drug, but has dissociative and anesthetic properties. Used primarily in veterinarian medicine, ketamine is used less frequently on humans because of its hallucinogenic properties. Recreational users describe some effects of the drug as similar to PCP (phencyclidine); many users take high doses in order to reach a state referred to as the "k-hole", which creates an out-of-body experience that mimics the effects of catatonic schizophrenia (Giannini, 1997).

Large-scale recreational ecstasy use was first reported in 1980, and use steadily increased until it peaked in 2001. At the peak of its use, 2.2% of those aged 12–17 and 9.2% of 12th graders had used MDMA in the last year (Maxwell, 2004). One explanation for the decline in MDMA use since 2001 is its decreased availability and purity. Monitoring the Future indicates that students perceived the availability of MDMA to be declining each year since 2001. Past-year use for ketamine, GHB, and flunitrazepam also peaked around this time, with 2.6%, 1.5%, and 1.6% of 12th graders reporting use (Johnston *et al.*, 2013; Maxwell, 2004).

One of the biggest concerns with club drugs is the threat of dehydration and over-heating, given that they are often used while dancing in warm environments. MDMA can interfere with the body's ability to regulate temperature and possibly lead to hyperthermia. Harm reduction approaches have tried to tackle this issue by educating club drug users, especially those who use MDMA, to drink plenty of water and to take breaks from dancing. Rollsafe.org has set up a web-based information guide to try to reduce MDMA-related harms. Recently, a new form of MDMA referred to as "molly" has become more popular and typically refers to a purified version of the substance in a concentrated powder or crystalline form (Kahn, Ferraro, & Benveniste, 2012).

Novel and emerging drugs

Over the last decade, a number of novel drugs have gained a foothold in society and a degree of popularity among adolescents and young adults. We refer to this group of compounds as "novel drugs" or "emerging drugs" because their recent introduction to the drug scene unites them more than their pharmacological effects. Many academics have referred to "legal highs" (Griffin, Miller, & Khey, 2008) or synthetic legal intoxicating drugs (Jerry, Collins, & Streem, 2012), but this nomenclature is inappropriate as many drugs that fall into the category are regulated in some way, and some are naturally occurring substances that are simply new to recreational use (Loeffler, Hurst, Penn, & Yung, 2012). Many of these drugs may represent a brief fad, and will no longer be a significant social concern following their regulation and diminishing novelty (Stogner, Khey, Griffin, Miller, & Boman, 2012). However, all commonly used drugs were at one point novel, and we have recently seen substances such as MDMA transition from a novel drug to a somewhat stable drug concern.

Two of the more publicized types of novel drugs are synthetic compounds that contain molecular structures similar to those of naturally occurring controlled substances (Loeffler *et al.*, 2012). Manufacturers created synthetic cannabinoids and synthetic cathinones in order to market compounds with effects similar to marijuana and stimulants, respectively, while avoiding legal penalties (Loeffler *et al.*, 2012). Synthetic cannabinoids, often referred to as "Spice" (the name of one of the more popular brands), are sold in packets containing dried inactive plant material that has been sprayed with the synthetic cannabinoids (Dresen *et al.*, 2010). When smoked, their effects are similar to that of marijuana. Synthetic cathinones are sympathomimetic compounds casually referred to as "bath salts" or "plant food" due to being labeled as such to avoid regulation as a food or drug product. They are typically manufactured as a powder and their effects are most similar to cocaine or methamphetamine (Loeffler *et al.*, 2012).

Another recent novel drug phenomenon is the increased use and retail sale of *Salvia divinorum*. Salvia can have a short-acting dissociative effect on users, although a variety of effects have been reported (Grundmann, Phipps, Zadezensksy, & Butterweck, 2007). Salvia, a naturally occurring plant, has long been used in the

Oaxaca region of Mexico in religious ceremonies and as a healing drink, but it emerged as a drug of concern in the late 1990s in the US. Partially responsible for this transition was it being smoked or inhaled as opposed to the more traditional chewing of leaves or brewing in teas (Dennehy, Tsourounis, & Miller, 2005). Additionally, manufacturers began to market packages of salvia that were impregnated with higher concentrations of salvinorin A, the main psychoactive compound.

The popularity of some novel drugs can be linked to their initial status as a "legal high". Most were initially inexpensive and readily available in gas stations, "head" shops, tattoo parlors, and online. Adolescents could purchase psychoactive products without associating with a street dealer or fearing legal ramifications. Additionally, they were initially not detected on standard drug screens, which may account for their use by athletes, probationers, and members of the armed services (European Monitoring Centre for Drugs and Drug Addiction, 2009). The US has taken steps to ban some novel drugs. Following several state bans, the Federal government scheduled some synthetic cannabinoids in 2011, and eventually scheduled all synthetic cannabinoids in 2012 (Food and Drug Safety and Innovation Act, 2012). Synthetic cathinones were also permanently scheduled in 2012 after a temporary scheduling that was implemented in August 2011. Salvia is federally legal, although the Drug Enforcement Agency has labeled it a "drug of concern" (Griffin *et al.*, 2008) and the majority of southeastern states have scheduled it (Stogner *et al.*, 2012).

The use of novel drugs appears to be most common among young adults; however, many of the data sources for adolescent drug use do not include novel drugs until their use is somewhat widespread. In 2011, Monitoring the Future added questions about synthetic marijuana (synthetic cannabinoids) to the study. At that time, 11.4% of seniors had used a synthetic cannabinoid in the last year. As a similar rate was noted in 2012 (11.3%; Johnston *et al.*, 2013), the study's authors suggest that the recent bans have had little effect on use. Synthetic cathinones or "bath salts" were added to MTF in 2012, but use was much more rare; only 0.8%, 0.6%, and 1.3% of 8th, 10th, and 12th graders, respectively, reported ever having used bath salts (Johnston *et al.*, 2013). Salvia use was reported by 4.4% of seniors in 2012 (Johnson *et al.*, 2013) and other studies suggest that use is more common among young adults in some geographic areas (Lange, Reed, Ketchie Croff, & Clapp, 2008; Khey, Miller, & Griffin, 2008). Use of novel drugs appears to be most common among men and users of other drugs (Stogner & Miller, 2013). As most studies that include measures of novel drugs are cross-sectional, it is not possible to determine whether novel drug use precedes, follows, replaces, or exacerbates use of other psychoactive substances.

Drugs and the Juvenile Justice System

At present, slightly over 17% of adolescent arrests can be directly attributed to violations of drug laws (OJJDP, 2013). However, it is likely that a much larger portion of adolescent arrests are drug-related due to many assaults being linked to their pharmacological effects, and many property crimes being linked to the economic demands of habitual drug use. Thus, substance use and abuse represent major strains on the juvenile justice system. Many have criticized the "war on drugs" for a bevy of reasons, but one of the most significant consequences has been the increased number of juveniles under the authority of the system (Gaudio, 2010). Between the 1980s and mid-1990s the incarcerated juvenile population grew prolifically, with incarceration and arrest rates more than doubling in a ten-year period (Schiraldi, Holman, & Beatty, 2000). This growth has largely been attributed to over-punitive reactions to drug-related offenses, and has contributed to less comprehensive or effective processing of both drug and non-drug offenses (Gaudio, 2010).

Fortunately, the juvenile arrest rates for most offenses have fallen significantly in the last decade. Despite lower levels of adolescent self-reported illicit drug use, the rates of juvenile drug-related arrests decreased by a smaller margin than other crimes. The rates of adolescent arrests for drug-related issues are still 42% above their 1980 levels, and will likely never return to those levels without significant policy reform. However, there is also good news: the rate of adolescent arrests for driving under the influence is currently lower than any time in the last 30 years (OJJDP, 2013). Given law enforcement's heightened attention to impaired driving, this finding suggests that the efforts of government and non-profit organizations to educate and deter juveniles from driving under the influence, and even stigmatize the behavior, have been somewhat successful.

The majority of adolescent drug offenses that result in citation or arrest can be attributed to either alcohol or marijuana. Though marijuana has been decriminalized in some jurisdictions, these areas typically still restrict adolescent possession. Apprehension of a juvenile for a drug-related offense may result in a citation, fine, or summons (likely only for limited quantities of alcohol or marijuana), arrest, or direct diversion to a drug treatment program (Walters, 2013). Diversion to a drug program may also occur after any number of points following an arrest or citation. One of the goals of diverting youth from the juvenile justice system is to avoid the stigmatizing label associated with formal processing. While the identification and apprehension may result in a label regardless of whether the youth is formally processed or not, diversion programs can be especially helpful in that they may be better equipped to handle drug dependencies (Gendreau, French, & Gionet, 2004). As they may be more efficient in assisting in recovery and cessation of drug use, diversion programs may more effectively reduce recidivism. A recent meta-analysis suggests that the diversion of drug offenders reduces their future drug use as well as their involvement in non-drug-related crimes (Harvey, Shakeshaft, Hetherington, Sannibale, & Mattick, 2007).

As a response to the surge in drug-related cases that filled the criminal justice system in the 1980s, many areas developed specialized courts to handle drug-related offenses. Drug courts both reduce the burden on traditional courts and provide specialized response to drug offenses. These courts are typically closely associated with treatment and monitoring programs as well as community programs. Research suggests that drug courts are very much more effective at reducing recidivism for adults, but only slightly so for juveniles (3–5% improvement in recidivism rates;

Harvey *et al.*, 2007). Policy-makers must remain careful to ensure that drug courts and diversion programs do not lead to net-widening, but should see each as a cost-efficient and potentially more effective alternative to the traditional court system.

A significant concern for law enforcement and the juvenile corrections system is the disparate treatment of racial and ethnic groups. Among those youth in custody for non-alcohol drug-related offenses, 39% are white, 36% are black, and 20% are Hispanic (OJJDP, 2013). These simple statistics may mask key racial differences in drug-related exposure to the juvenile justice system. The rate of arrest for a drug-related offense for black adolescents is approximately twice that of white adoles-cents, three times that of Native Americans, and over five times that of Asian adolescents. These disparities were most evident in the mid- to late-1990s and appear to be slowly dissipating (OJJDP, 2013); however, it is important to note that they were not fully driven by differences in drug use rates. A different story emerges for adolescent arrests related to alcohol. Over the last 30 years, white and Native American adolescents have consistently had higher rates of arrest for drunkenness, driving under the influence, and underage possession of alcohol compared with black and Asian adolescents (OJJDP, 2013).

For the future, many have predicted that adolescent substance use will be shifted from a criminal justice issue to a public health concern. As such, it is likely that attempts to educate youth, assist in reducing harms, and manage addictions will become more prevalent than punitive actions. Since it is unlikely that adolescents will ever completely abstain from using intoxicating substances, these interventions will likely focus on lim-iting consumption, reducing problematic use behaviors, and will target not only the drugs but also the negative environments that facilitate use.

References

Agnew, R. (1992). Foundation for a general strain theory of crime and delinquency. *Criminology, 30*(1), 47–87.

Agosti, V., Nunes E., Stewart, J.W., & Quitkin, F.M. (1991). Patient factors leading to early attrition from an outpatient cocaine research clinic: A preliminary report. *International Journal of the Addictions, 26*, 327–334.

Ahmadi, J., Kampman, K.M., Oslin, D.M., Pettinati, H.M., Dackis, C., & Sparkman, T. (2009). Predictors of treatment outcome in outpatient cocaine and alcohol dependence treatment. *American Journal on Addictions, 18*(1), 81–86.

Akers, R.L. (2009). *Social Learning and Social Structure: A General Theory of Crime and Deviance.* Brunswick, NJ: Transaction.

Amato, L., Minozzi, S., Pani, P.P., Solimini, R., Vecchi, S., Zuccaro, P., & Davoli, M. (2011). Dopamine agonists for the treatment of cocaine dependence. *Cochrane Database Syst Rev, 12.*

Ashley, R. (1975). *Cocaine, Its History, Uses and Effects.* New York: St. Martin's Press.

Bahr, S.J., Masters, A.L., & Taylor, B.M. (2012). What works in substance abuse treatment programs for offenders? *The Prison Journal, 92*(2), 155–174.

Brandt, A.M. (2007). *The Cigarette Century: The Rise, Fall, and Deadly Persistence of the Product that Defined America.* New York: Basic Books.

Breathes, W. (2013) Crazy-high times: The rise of hash oil, Meet the golden goop that gets you cosmically baked. *Rolling Stone,* June 20. Retrieved from http://www.rollingstone.com/culture/news/crazy-high-times-the-rise-of-hash-oil-20130610

Centers for Disease Control and Prevention. (2008). Smoking-attributable mortality, years of potential life lost, and productivity losses – United States, 2000–2004. *Morbidity and Mortality Weekly Report, 57*(45), 1226–1228.

Centers for Disease Control and Prevention. (2013a). *Alcohol and Other Drug Use.* Retrieved from http://www.cdc.gov/healthyyouth/alcoholdrug/

Centers for Disease Control and Prevention. (2013b). *Alcohol Use and Health.* Retrieved from http://www.cdc.gov/alcohol/fact-sheets/alcohol-use.htm

Centers for Disease Control and Prevention. (2013c). *Smoking & Tobacco Use Fast Facts.* Retrieved from http://www.cdc.gov/tobacco/data_statistics/fact_sheets/fast_facts/index.htm

Compton, W., & Volkow, N. (2006). Abuse of prescription drugs and the risk of addiction. *Drug & Alcohol Dependence, 83,* S4–S7.

Coronges, K., Stacy, A.W., & Valente, T.W. (2011). Social network influences of alcohol and marijuana cognitive associations. *Addictive Behaviors, 36*(12), 1305–1308.

Courtwright, D.T. (2001). *Forces of Habit: Drugs and the Making of the Modern World.* Cambridge, MA: Harvard University Press.

Creemer, H.E., Dijkstra, J.K., Vollebergh, W.A., Ormel, J., Verhulst, F.C., & Huizink, A.C. (2010). Predicting life-time and regular cannabis use during adolescence; the roles of temperament and peer substance use: the TRAILS study. *Addiction, 105*(4), 699–708.

Cullen, F., Wright, J., & Blevins, K. (2008). *Taking Stock: The Status of Criminological Theory* (Vol. *15*). Brunswick, NJ: Transaction.

Dennehy, C.E., Tsourounis, C., & Miller, A.E. (2005). Evaluation of herbal dietary supplements marketed on the Internet for recreational use. *Annals of Pharmacotherapy, 39,* 1634–1639.

Dresen, S., Ferreirós, N., Pütz, M., Westphal, F., Zimmermann, R., & Auwärter, V. (2010). Monitoring of herbal mixtures potentially containing synthetic cannabinoids as psychoactive compounds. *Journal of Mass Spectrometry, 45,* 1186–1194.

Drug Enforcement Agency (DEA). (2013). *Drug Fact Sheet: Kratom.* Retrieved from http://www.justice.gov/dea/druginfo/drug_data_sheets/Kratom.pdf

Dubey, A. (2012). Role of television in drug abuse prevention: an empirical study. *Pragyaan, Journal of Mass Communication, 10*(2), 31–35.

Durkin, S.J., Biener, L., & Wakefield, M.A. (2009). Effects of different types of antismoking ads on reducing disparities in smoking cessation among socioeconomic subgroups. *American Journal of Public Health, 99*(12), 2217–2223.

European Monitoring Centre for Drugs and Drug Addiction. (2009). *Understanding the "spice" phenomenon.* Retrieved from http://www.emcdda.europa.eu

Fernander, A., Resnicow, K., Viswanath, K., & Pérez-Stable, E.J. (2011). Cigarette smoking interventions among diverse populations. *American Journal of Health Promotion, 25* (sp5), s1–s4.

Fitzgerald, K.T., Bronstein, A.C., & Newquist, K.L. (2013). Marijuana poisoning. *Topics in Companion Animal Medicine, 28*(1), 8–12.

Food and Drug Safety and Innovation Act (2012). S. 3187, 112th Congress.

Freudenmann, R.W., Öxler, F., & Bernschneider-Reif, S. (2006). The origin of MDMA (ecstasy) revisited: the true story reconstructed from the original documents. *Addiction, 101*(9), 1241–1245.

Gaudio, C.M. (2010). A call to congress to give back the future: End the "war on drugs" and encourage states to reconstruct the juvenile justice system. *Family Court Review, 48*(1), 212–227.

Gendreau, P., French, S.A., & Gionet, A. (2004). What works (what doesn't work): The principles of effective correctional treatment. *Journal of Community Corrections, 13*(3), 4–6.

Giannini, A.J. (1997). *Drugs of Abuse*. Practice Management Information Corporation.

Goode, E. (2011) *Drugs in American Society*, 8th ed. New York: McGraw-Hill Higher Education.

Gottfredson, M.R., & Hirschi, T. (1990). *A General Theory of Crime*. Stanford, CA: Stanford University Press.

Griffin, O.H., III, Miller, B.L., & Khey, D.N. (2008). Legally high? Legal considerations of *Salvia divinorum*. *Journal of Psychoactive Drugs, 40*, 183–191.

Grinspoon, L., & Heblom, P. (1975). *The Speed Culture: Amphetamine Use and Abuse in America*. Cambridge, MA: Harvard University Press.

Grundmann, O., Phipps, S.M., Zadezensksy, I., & Butterweck, V. (2007). Pharmacology and analytical methodology of *Salvia divinorum*. *Planta Medica, 73*, 1039–1046.

Haines, M., & Spear, S.F. (1996). Changing the perception of the norm: A strategy to decrease binge drinking among college students. *Journal of American College Health, 45*, 134–140.

Hanson, G., Venturelli, P., & Fleckenstein, A. (2011). *Drugs and Society*. Burlington, MA: Jones & Bartlett Publishers.

Hatsukami, D.K., & Fischman, M.W. (1996). Crack cocaine and cocaine hydrochloride. *JAMA: the Journal of the American Medical Association, 276*(19), 1580–1588.

Harvey, E., Shakeshaft, A., Hetherington, K., Sannibale, C., & Mattick, R.P. (2007). The efficacy of diversion and aftercare strategies for adult drug-involved offenders: a summary and methodological review of the outcome literature. *Drug and Alcohol Review, 26*(4), 379–387.

Jerry, J., Collins, G., & Streem, D. (2012). Synthetic legal intoxicating drugs: the emerging 'incense' and 'bath salt' phenomenon. *Cleveland Clinic Journal of Medicine, 79*(4), 258.

Johnston, L.D., O'Malley, P.M., Bachman, J.G., & Schulenberg, J.E. (2011). *Monitoring the Future National Survey Results on Drug Use, 1975–2010. Volume I: Secondary School Students*. Ann Arbor: Institute for Social Research, University of Michigan.

Johnston, L.D., O'Malley, P.M., Bachman, J.G., & Schulenberg, J.E. (2012). The rise in teen marijuana use stalls, synthetic marijuana use levels, and use of 'bath salts' is very low. National press release, December 19. Ann Arbor: University of Michigan News Service.

Johnston, L.D., O'Malley, P.M., Bachman, J.G., & Schulenberg, J.E. (2013). *Monitoring the Future National Results on Adolescent Drug Use: Overview of Key Findings, 2012*. Ann Arbor: Institute for Social Research, University of Michigan.

Kahn, D.E., Ferraro, N., & Benveniste, R.J. (2012). 3 cases of primary intracranial hemorrhage associated with "Molly", a purified form of 3, 4-methylenedioxymethamphetamine (MDMA). *Journal of the Neurological Sciences, 323*(1), 257–260.

Kanavos, P., Ferrario, A., Vandoros, S., & Anderson, G.F. (2013). Higher US branded drug prices and spending compared to other countries may stem partly from quick uptake of new drugs. *Health Affairs, 32*(4), 753–761.

Khey, D.N., Miller, B.L., & Griffin, III, O.H. (2008). *Salvia divinorum* use among college students. *Journal of Drug Education 38*, 297–306.

Kinney, J. (2009). *Loosening the Grip: A Handbook of Alcohol Information* (9th ed.). New York: McGraw-Hill.

Kluger, R. (2010). *Ashes to Ashes: America's Hundred-Year Cigarette War, the Public Health, and the Unabashed Triumph of Philip Morris.* New York: Vintage.

Lange, J.E., Reed, M.B., Ketchie Croff, J.M. & Clapp, J.D. (2008). College student use of *Salvia divinorum. Drug & Alcohol Dependence, 94,* 263–266.

Loeffler, G., Hurst, D., Penn, A., & Yung, K. (2012). Spice, bath salts, and the US military: The emergence of synthetic cannabinoid receptor agonists and cathinones in the US Armed Forces. *Military Medicine, 177*(9), 1041–1048.

Maxwell, J.C. (2004). *Patterns of club drug use in the US, 2004.* The Gulf Coast Addiction Technology Transfer Center, University of Texas.

McAuliffe, W.E., & Gordon, R.A. (1975). Issues in testing Lindesmith's theory. *American Journal of Sociology, 81*(1), 154–163.

McCabe, S.E., Boyd, C.J., & Teter, C.J. (2009). Subtypes of nonmedical prescription drug misuse. *Drug and Alcohol Dependence, 102*(1), 63–70.

Merlin, M.D. (1984). *On the Trail of the Ancient Opium Poppy.* Rutherford, NJ: Fairleigh Dickinson University Press.

Musto, D.F. (1991). Opium, cocaine and marijuana in American history. *Scientific American, 265*(1), 40–47.

Musto, D.F. (1998). International traffic in coca through the early 20th century. *Drug and Alcohol Dependence, 49*(2), 145–156.

Office of Juvenile Justice and Delinquency Prevention. (2013). *OJJDP Statistical Briefing Book.* Retrieved from http://www.ojjdp.gov/ojstatbb/corrections/qa08205.asp?qaDate=2010

Perkins, H.W., & Berkowitz, A.D. (1986). Perceiving the community norms of alcohol use among students: Some research implications for campus alcohol education programming. *International Journal of the Addictions, 21,* 961–976.

Perkins, H.W., Haines, M., & Rice, R. (2005). Misperceiving the college drinking norm and related problems: A nationwide study of exposure to prevention information, perceived norms and student alcohol misuse. *Journal of Studies of Alcohol and Drugs, 66,* 470–478.

SAMHSA (Mental Health Services Administration). (2006). *Results from the 2005 National Survey on Drug Use and Health: National Findings.* Office of Applied Studies. Rockville, MD: Substance Abuse and Mental Health Services. Retrieved from http://www.oas.samhsa.gov/nsduh/2k5nsduh/2k5results.pdf

Schachter, R. (2012). A new prescription for fighting drug abuse. *District Administration, 48*(2), 41–42.

Schiraldi, V., Holman, B., & Beatty, P. (2000). *Poor Prescription: The Costs of Imprisoning Drug Offenders in the United States.* Justice Policy Institute.

Schneider, E.C. (2008). *Smack: Heroin and the American City.* Philadelphia, PA: University of Pennsylvania Press.

Stogner, J., Khey, D.N., Griffin, O.H., Miller, B.L., & Boman, J.H. (2012). Regulating a novel drug: An evaluation of changes in use of Salvia divinorum in the first year of Florida's ban. *International Journal of Drug Policy, 23,* 512–521.

Stogner, J., & Miller, B.L. (2013). A spicy kind of high: A profile of synthetic cannabinoid users. *Journal of Substance Use, 19*(1–2), 199–205.

Tang, Z., & Orwin, R.G. (2009). Marijuana initiation among American youth and its risks as dynamic processes: prospective findings from a national longitudinal study. *Substance Use & Misuse, 44*(2), 195–211.

Treatment Episode Data Set (TEDS). (2012). *2009 Discharges from Substance Abuse Treatment Services*. Available from http://www.samhsa.gov/data/DASIS.aspx?qr=t#TEDS

Ulmer, J.T., Desmond, S.A., Jang, S.J., & Johnson, B.R. (2012). Religious involvement and dynamics of marijuana use: Initiation, persistence, and desistence. *Deviant Behavior*, *33*(6), 448–468.

United States Surgeon General's Advisory Committee on Smoking. (1964). *Smoking and Health: Report of the Advisory Committee to the Surgeon General of the Public Health Service* (No. 1103). Washington, DC: US Department of Health, Education, and Welfare, Public Health Service.

van Amsterdam, J., Opperhuizen, A., & Hartgens, F. (2010). Adverse health effects of anabolic–androgenic steroids. *Regulatory Toxicology and Pharmacology*, *57*(1), 117–123.

Walters, G.D. (2013). *Drugs, Crime, and Their Relationship: Theory, Research, Practice, and Policy*. Burlington, MA: Jones & Bartlett Publishers.

Walters, S.T., Bennett, M.E., & Miller, J.H. (2000). Reducing alcohol use in college students: A controlled trial of two brief interventions. *Journal of Drug Education*, *30*(3), 361.

34

Maltreatment and Damaging Outcomes in Adolescence: Longitudinal Research and Policy

Timothy O. Ireland, Carolyn A. Smith,
and Jamie E. Walter

Introduction

Child abuse or maltreatment and damaging outcomes in adolescence have a long association in literature as well as research. Dickensian accounts of abused and abandoned children living as street urchins and thieves, and involved in criminal associations, have survived. However, only in the last three decades has the relationship been carefully examined. Today delinquency textbooks invariably devote a section or chapter to child maltreatment, generally as an important risk factor for delinquency (e.g., Hoffmann, 2011). As recently as the 1980s, the topic was only briefly mentioned in the context of a broader discussion on family relationships and delinquency. Its emergence is due to the confluence of several strands of research.

An early research connection between maltreatment and crime came from the study of psychopathy or psychopathic criminals, and evidence indicating that their early childhood involved serious family disturbance (Widom, 1997). More prominently for the study of maltreatment, and originating from the medical field, the early 1960s demonstrated a clinical condition, "battered child syndrome", in which parents or caretakers deliberately harmed children, often repeatedly, with serious consequences. Also in the 1960s the notion of a "cycle of violence" or intergenerational transmission of violent and aggressive behavior became a guiding idea (Curtis, 1963; Widom, 1989). Legal developments, developing terminology, and tracking mechanisms involving the maltreated followed in the 1970s, which enabled increasingly elaborate assessments of the nature and extent of child maltreatment. Subsequently, there has been a burgeoning research literature on links between maltreatment and delinquency or crime, as well as a range of other outcomes that

The Handbook of Juvenile Delinquency and Juvenile Justice, First Edition. Edited by Marvin D. Krohn and Jodi Lane.

increase the likelihood of contact with the juvenile justice system – for example, truancy, running away, dropping out, and alcohol and drug use. Historically, given available research designs, the relationships considered between maltreatment and adolescent negative behavioral outcomes were more often cross-sectional or correlational in nature. However, verifying and quantifying the extent of the risk for adolescent behavioral problems deriving from experiences of child maltreatment, and testing possible pathways between these phenomena, requires temporal ordering among constructs.

From about 1990, longitudinal research and strong research design features were increasingly used, and were better able to test the general questions posed above. Currently, the field of inquiry is interdisciplinary, sophisticated, and well developed empirically as well as theoretically, as this chapter will illustrate. We first discuss the definition and extent of child maltreatment; we then summarize applicable developmental theories and the research on maltreatment and adolescent behaviors that increase risk of juvenile justice intervention. In the final two sections of the chapter we outline future directions for both research and policy development.

Extent of the Problem

The federal government defines maltreatment in the Child Abuse and Prevention Treatment Act (CAPTA) of 1974 (re-authorized 2010) as "…any recent act or failure to act on the part of a parent or caretaker, which results in death, serious physical or emotional harm, sexual abuse or exploitation, or an act or failure to act which presents an imminent risk of serious harm" to a person under the age of 18. Generally, maltreatment encompasses physical abuse, sexual abuse, emotional abuse, as well as several different dimensions of neglect (e.g., NYS Family Court Act, 2012). Physical abuse refers to incidents of hitting, punching, kicking, burning, and otherwise inflicting physical harm. Nevertheless, there is definitional ambiguity about concepts of physical abuse, corporal punishment, and harsh discipline (Knutson & Heckenberg, 2006). Sexual abuse refers to a spectrum of behavior from fondling and touching to intercourse. Psychological or emotional abuse includes inadequate nurturing as well as criticism and rejection and other forms of mental cruelty that place children at risk of damaged development (Goldman, Salus, Wolcott, & Kennedy, 2003). Neglect refers to acts of omission of care including failure of parents to meet basic needs, including food, medical attention, and clothing, or to provide adequate protection and supervision. Neglect has proven much harder to define than abuse because it is more age-dependent in definition, and has historically received less research attention (Dubowitz, 2007; Straus & Kantor, 2005). In some jurisdictions, child witnessing of parental domestic violence is considered to be a form of child maltreatment (see Edleson, 1999); however, this has formed a different strand of research and is not the focus of this chapter.

Two sources provide national estimates on the extent of child abuse and neglect in the US – the National Child Abuse and Neglect Data System (NCANDS), which reports annually, and National Incidence of Child Abuse and Neglect studies (NIS). NCANDS data rely exclusively upon Child Protective Services (CPS) agency data from all states. The NIS is a congressionally mandated, periodic report with the most recent data collection in 2005–6, involving a representative sample of 122 US counties (NIS-4). The NIS reports rely upon estimates derived from information reported by a sample of sentinels who fill out data forms on child maltreatment encounters. Two other federal initiatives that have added to the national portrait of child maltreatment and outcomes are LONGSCAN (Longitudinal Studies of Child Abuse and Neglect) (Runyan *et al.*, 1998) and the National Study of Child and Adolescent Well-being, (NSCAW, 2007a).

NCANDS indicates that, in 2011, there were an estimated 3.5 million referrals of alleged abuse or neglect involving 6.4 million children (US Department of Health and Human Services, 2015). NIS-4 estimated that in 2005–6 slightly under 3 million children – or about 1 in every 25 children – were in danger of harm from maltreatment (Sedlak *et al.*, 2010). In both data sources the majority of cases involved neglect, and the typical perpetrator was a biological parent or parent figure. Finally, NCANDS reports that an estimated 1,640 children died in 2012 as a result of an injury cause by abuse or neglect (Child Welfare Information Gateway, 2014). Recently, Fang, Brown, Florence, and Mercy (2012) estimated that the total lifetime economic burden of maltreatment in the US from cases occurring in one year is approximately $124 billion. This assessment is surely an underestimate given the hidden nature of maltreatment and difficulties in estimating some costs. Moreover, it appears that more than half of adolescents reported for maltreatment may be at risk for emotional or behavioral problems including delinquency and status offending (NSCAW, 2007b). Child maltreatment is an extensive problem in American society, and the resulting costs are substantial.

Theoretical Orientation

The theoretical perspectives that link maltreatment to a multiplicity of damaging developmental consequences in adolescence are varied and incorporate models grounded in traditional criminological perspectives including social control, social learning, and strain theories (Smith & Ireland, 2009). In addition, several evolving perspectives embrace a dynamic developmental outlook, including Interactional theory (Thornberry, 1987; Thornberry & Krohn, 2005), which is broad-based and incorporates elements of individual development, the family microsystem, and the situational context in which the family operates (Bronfenbrenner, 1979, 1986). Interactional theory argues that antisocial behavior generally, and delinquency specifically, should be considered a behavioral trajectory that "unfolds over time" (Thornberry & Krohn, 2005, p. 188) and is influenced by other life-course trajectories that are also unfolding over developmental periods – family, schooling, and peer interactions, for example. This unpacking of life-course trajectories and their influences upon one another "emerge from interactions between the person and his or her environment and not simply from the environment acting upon the individual" (Thornberry & Krohn, 2005, p.189). Interactional theory views family processes as a critical starting point for prosocial and antisocial behavioral trajectories, and anti-social behavioral trajectories in adolescence in turn influence other domains in early adulthood, including subsequent family violence (Ireland & Smith, 2009; Thornberry, 2009). Therefore, in the context of maltreatment, interactional theory would antici-pate a disrupted developmental trajectory that influences and is influenced by school experiences and peer relationships, for example. These school experiences and peer relationships can either disrupt or reinforce the behavioral trajectory, such that a cascade of consequences flow, which may become embedded in adulthood.

The transactional–ecological perspective was specifically designed to address the developmental consequences of childhood exposure to maltreatment and community violence (Cicchetti & Lynch, 1993; Rogosch, Oshri, & Cicchetti, 2010). This perspec-tive also views the context of the child at multiple nested levels that interact with each other over time in a way that shapes individual development. Individual development is a process "whereby competencies and liabilities attained at successive stages of development are hierarchically integrated within and among developmental systems to influence subsequent development" (Rogosch *et al.*, 2010, p. 883). Therefore, mal-treatment is thought to compromise developmental competencies such that, over time, maltreated children will display a broad diversity of developmental liabilities cutting across several different spheres of functioning, including peer relationships, emotional regulation, romantic partnerships, and antisocial behavior.

A third developmental perspective that has its roots in the maltreatment and family violence literature is the social information processing (SIP) perspective (e.g., Dodge, Bates, & Pettit, 1990; Fite *et al.*, 2008; Lansford *et al.*, 2007). A child exposed to maltreatment develops "aggressive social-cognitive processing patterns" – learns and internalizes a worldview that regards the environment as a hostile place and therefore violence becomes a legitimate social response. Such children tend to develop a bias during benign interactions whereby they attribute hostility to other's actions, and employ aggressive responses during these interactions which are per-ceived as justifiable. This social information processing bias creates problems in school with teachers, problems with peers, and increases the risk of antisocial behavior and intergenerational violence (Berlin, Appleyard, & Dodge, 2011).

Longitudinal Research Linking Maltreatment to Damaging Adolescent Behaviors

In this section we summarize the research on negative outcomes primarily during adolescence that have been linked to experiences of maltreatment. Generally, we are interested in adolescent antisocial behavioral outcomes that increase the likelihood of contact with the juvenile justice system – which includes research on the effect of maltreatment on delinquency (including status offenses), illicit drug use and alcohol use, and risky sex.

Delinquency

Findings from the Rochester Youth Development Study (RYDS), a longitudinal study of 1,000 7th and 8th graders interviewed over time into adulthood, suggested a consistent relationship between reports of substantiated childhood maltreatment and later delinquency in sample members (Smith & Thornberry, 1995; Ireland, Smith, & Thornberry, 2002). The rate of substantiated maltreatment was high (21%) in this urban sample. Researchers found that childhood maltreatment was a risk factor for official delinquency, violent self-reported delinquency, and moderate self-reported delinquency. Overall, child maltreatment appeared to be a risk factor for more serious delinquency, such as assaults, but not lesser forms of delinquency, such as underage drinking (Kelley, Thornberry, & Smith, 1997). In another prominent study of a matched sample of 908 cases of substantiated child maltreatment with 667 matched cases of children who had not been maltreated, followed over time, abuse or neglect increased the likelihood of arrest as a juvenile by 59%, as an adult by 28%, and for a violent crime by 30% (Widom & Maxfield, 2001).

Additional studies with methodologically strong prospective research designs have documented a significant relationship between childhood maltreatment and delinquency (e.g., Grogan-Kaylor & Otis, 2003; Klika, Herrenkohl, & Lee, 2012; Lansford *et al.*, 2009; Mass, Herrenkohl, & Sousa, 2008; Verracchia, Fetzer, Lemmon, & Austin, 2010). For example, recently, Verracchia *et al.* (2010) examined the direct and indirect effects of maltreatment on youth offending using time-sequenced agency data. They found that supervisory neglect and maltreatment severity were either directly or indirectly related to delinquency referrals. In addition, Klika *et al.* (2012), utilizing data from the Lehigh Longitudinal Study, reported that physical child abuse predicted both childhood and adolescent antisocial behavior.

In much of the preceding research the focus has been on maltreatment that occurs in childhood, but a handful of studies have also considered the relationship between adolescent maltreatment and delinquency (e.g., Bright & Jonson-Reid, 2008; Eckenrode *et al.*, 2001; Ireland *et al.*, 2002; Mersky, Topitzes, & Reynolds, 2012; Stewart, Livingston, & Dennison, 2008). These longitudinal studies have consistently shown that adolescent maltreatment is at least as developmentally disruptive as childhood-limited maltreatment, and some have found that adolescent maltreatment is more disruptive than childhood-limited maltreatment, at least in terms of delinquency (Ireland *et al.*, 2002).

Under this heading we also consider two traditionally defined status offenses in most jurisdictions around the country – running away from home, and truancy/dropping out of school. Stouthamer-Loeber, Loeber, Homish, and Wei (2001) reported a significant relationship between substantiated maltreatment and authority avoidance, where authority avoidance includes truancy, running away, and staying out late. However, when considering the time order between maltreatment and authority avoidance, only about one third of the maltreatment cases had an onset prior to onset of authority avoidance behaviors.

Others have considered truancy and running away as separate outcomes. For example, Leiter (2007) considered school absenteeism trajectories before and after the first CPS report of maltreatment (substantiated or unsubstantiated) and discovered that "after the advent of reported maltreatment, the rate of increase in absenteeism mounted with increasing age" (Leiter, 2007, p. 374). Kim, Tajima, Herrenkohl, and Huang (2009) considered running away as a possible mediator linking maltreatment to later delinquency. Kaufman and Widom (1999) showed that experiences of abuse and neglect prior to age 12 predicted self-reported and officially measured running away in adolescence. However, they did not find that running away mediated the relationship between maltreatment and subsequent involvement in crime. Building on this research and using the Lehigh Longitudinal Study, Kim *et al.* (2009) estimated a structural equation model (SEM) showing that running away did partially mediate the relationship between physical/psychological abuse and delinquency.

Drug and alcohol use

Studies of adolescent substance users have generally estimated that 40–90% have been victimized (Dennis & Stevens, 2003). Grella and Joshi (2003) in conjunction with the Drug Abuse Outcome Study of Adolescents found of the 803 adolescents admitted into twenty-three treatment programs in the United States, 39% of males and 59% of females acknowledged a history of physical or sexual victimization. In comparison to their non-abused counterparts, abused adolescents have a greater likelihood of engaging in substance abuse (Funk, McDermeit, Godley, & Adams, 2003). In several longitudinal studies, maltreatment predicts later alcohol and drug use or related arrests (e.g., Funk *et al.*, 2003; Ireland & Widom, 1994; Lansford, Dodge, Pettit, & Bates, 2010; Lo & Cheng, 2007; Widom, Ireland, & Glynn, 1995). There also exists an established link between sexual abuse and early onset of alcohol and drug use, as well as higher levels of use (e.g., Hussey & Singer, 1993; Jarvis, Copeland, & Walton, 1998).

Rogosch *et al.* (2010, p. 884) provide a comprehensive review of the maltreatment–drug use hypothesis and conclude the "preponderance of the evidence supports the linkage between experiences of maltreatment and the development of adverse substance abuse outcomes among youth and adults." For example, Lansford *et al.* (2010), utilizing data from a prospective longitudinal multisite study of child development in 585 families, examined the parents' reports of child physical abuse in the first five years of a child's life as a predictor of substance abuse at ages 12, 16, and 24. They reported a significant association between physical abuse and substance abuse at each age for females but not for males.

Shifting from drug use to alcohol use, Shin, Miller, and Teicher (2013) consider heavy episodic drinking in early adolescence and adulthood and whether childhood maltreatment influences such behavior. Using AddHealth data and modeling longitudinal relationships, they find what others before them have reported: that maltreatment in childhood is related to alcohol use in adolescence and early adulthood.

> Compared to respondents who never experienced any maltreatment, respondents with a history of childhood neglect and physical abuse experienced a steeper increase in rates of HED (heavy episodic drinking) during adolescence and persistently higher HED beyond adolescence and throughout much of young adulthood. (Shin *et al.*, 2013, p. 34)

Teenage involvement in sex, pregnancy, and risky sex

Although the longitudinal research is limited on the relationship between maltreatment and teenage involvement in sex, pregnancy, or risky sex, the findings generally support a cross-sectional relationship when using retrospective reports with predominately adult samples (Blinn-Pike, Berger, Dixon, Kuschel, & Kaplan, 2002). Since some research in the juvenile justice arena indicates that the system is more likely to respond formally to female sexual activity in adolescence compared with male sexual activity, it is somewhat troubling that maltreatment may be, at least in part, a risk factor for precocious sexual activity and consequences such as teen pregnancy (e.g., Barnickol, 2000).

Smith (1996) reported a significant relationship between maltreatment occurring prior to age 12 and subsequent school-age pregnancy among the girls in the Rochester Youth Development Study. Smith (1997) also considered early initiation into sexual activity and found that maltreatment was related to early sexual activity among boys in the Rochester study, but not for girls. Widom & Kuhns (1996) found while a relationship between maltreatment and prostitution was identified, no relationship was identified between maltreatment and promiscuity or teenage pregnancy.

More recently, two studies using LONGSCAN data indicate that maltreatment experienced before age 12 is related to sexual intercourse at age 14 and age 16 (Black *et al.*, 2009), and sexual abuse trajectories estimated between 0–12 years of age predicted risky sex (alcohol use and intercourse) at 14 and 16. Finally, both Jones *et al.* (2010) and Black *et al.* (2009) report limited or no support for the hypothesis that the maltreatment–teenage sex relationship differs by gender (cf. Smith, 1997).

Multiple outcomes

In almost all of the preceding discussion the dependent variable focuses on a single outcome – whether the outcome is delinquency, drug use, or precocious sexual activity, for example. The implied conclusion flowing from the consideration of maltreatment and negative behavioral trajectories in adolescence is that any particular victim of maltreatment may respond with a specific maladaptive behavior: maltreatment increases the risk of drug use, for example.

Very few published studies explore whether or not maltreatment increases the risk of an array of negative behaviors instead of a single problem behavior. In other words, victims of maltreatment may be at risk for multiple problem behavioral adaptations, including alcohol use, drug use, delinquency, teenage sex, and other externalizing problems. To explore this issue, Thornberry, Ireland, & Smith (2001) created a multiple problem index that included the following items during late adolescence: school drop-out; teen pregnancy; externalizing behaviors; internalizing behaviors; depressive symptoms; alcohol-related problems; drug use; and delinquency. They found adolescent maltreatment was significantly related to experiencing multiple problems, reflecting the multiple pathways through which maltreatment might affect development.

Future Research

Longitudinal research over the past 20 years has, with a fair degree of consistency, shown linkages between maltreatment and damaging behavioral adaptations in adolescence that increase the risk for formal juvenile justice system intervention. Other arenas of investigation are not as mature and require further exploration, including the topics outlined below.

Developments in conceptualizing violence exposure

Much of the research, including a series of RYDS studies, considers maltreatment in isolation or considers various aspects of maltreatment – for example physical abuse – in isolation from other family dynamics. A growing literature is considering the effects of maltreatment in the context of exposure to other family and community violence, including harsh discipline, sibling conflict, violence between primary caregivers, and violence in the neighborhood. Finkelhor, Ormond, and Turner (2007) have coined the term "polyvictimization". The Juvenile Victimization Questionnaire (JVQ), the Adverse Childhood Experiences Scale (ACES) (Felitti *et al.*, 1998), and the Child Trauma Questionnaire (CTQ) (Paivio & Cramer, 2004) all represent multidimensional violence exposure measurement strategies. The relative impact of maltreatment in the face of other types of violence exposure in and outside the family is still an open question. A recent paper indicates that maltreatment may have relatively more impact on antisocial behavior than exposure to inter-parental violence (Park, Smith, & Ireland, 2012). However, there is some evidence that multiple experiences including both these forms of violence exposure produce equivalent harm in terms of antisocial behavior and arrest. Community violence also has a serious impact on adolescents and is often considered separately. Results from a meta-analysis of studies on childhood violence exposure and juvenile antisocial behavior suggest that "exposure to violence at home does not appear to have a greater impact on the development of antisocial behavior than exposure to violence outside the home" (Wilson, Stover, & Berkowitz, 2009, p. 775). To date, few studies have examined issues of relative impact, so this is an arena for continued research.

In addition to construction of multidimensional measures of family violence, it also seems reasonable to consider the dimensions of maltreatment itself. Very few longitudinal studies have considered characteristics of maltreatment that include chronicity, duration of the exposure, timing of maltreatment, services received, and the less familiar maltreatment types such as neglect, although these issues were highlighted at an earlier stage (Cicchetti & Barnett, 1991). For example, our research suggests that adolescent maltreatment has consequences that are at least as serious in terms of development disruption compared with childhood-limited maltreatment (Smith, Ireland, & Thornberry, 2005; Thornberry *et al.*, 2001). Findings from the NSCAW and LONGSCAN studies will bring additional information on these topics. The Federal Child Neglect Research Consortium headed by Cathy Widom (e.g., Widom, 2013) has brought new attention to the relatively overlooked topic of childhood neglect. We are beginning to understand more about how dimensions of exposure to family violence generally, and maltreatment specifically, are critical factors for understanding processes leading to problem behavioral outcomes in adolescence.

Exploring pathways

Research to understand pathways to antisocial and other outcomes is expanding. Researchers have documented a number of potential pathways from maltreatment or other family violence exposure to antisocial behavior in adolescence and early adulthood. These include mechanisms such as biased cognitive processing (Dodge, Pettit, Bates, & Valente, 1995), parental alienation and poor emotional regulation (Egeland, Yates, Appleyard, & Van Dulmen, 2002), and aggression and problem alcohol use (Widom, Schuck & White, 2006). Research on pathways is becoming more theoretically based, but understanding pathways and processes that lead from maltreatment to negative behavioral outcomes is critical for intervention. There has also been exponential research in the last decade on the neurobiology and genetics of maltreatment and pathways to adverse outcomes (summarized in McCrory, Brito, & Viding, 2010; Twardosz & Lutzker, 2010). The mechanisms that lead from child maltreatment to adverse outcomes including delinquency are still not clearly understood, but a picture is emerging that indicates a complex interaction between environmental experiences such as abuse, and genetic makeup. This then sets the stage for neurobiological development that affects emerging competencies, especially during sensitive periods. Neuroimaging studies have documented structural changes to the brain in response to maltreatment, consistent with attempts to manage stress. Efforts to understand these pathways in ways that inform policy and practice and promote more resilient and adaptive outcomes for children are critical (Perry, 2006).

As the focus on understanding consequences of maltreatment continues to evolve, systematic exploration of mediators becomes critical in trying to untangle the processes that result in some engaging in delinquency, others resorting to drugs or alcohol abuse, still others having multiple negative outcomes, and still others who apparently overcome their maltreatment experiences.

Investigating resilience

It is often overlooked that many maltreated children do not show ill-effects later in life. However, although research has investigated protective factors that promote resilient outcomes among stressed children more generally (e.g., Egeland, Carlson, & Sroufe, 1993; Garmezy & Masten, 1986; Kaufman & Zigler, 1987; Luthar, Cicchetti, & Becker, 2000), only a small body of research has explored protective factors for maltreated children (for reviews, see DuMont, Widom, & Czaja, 2007; McGloin & Widom, 2001). Herrenkohl, Sousa, Tajima, Herrenkohl, and Moylan (2008), in reviewing the research on resilience to child maltreatment, identified the following constructs as protective: high intelligence, high self-efficacy, high self-esteem, self-determination to be different from one's abusive parents, a positive relationship with a non-abusing adult, a supportive parent, a strong commitment to school, involvement in a religious community, and disapproval of violence from peers. The newest waves of resilience research focus on neurological protective factors, and also the role of interventions in elucidating processes that might link maltreatment to outcomes (Masten, 2007). This ongoing body of research continues to be challenged by a number of barriers common to studies of resilience that include difficulties in the conceptualization of resilience and in the appropriate strategies for investigating potential protective processes (e.g., see Luthar *et al.*, 2000; McGloin & Widom, 2001).

Directions for Policy and Practice

Somewhat consistent with the areas of research development outlined above, new developments in policy and practice are emerging. The current agenda for improved policy and practice in the light of new research includes strengthening maltreatment prevention; improving practices and services to assist maltreated youth, including a focus on resilience and protective factors; and changing service systems to attend to what are being called "crossover youth" (those in both child welfare and juvenile justice systems; Ryan, Herz, Hernandez, & Marshall, 2007).

In a very real sense, the manifested behavior – be it delinquency, drug use, or other problem behavior – that brings an adolescent into contact with the juvenile justice system may have its roots in abuse and neglect at home. Not understanding the life-experiences of the juveniles before apprehension and court experiences may result in missed opportunities for promoting healthier youth development, and may even lead to punishing the victim.

Prevention of maltreatment

The most important opportunity for delinquency prevention in this area is through preventing the occurrence or re-occurrence of maltreatment. Preventing maltreatment as part of the focus on violence and injury prevention among youth has been a federal policy initiative within the Centers for Disease Control and Prevention (CDC) since the 1980s (Centers for Disease Control and Prevention, 2012; Zimmerman & Mercy, 2010). Paired with this focus is developing and employing interventions that are evidence-based. There are a number of interventions that have an established track record in preventing maltreatment, including large-scale programs such as the Nurse–Family Partnership (Olds, 2006), and parent support programs such as Triple P (Prinz, Sanders, Shapiro, Whitaker, & Lutzker, 2009). Good summaries of tested prevention programs are widely available (e.g., Centers for Disease Control and Prevention, 2012; MacMillan *et al.*, 2009; World Health Organization & International Society for Prevention of Child Abuse and Neglect, 2006). However, such programs are often not available to child maltreatment victims and parents.

For example, it is estimated that a minority of children with substantiated maltreatment receive evidence-based services, although over 80% are identified as having service needs. Of those children and youth with a substantiated maltreatment report, only about half receive any services (Dolan, Smith, Vasanueva, & Ringeisen, 2012). It has been said that "in the second decade of the 21st century, evidence-based maltreatment prevention is a reality for at-risk groups; however, the research-to-practice and policy gap remains… [and many] children do not receive needed services because of service delivery and use barriers" (Wekerle, 2011, p. 159).

Importantly, there is a re-conceptualization of child maltreatment prevention underway within the CDC. The overall aim "is to promote safe, stable, and nurturing relationships (SSNRs) between children and caregivers" through strategies that include measuring impact; creating and evaluating new prevention approaches; applying and adapting effective practices, and building community readiness, including improving processes and partnerships (Centers for Disease Control and Prevention, 2008, p.1). The SSNR framework is also consistent with emerging neurobiological research on protective environments, including for stressed parents (Twardosz & Lutzker, 2010). Of course, these principles apply for children who have already experienced maltreatment.

Improving services for maltreated youth

Post-maltreatment services are important for children showing evidence of emerging difficulties such as antisocial behavior and delinquency, often in conjunction with serious emotional problems. Note also that many children who have experienced maltreatment are experiencing similar poor outcomes but are not accessing services (Smith, Ireland, Thornberry, & Elwyn, 2008). Here, too, evidence of effective programs is available, including evidence-based protocols that deal with multiple systems in a coordinated fashion, such as multisystemic therapy (Henggeler, Mihalic, Rone, Thomas, & Timmons-Mitchell, 1998) and multidimensional treatment foster care (Chamberlain & Mihalic, 1998).

New conceptualizations of interventions for maltreated youth are being developed consistent with emerging knowledge about risk and protective factors. The Administration on Children, Youth and Families (ACYF) administers the major federal programs that support child welfare services and promote the positive growth and development of at-risk children and youth and their families, as well as protective services and shelter (and adoption) for such children. A new protective factor framework based on emerging research on protective factors supports a focus on promoting well-being, as well as the objectives of safety and permanency (e.g., US Department of Health and Human Services, 2013).

About a third of those with substantiated maltreatment are placed in foster care (US Department of Health and Human Services, 2012) to improve their safety and security. However, whether out-of-home placements for maltreated children are a protective factor, a risk factor, or neither, remains a debated issue. For example, Lawrence, Carlson, and Egeland (2006, p. 71) reported that foster care placement may "lead to an increase in behavior problems that continues after exiting the system". However, Jonson-Reid and colleagues have also considered the effect of child welfare services, relying on agency data rather than self-report data (Jonson-Reid & Barth, 2000, 2003; Jonson-Reid, 2002). Generally, two groups are identified in Jonson-Reid's models: maltreated with services, and maltreated without services. Overall, foster care leads to improved outcomes, although factors such as placement stability, gender, race/ethnicity, as well as level of services, influence subsequent involvement in the juvenile justice system. DeGue and Widom (2009) found that placement of maltreated youth in foster care was associated with a significantly lower likelihood of adult arrest than remaining at home: almost half of the children who remained at home following sustained maltreatment were arrested as adults, compared to a third of those who were placed in foster care.

A number of factors appear to moderate outcomes. For example, group home care, often a placement of last resort, as compared to a family foster home, seems to be associated with more adverse outcomes (Ryan *et al.*, 2007). Programs of enhanced foster care are more clearly protective (Chamberlain & Mihalic, 1998; Kessler *et al.*, 2008). Since foster care can clearly provide protection for some youth, further clarity about how resilience can be promoted in such settings is important. Thus, these results remind us of the importance of service system accountability and policy shifts to promote better systems of care.

Changing service systems to address crossover youth

As was just discussed, the challenging experiences and criminal outcomes of maltreated youth indicate shortcomings in both child protection and evidence-based service provision, as well as new opportunities for improved approaches. Children who are involved with the child welfare system as well as with the juvenile justice system are referred to as crossover youth (Ryan *et al.*, 2007) or dually-involved youth (Huang, Ryan, & Herz, 2012).

For these youth, it seems appropriate to consider systems of care that provide a range of coordinated services to address both issues. Several jurisdictions are utilizing the Crossover Youth Practice Model, developed by the Center for Juvenile Justice Reform at Georgetown University in conjunction with Casey Family Programs (e.g., Herz *et al.*, 2012). This best-practice model proposes several strategies for cross-system identification, tracking and service provision for adolescents embedded in both the child welfare system and the juvenile justice system. Thus, positive steps are being made to reform practice and services for crossover youth, and technological developments will facilitate the gathering of information on program outcomes and further build the evidence base.

Conclusion

The distance travelled since identification of the battered child syndrome in 1962 – more than 50 years ago – is truly remarkable. We have much improved tracking systems to help understand the extent of maltreatment in American society, and longitudinal studies provide clear and fairly consistent results that indicate maltreatment has the potential to have developmentally damaging consequences across a broad array of behavioral outcomes during adolescence and early adulthood. Neurobiological studies are providing increasing evidence of internal mediators as well as risk and protective processes. In addition, evidence-based interventions have been developed and implemented that are designed to help prevent and address maltreatment. However, there is much work to be done. Considering maltreatment in the context of a broader conceptualization of exposure to violence, including in the family or in the neighborhood, will increase efforts to improve our understanding of the pathways that lead from maltreatment to delinquency and the mechanisms that act as protective factors. Finally, work is moving forward in the policy and service system to develop programs and policies that adequately address the needs of the maltreated children who are caught up in both the child welfare and juvenile justice systems.

References

Barnickol, L.A. (2000). The disparate treatment of males and females within the juvenile justice system. *Washington University Journal of Law and Policy, 2*, 429–457.

Berlin, L.J., Appleyard, K., & Dodge, K.A. (2011). Intergenerational continuity in child maltreatment: Mediating mechanisms and implications for prevention. *Child Development, 82*, 162–176.

Black, M.M., Oberlander, S.E., Lewis, T., Knight, E.D., Zolotor, A.J., ... English, D.E. (2009). Sexual intercourse among adolescents maltreated before age 12: A prospective investigation. *Pediatrics, 124*, 941–949.

Blinn-Pike, L., Berger, T., Dixon, D., Kuschel, D., & Kaplan, M. (2002). Is there a causal link between maltreatment and adolescent pregnancy? A literature review. *Perspectives on Sexual and Reproductive Health, 34*, 68–75.

Bright, C.L., & Jonson-Reid, M. (2008). Onset of juvenile court involvement: Exploring gender-specific associations with maltreatment and poverty. *Children and Youth Services Review, 30*, 914–927.

Bronfenbrenner, U. (1979). *The Ecology of Human Development.* Cambridge, MA: Harvard University Press.

Bronfenbrenner, U. (1986). The ecology of the family as a context for human development: Research perspectives. *Developmental Psychology, 22*, 723–774.

CAPTA (Child Abuse Prevention and Treatment Act). (2010). As Amended by P.L. 111-320 The CAPTA Reauthorization Act of 2010, 42 U.S.C. § 5106(g). Retrieved from http://www.law.cornell.edu/uscode/text/42/5106g

Centers for Disease Control and Prevention. (2008). *Strategic direction for child maltreatment prevention: Preventing child maltreatment through the promotion of safe, stable, and nurturing relationships between children and caregivers.* Retrieved from http://www.cdc.gov/violenceprevention/pdf/cm_strategic_direction--long-a.pdf

Centers for Disease Control and Prevention. (2012). *Child Maltreatment: Prevention Strategies.* Retrieved from http://www.cdc.gov/violenceprevention/childmaltreatment/prevention.html.

Chamberlain, P., & Mihalic, S.F. (1998). *Blueprints for Violence Prevention, Book 8: Multidimensional Treatment Foster Care.* Boulder, CO: Center for the Study and Prevention of Violence.

Child Welfare Information Gateway. (2014). *Child Abuse and Neglect Fatalities 2012: Statistics and Interventions.* Washington, DC: US Department of Health and Human Services, Children's Bureau.

Cicchetti, D., & Barnett, D. (1991). Toward the development of a scientific nosology of child maltreatment. In W. Gove, & D. Cicchetti (Eds.), *Thinking clearly about psychology, Essays in honor of Paul E. Meehl: Personality and Psychopathology (Vol. 2)* (pp. 346–377). Minneapolis: University of Minnesota Press.

Cicchetti, D., & Lynch, M. (1993). Toward an ecological/transactional model of community violence and child maltreatment: Consequences for children's development. *Psychiatry, 56*, 96–118.

Curtis, G.C. (1963). Violence breeds violence – perhaps? *American Journal of Psychiatry, 120*, 386–387.

DeGue, S., & Widom, C.S. (2009). Does out-of-home placement mediate the relationship between child maltreatment and adult criminality? *Child Maltreatment, 14*, 344–355.

Dennis, M.L., & Stevens, S.J. (2003). Maltreatment issues and outcomes of adolescents enrolled in substance abuse treatment. *Child Maltreatment, 18*, 3–6.

Dodge, K.A., Bates, J.E., & Pettit, G.S. (1990). Mechanisms in the cycle of violence, *Science, 250*, 1678–1683.

Dodge, K.A., Pettit, G.S., Bates, J.E., & Valente, E. (1995). Social information-processing patterns partially mediate the effect of early physical abuse on later conduct problems. *Journal of Abnormal Psychology, 104*, 632–643.

Dolan, M., Smith, K., Casanueva, C., & Ringeisen, H. (2012). *NSCAW II Wave 2 Report: Child and caregiver need and receipt of Child Welfare Services post-baseline.* OPRE Report #2013-08. Washington, DC: Office of Planning, Research and Evaluation, Administration for Children and Families, US Department of Health and Human Services.

Dubowitz, H. (2007). Understanding and addressing the 'neglect of neglect'. *Child Abuse & Neglect, 31,* 603–606.

DuMont, K.A, Widom, C.S., & Czaja, S.J. (2007). Predictors of resilience in abused and neglected children grown-up: The role of individual and neighborhood characteristics. *Child Abuse & Neglect, 31,* 255–274.

Eckenrode, J., Zielinski, D., Smith, E., Marcynyszyn, L.A., Henderson, Jr, C.R., Kitzman, H., … Olds, D.L. (2001). Child maltreatment and the early onset of problem behaviors: Can a program of nurse home visitations break the link? *Development and Psychopathology, 13,* 873–890.

Edleson, J.L. (1999). Children's witnessing of adult domestic violence. *Journal of Interpersonal Violence, 14,* 839–870.

Egeland, B., Carlson, E., & Sroufe, L.A. (1993). Resilience as process. *Development and Psychopathology, 5,* 517–528.

Egeland, B., Yates, T., Appleyard, K., & Van Dulmen, M. (2002). The long-term consequences of maltreatment in the early years: A developmental pathway model to antisocial behavior. *Children's Services: Social Policy, Research, and Practice, 5,* 249–260.

Fang, X., Brown, D.S., Florence, C.S., & Mercy, J.A. (2012). The economic burden of child maltreatment in the United States and implications for prevention. *Child Abuse & Neglect, 36,* 156–165.

Felitti, V.J., Anda, R.F., Nordenberg, D., Williamson, D.F., Spitz, A.M., Edwards, V., Koss, M.P., & Marks, J.S. (1998). Relationship of child abuse and household dysfunction to many of the leading causes of death in adults: The Adverse Childhood Experiences (ACE) Study. *American Journal of Preventive Medicine, 14,* 245–258.

Finkelhor, D., Ormond, R., & Turner, H.A. (2007). Polyvictimization and trauma in a national longitudinal cohort. *Development and Psychopathology, 19,* 149–166.

Fite, J.E., Bates, J.E., Holtzworth-Munroe, A., Dodge, K.A., Nay, S.Y., & Pettit, G.S. (2008). Social information processing mediates the intergenerational transmission of aggressiveness in romantic relationships. *Journal of Family Psychology, 22,* 367–376.

Funk, R.R., McDermeit, M., Godley, S.H., & Adams, L. (2003). Maltreatment issues by level of adolescent substance abuse treatment: The extent of the problem at intake and relationship to early outcomes. *Child Maltreatment, 8,* 36–45.

Garmezy, N., & Masten, A.S. (1986). Stress, competence and resilience: Common frontiers for therapist and psychopathologist. *Behavior Therapy, 17,* 500–521.

Goldman, J., Salus, M.K., Wolcott, D., & Kennedy, K.Y. (2003). *A Coordinated Response to Child Abuse and Neglect: The Foundation for Practice.* Washington, DC: US Department of Health and Human Services, Office on Child Abuse and Neglect.

Grella, C.E., & Joshi, V. (2003). Treatment processes and outcomes among adolescents with a history of abuse who are in drug treatment. *Child Maltreatment, 8,* 7–18.

Grogan-Kaylor, A., & Otis, M.D. (2003). The effect of childhood maltreatment on adult criminality: A tobit regression analysis. *Child Maltreatment, 8,* 129–137.

Henggeler, S.W., Mihalic, S.F., Rone, L., Thomas, C., & Timmons-Mitchell, J. (1998). *Blueprints for Violence Prevention, Book 6: Multisystemic Therapy.* Boulder, CO: Center for the Study and Prevention of Violence.

Herrenkohl, T.I., Sousa, C., Tajima, E.A., Herrenkohl, R.C., & Moylan, C.A. (2008). Intersection of child abuse and children's exposure to domestic violence. *Trauma, Violence and Abuse, 9,* 84–99.

Herz, D., Lee, P., Lutz, L., Stewart, M., Tuell, J., & Wing, J. (2012). *Addressing the needs of multi-system youth: Strengthening the connection between Child Welfare and Juvenile Justice.* Center for Juvenile Justice Reform. Retrieved from http://cjjr.georgetown.edu/pdfs/msy/AddressingtheNeedsofMultiSystemYouth.pdf

Hoffmann, J.P. (2011). *Delinquency Theories, Appraisals and Applications.* New York: Routledge.

Huang, S., Ryan, J.P., & Herz, D. (2011). The journey of dually-involved youth: The description and prediction of rereporting and recidivism. *Children and Youth Services Review, 34*, 254–260.

Hussey, D.L., & Singer, M. (1993). Psychological distress, problem behaviors, and family functioning of sexually abused adolescent inpatients. *Journal of the American Academy of Child and Adolescent Psychiatry, 32*, 954–961.

Ireland, T.O., & Smith, C.A. (2009). Living in partner-violent families: Developmental links to antisocial behavior and relationship violence. *Journal of Youth and Adolescence, 38*, 323–339.

Ireland, T.O., Smith, C.A., & Thornberry, T.P. (2002). Developmental issues in the impact of child maltreatment on later delinquency and drug use. *Criminology, 40*, 359–399.

Ireland, T.O., & Widom, C.S. (1994). Childhood victimization and risk for alcohol and drug arrests. *International Journal of Addictions, 29*, 235–274.

Jarvis, T.J., Copeland, J., & Walton, L. (1998). Exploring the nature of the relationship between sexual abuse and substance use among women. *Addiction, 93*, 865–875.

Jones, D.J., Runyan, D.K., Leiws, T., Litrownik, A.J., Black, M.M., Wiley, T., … Nagin, D.S. (2010). Trajectories of child sexual abuse and early adolescent HIV/AIDS risk behaviors: The role of other maltreatment, witnessed violence and child gender. *Journal of Clinical & Adolescent Psychology, 39*, 667–680.

Jonson-Reid, M. (2002). Exploring the relationships between child welfare intervention and juvenile corrections involvement. *American Journal of Orthopsychiatry, 72*, 559–576.

Jonson-Reid, M., & Barth, R.P. (2000). From maltreatment report to juvenile incarceration: The role of child welfare services. *Child Abuse & Neglect, 24*, 505–520.

Jonson-Reid, M., & Barth, R.P. (2003). Probation foster care as an outcome for children exiting child welfare foster care. *Social Work, 48*, 348–361.

Kaufman, J., & Zigler, E. (1987). Do abused children become abusive parents? *American Journal of Orthopsychiatry, 57*, 186–192.

Kaufman, J.G., & Widom, C.S. (1999). Childhood victimization, running away, and delinquency. *Journal of Research in Crime and Delinquency, 36*, 347–370.

Kelley, B.T., Thornberry, T.P., & Smith, C.A. (1997). *In the Wake of Childhood Maltreatment,* Juvenile Justice Bulletin. Washington, DC: Office of Juvenile Justice and Delinquency Prevention, US Department of Justice.

Kessler, R.C., Pecora, P.J., Williams, J., Hiripi, E., O'Brien, K., English, D., … Sampson, N.A. (2008). Effects of enhanced foster care on the long-term physical and mental health of foster care alumni. *Archives of General Psychiatry, 65*, 625–633.

Kim, M.J., Tajima, E.A., Herrenkohl, T.I., & Huang, B. (2009). Early child maltreatment, runaway youths and risk of delinquency and victimization in adolescence: A mediational model. *Social Work Research, 33*, 19–28.

Klika, J.B., Herrenkohl, T.I., & Lee, J.O. (2012). School factors as moderators of the relationship between physical child abuse and pathways of antisocial behavior. *Journal of Interpersonal Violence, 28*, 852–867.

Knutson, J.F., & Heckenberg, D. (2006). Operationally defining physical abuse of children. In M.M. Feerick, J.F. Knutson, P.K. Trickett, & S.M. Flanzer (Eds.), *Child Abuse and Neglect: Definitions, Classifications, and a Framework for Research* (pp. 69–106). London: Paul H. Brookes.

Lansford, J.E., Criss, M.M., Dodge, K.A., Shaw, D.S., Pettit, G.S., & Bates, J.E. (2009). Trajectories of physical discipline: Early childhood antecedents and developmental outcomes. *Child Development, 80*, 1385–1402.

Lansford, J.E., Dodge, K.A., Pettit, G.S., & Bates, J.E. (2010). Does physical abuse in early childhood predict substance use in adolescence and early adulthood? *Child Maltreatment, 15*, 190–194.

Lansford, J.E., Miller-Johnson, S., Berlin, L.J., Dodge, K.A., Bates, J.E., & Pettit, G.S. (2007). Early physical abuse and later violent delinquency: A prospective longitudinal study. *Child Maltreatment, 12*, 233–245.

Lawrence, C.R., Carlson, E.A., & Egeland, B. (2006). The impact of foster care on development. *Development and Psychopathology, 18*, 57–76.

Leiter, J. (2007). School performance trajectories after the advent of reported maltreatment. *Children and Youth Services Review, 29*, 363–382.

Lo, C.C., & Cheng, T.C. (2007). The impact of childhood maltreatment on young adults' substance abuse. *American Journal of Drug and Alcohol Abuse, 33*, 139–146.

Luthar, S.S., Cicchetti, D., & Becker, B. (2000). The construct of resilience: A critical evaluation and guidelines for future work. *Child Development, 71*, 543–562.

Maas, C., Herrenkohl, T.I. & Sousa, C. (2008). Review of research on child maltreatment and violence in youth. *Trauma, Violence and Abuse, 9*, 56–67.

MacMillan, H.L., Wathen, C.N., Barlow, J., Fergusson, D.M., Leventhal, J.M., & Taussig, H.N. (2009). Interventions to prevent child maltreatment and associated impairment. *The Lancet, 373*, 250–266.

Masten, A.S. (2007). Resilience in developing systems: Progress and promise as the fourth wave rises. *Development and Psychopathology, 19*, 921–930.

McCrory, E., Brito, S.A., & Viding, E. (2010). Research review: The neurobiology and genetics of maltreatment and adversity. *Journal of Child Psychology and Psychiatry, 51*, 1079–1095.

McGloin, J.M., & Widom, C.S. (2001). Resilience among abused and neglected children grown up. *Development and Psychopathology, 13*, 1021–1038.

Mersky, J.P., Topitzes, J., & Reynolds, A.J. (2012). Unsafe at any age: Linking childhood and adolescent maltreatment to delinquency and crime. *Journal of Research in Crime and Delinquency, 49*, 295–318.

NSCAW (National Survey of Child and Adolescent Well-Being). (2007a). *No. 16: A Summary of NSCAW Findings*. Washington, DC: Administration for Children and Families.

NSCAW (National Survey of Child and Adolescent Well-Being). (2007b). *No. 11: Adolescents Involved with Child Welfare: A Transition to Adulthood*. Washington, DC: Administration for Children and Families.

NYS (New York State) Family Court Act. (2012). Child Protection Proceedings, Article 10, Part 1 - §1012.

Olds, D.L. (2006). The nurse-family partnership: An evidence-based preventive intervention. *Infant Mental Health Journal, 27*, 5–25.

Paivio, S.C., & Cramer, K.M. (2004). Factor structure and reliability of the Childhood Trauma Questionnaire in a Canadian undergraduate student sample. *Child Abuse & Neglect, 28*, 889–904.

Park, A., Smith, C.A., & Ireland, T.O. (2012). Equivalent harm? The relative roles of maltreatment and exposure to intimate partner violence in antisocial outcomes for young adults. *Children and Youth Services Review, 34,* 962–972.

Perry, B.D. (2006). Applying principles of neurodevelopment to clinical work with maltreated and traumatized children: The neurosequential model of therapeutics. In N.B. Webb (Ed.), *Working With Traumatized Youth in Child Welfare* (pp. 27–57). New York: Guilford.

Prinz, R.J., Sanders, M.R., Shapiro, C.J., Whitaker, D.J., & Lutzker, J.R. (2009). Population-based prevention of child maltreatment: The U.S. Triple P System population trial. *Prevention Science, 10,* 1–12.

Rogosch, F.A., Oshri, A., & Cicchetti, D. (2010). From child maltreatment to adolescent cannabis abuse and dependence: A developmental cascade model. *Development and Psychopathology, 22,* 883–897.

Runyan, D.K., Curtis, P., Hunter, W.M., Black, M.M., Kotch, J.B., Bangdiwala, S., … Landsverk, J. (1998). LONGSCAN: A Consortium for Longitudinal Studies of Maltreatment and the Life Course of Children. *Aggression and Violent Behavior: A Review Journal, 3,* 275–285.

Ryan, J.P., Herz, D., Hernandez, P.M., & Marshall, J.M. (2007). Maltreatment and delinquency: Investigating child welfare bias in juvenile justice processing. *Child and Youth Services Review, 29,* 1035–1050.

Sedlak, A.J., Mettenburg, J., Basena, M., Petta, I., McPherson, K., Greene, A., & Li, S. (2010). Fourth National Incidence Study of Child Abuse and Neglect (NIS-4): Report to Congress. Washington, DC: US Department of Health and Human Services, Administration for Children and Families.

Shin, S.H., Miller, D.P., & Teicher, M.H. (2013). Exposure to childhood neglect and physical abuse and developmental trajectories of heavy episodic drinking from early adolescence into young adulthood. *Drug and Alcohol Dependence, 127,* 31–38.

Smith, C.A. (1996). The link between childhood maltreatment and teenage pregnancy. *Social Work Research, 20,* 131–141.

Smith, C.A. (1997). Factors associated with early sexual activity among urban adolescents. *Social Work, 42,* 334–346.

Smith, C.A., & Ireland, T.O. (2009). Family violence and criminology. In M. Krohn, A. Lizotte, & G. Penley-Hall (Eds.), *Handbook of Crime and Deviance,* 493–523. New York: Springer.

Smith, C.A., Ireland, T.O., & Thornberry, T.P. (2005). Adolescent maltreatment and its impact on young adult antisocial behavior. *Child Abuse & Neglect, 29,* 1099–1119.

Smith, C.A., Ireland, T.O., Thornberry, T.P., & Elwyn, L. (2008). Childhood maltreatment and antisocial behavior: Comparison of self-reported and substantiated maltreatment. *American Journal of Orthopsychiatry, 78,* 173–186.

Smith, C.A., & Thornberry, T.P. (1995). The relationship between childhood maltreatment and adolescent involvement in delinquency. *Criminology, 33,* 451–481.

Stewart, A., Livingston, M., & Dennison, S. (2008). Transition and turning points: Examining the links between child maltreatment and juvenile offending. *Child Abuse & Neglect, 32,* 51–66.

Stouthamer-Loeber, M., Loeber, R., Homish, D.L., & Wei, E. (2001). Maltreatment of boys and the development of disruptive and delinquent behavior. *Development and Psychopathology, 13,* 941–955.

Straus, M.A., & Kantor, G.K. (2005). Definition and measurement of neglectful behavior: Some principles and guidelines. *Child Abuse & Neglect, 29,* 19–29.

Thornberry, T.P. (1987). Toward an interactional theory of delinquency. *Criminology, 25*, 863–891.

Thornberry, T.P. (2009). The apple doesn't fall far from the tree (or does it?): Intergenerational patterns of antisocial behavior – The American Society of Criminology 2008 Sutherland Address. *Criminology, 47*, 297–325.

Thornberry, T.P., Ireland, T.O., & Smith, C.A. (2001). The importance of timing: The varying impact of childhood and adolescent maltreatment on multiple problem outcomes. *Development and Psychopathology, 13*, 957–979.

Thornberry, T.P., & Krohn, M.D. (2005). Applying interactional theory to the explanation of continuity and change in antisocial behavior. In D.P. Farrington (Ed.), *Integrated Developmental & Life-course Theories of Offending (Vol. 14)* (pp. 183–209). New Brunswick, NJ: Transaction.

Twardosz, S., & Lutzker, J.R. (2010). Child maltreatment and the developing brain: A review of neuroscience perspectives. *Aggression and Violent Behavior, 15*, 59–68.

US Department of Health and Human Services. (2015). *Child Maltreatment 2013*. Retrieved from http://www.acf.hhs.gov/programs/cb/research-data-technology/statistics-research/child-maltreatment

US Department of Health and Human Services. (2013). *Preventing Child Maltreatment and Promoting Well-Being: Network for Action 2013 Resource Guide*. Retrieved from https://www.childwelfare.gov/pubs/guide2013/guide.pdf

Verracchia, P.J., Fetzer, M.D., Lemmon, J.H., & Austin, T.L. (2010). An examination of direct and indirect effects of maltreatment dimensions and other ecological risks on persistent youth offending. *Criminal Justice Review, 35*, 220–243.

Wekerle, C. (2011). The dollars and senselessness in failing to prioritize childhood maltreatment prevention. *Child Abuse & Neglect, 35*, 159–161.

Widom, C.S. (1989). Does violence beget violence? A critical examination of the literature. *Psychological Bulletin, 106*, 3–28.

Widom, C.S. (1997). Child abuse, neglect and witnessing violence. In D.M. Stoff, J. Breiling, & J.D. Maser (Eds.), *Handbook of Antisocial Behavior* (pp. 159–170). New York: John Wiley and Sons, Ltd.

Widom, C.S. (2013). Translational research on child neglect: Progress and future needs. *Child Maltreatment, 18*, 3–7.

Widom, C.S., Ireland, T.O., & Glynn, P. (1995). Alcohol abuse in abused and neglected children followed-up: Are they at increased risk? *Journal of Studies on Alcohol, 56*, 207–217.

Widom, C.S., & Kuhns, J.B. (1996). Childhood victimization and subsequent risk for promiscuity, prostitution, and teenage pregnancy: A prospective study. *American Journal of Public Health, 86*, 1607–1612.

Widom, C.S., & Maxfield, M.G. (2001). *An update on the "Cycle of Violence"*. Research in Brief. Washington, DC: US Department of Justice, National Institute of Justice, NCJ 184894.

Widom, C.S., Schuck, A.M., & White, H.R. (2006). An examination of pathways from childhood victimization to violence: The role of early aggression and problematic alcohol use. *Violence and Victims, 21*, 675–690.

Wilson, H.W., Stover, C.S., & Berkowitz, S.J. (2009). Research review: The relationship between childhood violence exposure and juvenile antisocial behavior: a met-analytic review. *Child Psychology and Psychiatry, 50*, 769–779.

World Health Organization, & International Society for Prevention of Child Abuse and Neglect. (2006). Preventing child maltreatment: A guide to taking action and generating evidence. Geneva: World Health Organization.

Zimmerman, F., & Mercy, J.A. (2010). *A better start: Child maltreatment prevention as a public health priority: Zero to three.* Retrieved from http://www.zerotothree.org/maltreatment/child-abuse-neglect/30-5-zimmerman.pdf

35

Victimization and Fear of Crime Among Juveniles

David C. May

Actors in the juvenile justice system spend the majority of their time trying to apprehend and control individuals who violate the law. Nevertheless, there are important aspects of the study of juvenile justice that do not involve the apprehension or processing of the alleged delinquent. Two of these aspects involve crime victimization and fear of crime. In this chapter, I will discuss these two concepts in detail, examine the existing research around both topics, and close by offering strategies for expanding theory, policy, and practice in both of these areas.

Crime Victimization

According to the Merriam-Webster online dictionary, a victim is "one that is acted on and usually adversely affected by a force or agent"; thus a crime victim is an individual who is acted on and adversely affected by criminal act. The study of crime victimization, then, is the study of the adverse effects of crime on its victims and the causes and consequences of those effects. To have a full understanding of crime victimization, particularly victimization among juveniles, it is important to understand its prevalence. There are three primary sources of data about the extent of crime victimization among juveniles in the US: the Uniform Crime Reports, published annually by the Federal Bureau of Investigation; the National Crime Victimization Survey, published annually by the Bureau of Justice Statistics; and the Indicators of School Crime and Safety report, published annually by the Bureau of Justice

The Handbook of Juvenile Delinquency and Juvenile Justice, First Edition. Edited by Marvin D. Krohn and Jodi Lane.
© 2015 John Wiley & Sons, Inc. Published 2015 by John Wiley & Sons, Inc.

Statistics and the National Center for Education Statistics. Each of these sources of victimization data is discussed in detail below.

Uniform Crime Reports

One of the most important sources of data about crime victimization (particularly long-term trends in crime victimization) is the Uniform Crime Reports (UCR) produced annually by the Federal Bureau of Investigation (FBI). Each year, over 18,000 city, county, state, university, and tribal police agencies in the US voluntarily submit crime data about crimes known to the police from their jurisdiction to the FBI. The FBI then uses those data to compile the annual publication of the UCR. In 2011, the UCR indicated that there were 14,612 murders, 83,425 rapes, 354,396 robberies, 751,131 aggravated assaults, 2,188,005 burglaries, 6,159,795 larceny-thefts, and 715,373 motor vehicle thefts known to the police (Federal Bureau of Investigation, 2012).

Among the individuals arrested for these crimes, juveniles made up a small portion of these arrests, particularly for violent crime. Only 7.8% (651) of those arrested for murder, 14.1% (2,071) of those arrested for rape, 22.3% (18,377) of those arrested for robbery, and 10.2% (31,265) of those arrested for aggravated assault were juveniles. Juveniles were arrested for slightly larger percentages of serious property crime. Approximately one in five individuals arrested for larceny-theft, burglary, and motor vehicle theft was under the age of 18. More than two in five individuals arrested for arson (41%) in 2011 were juveniles. Of the less serious crimes, juveniles were most likely to be arrested for vandalism (28.5% of all those arrested were under 18) and disorderly conduct (23.6%) (Federal Bureau of Investigation, 2012).

Both UCR data and other data sources indicate that violent and property crime victimization among juveniles has decreased dramatically in the past few years, a fact that is both often unknown and unreported by various media outlets. In 2011, 9.3% of all murder victims (1,187) were under the age of 18 (Federal Bureau of Investigation, 2012). This figure is 15% lower than that same figure in 2001, when 1,402 murder victims were under the age of 18 (Federal Bureau of Investigation, 2002). In 2010, the total violent crime rate among juveniles was the lowest it had been in over three decades, and both the total violent crime rate for juveniles in 2010 (224.5 per 100,000) and the total property crime rate for juveniles (1,084.3 per 100,000) were less than half what they were two decades ago (449.9 per 100,000 for violent crime and 2,407 per 100,000 for total property crime in 1992) (National Center for Juvenile Justice, 2012).

Although the UCR provides important data about criminal offending and victimization in the US, there are two important limitations of the victimization data provided by the UCR that affect both adults and juveniles. First, and most importantly, with the exception of murder, the UCR provides no information about the victims of crime. Secondly, the UCR provides data only about victimizations reported to the police; thus, unreported crimes, or the "dark figure of crime", are not covered in the UCR (Meadows, 2014).

National Crime Victimization Survey

Over four decades ago, these limitations of UCR data motivated criminologists to attempt to develop more reliable measures of crime and victimization, with the hope of providing a more thorough picture of crime victimization in the US. As a result, criminologists developed the National Crime Victimization Survey (NCVS) to supplement the UCR by (1) providing data about victimizations not reported to the police and (2) providing more detailed information on situational factors (location and time of crime, etc.) and characteristics of victims of crime.

The NCVS is compiled by the Bureau of Justice Statistics and conducted by the US Census Bureau, and measures six of the eight index crimes examined by the UCR (rape, robbery, aggravated assault, burglary, larceny-theft, and motor vehicle theft). The NCVS does not compile data on murder or arson. Data on murder are not collected because the victim is dead, and arson is excluded because of the difficulty in determining whether the fire was intentionally set by the property owner or someone else (Bureau of Justice Statistics, 2013).

The NCVS originated in 1972 and is conducted every six months by the Department of Justice. The NCVS consists of household surveys of about 40,000 households, involving about 75,000 people each year. The NCVS tracks households for a three-year period. Each household is surveyed seven times: once upon entering the study and then at six-month intervals over the next three years. Participants are asked to report victimizations that have occurred in the previous six months. Information collected about victimizations includes: (1) the time and place of victimization; (2) the extent of the property damage or physical injury sustained; (3) the medical costs; (4) whether the victim engaged in self-defense; (5) whether the assailant was a stranger; (6) estimates of offender's race, gender, and approximate age; and (7) whether the victim reported the crime to the police (Bureau of Justice Statistics, 2013).

The NCVS relies on three types of respondents. A "knowledgeable adult" answers questions that pertain to the household. All household members aged 12 and over are then asked about their background characteristics and personal victimizations. "Proxy" respondents are used to answer the survey for household members not competent enough to answer on their own. The NCVS reports victimizations (number of people victimized) and incidents (number of criminal acts involving one or more victims) (Bureau of Justice Statistics, 2013).

Nevertheless, there are problems with NCVS data as well. One of the major problems facing the NCVS is "telescoping" – remembering incidents as occurring more recently than they actually occurred (forward telescoping) or as occurring in the more distant past than they actually occurred (backward telescoping). Results of the NCVS are also subject to interviewer effects; that is, some interviewers are able to uncover a larger number of victimizations from respondents than other interviewers. Another problem faced by the NCVS is related to the sampling design. Those respondents who have been interviewed before realize that if they answer a screen question about their criminal victimization affirmatively, they will be questioned much more extensively about the victimization incident. There is evidence to indicate that those who have been interviewed before report fewer victimizations, although this effect seems to be relatively small (O'Brien, 1985).

According to a recent report using NCVS data (White & Lauritsen, 2012), in 2010, juveniles in the US between 12 and 17 years of age experienced 873,449 violent crimes. The violent victimization rate for juveniles in 2010 (35.6 per 100,000) was slightly over half the 2002 rate (68.5 per 100,000) and far less than the 1994 rate (187.1 per 100,000). Since 1994, total violent crime victimizations among juveniles have declined over 80%; similar declines were found for rape/sexual assault (68%), robbery (77%), aggravated assault (80%), and simple assault (83%) (White & Lauritsen, 2012). Thus, juveniles are much less likely to be victimized by all types of violent crime today than two decades ago.

Indicators of School Crime and Safety

While both the UCR and the NCVS provide some data regarding victimization of juveniles, perhaps the most often cited source of victimization among juveniles is the Indicators of School Crime and Safety reports, published annually by the Bureau of Justice Statistics and the National Center for Education Statistics. Using data from a variety of sources, the report authors provide a variety of information about victimization of juveniles in school settings. The paragraphs below describe those findings for 2012.

Between July 1, 2010, and June 30, 2011, there were 31 school-associated violent deaths; of this number, 14 involved juvenile victims. Eleven of the 14 school-associated violent deaths were victims of homicide, while three were suicide victims. In 2011, students aged 12–18 were victims of 1.246 million non-fatal victimizations at school. These victimizations were distributed almost equally among thefts (648,600) and violent victimizations (597,500). Students were more likely to be victimized by property crime at school than away from school (49 per 1,000 at school vs. 38 per 1,000 away from school), but were equally likely to be victimized by non-serious violent crime at school as they were to be victimized away from school. Only 3% of students reported that they had been victimized by theft during the past six months at school; only 1% of students reported that they had been victimized by non-serious violence, and an even smaller proportion of students (0.1%) indicated that they had been the victim of serious violence during the past six months at school. In 2011, about 28% of students between the ages of 12 and 18 reported that they had been bullied at school during the past year; females were more likely than males to experience non-physical bullying (teasing, rumors, etc.) while males were more likely than females to be victims of physical bullying (being pushed, shoved, tripped, etc.). Students in 6th grade were more likely to be victimized by bullying than students in grades 7–12 (Robers, Kemp, Truman, & Snyder, 2013).

The three sources of data reviewed here suggest that juveniles are rarely victimized, either at school or away from school. Nevertheless, a number of studies have demonstrated that victimization among juveniles covaries with juvenile offending; in other words, victimization occurs most frequently among individuals engaged in delinquent behavior, particularly violent delinquency. In fact, a large body of research has determined that juveniles engaged in violent activity are much more likely to be victimized by crime than their counterparts who are not engaged in violence. This relationship has often been explained from a lifestyle/opportunity perspective, which argues that the lifestyles of certain youths make them more susceptible to victimization by crime. These youths engage in risky activities, such as joyriding, going to parties, staying out late at night, and various types of substance use and abuse. This lifestyle makes these youths more susceptible to victimization than their counterparts not engaging in these lifestyles (for review, see Vaske, Bosivert, & Wright, 2012).

Consequently, those theoretical perspectives that predict juvenile offending also predict juvenile victimization as well. While a detailed review of those theoretical perspectives is beyond the scope of this discussion, these studies generally indicate that (among other factors), youths with low self-control, weak bonds to conventional societal institutions, deviant friends, and whose family lives are dysfunctional, are both more likely to commit crime and be victimized by crime. Additionally, a number of demographic factors appear to influence juvenile victimization as well. In sum, non-white males from lower socioeconomic classes are those most likely to be victimized by crime. These demographic factors, and explanations for their relationship with increased likelihood of victimization, are discussed in detail below.

Gender and victimization

With the exception of rape/sexual assault, males are far more likely to be victimized by crime than females. In 2011, juvenile victims of murder were over twice as likely to be male as female (813 vs. 371 victims) (Federal Bureau of Investigation, 2012). For both adults and juveniles, males were slightly more likely than females to be victimized by violent crime in 2011 (Bureau of Justice Statistics, 2013), while females were over four times more likely than males to experience rape and sexual assault. Males are slightly more likely than females to be victimized by all other crimes for which the NCVS reports data (US Department of Justice, 2011).

Social class and victimization

The relationship between victimization and social class is also important. People with lower household incomes are much more likely to be victimized by violent crime (44.0 per 1,000 for those whose household income is less than $7,500 per year) than any other income group. In fact, there is a clear inverse relationship between household income and violent crime victimization. As household income increases, rates of violent victimization decrease. For the highest household income group ($75,000 and more), the total violent victimization rate is 12.9 per 1,000. The relationship between class and victimization for total property crime is also an inverse relationship, as households with household income less than $7,500 have the highest total property crime victimization rate (204.2 per 1,000), while those with household incomes between $50,000 and $75,000 and households whose income is over $75,000 have the lowest property crime victimization rates (US Department of Justice, 2011). Thus, juveniles from lower socioeconomic households are more likely to be victimized by crime than their more wealthy counterparts.

Race and victimization

Black people under the age of 18 were more likely than other racial groups to be murder victims in 2011 (572 black victims vs. 559 white victims and 36 victims of other races) (Federal Bureau of Investigation, 2012). For both adults and juveniles, victimization studies also indicate that blacks are more likely to be victimized by other violent crimes than whites and Hispanics (US Department of Justice, 2011).

Hawkins, Laub, Lauritsen, and Cothern (2000) suggested four explanations that highlight the interaction between class and race to explain the differential involvement of blacks in crime, particularly violent crime. The first explanation is that life courses of blacks are different than those of whites, as blacks are much more likely to grow up in poverty. Secondly, certain urban areas have persistent poverty and delinquency; blacks are much more likely to live in those areas. Thirdly, black male joblessness and incarceration causes family disruption, which has a significant effect on engagement in crime among adolescents, particularly violent delinquency. Finally, increased urbanization, inequality, and class segregation has differentially impacted blacks more than whites. Two in five blacks live in poverty, a percentage much higher than that for whites.

Age and victimization

As stated earlier, less than 1 in 10 murder victims each year is under the age of 18. For crime in general, however, adolescents are more prone to victimization than any other age group. Youths aged 12–15 (43.6 per 1,000) have the highest victimization rates for violent crime, followed closely by people aged 20–24 (38.4 per 1,000) and those aged 16–19 (37.4 per 1,000). Those aged 65 and older have the lowest victimization rates (3.5 per 1,000). The relationship between age and property crime mirrors that of violent crime, as the total property crime victimization rate for youths aged 12–15 is more than four times greater than the rate for adults aged 65 and over (267.9 per 1,000 and 62.4 per 1,000, respectively) (US Department of Justice, 2011).

Theories of Victimization

The scholarly study of crime victimization began in earnest in the 1940s. One of the first researchers to study victimization was Hans von Hentig, who studied the relationship between crime victims and offenders. Hentig argued that there were a number of personal factors associated with criminal victimization, and suggested that victims could be categorized into 12 categories. These categories included the young and the elderly (who were victimized because of their weakness and immaturity due to their underdeveloped physical statures, or their frailty); females (vulnerable to victimization because of less physical strength); the mentally defective (who were victimized because of their underdeveloped mental processes); immigrants (who were victimized because of their lack of experience with the new culture); minorities (who are forced to live where crime flourishes); "dull normals" (vulnerable because they are easily swindled due to their simple minds); depressed (vulnerable because of their psychological problems); "acquisitive" (greedy people susceptible to frauds and cheats); the "wanton" (males or females whose attempts at seduction of others make them more vulnerable to victimization); the lonesome and heartbroken (vulnerable to those that take advantage of their loneliness and sadness to commit crime against them); the tormentor (abusive individuals whose victim turns on them and victimizes them); and blocked, exempted, and fighting victims (individuals who become victims because of situations they have created for themselves (Hentig, 1948)).

Hentig's typology laid the foundation for future studies of victimization that further clarified his groups and attempted to explain why these groups were more likely to be victimized. Mendelsohn suggested a typology of victims that included six categories: the innocent victim (who is unaware of their potential for victimization) and five categories of victims who, in twenty-first century vernacular, would all be considered as categories of victim-precipitated crime. These categories include the victim with minor guilt (a victim who frequents high-crime areas); the victim as guilty as the offender (where the victim cooperates with the offender to commit a crime, then is victimized after the initial crime commission is ended); the victim more guilty than the offender (where the victim provokes someone else and is injured after the provocation); the most guilty victim (a victim killed by someone in self-defense); and the imaginary victim (those who pretend to be victims) (Doerner & Lab, 2012).

The works by Hentig and Mendelsohn are often referred to as the seminal works in the area of victimization. More recent work by Schafer built on Hentig's work and created a typology of victims that has come to be known as Schafer's Victim Precipitation Typology (Doerner & Lab, 2012). In this typology, Schafer focused on the responsibility of the different victims in their own victimization. These categories include the unrelated victim (no victim responsibility), the provocative victim (where the offender is reacting to some action by the victim), the precipitative victim (where the victim increases their vulnerability by being in dangerous places, or acting inappropriately), the biologically weak victim (the young, the old, the physically weak or disabled), the socially weak victim (immigrants, minorities, or others who are not successfully integrated in the larger society), self-victimizing (individuals involved in "victimless" crimes such as gambling and drug use), and political victims (individuals who are victimized because they oppose those in power). Schafer's typology began the exploration of what has come to be known as victim precipitation, or the study of the degree to which a victim is responsible for his or her own victimization (Doerner & Lab, 2012).

Meadows (2014) argues that victim precipitation theory suggests that victimizations occur because of a number of factors that combine to trigger the criminal act. One of these factors is the victim's own behavior. Victim precipitation can be either active (where the victim provokes the criminal encounter directly by their own words or actions) or passive (when the victim unknowingly provokes the criminal encounter because of their own attributes, such as race, beliefs, or sexual orientation). Although the suggestion that the victim could play a role in their own victimization was initially controversial, Doerner and Lab (2012) suggest that a more accurate definition of victim precipitation recognizes four major assumptions. They borrow from the work of Franklin and Franklin and outline four major assumptions of the victim precipitation argument, as follows (Doerner & Lab, 2012, p. 10):

1. The behavior of the victim helps explain the criminal act.
2. The offender initiated the criminal action only after the victim sent out certain signals.
3. A victim's behavior is sufficient and necessary to produce a criminal act.
4. The intent of the victim can be gauged by the victimization incident.

The study of crime victimization continues to evolve and will be a fruitful area of research for many years to come. As highlighted earlier, each year a relatively small number of people are directly impacted by crime victimization. A much larger percentage does not experience crime victimization directly but are fearful of crime; thus, any consideration of crime victimization must consider fear of crime as well. This area of research is discussed in detail in the following pages.

Fear of Crime

Fear can be defined as a "...usually unpleasant feeling that arises as a normal response to danger" (Scruton 1986, p. 30). Fear is often a rational response to a current or perceived threat and serves as a coping function because fear contributes to survival of a species. Just as they fear snakes, spiders, and public speaking, humans often fear that which they cannot control or do not understand. Crime fits both of those criteria.

Fear of crime has a variety of negative consequences. In fact, some scholars have argued that fear of crime may be a more severe problem than crime itself (Doerner & Lab, 2012), and the fear of crime is often incongruent with actual crime levels.

Even though the crime rate has declined dramatically since 1992 (Federal Bureau of Investigation, 2012), crimes such as the recent Sandy Hook elementary school mass murder (CNN, 2013) continue to make Americans fearful of crime, particularly violent crime.

Public opinion polls among adults provide evidence of the disjunction between fear of crime and the actual crime rate itself. For several decades, pollsters at Gallup have asked respondents "Is there any area right around here – that is, within a mile – where you would be afraid to walk alone at night?" In 2011, 38% of respondents answered yes; this percentage has remained stable over almost two decades, despite a dramatic reduction in crime in that same period (Gallup, 2012). Even though there is some controversy over whether this question is a valid measure of fear (see Ferraro, 1995), it is apparent that whatever the question is measuring, whether fear or perceived risk, Americans are just as concerned about crime as in previous years, despite dramatic reductions in violent crime.

One of the most controversial issues in recent studies examining fear of crime concerns the definition of fear of crime. Ferraro (1995) argued that many investigators apparently assume that the definition of fear of crime is obvious, and refrain from clearly delineating exactly what fear is. Ferraro (1995) defined fear of crime as "an emotional response of dread or anxiety to crime or symbols that a person associates with crime" (Ferraro, 1995, p. xiii). Ferraro's effort, while admirable, is obviously not the norm. Because of the difficulty in defining fear of crime, some authors believe that differences in defining and measuring fear of crime impede the ability to make generalizations about fear of crime (Ferraro & LaGrange, 1987).

Craske (1999) asserted that fear can be measured in three ways: verbally, behaviorally, and physiologically. The vast majority of studies measuring fear of crime use verbal self-reports where respondents are asked to indicate their level of fear through self-report surveys. Despite the fact that most fear of crime researchers use survey research techniques to measure fear of crime, there is little consensus about which survey question or questions are best to use to measure the phenomenon.

Until recently, fear of crime was measured most often with a single item indicator (much like the Gallup measure reviewed earlier) or a similar measure used by the National Crime Victimization Survey: "How safe do you feel or would you feel being out alone in your neighborhood at night?" (Ferraro & LaGrange, 1987). This single-item measure has received a wide variety of criticism. Because of the criticism levied at research using single-item indicators to measure fear of crime, several researchers began to use multiple item indices to assess fear. Lee (1982) was one of the first researchers to accomplish this when he constructed a general fear scale, using items such as "When I am away from home, I worry about the safety of my property"; "I worry a great deal about my personal safety from crime and criminals"; and "I worry a great deal about the safety of my loved ones from crime and criminals" (Lee, 1982, p. 659).

Although use of multiple items to measure fear was an improvement over previous research, Lee's measure did not specifically ask about "fear" or whether individuals were "afraid" of crime. Mark Warr (1984) was one of the first researchers to measure fear of crime by asking questions about individuals' fear of specific crimes in his analysis of data collected via mail survey from residents in Seattle in 1981. Ferraro and LaGrange (1987) and Ferraro (1995) determined that his scales are some of the best available and recommend that all fear of crime researchers use these types of measures to examine fear of crime. Due mainly to the efforts of Ferraro, LaGrange, and Warr, other fear of crime researchers have incorporated the use of questions asking about specific crimes to measure fear among their respondents as the most common measure of fear of crime in the twenty-first century.

Nevertheless, there is still not unanimous agreement regarding the measurement of fear of crime. One criticism that applies to fear of crime research applies to most self-report research: that fear of crime would be assessed more completely using open-ended rather than closed-ended questions. Fattah (1993) argued that fear cannot be measured using any type of self-report survey; he argues that fear needs to be measured by assessing physiological changes and reactions, and, as such, research using self-report assessments of fear of crime needs to be abandoned.

Despite the criticisms reviewed earlier, the most acceptable measurement of fear of crime is the use of multi item indices assessing respondent fears of specific crimes, using words such as "fear" and "afraid".

Perceived risk vs. fear of crime

Another recent critique of research in the area of fear of crime concerns the inattention given to the distinction between an individual's fear of criminal victimization and that same individual's perceived risk of victimization. Investigation into the distinction between perceived risk and fear of criminal victimization resulted from the persistent finding that women and the elderly are more fearful of criminal victimization than their younger and male counterparts, despite the fact that the elderly and women are much less likely to be victimized by crime (Ferraro & LaGrange, 1987; Warr, 1984).

Ferraro and LaGrange (1987) and Ferraro (1995) demonstrated that measures of risk of criminal victimization are often mistaken for measures of fear of crime. They argued that questions such as the single-item indicators listed earlier are asking people to judge their risk of victimization by crime, not their actual fear of crime. Ferraro (1995) argued that many researchers confuse fear and risk in their research, and that the two terms are conceptually distinct and thus must be measured separately; fear is an emotional response to a situation, while perceived risk is a cognitive judgment about one's likelihood of being victimized by crime in various situations. Ferraro argued that many researchers not only fail to make the distinction between fear of crime and perceived risk, they also fail to measure risk of criminal victimization at all. He suggested that there are two basic approaches to measuring risk. One method is to examine official crime statistics to provide an official or "objective" risk assessment, while a second method involved asking respondents to evaluate their own risk of victimization. He called this method "perceived risk" (Ferraro, 1995).

Using data collected by telephone from a national sample of respondents, Ferraro determined that, in general, perceived victimization risk correlates highly with official statistics on the prevalence of crime in an area (official risk). Ferraro also determined that perceived risk, as well as gender, race, education, and age, strongly affected fear of criminal victimization (Ferraro, 1995). A wide variety of research over the last two decades has concurred with his findings.

Measuring fear of crime among juveniles

The measurement problems around fear of crime are even more nuanced when considering fear of criminal victimization among juveniles. These problems are amplified by the fact that few published studies examine fear of crime among juveniles; among those that do, the vast majority use self-report data collected from small, local or regional samples of juveniles with specific measures of fear like those mentioned above, or national samples of juveniles with more general measures.

Despite the abundance of research examining fear of crime among adults, the examination of fear of crime among adolescents is much more recent and much less plentiful. In fact, Hale (1996), in an extensive review of the fear of crime literature, noted that adolescents have generally been ignored by fear of crime researchers, and recommend that fear of criminal victimization among this group be "an important research priority" (Hale, 1996, p. 100). Based on the discussion of perceived risk, and the previously highlighted increased likelihood of victimization for juveniles, it is plausible to suggest that adolescents may have higher levels of fear than young, middle-aged, or elderly adults. Youths may accurately sense that they are differentially exposed to criminal victimization, which might cause them to have higher levels of perceived risk. Following the aforementioned research, these higher levels of perceived risk would thus lead to higher levels of fear of crime.

According to the Indicators of School Crime and Safety data, the vast majority of students are not fearful of victimization at school, however. Only 1 in 25 students (4%) reported that they were afraid of attack or harm at school; an even smaller percentage (2%) was afraid of attack or harm away from school. Additionally, a small percentage of students (5%) reported that they had avoided one or more places at school because of fear of attack or harm (Robers *et al.*, 2013). Although studies using local or regional samples find higher levels of fear among juveniles, even those studies indicate that the vast majority of juveniles are not fearful of crime (Lane, 2006).

The vast majority of studies examining fear of crime among juveniles use one of two types of samples: (1) students that, as part of their school day, complete self-report surveys about their own fear of criminal victimization; and (2) juveniles that are either incarcerated in institutions or are under correctional supervision in the community. The primary reason these samples are used is a practical explanation; these locations are the most likely locations where juveniles will be a "captive audience" long enough for them to complete self-report instruments (or engage in interviews) about their fear of crime. The findings reviewed above derive from the first category of juveniles (in-school samples); a smaller but more recent body of research is developing using juvenile offenders. This body of research is discussed below.

Fear of crime among juvenile offenders

Recently, Lane and colleagues have begun to focus on fear of crime among juvenile offenders. Unlike the increased likelihood of victimization discussed earlier among juvenile offenders, Lane has found that, with the exception of being shot and/or murdered, juveniles who are engaged in criminal activity are not more fearful of crime than their less criminal counterparts. In fact, both May (2001a) and Lane have determined that only small proportions of juvenile offenders indicate they are fearful of crime at all (Lane, 2009). Additionally, the demographic factors found to predict fear of crime in school samples (gender, race, age, etc.) do not seem to be nearly as important in predicting fear among juvenile offenders as they are for in-school samples. Lane (2009) suggests that the diminished levels of fear among juvenile offenders may be due to the fact that these offenders are raised in environments where they are socialized not to be fearful (or admit fear) or they may really be "tougher" and not as afraid as their non-criminal counterparts. Whatever the case may be, the relationship between fear of crime and its predictors appears to be different for juvenile offenders than for non-offenders.

Correlates of Fear of Crime

In the four decades that have passed since fear of crime research became popular in the 1970s, several variables have emerged as predictors of fear of crime. These variables include gender, race, place of residence, and neighborhood incivilities. Although the vast majority of studies examining demographic differences in fear of crime use adult samples, with limited exceptions discussed below, the demographic predictors of fear of crime apply to both juveniles and adults.

Gender and fear of crime

The vast majority of studies investigating fear of crime among both adults and adolescents have determined that females are more fearful of crime than males for both adolescents and adults (for review see Hale, 1996). A number of explanations have been offered for women's higher levels of fear of crime. The oldest explanation for this relationship can best be described as the physical vulnerability hypothesis (Rader, Cossman, & Porter, 2012). According to this explanation, females feel more vulnerable than males because they believe they are physically weaker than men, and thus would be less able to physically fend off a would-be attacker.

The most often used explanation for gender differences in fear, however, is the "shadow of sexual assault" explanation (Ferraro, 1995, p. 86). This argument posits that females have an inordinate fear of sexual assault, especially rape, and this fear of rape pervades all aspects of their lives, causing them to express greater overall fear levels (May, 2001b). According to this argument, rape is a "perceptually contemporaneous offense" – an offense which people may associate with any victimization (Ferraro, 1995, p. 87). Thus, the shadow hypothesis suggests that females associate rape with myriad forms of crime (burglary, robbery, etc.) because they realize that, if victimized by any of these offenses, there is the possibility that they will be raped.

A third explanation for disproportionate fear of crime among females is the socialization hypothesis. This position argues that females are socialized to believe that males are necessary for their protection and that they are taught to be especially wary of strangers in public places (Rader *et al.*, 2012). More recent explanations of the differential levels of fear among men and women attribute this difference to: (1) a patriarchal society in which fear of crime serves as a mechanism to help control women by socializing them to believe that it is their responsibility to avoid criminal victimization (largely committed by men); (2) the "hidden victimization" perspective, which suggests that official statistics demonstrating that women are less likely to be victimized by crime than men hide the large number of victimizations of women that are unreported; and (3) the fact that women have higher levels of "altruistic fear" for their spouses and children than their male counterparts. Regardless of the explanation that one accepts, the finding that females are more fearful of crime than males is the strongest empirical relationship in this research area.

Race and fear of crime

The relationship between race and fear of crime is another heavily researched area in fear of crime. Almost without exception, in those studies where race is found to have a significant association with fear, blacks are more fearful of crime than whites (Hale, 1996). The most common explanation for the association between race and fear of criminal victimization seems to be the "social vulnerability" explanation. This argues that certain groups, primarily the poor and minorities, realize that they are frequently exposed to the threat of victimization. They also realize that if they are victimized by crime, they will suffer arduous economic and social consequences from victimization because they have fewer resources, both economic and emotional, to help them recover from the victimization. This realization makes them more fearful of crime (Evans & Fletcher, 2000; Ferraro, 1996; Mesch, 2000).

Social class and fear of crime

The overwhelming majority of studies using adult samples conclude that individuals of lower socioeconomic status are more fearful of crime than their counterparts of higher socioeconomic status (May, 2001a). This relationship between socioeconomic status and fear of crime may be explained by: (1) the limited exposure of higher socioeconomic groups to criminal conditions; (2) the additional security provided to members of higher socioeconomic status because of their additional financial, social, and political resources; and (3) their greater confidence in societal agencies of justice and security (May, 2001a).

Victimization and fear of crime

Intuitively, victims of crime should be more fearful of crime than their counterparts who have not been victimized. Unlike the variables discussed above, however, there is no consensus regarding the association between victimization and fear of crime. Some authors have suggested that victims of crime are more fearful than individuals who have not been victimized, while others have found the relationship between victimization and fear of crime to be weak or nonexistent.

Hale (1996) argued that the lack of consensus in the findings is due primarily to three factors: (1) the use of global measures of fear of crime, instead of specific measures of fear of criminal victimization discussed previously; (2) the failure of researchers to control for previous victimization experience when examining specific fear of crime; and (3) the failure to distinguish the type of victimization experience (property crime victimization vs. personal crime victimization) when examining the effect of victimization experience on fear of crime. Hale (1996) argued that the relationship between these two variables needs to be further explored to settle the present controversy. Despite the fact that Hale's argument is almost two decades old, and numerous studies have been conducted in this area since that time, the relationship between victimization and fear of crime still needs further examination.

Incivilities and fear of crime

In recent years, the focus has moved from individual-level predictors of fear to more structural-level predictors. One of the first to articulate this relationship was James Q. Wilson and George L. Kelling, who originated what has now become known as broken windows theory. Wilson and Kelling (1982), examining the effects of community disorder on crime, argued that "… if a window in a building is broken and is left unrepaired, all the rest of the windows will soon be broken" (Wilson & Kelling, 1982, p. 31). They argued that this unrepaired broken window: (1) indicates that no one cares enough about the neighborhood to repair the window; (2) the unrepaired broken window will lead to more vandalism, loitering, and eventually other types of crime to occur in the neighborhood; (3) the neighborhood will begin to deteriorate; (4) neighborhood residents will begin to think that crime is on the rise in their neighborhood; and (5) fear of criminal victimization among neighborhood residents will increase and they will modify their behavior accordingly.

The "broken windows" thesis has evolved into the neighborhood incivility hypothesis (Ferraro, 1995). The neighborhood incivility hypothesis argues that various features of the physical environment are related to criminal realities. LaGrange, Ferraro, and Supancic (1992, p. 312) define incivilities as "… low-level breaches of community standards that signal an erosion of conventionally accepted norms and values". Some areas develop reputations as being susceptible to crime because of features in the physical environment, such as trash, litter, graffiti, broken windows in buildings, abandoned houses and cars, and features in the social environment (drinking, rowdy youth, beggars, etc.) (LaGrange *et al.*, 1992).

Since the suggestion that neighborhood incivilities might lead to heightened levels of fear of criminal victimization, several researchers have examined this relationship. Nearly all the studies report a significant positive relationship between neighborhood incivility and fear of crime (May, 2001a) although some researchers argued that the effect of incivilities on fear of crime is indirect through elevated perceived risk of crime (Ferraro, 1995; LaGrange *et al.*, 1992). In other words, neighborhood incivility increases a person's perceived risk of victimization, thus increasing their fear of crime as well.

Correlates of fear of crime for adolescents

Although the research is limited in the area of adolescent fear of crime, May (2001a) and Lane (2006) argue that the predictors of fear for adolescents are somewhat different than those of adults. Blacks, females, those who perceive themselves at risk of victimization, and those from criminogenic neighborhoods are regularly found to be most fearful among both adolescents and adults. Additionally, there is little consensus regarding the relationship between victimization experience and fear of crime among adolescents. Nevertheless, while both age (older individuals are typically more fearful of crime) and socioeconomic status (those from lower socioeconomic classes are more fearful than their counterparts of higher socioeconomic status) are determinants of fear among adults, the effect of these two variables on fear of crime among adolescents is less well established (see May, 2001a, for review). While each of these findings may be an artifact of measurement, they point to the fact that predictors of adolescent fear of crime are somewhat different than those of adults, and thus need further exploration.

Consequences of fear of crime

A limited number of studies have attempted to examine the actions people take because of their fear of criminal victimization. These actions are generally grouped into two categories: avoidance behaviors and defensive behaviors (Ferraro, 1995).

Avoidance behaviors, or limitations people put on their activity as a result of their fear, are also commonly referred to as "constrained behaviors" (Ferraro, 1995).

Constrained behaviors include avoiding unsafe areas at night (the most common form of behavioral adaptation to fear or perceived risk of crime), avoiding unsafe areas during the day, avoiding places at school, and limiting or changing other daily activities (Ferraro, 1995).

Whereas with constrained behavior individuals place limitations on their conduct (e.g. avoiding unsafe areas), defensive behaviors involve an individual's rational decision to perform some type of action to allay their fear of crime. Examining defensive behaviors to fear of crime, Ferraro (1995) determined that adults attempted to reduce their risk of victimization in a variety of ways, including engraving identification numbers on their possessions, installing extra locks on windows or doors, adding outside lighting, or carrying a weapon or other object to protect themselves from victimization.

Among adolescents, however, defensive behavior options are not as readily available. Perhaps the most often-mentioned defensive behavior among juveniles is carrying a weapon for protection. Despite the fact that juveniles often argue that they carry weapons or join gangs for protection, May (2001a) determined that fearful students were no more likely than their counterparts to carry weapons or join gangs for protection. More recent studies have also supported that finding (Melde, Esbensen, & Taylor, 2009; Wilcox, May, & Roberts, 2006). Thus, fearful juveniles may be less likely than adults to use defensive behaviors and more likely to engage in constrained behavior because they have fewer available defensive options. More research is needed to unravel this relationship.

Theoretical models explaining fear of crime

Over the four decades of research in the area of fear of crime, three theoretical models have emerged as the best theoretical predictors of fear of crime: the vulnerability model, the disorder model, and the social integration model. The vulnerability and disorder models suggest that certain factors (many of which were described above) serve to increase fear, while the social integration model argues that social factors reduce or increase fear (Alper & Chappell, 2012). Each model is summarized below.

Theorists following the vulnerability model suggest that certain individuals (e.g., women, the elderly, those from lower socioeconomic classes, and victims of crime) feel that they are less able to defend themselves than their counterparts and thus have higher levels of fear of crime. Intuitively, juveniles would also be more fearful of crime than adults because of their smaller physical stature, their less mature emotional states, and their lack of social and political power that would help prevent or recover from crime victimization. May (2001b) argues that adolescents may rightly realize they are weaker than their older and stronger counterparts that may seek to victimize them, and may thus perceive that they do not have the power to resist attack; thus, this "shadow of powerlessness" causes them to be more fearful of crime than their more powerful counterparts. The disorder model follows the arguments outlined earlier by Wilson and Kelling; this model argues that neighborhood incivility is the best explanation of fear of crime, due to the fact that physical and social disorder in a neighborhood reduces informal (and often formal) social control. This reduced social control and increased disorder cause neighborhood residents to become more fearful and withdraw into their homes, and increase their fear of crime.

The third theoretical model is referred to as the social integration model. Theorists following this model argue that neighborhoods can respond collectively to reduce both crime and fear of crime. By responding collectively to a problem such as crime, neighborhood residents increase the collective efficacy, social cohesion, and social capital of the neighborhood and reduce their own fear of crime levels (Hale, 1996).

Suggestions for Future Research

Although scholarly research in the area of both juvenile crime victimization and fear of crime among juveniles has grown dramatically in the past two decades, there are still a number of areas that need further exploration. Future research should continue to explore both typologies of victims and victim precipitation factors using juvenile samples. While the idea that victims play a role in their own crime victimization is certainly not new, it is still somewhat controversial (Meadows, 2014) and thus needs further exploration, particularly among juveniles. Additionally, victimologists should continue to refine and develop other theoretical perspectives that explain victimization in the context of larger social, psychological, and sociobiological contexts. A number of recent works have begun to examine theoretical predictors of the intersection between victimization and offending among juveniles (Boutwell *et al.*, 2013); adapting traditional and emerging theories to explain juvenile victimization may be worthy of consideration as well.

Research in the area of fear of crime among juveniles also needs to be further developed. As mentioned earlier, despite the technological advances made throughout the twentieth century, the vast majority of fear of crime studies use either official data or survey data to attempt to understand the causes and consequences of fear, and most examine fear of crime among adults. Research examining physiological changes that occur as one is exposed to various criminogenic factors would be helpful, and with enough funding is certainly within the realm of possibility. In addition to physiological research, in-depth qualitative examinations of fear of crime would be helpful as well. Finally, and perhaps most importantly, it is essential that fear of crime researchers that use survey research strategies develop a consensus regarding what questions should be used to operationalize fear of crime. As various authors have highlighted, the method through which one operationalizes fear of crime is often the most important determinant of its correlates (Hale, 1996). Until consensus is reached on the measurement of the dependent variable, it is difficult to come to any consensus on the independent variables associated with fear of crime.

These improvements are even more relevant for juveniles. As mentioned earlier, relatively few studies examine fear of crime among juveniles at all, and among those that do, there is little consensus on the type of sample used by researchers and little consistency in the operationalization of fear of crime in those samples (Melde *et al.*, 2009). Future work should build on critiques of existing work and attempt to remedy that problem.

A final suggestion applies to both the study of crime victimization and fear of crime. With limited exceptions (Melde *et al.*, 2009; Wilcox *et al.*, 2006), research in both areas invariably uses cross-sectional data. Even when longitudinal data are used, the timeframe under consideration is relatively short, typically three years or less. In both areas, using longitudinal data to consider a life-course approach to fear and victimization would be helpful. This area is particularly appropriate for research with juveniles. Longitudinal research would help us understand at what stage of life fear of crime develops in individuals, whether fear of crime is maintained across one's life span, and what factors impact this fear of crime at various stages of life. Longitudinal research would also assist in understanding the factors that lead one to be victimized over their life course, and would help identify additional causes and consequences of crime victimization. Until this research is conducted, debates about both these topics will continue and will hamper any policy suggestions that might come from the research in these areas.

References

Alper, M., & Chappell, A.T. (2012). Untangling fear of crime: A multitheoretical approach to examining the causes of crime-specific fear. *Sociological Spectrum, 32*(4), 346–363.

Boutwell, B.B., Franklin, C.A., Barnes, J.C., Tamplin, A.K., Beaver, K.M., & Petkovsek, M.P. (2013). Unraveling the covariation of low self-control and victimization: A behavior genetic approach. *Journal of Adolescence, 36*(4), 657–666.

Bureau of Justice Statistics. (2013). *Data Collection: National Crime Victimization Survey (NCVS)*. Retrieved from http://www.bjs.gov/index.cfm?ty=dcdetail&iid=245# Methodology

CNN. (2013). Sandy Hook shooting: What happened? Retrieved from http://www.cnn.com/interactive/2012/12/us/sandy-hook-timeline/index.html

Craske, M.G. (1999). *Anxiety Disorders: Psychological Approaches to Theory and Treatment*. Boulder, CO: Westview Press.

Doerner, W.G., & Lab, S.P. (2012). *Victimology* (6th ed.). Burlington, MA: Elsevier.

Evans, D., & Fletcher, M. (2000). Fear of crime: Testing alternative hypotheses. *Applied Geography, 20*, 395–411.

Fattah, E.A. (1993). Research on fear of crime: Some common conceptual and measurement problems. In W. Bilsky, C. Pfeiffer, & P. Wetzels (Eds.), *Fear of Crime and Criminal Victimization* (pp. 45–70). Stuttgart: Ferdinand Enke Verlag.

Federal Bureau of Investigation. (2002). *Crime in the United States, 2001 – Table 2.3*. Retrieved from http://www.fbi.gov/about-us/cjis/ucr/crime-in-the-u.s/2001

Federal Bureau of Investigation. (2012). *Crime in the United States – 2011*. Retrieved from http://www.fbi.gov/about-us/cjis/ucr/crime-in-the-u.s/2011/crime-in-the-u.s.-2011

Ferraro, K.F. (1995). *Fear of Crime: Interpreting Victimization Risk.* Albany, NY: State University of New York Press.

Ferraro, K.F. (1996). Women's fear of victimization: 'Shadow of sexual assault.' *Social Forces,* 75(2), 667–690.

Ferraro, K.F., & LaGrange, R. (1987). The measurement of fear of crime. *Sociological Inquiry,* 57(1), 70–101.

Gallup. (2012). *The Gallup Poll: Crime.* Retrieved from http://www.gallup.com/poll/1603/%20Crime.aspx

Hale, C. (1996). Fear of crime: A review of the literature. *International Review of Victimology,* 4, 79–150.

Hawkins, D.F., Laub, J.H., Lauritsen, J.L., & Cothern, L. (2000). *Race, Ethnicity, and Serious and Violent Juvenile Offending.* NCJ 181202. Washington DC: United States Department of Justice.

Hentig, H. (1948). *The Criminal and His Victim.* Yale University Press.

LaGrange, R.L., Ferraro, K.F., & Supancic, M. (1992). Perceived risk and fear of crime: Role of social and physical incivilities. *Journal of Research in Crime and Delinquency,* 29(3), 311–334.

Lane, J. (2006). Explaining fear of general and gang crimes among juveniles on probation: The impacts of delinquent behaviors. *Youth Violence and Juvenile Justice,* 4(1), 34–54.

Lane, J. (2009). Perceptions of neighborhood problems, fear of crime, and resulting behavioral precautions: Comparing institutionalized girls and boys in Florida. *Journal of Contemporary Criminal Justice,* 25(3), 264–281.

Lee, G.R. (1982). Residential location and fear of crime among the elderly. *Rural Sociology,* 47(4), 655–669.

May, D.C. (2001a). *Adolescent Fear of Crime, Perceptions of Risk, and Defensive Behaviors: An Alternate Explanation of Violent Delinquency.* Lewiston, NY: Edwin Mellen Press.

May, D.C. (2001b). The effect of fear of sexual victimization on adolescent fear of crime. *Sociological Spectrum,* 21(2), 141–174.

Meadows, R.J. (2014). *Understanding Violence and Victimization* (6th ed.). Upper Saddle River, NJ: Pearson.

Melde, C., Esbensen, F., & Taylor, T.J. (2009). 'May piece be with you:' A typological examination of the fear and victimization hypothesis of weapon carrying. *Justice Quarterly,* 26(2), 348–376.

Mesch, G. (2000). Perceptions of risk, lifestyle activities, and fear of crime. *Deviant Behavior,* 21(1), 47–62.

National Center for Juvenile Justice. (2012). *Juvenile arrest rates by offense, sex, and race (1980-2010).* Retrieved from http://www.ojjdp.gov/ojstatbb/crime/excel/JAR_2010.xls

O'Brien, R. (1985). *Crime and Victimization Data.* Beverly Hills, CA: Sage.

Rader, N.E., Cossman, J.S., & Porter, J.R. (2012). Fear of crime and vulnerability: Using a national sample of Americans to examine two competing paradigms. *Journal of Criminal Justice,* 40, 134–141.

Robers, S., Kemp, J., Truman, J., & Snyder, T.D. (2013). *Indicators of School Crime and Safety, 2012.* NCES 2013-036/NCJ 241446. Washington, DC: Bureau of Justice Statistics and National Center for Education Statistics.

Scruton, D.L. (1986). The anthropology of an emotion. In D.L. Scruton (Ed.), *Sociophobics: The Anthropology of Fear* (pp. 7–49). Boulder, CO: Westview Press.

US Department of Justice. (2011). *Criminal Victimization in the United States, 2008 Statistical Tables.* NCJ 231173. Washington, DC: Bureau of Justice Statistics.

Vaske, J., Bosivert, D., & Wright, J.P. (2012). Genetic and environmental contributors to the relationship between violent victimization and criminal behavior. *Journal of Interpersonal Violence, 27*(16), 3213–3235.

Warr, M. (1984). Fear of victimization: Why are women and the elderly more afraid? *Social Science Quarterly, 65*, 681–702.

White, N., & Lauritsen, J.L. (2012). *Violent Crime against Youth, 1994–2010*. NCJ 240106. Washington, DC: United States Department of Justice, Bureau of Justice Statistics.

Wilcox, P., May, D.C., & Roberts, S.D. (2006). Student weapon possession and the 'fear and victimization hypothesis': Unraveling the temporal order. *Justice Quarterly, 23*(4), 502–529.

Wilson, J.Q., & Kelling, G.L. (1982). Broken windows. *The Atlantic Monthly, 249*(3), 29–38.

Index

parenting/childrearing (*cont'd*)
   antisocial behavior relating to 301
   attachment *see* attachment
   strengthening 360, 553
   progression from parents to peers 202
   reciprocal effects of delinquency and 170
   rejection by parents 167, 171, 240
   skills 165–6
     training programs 252
   styles 166–7, 175
   supervision 167, 246–8
   US 86, 93, 94, 96, 97
   see also abuse; family; foster care
parole, life imprisonment without 453–5, 502
Patane, Samuel (*US v. Patane* - 2004) 92
PATHE (Positive Action Through Holistic Education) project 379, 380
PATHS (Promoting Alternative Thinking Strategies) 191, 193, 381
patriarchy 105, 110–11, 115, 116, 613
peers 140–2, 152–3, 199–216
   adolescent development and 202–3
   associations with/ties with/influence of delinquent and deviant peers 122, 141–2, 143, 153, 182, 199, 200, 201, 203, 205, 208, 209, 210, 243, 245, 249, 252, 265, 323–4
   behavioral genetics and 148, 211
   co-offenders and 207–8
   delinquent coping and 242
   deviancy training (contagion effect) 210, 261, 423, 526
   future directions 211–12
   groups
     gangs and 541, 542
     homophily 152–3
     self-selection into 200–1
   in juvenile justice system 210–11
   methodological issues in research 209–10
   opportunity and 208–9
   pressure, and its reduction 382, 409
   in situational crime prevention 338
   social bonding 182
   weapon-carrying for a 548
   see also friendships
pejorative stereotypes 128, 130–1, 134

perceptions (public)
   delinquents 407–8
   of fear of crime 608–9, 610–11
   police
     in interventions 413–14
     in investigations 417
     in prevention 411–12
Perm Krai 47
Perry Preschool program 377–8
persistent offenders, life-course 142, 243–4, 246, 302, 303, 341
personnel/staff in juvenile justice system management 511
Pertsova (head of federal department for juvenile colonies) 46
pharmaceutical misuse 570–1
Philadelphia birth cohort study 292
physical abuse (child) 582, 587, 588
   girls 448
   youth with history as victim of 554
   see also trauma
physical security in schools 378
Pittsburgh
   gang problem trajectories 525
   One Vision One Life program 396
place (location) and crime 227
   gang violence 524–6
   see also proximity; relocation initiatives; space–time budgets
plasticity, developmental 294–5, 297, 298, 299, 301, 302, 303, 305, 307, 308
Plug Minas 35
pole-shackling 113
police, and policing/law enforcement 323, 405–21
   arrests *see* arrests
   Brazil 33, 34, 35–6
   community-assisted 394–5
   contacts/encounters with 412, 413–14
     impact later of 323, 323–4
     labeling and 318, 319, 323, 323–4, 325
   "hot spots" 396–7
   India 59–60
   intervening by 412–14
   investigations 414–17
   prevention by 409–12
   roles of police 409–12